Islas Baleares

Ibiza, Formentera, Mallorca,
Cabrera and Menorca

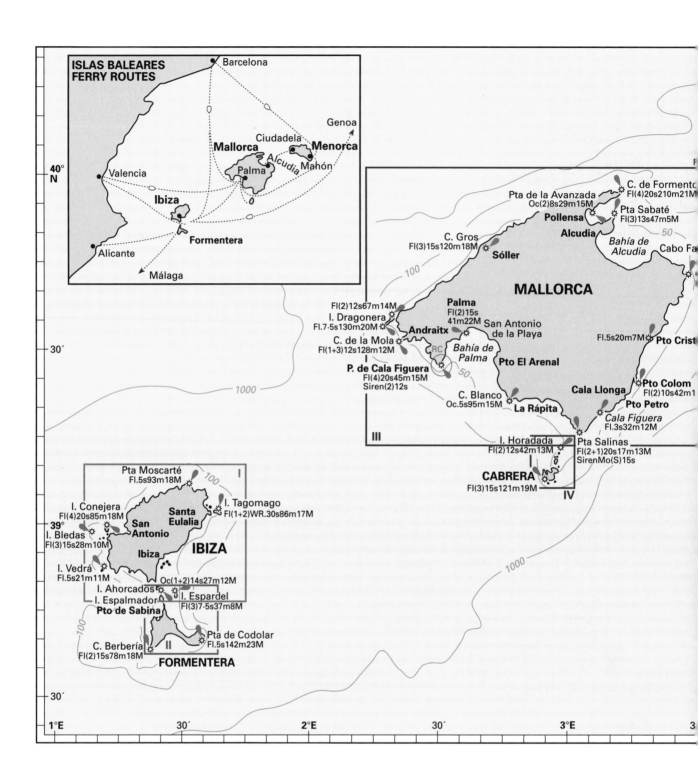

ISLAS BALEARES FERRY ROUTES

Barcelona

Genoa

Ciudadela
Mallorca   **Menorca**
Alcudia   Mahón

40°
N

Valencia
Palma

Ibiza

Alicante

Formentera

Málaga

30´

1000

Pta de la Avanzada
Oc(2)8s29m15M

C. de Formento
Fl(4)20s210m21M

Pta Sabaté
Fl(3)13s47m5M

Pollensa

Alcudia

Bahía de Alcudia

Cabo Fa

C. Gros
Fl(3)15s120m18M

Sóller

50

100

MALLORCA

Fl(2)12s67m14M
I. Dragonera
Fl.7·5s130m20M

Palma
Fl(2)15s
41m22M

San Antonio
de la Playa

Fl.5s20m7M   **Pto Crist**

C. de la Mola
Fl(1+3)12s128m12M

Andraitx

RC

Bahía de Palma

Pto El Arenal

Cala Llonga

☼ **Pto Colom**
Fl(2)10s42m1

P. de Cala Figuera
Fl(4)20s45m15M
Siren(2)12s

50

C. Blanco
Oc.5s95m15M

La Rápita

Pto Petro

Cala Figuera
Fl.3s32m12M

III

I. Horadada
Fl(2)12s42m13M

Pta Salinas
Fl(2+1)20s17m13M
SirenMo(S)15s

CABRERA
Fl(3)15s121m19M

IV

1000

Pta Moscarté
Fl.5s93m18M

I

100

I. Conejera
Fl(4)20s85m18M

Santa Eulalia

I. Tagomago
Fl(1+2)WR.30s86m17M

39°

San Antonio

I. Bledas
Fl(3)15s28m10M

IBIZA

I. Vedrá
Fl.5s21m11M

Ibiza

Oc(1+2)14s27m12M

I. Ahorcados
I. Espalmador

I. Espardel
Fl(3)7·5s37m8M

Pto de Sabina

Pta de Codolar
Fl.5s142m23M

100

C. Berbería
Fl(2)15s78m18M

II

FORMENTERA

30´

1°E   30´   2°E   30´   3°E   3

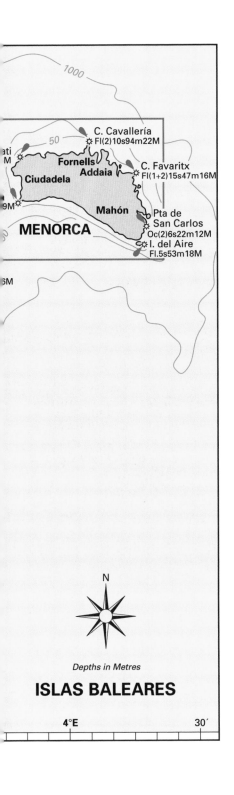

Islas Baleares

Ibiza, Formentera, Mallorca,
Cabrera and Menorca

ROYAL CRUISING CLUB
PILOTAGE FOUNDATION

Graham Hutt

Imray Laurie Norie & Wilson

Published by
Imray Laurie Norie & Wilson Ltd
Wych House The Broadway St Ives
Cambridgeshire PE27 5BT England
☎ +44 (0)1480 462114
Fax +44 (0)1480 496109
www.imray.com
2006

First edition 1977 (as *East Spain Pilot –*
   Chapter VII, Islas Baleares)
Second edition 1980
Third edition 1984
Fourth edition 1989 (including *East Spain Pilot chapter I,*
Introduction and General Information)
Fifth Edition 1991, updated 1995
Sixth Edition 1997
Sixth Edition revised 2000
Seventh Edition 2003
Eighth Edition 2006 (Reprinted with corrections, September)

ISBN 978 085288 915 2

British Library Cataloguing in Publication Data.
A catalogue record for this title is available from the British
Library.

Printed and bound in the UK by CPI Bath

CORRECTIONAL SUPPLEMENTS

This pilot book may be amended at intervals by the issue of
correctional supplements. These are published on the internet at
our website www.imray.com and also via www.rccpf.org.uk and
may be downloaded free of charge. Printed copies are also
available on request from the publishers at the above address.
Like this pilot, supplements are selective. Navigators requiring
the latest definitive information are advised to refer to official
hydrographic office data.

www.rccpf.org.uk includes a photo library for some ports in this
book. It shows additional material and will publish appropriate
updating photographs received in digital form from yachtsmen
or the authorities.

CAUTION

Whilst every care has been taken to ensure that the information
contained in this book is accurate, the RCC Pilotage Foundation, the
authors and the publishers hereby formally disclaim any and all
liability for any personal injury, loss and/or damage howsoever
caused, whether by reason of any error, inaccuracy, omission or
ambiguity in relation to the contents and/or information contained
within this book. The book contains selected information and thus is
not definitive. It does not contain all known information on the
subject in hand and should not be relied on alone for navigational
use: it should only be used in conjunction with official hydrographic
data. This is particularly relevant to the plans, which should not be
used for navigation.

The RCC Pilotage Foundation, the authors and publishers believe
that the information which they have included is a useful aid to
prudent navigation, but the safety of a vessel depends ultimately on
the judgment of the skipper, who should assess all information,
published or unpublished.

WAYPOINTS

This edition of the *Islas Baleares* pilot includes the introduction of
waypoints. The RCC PF consider a waypoint to be a position likely
to be helpful for navigation if entered into some form of electronic
navigation system for use in conjunction with GPS. In this pilot they
have been determined by actual observation. All waypoints are given
to datum WGS 84 and every effort has been made to ensure their
accuracy. Nevertheless, for each individual vessel, the standard of
onboard equipment, aerial position, datum setting, correct entry of
data and operator skill all play a part in their effectiveness. In
particular it is vital for the navigator to note the datum of the chart
in use and apply the necessary correction if plotting a GPS position
on the chart.

The attention of the navigator is drawn to the 'important note'
paragraph in the Introduction.

We emphasise that we regard waypoints as an aid to navigation
for use as the navigator decides. We hope that the waypoints in
this pilot will help ease that navigational load.

POSITIONS

Positions given in the text and on plans are intended purely as an
aid to locating the place in question on the chart.

PLANS

The plans in this guide are not to be used for navigation – they are
designed to support the text and should always be used together
with navigational charts. Even so, every effort has been made to
locate harbour and anchorage plans adjacent to the relevant text.

It should be borne in mind that the characteristics of lights may be
changed during the life of the book, and that in any case
notification of such changes is unlikely to be reported
immediately. Each light is identified in both the text and where
possible on the plans (where it appears in red) by its international
index number, as used in the *Admiralty List of Lights*, from which
the book may be updated when no longer new.

All bearings are given from seaward and refer to true N. Scales
may be taken from the scales of latitude. Symbols are based on
those used by the British Admiralty – users are referred to
Symbols and Abbreviations (NP 5011).

Contents

THE RCC PILOTAGE FOUNDATION

In 1976 an American member of the Royal Cruising Club, Dr Fred Ellis, indicated that he wished to make a gift to the Club in memory of his father, the late Robert E Ellis, of his friends Peter Pye and John Ives and as a mark of esteem for Roger Pinckney. An independent charity known as the RCC Pilotage Foundation was formed and Dr Ellis added his house to his already generous gift of money to form the Foundation's permanent endowment. The Foundation's charitable objective is 'to advance the education of the public in the science and practice of navigation', which is at present achieved through the writing and updating of pilot books covering many diffent parts of the world.

The Foundation is extremely grateful and privileged to have been given the copyrights to books written by a number of distinguished authors and yachtsmen including the late Adlard Coles, Robin Brandon and Malcolm Robson. In return, the Foundation has willingly accepted the task of keeping the original books up to date and many yachtsmen and women have helped (and are helping) the Foundation fulfil this commitment. In addition to the titles donated to the Foundation, several new books have been created and developed under the auspices of the Foundation. The Foundation works in close collaboration with three publishers – Imray Laurie Norie and Wilson, Adlard Coles Nautical and On Board Publications – and in addition publishes in its own name short run guides and pilot books for areas where limited demand does not justify large print runs. Several of the Foundation's books have been translated into French, German and Italian.

The Foundation runs its own website at www.rccpf.org.uk which not only lists all the publications but also contains free downloadable pilotage information.

The overall management of the Foundation is entrusted to trustees appointed by the Royal Cruising Club, with day-to-day operations being controlled by the Director. All these appointments are unpaid. In line with its charitable status, the Foundation distributes no profits; any surpluses are used to finance new books and developments and to subsidise those covering areas of low demand.

PUBLICATIONS OF THE RCC PILOTAGE FOUNDATION

Imray
The Baltic Sea
Faroe, Iceland and
 Greenland
Norway
North Brittany and
 the Channel Islands
Isles of Scilly
The Channel Islands
South Biscay
North Biscay
Atlantic Islands
Atlantic Spain & Portugal

Mediterranean Spain
 Costas del Sol & Blanca
Mediterranean Spain
 Costas del Azahar,
 Dorada & Brava
Islas Baleares
Corsica and North
 Sardinia
North Africa
Chile

Adlard Coles Nautical
Atlantic Crossing Guide
Pacific Crossing Guide
On Board Publications
South Atlantic Circuit
Havens and Anchorages for the South American Coast
The RCC Pilotage Foundation
Supplement to Falkland Island Shores
RCC PF Website www.rccpf.org.uk
Cruising Guide to West Africa
Supplements
Passage planning guides

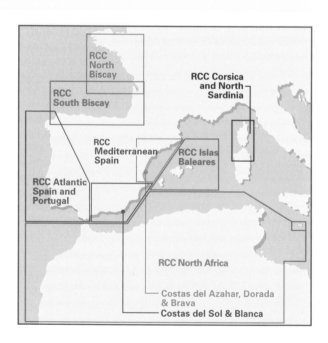

Foreword

Preface

The origins of this book go back to the late Robin Brandon's *East Spain Pilot*, in which *Islas Baleares* was first published as Chapter VII, after his detailed reconnaissance in 1977. When he revised his book in 1988 he commented on the rapid transition of the islands, and their harbours, as wealth and tourism took hold. The RCC Pilotage Foundation was honoured to take on the regular updating of his books – the two volumes of *Mediterranean Spain*, from Gibraltar to Denia and Denia to the French Border, being the others in this series.

The book has developed over the years and I was delighted that Graham Hutt agreed to carry out a major revision in 2005. With detailed explorations by land and sea, he built on his knowledge of the islands, recording the changes and opportunities which continue to take place. This has been a major task in this popular and still developing area. He has not only updated the facts, amply illustrated with new aerial photographs but, as far as is practicable, has verified the datum of the plans to WGS84 and added details of life ashore, to illustrate that tourism has not taken over the whole island group.

Islas Baleares may now be very busy in the height of summer but they remain important to the yachtsman, whether as a major source of technical support, for extended cruising or for use as a safe haven when cruising the Western Mediterranean. I am most grateful to Graham Hutt for his depth of research, continuing the line of dedicated authors who have maintained and extended Robin Brandon's original work; and to Willie Wilson and his team at Imray who have tackled the major restructuring of the work and the updating of the plans. This has been no mean task.

As always we welcome feedback from yachtsmen, so that we can continue to publish supplements on the Imray website where appropriate, or photographic updates on the Pilotage Foundation website.

Martin Walker
Director
RCC Pilotage Foundation
2006

Having sailed the Balearic Islands many times over the past few years, usually on my way to or from North Africa, it was an honour to be asked to revise this edition. It was the first opportunity to explore inland, as I had previously ventured little further from the coasts than to the airports. The island interiors were very different to what I expected.

I hear many complaints about the ruin of the islands by tourist development and have to wonder if those complaining have actually travelled further than the main busy ports. There has certainly been a lot of tourist development, as in all the Mediterranean, but the islands are far from spoiled by this.

In Mallorca fine pine forests still thrive and have not given way to concrete jungles. I found that most of the inland private developments are tastefully done. Even coastal developments compared favourably with those of the Costa del Sol and the coastlines of Greece and Italy, which I am also familiar with. Some areas along the coast of Mallorca actually resemble the beautiful Tuscany area of Italy, with their narrow winding roads through the pine forests. In Mallorca, these roads are again peaceful, thanks to a huge investment in motorways which keep vehicles away from the coast.

I could not better many of the *cala* (cove) descriptions given in the previous seven editions which had been honed over the years by my predecessors. However, it has been a thorough and complete revision and hopefully, an easier book to use.

There were many surprises during my visits. Unlike most of the Mediterranean mainland – both on the European and North African continents, where the internet is now widely used to convey information – in the Baleares much less use is made of this medium. The reason given by several port captains is that it is simply too much bother to keep the site updated. When I joked that it must indeed be hard to find time to keep up with the changing prices for a berth, one captain laughed and agreed that this was 'Indeed, sometimes a daily occurrence!'

Another surprise was to find German the first language heard ashore in many places. Shop workers often spoke German and English, but not Spanish or Catalan, no doubt a result of heavy investment by Air Berlin which has made its base in Palma, offering good package prices from Germany.

After working in other areas of the Mediterranean where officials are helpful and enthusiastic, it was also a surprise to find private marina authorities in the Baleares fairly uninterested and often unhelpful. Few wanted to part with any information, especially price lists. As with the websites, everything just seemed too much bother. Marinas are full: a sign of a successful maritime economy and one that shows no sign of weakening.

Graham Hutt
2006

Acknowledgements

I am indebted to those skippers living and working in the islands who contributed information and advice. Once again, as with my other books, Di Stoddard helped with every aspect in the preparation and checking, for which I am most grateful.

Mallorca

Garth and Beryl Alden aboard *At Last*, who provided valuable information on Palma and checked the proofs of the island.

Menorca

Bob Parker of *Antigua Meloussa* (www. menorca envelero.com/), who has been contributing information for some years from his base in Menorca and who checked the proofs for Menorca and Cabrera.

Ibiza

David Brooke, who checked the proofs for Ibiza and Formentera.

The Baleares Tourist Information Office for a wealth of brochures and information provided.

To Ros Hogbin and others behind the scenes at the Pilotage Foundation, who gave advice, help and checking of the text and layout to ensure that this edition is easier to navigate around and use.

The aerial photographers Patrick Roach and Geoff Williamson who provided many of the superb pictures. (Non-attributed pictures are the work of Patrick Roach. GW denotes Geoff Williamson.)

Graham Hutt
2006

Author's yacht *Safwana:* 14m Hartley Fijian   *Graham Hutt*

List of Ports

Introduction

The Islas Baleares (Llles Balears, Ballerics, Balearics, etc.) consist of four main islands: Mallorca, Menorca, Ibiza and Formentera, along with a number of smaller islets in three separate groups. They form one of the most attractive and varied cruising grounds in the western Mediterranean. There are hundreds of pleasant anchorages and many harbours, ranging from large cosmopolitan ports such as Palma de Mallorca, to completely deserted anchorages in exquisitely beautiful bays.

The islands are under Spanish sovereignty and therefore within the European Union. The distances between islands are not great and those between ports, harbours and anchorages, often only a few miles, making the islands suitable for cruising throughout the year with shelter never far away.

Although the islands – and Mallorca in particular – have become a byword for all that is worst in holiday development, in practice this applies only to a small percentage of the coastline, notably the beaches running W from Palma. In other areas it is possible to sail for hours past apparently untouched and frequently dramatic coastline. The same may be said of western and northern Ibiza, while Menorca, though possibly less spectacular, has managed to preserve a great deal of its rural charm. Driving along the coastal roads which wind their way inland around mountainous areas through thick pine forests, is very pleasant.

The western group of islands lies less than 50 miles E of the Spanish mainland. This includes Ibiza, Espalmador, Formentera and half a dozen smaller islets (*islotes*) separated from the mainland and Mallorca by deep channels. These islands were recognised as a separate group in Roman times when they were called *Pityusae* (Pine Islands) and are still sometimes referred to as the *Islas Pitiusas*. They offer many secluded bays and *calas* (coves) where it is possible to anchor. The northern islands are high and rocky whereas the south is low-lying with sandy bays.

The second group, consisting of Mallorca, Cabrera, Menorca and some small inshore islands, was known by the Romans as *Insulae Baleares*, possibly from the Phoenician *baal laaron* meaning 'a man who throws stones' (apparently the islanders' favourite method of resisting attack). The names Mallorca and Menorca are derived from the Latin 'Major' and 'Minor'. Mallorca, the largest island of the group, is approximately 45 miles NE of Ibiza. It has a major port, several harbours and many bays and *calas* where it is possible to anchor. The northern part is mountainous. There is one large offlying island to the S, Cabrera, which has a well protected bay, several *calas* and a number of offlying islets. It is a national park with restricted access. Anchoring is forbidden but mooring buoys have been laid. Menorca lies 25 miles NE of Mallorca and is much lower and flatter than its neighbour. It is some 30 miles long, with few harbours but numerous *calas* where anchoring is possible. As in Mallorca, the northern part is higher and more rugged than the south.

The islands are attractive, particularly away from 'developed' areas, and form an excellent cruising ground. However some coastal areas have suffered from the rapid growth of tourism in the same way as the coast of mainland Spain. The days of empty anchorages and uncrowded harbours are long gone, particularly during July and August, when it is difficult to find a mooring in any of the harbours. There is good reason for the cruising yachtsman to venture to quieter areas during July and August – if a quieter alternative can be found. Otherwise, simply expect disturbance from speed boats and jet-skis, and the occasional noisy disco as part of the cruise.

Cala Pinar: rich pine forests stretch from the sea to the mountains

Traditional farming: near Montuiri, Mallorca *GW*

CLIMATE AND SEASONS

For those accustomed to more northern latitudes a winter cruise has its attractions. There are many days with a good sailing breeze and the weather is warmer and sunnier than a normal English summer. Storms and heavy rain occur in winter, but in general the climate is mild and, particularly from January to March, reasonably pleasant most of the time.

Offshore, the Mediterranean weather in winter can be fearsome, but it is feasible to dodge bad weather and slip from harbour to harbour as they are seldom far apart. Sailing out of season not only has the great advantage that there are no crowds, but the shops and services are freer to serve the winter visitor. Local people can be met, places of interest enjoyed and the empty beaches and coves used in privacy. Many *club náuticos*, which in summer have to turn away cruising sailors, welcome visitors off-season.

LOCAL ECONOMY

Tourism is a significant contributor to the local economy, but agriculture and light industry manage to co-exist in the islands. An established boat building industry exists, drawing skilled labour from the industrial sectors. The yachting industry in the Balearic Islands generates almost half a billion Euros each year.

LANGUAGE

The islands have two official languages: Spanish Castilliano and Catalan. The latter is transformed into local dialects, referred to as *Mallorquín*, *Menorquín* and *Ibicenco*, in Mallorca, Menorca and Ibiza. Examples of Catalan alternatives for Castilliano Spanish phrases include: *bondia* – good morning (rather than *buenos días*), *bona tarde* – good afternoon (*buenos tardes*), *s'es plau* – please

(*por favor*). Many French and Italian words are integrated into the local dialects.

Many local people speak English or German, often learnt from tourists, and French is taught as a second language at school.

CULTURE AND RELIGION

Holidays and fiestas

As on the Spanish mainland, most inhabitants of the islands are Roman Catholic, though, as on many islands throughout the Mediterranean, practice may be more cultural than religious and quite different from that on the mainland. Perhaps the most overt manifestation of religious practice is the celebration of saints' days. There are literally hundreds of these throughout the islands and they can be a huge affair – always with a procession during which the saint, or an effigy of the Virgin Mary will be paraded down the main street or taken by boat, effectively closing down the town for several hours. One of the largest, *Fiesta del Virgen de la Carmen* is celebrated in many harbours during mid-July. When a national holiday falls on a Sunday it may be celebrated the following day.

Fiestas usually culminate with a firework display. Every city, town and village has its own saint's day and corresponding fiesta. Other celebrations are of historic events, commemorating the rich history of the islands.

A useful *Fiestas Guide* is published annually by the Balearic Tourist Institute and is available from tourist offices. There is also a monthly update including cultural events taking place locally, also available from tourist offices and from many hotel lobbies.

Addresses and websites for tourist offices in the Balearics are found later in this section, and overseas offices in the *Appendix*.

Ancient church in Banys de la Font Santa, Mallorca *Graham Hutt*

Maritime Information

METEOROLOGY

Regional weather in the Western Mediterranean

General

The weather pattern in the western Mediterranean basin is affected by many different systems and local topography. It is largely unpredictable, quick to change and often very different at places only a short distance apart (see *Appendix* for Spanish meteorological terms).

Winds most frequently blow from the W, NW, N and E but are considerably altered by the effects of local topography. The Mediterranean is an area of calms and gales and the old saying that in summer there are nine days of light winds followed by a gale, is very close to reality. Near to the coast normal sea and land breezes are experienced on calm days.

The winds in the Mediterranean have been given names dependent on their direction and characteristics. Those which affect this area are detailed below.

NW: tramontana

This wind, also known as the *mestral* or *maestral* near Río Ebro and the *mistral* in France (where it usually originates), is a strong, dry wind, cold in winter, which can be dangerous. It is caused by a secondary depression forming in the Golfo de León or the Golfo de Génova on the cold front of a major depression crossing France. The northwesterly airflow generated is compressed between the Alps and the Pyrenees and flows into the Mediterranean basin. In Spain it chiefly affects the coast to the N of Barcelona, the Islas Baleares, and is strongest at the northern end of the Costa Brava.

The *tramontana* can be dangerous in that it can arrive and reach gale force in as little as fifteen minutes on a calm sunny day, with virtually no warning. Signs to watch for are brilliant visibility, (sometimes two or three days in advance of a storm) clear sky – sometimes with cigar-shaped clouds, very dry air and a steady or slightly rising barometer. On rare occasions the sky may be cloudy when the wind first arrives, although it clears later. Sometimes the barometer will plunge in normal fashion, rising quickly after the gale has passed. If at sea and some way from land, a line of white on the horizon and a developing swell give a few minutes' warning. The only effective warning that can be obtained is by radio – Marseille (in French) and Monaco (in French and English) are probably the best.

The *tramontana* normally blows for at least three days and, on occasions, may last for a week or longer. It is very frequent in the winter months, blowing for a third of the time, and on occasions can reach Force 10 (50 knots) or above. In summer it is neither as strong nor as frequent.

W: vendaval

A depression crossing Spain or southern France creates a strong SW to W wind, the *vendaval* or *poniente*, which funnels through the Strait of Gibraltar and along the S coast of Spain. Though normally confined to the S and SE coasts, it occasionally blows in the NE of the area. It is usually short-lived and at its strongest from late autumn to early spring.

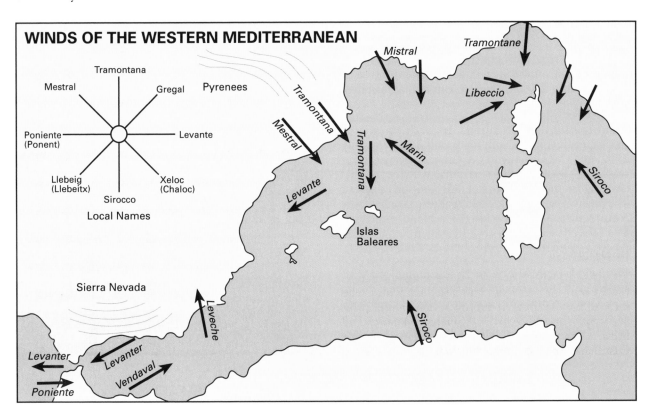

E: levante

Encountered from Gibraltar to Valencia and beyond, the *levante*, sometimes called the *llevantade* when it blows at gale force, is caused by a depression located between the Islas Baleares and the North African coast. It is preceded by a heavy swell *(las tascas)*, cold damp air, poor visibility and low cloud which forms first around the higher hills. Heavy and prolonged rainfall is more likely in spring and autumn than summer. A *levante* may last for three or four days or more. It is usually preceded two or three days in advance by brilliantly clear weather and the formation of cigar or huge layered saucer-shaped clouds.

S: sirocco

The hot wind from the S is created by a depression moving E along or just S of the North African coast. By the time this dry wind reaches Spain or the Islas Baleares it can be very humid, with haze and cloud. If strong it carries dust, and should it rain when the cold front comes through the water may be red or brown and the dust will set like cement. This wind is sometimes called the *leveche* in SE Spain. It occurs most frequently in summer, seldom lasting more than one or two days.

Precipitation

Annual rainfall is moderate, between 450mm and 500mm, and tends to be higher in the E of the area. It is heaviest in the last quarter of the year and lightest in the third quarter: July averages 4–5mm.

Thunderstorms

Thunderstorms are most frequent in the autumn – up to four or five each month, and can be accompanied by hail. High level cumulus clouds are frequent in winter.

Visibility

Fog is very rare in summer but may occur about three times a month in winter. On occasions dust carried by the southerly *sirocco* can reduce visibility.

Temperature

Temperatures drop to around 10°-15°C in winter, rising steadily after March to around 20°C, reaching 29°C in July and August. Afternoon temperatures reach 30°–33°C in these months, with occasional days higher, most likely in late July and early August. The usual afternoon sea breeze keeps the temperature from reaching mainland highs of around 40°C.

Humidity

With winds from W, NW, or N, low humidity can be expected. The *sirocco* southerly winds bring exceptionally dry air: these are rare. An easterly *levante* wind brings with it high humidity, often around 95%. The relative humidity increases throughout the night and falls by day.

A storm rolling past the anchorage in Colom   *Graham Hutt*

LOCAL WEATHER IN THE ISLAS BALEARES

The two main weather areas in the Islas Baleares lie either side of a line roughly bisecting Mallorca from N–NW to S–SE.

The southwestern area is influenced by the weather over mainland Spain – winds are variable but, in general, those from the SE semicircle prevail in summer and those from the NW in winter. Gales are rare in summer (though sudden short term squalls are becoming increasingly common), but may blow for 5–10% of the time in winter. These are generally the result of a *tramontana* though they may blow from anywhere between W through N to NE. Winds from the SE can bring clouds, rain and poor visibility, though these are more frequent in the winter months.

In the Menorca area, NW, N and NE winds are most common, especially in winter, though winds from other directions frequently occur. This area is influenced by the weather in the Golfo de León and is in the direct path of the NW *tramontana*, making it particularly important to listen to regular weather forecasts. Gales or increased winds forecast for the Golfo de León almost invariably mean stronger winds in the NE Baleares. Gales may be experienced for 10% of the time during the winter, dropping to 2% in July and August, sometimes arriving with little warning and rapidly building to gale force. Although there is more rain than in the SW sector of the archipelago, visibility is generally better. Menorca is sometimes described as 'The Windy Isle.'

Throughout the area, in calm weather a sea breeze (*brisa de mar*) will be experienced near the coast, blowing more strongly where it is channelled into a large bay such as the Bahías de Palma, Pollensa or Alcudia. It usually gets up at around 1300, is at its maximum between 1500 and 1600 and drops towards dusk. It can reach Force 5 (20 knots) or more at times. In spite of its name it seldom blows directly onshore – more often at 45° to the coast or even parallel to it.

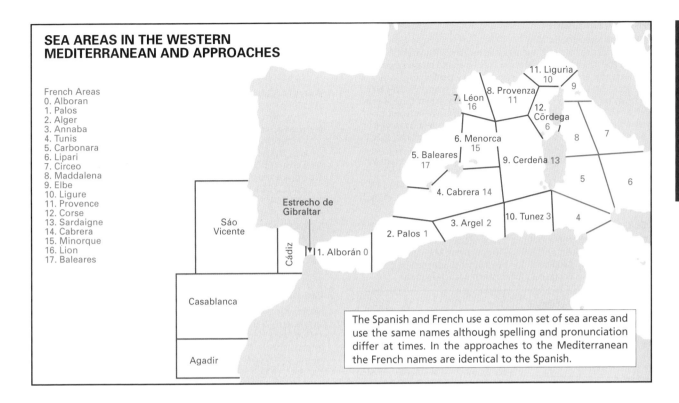

SEA AREAS IN THE WESTERN
MEDITERRANEAN AND APPROACHES

French Areas
0. Alboran
1. Palos
2. Alger
3. Annaba
4. Tunis
5. Carbonara
6. Lipari
7. Circeo
8. Maddalena
9. Elbe
10. Ligure
11. Provence
12. Corse
13. Sardaigne
14. Cabrera
15. Minorque
16. Lion
17. Baleares

The Spanish and French use a common set of sea areas and use the same names although spelling and pronunciation differ at times. In the approaches to the Mediterranean the French names are identical to the Spanish.

A land breeze is sometimes present during the latter half of the night and lasts until the sun has had time to warm the land. This breeze can be quite strong where there are valleys leading inland.

Precipitation and visibility

Annual rainfall at Palma averages 460mm, the wettest period being October to December. Fog sometimes occurs in winter but is almost unknown in summer.

WEATHER FORECASTS

It should be noted that visual signs and methods of forecasting using clouds and barometer, as is usual in Northern Europe, usually do not give the same indications in the Mediterranean. This is more noticeable as you travel E from the Strait of Gibraltar. It is common to see a fast falling or rising barometer, with no resulting change in conditions. Similarly, cloud formations that would normally indicate rain or storms approaching, often clear in minutes, leaving blue skies. Sudden winds or squalls can appear very quickly without any warning whatsoever. The good news is that these unannounced changes are normally short-lived.

Radio and other weather forecasts

Details of coast radio stations, weather forecasts, Weatherfax and Navtex follow. See individual harbour details for port and marina radio information. All times quoted are UT (universal time) unless otherwise specified. Only France Inter, Radio France International, BBC Radio 4 and one of the two Monaco stations observe local time (LT), thus altering the UT transmission times when the clocks change.

VHF

When calling a Spanish coast radio station on VHF use Ch 16. The station will then specify which channel to use for further communication. When calling a marina or another vessel, use Ch 09 unless stated otherwise in the text.

RADIO WEATHER FORECASTS IN SPANISH AND ENGLISH
Palma
Palma radio transmits a forecast on VHF in English and
    Spanish in Mallorca on Ch 10, in Ibiza on Ch 3 and in
    Menorca on Ch 85, announced on Ch 16 at about 0835,
    1135, 1635, 2135 LT
Valencia
Valencia radio transmits a forecast on VHF Ch 10,
    announced on Ch 16, in English and Spanish at 15
    minutes past every even hour.
Weather forecasts in French and English
Valencia
    VHF Ch 10 at 0835 covering all the coastal waters
    around Mallorca
Monaco (3AC)
VHF transmits and receives on Ch 20, 22, 25, 23 (Navimet),
    24 (winter 0600-2200; summer 0500-2100)
Weather messages
VHF Ch 20, 22 every H+03 and 0903, 1403, 1915 LT in French
    and English for areas 514-516
Navigational warnings
VHF Ch 20, 22 at 0803 LT
France Inter (Bulletin Inter-Service-Mer)
On 162kHz at 2003 LT for areas 514-516. May be worth
    tape recording by the less fluent.
Radio France-Internationale
On 6175kHz at 1140 UT (gale warnings, synopsis,
    development, 24 hr forecast, in French)
Alger (7TA), Algeria (36°40′N 03°18′E)
On 1792kHz SSB at 0903, 1703 UT (12h forecast in French
    for area 3, followed by gale warnings, synopsis, 12h
    forecast and further 12h outlook, in French, for all areas
    (see diagram)

ENGLISH LANGUAGE

UK Maritime Mobile Net

In addition to 'official' weather forecasts, information given by the UK Maritime Mobile Net covering the Eastern Atlantic and Mediterranean are very useful, especially in forming an opinion from the general synopsis. The Net can be heard on 14303kHz SSB on the Upper Side Band at 0800 and 1800 UT daily, the full forecast following about 30 minutes later. On Saturday there is usually a preview of the coming week's weather prospects. It is not necessary to have a licence to listen to the Net, though an amateur radio licence is required to transmit.

BBC Radio 4, UK on 198kHz at 0048, 0555, 1355, 1750 LT. Occasionally the synopsis provides advance warning of the approach of an Atlantic depression which could lead to a NW tramontana.

GERMAN LANGUAGE

Offenbach (Main)/Pinneberg (DDH)(DDK), Germany
On 4583, 7646kHz at 0415, 1610 for areas M1-M9; 1015, 2215. 2 day prognosis for Western Mediterranean; 1115, 2315. 2 day prognosis for Eastern Mediterranean.

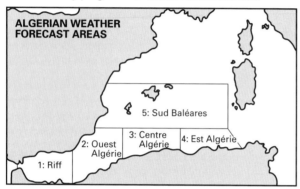

ALGERIAN WEATHER FORECAST AREAS

5: Sud Baléares
3: Centre Algérie
2: Ouest Algérie
4: Est Algérie
1: Riff

Non-radio weather forecasts

A forecast in Spanish can be obtained from the airport Met Office on each island (ask for *meteorologia*). Alternatively a pre-recorded marine forecast – the 'High Seas Bulletin' – includes the Islas Baleares and is available by telephoning Teletiempo (telephone numbers for meteorological maritime weather). By dialling the numbers below, a list of options will be given covering all Spanish sea areas.

Baleares   ☎ 807 17 03 70
Mediterranean   ☎ 807 17 03 71

An excellent forecast is given on all Spanish TV channels following the main morning and evening news. This is produced by the meteorological department of the Spanish military and are generally accurate. Channel TV1 gives best coverage with a full synoptic forecast, wind direction and 3-day outlook. News broadcast times vary depending on which channel is used and the length of the preceding adverts. Most national and local newspapers also carry some form of forecast.

All marinas and yacht harbours display a synoptic chart and forecast, generally updated daily (though often posted rather late to be of use if you want to get away early).

Weatherfax

Rome broadcast weatherfax transmissions covering the Islas Baleares and suitable for reception via SSB and computer or dedicated weatherfax receiver. Refer to the *Admiralty List of Radio Signals Vol 3 Part 1* (NP 283(1)) for times and frequencies.

Navtex

Navtex is transmitted on the standard frequency of 518kHz. The Mediterranean and Black Sea fall within NAVAREA III.

Valencia (Cabo de la Nao), Spain (Identification letter X)
Weather messages: 0750, 1950 (gale warnings, synopsis and 24-hr forecast, in English, for areas 8-12.
Navigational warnings: 0350, 0750, 1150, 1550, 1950, 2350 in English, for the Mediterranean coast of Spain and Islas Baleares.

La Garde (CROSS), France (Identification letter W)
Storm warnings: On receipt and at 0340, 0740, 1140, 1540, 1940, 2340, in English, for areas 514 (eastern part)-523, 531-534.
Weather messages: 1140, 2340 (gale or storm warnings, synopsis and 24-hr forecast, in English, for areas 514 eastern part-523, 531-534): see diagram for areas covered.
Navigational warnings: in English, for the northwestern Mediterranean only.

Weatherfax and RTTY

Northwood (RN) broadcasts a full set of UK Met Office charts out to 5 days ahead on 2618.5,4610,8040 and 11086.5kHz. (Schedule at 0236, surface analysis at 3 hourly intervals from 0300 to 2100 and 2300.)

Deutscher Wetterdienst broadcasts German weather charts on 3855,7880,13882.5kHz. (Schedule at 1111, surface analysis at 0430, 1050,1600,2200.)

DWD broadcasts forecasts using RTTY on 4583, 7646, and 10001.8kHz (in English at 0955 and 2155) 11039 and 14467.3kHz (in German at 0820, 1429, 2020). Alternatively, a dedicated receiver will record automatically – see 'weatherman' on www.nasamarine.com

Inmarsat

Broadcast times for weather for METAREA III are 1000 and 2200.

GRIB

This service enables arrow diagram forecasts for up to 5 days ahead, and other information, to be obtained in email form (or by marine HF and HAM radio). The data is highly compressed so that a great deal of information can be acquired quickly, even using a mobile phone connected to a laptop. For details of one popular service email query@saildoc.com subject 'any'.

Internet forecasts

Many internet sites give excellent forecasts. These are too numerous to mention and are added to daily. Few yacht skippers will be unfamiliar with these sites, but by typing into a search engine 'weather Med' many options will result. The Italian 'meteomar' is one of the best and http://meteonet.nl/aktueel/brackall.htm gives the latest UK Met office Bracknel synoptic chart of the whole Mediterranean. See also www.bbc.co.uk/weather/coast/pressure/ and www.inm.es Of particular note are the sites:

http://www.inm.es/web/infmet/predi/metmar/bolmet.html
http://www.inm.es/web/infmet/predi/metmar/indpuer1.html

which give useful maps showing the wind speeds and wave heights for all of the coastal areas of Spain including the Balearic Islands and the Canaries).

See list of weather terms in English and Spanish in the *Appendix*.

SEA CONDITIONS

Currents

The current around the islands normally sets SE, S or SW at a rate of 0.5 to 1 knot, though stronger in the channels between them and off promontories. Its direction and strength can also be modified by the effects of strong or prolonged winds, those from the S tending to reduce or reverse the current and those from the N increasing the rate of flow.

Tides

Even at springs, tidal range is less than 0.3m, so can be disregarded. Sea level is more affected by the strength, direction and duration of winds and by variations in barometric pressure. In general, winds from the N combined with high pressure cause a fall in sea level and those from the S with low pressure cause a rise in the level. In addition, the levels in harbours or *calas* facing an onshore wind will be higher than in those experiencing offshore winds.

Even with these factors, the range of sea level is unlikely to exceed 1m, other than during a phenomenon known as *resaca* or *seiche*. This occurs rarely: usually when a depression and spring tide coincide. This causes a rise and fall of sea level by as much as 1.5m every ten or fifteen minutes; an oscillation which may last for several days. *Resaca* most often affects Puerto de Ciudadela, Menorca and the deeply indented harbours and *calas* on the SE coast of Mallorca, but has also been experienced as far W as Puerto de Arenal in the Bahía de Palma.

For interest: an earthquake during 2004 in Al Hociema, Morocco, 400 miles away, caused a lot of damage in several marinas in the islands. Advance warning was given – though few understood its significance – when some harbours and the Mahón river suddenly dried out. The resultant surge of incoming water half an hour later was traumatic, leaving some boats several hundred metres inland and many trapped under pontoons.

Swell

Swell is not usually a problem in summer: winds are local and form a daily pattern of sea or land breezes, dropping at sunset. However, there are occasional gales which can quickly whip up high steep seas, though these usually are short lived. In early 2005, a large passenger ferry encountered 40-foot seas between Menorca and Corsica and sustained severe damage when the bridge windows were smashed and electrics disabled, but these conditions are rare. In July and August periods of flat calms are more often experienced. Swell from any direction can affect the Islas Baleares, and particularly the *cala* anchorages. A gale in the Golfo de León – common in winter – is likely to send a N or NE swell of up to 2m down into the islands, possibly before the wind itself arrives. E or NW winds can set in for days, making the E and N facing *calas* uncomfortable.

Scouring and silting

In passages and anchorages where the bottom is of loose sand, depths may change due to the effects of rainfall and wind.

Sea temperature

Sea temperature ranges from around 14°C in February to 25°C or more in August. Winds from the S and E tend to raise the temperature and those from the W and N to lower it.

Waterspouts

Waterspouts may occasionally be encountered in spring and autumn, usually near promontories and often associated with thunderstorms.

FLORA AND FAUNA ON THE ISLANDS

Much as on the Spanish mainland, pine trees and lavender can be smelled from miles offshore. Olive trees and several species of orchid, along with honeysuckle, abound. *Adelfa* (oleander) grow well in riverbeds, bringing colour throughout the summer season.

Birds

The Audouins Gull (rare elsewhere) can often be seen, particularly at San Antonio (Ibiza), Puerto de Andraitx, Puerto de Pollensa and Porto Colom (Mallorca), around Cabrera, and Mahón (Menorca). They are somewhat smaller than herring gulls, and have a large red beak with black tip and dark legs. Viewed from below in flight, the wingtips appear considerably blacker than those of a herring gull. The cry is a nasal 'gee-ow'. Herring gulls are common (though with yellow legs rather than the pink of their northern relatives), together with shearwaters and many land birds.

Poppies and daisies carpeting the earth in spring.
SE Mallorca   *GW*

An abundance of wildlife lives in the forests, here near Sóller   *Graham Hutt*

Birds of prey such as osprey and both species of peregrine and the very rare Eleanora's falcon favour the more wild and rocky stretches, including parts of Mallorca's N coast and that of the Cabrera group. Several species of owl, eagles, hawks and kites and the rare black vulture can be seen on the Formentor peninsula ridges.

The Albufera Nature Reserve, 4km S of Alcudia, is home to many rare waders and other water birds; a visit is recommended (and it is free!).

The publication *Essential Mallorca, Ibiza and Menorca* includes a particularly interesting section entitled 'Countryside and Wildlife on the Balearic Islands', detailing bird migration as well as the flora and fauna of the various habitats.

Animals

You can see sheep, goats, rabbits and horses throughout the islands. A rare frog-ferret can be found only on Formentor, Mallorca. Several different species of lizard abound on the islands, some being rare or none existent elsewhere.

Marine life

Several parts of the islands have been declared nature reserves and fishing is not permitted in those areas. This has done a lot to preserve fish stocks. Tuna and dolphins are often seen, along with grouper and sunfish.

NAVIGATIONAL INFORMATION

Buoyage

Buoys in the Balearics adhere to the IALA A system, based on the direction of the main flood tide. Yellow-topped black or red rusty buoys some 500m offshore mark raw sewage outlets.

Yellow or white buoys in line mark the seaward side of areas reserved for swimming. Narrow lanes for water-skiing and sailboarding, also buoyed, may lead out from the shore.

Harbour traffic signals

Traffic signals are rare, and in any case are designed for commercial traffic and seldom apply to yachts except in Ciudadela where everyone, including pleasure craft, must comply with the signals.

Storm signals

The signal stations at major ports and harbours may show storm signals, but many do not. With minor exceptions they are similar to the International System of Visual Storm Warnings.

Lights

The four-figure international numbering system has been used to identify lights in the text and on plans, the Mediterranean falling into Group E. As each light has its own number, correcting from *Notices to Mariners* or the annual *List of Lights and Fog Signals*, whether in Spanish or English, is straightforward.

Positions correspond to the largest-scale British Admiralty chart of the area currently available. All bearings are given from seaward and refer to true N. Where a visibility sector is stated this is always expressed in a clockwise direction.

Harbour lights, which in the Islas Baleares adhere to the IALA A system, are normally listed in the order in which they become relevant upon approach and entry.

Radio beacons

Many radio beacons are no longer maintained. Since the accuracy of GPS – even given the cautions below – is well above that which can be derived from radio beacons, this information is no longer included.

Depths around harbour entrances

Depths where known are shown on the harbour plans. It should be noted, however, that these can and do change, especially following onshore gales and if harbour entrances are open towards the prevailing wind sector. It also applies near rivers. Although most ports and harbours are dredged, there is no certainty about the depth to which dredging has taken place or when it was last done. Always proceed with caution, paying attention to the depth sounder on entry to any harbour.

Caution: important note on waypoints and location coordinates

Waypoints have been added in this edition to assist with passage planning and harbour approach. These should always be treated with caution.

The World Geodetic System 1984 is now the standard datum for all new charts and is used for all coordinates throughout this volume. Note, however, that many charts are in use with various datum systems. Ensure your GPS receiver is set to whatever datum the chart is using, or apply the appropriate correction as stated on the chart.

Positions given in the text and on plans are intended purely as an aid to locating the place in question on the chart.

Waypoint placements

Waypoints are named by the nearest charted point – usually a headland, harbour or *cala*. The coordinate given is usually located at least half a mile off the named point to act as a clearing coordinate or an approach coordinate.

Magnetic variation

Magnetic variation throughout the Balearics is now less than 001°W and decreasing further.

Charts

Current British Admiralty information is mostly obtained from Spanish sources. The Spanish Hydrographic Office re-issues and corrects its charts periodically, and issues weekly *Notices to Mariners*. Corrections are repeated by the British Admiralty, generally some months later. Spanish charts tend to be short on compass roses, so carry a chart plotter or rule which incorporates a protractor.

Before departure

Spanish charts can be obtained through certain British agents, notably

Imray Laurie Norie & Wilson Ltd, Wych House, The Broadway, St Ives, Cambs PE27 5BT
☎ +44 (0)1480 462114 *Fax* +44 (0)1480 496109
Email orders@imray.com

Orders can be made direct from

Instituto Hidrográfico de la Marina, Tolosa Latour 1, DP 11007 Cádiz ☎ +34 956 59 94 12 *Fax* +34 956 25 85 84
Suisca SL, Avda Blas, Infante, Centro Blas Infante Local 1,11201 Algeciras, Spain ☎ +34 902 22 00 7 *Fax* +34 902 22 00 08 *Email* admiraltycharts@suiscasl.com

In Spain and Islas Baleares

The only British Admiralty chart agent in the Islas Baleares is

Rapid Transit Service SL, Network Yacht Team, Edificio Torremar, Paseo Marítimo, 44 – 07015, Palma de Mallorca ☎ 971 40 12 10 *Fax* 40 45 11
Email rts@rapidtrans.com

In Mallorca, Spanish charts are stocked by

Libreria Fondevila, C/Costa de las Pols 18 Palma
☎ 971 72 56 16 *Fax* 971 71 33 26
Email pedidos@www.libfondevila.com
Casa del Mapa, Empresa Munic Informatica SA, Joan Maragall No 3, Palma ☎ 971 466061 *Fax* 971 77 16 16
Valnautica SL, Miquel Santadreu 10, Palma ☎ 971 46 49 90 *Fax* 971 46 54 22

In Ibiza, Spanish charts of the islands are held by

Valnautica SL, Ibinave, Travesia del Mar, s/n, local 2, San Antonio ☎ 971 34 52 51 *Fax* 971 34 67 32
Email ibinave@wanadoo.es

There is currently no approved Spanish chart stockist in Menorca.

Listing of a chart under both *Approach* and *Harbour* headings normally implies that a large-scale harbour plan appears as an insert on a smaller-scale approach chart. A complete list of available charts is included in the *Appendix*.

Pilot books

Details of principal harbours and some interesting background information appear in the British Admiralty Hydrographic Department's *Mediterranean Pilot Vol 1* (NP 45), updated and reissued in mid 2005. Harbour descriptions are also to be found in *Guia del Navegante – La Costa de España y el Algarve* (PubliNáutic Rilnvest SL) written in colloquial English with a Spanish translation. Published annually, it carries many potentially useful advertisements for marine-related businesses.

For French speakers, *Votre Livre de Bord – Méditerranée* (Bloc Marine) and *Les Guides Nautiques-Baléares* (Edition Eskis) may be helpful. In German there are *Spanische Gewässer, Lissabon bis Golfe du Lion* (Delius Klasing), *Die Baleares* (Edition Maritim) and others, though possibly out of date in some aspects. See *Appendix* for further details.

Presentation of information

Chart information

Much of the navigational information – lights, buoys, etc. – is better conveyed in the plans than by text. The text information has therefore been moved to the *Appendix* for those who want it.

Charts are the same for many adjacent ports. To avoid repeated lists of the same information, chart lists are given in the *Appendix* both by name and on island plans showing areas covered. Included are British Admiralty charts and those of the Spanish and French Hydrographic authorities. Imray M3 also covers the Balearic Islands.

Chart spellings, nomenclature and language

Charts and pilots are inconsistent in their spellings. Names appear in Castilliano, French, Catalan and English, often mixed or transliterated on the same chart.

An attempt has been made to standardise spellings to appear in Castilliano Spanish form where possible – the spelling normally used on British Admiralty charts – with local alternatives in brackets. Where there is no Castilliano form, the local name is used.

Many enterprises, including marinas, use different nomenclature to describe themselves. So, 'Puerto, Puerta and Port' can all be found along with 'Marina'. Since these are commercially registered names, these have been used. Many marine commercial enterprises are not quite what they seem. Several 'Marinas' are no more than a pontoon or two, with few facilities other than water and electricity. Some open beaches or *calas* (bays or coves) are also titled harbour, puerto or even sometimes, marina. To avoid confusion, since these are official names, they are named likewise here regardless of what they offer.

Words used to describe nautical locations are also variable, depending on which chart is used and even within the same chart. A cape may be called a 'point, punto, punta, pta, cabo, c', etc. As with island, which may be isl, isla, isloto, islota, the title used is as per the chart.

Information layout

Port information begins at the relevant capital, Palma, Puerto de Ibiza and Mahón, and moves in a clockwise direction around the island. With excellent international airports located close to these ports, this will be a natural starting point for the many who charter from, or keep their yachts in the islands.

Waypoints are noted in the text as they appear.

Harbour information

1. Co-ordinates of ports are usually taken from about midway in the entrance and given under *Location*. These should not be taken as waypoints.
2. Description of lights is sometimes changed from the *Admiralty List of Lights* if their description is not clear or is simply incorrect.
3. When two charts are listed for a port the first one is to scale (1:300,000) and the second to scale (1:60,000).
4. Some Admiralty charts give the tides as 'not exceeding 0.6m.' In practice the tides are usually less and are omitted.
5. Prices for harbour dues and hauling out, etc. are usually available on websites. Where known, web addresses are included.
6. Bearings are true and from seaward.
7. Depths are in metres.

PLANNING YOUR CRUISE

Time zone

Spain keeps Standard European Time (UT+1), advanced one hour in summer to UT+2 hours. Changeover dates are now standardised with the rest of the EU as the last weekends in March and October respectively.

Budgeting and finance

Though the islands are not cheap if harbours and marinas are used, most anchorages are free and cheap eating places can be found everywhere ashore. A Spanish custom, written into law, is that every restaurant must offer a *menu del dia* (lunch at a reasonable price). This is often a substantial meal with a set menu for less than €8, including wine. This law goes back to the Franco era when the country was poor. The islands' facilities cater for cruising yachtsmen on a tight budget to super-yachts, the latter abounding in places like Palma and Puerto Portals.

Credit cards can be used almost everywhere to draw cash from banks on presentation of a passport. ATM machines are fitted in most banks. Travellers cheques are taken in most banks. Cash in Dollars, Pounds Sterling and Euros is acceptable almost everywhere in banks and in many shops. €500 notes are not always accepted.

The unit of currency is the Euro, though prices are still often displayed using both the Euro and Peseta (€1=166.396 pesetas). Major credit cards are widely accepted. Bank hours are normally 0830 to 1400, Monday to Friday, with a few also open 0830 to 1300 on Saturday.

Medical advice

Vaccinations are not required. Take along any personal medicines or enquire about generic availability abroad via the internet. Many drugs normally restricted abroad are available here without prescription.

Though not a requirement, limited health insurance can be inexpensive and many yacht insurance policies include health cover for crew, particularly in the event of injury while on board. This can include repatriation to your home country for treatment.

Minor ailments may best be treated by consulting a *farmacía*, or by contacting a doctor (recommended by the *farmacía*, marina staff, a tourist office, the police or possibly a hotel). Medicines are expensive in Spain and often have different brand names from those used in Britain.

Apart from precautions against the well recognized hazards of sunburn and stomach upsets, heat exhaustion (or heat stroke) is most likely to affect newly joined crew not yet acclimatised to Mediterranean temperatures. Carry Dioralyte or similar to counteract dehydration. Insect deterrents, including mosquito coils, can be obtained locally.

Emergency medical treatment for EU/EEA nationals.

As from 1st June 2004 the form E111 was replaced by a European Health Insurance card (EHIC) which is valid for up to 5 years. (The old E111 forms became obsolete as from 1st January 2006.) This facilitates reduced cost or free emergency medical treatment under a reciprocal agreement between the countries of the EEA which in 2005 include the 25 EU member states plus Iceland, Norway and Lichtenstein.

If you are an EU/EEA national and qualify for a card, which is free, contact your Health Department several weeks before your planned departure date. UK nationals may apply to the Department of Health (DH) by post (forms available from post office branches), or phone ☎ 0845 606 2030, but the quickest method is via the DH website below (which also contains comprehensive information about the card and how to apply for it) whereby you should receive your EHIC within 7 days:

www.dh.gov.uk/PolicyAndGuidance/
HealthAdviceForTravellers/fs/en

(Other nationalities can run a Google search: EHIC plus your country e.g. EHIC Italy.) For further enquiries, UK nationals may phone 08702 40 01 00 or from outside UK ☎ 0044 191203 55 55 or *Email* generalenquiries@cfsms.nhs.uk

For further details of Spanish medical protocols and emergency treatment access the DH web page and click on: 'getting medical treatment around the world', followed by 'EEA and Switzerland', 'Country by country guide' and then select 'Spain (including the Canaries and Balearics Islands)'.

Medical emergency telephone numbers are ☎ 112 and ☎ 061. If you have an EHIC card, be sure to inform the medical authorities of this when first contacting them for emergency treatment or you may have to pay full private rates which might not not be reimbursed.

CRUISING THE ISLANDS

The whole island chain is a suitable cruising ground, though some areas have restricted access having been declared conservation zones. The island of Cabrera is one such place where buoys have been laid which must be used in lieu of anchoring in restricted zones, as is the National Park zone in Palma Bay. These zones are noted on the plans.

Anchorages

One of the main charms of the islands is the large number of attractive *cala* anchorages, although many are often crowded in summer. A down-sun approach using eyeball navigation with a lookout on the bow, equipped with Polaroid sunglasses greatly assists anchoring. Note that most of the anchorage plans (as opposed to those of marinas and commercial harbours) are derived from observation and virtually no official data is available. Depths, shapes, distances, etc. should be taken as approximate.

A number of *calas* have more than one name, whilst popular names, such as Cala Figuera, crop up several times.

The weather in the Islas Baleares can be unexpectedly changeable and can deteriorate very quickly. During the day the sea breeze can be strong, especially if there is a valley at the head of an anchorage. Similarly a strong land breeze can flow down a valley in the early hours of the morning. If anchored near the head of a *cala* backed by a river valley, should there be a thunderstorm or heavy downpour in the hills above, take precautions against the flood of water and debris which will descend into the *cala*.

Many *cala* anchorages suffer from swell even when not open to its apparent direction. This is because swell tends to run along the coast, curling around all but the most prominent headlands into the *cala* behind. Wash from boats entering and leaving, as well as from larger vessels passing outside, adds to the discomfort. If considering a second anchor or a line ashore in order to hold the yacht into the swell, first calculate the swinging room required by yachts on single anchors should the wind change.

In a high-sided *cala*, winds are often fluky and a sudden blow, even from the land, may make departure difficult. Plans for a swift and orderly exit – possibly in darkness – should be considered. This type of anchorage should only be used in settled weather and left in good time if swell or wind rise. It is unwise to leave an anchored yacht unattended for any length of time.

Anchoring technique

Choice of anchor: many popular anchorages are thoroughly ploughed up each year by the hundreds of anchors dropped and weighed by visiting yachts.

Puerto de Antraitx anchorage   *Graham Hutt*

Others are of weed-covered compacted sand and, not without reason, the four-pronged grab is the favourite anchor of local fishermen, though difficult to stow. A fisherman-type anchor is easier to stow and a useful ally. If using a patent anchor – Danforth, CQR, Bruce, Fortress, etc. – an anchor weight (or Chum) is a worthwhile investment, encouraging the pull to remain horizontal.

Once in a suitable depth of water, if clarity permits, look for a weed-free patch to drop the anchor. In rocky or otherwise suspect areas, including those likely to contain wrecks, old chains, etc., use a sinking trip line with a float (an inviting buoy may be picked up by another yacht). Chain scope should be at least four times the maximum depth of water, for nylon scope double this. It is always worth setting the anchor by reversing slowly until it holds, but on a hard or compacted bottom this must be done very gently in order to give the anchor a chance to bite – over-enthusiasm with the throttle will cause it to skip without digging in.

Rescue and emergency services

In addition to VHF Ch 16 or 2182kHz on MW (MAYDAY or PAN PAN as appropriate) the marine emergency services can be contacted by telephone at all times on 900 202 202

The National Centre for Sea Rescue is based in Madrid but has a string of communications towers, including one at Palma, Mallorca. On-the-spot

Harbours of refuge

The following harbours and anchorages can be entered in severe weather, albeit with some difficulty. They are listed below with nearest waypoints.

Isla de Ibiza
Puerto de Ibiza	⊕2	38°53′.9N 01°26′.7E
Puerto de San Antonio	⊕10	38°58′.8N 01°17′.0E

Isla de Mallorca
Puerto de Palma	⊕31	39°33′.4N 02°38′.5E
Puerto Portals	⊕34	39°31′.5N 02°33′.8E
Puerto de Andraitx	⊕39	39°31′.6N 02°21′.4E
Puerto de Sóller	⊕44	39°48′.0N 02°41′.2E
Anchorage NW of Punta de la Avanzada, Bahía de Pollensa	⊕49	39°55′.0N 03°09′.0E
Puerto de Alcudia	⊕52	39°49′.9N 03°10′.3E
Porto Colom	⊕62	39°24′.7N 03°16′.2E
Cala Llonga	⊕63	39°22′.0N 03°14′.2E

Isla de Cabrera
Puerto de Cabrera (other than in a northwesterly gale)	⊕73	39°09′.5N 02°55′.6E

Isla de Menorca
Puerto de Mahón	⊕81	39°52′.0N 04°18′.6E
Puerto de Fornells	⊕96	40°04′.0N 04°08′.0E

Many other harbours and anchorages can safely be entered in strong offshore winds and even gales, and even more provide excellent shelter from most directions once inside.

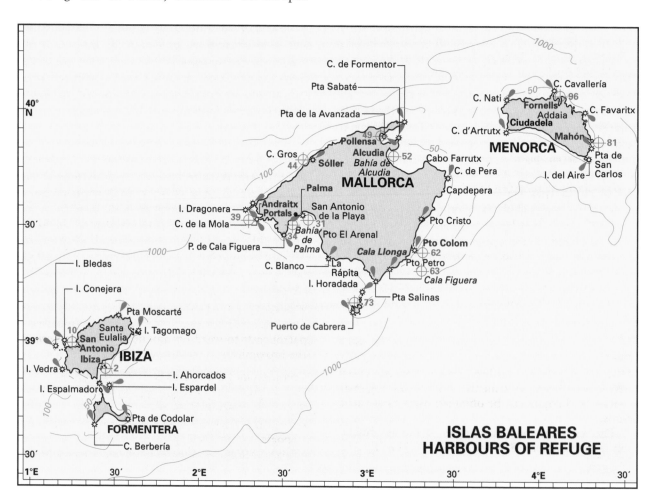

ISLAS BALEARES
HARBOURS OF REFUGE

responsibility for co-ordinating rescues lies with the Capitanías Marítimas with support from the Spanish Navy, Customs, Guardia Civil, etc. Lifeboats are stationed at some of the larger harbours but the majority do not appear to be all-weather boats.

The other emergency services can be contacted by dialling 003 for the operator and asking for *policía* (police), *bomberos* (fire service) or *Cruz Roja* (Red Cross). Alternatively the police can be contacted direct on 091.

Sea rescue/Rescate en alta mar emergency Salvamento notes

Search, rescue and salvage services at sea, as well as clean-up operations and the prevention of pollution, are undertaken by the National Society for Maritime Rescue and Safety (Salvamento y Seguridad Marítima: SASEMAR). SASEMAR is co-ordinated by joint collaboration agreements between the following bodies:

The Spanish Navy, the Air Force SAR service – the Customs Coastguard Service, the Guardia Civil Maritime Services, the regional governments, the national telephone company's Maritime Service and the Spanish Red Cross.

SASEMAR works in close collaboration with the coastal stations of each town around the coast. These are equipped with rescue launches, 15m and 20m rapid intervention craft, small sized antipollution craft and rescue helicopters.

Anyone on shore who sees a boat in difficulties (signalling by waving arms or setting off flares, smoke or fire, etc.) should report to the appropriate rescue centre by calling Freephone ☎ 900 2002 202

Persons on board a ship in distress should radio for help on VHF Ch 16 or 2182kHz on MW. The correct procedure in Spanish is as follows:

1. MAYDAY. . . MAYDAY . . . MAYDAY . . .
2. AQUI LA EMBARCACION . . . (The name of your boat repeated three times)
3. ESTA EN LA SITUACION . . . (Give your position) or ME ENCUENTRO A . . . MILLAS DE . . . (Give position as regards distance in miles or in journey time from any given point) Una (1), dos, tres, cuatro, cinco, seis, siete, ocho, nueve, diez (10))
4. NECESITO AYUDA URGENTE A CAUSA DE . . . (Indicate nature of emergency)
   fire – *tengo fuego en mi barco*
   sinking – *mi barco esta hundimiento*
   man overboard – *hombre en agua*
   medical emergency – *urgencia medical*

The rescue centres lay particular emphasis on proper preparation as the best means of avoiding dangerous situations. It is essential to have the correct equipment, to have the necessary skill and experience, and to keep informed about weather conditions.

A shipping forecast is broadcast in Spanish, every two hours from Salvamento Marítimo's regional centres, and copies can be obtained from most yacht clubs.

The telephone and fax details of the sea rescue centre in Palma are ☎ 971 728322/722011 *Fax* 971 728352.

HAZARDS

Restricted areas

Anchoring and fishing is banned in the following areas due to submerged cables: Cala de Puerto Roig, Punta Grosa and N of Isla Vedrá in Ibiza, S of Cabo de Pera on the E coast of Mallorca and off Cabo Dartuch in SW Menorca. Spanish naval vessels and submarines exercise around Isla de Cabrera and in the Bahía de Pollensa, Mallorca.

Night approaches

Approaches in darkness are often made more difficult by the plethora of background lights – fixed, flashing, occulting, interrupted – of all colours. Though there may be exceptions, this applies to nearly all harbours backed by a town of any size. Powerful shore lights make weaker navigation lights difficult to identify and mask unlit features such as exposed rocks or the line of a jetty. If at all possible, avoid closing an unknown harbour in darkness. A particular hazard is the green flashing light of the local pharmacy, which can be very confusing.

Skylines

Individual buildings on these developing islands – particularly prominent hotel blocks – do change with surprising frequency. With the greater use of waypoints and a more reliable accuracy of port coordinates, this should present no great problem these days.

Swimming areas

Many *calas* and beaches have large areas up to 50 metres from the shoreline roped and buoyed off during the summer. These areas are exclusion zones for all vessels and large penalties are extracted in fines for crossing them.

Tunny nets

In the past during summer and autumn, these nets anchored to the sea bed and up to 6 miles long, were a substantial hazard to yachts. Due to dwindling fish stocks and conservation zones, they no longer seem to be a problem around the Baleares Islands.

If found, they are normally laid inshore in depths of 15–40m but may extend several miles offshore. The outer end should be marked by a float or a boat carrying a white flag with an 'A' (in black) by day, and two red or red and white lights by night. There should also be markers along the line of the net. These nets, capable of stopping a small freighter, are expensive and are almost always accompanied by a patrol craft to ward off any unsuspecting vessels in the proximity.

Commercial fishing boats

Commercial fishing boats should be given a wide berth. They may be:
- trawling singly or in pairs with a net between the boats
- laying a long net, the top of which is supported by floats

- picking up or laying pots either singly or in groups or lines
- trolling with one or more lines out astern
- drifting, trailing nets to windward.

Do not assume they know, or will observe, the law of the sea – keep well clear on principle.

Small fishing boats

Small fishing boats, including the traditional double-ended *llauds*, either use nets or troll with lines astern and should be avoided as far as possible. At night many *lámparas* put to sea and, using powerful electric or gas lights, attract fish to the surface. When seen from a distance these lights appear to flash as the boat moves up and down in the waves and can give the appearance of a lighthouse.

Speedboats, etc.

Para-gliding, water ski-ing, speed boats and jet-skis are all popular, and are sometimes operated by unskilled and thoughtless drivers with small regard for collision risks. In theory they are not allowed to exceed 5 knots within 100m of the coast or within 250m of bathing beaches. Water-skiing is restricted to buoyed areas.

Scuba divers and swimmers

A good watch should be kept for scuba divers and swimmers, with or without snorkel equipment, particularly around harbour entrances. If accompanied by a boat, the presence of divers may be indicated either by International Code Flag A or by a square red flag with a single yellow diagonal, as commonly seen in North America and the Caribbean.

PREPARATION AND PRACTICAL TIPS

Yacht and equipment

The type of yacht suitable depends entirely on the type of sailing envisaged, from a small motor yacht for coast hopping in good weather, to more adventurous voyages around the islands and to the mainland. Do bear in mind that there are often light winds, decreasing to no wind at night, or the occasional possibility of sudden strong or gale force winds, even in summer.

A yacht properly equipped for cruising in northern waters should need little extra gear, but the following items are worth considering if not already on board.

Batteries With sun all the year round, solar panels to keep the batteries charged will be useful, especially in summer if you cannot find a berth in a marina with services available.

Radio equipment In order to receive weather forecasts and navigational warnings from Coast Radio Stations, a radio capable of receiving short and medium wave Single Sideband (SSB) transmissions will be needed. Do not make the mistake of buying a radio capable only of receiving the AM transmissions broadcast by national radio stations, or assume that SSB is only applicable to transmitting radio tranceivers.

Most SSB receivers are capable of receiving either Upper Side Band (USB) or Lower Side Band (LSB) at the flick of a switch. Which band to use is determined by the frequency in use, as promulgated by international law and published by the UK Maritime Communications Agency. The UK Maritime Mobile Net covering the Eastern Atlantic and Mediterranean uses USB, and it is not necessary to have any licence to listen in. All Coast Radio Stations broadcast on SSB – whether on USB or LSB should be easy to determine by trial and error.

Digital tuning is very desirable, and the radio should be capable of resolving tuning to a minimum of 1kHz and preferably to 0.1kHz. Several companies (including Sony, Grundig and Roberts) market suitable SSB receivers in the UK via high street retailers and marine outlets. ICOM and Yaesu make more expensive marine receivers.

Ventilation Modern yachts are, as a rule, better ventilated than their older sisters though seldom better insulated. Consider adding an opening hatch in the main cabin, if not already fitted, and ideally another over the galley. A wind scoop for the forehatch helps increase the draught, particularly if the open hatch is not forward facing.

Awnings An awning covering at least the cockpit provides shade and protection for the crew, while an even better combination is a bimini which can be kept rigged whilst sailing, plus a larger 'harbour' awning, preferably at boom height or above and extending forward to the mast.

Cockpit tables It is pleasant to eat in the cockpit, particularly while at anchor. If nothing else can be arranged, a small folding table is an advantage.

Refrigerator/ice-box If a refrigerator is not fitted it may be possible to build in an ice-box (a plastic picnic coolbox is a poor substitute), but this will be useless without adequate insulation. An ice-box designed for northern climes will almost certainly benefit from extra insulation, if this can be fitted – 100mm (4in) is a desirable minimum, 150mm (6in) even better. A drain is also essential.

If a refrigerator is fitted but electricity precious, placing ice inside will help minimise battery drain.

Mosquito nets Some advocate fitting screens to all openings leading below. Others find this inconvenient, relying instead on mosquito coils and other insecticides and repellents. For some reason mosquitoes generally seem to bother new arrivals more than old hands, and anchoring well out will often decrease the problem.

Water A large extra water container or two should be carried in summer in case harbours are unable to offer a berth. Low cost watermakers are now available and could be considered.

Hose At least 25 metres. Standpipes tend to have bayonet couplings of a type unavailable in the UK so purchase them on arrival. Plenty of 5- or 10-litre plastic carriers will also be useful.

Deck shower If no shower is fitted below, a black plastic bag or even a bucket of water heats very quickly when hung in the rigging. (At least one proprietary model is available in the UK).

Communications

The GSM mobile phone system often functions several miles out to sea – particularly using one of the older types of handset – providing a link to the world even some miles offshore. With a computer interface, this can also provide Internet and email facilities. Ensure that the International Roaming facility is activated for use abroad. GSM call rates are usually cheaper than using local hotel phones.

Carry

Tools and equipment to hook up to continental-type electrical fittings. A selection of fittings and jubilee clips.

All charts, maps, guidebooks, and a Spanish dictionary.

Fenders and Warps

In marinas, mooring is usually bows or stern-to a quay or pontoon with a line tailed from the quay, so good clean fenders are required as it is often a tight squeeze.

PREPARATION – THE CREW

Clothing

The sun's rays at sea, especially in summer, are easy to underestimate and present a serious risk of burning. Direct sunlight, reflected light from the sea combined with salt air and wind, constitute a hazard to be avoided.

Lightweight, patterned cotton clothing is handy in this context – it washes and dries easily and the pattern camouflages the creases! Non-absorbent synthetic materials are best avoided. Until a good tan has been built up it may be wise to wear a T-shirt when swimming, while shoes give necessary protection against sea-urchin spines.

Some kind of headgear, preferably with a wide brim, is essential. A genuine Montecristi hat can be rolled up, shoved in a pocket and doesn't mind getting wet (they come from Ecuador, not Panama, which has usurped the name). A retaining string, tied either to clothing or around the neck, is a wise precaution whilst on the water.

Footwear at sea is a contentious subject. Many experienced cruisers habitually sail barefoot, but while this may be acceptable on a familiar vessel it would be courting injury on a less intimately known deck. In either case, proper sailing shoes should always be worn for harbour work or anchor handling. Decks (especially teak decks) may become

unexpectedly hot and very painful to unprotected feet. If wearing sandals ashore, the upper part of the foot is a prime area for sunburn.

Winters can be wet and cold, and foul weather gear as well as warm sweaters, etc. will be needed. Even night sailing in summer can be unexpectedly cold due to precipitation.

Shore-going clothes should be on a par with what one might wear at home – beachwear is not usually acceptable in restaurants and yacht clubs.

AVAILABILITY OF SUPPLIES AND PROVISIONS

Fuel

Diesel (*gasoleo*, *gasoil* or simply *diesel*) is available in most marinas and yacht harbours in the Islas Baleares. A limited number also have a pump for petrol (*gasolina*). *Petróleo* is paraffin (kerosene). Credit cards are widely, but not universally, accepted – if in doubt, check before filling.

A concession for fishing boats that benefited yachts, was the provision of Gasoleo B. This carried a lower rate of tax making it considerably cheaper than the usual Gasoleo A. However, this tax exemption is being phased out to comply with EC tax laws.

Water

In many places drinking water (*agua potable*) is scarce and becoming increasingly more so each year. It is available at every berth, but expect to pay for it, particularly if supplied by hose, and do not wash sails and decks before checking that it is acceptable to do so. Many marinas insist on hoses being connected to a 'pistol' rather than being open-ended. In those harbours where a piped supply is not available for yachts a public tap can often be found.

Water quality in Mallorca and Menorca is generally good, less so in Ibiza, particularly at San Antonio. However, water quality throughout all the islands varies from year to year. Locals nearly always drink bottled water, not so much because the *agua potable* is contaminated, but because it tastes better. Always check verbally and taste for salinity or over-chlorination before topping up tanks – the ideal is to have a tank specifically reserved for drinking water, with other tanks for general use. Failing this, earmark some cans for the purpose, but stow them in a dark locker to discourage algae. As most of the water in the islands is desalinated it can be quite corrosive, especially to stainless steel tanks and pumps, and a pre-tank in-line filter is highly recommended.

Bottled water is readily available in bars and supermarkets.

Ice

Block ice for an icebox is widely obtainable – use the largest blocks that will fit – while chemical ice is sometimes available in blocks measuring 100 x 20 x

20cms. The latter must not be used in drinks, the former only after close inspection. Cube or 'small' ice is widely obtainable and generally of drinks quality, particularly if bought in a sealed bag. An increasing number of marinas and yacht clubs now have ice machines.

Gas

Camping Gaz is widely available from marinas, supermarkets or *ferreterias* (ironmongers); the 1.9kg bottles are identical to those in the UK. Its availability is therefore not usually listed in the text under individual harbour facilities.

REPSOL/CAMPSOL depots in Mallorca will not refill any UK (or any other country's) Calor Gas bottles even with a current test certificate. It is therefore essential to carry the appropriate regulator and fittings to permit the use of Camping Gaz bottles. Yachts fitted for propane systems should certainly follow this course. If in doubt, consult the Calor Gas Boating Industry Liaison Officer ☎ +44 (0)1753 540000 *Fax* +44 (0)1753 586037.

Electricity

It is a good idea to be self-sufficient with solar panels and an inverter if planning to anchor a lot, or be prepared to run your engine on a regular basis.

Electricity is provided at every marina berth, the standard being 220V, 50Hz, generally via a two-pin socket for which an adapter will be needed. Some marinas provide 380V supplies to berths for yachts over 20m. If using 110V 60Hz equipment seek advice – cycles may be a greater problem than volts for some equipment, particularly those using motors. Even if the yacht is not wired for mains, a 25m length of cable and a trickle charger may be useful.

PROVISIONS

Food and drink

There are many well stocked stores, supermarkets and hypermarkets in the larger towns and cities and it may be worth doing the occasional major stock-up by taxi. Conversely, some isolated anchorages have quite literally nothing. As a rule, availability and choice varies in relation to the size of the town. Even the smallest has something and most older settlements (though not all tourist resorts) have a traditional-style market offering excellent local produce at very reasonable prices. Alcohol is cheap by UK standards with, not surprisingly, Spanish wines and spirits of particularly good value. Shop prices generally are noticeably lower away from tourist resorts.

Most shops, other than the largest supermarkets, close for siesta between 1400 and 1700 and remain closed on Sunday, though some smaller food shops do open on Sunday mornings. In larger towns the produce market may operate from 0800 to 1400, Monday to Saturday; in smaller towns it is more often a weekly affair.

Local gastronomic specialities include *ensaimadas*, flat spirals of flaky pastry ranging from one-person size to family-size – nearly two feet across! Everyone is familiar with *mahonésa* (mayonnaise), but possibly not with its cousin *aïoli* or *alioli*, a more powerful version made with garlic. An excellent way to sample unfamiliar delicacies in small portions is in the form of bar snacks or tapas, once served gratis but now almost invariably charged for, sometimes heavily.

Mallorca produces some local wines, including Binisalem and Felanitx, but most wine is imported from the mainland. Each island has its own apéritifs and liqueurs. Ibiza produces Hierbas, Rumaniseta and La Frigola, all made from herbs. Mallorca makes Palo from carob nuts, and Menorca specialises in gin: Bertram and Lord Nelson are the best known brands and are 70° proof.

EATING OUT

Every marina, port, harbour, village and even most semi-deserted bays have eating facilities too numerous to mention. In summer, *chiringhitos* spring up on every beach, offering fresh fish at decent prices.

Do consult some of the excellent guidebooks on the Balearics for more information.

HARBOURS AND MARINAS

The rapid growth of marinas in the 1990s was suddenly halted in 2000 because of environmental concerns. There are nearly 30,000 yacht berths in the islands and around 36,000 boats are cruising there in summer. During July and August, it is almost impossible to find a mooring in any of the harbours. The fact is that there are many more local yachts than berths available. Thus it is essential to radio (VHF Ch 09) or phone before arrival at a port to check if a berth may be available.

Future plans for new marinas or extensions

It is unlikely that any further major developments or new marinas will be permitted in the foreseeable future, though works are going on in several places to improve existing facilities.

Berthing

Due to the vast numbers of yachts and limited space available, berthing stern-to the quays and pontoons is normal (and allows easiest shore access). For greater privacy berth bow-to, which has the added advantage of keeping the rudder away from possible underwater obstructions near the quay and making the approach a much easier manoeuvre. An anchor may occasionally be needed, but more often a bow (or stern) line will be provided, usually via a lazyline to the pontoon, though sometimes buoyed. This line may be both heavy and dirty and gloves will be useful. Either way, have plenty of fenders out and lines ready.

Most cruising skippers will have acquired some expertise at this manoeuvre before reaching the Islas Baleares, but if taking over a chartered or otherwise unfamiliar yacht it would be wise both to check handling characteristics and talk the manoeuvre through with the crew before attempting to enter a narrow berth. Detailed instructions regarding Mediterranean mooring techniques will be found in Imray's *Mediterranean Almanac*.

Mooring lines Surge in harbours is not uncommon and mooring lines must be both long and strong. It is sometimes useful to have a loop of chain made up at the shore end to slip over bollards, though in other places rings are in use. Carry plenty of mooring lines, especially if the boat is to be left unattended for any length of time.

Gangplanks If a gangplank is not already part of the boat's equipment, a builder's scaffolding plank, with a couple of holes drilled at either end to take lines, serves well. As it is cheap and easily replaced it can also be used outside fenders to deal with an awkward lie or ward off an oily quay. A short ladder may also have its uses, particularly if berthing bow-to.

Moorings

As stated on page 17, in order to capitalise on cash to be earned from anchoring space, many marinas and harbours are laying moorings in the vicinity. A daily charge is made for their use. Some are well served with rubbish collection and a water-taxi service. Anchoring in these areas is prohibited. Due to restrictions in extending marinas, it is likely that most areas around ports will have moorings laid.

All other moorings are privately owned and if one is used it will have to be vacated should the owner return. There are often no markings to give any indication as to the weight and strength of moorings so they should be used with caution.

Yacht clubs

Most harbours of any size support at least one *club náutico*. However, the grander ones in particular are basically social clubs – often with tennis courts, swimming pools and other facilities – and may not welcome the crews of visiting yachts. There is usually both a marina and a club, and unless there are special circumstances, the first option for a visitor is the marina. That said, many *club náutico*s have pleasant bars and excellent restaurants which appear to be open to all, while a few are notably helpful and friendly to visitors. The standard of dress and behaviour often appears to be somewhat more formal than that expected in a similar club in Britain.

Harbour charges

All harbours and marinas charge, at a scale which varies from season to season and year to year: sometimes even from day to day! Several marinas admit that prices increase if a regatta or some special event is in progress. July and August are normally considered to be 'high season', with some harbours citing May, June and September as 'mid-season' while others go directly to 'low-season' rates. During the low season, large discounts can often be negotiated, especially if paying in advance and with cash.

High-season charges vary from €35 to €200 per day for a 15m yacht and €20 to €70 for a 10m yacht but with berths at a premium in the islands, these figures may be greatly exceeded in some places. A banding system was used in the past to indicate prices, but it is so inaccurate and of little practical use, that it is now omitted. Many harbours and marinas have a website which gives up-to-date information of facilities, availability and prices. Use the web addresses supplied, 'Google' the name, or phone the marina for up-to-date information.

Public quays and club moorings

Many harbours have public quays, buoys or pontoons, administered by the port authority, rather than by the local *club náutico*. These are usually (though not always) charged at a lower rate. Anchoring is now prohibited or actively discouraged in all commercial (and some smaller) harbours. Where it is allowed, a charge will almost always be made.

Payment

Nearly all harbours accept payment by major credit cards (Amex, Visa, etc.) but where this is not the case it will be noted in the text. Multihulls are frequently charged up to 50% more than monohulls and some places are now charging by the (LOA x Beam) factor.

Large yachts

Many harbours in the Islas Baleares are too small, or too shallow for a large yacht, which must anchor outside whilst its crew visit the harbour by tender. It is essential that the skipper of such a yacht wishing to enter telephones or radios the harbour authorities well in advance to reserve a berth (if available) and receive necessary instructions.

Laying up

Laying up either afloat or ashore is possible at most marinas, though a few have no hard standing. Facilities and services provided vary considerably, as does the cost, and it is worth seeking local advice as to the quality of the services provided and the security of the berth or hard standing concerned.

The northwesterly *tramontana* (*mestral*) can be frequent and severe in winter and early spring, and this should be borne in mind when selecting the area and site to lay up. Yachts with wooden decks and varnished brightwork will need protection from the winter sun, and ideally arrangements should be made for the former to be hosed down each evening or covered with a tarpaulin. It may well prove cheaper to return to mainland Spain rather than to lay up in the Islas Baleares.

INTRODUCTION

Repairs and chandlery

Many marinas are equipped to handle all aspects of yacht maintenance from laying up to changing a washer. Nearly all have travel-hoists and the larger marinas have specialist facilities – GRP work, electronics, sailmaking, stainless welding, etc. Charges may differ widely so, if possible, shop around.

The best-equipped chandleries will be found near the larger marinas, where they may equal anything to be found in the UK (though generally with higher prices). Smaller harbours or marinas are often without a chandlery, though some requirements may be found in the associated town. Basic items can sometimes be found in *ferreterias* (ironmongers).

Chartering

Chartering is a well-regulated business in the Islas Baleares with somewhat different regulations to those applied in mainland Spain: notably that there is no blanket restriction on foreign-owned and/or skippered vessels applying for charter authorisation. However the necessary paperwork is time-consuming and involved. See *Appendix* for further information.

Security

Crime afloat is not a major problem in most areas, and regrettably much of the theft which does occur can be laid at the door of other yachtsmen. It is sensible to take much the same precautions as at home: lock up before leaving the yacht, padlock the outboard to the dinghy, and secure the dinghy (particularly if an inflatable) with chain or wire rather than line. Folding bicycles are particularly vulnerable to theft, and should be chained up when not in use, even when on deck.

Ashore, the situation in the big towns is certainly no worse than in the UK, and providing common sense is applied to matters such as how handbags are carried, where not to go after the bars close, etc. there should be no problems.

The officials most likely to be seen are the *Guardia Civil*, who wear olive green uniforms and deal with immigration as well as more ordinary police work, the *Aduana* (customs) in navy blue uniforms, and the *Policía*, also in blue uniforms, who deal with traffic and civil disturbances rather than criminal matters.

FORMALITIES AND DOCUMENTATION

Formalities vary from place to place, but in general, if coming from another EC port, no formalities are expected other than checking in with the marina and officials, who are generally uninterested. If a vessel is entering from a non-EC country, or carrying non-EC nationals onboard, it is necessary to inform the local authorities, clear customs and complete immigration formalities when first entering the islands. Passports and the ship's registration papers will be required. A certificate of competence (or equivalent) and evidence of VAT status may also be requested.

Other documents sometimes requested are a crew list with passport details, the radio licence and evidence of insurance. Subsequently, at other ports, clearance need not be sought but the *Guardia Civil* (military police) may wish to see papers, particularly passports. Marina officials often ask to see yacht registration documents and the skipper's passport, and sometimes evidence of insurance.

Flag etiquette

A yacht in commission in foreign waters is legally required to fly her national maritime flag, normally the Red Ensign for a British yacht. If a special club ensign is displayed, it must be accompanied by the correct burgee. The courtesy flag of the country visited should be flown from the starboard signal halliard – note that in Spain, as in the UK, the maritime ensign and national flags are not the same. The Islas Baleares have their own regional flags which may be flown below the national courtesy flag if desired.

Under EU regulations, EU-registered vessels are not required to fly the Q flag on first arrival unless they have non-EU nationals or dutiable goods aboard. Nevertheless, clearance should be sought either by a visit to or from officials or through the offices of the larger marinas or yacht clubs.

Visas

As Spain is a member of the European Union, other EU nationals may now stay indefinitely. The requirement for a residence permit or visa was officially abolished as of 1 May 2006. However, some local authorities seem unaware of the changes and doubts have been raised about the working of the directive by some authorities.

Non-EU nationals wishing to remain in Spain may apply for a *permiso de residencia* and subsequent 90-day extensions.

With the high rate of illegal immigration and smuggling taking place throughout the Mediterranean, all yachts are now tracked by satellite. On entering harbour, a form is completed which often serves as the entry formality, with no officials involved.

Pet 'passports', along with up-to-date health check documents, are required but are rarely asked for.

Certificate of Competence

Like the pet 'passport', a Certificate of Competence, though a requirement by skippers of all Spanish vessels, is rarely asked of foreign visitors. Production of the RYA Yachtmaster's certificate is sufficient in most marinas for the form-filling. Note, however, that things are tightening up, principally as a result of the many jet-ski accidents, which has drawn attention to incompetent and unlicensed skippers of pleasure craft. The RYA will issue an internationally recognised Certificate of Competence on production of a Yachtmaster's certificate.

1. Given below is a transcription of a statement made by the Counsellor for Transport at the Spanish Embassy,

London in March 1996, but which is still current advice (2006). It is directed towards citizens of the UK but doubtless the principles apply to other EU citizens. One implication is that in a particular circumstance (paragraph 2a below) a UK citizen does not need a Certificate of Competence during the first 90 days of his visit.

2. a. British citizens visiting Spain in charge of a UK registered pleasure boat flying the UK flag need only fulfil UK law.
    b. British citizens visiting Spain in charge of a Spanish registered pleasure boat flying the Spanish flag have one of two options:
    i. To obtain a Certificate of Competence issued by the Spanish authorities. See *Normas reguladores para la obtención de titulos para el gobierno de embarcaciones de recreo* issued by the Ministerio de Obras Publicas, Transportes y Medio Ambiente.
    ii. To have the Spanish equivalent of a UK certificate issued. The following are used by the Spanish Maritime Administration:
    Yachtmaster Ocean: *Capitan de Yate*
    Yachtmaster Offshore: *Patron de Yate de altura*
    Coastal Skipper: *Patron de Yate*
    Day Skipper: *Patron de Yate embarcaciones de recreo*
    Helmsman Overseas:* *Patron de embarcaciones de recreo restringido a motor*
    *The Spanish authorities have been informed that this certificate has been replaced by the International Certificate of Competence.

3. The catch to para 2(a) above is that, in common with other EU citizens, after 90 days, a UK citizen is technically no longer a visitor, must apply for a *permiso de residencia* and must equip his boat to Spanish rules and licensing requirements.
    In fact, many authorities refuse to grant residence to those living afloat because they are considered temporary. By the same token, the requirement for a British skipper in charge of a UK-registered pleasure boat flying the UK flag to carry a Certificate of Competence after their first 90 days in Spanish waters, also appears to be waived.

4. The RYA suggests the following technique to obtain an equivalent Spanish certificate:
    a. Obtain two photocopies of your passport
    b. Have them notarised by a Spanish notary
    c. Obtain a copy of the UK Certificate of Competence and send it to the Consular Department, The Foreign and Commonwealth Office, King Charles Street, London SW1A 2AH, with a request that it be stamped with the Hague Stamp (this apparently validates the document). The FCO will probably charge a fee so it would be best to call the office first ☎ 020 7008 1500/0210 8438 www.fco.gov.uk
    d. Have the stamped copy notarised by a UK notary
    e. Send the lot to the Spanish Merchant Marine for the issue of the Spanish equivalent.

It may be both quicker and easier to take the Spanish examination!

VAT on yachts

Value Added Tax IVA – (*Impuesto sobre el valor añadido*), subject to certain exceptions, is levied at 16% of the value of the vessel unless it can be shown to have been paid or has an exemption certificate. To qualify for exemption, the vessel must have been launched before 1st January 1985 and have been in EU waters on 31st December 1992 (or, in the case of Austrian, Finnish and Swedish waters, 31 December 1994), with documents to verify these facts. A Single Administrative Document (SAD) certificate is issued if these credentials are ascertained.

Note that for VAT purposes the Canaries, Gibraltar, the Channel Islands and the Isle of Man are outside the EU fiscal area. See *Temporary import and laying up* below.

Any boat purchased outside the EU by an EU resident is liable for VAT on import to the EU.

EU owners of boats built within the EU, exported by them and which were outside EU fiscal waters at the cut-off date, may be entitled to Returned Goods Relief. In the latter case, HM Customs and Excise may be able to issue a 'tax opinion letter'. It is not, however, possible to obtain it from the UK authorities if the vessel is outside UK waters. All the rules change when a yacht is used commercially, most commonly for chartering.

Contact HM Customs & Excise ☎ 0845 010 9000 or +44 208929 0152 from outside UK.
http://customs.hmrc.gov.uk

A boat registered outside the EU may stay in an EU port for up to six months before VAT must be paid, although this time period can often be extended.

All the above rules are open to differing interpretations and flexibility and the practices vary considerably from one country to another, and often from one harbour to another in Spanish waters. Generally, Spanish authorities are pragmatic and more concerned to retain the goodwill of the visiting yachting community, than to frighten them away by imposing once-only taxes.

Temporary import and laying up

A VAT paid or exempt yacht should apply for a *permiso aduanero* on arrival in Spanish waters. This is valid for twelve months and renewable annually, allowing for an almost indefinite stay. As well as establishing the status of a foreign-owned vessel, possession of a *permiso aduanero* should enable the owner to import equipment and spares from other EU countries free of duty.

A boat registered outside the EU fiscal area on which VAT has not been paid may be temporarily imported into the EU for a period not exceeding six months in any twelve before VAT is payable. This period may sometimes be extended by prior agreement with the local customs authorities (for instance, some do not count time laid up as part of the six months). While in EU waters the vessel may only be used by its owner, and may not be chartered or even lent to another person, on pain of paying VAT but see *Appendix* for further details. If kept in the EU longer than six months the vessel becomes liable for VAT, but there are huge differences in the way the rules are applied from one harbour to the next and in different countries, so check the local situation on arrival.

Insurance

Many marinas require vessels to have insurance cover, though third party only is usually all that is required. Many UK companies are willing to extend home waters cover to the Mediterranean, sometimes excluding certain areas.

On 1 July 1999 a requirement was introduced for all foreign yachts sailing in Spanish waters to carry third party insurance cover of at least £1,000,000 with all the details on the correct form in Spanish. UK insurance companies are aware of this requirement, and will issue, on request, the relevant document in Spanish. All kinds of unpleasantness, from a heavy fine to confiscation of the yacht can technically result from non-compliance. The law is not enforced currently, but would probably be in the event of an accident resulting in a claim.

Light dues

A charge known as Tarifa G5 is supposedly levied on all vessels in the islands. Locally based pleasure craft pay at the rate of €5 per square metre per year (area being calculated as LOA x Beam). Visiting pleasure craft pay one tenth of that sum on arrival, which covers a ten-day period, after which it is again due. Visiting vessels of less than 7m LOA and with engines of less than 25hp make a single payment of €30 per annum. The status of a charter yacht is not clear. In practice, this levy appears seldom to be requested and it is unclear to whom it should be paid.

MARITIME REGULATIONS AND RESTRICTIONS

Speed limit

All harbours have speed limits, usually 3 knots or less. There is a blanket 5 knot speed limit along the whole coast extending 100m offshore, increasing to 250m off bathing beaches.

Buoys

Yellow (usually) buoys are placed parallel to beaches in summer to indicate swimming areas. These can extend up to 100m off the beach, but are usually much closer. Anchoring or venturing beyond these towards the beach is strictly prohibited with heavy fines levied if contravened.

Water-skiing and jet-skis

There has been an explosive increase in the use of high powered outboards for water-skiing over the past decade, accompanied by a significant increase in accidents. In most of the main ports and at some beaches it is now controlled and enquiries should be made before skiing.

It is essential to have third party insurance and, if possible, a bail bond. If bathing and water skiing areas are buoyed, yachts are excluded.

Due to the number of fatal accidents in recent years, the use of jet-skis is now prohibited without a specific license to operate one.

Cala Tuent, Mallorca *GW*

Snorkelling

Spearfishing while using a snorkel is controlled and, in some places, prohibited.

Scuba diving

Inshore scuba diving is strictly controlled and a licence is required from the Comandancia Militar de Marina. This involves a certificate of competence, a medical certificate, two passport photographs, the passport itself (for inspection), knowledge of the relevant laws and a declaration that they will be obeyed. The simplest approach is to enquire through marina staff. Any attempt to remove archaeological material from the seabed will result in serious trouble.

Garbage

It is an international offence to dump garbage at sea and, while the arrangements of local authorities may not be perfect, garbage on land should be dumped in the proper containers. Many marinas now have facilities for the removal of holding tank waste (*agua negra*) and old engine oil.

Anchoring

It is prohibited to anchor within the confines of most harbours (except in an emergency or for a short period while sorting out a berth) and many authorities extend this prohibition to the bay areas outside. See under *Moorings* on p. 17.

COMMUNICATIONS

Internet facilities

Internet cafés are located all over the islands with facilities also in many of the marinas. Modern mobile phones – especially those with GPRS access – can either connect to the internet directly, or through a computer.

Telephone and Fax

International code +34
Local code for Balearics 971

Telephone kiosks are common, both local and *teléfono internacional*, and most carry instructions in English. Both coins and phonecards (available from tobacconists) are used – most kiosks accept either. American Express and Diners Club cards can also be used in some phone boxes, though oddly enough not VISA or Access. Mobile phones work throughout the islands.

Calls to the United Kingdom begin with the prefix 0044, followed by the area code (without the initial zero) and number; calls to North America with the prefix 001, plus area code and number. It may be necessary to pause after dialling the initial 00 to await a second dialling tone. The European International Operator can be accessed on 1008 and the Worldwide International Operator on 1005.

To call a Spanish number from abroad, dial that country's international access code (00 in the UK, 011 in North America) followed by 34, plus area code and number. If dialling within Spain it should be noted that the area code forms part of the number, with no digits dropped when dialling from abroad. A number prefixed with 6 denotes a mobile phone, e.g. 608 or 609.

Mail

Letters may be sent *poste restante* to any post office (*oficina de corréos*). They should be addressed with the surname of the recipient followed by *Lista de Corréos* and the town, island and Islas Baleares. Addresses of harbours can be found on the internet using the web address given in the text. Collection is a fairly cumbersome procedure and a passport is likely to be needed. Alternatively, most marinas and some *club náutico*s will hold mail for yachts, but it is always wise to check in advance if possible. Uncollected letters are seldom returned.

Mail to and from the UK should be marked 'air mail' (*por avión*) but even so may take up to ten days, so if speed is important it may be better to arrange fax contact. Generally, mail speed in Spain is excellent, though some pockets of poor service remain. It takes much longer for mail sent locally to reach its desination than overseas mail. Post boxes are yellow, and stamps are available from tobacconists (*Estancos* or *Tabacos*) as well as post offices. Every town has a post office, so these are not listed under individual harbour facilities in the text.

Tourist offices

There is at least one tourist office in every major town or resort. They are graded as Provincial Tourist Office, one only in the Islas Baleares, at Plaça de la Reina 2, 07012 Palma de Mallorca ☎ 971 71 22 16 *Fax* 971 17 39 94 www.infomallorca.net; Insular Tourist Office, generally at the airport and well stocked with literature, maps, etc; and Municipal

Tourist Office, to be found in most towns and usually listed at www.illesbalears.es

Of the many free handouts available, the A4-sized *I'd like to see you!* series published by The Balearic Institute for the Promotion of Tourism (IBATUR) is worth seeking out. Four beautifully illustrated booklets cover the main islands, giving a smattering of history, places to visit, fiestas, local folklore, island statistics and useful telephone numbers. Excellent value!

See *Appendix* for national tourist offices abroad.

Transport and travel

International airports Information is given in each island section. The three larger islands each have an international airport, Mallorca's being one of the busiest in Europe during the holiday season. There are still some real bargains to be found amongst charter flights from the UK.
Ferries Listed under each island. Ferries run to mainland Spain, France and Italy and there are frequent inter-island ferry and hydrofoil services. The largest ferry company is Trasmediterránea with offices at Palma, Ibiza and Mahón.

Almost every community has some form of public transport, if only one *autobús* a day.
Trains Surprisingly, Mallorca boasts two railway lines – one is narrow-gauge, dating back to Victorian times, which links Palma to the town of Sóller in the N, the final connection to Puerto de Sóller being completed by vintage tram. The other line runs from Palma to Inca, about halfway to Alcudia. Both are recommended for the experience and as a means of seeing some of Mallorca's unspoilt interior.
Taxis Are easily found in the tourist resorts though less common outside them, but can always be ordered by telephone. Car hire is simple, but a full national driving licence, preferably the new one with photo, must be shown.

Embassies

See *Appendix* for listing of British and American representation in the Balearics and Spain.

The spectacular caves at Campanet are well worth a visit with 50-million-year-old stalactites and stalagmites   *GW*

INTRODUCTION

Approaches to the Islas Baleares

General

With the exception of a few inshore rocks and islands, and shallow water at the heads of bays, there is generally deep water up to the coast with few offshore dangers. The islands, by virtue of their height and the usual good visibility, can often be seen from many miles away and are well lit at night. The channels between the islands are free from obstructions, but in the strong winds that blow between Mallorca and Menorca, the sea can be rough due to a shallow and uneven bottom. The passage from the mainland to the islands presents no particular problems with the one exception of the N or NW *tramontana* or *mestral* which can be dangerous in winter and unpleasant in summer.

From the Spanish coast

From W and SW The shortest passage from mainland Spain is from Puerto de Jávea or Puerto de Denia to Puerto de San Antonio, Ibiza, at about 55 miles. Should a *tramontana* arise during the crossing it will be on the beam or the quarter and San Antonio can, if necessary, be entered under gale conditions. For a flatter approach and better protection once in harbour, it would be wise to continue around the island to Puerto de Santa Eulalia or Puerto de Ibiza.

From NW and N From the Spanish coasts between Valencia and Barcelona, a choice of islands is offered at distances of 80 miles plus. The usual route is to leave the Spanish coast near Barcelona and to sail for Puerto de Andraitx (110 miles). If the *tramontana* or *mestral* blows it will be on the stern or quarter. Puerto de Andraitx can be entered in almost any conditions. In good and settled weather Puerto de Sóller is nearer but, because the coast on either side is very dangerous, accurate navigation is vital. Note also the *Caution* on the following page.

DISTANCES BETWEEN PORTS IN NAUTICAL MILES

MALLORCA	MENORCA Ciudadela	MENORCA Fornells	MENORCA Mahón	IBIZA Ibiza	IBIZA S Antonio	FORMENTERA Puerto de Sabina
Palma	87	106	100	69	77	78
Cala Bona	32	50	49	106	115	112
Cala d'Or	47	65	61	90	99	96
Cala Figuera	66	85	79	74	84	82
Cala Gamba	85	104	98	70	78	79
Cala Nova	87	106	100	67	75	76
Cala Ratjada	25	43	44	112	121	118
Ca'n Pastilla	84	103	97	70	78	79
Ca'n Picafort	34	51	56	121	125	129
Colonia San Jordi	63	82	76	77	87	85
Colonia San Pedro	32	49	54	122	126	130
El Arenal	82	101	95	71	79	80
Bonaire	35	51	62	119	123	127
Molinar de Levante	86	105	99	69	72	78
Islote El Toro	84	108	102	60	69	69
Estanyol	70	89	83	70	80	79
Palma Nova	87	106	100	65	73	74
P. d'Alcudia	35	51	60	119	123	127
P. Andraitx	81	96	108	59	63	67
P. Pollensa	35	61	62	119	123	127
P. Sóller	56	71	83	81	85	89
Portals Vells	86	105	99	61	69	70
Portixol	86	105	99	69	77	78
Porto Colom	44	62	60	93	101	99
Porto Cristo	36	54	52	101	110	107
Porto Petro	48	66	62	89	98	95
P. de la Rapita	67	86	80	74	84	82
Sta Ponsa	92	111	105	61	69	70
Serra Nova	32	49	54	122	126	130
Ciudadela		22	33	136	147	144
Fornells			20	155	166	163
Mahón				149	160	157
Ibiza					27	11
S. Antonio						25
Puerto de Sabina						

From the French coast

Menorca is the nearest island to the French coast, being 170 miles from Port Vendres, 210 miles from Sète and Toulon and 270 miles from Nice. Probably the safest route is from the area of Cap Béar to Mahón, which can safely be entered in gale conditions. Should a *tramontana* blow it will be on the stern or quarter, and should this occur in the early part of the voyage the Spanish coast can be closed for shelter. Again, note the *Caution* below.

From the eastern Mediterranean

For yachts on passage from Sardinia, Tunisia, Malta or further E, Mahón is the obvious choice for arrival. Distances are approximately 200 miles from the W coast of Sardinia, 360 miles from Tunis and 550 from Valletta, Malta. Should a *tramontana* affect the last part of the passage it will of course be directly on the nose but the landfall will be relatively sheltered. Conversely a southerly *sirocco* will be on or aft of the beam but may give rise to poor visibility.

Caution

The two lights marking the N end of the channel between Mallorca and Menorca have similar characteristics and are easy to confuse. Cabo Formentor (Mallorca) shows Fl(4)20s while Cabo Nati (Menorca) is Fl(3+1)20s. When running towards the islands in a *tramontana*, mistaken identification could lead to a dangerous situation.

The Almudaina palace displaying splendid Arab-style architecture from a bygone era   *GW*

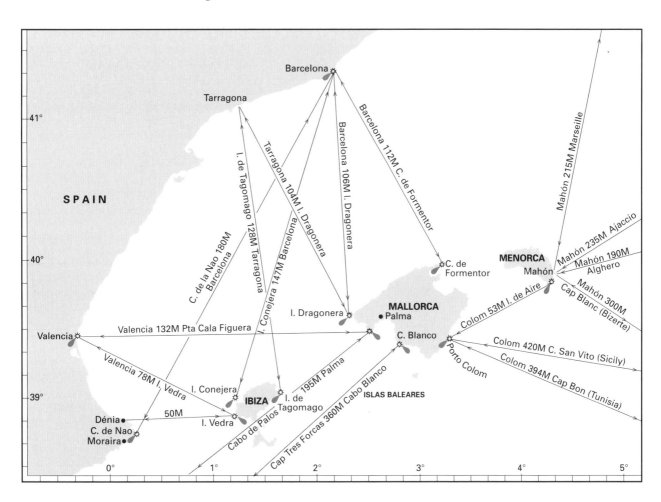

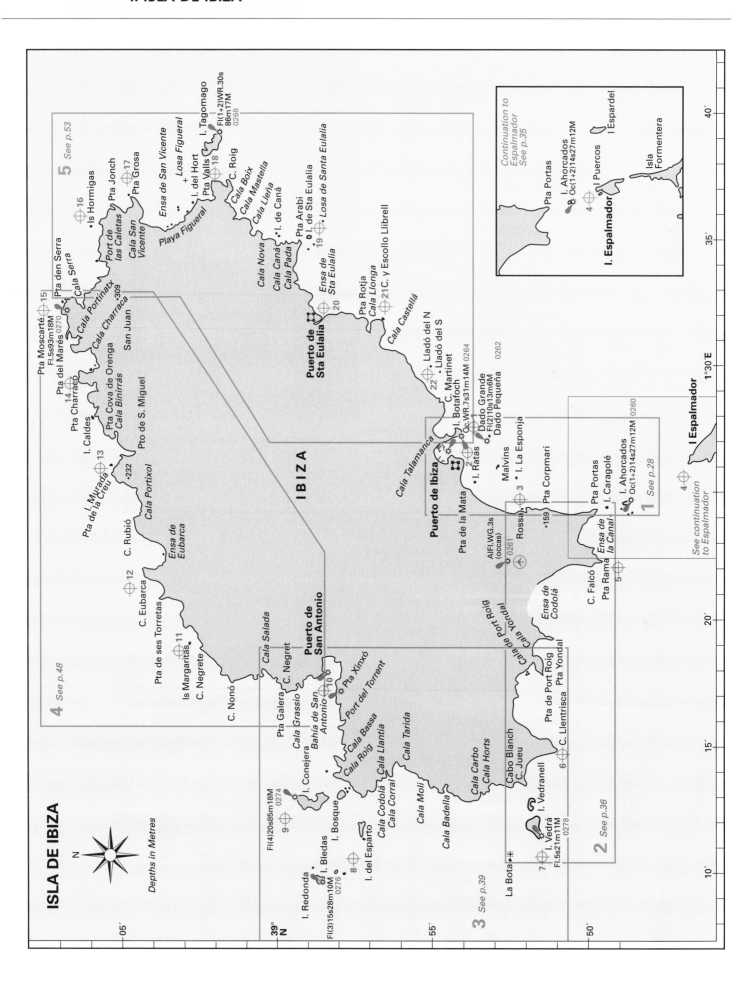

ISLA DE IBIZA

N

Depths in Metres

39°
N

See p.48 4

See p.53 5

Pta Moscarté 15
Fl.5s93m18M 0270
Pta del Marés
Pta Charraco 14
I. Caldes
Pta Cova de Orenga 13
I. Murada
Pta de la Creu
C. Rubió
C. Eubarca 12
C. Eubarca
Pta de ses Torretas
Is Margaritas 11
C. Negrete
C. Nonó

Pta den Serra
Cala Serra
Cala Portinatx
Cala Charraca 309
San Juan
Cala Binirrás
Pto de S. Miguel
Cala Portixol
Ensa de Eubarca

Is Hormigas 16
Pta Jonch
Pta Grosa 17
Ensa de San Vicente
Cala San Vicente
Port de las Caletas
Playa Figueral
Losa Figueral
I. del Hort
Pta Valls 18
Cala Boix
C. Roig
Cala Mastella
Cala Lleña
I. de Caná
Cala Nova
Cala Caná
Cala Pada

I. Tagomago Fl(1+2)WR.30s
86m17M 0268

Pta Arabi
I. de Sta Eulalia 19
Losa de Santa Eulalia
Ensa de Sta Eulalia 20
Pta Rotja
Cala Llonga
21 C. y Escollo Llibrell
Cala Castellá

Puerto de Sta Eulalia

Lladó del N
22 Lladó del S
C. Martinet
C. Botafoch
Oc.WR.7s31m14M 0264
I. Rates
Dado Grande Fl(2)10s13m6M
Dado Pequeña 0262

Cala Talamanca

Puerto de Ibiza

Pta de la Mata
2 I. La Esponja
Malvins
3 0261
Rossa AIFl.WG.3s (occas)
•159
Pta Corpmari
Pta Portas
I. Caragolé
1 See p.28 I. Ahorcados
Oc(1+2)14s27m12M 0260

IBIZA

Cala de Port Roig
Cala Yondal
Ensa de Codolá
C. Falcó
Pta Rama 5
Ensa de la Canal

Puerto de San Antonio
Cala Salada
C. Negret
Pta Galera C. Grassio
Bahía de San Antonio 10 Pta Xinxó
Port del Torrent
Cala Bassa
Cala Roig
Cala Llantia
Cala Corral
Cala Codolá
Cala Moli
Cala Badella
Cala Tarida
Cala Carbo
Cala Horts
Cabo Blanch
C. Jueu
I. Vedranell 6 C. Llentrisca
I. Vedrá Pta de Port Roig
Fl.5s21m11M Pta Yondal
0278
7 La Bota

Fl(4)20s85m18M 0274 9
I. Conejera
I. Bosque
I. del Esparto
I. Bledas 8
I. Redonda
Fl(3)15s28m10M 0276

3 See p.39
2 See p.36

Continuation to Espalmador See p.35

Pta Portas
I. Ahorcados Oc(1+2)14s27m12M
I. Puercos 4
I. Espardel
I. Espalmador
Isla Formentera

I. Espalmador

05' 40' 35' 1°30'E

I. Ibiza

Ensenada Codolar

Although a magnet for young nightclubbers and hordes of summer holiday makers, Ibiza has much to offer the yachtsman year-round. Scenic anchorages abound and all facilities are available at the major marinas of Puerto de Ibiza and the breathtaking Puerto de San Antonio. The pine forests inland inspired the Romans to name the group Pityusae: the Pine Islands

SECTION HEADINGS

The coastline is considered in a clockwise direction around the island beginning at Puerto de Ibiza

1. **Puerto de Ibiza to Punta Portas (including Espalmador)** *28*

2. **Ensenada de la Canal to Isla Vedrá** *36*

3. **Cabo Jueu to Puerto de San Antonio** *39*

4. **Cala Grassió to Pta Moscarté** *48*

5. **Pta Den Serra to Islote Botafoch** *53*

IBIZA WAYPOINTS

⊕1	E Approach to Puerto de Ibiza	38°53´.7N 01°27´.5E
⊕2	Puerto de Ibiza	38°53´.9N 01°26´.7E
⊕3	Isla Sal Rossa	38°52´.2N 01°24´.8E
⊕4	Freu Grande channel	38°48´.6N 01°25´.6E
⊕5	Punta Rama	38°49´.5N 01°22´.0E
⊕6	Cabo Llentrisca	38°51´.0N 01°14´.7E
⊕7	Isla Vedrá W	38°51´.7N 01°10´.8E
⊕8	Isla del Esparto W	38°57´.5N 01°10´.4E
⊕9	Isla Conejera NW	38°59´.7N 01°12´.5E
⊕10	Puerto de San Antonio	38°58´.8N 01°17´.0E
⊕11	Islas Margaritas (Margalides) W	39°03´.0N 01°18´.6E
⊕12	Cabo Eubarca	39°04´.6N 01°21´.4E
⊕13	Isla Murada	39°05´.8N 01°25´.9E
⊕14	Punta Charracó	39°06´.7N 01°29´.4E
⊕15	Punta Moscarté	39°07´.4N 01°32´.0E
⊕16	Islas Hormigas	39°06´.3N 01°35´.5E
⊕17	Punta Grosa	39°05´.0N 01°37´.0E
⊕18	Between Punta Valls and Isla Tagomago	39°02´.2N 01°37´.7E
⊕19	Isla de Santa Eulalia	38°58´.8N 01°35´.3E
⊕20	Puerto de Santa Eulalia	38°58´.6N 01°32´.5E
⊕21	Cabo y Escollo Llibrell	38°56´.6N 01°32´.0E
⊕22	Lladó del Norta W	38°55´.4N 01°29´.5E

Navigational information for approaches to Ibiza

All offlying dangers, including Islas Bledas and Isla Vedrá to the W and Isla Tagomago to the E are well covered in this chapter.

Magnetic variation

Ibiza – Now less than 1°W, decreasing (2005)

Approach and coastal passage charts

(See *Appendix* for full list of Balearic charts)

Imray	M3, M12, M13
Admiralty	1701, 1702, 2834
Spanish	7A, 478, 479
French	5505, 7114

Approach lights

0261 **Aeropuerto** 38°52´.7N 01°22´.3E Aero AlFl.WG.3s16m Control tower 9m Occas Situated 1M inland

0278 **Isla Vedrá** 38°51´.9N 01°11´.5E Fl.5s21m11M White conical tower 3m 262°-vis-134°

0276 **Islote Bleda Plana** 38°58´.9N 01°10´.5E Fl(3)15s28m10M White round tower 8m 349°-vis-239°

0274 **Isla Conejera** 38°59´.7N 01°12´.9E Fl(4)20s85m18M White tower and building 18m

0268 **Islote Tagomago** 39°02´.1N 01°38´.9E Fl(1+2)WR.30s86m17M White octagonal stone tower on building 23m 043.5°-W-037°-R-043.5° (red sector covers Losa de Santa Eulalia)

0270 **Punta Moscarté** 39° 06´.8N 01°32´E Fl.5s93m18M White round tower, black diagonal stripes 52m 074°-vis-294°

INTRODUCTION

Ibiza, the most westerly of the Islas Baleares, lies 50 miles off Cabo de la Nao on the Spanish mainland. It is 26 miles long and 16 miles wide and covers an area of 22 square miles. The northern half and the southwestern extremity are mountainous, the highest point being Atalayasa at 475m. There are three true harbours and hundreds of small anchorages around the coast which, with the exception of some stretches of low sandy beaches on the S and SE sides, is very rugged and broken. Rocky cliffs are interspersed with numerous *calas* (literally coves, but in practice often wide bays), many with small sandy beaches at their heads.

The Romans named the island group the Pityusae (Pine Islands), which is as appropriate today as it was 2,000 years ago. Inland, Ibiza is green and fertile with carpets of flowers in the spring and many pine forests throughout. In common with the rest of the archipelago, Ibiza receives huge numbers of holidaymakers each summer and many of the formerly deserted and exquisitely beautiful *calas* are now surrounded by hotels and holiday apartments as in all the Mediterranean. The permanent population of Ibiza is around 72,000, more than a third of whom live in the capital, Ibiza (Eivissa). Hotels, apartments and guest houses throughout the island have the capacity to accommodate a further 65,000 visitors.

The ancient Moorish castle at the head of Ibiza port *GW*

HISTORY

Like many parts of the Mediterranean, Ibiza has experienced waves of invasion and settlement throughout its history.

Neolithic pottery discovered in a cave near Cala Vicente indicates that the inhabitants at the time of the Early Bronze Age were Iberian; this is borne out by drawings on the walls in a cave at the foot of Cabo Nono. But by 1200BC the civilisations of the eastern Mediterranean were spreading westwards and there are many objects of Phoenician and Carthaginian origin, such as bronze axes and discs from San Juan, Salinas and Formentera, as well as figures from the Cave of Es Cuyeram, once a temple dedicated to the goddess Tanit.

The city of Ibiza was founded during the 6th century BC by the Carthaginians, who are thought to have fortified the hill now known as D'Alt Vila (the old town) and to have given both town and island the name Ibasim. There is evidence to show that agriculture was improved, tunny fishing and olive cultivation were introduced and the manufacture of purple dye from murex molluscs commenced. By the 3rd century BC the island was minting its own coinage.

It is claimed that Isla Conejera, off the W coast of Ibiza, was the birthplace of the Carthaginian general Hannibal. Certainly the inhabitants of the Islas Planas, part of the Islas Bledas group, were known for their skill at stone slinging and a number of slingers were recruited for the armies of Hannibal in his fight against Rome. As Rome gradually became the victorious power, both Ibiza and Formentera recognised her sovereignty and became city states within the Roman Empire under the name Pityusae (the Pine Islands), as mentioned above.

Other than the name Ebysos there is little remaining evidence of the Greeks in Ibiza, but the Romans brought prosperity to the island, later renamed Ebusus, founding saltworks at Salinas and lead mines at San Carlos. They boosted agriculture by taking shipments of corn to Rome, also built an aqueduct, and a new citadel on the site of the old Carthaginian fortress.

With the fall of Rome, Ibiza suffered the same fate as other satellite countries, being occupied throughout the centuries by various different groups. Raids by the Vandals drove many inhabitants away to seek refuge on the mainland. In AD426 a Barbarian tribe called the Gunderic occupied the island until the great Byzantine sailor Admiral Belisarius captured it in 535.

The Moors, who at first found the island useful as a base for raids on shipping and the mainland, arrived from North Africa in 707 and remained for more than 500 years. To them the island was

Yebisah. The Vikings attempted an invasion in 857 as did Charlemagne in 798-801, but the Moors managed to hold on until 1235 when Ibiza was eventually reconquered by a force under Guillem de Montgrí, Bishop of Tarragona, backed by King Jaime I of Catalonia. The Moorish influence is still evident in the architecture, customs and traditional dress of the islanders and the presence of Catalonian in their language, from which the Ibizan dialect is derived and the origin of the island name Eivissa.

Ibiza's return to Christian rule failed to bring peace, and the island was subject to much fighting during the period of Spanish internal strife. In 1492 the whole of Spain, including Ibiza, became united under King Ferdinand and Queen Isabella, but for another two centuries attacks on the island by Barbary pirates, Moors and Turks were frequent. Watchtowers were kept permanently manned, the present city walls were built and cavalry patrols were established. Even village churches were fortified.

After a period being part of the Kingdom of Mallorca, Ibiza reverted to Catalonian rule, but then backed the losing side in the War of the Spanish Succession (1702-14) and was made into a Spanish province as a result. It gradually became a cultural and economic backwater, emigration adding to a population decline begun by the Black Death 400 years earlier.

Recent history

During the Spanish Civil War Ibiza declared allegiance to Franco, only to be rebuffed by the Republicans and was occupied for a six-week period when considerable damage was done to churches and other buildings.

In the past, Ibiza's main wealth came from the export of 'red' salt which was particularly valued. Even today over 100,000 tons are exported each year. Fruit, grain and shellfish are other exports of importance. During the last fifty years the tourist trade has expanded into a major industry and the island, which was in the past a haven for the simple life and values, has been dragged into the 21st century. In particular both Ibiza and Formentera became favourites with the so-called 'hippie' culture, a legacy still evident in a marked tolerance towards unusual clothes and non-mainstream lifestyles. The construction of apartment blocks for tourists is finally slowing, together with large numbers of tourist shops, cafés, bars, restaurants and related services. The local authorities have realised, perhaps a little late, that ever-expanding tourism brings with it a heavy environmental price. It is hard, though, to dent the pleasure and joy the sea brings. Little changes that fact.

TOURIST INFORMATION

Places of particular interest on Ibiza

The church of Nostra Señora in the small village of Jesús just N of Ibiza city contains a famous (and very beautiful) altarpiece dating back to the early 16th century.

In the northern part of the island lie Balafia, a fortified Moorish village just outside San Lorenzo, and the Es Cuyeram cave which was once a Carthaginian temple to the goddess Tanit (also accessible from the anchorage at Cala de San Vicente). In the SW, the Carthaginian and Roman remains at Ses Païses de Cala d'Hort (near Cala Horts) make an interesting visit. Inland lies Ibiza's highest point, Atalayasa, near the village of San José. Further E, on the road to Ibiza, are the caves of Cova Santa, also accessible via a track from Cala Yondal. For details of tourist offices see above in the *General Introduction*.

Embassies

See *Appendix*.

Cala Llonga. A sheltered anchorage in all but E winds, on the SE side of the island   *GW*

1. Puerto de Ibiza to Punta Portas, including passages between Ibiza and Espalmador

PUERTO DE IBIZA
TO PUNTA PORTAS

WAYPOINTS

⊕1	E Approach to Puerto de Ibiza	38°53′.7N 01°27′.5E
⊕2	Puerto de Ibiza	38°53′.9N 01°26′.7E
⊕3	Isla Sal Rossa	38°52′.2N 01°24′.8E
⊕4	Freu Grande channel	38°48′.6N 01°25′.6E

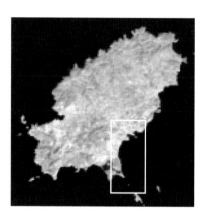

View along the SW harbour wall towards the ancient town of Ibiza and the Cathedral of Our Lady of the Snows   *GW*

IB1 Puerto de Ibiza (Eivissa)

An easy-to-enter harbour in almost any conditions, offering good shelter, with several commercial yachting facilities. Berthing for over 1,200 yachts up to 30m

Location
38°54′.7N 01°26′.7E

Communications
Pilots (*Ibiza Prácticos***)** VHF Ch 12, 13, 14, 16
Port Authority Ch 09,16
☎ 971 31 06 11/31 33 63 *Fax* 971 31 04 00
See text for further internet information on other options

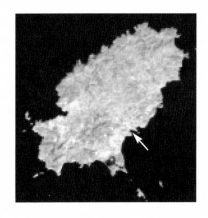

The port

Puerto de Ibiza is a large port offering excellent facilities for over 1,200 yachts. The harbour is easy to enter under most conditions, giving good shelter. Swell which used to enter the port has been considerably reduced by the extension of the breakwater extending WSW from Islote Botafoch. The harbour is expensive and in season a berth will be hard to find.

Puerto de Ibiza looking NW. Marina Botafoch

PILOTAGE

Approach

⊕2 38°53′.9N 01°26′.7E Puerto de Ibiza

From S Several potential hazards litter the southern approach. These are: Islote La Esponja (10m), one mile E of Isla Sal Rossa; Malvins del Sur (20m) and Malvins del Norte (12m), 1.1 and 0.9 miles S of Pta Marloca; Dado Grande (7m) and Dado Pequeño (9m) about 0.8 miles S of Isla Botafoch. All lie near or outside the 20m contour and in daylight can be left on either hand.

I. IBIZA

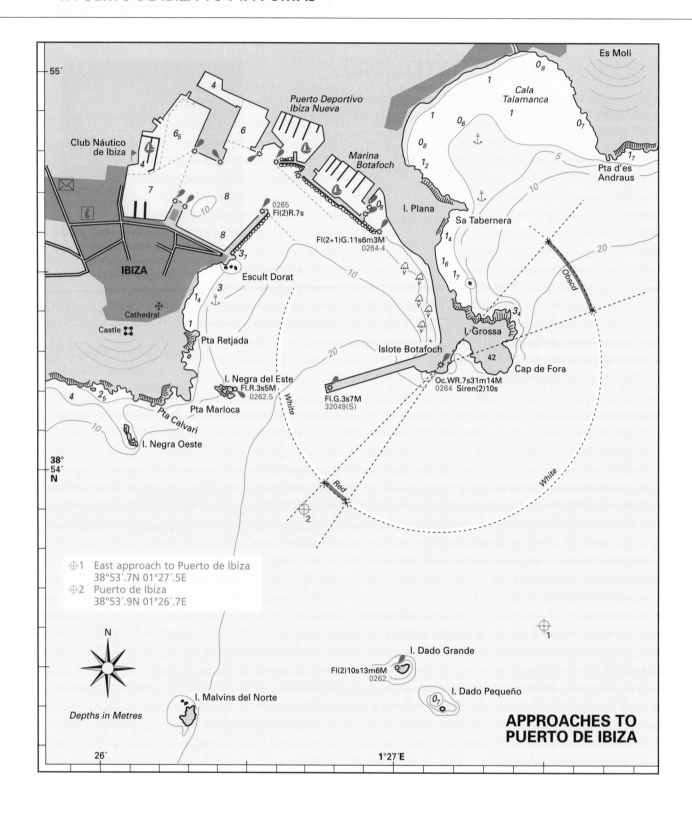

APPROACHES TO PUERTO DE IBIZA

⊕1 East approach to Puerto de Ibiza
38°53'.7N 01°27'.5E
⊕2 Puerto de Ibiza
38°53'.9N 01°26'.7E

Depths in Metres

⊕1   E Approach to Puerto de Ibiza   38°53′.7N 01°27′.5E

If approaching at night it is wise to pass outside (E) of all these hazards – a bearing of 345° or less on Islote Botafoch ensures safe water. There is a Fl.G.3s5m7M light at the head of the newly extended breakwater.

From NE Coastal sailing from the NE end of the island, or approaching from the direction of Mallorca, see page 55 for details of the passage inside Isla Tagomago and page 58 for Isla de Santa Eulalia. After passing Puerto de Santa Eulalia, Cabo Llibrell should be given a least offing of 200m, then the two small islands Lladó del Norte (10m), and Lladó del Sur (6m) identified just under a mile NE of Cabo Martinet. Once spotted they can safely be passed on either side. Cabo Martinet, Isla Grossa and Isla Botafoch are all steep-to, though the latter now has a 400m breakwater running WSW from the lighthouse, which must be rounded to starboard.

Anchorages in the approach

In fine weather it is possible to anchor 200m off the cliff, E of the cathedral, in 6m over sand and weed but it is shallow close in.

Entrance

The outer harbour is entered on passing between the extended breakwater and Islote Negra del Este. An inner harbour half a mile further N, wherein lies the *club náutico* and Puerto Deportivo, is formed by another mole on the W side and Marina Botofach to the NE.

Large commercial ships and many ferries use the harbour; they have right of way and must not be obstructed. For this reason it is advisable to keep to the starboard side of the entrance but there are no other navigational hazards. Islote Negra del Este and the breakwater head are both steep-to and there are good depths (i.e. more than 5m) in the entrance and throughout the commercial harbour.

Berthing

Once in the harbour there are several options for berthing, though all are likely to be crowded in the high season.

1. **Marina de Botafoch.** An upmarket marina with 428 berths, able to take yachts of up to 30m, with excellent facilities (see below). The office staff are helpful and several speak English.

   The entrance lies outside the harbour proper, some 0.4M N of the Islote Botafoch, from which it takes its name. Although reasonably wide, the entrance does not open up until well inside a line from Islote Botafoch to the end of the NE (Marina Botafoch) breakwater and can therefore be difficult to identify. The fuel and reception berth is on the starboard side on entry, with the marina offices nearby. When berths are not available, secure alongside the fuel dock when it closes at 1430, so long as you are away before it opens again at 0900 the next morning. A ferry plies across the harbour into town every half hour.

VHF Ch 09
☎ 971 31 17 11/31 30 13/31 22 31 *Fax* 971 31 15 57
Email info@marinabotafoch.com
www.marinabotafoch.com

2. **Puerto Deportivo Ibiza Nueva** Extending into the old commercial basin to the W has made Ibiza Nueva the largest marina in the port with 536 berths for yachts of up to 40m. Facilities are good, though some of the berths are rather remote.

   The dogleg entrance to the right of a large yellow building presents no particular problems and has 3.5–4m depths. Secure on the N side of the N mole (where fuel is also available) to await allocation of a berth. There is a ferry service into town.
   Note 1. Several reports of boats being robbed at this marina and at the town quays have emerged over the past few years. Do not leave a vessel unattended if possible.
   Note 2. Berths near the commercial mole can be noisy with ships sometimes unloading all night.

Puerto Deportivo Ibiza Nueva VHF Ch 09
☎ 971 31 20 01/31 40 50 *Fax* 971 31 35 23
Email Ibiza.nueva@pmi.servicom.es

3. **Club Náutico de Ibiza** Situated at the head of the harbour and small compared to its neighbours, has berthing for 300 vessels. The club normally reserves twenty outside berths for visiting yachts (berths inside the harbour are private). These can be oily and are exposed to ferry wash, so the use of 'spring coil'-type shock absorbers is recommended or use the *club náutico* lines which have car tyres as springs.

Club Náutico de Ibiza VHF Ch 09
☎ 971 33 97 54/31 33 63 *Fax* 971 33 28 10
Email info@clubnauticoibiza.com
www.clubnauticoibiza.com

4. **Port Authority pontoons** The two pontoons situated in the extreme SW of the harbour, S of the *club náutico*, are now exclusively reserved for local vessels with card access to the pontoons. There is a further pontoon just inside the SW breakwater but this is shallow and is only for small boats.

   The area between the SW breakwater and the inner mole (now the ferry station) is devoted to RoRo ferries. On the W side of this mole there are some moorings for larger (20m+) craft which may be booked through the Port Authority's office. Lazy lines, water and electricity are laid on.

Facilities

Water At all berths listed above. The water in Ibiza is of variable quality, so if possible consult other yachtsmen before filling tanks.
Electricity At all berths. Normally 220v, but 380v available at large yacht (25m) berths in the two marinas.
Fuel At both marinas. Ibiza Nueva has two fuelling points.
Bottled gas Camping Gaz exchanges at chandleries or in town. Note that Calor Gas bottles are not refillable on the islands now.

I. IBIZA

Puerto de Ibiza looking S. Isla Botafoch light top left of picture

Provisions Supermarkets at both marinas plus excellent choice in the town. There is an all-day market on Fridays in summer.

Ice In the supermarkets at the marinas and in the *club náutico* bar.

Chandlery Well-stocked chandleries at the Marina Botafoch and across the road from the *club náutico*.

Repairs The largest boatyard is situated just N of the *club náutico* but is actually part of the Puerto Deportivo Ibiza Nueva, as is the yard at the head of their W basin. A smaller concern at Marina Botafoch. There are 100-tonne and 27-tonne travel-lifts at Ibiza Nueva yards, 62-tonnes at Marina Botafoch and a slipway close N of the *club náutico*.

Engineers Marina Botafoch and Ibiza Nueva boatyards, also Yates Ibiza ☎/*Fax* 971 19 03 26 just N of the *club náutico* and Ibiza Yacht Service ☎ 971 31 06 17 *Fax* 971 31 06 56 at the head of the Ibiza Nueva W basin.

Official service agents include: Auto Recambios Isla ☎ 971 31 10 12, 31 37 00 *Fax* 971 31 69 66 – Yamaha; Ibiza Yachting ☎ 971 341159 – Johnson; Marina Marbella Ibiza SA ☎ 971 3 08 11 – Mercury/MerCruiser, Volvo Penta; Motonautica ☎ 971 30 66 65 *Fax* 971 30 66 62 – Honda, Mercury/MerCruiser, Soler, Suzuki, Yanmar; Servinautic ☎/*Fax* 971 31 19 63 – Mariner, MerCruiser, Volvo Penta. ☎ 971 19 19 59 – Englishman located by the casino N of the Nueva Marina.

Electronic and radio repairs Both marina boatyards, Nautronic at Marina Botafoch, Yates Ibiza and Ibiza Yacht Service. Dews Marine.

Sailmaker At the Polígono Eurocentro ☎ 971 31 16 60. Also services inflatable dinghies and liferafts.

Yacht club The Club Náutico de Ibiza has a bar, lounge, terrace, showers and restaurant.

Showers At both marinas and the *club náutico*.

Launderettes At both marinas and in the town.

Banks In the town, many with credit card facilities.

Post office In the town.

Hospital/medical services In the town.

Transport

Car hire/taxis In the town, or arrange through marina offices.

Buses Regular services over most of the island.

Ferries Car ferries to mainland Spain and Mallorca. Frequent tourist ferries and hydrofoils to Formentera and various beaches.

Air services International airport 3 miles S of the harbour. The hourly bus service from the airport to the terminus on Avenida Isidoro Macabich in the centre takes 20 minutes and runs between 0730–2230 from the airport.

Sights ashore locally

Although a small part of the old town and citadel is still unspoilt, the city has become an international tourist centre, very overcrowded in the summer, and even in winter the locals are outnumbered by foreign visitors and residents.

It was founded during the 6th century BC by the Carthaginians, who are thought to have occupied the hill now known as D'Alt Vila (the old town) and to have referred to both town and island as Ibasim.

The city is well worth a visit and contains, amongst many other interesting buildings, the cathedral and the Archaeological Museum.

On the western slopes of the hill is the Puig des Molins necropolis, a subterranean burial place which served the city from the Phoenician era (7th century BC) until Roman times. It is open to the public, together with a museum. Parts of the cathedral date back to the 13th century, shortly after the island was reconquered for Spain, but the great citadel walls were built in the late 16th century and bear the arms of King Phillip II.

If travelling by car, take the road N from Ibiza city towards San Juan Bautista and Cala Portinatx or to the tranquil Cala San Vicente, a pleasant drive along windy coastal roads, where you will find a shrine to the goddess Tanit who was worshiped by the Phoenicians at the Cueva Culleram.

Local events

Fiestas are held on the Friday night of Holy Week (Good Friday), on 24 June to celebrate the king's name saint (San Juan), and 1 August in honour of La Virgen de las Nieves, patron saint of the island. On 16 August there is a sea procession as part of the Fiesta del Virgen del Carmen.

Eating out

Restaurants, cafés and bars at both marinas plus vast numbers in the town.

Islets S of Puerto de Ibiza

Several small islets lie in the bay S of Puerto de Ibiza (see *Approach* above). From N to S these are: Dado Grande (Dau Gran) (7m) and Dado Pequeño (Dau Petit) (9m) about 0.8 miles S of Islote Botafoch; Malvins del Norte (12m) and Malvins del Sur (20m) 0.9 and 1.1 miles S of Pta Marloca; and Islote La Esponja (10m), one mile E of Isla Sal Rossa. All lie near or outside the 20m contour and can be left on either hand.

ANCHORAGES AND FEATURES S OF PUERTO DE IBIZA

⚓ PUNTA DE LA MATA (PLAYA D'EN BOSSA)
38°53′.7N 01°25′E

A small and shallow harbour of little use to yachts about 1 mile SW of Puerto de Ibiza, tucked SW of the *punta* and partially enclosed by a rough breakwater and short jetty. Small fishing boats and motor boats lie to crowded moorings in ±1m over sand and weed.

It is overlooked by hotels and high-rise tourist apartments, with a main road nearby.

⊕3 38°52′.2N 01°24′.8E Isla Sal Rossa

⚓ CALAS DE SAL ROSSA
38°52′.3N 01°24′.4E

Two small anchorages either side of Isla Sal Rossa, open NE–E–SE. Anchor in 2–3.5m over weed, sand and rock. The conspicuous (28m) Torre Sal Rossa stands to the NW.

The area is still unspoilt, with only some local fishing craft and net stores ashore. Ibiza airport is little more than a mile away but noise is not really a problem. There is a rough track to the main road.

⚓ PLAYA D'ES CABALLET (ES CAVALLET)
38°50′.7N 01°24′.3E

A long sandy beach open from N–E–S. There are developments at either end, a small jetty to the N and a track to the road. Anchor in 5m or less over sand and rock.

ISLA ESPALMADOR
38°47′.8N 01°25′.3E (N tip)

This 1.5M long rocky island is the largest of a chain forming the long SSE-going reef that connects (with passages between) Ibiza with the island of Formentera. Anchorages and features around Espalmador and Espardel are described separately under *Formentera* below.

Ibiza viewed SW across Marina Botafoch and the ferry terminal towards the old town   GW

I. IBIZA

Passages between Ibiza and Espalmador

PILOTAGE

This whole area is a marine reserve (effectively meaning no fishing or anchoring) and marked by six yellow conical buoys Fl.Y.5s with × topmark. Three are to the E and three to the W of the chain of islands.

There are three possible passages (*freus*) between Isla de Ibiza and Isla Espalmador, which are separated by a series of small islands and rocky banks strung along a ridge running S from Ibiza through Espalmador to Formentera.

Only one, the Freu Grande, is usable in all conditions, day or night though the northern Freu Mediano makes a useful short cut in good weather in daylight. The lights in the area are reliable and a night passage through Freu Grande should not present any problems.

Approach

From E or NE Approach the *freus* on a SW course following the coast of Ibiza and leaving Isla Espardel (lit) to port. Two hills, Corpmari (159m) and Falcón (145m), lie near the southern extremity of Ibiza though Punta Portas itself is low. The black-and-white-banded lighthouses of Isla Ahorcados and Isla Puercos (or Los Pou) are unmistakable, with the lit N cardinal beacon of Bajo d'en Pou between them.

From W or NW If approaching the passages from the Spanish mainland, the mountains of southern Ibiza will be first to rise above the horizon, followed by the spectacular cliffs of Isla Vedrá (lit). On closer approach the higher southern parts of Formentera will be seen, but the smaller islands of the freus will not become visible until much closer in, when the black-and-white-banded lighthouses of Isla Ahorcados and Isla Puercos (or Los Pou) can be identified with the lit N cardinal beacon of Bajo d'en Pou between them.

TRANSITING THE PASSAGES

FREU GRANDE
38°48´.5N 01°25´E
⊕4 38°48´.6N 01°25´.6E E entrance to Freu Grande channel

Freu Grande is located between the lighthouses of Isla Ahorcados to the N and Isla Puercos (or Los Pou) to the S and is just over a mile wide and 6–7m deep. Slightly to the S of its centre is the N cardinal beacon marking Bajo d'en Pou, also lit. In heavy seas keep clear of Bajo Ahorcados, 550m SW of Isla Ahorcados, and pass just N of Bajo d'en Pou. It is the only passage recommended for use after dark, but in that case be careful to avoid the two Islas Negras del Freu, about 500m W of Isla Ahorcados, unlit, and only 2m and 4m high.

FREU MEDIANO
38°49´.4N 01°24´.6E

Freu Mediano lies between Isla Ahorcados to the S and Islote Caragolé, a small rock 8m high, to the N. Watch out for La Barqueta, an unmarked rock awash 500m WSW of Islote Caragolé: though often indicated by breaking seas, in calm weather it does not show clearly. Depths of 3–4m are to be found in the centre of the channel. Isla Ahorcados was once the site of the gallows where condemned prisoners were executed.

FREU CHICO
38°49´.8N 01°24´.4E

The furthest N, narrowest and shallowest of the northern *freus*, for use only by shallow-draught vessels in calm weather and with care. Depths may shoal to less than 1m. Careful eyeball navigation is required in order to avoid a rocky patch N of Islote Caragolé; a course a little N of halfway between Islote Caragolé and Punta Portas appears the optimum. La Barqueta rock (see *Freu Mediano* above) is also a potential hazard when using this *freu*.

Freu Grande passage from the SW. Lighthouses on Isla Puercos (right) and Isla Ahorcados (left) are clear for a night passage

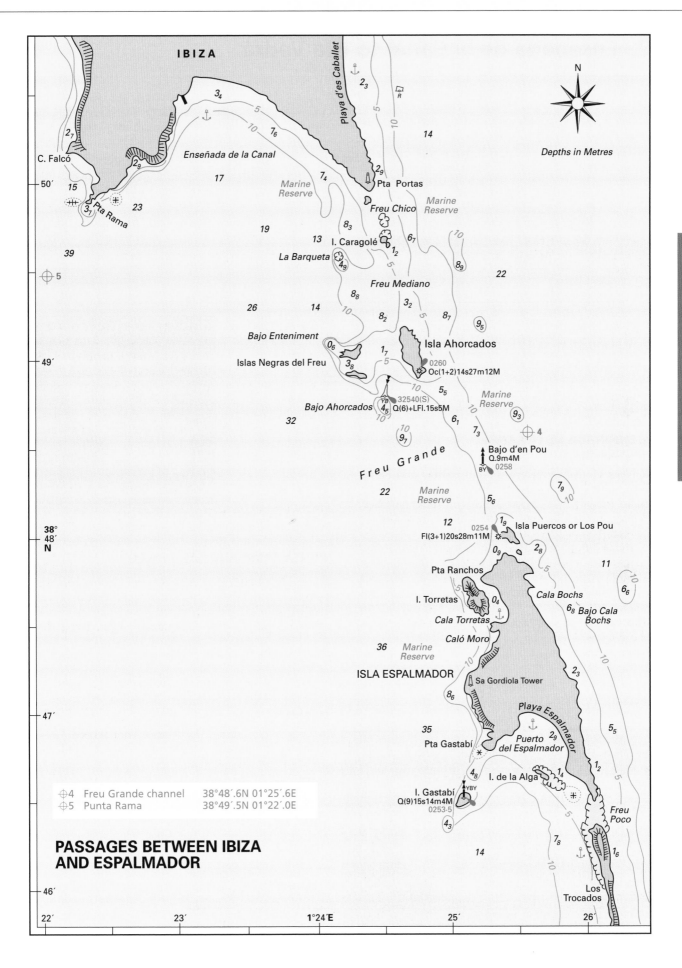

IBIZA

Playa d'es Caballet

N

Depths in Metres

C. Falcó

Pta Rama

Enseñada de la Canal

Marine Reserve

Pta Portas

Freu Chico

Marine Reserve

I. Caragolé

La Barqueta

Freu Mediano

Isla Ahorcados

0260
Oc(1+2)14s27m12M

Bajo Enteniment

Islas Negras del Freu

32540(S)
Q(6)+LFl.15s5M

Bajo Ahorcados

Marine Reserve

Freu Grande

Bajo d'en Pou
Q.9m4M
0258

Marine Reserve

Isla Puercos or Los Pou

0254
Fl(3+1)20s28m11M

Pta Ranchos

I. Torretas

Cala Bochs

Cala Torretas

Bajo Cala Bochs

Caló Moro

Marine Reserve

ISLA ESPALMADOR

Sa Gordiola Tower

Playa Espalmador

Pta Gastabí

Puerto del Espalmador

I. de la Alga

I. Gastabí
Q(9)15s14m4M
0253·5

Freu Poco

Los Trocados

| ⊕4 | Freu Grande channel | 38°48′.6N 01°25′.6E |
| ⊕5 | Punta Rama | 38°49′.5N 01°22′.0E |

PASSAGES BETWEEN IBIZA AND ESPALMADOR

I. IBIZA

2. Ensenada de la Canal to Isla Vedrá

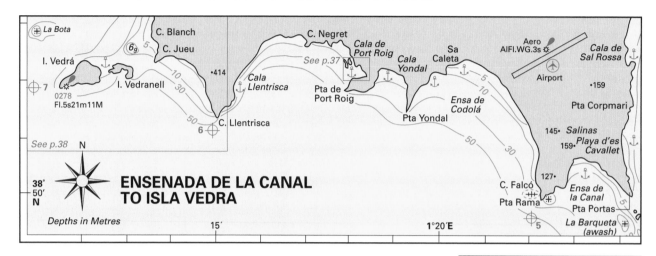

WAYPOINTS

⊕5 Punta Rama   38°49′.5N 01°22′.0E
⊕6 Cabo Llentrisca   38°51′.0N 01°14′.7E
⊕7 Isla Vedrá W   38°51′.7N 01°10′.8E

⚓ ENSENADA DE LA CANAL

38°50′.4N 01°23′.2E

A large sandy bay between Punta Portas and Punta Rama, on the S tip of Ibiza. Anchor to suit conditions in 2–10m over sand with rocky patches. A pier for loading salt is sited in the NW corner, backed by a factory complex ashore.

Relatively undeveloped ashore other than a few beach restaurants, but the beach itself (the Playa de Mitjorn) can get very crowded, due to frequent ferries and buses from Ibiza. The nearby *salinas* (salt pans) are a protected area, attracting many migrating birds in spring and autumn.

Ensenada de la Canal anchorage. Note the salt loading pier

PUNTA RAMA AND CABO FALCÓ

38°50′.1N 01°22′.3E
⊕5 38°49′.5N 01°22′.0E Punta Rama

A prominent double headland with various offlying hazards. The isolated Bajo Morenallet lies 350m E of Punta Rama, several islets to the S and a wreck some 100m W of the punta. Allow an offing of at least 500m.

⚓ ENSENADA DE CODOLÁ (SA CALETA)

38°51′.8N 01°20′.3E

A long bay shielded by Punta Yondal and Cabo Falcó at either end. Anchor in 10m over sand and weed off the sand and stone beach. The village of Sa Caleta lies at the NW end, backed by several tower blocks.

The centre of the bay lies under the airport flight path, making the area noisy – it is 1.5 miles from Sa Caleta to the terminal buildings. The southern part of the beach is backed by salt pans.

PUNTA YONDAL (DES JONDAL)
38°51′.4N 01°19′.3E

A serrated headland running out to a low promontory with a hole through it. Rocks extend up to 300m S of the point. Phoenician remains have been found on the peninsula W of Sa Caleta, including the foundations of a village dated at around the 7th century BC.

⚓ CALA YONDAL (DES JONDAL)
38°51′.8N 01°18′.9E

A wide but relatively sheltered bay lying between Punta de Port Roig and Punta Yondal, open S and SW. Anchor about 100m off the beach in 6–10m over sand and weed. Beach café and other buildings inland, and a track to the road.

Cala Port Roig: a remarkably tranquil place to anchor

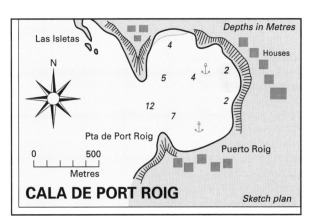

CALA DE PORT ROIG

Cala Yondal

PUNTA DE PORT ROIG (PUNTA PORROIG)
38°51′.7N 01°17′.9E

A low flat point with a hole through it and some scattered buildings on the summit.

⚓ CALA DE PORT ROIG (CALA PORROIG)
38°52′.1N 01°18′.3E

In no way a port, but rather a delightful sheltered anchorage between Punta de Port Roig and Las Isletas, surrounded by sloping reddish cliffs and well protected from all winds except SW. Anchor in 6–10m over sand, weed and rock, taking care to avoid cables from the Spanish mainland which come ashore in the bay.

Fishermen's huts line the eastern shore but otherwise there are few buildings and currently no bars or restaurants, though a small beach bar will be found under Cabo Negret about a mile to the NW (best reached by dinghy).

⚓ CALA LLENTRISCA
38°51′.8N 01°15′.4E

A small anchorage with a stony beach tucked under scrub-covered cliffs, Exposed from NE to SE and to swell from the S. Anchor in 4–6m over sand and

Cala Llentrisca. a small sheltered anchorage W of Cape Llentrisca

stone, though there are depths of up to 23m off the entrance. Boats and fishermen's huts line the beach, with a steep track up to the road.

This is a useful anchorage while awaiting favourable weather for the passage to the mainland but keep well clear of the fishermen's moorings.

CABO LLENTRISCA

38°51′.4N 01°15′E

⊕6 38°51′.0N 01°14′.7E Cabo Llentrisca

A steep, white-cliffed headland (148m) free of offlying dangers.

⚓ ISLA VEDRÁ

38°51′.7N 01°11′.3E (light)

⊕7 38°51′.7N 01°10′.8E Isla Vedrá

A lofty (382m), spectacular, rocky island, steep sided and steep-to, of a reddish colour. The lighthouse (Fl.5s21m11M, white conical tower 3m) is on the S coast and obscured when bearing between 134° and 262°.

There are two possible anchorages: one close N of the island in 12m, with landing feasible in a small inlet, the other off the NE coast in 15m, just W of a group of rocks. Both have poor holding over stone and rock. Approach with care, and only in good conditions. The island was used as the location for the *South Pacific* 'Bali Hai' photography.

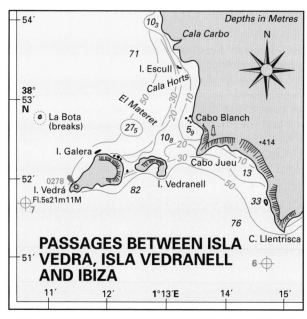

Isla Vedra, Isla Vedranell and the passages to the mainland
GW

⊕6 Cabo Llentrisca   38°51′.0N 01°14′.7E
⊕7 Isla Vedrá W   38°51′.7N 01°10′.8E

Isla Vedranell and Isla Vedrá. However, attention must be paid to the following dangers:

- La Bota, a breaking rock 1M NNW of Isla Vedrá light
- A series of small rocky islets on the NE and E coasts of Isla Vedrá
- El Materet, 10.8m deep, 800m SW of Cabo Blanch.

A course of 125°/305° down the centre of the passage between Isla Vedranell and Cabo Jueu, keeping the point of Cabo Llentrisca equidistant between the two, clears El Materet. The inside passage is prone to sudden, strong gusts, and in heavy weather it is advisable to pass well outside Isla Vedrá and La Bota.

⚓ ISLA VEDRANELL

38°52′.4N 01°12′.8E

Considerably lower (125m) and smaller than its neighbour, but equally steep-to, particularly to the S. Anchor in 12m over sand and rock close off the N coast. Again, a strictly fair weather spot.

Passages between Isla Vedrá, Isla Vedranell and Ibiza

A channel 750m wide and with a minimum depth of 10.8m runs between Isla Vedranell and Cabo Jueu on the mainland. A much narrower passage, some 200m wide but also carrying a good 10m, separates

Isla Vedranell with deep-water passages either side

3. Cabo Jueu to Puerto de San Antonio

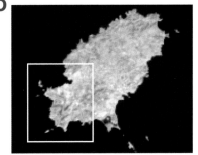

WAYPOINTS
⊕6   Cabo Llentrisca   38°51′.0N 01°14′.7E
⊕7   Isla Vedrá W   38°51′.7N 01°10′.8E
⊕8   Isla del Esparto W   38°57′.5N 01°10′.4E
⊕9   Isla Conejera NW   38°59′.7N 01°12′.5E
⊕10 Puerto de San Antonio   38°58′.8N 01°17′.0E

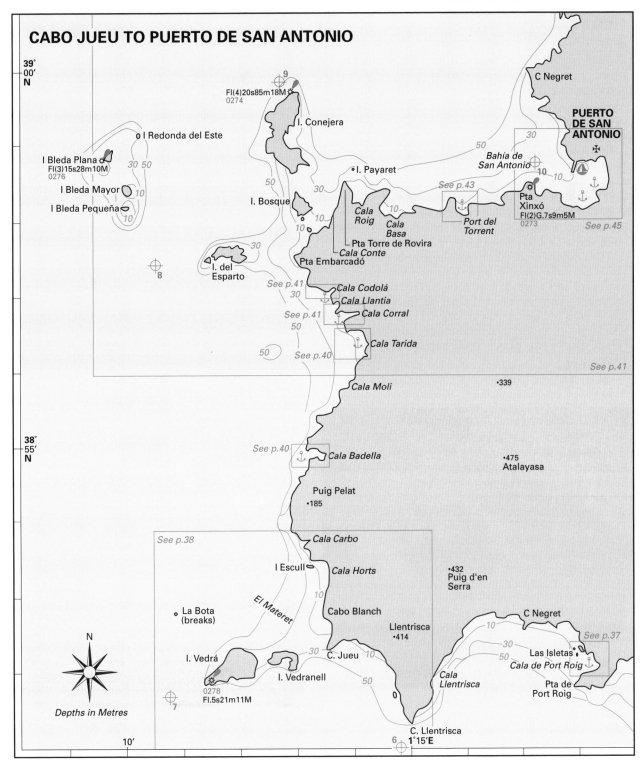

⚓ CALA HORTS (D'HORT)

38°53′.3N 01°13′.4E

A popular anchorage in 5–10m over sand, open to S and SW, but sheltered by high cliffs and the two offshore islands. The long stony beach has two beach restaurants, one high-rise building and some smaller buildings.

Remains from the Carthaginian and Roman periods, including the foundations of a substantial villa, have been excavated at ses Païses de Cala d'Hort, a short distance inland.

⚓ CALA CARBO

38°53′.7N 01°13′.0E

A small angled *cala* between low reddish headlands, which may be difficult to identify from offshore. Sound-in carefully to anchor in ±3m over sand and weed, off a fine sandy beach sporting the usual beach restaurant.

⚓ CALA BADELLA (VADELLA)

38°54′.9N 01°13′.2E

A deep and attractive *cala* with an excellent beach, well protected by high wooded cliffs and offering a safe but often crowded anchorage with many permanent moorings. The N headland extends underwater and should be given minimum clearance of 25m, otherwise depths are considerable until well inside the *cala*. Anchor in 3–10m as space permits over sand and weed; it may be necessary to use two anchors to limit swinging. Larger yachts sometimes moor with a line to the rocks on the southern headland. No shortage of restaurants, cafés and bars behind the beach, plus a small supermarket in the village.

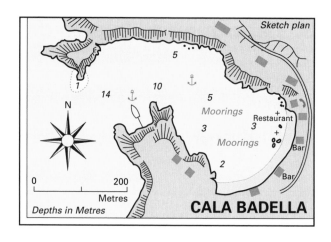

⚓ CALA MOLI

38°55′.9N 01°13′.8E

A small *cala* with a fine sandy beach, open to SW through NW but otherwise well protected by high cliffs. A distinctive pink building stands on the southern headland, its curved façade supported by columns. Anchor in 5m over sand. A beach restaurant ashore, catering for the tourist boats from San Antonio, plus some new development to the N.

⚓ CALA TARIDA

38°56′.4N 01°14′E

A long bay with sandy beaches separated by rocky outcrops, and with two low, inshore islands. Cala Tarida is easily identified by the extensive tourist developments to both N and S. Anchor in 4–5m over sand, weed and rock. There are many beach restaurants and cafés ashore, together with some shops.

Cala Badella: fine anchorage with restaurant on the beach

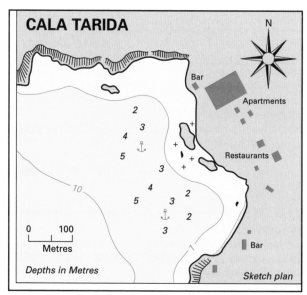

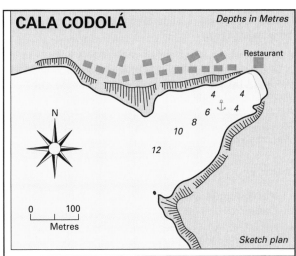

CALA CODOLÁ — *Depths in Metres*

Restaurant

N

0   100
Metres

Sketch plan

Cala Tarida

⚓ CALA CORRAL
38°56′.8N 01°13′.8E

A rocky-sided *cala* open SW through NW and with a small and shallow private harbour (Coralmar) tucked behind a rocky wall at its head. Anchor in 5–6m over sand and rock. A large tourist development stands behind and somewhat above the beach, itself fringed by fishermen's huts. A restaurant and supermarket will be found amongst the buildings to the N.

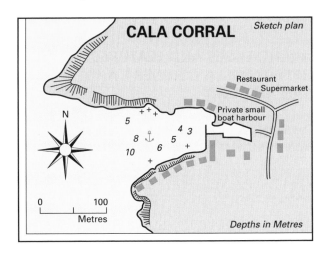

CALA CORRAL — *Sketch plan*

Restaurant
Supermarket
Private small boat harbour
N
0   100
Metres
Depths in Metres

⚓ CALA LLANTIA
38°56′.8N 01°13′.7E

A rocky-sided *cala* open SW and W, with a beach at its head and a line of white houses on a cliff to the NW. Anchor off the beach in 5m over sand.

⚓ CALA CODOLÁ (CODOLAR)
38°57′N 01°13′.5E

A cliff-sided *cala* with a stony beach at its head, open to SW through NW. Anchor in 4–6m over sand and

weed near the head of the *cala*, where a restaurant and beach bar will be found. Low-rise white houses line the clifftop to the N, together with a few shops. Tourist boats visit daily in season.

Passage between Isla del Esparto (Illa de s'Espart) and Ibiza

The N–S passage between Isla del Esparto (68m) and Ibiza is more than 1,000m wide with a minimum depth of 30m. A small rocky islet stands just off the NE point of the island.

⊕ 8 38°57′.3N 01°10′.4E Islote Espardel W (off Isla Esparto)

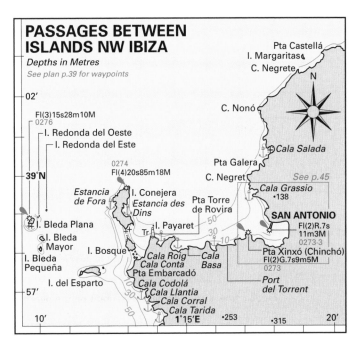

PASSAGES BETWEEN ISLANDS NW IBIZA
Depths in Metres
See plan p.39 for waypoints

I. IBIZA

Islas Bledas (Ses Bledes)

38°58′.8N 01°09′.6E

A group of five uninhabited rocky islets lying 2 miles NW of Isla del Esparto. At their centre is Isla Bleda Plana (23m), which has offlying rocks to the SW. There is a lighthouse (Fl(3)15s28m10M, white round tower 8m) on the NW side of this island, obscured when bearing between 239° and 349°. The other islands, taken from N to S, comprise:

- Isla Redonda del Este (13m), 1,000m NE of Isla Bleda Plana
- Isla Redonda del Oeste, close NE of Isla Bleda Plana
- Isla Bleda Mayor (Na Bose) (39m), 1,000m SSE of Isla Bleda Plana
- Isla Bleda Pequeña (Na Gorra) (29m), sometimes referred to as Porros, about 400m S of Isla Bleda Mayor and with foul ground between the two.

Explore the area with care and a bow lookout. In settled conditions it is reported possible to anchor in 5m near the lighthouse landing on Isla Bleda Plana, taking a sternline ashore.

Passage between Isla Conejera (Sa Conillera) and Isla Bosque (de Bosc)

⊕9 38°59′.7N 01°12′.5E Isla Conejera (NW)

A passage 200m wide exists between Isla Conejera (69m) and Isla Bosque (67m). It is generally deep, other than where a narrow (15m) bar carrying some 3–4m links the two islands (see plan). In good light the paler colours of the bar should be clearly visible. Rocks extend from both islands, those off Isla Conejera barely breaking while those off Isla Bosque stand well above the water (though with a few breaking outliers).

Isla Conejera (larger island) and Isla Bosque: the bar clearly visible

Isla Bosque: the rocky reef between Ibiza and mainland is clear

Take the passage in an E–W direction halfway between the two islands with a bias towards Isla Bosque. It becomes unsafe with any sea running, when it would be wise to pass outside Isla Conejera (⊕9).

Passage between Isla Bosque and Ibiza

The passage between Isla Bosque and Ibiza is a dangerous mass of awash and barely-covered rocks (see photo) and really only suitable for dinghies in calm conditions, though a 2m passage is said to exist.

ANCHORAGES AND FEATURES BETWEEN ISLA CONEJERA AND SAN ANTONIO

⚓ ESTANCIA DE FORA, ISLA CONEJERA

38°59′.1N 01°12′.4E

A small *cala* on the W side of Isla Conejera. Strictly a fair-weather spot. Anchor in 5–7m over sand and rock.

⚓ ESTANCIA DES DINS, ISLA CONEJERA

38°59′.0N 01°12′.6E

A large sandy bay on the E of the island, open to the NE and with a 3 mile plus fetch to E and SE. Anchor in 3m or more over sand and rock. There is a landing and miniature boat harbour at the N end of the bay, with a track to the lighthouse (Fl(4)20s85m18M, white tower and building 18m) which stands at the N end of the island.

There are no facilities ashore, though temporary beach restaurants do set up in summer when the island is a popular destination with tourist boats. The protected green lizard abounds.

⚓ CALA CONTA (COMTE)

38°57′.9N 01°13′.4E

A small *cala* on the mainland shore just N of the shoals running out to Isla Bosque, but exposed. Anchor in 5–6m over sand, off a fine beach fringed by fishermen's huts.

⚓ CALA ROIG (ROJA)

38°58′.3N 01°14′.1E

A rocky-sided *cala* open to the N sector, not recommended unless conditions are good. The impressive Torre de Rovira, built in 1763 to protect Ibiza's W coast, stands on the headland of that name W of the *cala*. Shoals run out towards Isla Payaret some 200m NE of the point.

⚓ CALA BASA

38°58′.2N 01°14′.6E

A large and attractive *cala* with a sandy beach at its head, surrounded by pine woods and low cliffs, open to N and NE. Anchor in 5–8m over sand. There is a landing stage used by tourist boats, several beach restaurants and cafés, and a nearby camp site. Though often crowded during the day, the beach is usually deserted by evening.

Cala Basa: yachts anchored on W side. Note the swimmers' buoys   *GW*

⚓ PORT DEL TORRENT

38°58′.2N 01°15′.9E

A large angled *cala* with low rocky sides and a sandy beach at its head, open to the N sector. Anchor in 4–6m over sand, rock and weed. Small yachts may be able to tuck into the sheltered E arm, though this is now partly occupied by permanent moorings. A careful watch should be kept for swimmers and water-skiers, as well as on the depth. Larger vessels should anchor further NW (see plan) where the holding is also somewhat better, but be ready to depart at the threat of onshore winds.

Port del Torrent: only a *cala*, but offering shelter deep inside

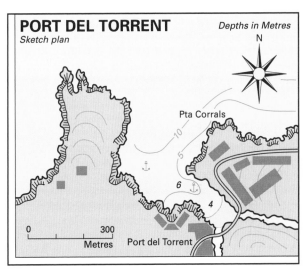

Beach bars and restaurants abound, with a supermarket some 100m to the S. Hotels and apartment blocks fringe the bay to the E and S.

PUNTA XINXÓ (Chinchó)

38°58′.5N 01°17′.1E

A very low, rocky-cliffed promontory, difficult to identify except for the lighthouse on the point (Fl(2)G.7s9m5M green column on white base displaying a green triangle). A road and buildings lie behind.

IB2 Puerto de San Antonio (Sant Antoni de Portmany)

A harbour easy to enter in all conditions, tucked into the N end of a large bay, with berthing for 330 yachts at Club Náutico, San Antonio, though all usually occupied

Location
38°58′.5N 01°17′.9E

Communications
Yacht harbour (San Antonio Náutico) VHF Ch 09 (0830–1330 and 1600–2100).
Port Authority ☎ 971 340503
Club Náutico San Antonio ☎ 971 340645
Fax 971 345607
Email Info@nauticsantantoni.com
www.nauticsantantoni.com

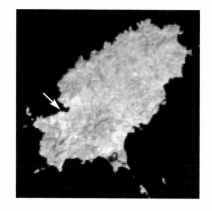

The harbour

A yachting and fishing harbour in a deep bay partially protected by a breakwater. Several private moorings line the shore but it is difficult to get a berth or find space here at any time.

Bahía de San Antonio

PILOTAGE

Approach

⊕10 38°58′.8N 01°17′.0E Puerto de San Antonio

From NE and N Cabo Eubarca, which has a cone-shaped top, and Cabo Nonó, which is covered with pine woods, are high, steep headlands and easy to identify. The Islas Margaritas can be left on either side. Enter the bay of San Antonio on a southerly course, steering initally towards a group of distant

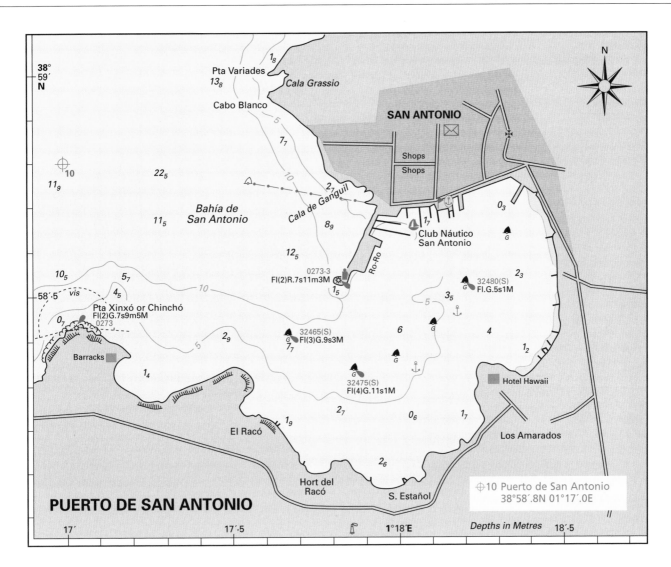

mountains. When well inside the bay the head of the breakwater with its red column and white base will open up.

From W and S Isla Conejera with its conspicuous lighthouse is easily seen. In bad weather it is advisable to pass outside this island with an offing of at least 200m before setting a SE course towards the harbour. In settled conditions the passage between Isla Conejera and Isla Bosque can be used. If approaching from the Iberian mainland note that the Islas Bledas lie some 2½ miles W of Isla Conejera, only the largest having a lighthouse.

Anchorage in the approach

There are several possible *cala* anchorages on the S side of the Bahía de San Antonio, as detailed in the preceding pages.

Entrance

Underwater obstructions extend a short distance beyond the end of the breakwater, so allow at least 50m. Otherwise the entrance is wide and without hazards, though shoals run out a short way beyond Punta Xinxó (Chinchó) and its equally inconspicuous eastern neighbour: keep at least the first two starboard-hand buoys to starboard.

Berthing

Club Náutico San Antonio has 330 berths, but even with the latest extension, vacant berths are seldom available in high season.

A small dinghy quay administered by the Port Authority exists in the extreme NE of the bay. It is forbidden for yachts to berth alongside the breakwater.

Anchorage in the bay

Anchor to the S and E of the green buoys marking the access channel in 5m or less, in sand and weed. Holding is poor in patches, with the best holding in the N of the bay.

Ro-Ro ferries which berth near the root of the breakwater and on the widened area must not be impeded, and a channel must also be left for the fishing boats and tourist ferries which berth E of the *club náutico* pontoons. As much of the bay is occupied by moorings this leaves limited space for anchoring in the northern part of the bay but even in the height of summer there is usually room to be found further S.

Puerto de San Antonio

Moorings

There are a few private moorings, some of which may be available. However one can never be sure of intended maximum tonnage, state of repair, or when the owner will return. Certainly a yacht on a borrowed mooring should never be left unattended.

Facilities

Water Taps on the pontoons and at the *club náutico*, available 1000-1300 on payment of a fee. It is very brackish and unsuitable for drinking.

Electricity On the pontoons.

Fuel Diesel and petrol from pumps on the breakwater. Diesel at the *club náutico*.

Provisions A wide range of shops and supermarkets in the town, several on the road leading from opposite the *club náutico*. Also two small supermarkets behind the prominent Hotel Hawaii on the SE shore of the bay. A produce market on the Carrer Vara del Rey.

Ice From the *club náutico* bar.

Chandlery On the road opposite the *club náutico*.

Charts The only agent for Spanish charts on the island is Valnautica SL, Ibinave, Travesia del Mar s/n, local 2, San Antonio ☎ 971 34 52 51 *Fax* 971 34 67 32 *Email* ibnave@wanadoo.es.

Repairs A small yard at the *club náutico* able to handle routine maintenance, painting, etc. and other craftsmen and engineers are also available – enquire at the club. A 6.5-tonne mobile crane.

San Antonio: a view along the promenade *GW*

Yacht club The Club Náutico San Antonio welcomes visiting yachtsmen, including those anchored off. It has a pleasant bar/restaurant, and an excellent view from its terrace. Several of the staff speak English. ☎ 971 34 06 45.

Showers At the *club náutico*. The crews of yachts anchored off are charged a small fee.

Banks In the town, most with credit card facilities.

Hospital/medical services In the town.

Transport

Car hire/taxis In the town, or arrange through the *club náutico*.

Buses Regular bus service to Ibiza and elsewhere.

Ferries Ferry service to the Spanish mainland.

History

The harbour has probably been in use since prehistoric times, and certainly since the Phoenician and Carthaginian eras. In Roman times it was called Portús Magnus, changed by the Ibizencos to Portmany (meaning 'big bay'). It is claimed that Isla Conejera ('rabbit's burrow') was the birthplace of the Carthaginian warrior Hannibal – not impossible, since the island was in the hands of the Carthaginians at the time. Certainly, many of the stone-slingers in his army came from the nearby Islas Bledas.

Sights ashore locally

Little is now evident of the original fishing village, which has given way to tourist development and the bay is now lined with high-rise apartment buildings and hotels, mainly for young English tourists. Although the town itself is without charm, the bay is still surprisingly attractive and largely surrounded by rolling, tree-covered hills.

In spite of its reputation as a noisy and crowded holiday resort, San Antonio still makes a good base for exploring the western and northern coasts.

There are cave paintings of disputed date at the cave 'des Vi' near Cabo Nonó, and a subterranean chapel dedicated to Santa Inés (Santa Agnès in Ibicenco) close N of the town. The church of San Antonio de Portmany, parts of which date back to 1305, is also worth a visit.

Local events

On 17 January a fiesta is held in honour of San Antonio (patron saint), while on 16 July there is the fiesta of Our Lady of Mont Carmel, with a regatta on the following Sunday. 24 August sees the fiesta of San Bartolomé.

Eating Out

An enormous range of cafés and restaurants to suit all purses.

I. IBIZA

View across Bahía de San Antonio   *GW*

4. Cala Grassió to Punta Moscarté

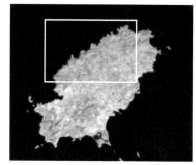

WAYPOINTS
⊕11 Islas Margaritas
     (Margalides) W   39°03′.0N 01°18′.6E
⊕12 Cabo Eubarca   39°04′.6N 01°21′.4E
⊕13 Isla Murada   39°05′.8N 01°25′.9E
⊕14 Punta Charracó   39°06′.7N 01°29′.4E

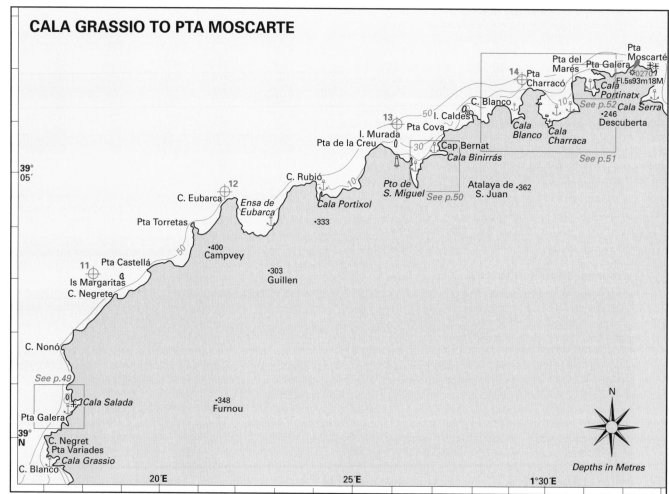

⚓ CALA GRASSIÓ (GRACIÓ)

38°59′.5N 01°17′.3E

A *cala* surrounded by low cliffs, splitting into two branches near its head, both with sandy beaches. Open to W and SW. Anchor in 4–6m over sand. The immediate surroundings are wooded, with houses and apartments set further back. Both beaches are popular with tourist boats and the usual bars and restaurant will be found ashore.

Looking N over Pto Variades from Cala Grassio towards Pto Galera

Cala Salada: still an unspoilt spot to anchor

⚓ CALA SALADA
39°00′.6N 01°17′.8E

A narrow, largely unspoilt *cala* with steep rocky sides and woods above. The small island of S'Illeta lies close inshore to the N. Anchor in 4–8m over sand and thin weed, taking care to avoid an unmarked rock carrying some 2.8m in the N of the *cala*. Fishermen's huts line the S side where there is a small quay.

The beaches are popular with day tourists from San Antonio, and there are beach bars and restaurants ashore. Part of the beach, marked by a line of white buoys, is marked off for swimmers as a defence against the many water-skiers.

⊕11 Islas Margaritas (Margalides) W 39°03′.0N 01°18′.6E

ISLAS MARGARITAS (SES MARGALIDES)
39°03′N 01°19′E

A horseshoe-shaped group of rocks with a low arch through their centre. They can be left on either side when coastal sailing, an offing of 350m ensuring good water.

PUNTA TORRETAS
39°04′.0N 01°20′.6E

A relatively low promontory running out as an apparent afterthought from the surrounding 150-200m cliffs. From some directions it appears as two towers or a small fort. A natural arch runs through the point.

CABO EUBARCA (CAP DES MOSSONS)
39°04′.5N 01°21′.5E

A high, steep-cliffed promontory topped by a regular cone (262m).

⊕12 39°04′.6N 01°21′.4E Cap Eubarca

⚓ ENSENADA DE EUBARCA (D'ALBARCA)
39°04′.0N 01°22′.4E

A large, high-cliffed bay with shallowish rocky sides, sheltered by Cabo Eubarca to the W and Cabo Rubió to the E. The holding is mostly rock with sand patches; use with care. The *cala* itself is deserted, but there is a village up the track leading inland.

CABO RUBIÓ
39°04′.8N 01°23′.8E

A high, steep-cliffed promontory.

Punta Torretas: a rugged coastline

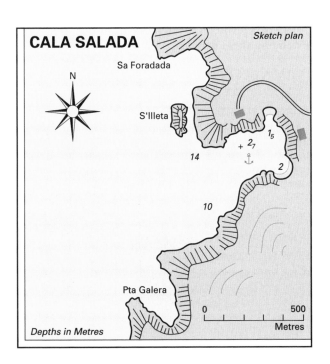

Cala Portixol: a bay cut into rugged scenery

⚓ CALA PORTIXOL
39°04´.6N 01°23´.9E

A very small horseshoe *cala* just E of Cabo Rubió, open to N and NE but otherwise surrounded by high cliffs. Anchor in 4–5m over sand and rock (there is a sand patch near the centre of the *cala*) off the sand and stone beach.

⊕ 13 39°05´.8N 01°25´.9E Isla Murada

⚓ PUERTO DE SAN MIGUEL
39°05´.2N 01°26´.5E

Not a true port but a deeply indented *cala*, well protected by Isla Bosch (a rocky peninsula stretching nearly halfway across the inner entrance on the W

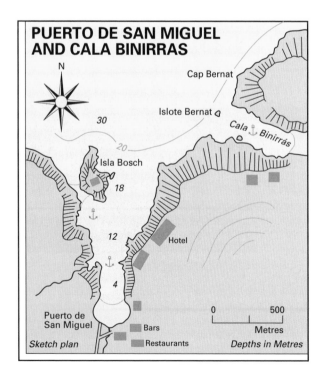

side) and surrounded by cliffs. If approaching from the W and planning to pass inside Isla Murada, (⊕13) watch out for an isolated rock 1.5–2m high which lies in the passage between the island and the shore towards Punta de la Creu.

Anchor in 4–8m over sand behind the peninsula or off the larger of the two beaches, open only to N and NE. There are some permanent moorings and a buoyed-off area reserved for the water-ski school.

At the head of the *cala* are apartment blocks and hotels. The beach is usually crowded in season, with beach bars and restaurants flourishing. There is a good supermarket on the W side of the *cala*.

⚓ CALA BINIRRÁS (BENIRRÁS)
39°05´.3N 01°27´.1E

A small *cala* between steep cliffs, less than 1000m E of Puerto de San Miguel. The rocky, pinnacled Islote Bernat (27m) lies in the middle of the entrance, from some angles looking uncannily like the elderly Queen Victoria on her throne! It is without outliers and can safely be passed on either hand.

Anchor in 5–8m over sand near the head of the *cala*, avoiding some rocky shallows in the SE corner. Although as yet still undeveloped other than a few bars and restaurants, the beach is often crowded.

PUNTA COVA DE ORENGA
39°05´.8N 01°27´.2E

A high, cliffed point with a cave at its foot.

ISLAS CALDES (D'EN CALDERS)
39°06´.2N 01°27´.8E

A group of rocky islands close off Punta Caldes, itself between Punta Cova de Orenga and Cabo Blanco, with offliers up to 350m offshore.

CABO BLANCO
39°06´.3N 01°28´.5E

A spit is reported to stretch NE from this headland, extending some distance offshore.

⚓ CALA BLANCO
39°06´.2N 01°29´E

A small, attractive *cala* E of Cabo Blanco, open to the N sector and with two distinct 'corners'. Anchor in either corner over sand; some 5–6m will be found to the SW with 4–5m to the SE. Apart from two private houses the *cala* is deserted, and much of the surrounding land is private.

⊕ 14 39°06´.7N 01°29´.4E Pta Charracó

PUNTA CHARRACÓ (XARRACA)
39°06´.6N 01°29´.4E

A high (73m) cliff-edged headland, covered by trees.

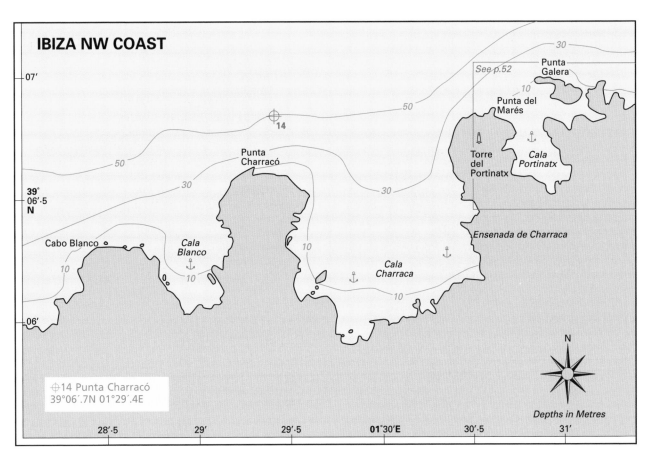

See p.52

⊕14 Punta Charracó
39°06′.7N 01°29′.4E

Depths in Metres

⚓ CALA CHARRACA (XARRACA)

39°06′.2N 01°30′E

A large, square bay surrounded by forested cliffs and offering several possible anchorages, open N–NE. There are two small rock-fringed islands near the W side of the *cala* plus a rock awash in the centre of the SW cove, so approach slowly with a lookout on the bow. The SE corner is without dangers. Anchor in 5–6m over stones and sand to suit wind direction.

A road runs down to the SW corner where there are fishermen's huts, a few houses and a restaurant.

PUNTA DEL MARÉS

39°06′.9N 01°30′.7E

A 54m headland crowned by a 9m watchtower. The 'cliffs' are set well back from the present shoreline.

⚓ CALA PORTINATX

39°06′.8N 01°30′.8E

An attractive multiple *cala* against a backdrop of wooded mountains, Cala Portinatx has seen considerable tourist development over recent years. There are three arms, each with a sandy beach.

Cala Portinatx: looking NE over Punta Moscarté and its unusual lighthouse

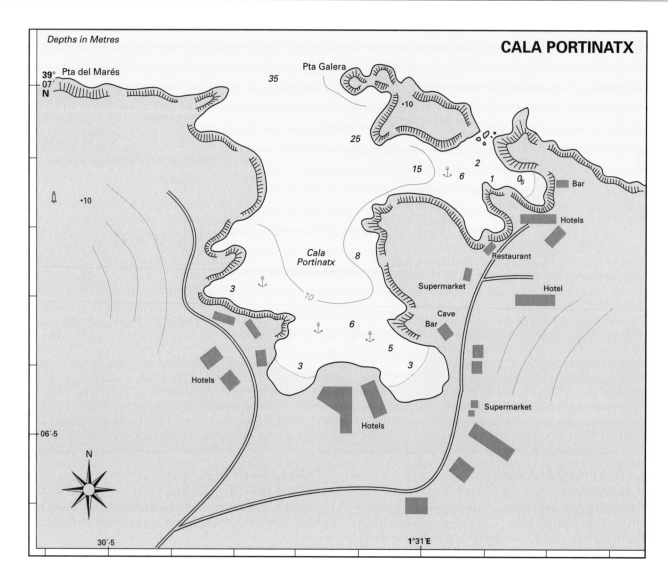

CALA PORTINATX

Depths in Metres

There are bars, restaurants and discos at night (and sometimes during the day).

Anchor in 3–15m over sand and weed as space permits (but note that holding is patchy and very poor in places) open to NW and N. There are some private moorings, mostly in the eastern arm, and each beach has an area roped off for swimmers.

Amongst the surrounding hotels and apartment blocks are many restaurants, supermarkets and other shops, plus a dive centre on the central beach where scuba bottles can be refilled.

The Torre de Portanix (or Torre de sa Plana) stands on Punta del Marés to the W of the *cala*. Like most of Ibiza's defensive towers it was built in the second half of the 18th century, but was never fitted with artillery and was later used as a dwelling.

⊕ 15 39°07′.4N 01°32′.0E Pta Moscarté

PUNTA MOSCARTÉ (DES MOSCARTER)
39°07′.2N 01°32′.1E

A prominent rocky headland topped by an unusual lighthouse (Fl.5s93m18M, white round tower with black diagonal stripes 52m: see photo).

Pta Moscarté light with its strange diagonal black stripes

5. Punta Den Serra to Islote Botafoch

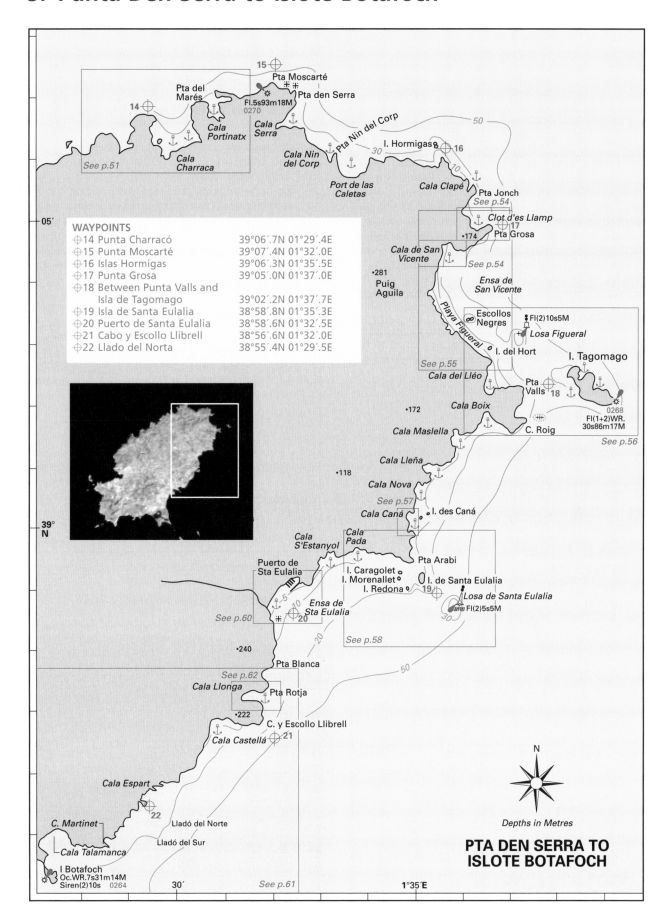

WAYPOINTS

⊕14	Punta Charracó	39°06′.7N 01°29′.4E
⊕15	Punta Moscarté	39°07′.4N 01°32′.0E
⊕16	Islas Hormigas	39°06′.3N 01°35′.5E
⊕17	Punta Grosa	39°05′.0N 01°37′.0E
⊕18	Between Punta Valls and	
	Isla de Tagomago	39°02′.2N 01°37′.7E
⊕19	Isla de Santa Eulalia	38°58′.8N 01°35′.3E
⊕20	Puerto de Santa Eulalia	38°58′.6N 01°32′.5E
⊕21	Cabo y Escollo Llibrell	38°56′.6N 01°32′.0E
⊕22	Llado del Norta	38°55′.4N 01°29′.5E

Depths in Metres

PTA DEN SERRA TO ISLOTE BOTAFOCH

I. IBIZA

⚓ CALA SERRA

39°06′.5N 01°32′.5E

An attractive rocky *cala* open to NE and E and surrounded by wooded hills. Anchor in 4–5m over sand and rock close to the small stony beach, possibly taking a line to the rocks to limit swinging. Deserted until recently, a tourist development has taken shape to the NW of the *cala*, this has done little to disturb the remoteness of this bay.

⚓ CALA NIN DEL CORP

39°06′N 01°33′.2E

A small, narrow *cala* to the W of Punta Nin del Corp, which can be difficult to identify from offshore. Anchor in 3–4m near the head of the *cala* over rock, stones and weed, open to the N sector. A second anchor or a line ashore may be needed to limit swinging. Some fishermen's huts will be found on the beach but there are no other buildings.

⚓ PORT DE LAS CALETAS (RACÓ DE SA TALAIA)

39°05′.9N 01°33′.6E

Another misnomer, being a wide but undeveloped *cala* lying beneath high rocky cliffs and open to the N sector. Houses line the zigzag road up from the small beach. Anchor in the W part of the *cala* close inshore in 10m over rock, stone or sand; a breaking shoal lies between this anchorage and the beach.

⊕ 16 39°06′.3N 01°35′.5E Islas Hormigas

⚓ CALA CLAPÉ (CALA JONE)

39°05′.5N 01°36′.2E

A small *cala* NW of Punta Jonch (Punta Jone), open to N sector and fringed by rocks on its S side. Anchor in the middle of the *cala* over sand.

⚓ CLOT D'ES LLAMP

39°04′.9N 01°36′.4E

A coastal anchorage on the N side of Punta Grosa, useful for the crossing to and from Mallorca. Anchor inshore in 4–6m over sand and stone. Open to the N sector and the E, but protected from other directions by high cliffs containing some fantastic rock formations, including a large stalactite cave. Landing can be difficult, but once ashore there are steps up to some hotels and a supermarket.

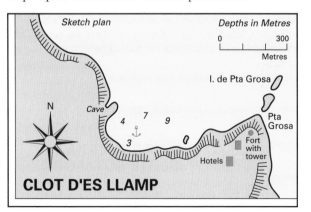

⊕ 17 39°05′.0N 01°37′.0E Pta Grosa

PUNTA GROSA

39°04′.9N 01°36′.7E

A high (174m), rocky, cliffed point with two offlying islands. A small square fort with a distinctive single tower stands on the headland.

⚓ CALA DE SAN VICENTE (SANT VICENC)

39°04′.5N 01°35′.6E

A well-protected anchorage at the N end of a long bay, the Ensenada de San Vicente, open to the SE and with some fetch from the S. Anchor close inshore in 3–6m over sand and weed, being careful to avoid an underwater cable from Palma which terminates near the road (see plan). The beach is lined by hotels and tourist apartments against a backdrop of high wooded hills. The beach gets crowded in season and the usual bars and restaurants will be found ashore.

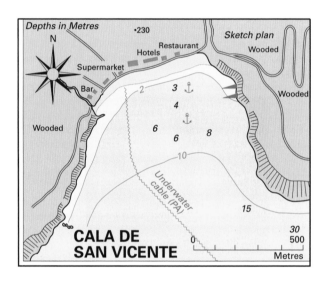

Cala de San Vicente: again showing the spectacular countryside

The cave temple of Es Cuyeram, dating back to the 5th century BC and later dedicated to the Carthaginian goddess Tanit, lies in the hills to the N. Excavated in 1907, most of the artefacts have now been moved to the Archaeological Museum of Ibiza.

PLAYA FIGUERAL

Centred on 39°03'.4N 01°36'E

A long stony beach occupying the S part of the Ensenada de San Vicente and with various offlying dangers. Taken from N to S these are:

- The Escollos Negres, three small, low, black, rocky islands lying up to 0.4 miles offshore
- Losa Figueral (39°03'.1N 01°37'.3E), is an awash rock 0.6 miles off the beach. An isolated, lit (Fl(2)10s5M), danger pillar buoy has been laid nearby with ⁞ topmark. Note that dangerous, rocky shoals extend 500m N and S of the Losa itself
- Isla del Hort, 20m in height, lying 200m off the coast inshore of Losa Figueral.

Small inshore rocky islets line much of the playa, in addition to the above.

⚓ CALA DEL LLÉO (CALA SAN CARLOS)

39°02'.3N 01°36'.6E

An open bay anchorage under high cliffs, S of Playa Figueral and NW of Punta Valls. There are dangerous rocks on either side of the bay – approach the centre of the sandy beach on a bearing of 220° to anchor in 4–6m over sand and rock. A few fishermen's huts will be found at the head of the *cala* with a café a short walk inland.

PUNTA VALLS

39°02'.3N 01°37'.3E

A 67m cliffed promontory with a 9m stone tower.

ISLA TAGOMAGO

39°01'.9N 01°39'.0E (lighthouse)

A very conspicuous island nearly one mile long which resembles a huge dolphin heading out to sea. The lighthouse at its SE tip (Fl(1+2)WR.30s 86m17M White octagonal tower on building 23m) has a red sector 037° to 043.5°over Losa de Santa Eulalia and is obscured from the W by a 114m hill. A large white house occupies the centre of the island.

Passage between Isla Tagomago and Ibiza

⊕18 39°02'.2N 01°37'.7E Between Pta Valls and Isla Tagomago

A clear passage 0.8 miles wide and around 40m deep separates Isla Tagomago from Ibiza. However, be aware of the unmarked wreck off Cabo Roig (see plan below).

⚓ ISLA TAGOMAGO, NE ANCHORAGES

39°02'.4N 01°38'.5E and 39°02'.2N 01°38'.8E

Two small *calas* open to the NE sector, the NE *cala* tucked in behind breaking rocks. Approach with care: the water is deep until very close in, so anchor close inshore in 8–10m over rock with a few sand patches.

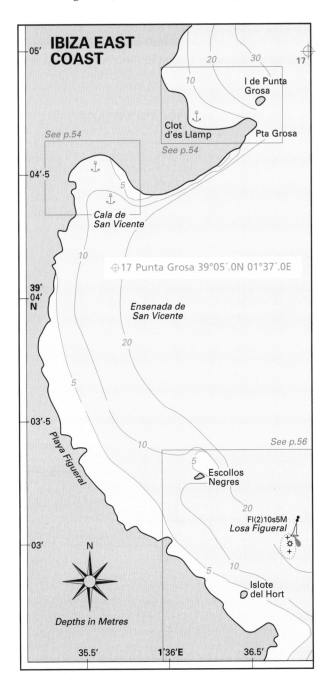

IBIZA EAST COAST

⊕17 Punta Grosa 39°05'.0N 01°37'.0E

Depths in Metres

Isla Tagomago: looking ESE into the W anchorage

Looking NW across Isla Tagomago towards Cala de San Vicente

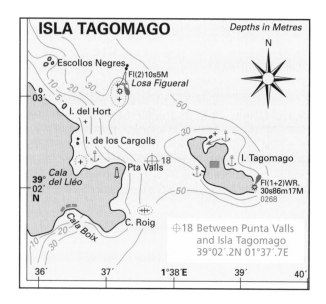

Isla Tagomago: SW anchorage

⚓ ISLA TAGOMAGO SW ANCHORAGE
39°02′.2N 01°38′.4E

A small *cala* open to the S and W sectors and susceptible to swell. Anchor close inshore in 5m over sand – a line to a rock may be required – or further off in 8–10m over weed. There are two landing places used by daily tourist boats in season, and a beach bar. A track leads up to the lighthouse.

CABO ROIG
39°01′.5N 01°37′.0E

A grey and reddish rocky cliffed headland (138m). A dangerous wreck, awash but unmarked, lies some 350m NE of the point. It should be given a wide berth.

Cala Boix: the fertile plain highlighted in the sun

⚓ CALA BOIX
39°01′.7N 01°36′.5E

A good anchorage W of Cabo Roig, surrounded by high rocky cliffs and open to the S sector. Anchor off the sandy beach in 3–8m over sand. There is a small jetty, a beach bar and a few houses ashore, plus a track to the main road.

⚓ CALA MASTELLA
39°01′.3N 01°35′.8E

A pleasant little *cala* with a beach at its head, surrounded by trees and some houses. Anchor in the centre of the *cala* in 2–4m over sand, weed and occasional rock patches. There is a beach bar and fish restaurant ashore, and the village of Ca'n Jordi about ½ mile away.

Cala Mastella: a tiny *cala* with a development at its head

Cala Lleña: An attractive beach

⚓ CALA LLEÑA (LLENYA)
39°00′.9N 01°35′.4E

A wide *cala* with an attractive beach, often crowded, in an outcrop of square white hotels and apartment buildings – the Club Cala Lleña – amongst the pine trees to the S. Anchor off the beach in 5m over sand, open to the E–SE–S.

⚓ CALA NOVA
39°00′.5N 01°35′.1E

Another wide *cala* with a long beach and pine trees, but somewhat less built up than Cala Lleña. Even so there are beach bars, etc. to cater for the tourists staying in nearby resort of Es Caná. Anchor in 4–6m over sand. If approaching from the S be sure to avoid the Islas des Caná, described below.

ISLAS DES CANÁ
39°00′.2N 01°35′.2E

The Islas des Caná comprise Isla de Caná (2.3m) and the smaller Sa Galera, plus some offlying rocks. Shoals run out from the headland N of Cala Caná to about halfway to the islands, and the inside passage should not be attempted without local knowledge.

⚓ CALA CANÁ (CANAR)
39°00′.1N 01°34′.7E

A popular open *cala* with a sandy beach and low rocky sides, surrounded by hotels and apartment blocks. There is a tiny harbour for speedboats and small fishing craft on the S shore. Anchor off the centre of the beach in 4–6m over sand as fringing rocks covered to a depth of 2m or so extend from either side. The Islas des Caná lie some 600m offshore due E of the *cala*, but are easily seen on approach.

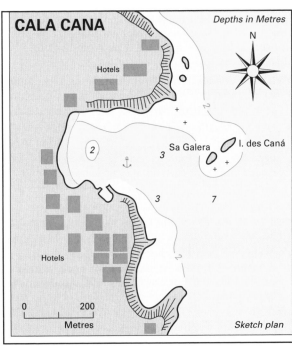

CALA CANA
Depths in Metres
N
Hotels
2
2
Sa Galera
I. des Caná
3
3
7
2
Hotels
0   200
Metres
Sketch plan

I. IBIZA

Cala Caná: surrounded by the usual tourist development, but still a good anchorage

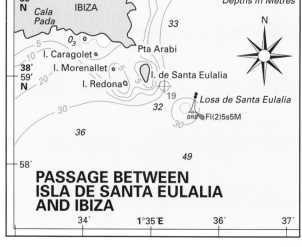

PASSAGE BETWEEN
ISLA DE SANTA EULALIA
AND IBIZA

⊕19 Isla de Santa Eulalia 38°58´.8N 01°35´.3E

PUNTA ARABI

38°59´.4N 01°35´E

A low (22m) whitish rocky point surmounted by buildings and dark trees.

ISLA DE SANTA EULALIA

38°59´.1N 01°35´.2E

A peardrop-shaped island, 37m in height and measuring some 350m along its N/S axis.

Passages between Isla de Santa Eulalia and Ibiza

⊕ 19 38°58´.8N 01°35´.3E E of Isla de Santa Eulalia

The passage itself should present no problems, being at least 400m wide and with depths of more than 5m throughout. However, a possible hazard is posed by four small rocky islands which straddle the western approach/exit (see plan). Taken from NE to NW these comprise:

- Isla Redona (22m), 400m SW of Isla de Santa Eulalia and easily seen. Close in it is foul to E and S. It can be left on either side.

- Isla Morenallet, a low, black, rocky islet usually surrounded by breaking seas, some 650m W of Isla de Santa Eulalia and 550m NW of Isla Redona. Easily seen in daylight but difficult to spot at night. Again, it can be left on either side.

- Isla Caragolet, similar in appearance to Isla Morenallet but 450m to the NW and about that distance offshore. On no account attempt to pass inside Isla Caragolet, due to shoals.

- A small unnamed island close inshore, which is surrounded by rocky shallows and should not be approached.

LOSA DE SANTA EULALIA

38°58´.8N 01°35´.7E

This rocky patch 1.7m deep lies 1000m SE of Isla Santa Eulalia and is often marked by broken water. A buoy has been laid 350m at 290° from the rock at 38°58´.7N 01°35´.5E, (Fl(2)5s5M Pillar buoy with topmark).

Other than a few nearby rocks the Losa de Santa Eulalia is surrounded by clear water, and a 32m deep passage separates it from Isla Santa Eulalia. It is covered by the red sector of the Islote Tagomago light.

⚓ CALA PADA

38°59´.5N 01°33´.7E

A very small anchorage in a tiny *cala*, surrounded by trees and open SE–S–SW. The eastern part of the bay is reserved for boardsailors. Anchor in 3m over sand off the small beach, avoiding the many permanent moorings. A beach restaurant lies directly behind the short wooden jetty.

⚓ CALA S'ESTANYOL

38°59´.5N 01°33´.2E

A small, wooded anchorage near the mouth of a river, off a sand and stone beach. Anchor in 3m over sand, stones and weed, open to E–SE–S. Two large white hotel or apartment buildings mark the southern end of the beach.

IB3 Puerto de Santa Eulalia del Río (Santa Eulària des Riu)

A safe and friendly harbour, 50M from Mallorca, easy to enter in most conditions, with berths for 755 vessels up to 25m

Location
38°58′.9N 01°32′.3E

Communications
Puerto Deportivo de Santa Eulalia VHF Ch 09
Club náutico ☎ 971 339754/336161 *Fax* 971 332810
Email ptostaeulalia@interbook.net

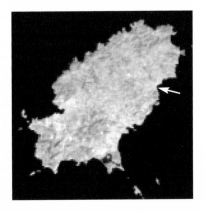

The marina

Santa Eulalia Marina is a large (755-berth) marina completed in 1991, with an easy approach and entrance other than in strong winds from SE and S. The staff are helpful and several speak good English.

PILOTAGE

Approach

⊕20 38°58′.6N 01°32′.5E Puerto de Santa Eulalia

From SW If coming from Puerto de Ibiza or Formentera be sure to identify the two small islands Lladó del Sur (6m), and Lladó del Norte (10m), which lie 0.8 and 1 mile respectively NE of Cabo Martinet, near the 30m contour. Once identified, they can safely be passed on either side. Cabo Llibrell can be rounded at 200m, after which the houses and high-rise buildings of Santa Eulalia will be seen. The harbour lies at the northern end of the town, near the middle of the wide bay.

From NE If approaching the island from the direction of Mallorca and intending to make Puerto de Santa Eulalia the first port of call, Isla Tagomago may be passed on either side. However, if taking the inshore passage give a wide berth to the wreck, awash but unmarked, 350m NE of Cabo Roig. The

Puerto de Santa Eulalia viewed from SE

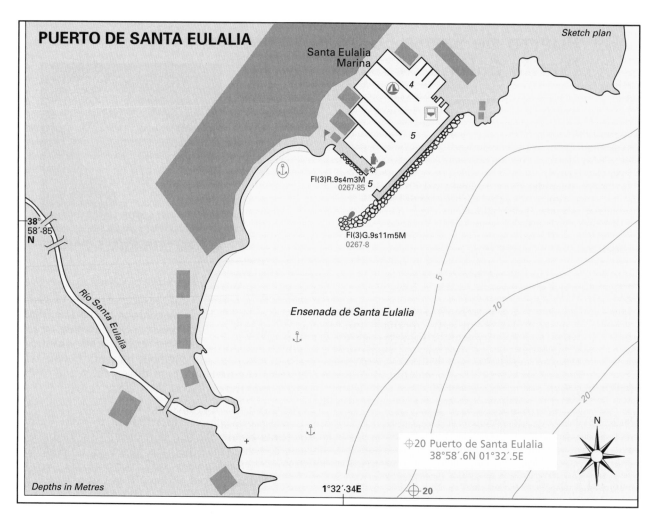

PUERTO DE SANTA EULALIA

Santa Eulalia Marina

Sketch plan

Fl(3)R.9s4m3M
0267·85

Fl(3)G.9s11m5M
0267·8

38° 58'·85 N

Río Santa Eulalia

Ensenada de Santa Eulalia

⊕20 Puerto de Santa Eulalia
38°58'.6N 01°32'.5E

Depths in Metres

1°32'·34E

⊕ 20

headland itself is steep-to. Off Punta Arabi, either set a course between Isla de Santa Eulalia and Losa de Santa Eulalia, or take one of the passages between Isla de Santa Eulalia and the mainland as described earlier. The harbour lies at the N end of the town, near the middle of the wide bay.

Anchorage in the approach

There are two small calas, Cala Pada and Cala S'Estanyol (detailed above and marked on the plan on page 53), in the N part of the bay. However, the anchorage most convenient for the town is that in the SW corner of the bay, near the mouth of the Río Santa Eulalia (see *Ensenada de Santa Eulalia* anchorage below). Anchoring outside the marina entrance is forbidden.

Entrance

At the end of the W mole is situated a round, white, three-storey tower which houses, amongst other things, the marina offices. Approach from anywhere in the bay keeping well clear of the end of the SE breakwater. The marina entrance is kept dredged to at least 5m.

Berthing

Berth alongside the fuel/reception pontoon, beneath the white tower, to be allocated a berth. There is a 3-knot speed limit. The marina can accommodate

yachts of up to 25m LOA and 4.5m draught. However, like many marinas in the Islas Baleares it is frequently full to capacity during the high season.

Facilities

Water Taps on pontoons and quays. The water in Ibiza is of variable quality so if possible consult other yachtsmen before filling tanks.

Electricity 220v AC points on pontoons and quays.

Fuel Diesel and petrol pumps close beneath the tower on the W mole.

Provisions Shops and supermarkets in Santa Eulalia del Rio nearby, where most requirements can be met. All-day market on Wednesdays in summer. There is also a supermarket at the harbour.

Ice From the marina office.

Chandlery In the marina complex.

Repairs Marina Río boatyard can handle all usual work including GRP repairs ☎ 971 33 04 53 *Fax* 971 33 21 11. Travel-lift 60 tonnes.

Engineers At Marina Río, Boat Service Germany ☎/*Fax* 971 33 01 21 is a local service agent for Volvo Penta.

Showers In the 'control tower' building and behind the diving school at the NW end of the marina.

Launderette In the town.

Banks In the marina complex and in town.

Hospital In the town.

Transport

Car hire/taxis Can be arranged via the marina office.
Buses Regular service to Ibiza town (15 minute journey) and elsewhere.
Ferries Tourist ferries berth outside the harbour, near the root of the W mole.
Air services Ibiza airport 15 miles.

Sights ashore locally

Previously a fishing village and market centre based on the fortified 16th-century church at Puig de Missa, the hill above the river mouth, Santa Eulalia later became a centre for artists but is now a major tourist resort. The bay has been overwhelmed by hotels and other buildings in recent years, but still offers good, if crowded, sand and rock beaches.

There are many interesting buildings in the old town, plus the remains of a Roman aqueduct across the Río Santa Eulalia. The Ethnological Museum of the Pitiusan Islands is situated in the town.

Local events

Santa Eulalia's day is celebrated on 12 February. There is a Holy Week procession on the afternoon of Good Friday and a Festival of Flowers on the first Sunday in May. The Fiesta de Jesus is held on 8 September.

Eating out

Many, cafés and restaurants of all grades, including several in the marina itself.

Paella chef near Santa Eulalia   *GW*

ANCHORAGES AND FEATURES FROM PUERTO STA EULALIA TO PUERTO IBIZA

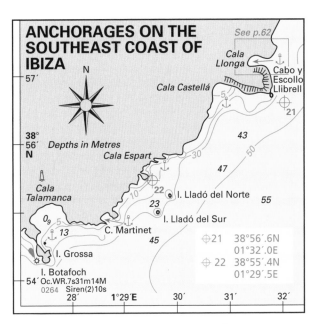

⚓ ENSENADA DE SANTA EULALIA (SANTA EULÀRIA)

38°58′.7N 01°32′.1E

Anchor in the SW corner of this large bay, near the mouth of Río Santa Eulalia, in 3–5m over sand and mud. A sandy beach runs NE, with several large hotels a short distance inland. All the facilities of Puerto de Santa Eulalia are available within half a mile. There are rocks awash near the shore S of the river mouth.

PUNTA ROTJA (ROJA)

38°57′.4N 01°31′.9E

A high (100m) red and whitish cliffed point with houses on the top.

⚓ CALA LLONGA

38°57′.2N 01°31′.6E

A long, high-sided *cala* with an excellent but often crowded beach at its head. The entrance can be difficult to spot until almost due E of the *cala*, when the huge blocks of flats and other buildings which line the wooded cliffs will be seen.

Anchor in 4–6 m over sand about halfway up the *cala* but keep clear of the swimmers' buoys at the W end of the *cala*. Although open only to the E and offering good protection, it can be gusty at times when W winds funnel down the valley. Swell from the E quadrant also works in, rebounding off the sides and setting yachts rolling.

Daily tourist boats visit from Santa Eulalia, causing some swell. Bars, restaurants and a supermarket will be found ashore. Buses run to Santa Eulalia. On 15 August Cala Llonga celebrates the anniversary of its patron saint.

I. IBIZA

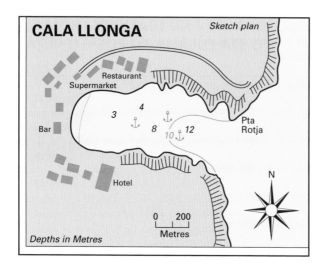

CALA LLONGA

Sketch plan

Restaurant
Supermarket

3   4

8   12

Bar

10

Pta
Rotja

Hotel

0   200

Metres

N

Depths in Metres

⊕ 21 38°56′.6N 01°32′.0E Cabo y Escollo Llibrell

CABO Y ESCOLLO LLIBRELL
38°56′.8N 01°31′.8E

A high (220m) headland of whitish rock with a small outlying islet.

⚓ CALA CASTELLÁ (SÓL D'EN SERRA)
38°56′.8N 01°30′.9E

A wide bay just S of Cabo y Escollo Llibrell, open to E through S to SW. Anchor in 5m over sand off the long sandy beach.

⚓ CALA ESPART
38°55′.6N 01°29′.4E

A small open bay with a sandy beach track to the road. Anchor in 5m over sand off the beach.

⊕ 22 38°55′.4N 01°29′.5E Between Lladó del Norte and the mainland

Cala Llonga: a popular anchorage in summer

LLADÓ DEL NORTE AND LLADÓ DEL SUR
38°55′.2N 01°29′.8E

Two small islands, 10m and 6m high respectively, which lie 0.5 and 0.7 miles S of Cala Espart, near the 30m contour. They may be left on either side.

⚓ CALA NE OF CABO MARTINET
38°54′.9N 01°28′.6E

A small unnamed *cala* on the NE side of the cape, to be used with care. Anchor off the small beach in 5m over sand and rock, open to E through S. There is a road at the top of the cliff.

CABO MARTINET
38°54′.8N 01°28′.7E

A low headland of dark rock with trees and houses on the top. An aero radiobeacon, inconspicuous, lies 700m to the WNW.

⚓ CALA TALAMANCA
38°54′.9N 01°27′.6E

A large open *cala* with a long sandy beach at its head. The head of the *cala* is shallow and has some reefs; anchor with care off Punta Sa Tabernera in 3–6m over sand and weed, although with careful sounding, a spot can be found further N in the middle of the *cala* (see plan on page 61).

Land in the NW corner of the bay – from which it is about 20 minutes' walk into Ibiza or a mere 350m to the facilities of Marina Botafoch – or on the isthmus leading to Isla Grossa.

Ibiza Town, viewed towards Marina Botafoch and Cala Talamanca *GW*

I. IBIZA

II. Formentera

Smaller than Ibiza and without an airport, Formentera is less developed and enjoys a slower pace of life. Nudism is an accepted feature. The low-lying plain in the north with its associated saltpans and lagoons are of interest. The only port, Puerto de Sabina, has limited facilities. There are a few pleasant anchorages around the island, and a large bay in which to drop anchor in the adjacent Isla Espalmador, linked to Formentera via a long sandy spit, broken by a rocky passage.

FORMENTERA WAYPOINTS
⊕4   Freu Grande channel   38°48'.6N 01°25'.6E
⊕23 Puerto de Sabina   38°44'.2N 01°25'.3E
⊕24 Isla del Gastabí (SW) 38°46'.3N 01°24'.7E
⊕25 Pta Single Mal   38°39'.8N 01°36'.0E
⊕26 Cabo Berbería   38°37'.7N 01°23'.2E
⊕27 Pta Gabina   38°43'.1N 01°22'.1E

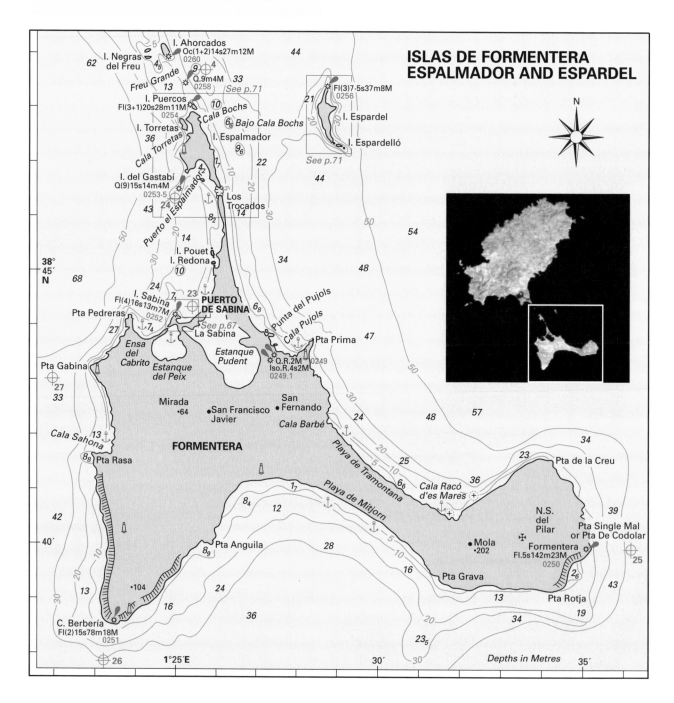

ISLAS DE FORMENTERA
ESPALMADOR AND ESPARDEL

NAVIGATIONAL INFORMATION FOR APPROACHES TO FORMENTERA

Coming up from North Africa or the Eastern Mediterranean and heading for Spain, Formentera is a good first landfall if W winds have hindered a westerly passage. In which case, head either for one of the anchorages described on the E side of the island, or for the only port on the island, Puerto de Sabina.

Magnetic variation

Formentera –00°42′W (decreasing 6′E annually).

Approach and coastal passage charts
(See *Appendix* for a full list of Balearic charts)

Imray	M3, M12, M13
Admiralty	1701, 1702, 2834
Spanish	7A, 478, 479, 479A
French	5505, 7114

Approach lights
0256 **Isla Espardel, N point** 38°48′.2N 01°28′.6E
Fl(3)7.5s37m8M White truncated conical tower 16m
0250 **Formentera (Punta Single Mal or Punta de Codolà)**
38°39′.7N 01°35′E Fl.5s142m23M White tower on white building 22m 150°-vis-050°
0251 **Cabo Berbería** 38°38′.4N 01°23′.3E Fl(2)15s78m18M White round tower 19m 234°-vis-1701°
0252 **Isla Sabina** 38°44′.1N 01°24′.9E Fl(4)16s13m7M White truncated conical tower 11m
0253.5 **Isla del Gastabí** 38°46′.5N 01°25′.1E Q(9)15s14m4M W cardinal tower, ⌶ topmark 8m

Buoys in the approach to Puerto de Sabina
32841(S) **Buoy 1** 38°44′.2N 01°25′.1E Fl.G.4s5M lateral starboard, green cylindrical buoy.
32842(S) **Buoy 2** 38°44′.3N 01°25′.5E Fl.R.4s5M lateral port, ■ topmark

Introduction

Formentera and the small island of Espalmador to its N, lie 2 miles S off Punta Portas, the most southerly tip of Ibiza. These islands remain underdeveloped as compared with the rest of the Balearic Islands, with just one harbour serving Formentera.

Espalmador, by far the smaller of the two and virtually deserted, is 1.5 miles long and less than a mile wide, rising to a height of 24m on its W side where there is a conspicuous tower. It is joined to Formentera by a long sandy spit broken by a shallow rocky passage, the Freu Poco, which separates the two islands.

Formentera is 10 miles long and 8 miles wide at its extremes, but being an elongated S-shape, covers an area of only 37 square miles. It comprises two high features: La Mola (192m), an island-like area to the E, and the peninsula running out to Cabo Berbería (107m) to the SW. These two higher regions are attached by a long, low neck of land. There is a large, low-lying plain in the northern part of the island, the greater part of it occupied by lagoons and salt pans. Salt has long been a major export. Around the two high features the coast is made up of rocky cliffs, but in the N and NE it is flat and sandy. Much of the island is cultivated and there are pine forests around La Mola.

There is a permanent population of around 5,000 (according to some sources, favoured with the longest life expectancy in Spain), most of whom are involved in some aspect of the tourist industry. Nudism has long been accepted on the beaches of Formentera. Do not be surprised to see sailboarders, waterskiers and yacht crews sailing around naked.

HISTORY

The history of Formentera and Espalmador parallels that of Ibiza. The oldest evidence of human occupation is the 2000BC megalithic tomb at Cana Costa. In Roman times they formed part of the Pityusae (Pine Islands): Espalmador was known as Ophioussa and Formentera as Frumentum or Frumentaria (a reference to the large amount of wheat it supplied), since corrupted into Formentera. During the hundreds of years following the downfall of Rome the island became depopulated as it was frequently raided by Barbarians, Moors, Saracens and even Scandinavians on their way home after taking part in one of the Crusades. It was not until 1697 that the island was repopulated, but even so was still subject to raids by pirates. The local inhabitants even turned to piracy themselves on occasion, and in 1806 captured the British 12-gun brig *Felicity* and sailed her into Ibiza.

TOURIST INFORMATION

Places of interest

San Francisco Javier is an attractive small town with a fortified church which once mounted guns on its tower, from which fine views can now be enjoyed. The ravine running down to Cala Sahona on the W coast and the area around La Mola in the E are worth visiting if time permits, with the caves of d'en Xeroni also of interest.

For details of tourist offices see the *General Introduction*.

Embassies

See *Appendix* for list of embassies.

One of the many anchorages around Formentera

F1 Puerto de Sabina (Port de sa Savina)

Puerto de Sabina is the only harbour on Formentera. It provides good protection from swell but not from the wind as it is a low-lying island. The two marinas within the harbour provide just over 200 yacht berths between them, for yachts up to 22m. Both are always full during the summer

Location
38°44´.1N 01°25´.1E

Distance from Spanish mainland
Javier 60M

Buoys
32843(S) **Buoy 3** 38°44´.2N 01°25´.4E Fl(2)R.15s3M lateral port, ∎ topmark
32844(S) **Buoy 4** 38°44´.1N 01°25´.4E Fl(3)R.19s3M lateral port, ∎ topmark

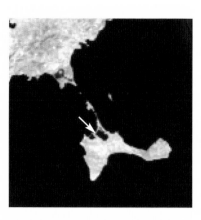

Communications
Marina de Formentera VHF Ch 09
Port Authority ☎ 971 32 31 32 *Fax* 971 32 32 52
www.marinadeformentera.com
Email info@marinadeformentera.com
Marina Formentera Mar
☎ 971 32 32 35/32 29 63
Fax 971 32 22 22
Email info@formenteramar.com
www.formenteramar.com

The port

Puerto de Sabina is the only harbour on Isla de Formentera and is in constant use by ferries, commercial shipping and fishing craft. Even so, it has maintained an attractive atmosphere and is not yet overrun with tourists. No room will be found for visiting yachts during the summer season. Even getting water may take a day or two of waiting at the anchorage. The harbour is easy to approach and enter, well sheltered once inside, though the breakwaters offer little protection from the wind. As with many harbours in the Islands, more than one marina operates within the same basin.

Formentera viewed from NW across Puerto de Sabina

PILOTAGE

Approach

⊕23 Puerto de Sabina 38°44´.2N 01°25´.3E

From E and NE Approach to the marina can be made either through the Freu Grande between Ibiza and Espalmador (see *Passages between Ibiza and Espalmador* on page 34) or around the S side of the island.

From W Approach from the Spanish mainland is straightforward with no offlying dangers.

From W, NW and N There are no hazards in the approach to Puerto de Sabina over an arc between Punta Pedreras (unlit) to the W and Isla Gastabí (lit) to the N. The white buildings behind the harbour show up well, as does the white tower of Isla Sabina lighthouse. Note that this lighthouse is situated near the end of a projecting rocky spur with shallow water to either side.

Entrance

Entrance to the main harbour is generally straightforward, though it can become dangerous in strong northerly or northwesterly winds due to shoaling depths. This has been alleviated with the aid of the four laid buoys noted above and shown on the plan below, but care is still needed in the entrance in rough weather. Normally the greatest hazard is posed by the many ferries which enter and leave at speed. Both Marina de Formentera in the SW corner of the basin and Marina Formentera Mar to the E are reached through relatively narrow inner entrances.

Berthing

Marina de Formentera at the SW end of the harbour. 108 berths up to 20m.

VHF Ch 09
☎ 971 32 31 32 *Fax* 971 32 10 33
Email reservas@marinadeformentera.com
www.marinadeformentera.com

Marina Formentera Mar to the E end berths 90 vessels.

Contact the marina office on approach or occupy any convenient vacant berth until allocated a spot by marina staff. Staff are usually prompt at any time of the day or night in summer, turning away most new arrivals!

☎ 971 32 32 35/32 29 63 *Fax* 971 32 22 22
Email info@formenteramar.com
www.formenteramar.com

Facilities

Water Metered taps on pontoons and quays.
Electricity 220v AC points on pontoons and quays, charged by the day.
Fuel Diesel pump on the central mole (see plan).
Repairs A small boatyard centred around the travel-lift and slipway. Boat repairs and engineering services can be arranged via the marina office. A 35-tonne travel-lift and slipway near the office. Oil collection facility.
Chandlery To the W of the main harbour.

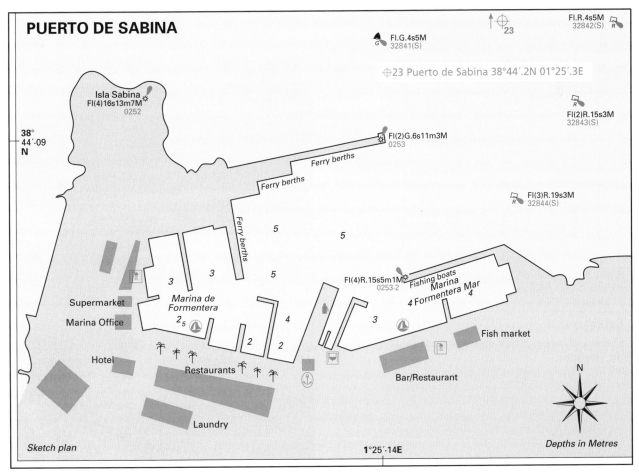

Provisions Two supermarkets near the harbour, plus more in San Francisco Javier a couple of miles inland. A fish market near the E basin.

Ice From the supermarket.

Yacht club The Club Náutico Formentera, formerly located opposite the marina office tower, was no longer in evidence in 2005/6.

Showers Blocks serving both marina basins, a small charge is made.

Laundry S of the harbour near the Estanque Peix.

Banks and post office None closer than San Francisco Javier, ATMs on the parade of shops and restaurants overlooking the harbour. Post office facililities in the marina.

Hospital/medical services Small hospital in San Francisco Javier.

Transport

Car hire/taxis Car hire from an office to the W of the main harbour ☎ 971 32 20 02. Bicycle hire is also popular and widely available. Motor scooters may also be rented from the marina.

Buses Bus service to San Francisco Javier.

Ferries Very frequent ferries (including hydrofoils) to Ibiza.

Eating out

Several pleasant cafés and restaurants overlooking the harbour.

Puerto de Sabina. Good protection from the seas, but the low-lying surroundings give little shelter from the wind

La Sabina, looking W. Ensenada del Cabrito at top of photo *GW*

ANCHORAGES AND FEATURES AROUND FORMENTERA

⚓ CALA SABINA
38°44′.2N 01°25′.4E

A wide *cala* E of Puerto de Sabina has been encroached by the extended harbour development, but leaves an anchorage extending to the beach, Playa del Cabali Borras. Anchor in 3–5m over sand and rocky beach. This area is open to W and N. There is a restaurant in the ruined windmill at the northern end of the beach.

⚓ ISLAS REDONA AND POUET (PONET)
38°45′.2N 01°25′.9E

Two small islands which, together with three even smaller islets, give some shelter to a shallow (2–3m) anchorage in a sandy bay otherwise open W–NW–N. The restaurant in the old windmill to the S is near a landing pontoon for local tourist ferries.

⚓ PLAYA TROCADOS (TROCADORS)
38°45′.7N 01°25′.9E

A long sand and rock beach open SW-W-NW. Anchor near the centre of the beach in 5m or less over sand: there are rocky outcrops near each end. A nature reserve has been enforced at the N end of the beach. Playa Trocados is popular with local boats and tourist ferries.

⚓ FREU POCO (PAS DE TROCADORS)
38°46′.5N 01°26′E

A very shallow channel separating Espalmador from Formentera, Freu Poco lies at the N end of the Playa Trocados, W of Isla Gastabí.

⊕24 38°46′.3N 01°24′.7E Isla del Gastabí

Espalmador looking NE. The shallow Freu Poco passage right and Freu Grande left of picture above Isla del Gastabí

The channel can only be transited by dinghy and sometimes it is possible to wade between the islands, though either of these would be unwise if any swell is breaking.

⚓ CALA PUJOLS
38°43′.6N 01°28′.1E

A rocky-sided *cala* on the NE coast, tucked between the Punta and Islas del Pujols, and Punta Prima; littered with shallows, and with rocks on its NW side. Approach with care and anchor in the SE corner in 8m over sand, NW of the old watchtower. There is a large holiday village nearby, complete with supermarkets and restaurants. There are leading marks for the fishing boat slipway NW of the anchorage, but these are not relevant for deep keeled vessels.

⚓ PLAYA DE TRAMONTANA
Centred on 38°41′.4N 01°30′.2E

A long sand and rock bay (more rock than sand) stretching for 3 miles between Cala Barbé and Cala Racó d'es Mares. Open to N and E sector. There are some interesting sea caves. Anchor close inshore in 5–10m over sand.

⚓ CALA RACÓ D'ES MARES (RECO DEL CALÓ)
38°40′.6N 01°31′.6E

A small fishing-boat *cala*, with steep rocky sides and a 1.5m deep rock 100m N of the entrance. There is a small jetty and a beach restaurant ashore.

⊕25 38°39′.8N 01°36′.0E Pta Single Mal

PUNTA SINGLE MAL (PUNTA DE CODOLAR OR DE SA RUDA)
38°39′.9N 01°35′.1E

The headland is 120m high with a tall white lighthouse (Fl.5s142m23M, white tower on white building 22m). It has steep rocky cliffs, as do Punta de la Creu to the N and Punta Rotja to the S. The light is obscured when bearing between 50° and 150°.

⚓ PLAYA DE MITJORN (MIGJORN)

Centred on 38°40´.6N 01°29´E

A 4-mile long sandy beach which is open to the S sector. Anchor in 5m over sand and rock in settled weather only. Unsuitable for an overnight stay.

CABO BERBERÍA

38°38´.5N 01°23´.5E

⊕26 38°47´.7N 01°23´.2E Cabo Berbería

A steep-to, rocky cliffed headland (55m) with a lighthouse (Fl(2)15s78m18M, round white tower 19m) and a watchtower 650m to the NE. The light is obscured when bearing between 170° and 234°.

⚓ CALA SAHONA (SAONA)

38°41´.8N 01°23´.3E

An excellent anchorage off a sandy beach with rocky sides, somewhat spoilt by a large hotel and other buildings ashore. Open to W–NW–N but protected from the S by Punta Rasa. Anchor off the beach in 3–5m over sand. There is a beach bar and restaurant ashore, and fishermen's huts to the S.

⊕27 38°43´.1N 01°22´.1E Pta Gabina

PUNTA GABINA (GAVINA)

38°43´.1N 01°22´.9E

A 14m cliffed headland topped by a 9m tower.

⚓ ENSENADA DEL CABRITO

38°43´.8N 01°24´.2E

Just W of the marina lies a large bay between Isla Sabina and Punta Pedreras: Ensenada del Cabrito. This offers a quiet anchorage in 3–5m over sand, rock and weed. It is open to the NNW through NE, but gives good protection from the S and W. Tucked in behind Pta Pedreras, swell is usually not a problem unless the wind turns to the N. This is a good spot if the marinas are full, while waiting for fuel or water.

⚓ ESTANQUE DEL PEIX (ESTANY DES PEIX)

38°43´.9N 01°24´.8E (entrance)

A large saltwater lagoon with a narrow entrance, carrying a scant 1m depth. Once inside depths are reported to increase, and many dinghies and other small pleasure and fishing craft are moored there. The larger Estanque (Estany) Pudent further E has no outlet to the sea.

Espalmador: looking NNE. Puerto El Espalmador centre, Ibiza top, with a yacht passing through Freu Grande passage

ISLA ESPALMADOR

⊕24 Isla del Gastabí (SW)
38°46′.3N 01°24′.7E

CALÓ MORO (CALA MORROS)
38°47′.4N 01°25′.3E

A tiny anchorage capable of taking one yacht in fair weather. Open to the S through to W. Anchor in 4m over rock and sand with a line ashore.

CALA BOCHS (CALA BOC OR CALA ROJA)
38°47′.6N 01°25′.6E

A small and shallow anchorage near the northern end of Espalmador. Anchor in 1.5m over sand off the small beach; otherwise, the shore is mostly rock.

ISLA ESPARDEL

The island is a mile long with an elevation of 29m. It is low to the W and cliffed to the E, with outlying rocks and islets extending 300m northwards (Piedra Espardelló Tramontana awash) and 500m SE from Punta Mitjorn to Islote Espardelló. There is no navigable passage between the latter. This island is now a nature reserve and marked by four yellow conical buoys Fl.Y.5s5M with × topmark. No swimming or fishing is allowed and the passage of any pleasure craft is prohibited inside the buoys.

ISLA ESPALMADOR

PUERTO EL ESPALMADOR
38°46′.8N 01°25′.7E

Puerto and *marina* in Spanish can mean any place to accommodate a vessel, even, sometimes, an anchorage off a beach. This bay is by no means a port, but it does give excellent shelter from the N and E, though it is open to the SW.

From the S, enter between Isla del Gastabí (lit) and Isla de la Alga. Do not attempt to cut between Isla de la Alga and Espalmador itself. From N or W, enter between Punta Gastabí and Isla del Gastabí, keeping at least 200m off Punta Gastabí to avoid shoals. Anchor in 3–5m over sand and weed.

This popular anchorage – often containing up to a hundred yachts as well as tourist ferries and local craft – gets very ploughed up towards the end of the season, when holding can be poor. However, it is large enough to cope with these numbers. It remains a tranquil and sheltered spot, probably because it is privately owned. There appears to be no serious attempt to prevent visitors using the beaches, though the owners' privacy should be respected.

SA GORDIOLA TOWER (TORRE ESPALMADOR)
38°47′.1N 01°25′.1E

A large (9.6m) and very conspicuous stone tower standing near the cliff edge (at a total elevation of 34m) on the W coast of Espalmador.

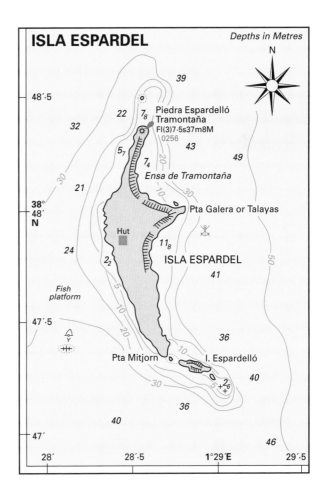

II. FORMENTERA AND ESPALMADOR

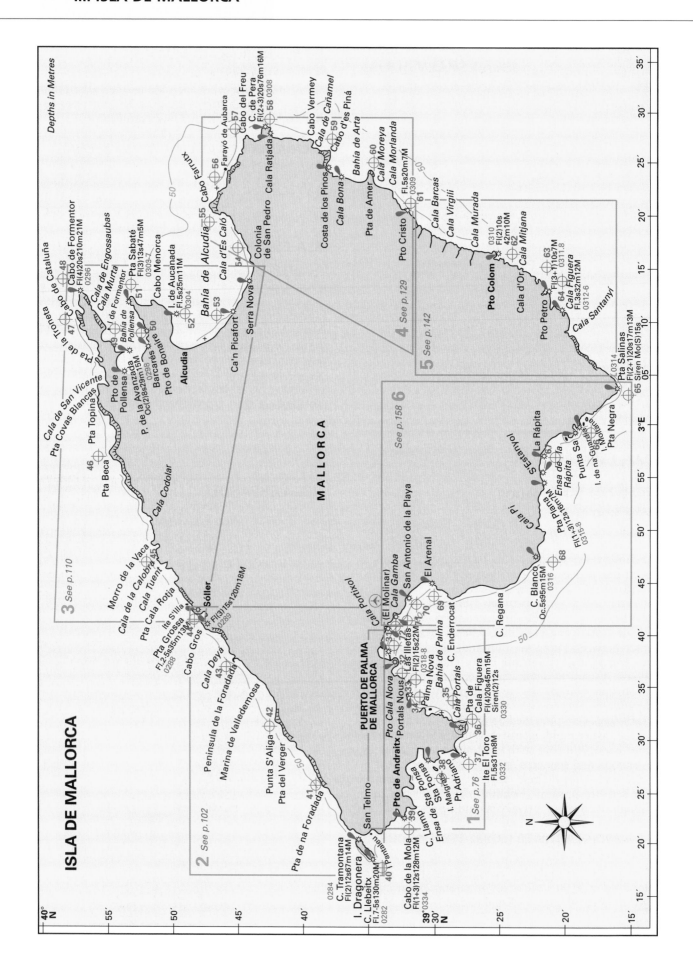

ISLA DE MALLORCA

MALLORCA

Depths in Metres

2 *See p.102*

3 *See p.110*

4 *See p.142*

5 *See p.129*

6 *See p.158*

1 *See p.76*

Cabo de Formentor
FI(4)20s210m21M
0296

Cabo de Formentor

Cala de Engossaubas
Cala Murta

P. de Formentor

Pta Sabaté
FI(3)13s47m5M
0303-7

Cabo Menorca

I. de Aucanada
FI.5s25m11M
0304

Bahía de Alcudia

55 Cabo
de Alcudia

Cala d'Es Caló

Farayó de Aubarca

Cabo del Freu
FI(2+3)20s76m16M
58 0308

C. de Pera

Cabo Vermey

Cala de Cañamel
59
Cabo d'es Piná

Bahía de Arta

Cala Moreya
60
Cala Morlanda

Pta de Amer

Pto Cristo
FI.5s20m7M
0309
61

Cala Barcas

Cala Virgili

Cala Murada

Cala Mitjana
0310
FI(2)10s
42m10M
62

Pto Colom
FI(3+1)10s7M
63
0311.8

Cala Figuera
FI.3s32m12M
0312-6

Pto Petro
64
0312-6

Cala d'Or

Cala Santanyi

Pta Salinas
FI(2+1)20s17m13M
Siren Mo(S)15s
65 0314

Serra Nova

Ca'n Picafort

Colonia
de San Pedro

Cala Ratjada

Cabo Fenaux

Costa de los Pinos

Cala Bona

Pta Negra

Pta Plana
FI(1+3)12s16m7M
0315-8

Ensa de la
Rápita

La Rápita

S'Estanyol

Punta Sa

I. de na Guardia
Molinar

I. de na Guardia

C. Regana

C. Blanco
Oc.5s96m15M
0316
68

El Arenal

San Antonio de la Playa

Cala Gamba

(El Molinar)

Cala Pi

Cala Portixol

Bahía de Palma

C. Enderrocat
69

70

Las Illetas
FI(2)15s22M
0318-8

Palma Nova

Cala Portals

Pta de
Cala Figuera
FI(4)20s45m15M
Siren(2)12s
0330
36

Portals Nous
Pto Cala Nova
FI(2)15s22M

Cala Nova

PUERTO DE PALMA
DE MALLORCA

Ite El Toro
FI.5s31m8M
0332
37

I. Malgrats
38

Pt Adrian
39 0334

C. Llamp
Ensa de Sta
Sta
Pta de Sta Ponsa

Pto de Andraitx

San Telmo

Cabo de la Mola
FI(1+3)12s128m12M
0334

C. Llebeitx
FI.7.5s130m20M
0282

C. Tramontana
FI(2)12s67m14M
0284

I. Dragonera

Pantaleu

Pta de na Foradada

Pta del Verger

Punta S'Aliga
42

Marina de Valledemosa

Peninsula de la Foradada
41

Cala Deyá
43

Cabo Deyá

Cabo Gros

Pta Grossa
FI.2.5s35m13M
0288

Ite S'Illa
44

Sóller
FI(3)15s120m18M
0289

Pta Cala Rotja

Cala Tuent

Cala de la Calobra
45

Morro de la Vaca

Cala Codolar

Pta Beca
46

Cala de San Vicente

Pta Covas Blancas

Pta de la Troneta de Cataluña

Pta Topinas

Cabo 47
48

Barcarés
Pto de Bonaire
50

Pto de
Pollensa

P. de la Avanzada
Oc(2)8s29m15M
0298

Bahía de
Pollensa
49

Alcudia

51
FI(3)13s47m5M

52
53
54

56
57

Cala Menorca

III. Mallorca

Mallorca, the capital of the Balearics, is the largest and most cosmopolitan of the group. There are many historical sites to visit, including the capital port of Palma which provides excellent berthing and every nautical requirement, including the necessary permits for the neighbouring island of Cabrera. There are many superb ports and anchorages around its coasts. Puerto de Sóller is of particular interest with its vintage tramway and Victorian train linking the port with Palma. Inland there are orange groves and pine forests, and restored windmills: a unique feature of the island.

SECTIONS

The coastline is considered in a clockwise direction around the island beginning at Palma. Cabrera is dealt with in Chapter IV.

NAVIGATIONAL INFORMATION ON APPROACHES TO MALLORCA

Coming from the S from North Africa or the eastern Mediterranean and heading for northern Spain or France, or a crew change, Mallorca may be the preferred landfall because of its size, international airport or the safe port of Palma. With many ports and anchorages to choose from and the huge Bahía de Palma, calmer waters in any weather conditions are assured. Passages to and from the other islands are described.

Magnetic variation

Mallorca – 0°47′W (decreasing 6′E annually) (2005)

MALLORCA WAYPOINTS

⊕31	Puerto de Palma	39°33′.4N 02°38′.5E
⊕32	Puerto de Cala Nova	39°32′.8N 02°36′.1E
⊕33	Las Illetas	39°31′.8N 02°35′.5E
⊕34	Puerto Portals	39°31′.5N 02°33′.8E
⊕35	Isla del Sech	39°28′.7N 02°32′.8E
⊕36	Punta de Cala Figuera	39°27′.2N 02°31′.5E
⊕37	Islote el Toro	39°27′.5N 02°28′.0E
⊕38	Isla Malgrats	39°29′.5N 02°26′.5E
⊕39	Cabo de la Mola	39°31′.6N 02°21′.4E
⊕40	Isla Dragonera (S)	39°33′.8N 02°18′.5E
⊕41	Punta de na Foradada	39°38′.5N 02°25′.2E
⊕42	Punta S'Aliga	39°42′.4N 02°31′.5E
⊕43	Peninsula de la Foradada	39°45′.6N 02°37′.2E
⊕44	Approach to Sóller	39°48′.0N 02°41′.2E
⊕45	Morro de la Vaca	39°52′.0N 02°48′.3E
⊕46	Punta Beca	39°55′.6N 02°57′.0E
⊕47	Cabo de Cataluña	39°58′.0N 03°10′.7E
⊕48	Cabo de Formentor	39°57′.8N 03°13′.0E
⊕49	Isla de Formentor (S)	39°55′.0N 03°09′.0E
⊕50	Puerto de Bonaire	39°52′.2N 03°08′.5E
⊕51	Cabo del Pinar	39°53′.5N 03°12′.7E
⊕52	Isla de Aucanada (S)	39°49′.9N 03°10′.3E
⊕53	Off C'an Picafort	39°46′.2N 03°09′.5E
⊕54	Off Puerto de Colonia de San Pedro	39°44′.5N 03°16′.3E
⊕55	SW of Cala Es Calo	39°46′.3N 03°19′.8E
⊕56	Farayó de Aubarca (W)	39°46′.2N 03°24′.3E
⊕57	Cabo del Freu	39°45′.0N 03°28′.0E
⊕58	Cabo de Pera	39°43′.0N 03°29′.2E
⊕59	Cabo d'es Piná (Del Pinar)	39°38′.0N 03°26′.5E
⊕60	Punta de Amer	39°34′.8N 03°24′.5E
⊕61	Cala Manacor (Porto Cristo)	39°32′.2N 03°20′.5E
⊕62	Punta de ses Crestas (Approach to Puerto Colom)	39°24′.7N 03°16′.2E
⊕63	Cala Llonga (Approach to Puerto de Cala D'or)	39°22′.0N 03°14′.2E
⊕64	Off Porto Petro	39°21′.3N 03°13′.2E
⊕65	Punta Salinas	39°15′.5N 03°03′.2E
⊕66	Off Puerto Colonia de Sant Jordi	39°18′.5N 02°59′.7E
⊕67	Puerto de la Rápita	39°21′.7N 02°57′.3E
⊕68	Cabo Blanco	39°21′.6N 02°47′.0E
⊕69	Off El Arenal	39°30′.3N 02°44′.5E
⊕70	Puerto de San Antonio	39°31′.7N 02°43′.0E
⊕71	Puerto de Cala Gamba	39°32′.7N 02°41′.7E
⊕72	Off Puerto de Cala Portixol	39°33′.4N 02°40′.1E

Approach and coastal passage charts
(See *Appendix* for a full list of Baleares charts)

Imray	M3
Admiralty	1702, 1703, 2831, 2832
Spanish	48E, 900, 965, 970, 421, 422, 423, 424, 425, 426, 427
French	5505, 7115, 7116, 7118

Approach lights

0318.8 **Puerto de Palma** 39°33′N 02°37′.5E Fl(2)15s41m22M Square brown stone tower, visible outside Bahía de Palma 327°-040°

0330 **Punta de Cala Figuera** 39°27′.5N 02°31′.4E Fl(4)20s45m15M Siren(2)12s White round tower, black diagonal stripes, on building 24m

0334 **Cabo de la Mola** 39°32′N 02°21′.9 Fl(1+3)12s128m12M White column, black bands, on white square tower 10m

0282 **Cabo Llebeitx** 39°34′.5N 02°18′.3E Fl.7.5s130m20M Masonry tower on stone building with red roof 15m 313°-vis-150°

0284 **Cabo Tramontana** 39°36′N 02°20′.4E Fl(2)12s67m14M
Round masonry tower on stone building with red roof
15m 095°-vis-230° and 346°-vis-027°

0289 **Cabo Gros** 39°47′.9N 02°41′E Fl(3)15s120m18M White
tower and house, red roof 22m 054°-vis-232°

0296 **Cabo Formentor** 39°57′.7N 03°12′.8E Fl(4)20s210m21M
White tower and house 22m

Note The characteristics of Cabo Formentor are almost
identical to those of Cabo Nati, Menorca

0303.7 **Punta Sabaté (Cabo del Pina)** 39°53′.6N 03°11′.8E
Fl(3)13s47m5M White triangular tower, black band 12m

0308 **Cabo de Pera** 39°43′N 03°28′.7E Fl(2+3)20s76m16M
White tower on white building with dark corners and
red roof 21m 148°-vis-010°

0310 **Punta de ses Crestas/Punta de la Farola** 39°24′.9N
03°16′.3E Fl(2)10s42m10M White round tower, three
black bands, on white building with red roof 25m 207°-
vis-006°

0312.6 **Torre d'en Beu** 39°19′.8N 03°10′.7E Fl.3s32m12M
White octagonal tower, vertical black stripes 6m

0314 **Punta Salinas** 39°16′N 03°03′.3E Fl(2+1)20s17m13M
SirenMo(S)15s White tower and building 17m 265°-vis-
116°

0316 **Cabo Blanco** 39°21′.9N 02°47′.3E Oc.5s95m15M White
tower and building 12m 336°-vis-115°

INTRODUCTION

Isla de Mallorca (also spelled Majorca and
pronounced as Mayorca) is the largest island of the
Baleares group, being some 62 miles long and 47
miles wide. The N and E coasts are mountainous
with numerous coves, whilst the S coast has rolling
hills and sandy beaches. The central plain is flat with
huge expanses of fertile agricultural terrain.
Mallorca has a very large port, several harbours and
many anchorages in *calas*. There is one large offlying
island to the south (Cabrera), described in the next
chapter.

The mountain range that fringes the NW-facing
coast is high, culminating in the 1,445m peak of
Puig Mayor. This stretch of coast is very rugged,
with steep rocky cliffs broken by a number of
indentations, nearly all located in the northeastern
section and providing some spectacular anchorages
for use in settled weather. Puerto de Sóller offers the
only harbour on the NW coast and a refuge in the
event of a NW *tramontana* or *mestral*, turning the
entire coastline into one long leeshore.

The coast that faces NE towards Menorca
consists of two large sandy bays, each with a major
harbour and a number of anchorages and smaller
harbours. While not as dramatic as the NW coast,
parts are attractive and safe harbours and
anchorages can be found in most conditions.

The SE coastline comprises the coast of the calas.
In general this 35 mile section has low rocky cliffs
with ranges of hills several miles inland. The
relatively straight run of the coast is broken by
numerous inlets in which lie small harbours and
anchorages, the majority very attractive. Notable on
this coast is the large but relatively shallow inlet of
Porto Colom, the best natural harbour and
anchorage in Mallorca and possibly in the whole
Islas Baleares. It was also the cheapest until now.

The remaining coast, facing the SW, is centred
around the large Bahía de Palma, where the majority
of the industry and population of the island is
situated. Palma de Mallorca, the capital and a major
port, can supply most material, cultural and holiday
requirements but, like all cities, it is busy, crowded
and noisy. On the SE side of this bay are high, white
cliffs and on the opposite side high, rocky cliffs
broken by a number of small bays and calas.

With the exception of the heads of the large sandy
bays, deep water can generally be carried very close
to the shore. Other than Isla de Cabrera and Isla
Dragonera there are no offshore dangers, and the few
smaller islands that exist are generally very close in.

Inland, Mallorca is unexpectedly beautiful, with
large areas, of fruit orchards in addition to olive
groves and fields of wheat and vegetables. In the
more hilly areas Moorish methods of terraced
cultivation are still to be seen. The mountains of the
NW provide dramatic views and some challenging
hill walks. Away from the coast – and particularly in
the eastern half of the island – many of the smaller
walled towns remain relatively unspoilt. One feels
saddened, and at the same time relieved, that so few
tourists appear to venture far beyond the nearest
beach and their package holiday hotel.

Two factors have tended to make the Mallorcans
more cosmopolitan and subtly different from the
inhabitants of the other islands in the group – firstly,
wide intermarriage with the Moors, who remained
in greater numbers than on the other islands, and,
secondly, the rise in power and prosperity of Palma
in the 14th and 15th centuries, which brought a flow
of riches and contact with the outside world which
the other islands lacked. Palma is still the seat of the
government and parliament of the Autonomous
Community of the Balearic Islands, and home to
well over half of the island's current population of
around 530,000 people.

HISTORY

Mallorca appears to have been inhabited for at least
6,000 years, with some of the earliest human traces
found in a cave near Sóller on the N coast. Later,
from around 1200BC, the bronze age *talayot* (tower)
culture flourished in both Mallorca and Menorca,
with sites near Artá on the E coast and Lluchmayor
further south. Little is known about these early
peoples, though successive invasions by Phoenicians,
Carthaginians and Greeks have left some traces.
According to the 1st century BC Greek writer
Diodorus, the inhabitants of both Mallorca and
Menorca wore few clothes and were called *gymnetes*
('naked men'), their islands being collectively known
as Gymnesia.

The Romans conquered Mallorca in 123BC and
remained until the 5th century. It was known to
them as Major, as opposed to Menorca, which was
called Minor, and these two formed, together with
Cabrera, the Insulae Baleares. The city of Pollentia,
now called Alcudia, became their capital, and they
also founded the harbours of Palma and Pollensa.
However, the Romans used the island more as a
staging post than as a permanent settlement and

there are few remains of buildings to be found. A notable exception is the Roman theatre at Alcudia, easily reached from the yacht harbour. After the departure of the Romans the island entered the dark ages, overrun by the Vandals and a favoured base for pirates and Corsairs.

Mallorca's next taste of prosperity was under the Moors, who arrived early in the 10th century. Roman Palma was renamed Medina Mayurqa and grew into a bustling city of some 25,000 inhabitants, while throughout the island agriculture was improved and irrigation canals built. However, almost equally little remains of this period, other than the delightful Arabian Baths and the Almudaina arch in Palma.

The destruction of Moorish Palma can fairly be laid at the door of King Jaime I (Rey Jaime Conquistador), who drove the Moors out in 1229, backed by the combined armies of Catalonia and Aragon. A monument to their landing stands on the headland overlooking Puerto de Santa Ponsa on the SW coast. With them the conquering army brought the Catalan language, which gradually evolved into the Mallorquín dialect spoken by many islanders today.

The 13th to 15th centuries were a golden age, with a vast increase in population and wealth. Palma, with its imposing Gothic cathedral, new castle and growing dock system, became a centre for trade inside the Mediterranean. However, as Spain gradually turned her attention westward towards the New World, her Mediterranean possessions became something of a backwater. Frequent attacks by

pirates resulted in coastal villages and towns being rebuilt several miles inland, with only a few huts on the shore or at the harbour. In this way the damage and loss caused by surprise raids were minimised. During the next few centuries little of historical importance took place in Mallorca, other than the building of many churches and of houses for the nobility.

Recent history

During the Spanish Civil War the island supported the Nationalists and suffered little damage. Greater changes have come about with the post-war advent of mass tourism. Not only are there now areas in which the ground can barely be seen for high-rise hotels or the beach for sunbeds, but the many support services, from tourist shops to smart restaurants, have revived Mallorca's fortunes and changed its former agricultural-based economy for ever.

TOURIST INFORMATION

Places of interest

In addition to places of interest described in the harbour sections, there are many other sites further inland which can be visited by taxi, bus or, in some cases, rail from almost any port. Mallorca is one place where it is well worth hiring a car. Car rental in the town centres is considerably cheaper than at the airports. There are spectacular mountain ranges and old *pueblos* (towns) to visit, along with the ancient remains of Moorish and Roman architecture.

High in the mountains near the NW coast is the Carthusian monastery at Valldemosa, which was once the palace of the Kings of Mallorca and has fine views. The road running E towards Sóller passes the Peninsula de la Foradada and the Son Marroig estate (once owned by Archduke Luis Salvador of Austria), before winding through Deya, famous for its associations with the writer Robert Graves. Further NE, Lluch boasts a monastery built in the 14th century, 305m high and with excellent views.

In the southern part of the island, Campos has Roman baths and a 15th-century church, while nearby Lluchmayor has prehistoric and Roman remains and is also the site of the battle where Mallorca lost her independence.

Look up the tourist information offices, where a wealth of information will be found on all the sites of interest. These are listed in the *General Introduction* and at www.illesbalears.es See also www.infomallorca.net for current events. Many books have been published on the sites of the island, a number of which are available at airports throughout Europe.

Embassies

For details of embassies see that section in the *Appendix*.

Roman bridge in Pollensa, NE Mallorca   GW

1. Puerto de Palma to Puerto de Andraitx

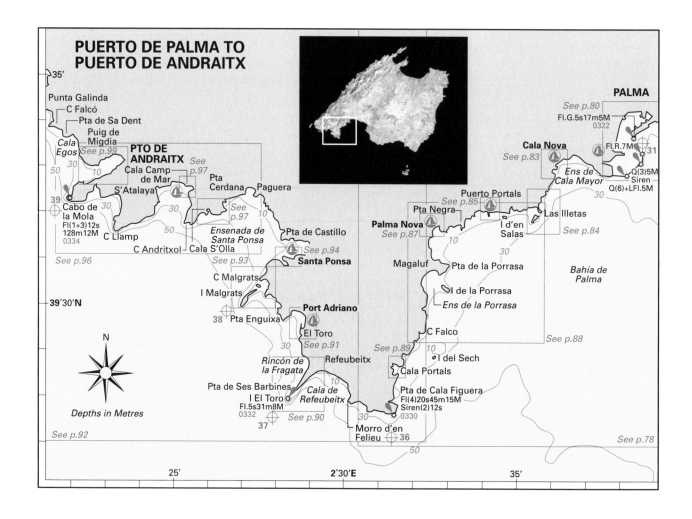

PUERTO DE PALMA TO
PUERTO DE ANDRAITX

35'

Punta Galinda
C Falcó
Pta de Sa Dent
Puig de
Migdia
Cala
Egos   See p.99   PTO DE
ANDRAITX   See
Cala Camp   p.97
de Mar
S'Atalaya
39   Cabo de
la Mola
Fl(1+3)12s
128m12M
0334

C Llamp
C Andritxol — Cala S'Olla
See p.96

39°30'N

N

Depths in Metres

See p.92

25'

PALMA
See p.80
Fl.G.5s17m5M
0322
Cala Nova   Fl.R.7M   31
See p.83
Ens de   Q(3)5M
Cala Mayor   Siren
Puerto Portals   Q(6)+LFl.5M
See p.85   30
Pta Negra   Las Illetas
Palma Nova   I d'en   See p.84
See p.87   Salas
10
Magaluf   Pta de la Porrasa   Bahía de
Palma
30
I de la Porrasa
Ens de la Porrasa

C Falco   See p.88
See p.89   10
I del Sech
Cala Portals
Pta de Cala Figuera
Fl(4)20s45m15M
Siren(2)12s
30   0330
Morro d'en
Felieu   36
50   See p.78

Pta
Cerdana   Paguera
See
p.97   10
Ensenada de
Santa Ponsa   Pta de Castillo
See p.93   See p.94
50
Santa Ponsa
C Malgrats
I Malgrats   Port Adriano
38   Pta Enguixa   El Toro
30   See p.91
Rincón de   Refeubeitx
la Fragata
Pta de Ses Barbines   Cala de
I El Toro   Refeubeitx
Fl.5s31m8M
0332   See p.90
37

2°30'E   35'

WAYPOINTS:
⊕31 Palma   39°33'.4N 02°38'.5E
⊕36 Punta de Cala Figuera   39°27'.2N 02°31'.5E
⊕37 Islote el Toro   39°27'.5N 02°28'.0E
⊕38 Isla Malgrats   39°29'.5N 02°26'.5E
⊕39 Punta de la Mola   39°31'.6N 02°21'.4E

Palma: looking over Muelle Viejo the ancient cathedral is
still well able to dominate the skyline after hundreds
of years   GW

M1 Puerto de Palma de Mallorca

Within this major commercial port lie several marinas with facilities for several thousand yachts of any size, including super-yachts. However, it is difficult to find a place to berth during July and August. Safe to enter in any weather

Location
39°33.5N 02°38´E

Distances
Ibiza 60M
Barcelona 120M

Communications
VHF Ch 6, 7,9, 14,16.
Port office ☎ 971 72 68 48 *Fax* 71 86 36
Pilots (Palma Prácticos) 971 71 19 37
Email rcnp@pml.servicom.es or
club@realclubnauticopalma.com
www.realclubnauticopalma.com
See text for further internet information on other options

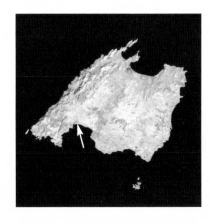

The port

Puerto de Palma shelters several yachting facilities, most called marinas even if only a pontoon. Set in a huge bay, it is one of the largest collective yachting centres in the Mediterranean, with berthing for several thousand yachts.

The port comprises naval, commercial, fishing and yachting harbours, which are clean and can be entered in all weathers, providing good shelter. Amenities are excellent and there is an attractive town nearby with extensive shops and markets. There are two large principal yacht marinas, both with palatial clubhouses and all facilities. Pier 46 and a Port Authority quay, along with several more 'marinas' – some offering not much more than a berth with water and electricity – complement the

The commercial mole of Palma de Mallorca harbour, with several of the inner harbours visible

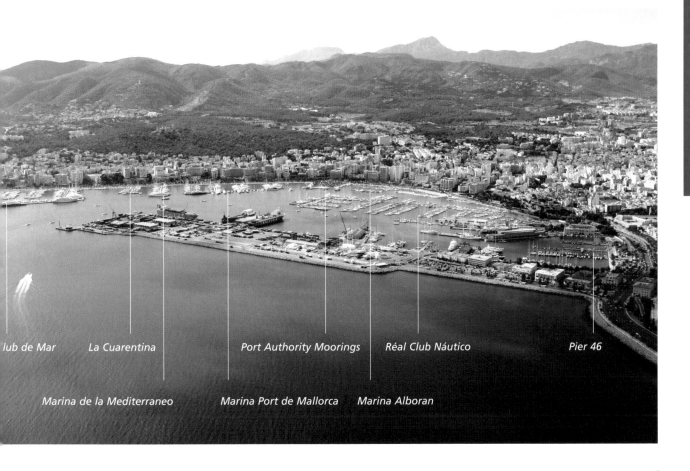

Club de Mar   La Cuarentina   Port Authority Moorings   Réal Club Náutico   Pier 46

Marina de la Mediterraneo   Marina Port de Mallorca   Marina Alboran

III. MALLORCA

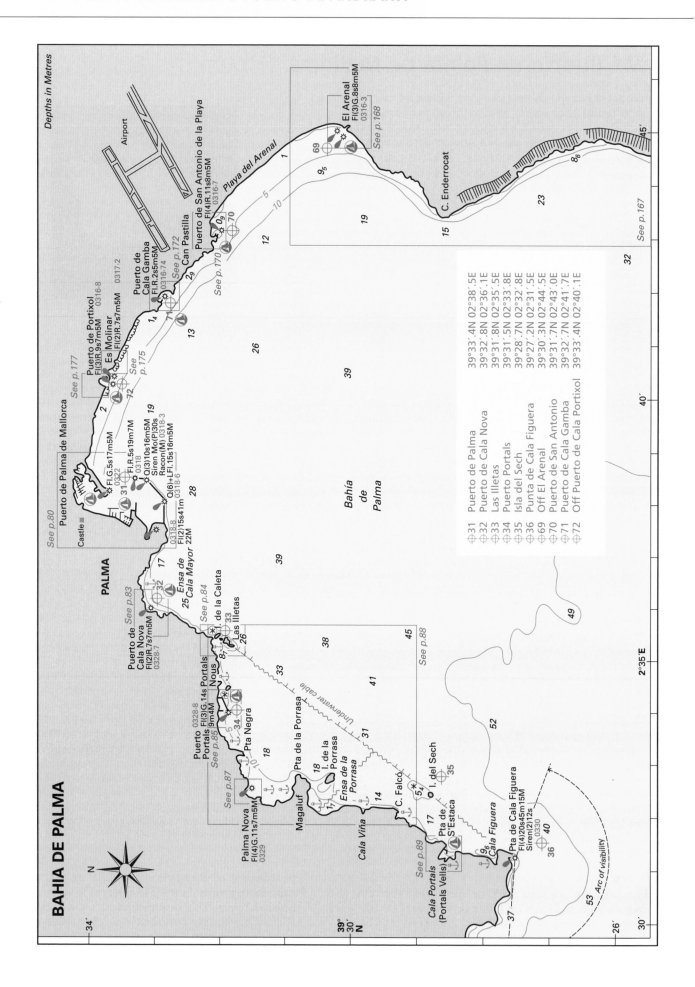

Depths in Metres

BAHIA DE PALMA

Airport

Playa del Arenal

El Arenal
Fl(3)G.8s8m5M
0316.3
See p.168

C. Enderrocat

See p.167

Puerto de San Antonio de la Playa
Fl(4)R.11s8m5M
0316.7

Can Pastilla
See p.172

See p.170

Puerto de
Cala Gamba
Fl.R.2s5M
0316.74
0317.2

Puerto de Portixol
0316.8
Fl(3)R.9s7m5M

Es Molinar
Fl(2)R.7s7m5M
See
p.175

See p.177

Bahía
de
Palma

Puerto de Palma de Mallorca

See p.80

Fl.G.5s17m5M
0322

Fl.R.5s19m7M
0318

Q(3)10s16m5M
Siren Mo(P)30s 0318.2
Racon(M) 0318.3
Q(6)+LFl.15s16m5M
0318.6

Fl(2)15s41m 22M
0318.8

Ensa de
Cala Mayor

Castle ■

PALMA

See p.83

Puerto de
Cala Nova
Fl(2)R.7s7m5M
0328.7

I. de la Caleta

I. de las Illetas

Puerto
Portals
0328.8
Fl(3)G.14s Portals
9m4M Nous

Pta Negra

Underwater cable

Pta de la Porrasa

I. de la
Porrasa

Ensa de la
Porrasa

C. Falcó

I. del Sech

See p.87

See p.85

Magaluf

Cala Viña

Pta de
S'Estaca

Palma Nova
Fl(4)G.11s7m5M
0329

See p.89

Cala Portals
(Portals Vells)

Cala Figuera

Pta de Cala Figuera
Fl(4)20s45m15M
Siren(2)12s
0330

Arc of visibility

See p.88

⊕31	Puerto de Palma	39°33'.4N 02°38'.5E
⊕32	Puerto de Cala Nova	39°32'.8N 02°36'.1E
⊕33	Las Illetas	39°31'.8N 02°35'.5E
⊕34	Puerto Portals	39°31'.5N 02°33'.8E
⊕35	Isla del Sech	39°28'.7N 02°32'.8E
⊕36	Punta de Cala Figuera	39°27'.2N 02°31'.5E
⊕69	Off El Arenal	39°30'.3N 02°44'.5E
⊕70	Puerto de San Antonio	39°31'.7N 02°43'.0E
⊕71	Puerto de Cala Gamba	39°32'.7N 02°41'.7E
⊕72	Off Puerto de Cala Portixol	39°33'.4N 02°40'.1E

harbour. The Port Authority moorings (there are 2,300 of them) were traditionally a cheaper alternative to the marinas, but are now about the same price, despite their lack of security or services. The harbour becomes very crowded in summer and vacant berths may be difficult to find but there are other yacht harbours in the Bahía de Palma where berths are usually available, and many possible anchorages can be found.

This is one of the few places where a major expansion plan for the commercial port is planned and work is already underway to almost double the size of 'Muelles Commerciales', the main commercial mole.

PILOTAGE

Approach

⊕ 31 39°33′.4N 02°38′.8E Puerto de Palma

From W Round the very prominent Punta de Cala Figuera which has a lighthouse, (Fl(4)20s45m15M white round tower with black diagonal stripes on building 24m) and radio masts on its steep cliffs. Cross the Bahía de Palma heading NE towards Palma Cathedral, a very large building with small twin spires. Castillo de Bellver (140m) is also conspicuous. The breakwaters will be seen on closer approach. There are no offlying dangers for day or night entry, except shipping in the entrance to beware of.

From E Round Cabo Blanco, which is high with steep light brown cliffs topped by a lighthouse (Oc.5s95m15M, white tower and building 12m) and an old watchtower. Follow the coast NW until the buildings of Palma, including the cathedral and Castillo de Bellver, described above, come into view. The breakwaters will be seen on closer approach.

Anchorage in the approach

Anchor in 10–12m over mud and sand S of the NE breakwater, exposed to the southerly quadrant. Keep well out of the channel, and display an anchor light at night. Note that anchoring within the harbour is prohibited.

Entrance

Puerto de Palma is a busy harbour in which ferries and other commercial vessels have right of way. Round the end of the S breakwater with an offing of at least 100m. The Club de Mar will be seen ahead with the Réal Club Náutico de Palma to starboard behind the NE breakwater (which should be given a similar offing).

There is a 5-knot speed limit in the harbour, decreasing to 3 knots in the marinas.

In fog

If navigating without GPS or the equivalent, the radiobeacon and siren on Punta de Cala Figuera (the siren at the outer elbow of the S breakwater and the racon at Puerto de Palma lighthouse), may be of assistance.

Berthing (see plan p. 80)

Although there are so many moorings, the harbour still becomes very crowded in high season and it is essential to book ahead in one or other of the available amenities. Going clockwise from the SW corner, moorings are as follows.

1. **Darsena de Porto Pi**
   A commercial quay tucked into the SW corner of the harbour, which allows yachts to moor on the S side. It offers few facilities.

2. **Club de Mar**
   A very large and well equipped marina due W of the entrance, offering more than 600 berths ranging in size from 8m up to 120m. Facilities are excellent, with charges to match. There is no reception pontoon; call on VHF Ch 09 to be allocated a berth. Note that the marina is divided into two sections with separate entrances (see plan).
   ☎ 971 40 36 11 *Fax* 971 40 36 18
   Email secretaria@clubdemar-mallorca.com
   www.clubdemar-mallorca.com

3. **Pontelle/Pantelan de la Cuarentina**
   A long single pontoon located just N of Club de Mar. It is prone to surging during winds from the W sector.
   ☎ 971 45 43 95/971 73 07 50 *Fax* 971 28 84 14

4. **Marina del Mediterraneo**
   A single long pontoon just N of Pontelle Cuarentina, offering little protection during winds from the W sector.
   www.mallorcaonline.com

5. **Marina Port de Mallorca**
   Just N of the Port Authority pontoon on the Paseo Marítimo, in front of Hotel Melia Victoria, with berthing for 152 yachts. Although privately owned with all berths being used by locals, visitors are welcome to use any vacant berths. It is expensive but has water and electricity on the pontoons and free showers, with the office on the SE corner of the shore pontoon. Security is excellent but there is no fuel or reception dock. The concrete pontoons are unusually high, the lower edge of their sides being some 1.25m above water. Thus even quite large craft are in danger of being pushed under the pontoons in a crosswind as fending off may not be possible. Also, despite addition of extra wave breaks under the N/S pontoon, swell and wash from passing craft is still a problem.
   ☎ 971 28 96 93 *Fax* 971 28 63 11
   Email recepcion@portdemallorca.com or
   comercial@portdemallorca.com
   www.portdemallorca.com

6. **Marina Alboran**
   This consists of 2 pontoons on the N Paseo Marítimo (opposite Hotel Miramar) which runs around the port. This new facility offers security and parking via the use of a large glass sliding door frontage accessed by an electronic key.

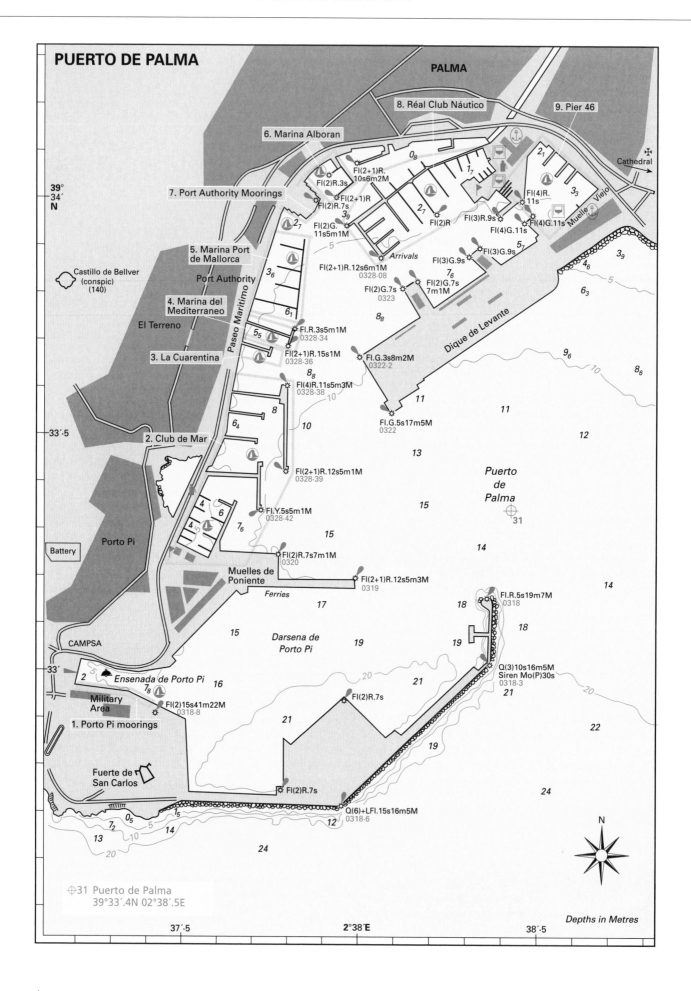

PUERTO DE PALMA

PALMA

8. Réal Club Náutico

9. Pier 46

6. Marina Alboran

7. Port Authority Moorings

Fl(2+1)R. 10s6m2M

Fl(2)R.3s

0_8

2_1

Cathedral

Fl(2+1)R

Fl(2)R.7s

Fl(4)R. 11s

3_3

Fl(2)G. 11s5m1M

3_9

Fl(2)R

Fl(3)R.9s

Fl(4)G.11s

Fl(4)G.11s

Muelle Viejo

2_7

5. Marina Port de Mallorca

Fl(2+1)R.12s6m1M 0328·08

Arrivals

Fl(3)G.9s

Fl(3)G.9s

5_7

3_9

4_6

Port Authority

3_6

Fl(2)G.7s 0323

Fl(2)G.7s 7m1M

7_6

6_3

5

4. Marina del Mediterraneo

6_1

8_8

Dique de Levante

El Terreno

5_5

Fl.R.3s5m1M 0328·34

Fl.G.3s8m2M 0322·2

9_6

10

8_6

3. La Cuarentina

Fl(2+1)R.15s1M 0328·36

8_8

11

Fl(4)R.11s5m3M 0328·38

Fl.G.5s17m5M 0322

11

12

8

10

6_4

13

2. Club de Mar

Fl(2+1)R.12s5m1M 0328·39

15

Puerto de Palma

14

Castillo de Bellver (conspic) (140)

15

Porto Pi

4

6

Fl.Y.5s5m1M 0328·42

7_6

4

15

14

Battery

Fl(2)R.7s7m1M 0320

15

Muelles de Poniente

Fl(2+1)R.12s5m3M 0319

Fl.R.5s19m7M 0318

17

18

18

Ferries

15

Darsena de Porto Pi

19

19

CAMPSA

Q(3)10s16m5M Siren Mo(P)30s 0318·3

21

2

5

Ensenada de Porto Pi

16

20

21

21

22

7_8

Military Area

Fl(2)15s41m22M 0318·8

Fl(2)R.7s

1. Porto Pi moorings

21

19

24

Fuerte de San Carlos

Fl(2)R.7s

Q(6)+LFl.15s16m5M 0318·6

0_5

1_5

12

7_2

10

5

14

13

10

24

20

N

⊕31 Puerto de Palma
39°33'.4N 02°38'.5E

Depths in Metres

37'·5

2°38'E

38'·5

Port de Mallorca: one of the many facilities within Puerto de Palma   *GW*

7. Port Authority berthing: Paseo Marítimo

For many years yachts have anchored and moored bow or stern-to along the main thoroughfare: the Paseo Marítimo. The entire length of the Paseo Marítimo has been paved, giving it a clean look and increased security by the addition of a stainless steel fence. It is convenient for the town but lacks the security of the marinas. There are no facilities, though buoys have been laid along the entire length of the Paseo providing moorings for 2,300 yachts. In strong E or SE winds surging is evident, but some protection is afforded by the several marina pontoons which now run parallel to the quayside.

Palma: Overlooking Castillo de Bellver into Réal Club Náutico de Palma and Pier 46 (top end of commercial quay)   *GW*

PA berthing includes most of the quay areas W of all the marinas and includes a large quay marked 'Terminal para pasajeros de la trafico local' (passenger quay) just N of the marina Port de Mallorca. This is a large car park around which boats engaged in local chartering moor. It also includes a single pontoon just E of Marina Alboran for fishing boats.

☎ 971 71 51 00/72 47 49 *Fax* 971 72 69 48

8. Réal Club Náutico de Palma

Situated in the NE of the harbour at the root of a long mole with many side spurs, this huge marina has berthing for 850 yachts from 8m to 20m. There is a reception quay on the outside of the SW arm (see '*Arrivals*' on plan) and visiting yachts usually lie alongside or bow/stern-to on one of the fingers in the basin to the N. A splendid backdrop is the ancient cathedral a short distance away.

Harbourmaster VHF Ch 07 or 09
Marina ☎ 971 72 68 48 *Fax* 971 71 86 36
Email rcnp@pmi.servicom.es or
club@realclubnauticopalma.com
www.realclubnauticopalma.com

9. Pier 46

This marina has moved to the NE corner of Dique de Levante, just E of Réal Club Náutico from its former position along the Paseo Marítimo. This is one of the most sheltered positions within the harbour.

☎ Pier 46 971 72 49 49 *Fax* 971 72 52 08

Facilities

Palma de Mallorca has by far the best facilities for yachts in the Islas Baleares and many of the services listed are not readily available elsewhere in the islands.

Water Water points at all yacht berthing locations including the Port Authority jetties and intervals along the Paseo Marítimo.

Electricity 220v and 380v AC available at both marinas and the two Pier 46 berthing areas. Some power points on the Port Authority jetty.

Fuel Diesel and petrol pumps at the Club de Mar and on the quay. The Réal Club Náutico has a fuel berth near the end of the main NW going pontoon.

Bottled gas It is understood that CAMPSA will not now fill any gas bottles, even with a current test certificate. Camping Gaz is, however, widely available.

Repairs See *Appendix* for list of chandleries and repair facilities.

Provisions A massive Carrefour hypermarket in the Porto Pí shopping centre five minutes' walk from the Club de Mar, with another of similar size on the road to the airport. Small supermarket at Club de Mar. Wide variety of other shops, as one would expect of a major city. A produce market at Santa Catalina, ten minutes from the Réal Club Náutico and Pier 46 berths.

Ice Cube ice from the Réal Club Náutico, the fuel berth at the Club de Mar and many supermarkets. Block ice (not for use in drinks) from *la lonja*.

Yacht clubs The Réal Club Náutico de Palma was founded nearly fifty years ago and has bars, a restaurant, bedrooms, a swimming pool, showers, repair workshops, etc. The Club de Mar is a much newer 'marina' yacht club with similar facilities. Apply to the secretary before using either club.

III. MALLORCA

Showers At both marinas and Port de Mallorca. No showers on public jetties.

Banks One in the Club de Mar complex, with many more throughout the city. Most (including the Club de Mar unit) have ATMs.

Launderettes Facilities at both marinas and others in the city.

Hospital/medical services Medical Office in Club de Mar and several in the city.

Transport

Car hire A wide choice, with the cheapest rates to be found around the Paseo Marítimo.

Taxis Can be found everywhere.

Buses and trains Bus service throughout the island plus trains to Sóller (recommended) and Inca. Timetables available from tourist offices.

Ferries Car ferries to mainland Spain, Ibiza and Menorca. (See *General Introduction*.)

Air services Busy international airport 4 miles E of the city and the hub for Air Berlin. (A bus links Plaza de España in the city centre to the airport four times an hour. Times from the airport are between 0610–0215.)

History

The city of Palma is thought to have been founded by the Romans, who knew it as Palmaria and built its first city walls during the 4th century. It flourished under the Moors, who renamed it Medina Mayurqa and whose legacy includes the Arabian Baths and the Almudaina arch. Subsequently it became the Spanish capital of the islands and the centre of a Mediterranean trading empire, giving rise to the first proper harbour works some time in the 14th century.

Sights ashore locally

First amongst Palma's treasures must be its soaring Gothic cathedral, begun in 1230 and still able to dominate the eastern part of the city at the N end of the port. Opposite is the Almudaina palace, built by the Moors but swiftly taken over by their Christian conquerors. Behind and slightly inland lies the oldest and most fascinating part of the city, where narrow flagged alleyways lined by shops, bars and restaurants can only be explored on foot. All are within comfortable walking distance of the harbour. Further out of the city on a hillside to the NW stands the Castillo de Bellver, also built in the 13th century and entered by a drawbridge across the moat. As with any major city there are museums, churches and historic buildings by the score. Do refer to the list of guide books (see *Appendix*) or visit the tourist office for information or you will miss a lot.

Local events

Fiestas are held on 5 January with the Procession of the Three Kings and on 17 January to celebrate the Blessing of St Anthony. Two days later are the Revels of St Sebastian. February sees Carnival Week and March or April the Fair of Ramos. Religious processions are held during Easter Week, with the Fiesta of the Angel on the first Sunday after Easter. The Fiesta de Santa Catalina Tomás, the island's own saint, is held on the first Sunday after 28 July,

with the Procession of Sta Beateta on 28 October. On 31 December the old year is rounded off with the Fiesta of the Standard.

Many of the elegant courtyards, which are a feature of the Old Town, are open to the public over the summer and some host musical events.

Eating out

Bars, cafés and restaurants abound all around the harbour and in the city. Of the latter, some of the most intriguing are in the old part of the city behind the cathedral. Many specialist high class Indian, Sushi, Chinese, Malasian, Thai and French restaurants can be found. Both main marinas have their own restaurants and indoor/outdoor bars.

ANCHORAGE W OF PUERTO DE PALMA

⚓ ENSENADA DE CALA MAYOR
39°33'.0N 02°36'.23E

An open bay close to and W of Puerto de Palma, with Puerto de Cala Nova yacht harbour tucked in on its western side. Anchor in 5m+ over sand and stone about 200m NE of the harbour entrance and well clear of the approach, open to SE through SW. Five underwater cables run in a S–SE direction from a point near the centre of the bay, where anchoring is prohibited. The anchorage is backed by large apartment blocks, houses and shops.

Famous ancient train provides a service from Palma to Sóller in the N   *GW*

M2 Puerto de Cala Nova

A small friendly harbour a short distance W of Palma but with doubtful space for visitors. It has berths for 215 yachts, most of which are taken up by locals all year round

Location
39°33′N 02°36′E

Communications
Escola Nacional de Vela Cala Nova VHF Ch 09
☎ 971 40 25 12 *Fax* 971 40 39 11

The harbour

A small and rather shallow artificial harbour, built by the Balearic authorities as a base for the national sailing school, the Escola Nacional de Vela, where children and adults learn windsurfing, dinghy and keelboat sailing. Although technically a private harbour, visitors' berths are occasionally available. Cala Nova is pleasant with good facilities. It is easy to enter with good protection once inside, though a swell works in with strong E or SE winds.

PILOTAGE

Approach

⊕32 39°32′.8N 02°36′.1E Puerto de Cala Nova

For outer approaches see *Puerto de Palma*.

From W After rounding Punta de Cala Figuera cross the Bahía de Palma heading NE, leaving the low-lying Isla del Sech to port. When past Las Illetas follow the coast at 200m for one mile when Puerto de Cala Nova will easily be seen.

From E Leave Puerto de Palma's long south breakwater to starboard to enter the Ensenada de Cala Mayor. Puerto de Cala Nova will be seen in the NW corner.

Anchorage in the approach

In the Ensenada de Cala Mayor (see above).

Entrance

Keep to the middle of the 55m-wide entrance maintaining a careful watch for sailing school craft (novices) entering or leaving. There is a 2-knot speed limit inside the harbour.

Berthing

Secure to the inside of the south breakwater unless a berth has already been allocated.

Facilities

Water Taps on quays and pontoons.
Electricity 220v AC points on the quays and pontoons.
Fuel For the sailing school's use only, and not on public sale.
Provisions All normal supplies are available from supermarkets and shops in Cala Nova and nearby San Augustin.
Ice From the *club náutico* bar.
Chandlery By the harbour.
Repairs A 35-tonne travel-lift at the W end of the harbour and a 2.5tonne crane. A wide but shallow dinghy slipway backed by an area of hard standing.
Engineers Available: enquire at the *club náutico* or the Escola Nacional.

Puerto de Cala Nova from S

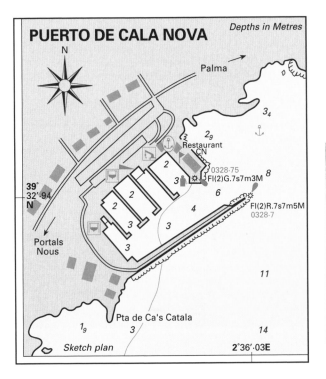

Yacht clubs The Club Náutico de Cala Nova has a pleasant clubhouse on the N mole with a restaurant, bar, terrace, swimming pool, showers, etc.

Showers At the *club náutico*.

Launderette Near the harbour.

Hospital/medical services In Palma.

Transport

Car hire/taxis ☎ 971 75 54 40 or from Palma.

Buses To Palma and elsewhere regularly pass the port.

Sights ashore locally

As for Palma.

Eating out

Many eating places of all grades, including a restaurant and bar at the *club náutico*.

ANCHORAGES W OF CALA NOVA

⊕33 39°31′.8N 02°35′.5E Las Illetas

⚓ LAS ILLETAS ANCHORAGES

39°31′.5N 02°35′.5E

An attractive group of anchorages best viewed on the chart, surrounded by the exclusive Bendinat holiday development. There are a few dangerous rocks awash between Islote de s'Estenedor (actually a low peninsula) and Illeta, and SW of Islote de la Caleta. Islote de s'Estenedor is a military area and landing on the beach may not be permitted. Fishing nets supported by lines of floats are sometimes laid in the approaches.

Note From Las Illetas S to Cabo Falcó there are several fish farms, noted on Spanish charts as obstructions. All are easily seen.

⚓ N anchorage Enter heading W or SW to anchor in 3m over sand, open NE through E to SE.

⚓ Central anchorage Enter from NE (inside Islote de la Caleta) or SE, in which case take care to avoid Bajo Calafat and other rocks SW of the island. Anchor in 2–3m over sand, open to NE and SE, off a small beach.

⚓ S anchorage A small, well protected anchorage between Islote de s'Estenedor and Illeta, open only to the E and to swell from NE and SE. Anchor in 3–5m over sand.

⚓ W anchorage The largest of the four anchorages, off a good beach (the property of the holiday complex and technically private). Enter heading NE to anchor in ±5m over sand, open to SW and W.

⚓ PORTALS NOUS

39°31′9.N 02°34′.6E

A deeply indented *cala*, close E of Islote d'en Salas. Anchor in 5m over sand, open to S and SW. There are shops, restaurants, etc. ashore.

LAS ILLETAS

N

Playa de Illetas

⚓ N
2₆

7

5

1₁

⚓ C

I. de la Caleta

8

6₄

11

39°32′N

1₂

0₉

⚓ W

Bajo Calafat

0₇

I. de s'Estenedor

12

4₅

6₄

1₅

0

⚓ S

Pta del Bufadó

2₈

⊕ 33

Illeta

Tr

16

4₄

0₈

1₂

7₆

5

⊕33   Las Illetas
      39°31′.8N 02°35′.5E

0   300

18

26

Metres

Depths in Metres

35′·3

2°35′·5E

Puerto Portals foreground, looking E over Isla D'En Salas and Las Illetas to Cala Major and the Bay of Palma   *GW*

M3 Puerto Portals

One of the most luxurious and expensive marinas in the Mediterranean with facilities for 670 yachts from 8 to 80m

Location
39°31´46.N 02°35´50.E

Communications
VHF Ch 09
Puerto Portals ☎ 971 17 11 00 *Fax* 971 17 11 17
Email marina@puertoportals.com and
puertoportals@oninet.es
www.puertoportals.com

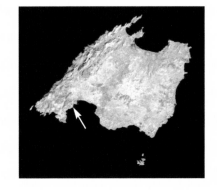

The marina

Opened in 1986 Puerto Portals is, in the words of its brochure 'modern and sophisticated' – as are many of the 670 yachts berthed there. Like Puerto de Palma 4 miles to the NW, it is capable of taking super-yachts up to 80m overall, and claims to have minimum depths of 4–5m throughout. Staff here are quite indifferent to visitors, though I suspect they would be more accommodating to a super-yacht arrival.

The immediate surroundings include restaurants, cafés, boutiques and various marine-related businesses, against a backdrop of bare sandy cliffs topped by white apartment blocks and hotels. Approach and entrance are straightforward except with a southeasterly gale when care must be taken.

PILOTAGE

Approach
⊕34 39°31´5.N 02°33´.8E Porto Portals

For details of the outer approaches see *Puerto de Palma* and page 79.

From W After rounding Punta de Cala Figuera follow the coast N-NE, leaving the low-lying Isla del Sech on either side but then maintaining an offing of about ½ mile. Isla and Punta de la Porrasa are unmistakeable, while Portals Nous's orange cliffs surmounted by white buildings can be seen from afar. In the close approach the long S breakwater will be seen, as will the distinctive square tower on the N mole, which houses the marina offices.

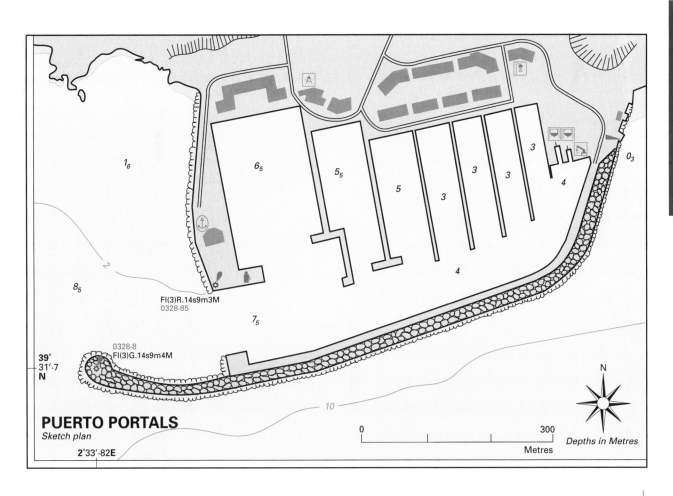

PUERTO PORTALS
Sketch plan

Fl(3)R.14s9m3M
0328·85

0328·8
Fl(3)G.14s9m4M

39°
31´·7
N

2°33´·82E

0   300
Metres

Depths in Metres

From E Round Cabo Blanco onto a NW course across the Bahía de Palma. See above for the final approach.

Anchorage in the approach

Anchor 200m W of the tower in 5m over sand, taking care not to impede the entrance channel. Watch for buoys off the beach.

Entrance

Swing wide around the head of the S breakwater onto an easterly heading, ready to berth alongside the reception quay at the S end of the N mole. There is a 3-knot speed limit in the harbour.

Berthing

The harbour is frequently full to capacity in summer, and it is wise to call before arrival (telephone or VHF) to ascertain that a berth will be available.

Facilities

Water Taps on all quays and pontoons. Check for quality before filling tanks.
Electricity 220v and 380v AC points on all quays and pontoons.
Fuel Diesel and petrol from pumps at the head of the N mole. Direct supply available to yachts over 18m requiring more than 1,000 litres.
Provisions The shops on the N side of the harbour include a small supermarket. More shops in Portals Nous a short distance inland.
Ice At the fuel berth.
Chandlery Multi-Marine ☎ 971 67 56 62/67 72 29 *Fax* 971 67 72 44 and Nauti Parts ☎ 971 67 77 30 *Fax* 971 67 74 95.
Repairs Mundimar Boatyard: Portals SA ☎ 971 676369 *Fax* 971 676409 at the NE end of the harbour can handle most jobs on yachts up to 80 tonnes. It has two travel-lifts 80 and 30 tonnes, with 2 and 10-tonne cranes near the travel-lifts. A dinghy slip at the root of the S breakwater.
Engineers Danbrit ☎ 971 67 72 01 *Fax* 971 67 73 28. Official service agents include: Danbrit – Lugger; Motornautica Portals Nous ☎ 971 67 77 95 *Fax* 971 67 77 94 – Mercury/MerCruiser, Quicksilver, Volvo Penta; Mundimar Portals SA (see *Repairs*) – Volvo Penta.
Electronic & radio repairs Danbrit ☎ 971 72 39 77.
Showers Two shower blocks in the marina complex, for which a key is required.
Launderette In Portals Nous.
Banks Bank with ATM in the marina complex.
Hospital/medical services In Portals Nous and Palma.

Transport

Car hire Four car hire firms around the harbour.
Taxis Via the marina office or ☎ 971 68 09 70.
Buses Bus service along the coast.

Sights ashore locally

As for Palma.

Eating out

Many restaurants and a few cheaper eating houses in the vicinity. There are more than twenty restaurants, cafés, bars and ice cream parlours around the harbour alone. Some of the most expensive restaurants in Mallorca are in this harbour.

ANCHORAGE SW OF PUERTO PORTALS

⚓ ANCHORAGE PUNTA NEGRA
39°31′.8N 02°33′.4E & 02°33′.1E

Anchor on either side of the headland in 2–3m over sand and stone. Punta Negra is remarkably unspoilt, with few houses ashore.

Puerto Portals: one of the most expensive marinas in the Mediterranean

M4 Puerto de Palma Nova

A small harbour with 82 berths and a restricted entrance due to silting. Hardly worth a mention, but it may spring to life if dredged

Location
39°31´.5N 02°32´.6E

Communications
Club Náutico Palma Nova ☎ 971 68 10 55
Fax 971 68 24 37

The harbour

This very small harbour has been partially silted up for years and does not seem to have the funds to dredge. At present it can only be used by shallow-draught vessels. Depths in the entrance are reported (Nov 2005) to be around 1 to 1.5m. Harbour facilities for the 82 boats it can accommodate are very limited.

PILOTAGE

Approach

Details of the outer approaches as for Puerto de Palma.

From W After rounding Punta de Cala Figuera follow the coast N–NE, leaving the low-lying Isla del Sech on either side. Round Isla and then Punta de la Porrasa, after which Puerto de Palma Nova will been seen at the N end of the long beach, Playa de Palma Nova.

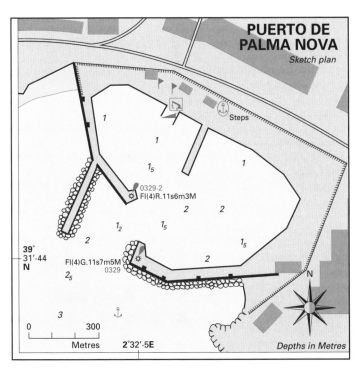

PUERTO DE PALMA NOVA
Sketch plan

Depths in Metres

From E Round Cabo Blanco onto a northwesterly course across the Bahía de Palma. Puerto de Palma Nova will be seen at the N end of the long beach.

Anchorage in the approach

Anchor in 3–5m over sand S of the harbour, open to SE.

Entrance

Due to the silting problem (sand rather than mud) it would be unwise to enter the harbour in any boat drawing more than 1m without first making a recce by dinghy. The water is generally too cloudy to read depths visually. There is a 2-knot speed limit.

Berthing

Secure in an empty berth and report to the harbour office by the slipway (closed Thursday and Saturday, otherwise open 0930–1300 daily).

Facilities

Water Taps around the harbour.
Electricity A few 220v AC points.
Fuel By can from a filling station on the road to Palma.
Provisions Supermarket and other shops nearby.
Repairs A 6-tonne crane beside the slipway at the N of the harbour, which has1m depth.
Yacht club The Club Náutico Palma Nova ☎ 971 68 10 55 has a small clubhouse and bar near the slipway.
Banks In Palma Nova.
Hospital/medical services In Palma Nova and Palma itself.

Transport

Car hire/taxis In Palma Nova or taxi ☎ 971 68 07 80
Buses Bus service along the coast.

Eating out

A vast number of restaurants and cafés (Palma Nova is at the northern end of the Magaluf holiday area.)

III. MALLORCA

ANCHORAGES BETWEEN PALMA NOVA AND PORT ADRIANO

⚓ PLAYA DE PALMA NOVA

39°31′.0N 02°32′.5E

A long and often crowded sandy beach, broken into three by a pair of low rocky promontories, each occupied by a large hotel. Anchor in 2–4m over sand, open to the eastern quadrant. Behind the beaches there are many hotels, restaurants and shops.

View over Torre Nova and Playa de Palma Nova, with Magaluf behind   *GW*

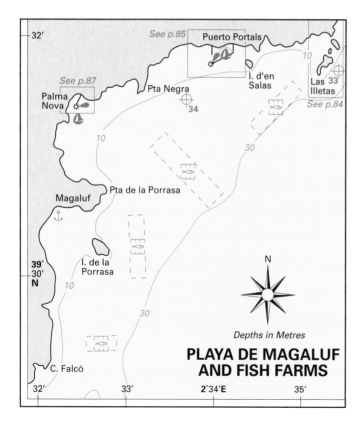

Depths in Metres

**PLAYA DE MAGALUF
AND FISH FARMS**

⚓ PLAYA DE MAGALUF

39°30′.3N 02°32′.3E

An anchorage off a long beach in the northern part of the Ensenada de la Porrasa, tucked in behind Isla de la Porrasa. The beach is lined with apartment blocks, hotels, beach cafés, shops, etc. but the island is deserted and landing is possible on the SW coast. The island (which is unlit) can be left on either side on entry, though 2.5m shoals extend NW for 200m. Anchor in 3–5m over sand, open to the E and SE. Holding is reported to be poor. A submarine cable runs SE from a point just S of the centre of the bay.

A marina with 1,500 berths is supposedly planned for this bay, but it appears unlikely to be built in the foreseeable future.

Isla de la Porrasa is rocky and scrub-covered: 425m long, 220m wide and 36m high. The SE point is steep-to, but the NW end of the island has a 2.5m shoal extending as described above. There is a 200m passage with 5–6m depths between Isla de la Porrasa and Punta de la Porrasa to the N.

Long fishing nets supported by small white or pink floats are sometimes laid near the island.

⚓ CALA VIÑA

39°29′.6N 02°32′.2E

A small, narrow *cala* surrounded by high-rise buildings, with a small sandy beach. The inner half of the bay is roped off for swimmers. Anchor in 4–5m over sand, open to the E.

⚓ SOUTH OF CABO FALCÓ

39°29′.1N 02°32′.1E

Two very small *calas* lie S of Cabo Falcó (note the 0.4m shoal 100m SE of the headland). Both anchorages are in 3m over sand, open to the eastern quadrant, with small sandy beaches and a few houses.

ISLA DEL SECH

Bisected by 39°28.8′N 02°32′.5E

⊕35 39°28.7′N 02°32′.8E Isla del Sech

A low (10m) flat black rocky islet with 4 to 6m and 4m shoals extending 500m to the NE, but with a 0.5M wide passage with depths of more than 10m between it and the shore.

Unlit buoys are laid in February 150m W and N of the island, marking the dive area used by the tourist submarine *Nemo I* (based in Puerto Portals). These are removed during the winter months.

⊕33   Las Illetas   39°31′.8N 02°35′.5E
⊕34   Puerto Portals   39°31′.5N 02°33′.8E

⚓ CALA PORTALS (PORTALS VELLS)
39°28′.4N 02°31′.5E

An attractive triple *cala* a mile N of Punta de Cala Figuera, approached between steep-to cliffs and popular with the tourist operators who visit by ferry (road access is poor). The tiny private harbour is lit (Fl.G.2s5m5M: 39°28′.9N 02°31′.5E, green column on white base). The harbour is shallow and can only take craft of less than 9m overall. There are water taps on the quay.

Anchor as space permits in 2–8m over sand and weed, with poor holding. Open to E.

There are tombs dating back to Phoenician times cut into the caves in the southern cliffs, one of which has been turned into a small shrine (take a torch). Several beach cafés and restaurants, some of which close for the evening after the tourists depart, overlook the bay. Parts of the beach are designated nudist areas.

Harbour ☎ 971 68 05 56.

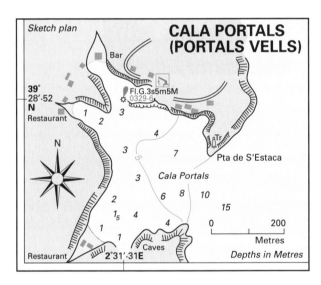

Cala Portals (Portals Vells)

⚓ CALA FIGUERA
39°27′.8N 02°31′.4E

A small *cala* close N of Punta de Cala Figuera. Its steep sides are wooded, with few houses. Anchor in 5m over sand and rock, open to NE and E.

⊕36 39°27.2′N 02°31′.5E Pta de Cala Figuera

PUNTA DE CALA FIGUERA
39°27′.5N 02°31′.4E

A very prominent headland with a lighthouse (Fl(4)20s45m15M, white round tower with black diagonal stripes on building 24m) and radio masts on its steep cliffs. The light is only visible when bearing between 293° and 094° – not from within the Bahía de Palma.

⊕37 39°27′.5N 02°28′.0E Islote el Toro

View over Punta de Cala Figuera looking NE into the Bay of Palma *GW*

Passage between Islote El Toro and Punta de Ses Barbines
39°27′.9N 02°28′.4E

A passage 200m wide and carrying 3m+ depths leads on a NW–SE axis between a small rock just NE of Islote El Toro (Fl.5s31m8M, white round tower 7m) and the double-humped Islote Banco de Ibiza off Punta de Ses Barbines. This latter promontory is very low and difficult to see from a distance, which can be confusing on the approach. Best depths (±4m) are reported about two-thirds of the way from Islote Banco de Ibiza out towards the rock.

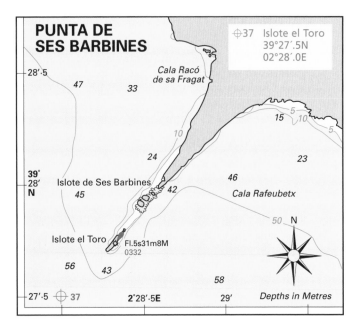

Islote El Toro and Punta de Ses Barbines showing clearly the bar. Port Adriano is tucked inside the bay on the far side of the peninsula

⚓ CALO RACÓ DE SA FRAGAT

39°28′.5N 02°28′.7E

An attractive anchorage close inshore at the root of the long promontory leading to Punta de Ses Barbines, exposed to W and S sector. The cliffs are steep-to. Anchor in 10–15m over sand and rock, open from SW to NW. A trip line is advisable.

M5 Port Adriano

A large yet quiet and pleasant harbour with berthing for over 400 yachts up to 18m. Set in the E side of the Cala de Peñas Rojas, it is easy to enter in most conditions and safe inside

Location
39°29′.5N 02°28′.7E

Communications
VHF Ch 09 and 16
☎ 971 23 24 94 *Fax* 971 23 25 66
Email info@portadriano.com
www.portadriano.com

The marina

A large marina with 404 berths for yachts up to 18m. Above is the luxury holiday development of El Toro, with the 5-star Hotel Port Adriano giving a good landmark N of the port. Port Adriano is simple to approach and enter with reasonable protection once inside, though water has been known to come over the breakwater during westerly gales.

The backdrop of bare reddish cliffs, hotels and apartment buildings is somewhat barren but the marina itself is quite attractive.

It is often very full and if possible, contact should be made before arrival to check that a berth will be available.

The diving school Escuela Buceo in the marina complex covers all aspects of the sport including beginners' tuition. It stocks diving equipment, and has full decompression facilities.

PILOTAGE

Approach

From the NW Round Cabo de la Mola, a high headland terminating in sheer cliffs topped by a lighthouse (Fl(1+3)12s128m12M, white column with black bands on a square white tower 10m) and Cabo Llamp (unlit). Then steer SE across the wide mouth of Ensenada de Santa Ponsa towards Islote El Toro leaving Isla Malgrats to port. Port Adriano will open up on rounding Punta Enguixa.

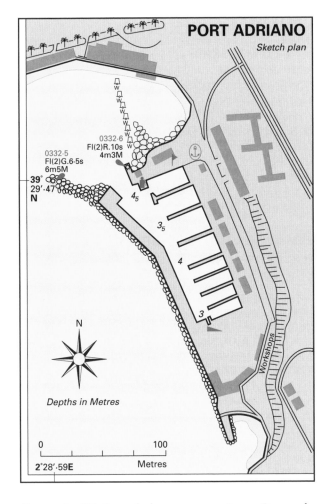

PORT ADRIANO
Sketch plan

0332·6
Fl(2)R.10s
4m3M

0332·5
Fl(2)G.6·5s
6m5M

39°
29'·47
N

4₅

3₅

4

3

Workshops

N

Depths in Metres

0   100

2°28'·59E   Metres

From the SE Round the very prominent Punta de Cala Figuera which has a lighthouse (Fl(4)20s 45m15M, white round tower with black diagonal stripes on building 24m) and radio masts on its steep cliffs, continuing W to leave Islote El Toro (Fl.5s31m8M, white round tower) to starboard, or see previous page for details of the passage between Islote El Toro and the peninsula. Port Adriano will then be visible just under 2 miles N, tucked well into the aptly named Cala de Peñas Rojas, 'the bay with red cliffs'.

Anchorage in the approach

Anchor off the beach close N of the entrance in 3m+ over sand, open to the westerly quadrant, or see *Cala de Peñas Rojas* below.

Entrance

Entrance is straightforward, but do not cut the W breakwater too closely as stones slope downwards from its end. There is a reception pontoon at the end of the E mole, near the large brown and cream office building. There is a 2-knot speed limit in the harbour. After strong S or W winds have been blowing there is a possibility that the entrance depth may be reduced due to silting; careful sounding in the approach is needed following these strong onshore winds.

Berthing

The marina is often very full and if possible contact should be made before arrival to check that a berth will be available.

Secure port side-to at the reception pontoon until a berth is allocated.

Facilities

Water Water points on the pontoons and breakwater.

Electricity 220v and 380v AC points on the pontoons and breakwater.

Fuel Diesel and petrol pumps at the fuel berth on the E mole (by the reception pontoon).

Provisions Small supermarket in the marina complex and another at the top of the steep hill up from the marina, but otherwise mainly tourist shops.

Ice Cube ice from bars and supermarkets.

Chandlery In the marina complex.

Repairs Boatyard Mar Adriano (☎ 971 10 26 65) at the southern end of the harbour is able to handle all normal work. A 50-tonne lift and slipway in the boatyard.

Engineers At Mar Adriano (see *Repairs* above).

Electronic & radio repairs At Mar Adriano (see *Repairs* above).

Yacht club The Club Náutico Porto Adriano has good facilities including a large restaurant and a swimming pool.

Showers In the marina office building.

Launderette In El Toro.

Bank/bureau de change In the nearby holiday town of El Toro.

Hospital/medical services In El Toro and Palma (the latter about 8 miles by road).

The port also owns moorings in Ibiza:

Ibizamagna ☎ 19 38 70/19 38 90

Email info@ibizamagna.com

www.ibizamagna.com

Port Adriano marina looking SE   *GW*

Transport

Car hire/taxis Arrange via the marina office or taxi ☎ 68 09 70

Buses Bus service to Santa Ponsa and Palma from a stop near the top of the marina access road.

Sights ashore locally

Spectacular countryside with huge expanses of pine forests, especially to the NE. See *Palma* for attractions.

Eating out

Restaurants and cafés overlooking the marina; hotels and more restaurants in the surrounding tourist development.

ANCHORAGES NW OF PORT ADRIANO

CALA DE PEÑAS ROJAS
39°29′.6N 02°28′.5E

Less than 0.5M NW of Port Adriano it is possible to anchor under steep cliffs in the NW part of the *cala* in 5m+ over sand, open from S round to W. Watch for rocks close inshore. The *cala* is shown on the photo of *Punta de Ses Barbines* above.

⊕38 39°29′.5N 02°26′.5E Isla Malgrats

⚓ CABO MALGRATS
39°30′.2N 02°27′.5E

There is a settled-weather anchorage between Cabo Malgrats and Punta Negra sheltered by Isla de los Conejos. Anchor in 4–5m over rock and sand, open to S and W and to swell from NW and SE. The bay is surrounded by cliffs, behind which is a tourist development. Although the beach is poor, the area is popular with day tourist boats. In favourable conditions it is also possible to anchor S of Isla Malgrats in ±10m over rock and sand.

Passages either side of Isla de los Conejos
39°30′.2N 02°27′.4E

Spectacular passages 100m wide exist either side of Isla de los Conejos. The southern passage has a minimum of 6m and should be taken on a NW-SE axis keeping to the centre of the channel. For the northern passage, less than 5m deep, and approaching from the S, leave Punta Negra some 100m to starboard and steer N for Cabo Malgrats.

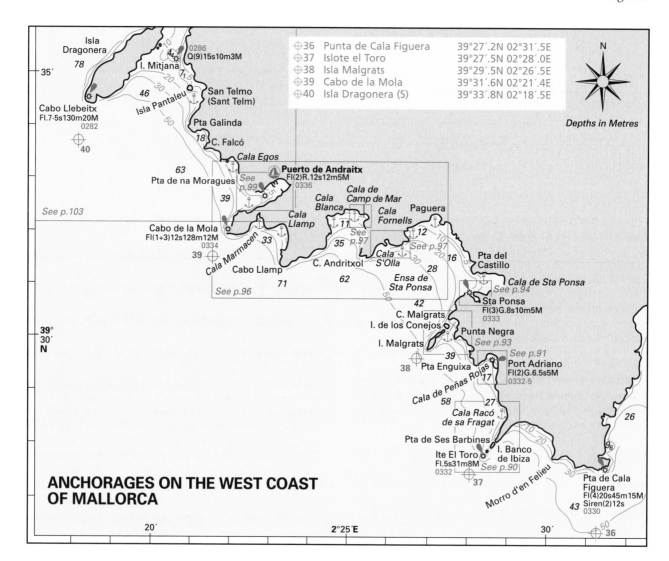

⊕36	Punta de Cala Figuera	39°27′.2N 02°31′.5E
⊕37	Islote el Toro	39°27′.5N 02°28′.0E
⊕38	Isla Malgrats	39°29′.5N 02°26′.5E
⊕39	Cabo de la Mola	39°31′.6N 02°21′.4E
⊕40	Isla Dragonera (S)	39°33′.8N 02°18′.5E

ANCHORAGES ON THE WEST COAST OF MALLORCA

When the NE point of the island is about 100m on the port beam, steer to follow the island's coast keeping 100m off until a course of NW is attained and then depart on that course. Coming from the N use the reciprocal.

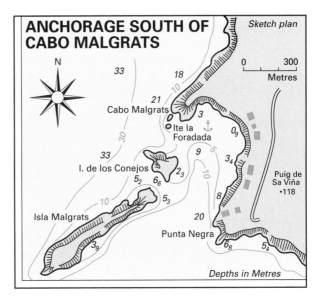

Restored traditional windmill, Santa Ponsa

M6 Puerto de Santa Ponsa

A very attractive harbour with berths for over 500 yachts up to 20m

Location
39°30′.8N 02°28′E

Communications
VHF Ch 09
Club Náutico Santa Ponsa ☎ 971 69 49 50
Fax 971 69 44 88
Email cnsp@sertebal.com or cnsp@arrakis.es

The harbour

On an island with so many attractive harbours, Santa Ponsa (Santa Ponça) must be one of the most picturesque, in spite of the many surrounding buildings. Long and narrow, guarded at its northwestern end by a curved breakwater, the inlet gives excellent protection, though it can get rather hot and airless in summer. There are 522 berths for yachts up to 20m, but even so it is necessary to contact the *club náutico* before arrival as most of the berths are permanently occupied and there is often no room for visitors.

Approach and entry are straightforward, but care should be taken in strong winds from the westerly quadrant. Space for manoeuvring larger yachts is very restricted once inside the harbour.

PILOTAGE

Approach

From NW Round Cabo de la Mola, a high headland terminating in sheer cliffs topped by a lighthouse (Fl(1+3)12s128m12M, white column with black bands on a square white tower 10m) and Cabo Llamp (unlit). Then head E towards the long Playa de Santa Ponsa – the tall stone memorial to Jaime I and the breakwater below will be seen to starboard, near the mouth of the bay, on closer approach. A fish conservation area has been created near the entrance to the *cala* which is clearly visible when in place.

From SE Round the very prominent Punta de Cala Figuera which has a lighthouse (Fl(4)20s45m15M, white round tower with black diagonal stripes on building 24m) and radio masts on its steep cliffs, continuing W to leave Islote El Toro (Fl.5s31m 8M, white round tower) to starboard. Settle onto a NW course to round Isla Malgrats (or in good weather use the inshore passage as previously described), then follow the coast NE. Soon after rounding Morro d'en Grosser, the tall stone memorial to Jaime I and the breakwater below will be seen to starboard.

Anchorage in the approach

See *Cala Santa Ponsa* under *Anchorages* below.

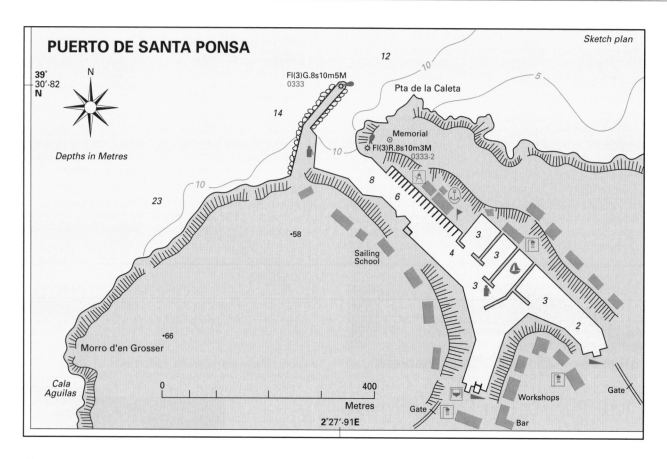

Entrance

Approach the head of the NW breakwater on a S or SE course. Enter keeping to the starboard side of the channel, ready to berth starboardside-to on the reception quay at the root of the breakwater. There is a 2-knot speed limit.

Berthing

It is advisable to contact the *club náutico* before arrival as most of the berths are permanently occupied and there is often no room for visitors.

A berth will be allocated (if available). The marina office can be contacted on VHF Ch 09, or by dialling 9 at one of the four telephone booths around the inlet (the nearest one to the reception pontoon is situated by the sailing school).

Facilities

Water Taps on quays and pontoons.
Electricity 220v AC points on quays and pontoons. 380v AC available in the boatyard.
Fuel Pumps on the reception quay at the root of the breakwater and on one of the inner pontoons.
Provisioning Small supermarket near the *club náutico* and many shops in Santa Ponsa less than a mile away.
Ice At the fuel berth.
Chandlery In the block containing the *club náutico* and marina office.
Repairs Boatyard at the head of the SW arm with a 50-tonne lift. A 2.5-tonne crane at the sailing school. Three slipways, one in each of the southern arms of the harbour and one at the sailing school.
Engineers At the boatyard and Port Fairline Santa Ponsa ☎ 971 69 07 17 (official service agents for Volvo Penta).

Metalwork Metalnox SL ☎ 971 69 40 11 *Fax* 971 69 56 91.
Electronic & radio repairs Can be organised via the boatyard or *club náutico*.
Sail repairs In the block containing the *club náutico* and marina office.
Yacht club The Club Náutico de Santa Ponsa has a palatial clubhouse on the NE side of the harbour with lounge, terrace, restaurant, bar, etc.
Showers Below the *club náutico* and at the heads of both the southern arms.
Launderette At the *club náutico*.
Banks Several in Santa Ponsa.
Hospital/medical services In Santa Ponsa and Palma (about 7M by road).

Transport

Car hire/taxis At the marina office or in Santa Ponsa.
Buses Bus services from Santa Ponsa to Palma and elsewhere.

History

This is a site of great historical interest. The area is celebrated for the fact that the combined fleets of Catalonia and Aragon dropped anchor here in 1229 under the command of King Jaime I (Rey Jaime Conquistador), landing an army which eventually drove the Moors from Mallorca.

Sights ashore locally

A stone cross with scenes commemorating the events above stands on Punta de la Caleta, just inside the harbour entrance and is well worth the short stroll

Santa Ponsa Marina looking SE: a well-sheltered harbour in pleasant surroundings   *GW*

for closer inspection. A fiesta to celebrate the anniversary is held from 9–16 September.

Eating out
Many eating establishments of all grades, including a restaurant at the *club náutico*.

ANCHORAGES AROUND ENSENADA DE SANTA PONSA

⚓ CALA DE SANTA PONSA
39°31′N 02°28′.3E

There are several good anchorages in Cala de Santa Ponsa, a wide bay to the NE of the harbour surrounded by apartments, houses and hotels. It is shallow around the sides and near the head – where there is a long but often crowded beach – with two 0.5m shoal patches (Las Secas) near the centre, marked by a W card light buoy YBY(9)15s at its seaward end and an unlit E card beacon BYB 250m to the E.

Cala de Santa Ponsa looking across the harbour entrance. Note shoal patch markers just visible centre of *cala*   *GW*

An underwater cable runs from the southern end of the beach towards Las Secas before continuing westward.

Anchor about 200m N of Caló de Pellicer on the southern shore in 2–4m over sand, open to W and NW, or on the N side in 4–6m over sand, open to W and SW. Shallow-draught yachts may be able to work closer in towards the head of the bay but a careful watch on the depth will be necessary.

Routine shopping requirements can be met in the tourist developments surrounding the bay, and there are many restaurants, cafés and bars. If anchored on the N side, a walk out to the fortified Gothic tower and the smaller watchtower on the northern headland might be enjoyed.

⚓ PLAYA DE PAGUERA
39°32′.2N 02°27′.1E

A large semicircular bay with an excellent beach, backed by apartment buildings and hotels. Rocks run out some distance from the SE side of the entrance. Anchor as space permits in 3–5m over sand, open to S and SW.

⚓ CALA FORNELLS (PUERTO DE PAGUERA)
39°32′N 02°26′.4E

An attractive anchorage just N of Pta Cerdana, but not in any sense a port, the most sheltered part is occupied by moorings. It is open to E and SE and from swell from the S. The *cala* is surrounded by wooded cliffs and a growing number of low-rise apartment buildings plus a few shops. The small sandy beach at the head of the *cala* is often crowded. A fish conservation farm is usually laid just off Pta Cerdana running SE, but was not in position in summer 2005. Anchor as space allows in 5–10m over sand and weed. A tripline is advised as there is reported to be considerable debris on the bottom.

⚓ CALA S'OLLA
39°31′.7N 02°26′E

A fascinating small *cala* between rocky cliffs, surrounded by unspoilt woodland. Approach with a lookout on the bow to anchor near the entrance in 3–5m over sand as there are several isolated rocks further in. Space is very restricted and two anchors will probably be required. Although open only to the S, the *cala* would quickly become dangerous in any wind from this direction and should be vacated immediately.

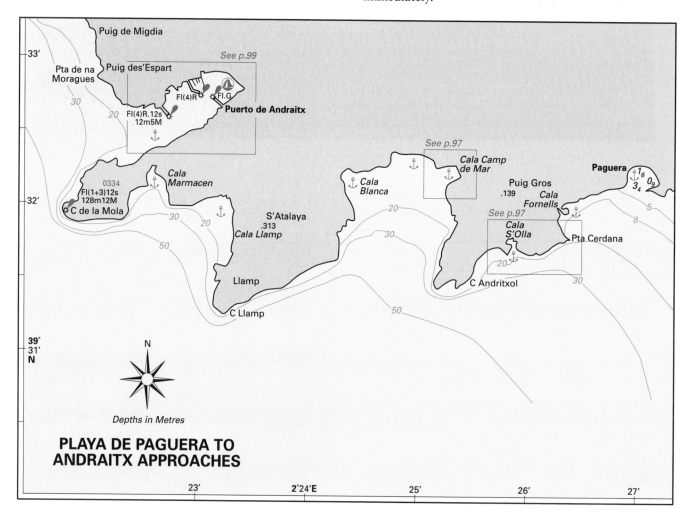

PLAYA DE PAGUERA TO
ANDRAITX APPROACHES

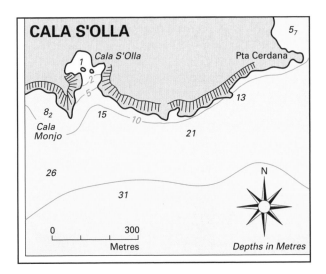

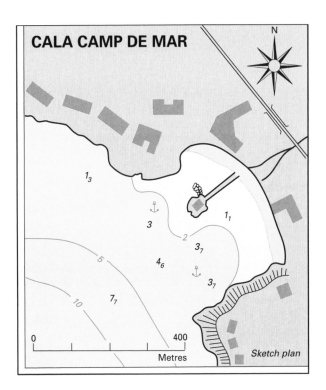

Cala S'Olla from the S. Submerged rocks further in can be clearly seen

Cala Camp de Mar island and restaurant   *GW*

⚓ CALA CAMP DE MAR
39°32′.3N 02°25′.4E

A pleasant bay which has become a popular tourist resort, partly due to a small island in its centre reached by a narrow wooden bridge and housing an outdoor bar/restaurant. A tourist ferry is often moored stern-to the restaurant island. There are several high-rise hotels behind the beach and more close NW, plus a few tourist shops.

Anchor SE of the island in 2–4m over sand and rock (shoals extend northwards from the heel of the island towards the white hotel), open to S and SW.

Cala Camp de Mar viewed from W. Note island and restaurant left   *Graham Hutt*

III. MALLORCA

View over Cala Marmacen and Cabo de la Mola to Andraitx harbour

Cala Blanca: a pleasant but very busy bay in the high season
GW

⚓ CALA BLANCA
39°32′.2N 02°24′.5E

A small *cala* with cliffed sides and a sand and stone beach, as yet undeveloped. Anchor in 2–3.5m over sand off the beach, open to E through S.

⚓ CALA LLAMP
39°32′N 02°23′.3E

A somewhat unappealing anchorage, very open and with much development despite having no beach. Anchor close to the NE corner in 4m over sand and stone, open S through SW to W. (See plan of *Approaches to Andraitx* on page 96.)

⚓ CALA MARMACEN
39°32′.2N 02°22′.7E

A spectacular anchorage surrounded by cliffs in the approach and narrow at its head. Anchor in 5m over sand and stone near the head of the *cala*, open to the southern quadrant. Much new development surrounds the *cala*.

⊕39 39°31′.6N 02°21′.4E Cabo de la Mola

CABO DE LA MOLA
39°32′N 02°21′.9E

A high headland terminating in sheer cliffs topped by a rather inconspicuous lighthouse (Fl(1+3)12s 128m12M, white column with black bands on a square white tower 10m). The light is only visible when bearing between 304.4° and 158.2° and is obscured during the final approach to Puerto de Andraitx.

⚓ SE OF PUNTA DEL MURTÉ
39°32′.3N 02°22′.4E

A small anchorage under steep cliffs, suitable for use in settled southerly weather. Anchor off the beach in 3m over sand and stone, open to N and NE.

M7 Puerto de Andraitx (Club de Vela)

One of the oldest yachting marinas in Mallorca, in a fine setting. It offers nearly 500 berths for yachts up to 25m, with easy access through a buoyed channel. The harbour is often full

Location
39°32′.7N 02°22′.8E

Communications
Call *Andraitx Vela* VHF Ch 10 to avoid confusion with Puerto de Santa Ponsa (Ch 09)
Port Authority ☎ 971 46 62 12
Club de Vela Puerto de Andraitx
☎ 971 67 17 21 *Fax* 971 67 42 71
Email cvpa@sertebal.com
www.cvpa.es

The harbour

A yachting and fishing harbour set in most attractive surroundings with a pleasant village nearby and a larger (and much more atmospheric) town some 2 miles inland. Inevitably a good deal of housing development is taking place around the bay, but this has not ruined its beauty and charm.

The harbour is easy to approach and enter and offers good protection, though strong gusts of wind can flow down from the surrounding hills. A heavy swell sets in with strong winds from W and SW. Very occasionally the phenomenon known as *resaca* or *seiche* occurs (see *Tides* section in the *General Introduction*): particularly dangerous to yachts berthed on the quays.

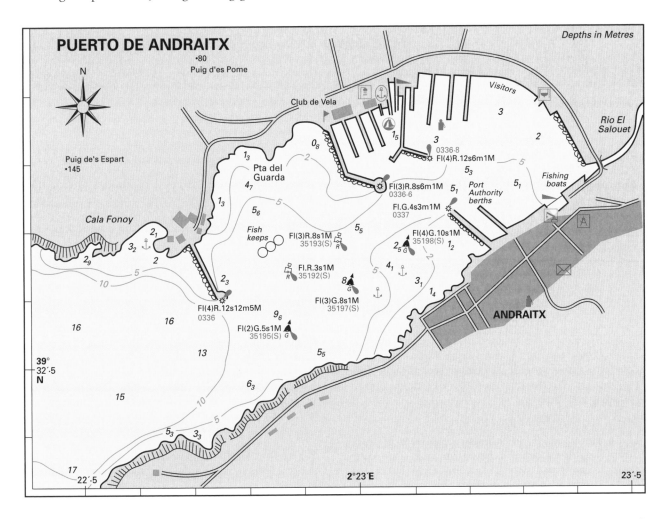

III. MALLORCA

Andraitx Harbour viewed from SE

PILOTAGE

Approach

From N Pass either side of Isla Dragonera (see separate plan of island below) towards Cabo de la Mola, a high headland terminating in sheer cliffs topped by a lighthouse (Fl(1+3)12s128m12M, white column with black bands on a square white tower 10m). The entrance to Puerto de Andraitx lies to the N of the headland and will come into view on rounding Punta de las Brescas, which has a massive housing development on its sloping face.

From SE Cross the wide mouth of Ensenada de Santa Ponsa towards Cabo Llamp (high and pine-covered) and Cabo de la Mola (see above). The entrance to Puerto de Andraitx will open up on rounding the latter.

Anchorage in the approach

In northerly winds, anchorage is possible in Cala Fonoy on the N side of the entrance in 2m+ over sand. In southerly winds, tuck in SE of Punta del Murté in 3m over sand and stone. These anchorages should only be used in good conditions and neither gives much protection. Anchoring in the outer harbour is discouraged by the authorities (keep out of the buoyed channel), and in the inner harbour it is prohibited.

Entrance

Approach down the centre of the bay leaving the head of the outer breakwater some 50m to port. Keep to the buoyed channel, taking care to avoid the shoal area close SW of the S mole. Note that the original buoys listed in the *Appendix* may have been moved. There is a speed limit of 5 knots in the outer harbour decreasing to 3 knots in the inner harbour.

The fish keeps (see photographs) may be marked by one or more yellow lights (Fl.Y.4s) and several unlit reflectors, but are out of the channel to the N.

Note

Where 4m depths at the NE end of the harbour are shown, information indicates that it is now reduced to 2.3m.

Berthing

If intending to stay in the yacht harbour run by the Club de Vela Puerto de Andraitx, secure to the inner side of the head of the N mole until a berth is allocated (assuming one is available – the Club de Vela has 475 berths for yachts up to 25m, but is often full). Visitors are often allocated berths on the quay in the NE of the harbour, between the pontoons and the travel-lift (which is near the end of the stone wall). Yachts lie bow or stern-to, and a mooring line is provided tailed to the quay.

Alternatively, the Port Authority oversees an area on the S side of the harbour, with berthing bow or stern-to along the inside of the end section of the S mole (no mooring lines, so an anchor will be needed) or on the floating pontoon just beyond it (mooring lines provided, tailed to the pontoon). About 125 Port Authority berths are available, nominally able to take yachts to 25m but these are mainly taken by local residents.

Note that there are 3m depths along the visitors' quay itself but care should be exercised at the far eastern end where the depth is reported to be less than 2.3m.

Moorings

The area between the outer breakwater and the N mole is filled with moorings, but it is unlikely that any will be free.

Facilities

Water On the Club de Vela pontoons and at the fuel berth. The quality is reported to be poor – brackish and over-chlorinated.

Electricity 220v AC points at the Club de Vela and on the S mole and adjacent pontoon.

Diesel and petrol At the fuel berth on the furthest but one pontoon at the Club de Vela. There is a diesel pump on the fish quay but it is for fishing vessels only.

Provisions Good supermarket just behind the fuel berth on the fish quay with other food shops nearby, plus many tourist shops. Two small supermarkets N of the harbour. The town of Andraitx 2 miles inland has many more shops and a good market. Good fish market in the SE corner of the harbour after the boats return each day. Regular Wednesday market at Andraitx, 2½ miles inland.

Ice From Tim's Bar close SW of the S mole and from some supermarkets.

Chandlery One at the Club de Vela plus a chandlery/hardware store S of the harbour.

Repairs Can be carried out at the yacht harbour boatyard – enquire at the Club de Vela office. A 50-tonne capacity lift and a 3-tonne crane in the yacht harbour. A large slipway at the yacht harbour and another at the SE corner of the inner harbour.

Engineers Phoenix Marine ☎ 971 67 20 12 *Fax* 971 67 29 66 are official service agents for Mercury/MerCruiser and Volvo Penta. Taller Náutico Toni Mas ☎ 971 67 36 03, 105565 *Fax* 971 67 36 03 are official service agents for Mercury/MerCruiser and Yanmar.

Electronic & radio repairs Enquire at the Club de Vela office.

Yacht club The Club de Vela Puerto de Andraitx ☎ 971 67 23 37 *Fax* 971 67 42 71 occupies an impressive

View down *cala* hosting Andraitx harbour. Note circular fish keeps   *GW*

building N of the yacht harbour with lounge, bar, restaurant, swimming pool and showers.

Showers At the Club de Vela, free to those staying in their marina but with restricted hours.

Laundry/launderette In the town.

Banks In the town S of the harbour.

Hospital/medical services In Andraitx and Palma (about 15 miles by road).

Transport

Car hire/taxis In the town or arranged through the Club de Vela.

Buses Frequent buses to Andraitx 2½ miles inland and several each day to Palma.

Ferries A tourist ferry makes the trip to Isla Dragonera via San Telmo.

Sights ashore locally

In addition to the old town, where there is an interesting church, a walk along the upper roads and tracks on either side of the harbour is rewarded with excellent views.

Local Events

Fiestas are held on or about 29 June (a public holiday), in honour of San Pedro, with waterborne processions; 15–16 July, Fiesta de la Virgen del Carmen, again with waterborne processions, and the two weekends around 19–20 and 26–28 August, S'Arracó El Santo Cristo (also a public holiday).

Eating out

Many eating places around the harbour, with the southern waterfront seemingly wall-to-wall with cafés and restaurants.

III. MALLORCA

2. Cala Egos to Sóller

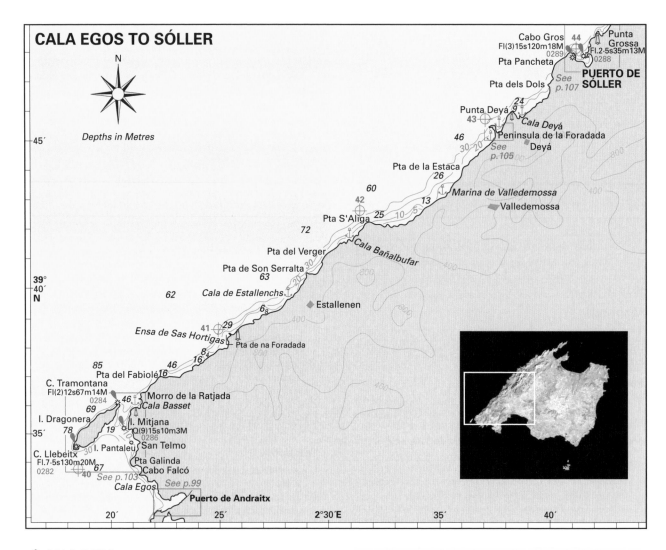

CALA EGOS TO SÓLLER

N

Depths in Metres

45′

39°
40′
N

39°
40′
N

35′

Cabo Gros
Fl(3)15s120m18M
0289
Pta Pancheta
Pta dels Dols
See p.107
PUERTO DE SÓLLER

Punta Grossa
Fl.2-5s35m13M
0288

44

Punta Deyá
43
Cala Deyá
Peninsula de la Foradada
Deyá

24

46
30 20
See p.105

Pta de la Estáca
26
Marina de Valledemossa
Valledemossa

60
42
13
25 10 5

Pta S'Aliga
72

Pta del Verger
Cala Bañalbufar

Pta de Son Serralta
63
62
Cala de Estallenchs
♦ Estallenen

Ensa de Sas Hortigas
41 29
Pta de na Foradada

85
46
16
*Pta del Fabiolé*16

C. Tramontana
Fl(2)12s67m14M
0284
69
I. Dragonera
78
C. Llebeitx
Fl.7-5s130m20M
0282
40
See p.103
Cala Egos
Puerto de Andraitx

46
Morro de la Ratjada
Cala Basset
I. Mitjana
Q(9)15s10m3M
0286
19
I. Pantaleu
San Telmo
Pta Galinda
Cabo Falcó
See p.99

20′   25′   2°30′E   35′   40′

CALA EGOS
39°33′.2N 02°22′E

A small, unspoilt *cala* and beach surrounded by rocky cliffs SE of Pta de sa Dent. Anchor in 4m over sand and rocks off the beach, open to S through W.

PLAYA DE SAN TELMO (SANT TELM OR SAN ELM)
39°34′.7N 02°21′.1E

A pleasant bay with sandy beaches and a small tourist resort. Isla Pantaleu (29m) 220m long by 200m wide in the mouth of the bay gives protection from the W, as does Isla Dragonera further offshore. Parts of the beach are buoyed off for swimmers.

Enter the bay from the SW and anchor off San Telmo in 2–5m over sand, weed and clay (holding is patchy), open to SW and with a mile or more's fetch to the NW. The winds can also funnel down from the mountains causing local disturbances on the water so care should be taken to anchor clear of

WAYPOINTS:
40	Isla Dragonera (S)	39°33′.8N 02°18′.5E
41	Punta de na Foradada	39°38′.5N 02°25′.2E
42	Punta S'Aliga	39°42′.4N 02°31′.5E
43	Peninsula de la Foradada	39°45′.6N 02°37′.2E
44	Approach to Puerto Sóller	39°48′.0N 02°41′.2E

weed and/or ensure the anchor is well dug in. The approach from the NW is shallow, and may be obstructed by the stern anchors of tourist ferries lying bows-on at the quay as well as moored smallcraft. Several years ago plans were drawn up to construct a large yacht harbour in the bay N of Isla Pantaleu but these appear to have been dropped along with most expansion plans for the island, due to environmental considerations.

Isla Pantaleu was the first landfall of King Jaime I of Aragon on his way to liberate Mallorca from the Moors in 1229, though his troops were finally disembarked near Santa Ponsa.

San Telmo from SW. Isla Pantaleu centre, N tip of Isla
Dragonera left

Isla Dragonera and the Dragonera Passage

Location
39°35′.3N 02°20′.2E

⊕40 39°33′.8N 02°18′.5E Isla Dragonera (S end)

The island

Isla Dragonera is an island of spectacular and unique
shape, being almost sheer on the NW side and
steeply sloping to the SE. It is just over 2 miles long
but only 0.6 miles wide with an old signal station
and tower on Puig de Sa Popi, the pyramid-shaped
360m summit. Lighthouses mark each end of the
island.

ISLA DRAGONERA AND THE
DRAGONERA PASSAGE

III. MALLORCA

The passages

The passage between Isla Dragonera and Mallorca should present no problems to yachtsmen: the height of the surrounding hills make it appear much more alarming than it really is. The passage is funnel-shaped, opening to the S, with shoals and small rocky islets on either side of the narrows at the northern end. There are effectively two passages, either side of the 8m Isla Mitjana. The main channel is that to the W, which although wider has unmarked foul ground on both sides stretching some 200m from both Isla Mitjana and Isla Dragonera, leaving a passage 350m wide and 19m deep. The eastern channel, though much narrower at less than 200m, has a good depth of water (10m+) close to both Isla Mitjana and Mallorca.

Heavy gusts can descend from the high land around the passage without warning, while strong currents may flow through it in either direction after a gale, the direction dictated by the wind. Fishing nets supported by small white or pink buoys may be laid from either shore of the passage. The area between the island and mainland is marked on Spanish charts as an exercise ground, though no prohibitions seem to be effected.

PILOTAGE

Approach and passages

From NE Following the coast southwestwards from Puerto de Sóller or beyond, Isla Dragonera will be seen from afar. (Light Cabo Tramontana 39°36′N 02°20′.4E Fl(2)12s67m14M. Round masonry tower on stone building with red roof 15m). The Mallorcan coast is steep-to and can be followed close inshore past Punta Galera, with its prominent watchtower into the N entrance to the passage. Then work 200m offshore to take the eastern passage between Isla Mitjana and Mallorca in a N–S direction, approximately down the centre. There are no further hazards once the island has been passed. Alternatively the western passage can be used, passing equidistant between Isla Mitjana and the coast of Isla Dragonera (note the offlying rocky islands) on a S-SW heading.

From SE Round Punta Galinda and then Isla Pantaleu, leaving the latter 300m to starboard. To take the E channel pass halfway between Isla Mitjana (39°35′.2N 02°20′.6E Q(9)15s10m3M Y beacon, black band 5m) and the Mallorcan coast, then follow this coast past Punta Galera with its prominent watchtower, into the open sea.

The W channel can be used by standing out into the centre of the passage to pass equidistant between Isla Mitjana and the coast of Isla Dragonera (note the offlying rocky islands) on a N–NE bearing before heading NE to round Punta Galera.

At night

Transiting either passage after dark is not recommended unless the area is already familiar. It would be safer to sail the extra few miles around Cabo Llebeitx at the SW end of Isla Dragonera.

Sites ashore locally

There is very little ashore, but tracks link Cala Lladó to the lighthouses and the NW coast and offer some memorable walks.

ANCHORAGES AROUND ISLA DRAGONERA

There are several possible daytime anchorages on the SE coast of Isla Dragonera, all framed by spectacular cliffs. Without exception they are small with sand and rock bottoms, and tenable only in settled conditions. Taken from NE to SW they are as follows.

⚓ CALA ENRENGAN
39°35′.6N 02°20′.1E

Reasonable shelter for one yacht, open only to NE and E. A small island lies off the southeastern promontory.

⚓ COVA DELS BOSCH
39°35′.3N 02°20′.0E

A wide open, cliffed *cala*, open from E round to S and to swell from SW. Careful eyeball pilotage is called for. There is a low, isolated rock to the E.

⚓ CALA LLADÓ
39°35′.2N 02°19′.7E

A narrow *cala* with a 2m rock in the centre. A stone watchtower stands on the promontory to the SE, with a small quay (reserved for lighthouse officials and tourist ferries) opposite. Anchor in 2m+ over sand and rock, open to SE through S to SW.

⚓ CALA COCÓ
39°34′.9N 02°19′.4E

Anchor close inshore under steep cliffs, open to NE through E to SE.*f*

⚓ CALA EN BAGUR
39°34′.7N 02°19′.2E

Again anchor close inshore under steep cliffs, open to NE through E to SE.

⚓ CALA LLEBEITX
39°34′.4N 02°18′.5E

Slightly larger than Cala Cocó or Cala En Bagur, but still very small. Anchor under steep cliffs near the head of the *cala*, open E round to S.

Dragonera Island light with San Telmo behind   *GW*

ANCHORAGES FROM ISLA DRAGONERA TO SÓLLER

There are a small number of rocky anchorages on this stretch of the NW coast of Mallorca, only suitable for use with great care in settled conditions. The only shelter is the port of Sóller in the event of sudden weather deterioration. The mountains and sheer cliffs which form much of the Costa Mirador offer spectacular scenery but also a totally unforgiving lee shore in the wrong conditions – in particular the NW *tramontana* (see *General Introduction* above). The mountains and narrow valleys influence the wind in both strength and direction, and a generous offing must be allowed in these conditions.

⚓ CALA BASSET
39°35′.8N 02°21′.3E

Close N of Punta Galera, which has a tower, a small house and track to the road. Enter with a lookout forward as there are several isolated breaking rocks. Open W–N. Holding is reported to be poor.

⊕41 39°38′.5N 02°25′.2E Pta de na Foradada

⚓ CALA DE ESTALLENCHS
39°39′.7N 02°28′.3E

A very open *cala* under the village of the same name, totally exposed to the entire W sector. There is a track up to the village. Reports mention a small rock awash close NE of the small stone jetty.

⚓ CALA BAÑALBUFAR
39°41′.6N 02°31′E

Another open *cala*, exposed to the W sector, with a track up to the village.

⊕42 39°42′.4N 02°31′.5E Pta S'Aliga

⚓ CALA DE VALLEDEMOSSA
39°43′.2N 02°35′.3E

Very little shelter, but there is a tiny quay backed by a small village, both dwarfed by breathtaking pine-covered mountains. Worth a detour inshore if time and weather conditions permit.

Peninsula de la Foradada
39°45′.4N 02°37′.3E (N tip of peninsula)
⊕43 39°45′.6N 02°37′.2E Peninsula de la Foradada

This extraordinary inverted boot-shaped promontory 600m in length has anchorages on either side, though the most sheltered area is now full of moorings. It is possible to land at the NW corner where there is a path up to a white house. A track inland leads to a large and conspicuous house known as Son Marroig, once owned by Archduke Luis Salvador of Austria who kept his steam yacht in the anchorage below.

⚓ W anchorage

The most sheltered area, in the angle of the 'L', is now occupied by moorings; anchor as close in as these permit in 5–10m over rock and weed with a few sand patches, open (depending on position) to SW–W–NW. Holding is generally poor. The spectacular hole through the end of the outcrop is best seen from this angle.

⚓ E anchorage

This anchorage, tucked between the peninsula and the coast, is open through NW-N-NE. Approach from the NW, following the coast of the peninsula, to avoid a line of breaking and submerged rocks which extend 100m or so from the mainland coast. The easternmost rock is about 100m from the anchorage. Anchor in 7–10m over rock and sand. There is a track uphill to the road.

⚓ CALA DEYA (DEIA)
39°45′.8N 02°38′.5E

A small, picturesque *cala* NE of the Peninsula de la Foradada, with a tiny quay at its head. Anchor near the middle in 4–6m over sand and rock, open to the northerly quadrant. There are fishermen's huts and several restaurants near the water, but little else. Deya itself, about a mile inland, is celebrated as the home of Robert Graves for many years prior to his death in 1985. It is also amongst the loveliest of Mallorca's villages and the antithesis of the tourist resorts that abound on much of the coastline.

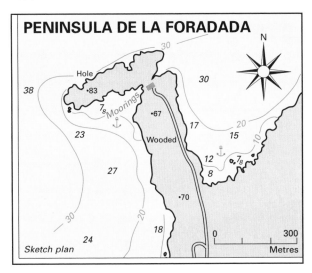

PENINSULA DE LA FORADADA

III. MALLORCA

M8 Puerto de Sóller

A very attractive harbour with a long history, tucked well inside a large *cala*. It is surrounded by mountains and pine forests. This is the only harbour on this stretch of coast and easy to enter in most conditions

Location
39°47′.7N 02°41′.6E

Communications
Port Authority ☎ 971 63 13 26 or ☎/*Fax* 971 63 33 16
Email webmaster@solleronline.com
www.SollerOnline.com

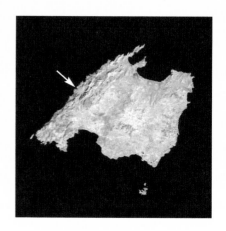

The port

Lying at the NE end of a beautiful bay, in the midst of spectacular mountainous scenery, Puerto de Sóller is a commercial and fishing harbour with some space for yachts. Works were still in progress towards the end of 2005 on the quay vacated by the navy some years ago.

This is the only harbour of refuge on the whole 50 mile stretch of the rugged, inhospitable NW coast of Mallorca, although there are a number of fair-weather anchorages. Facilities for yachtsmen are somewhat limited and it is often difficult to find a vacant space on the commercial mole.

PILOTAGE

Approach

⊕44 39°48′.0N 02°41′.2E Approach to Sóller

The approach and entrance present no problems in normal conditions, but could become difficult and perhaps dangerous in a gale from the NW, N or NE.

From NE From Cabo de Formentor, which can be recognised by its lighthouse (Fl(4)20s210m21M, white tower and house 22m), the coast comprises high rocky cliffs, very rugged and broken. Careful pilotage is necessary because many of the headlands

Puerto de Sóller, set in mountainous surroundings, looking NNE

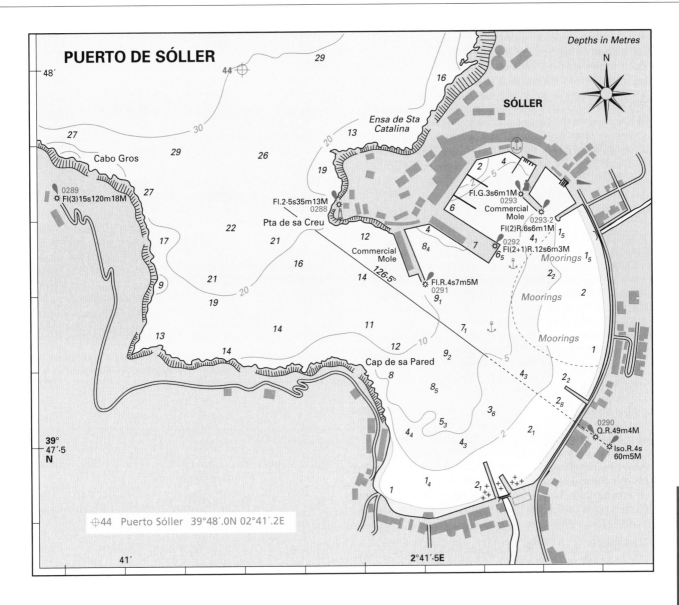

PUERTO DE SÓLLER

Depths in Metres

SÓLLER

Ensa de Sta Catalina

Cabo Gros

0289 Fl(3)15s120m18M

Fl.2·5s35m13M
0288

Pta de sa Creu

Commercial Mole

126·5°

Commercial Mole

Fl.G.3s6m1M

0293
Fl(2)R.6s6m1M
0293·2

0292
Fl(2+1)R.12s6m3M

Moorings

Moorings

Moorings

Fl.R.4s7m5M
0291
9₁

Cap de sa Pared

0290
Q.R.49m4M

Iso.R.4s 60m5M

⊕44 Puerto Sóller 39°48'.0N 02°41'.2E

2°41'·5E

---

are similar. The following may be recognised: Cala de San Vicente, which has a tourist development at its head, Punta Beca with a long beak-like extension, and Morro de la Vaca, looking like the head of a cow from some directions. In the last 3 miles two conspicuous watchtowers and the small Islote S'Illa will be seen and, in the close approach, the two lighthouses at the harbour entrance. Puig Mayor (1,445m), the highest point on Mallorca with radio towers (F.R) and two radomes on its summit, is just under 5 miles E of the entrance.

From SW From Isla Dragonera, a large, high and conspicuous island with two lighthouses (Fl.7.5s130m20M and Fl(2)12s67m14M), the coast is very high with broken rocky cliffs backed by mountains inland. The unmistakable Peninsula de la Foradada will be seen if coasting close inshore, with Cabo Gros and its white lighthouse 3.8 miles beyond. Punta de Sa Creu on the E side of the entrance is considerably lower and will not open until Cabo Gros has been rounded.

Anchorage in the approach

Anchor as space permits in 5–10m over mud and sand. Moorings extend to the 5m line, but appear too light for all but the smallest yachts. In summer the anchorage may become very full.

Entrance

Enter on a southerly course between Cabo Gros and Punta de sa Creu, swinging SE and then E to remain near the centre of the channel. There is a 4 knot speed limit. Keep well clear of the two naval moles if looking for a berth on the commerical mole.

Entrance at night should not present problems in reasonable weather: follow the leading lights into the anchorage.

Berthing

Visitor berths are restricted to rafting up at the outer extremity of the commercial mole, the inside end of the SW mole or the end of the pontoon in the W corner. There is very little room as local boats, ferries and tripper boats fill most of the available quay space. Visitors should come to Sóller expecting to anchor and then if they find a billet it is a bonus. Both moles on the NW side of the harbour are in the naval zone and should not be approached.

Facilities

Water Taps on the commercial mole, but only operational for a few hours each day (currently 0900-1100 weekdays). Also from a public water fountain up the hill behind the commercial mole. Reports regarding quality vary: taste before filling tanks.

Electricity 220v and 375v AC points on the commercial mole.

Fuel Diesel and petrol from pumps at the angle of the commercial mole.

Provisions Shops and supermarkets in the village around the harbour, with a much greater selection in the town 2 miles inland. Produce/fish market every morning except Sunday in Sóller town.

Ice From the fishermen's quay, bars and supermarkets.

Chandlery Small chandlery/fishing tackle/hardware shop up the hill behind the commercial mole.

Repairs There is no boatyard, but local craftsmen are available and should be able to carry out minor work. Three small slipways either side of the commercial mole, one of which has a cradle. However, there is no more than 2m depth at its foot. A 1-tonne crane near one of the slipways.

Engineers Available, but more accustomed to fishing boats.

Yacht club There is a small *club náutico*.

Launderette In the village.

Banks In the village and at Sóller town.

Hospital/medical services In Sóller town. Medical Emergencies ☎ 971 63 30 11 or 63 30 50. Other emergency and useful local numbers on the marina website.

Transport

Car hire/taxis In Sóller town.

Buses Bus service to Sóller and elsewhere.

Trams A quaint old wooden tram provides transport between the port and the town. The 2-mile journey takes about 20 minutes.

Trains Rail link from Sóller town to Palma by Victorian train (1 hour).

Ferries Tourist ferries to several of the *calas* along the coast to the NE.

History

Several prehistoric artifacts have been found in the town indicating its ancient past. In the 13th century under Moorish Arab power it was known as Puerto de Santa Catalina. Some years later King Jaime I Conquered the island and the port was renamed Puerto de Sóller.

The port has been of crucial importance since the thirteenth century when it was the only stopover on this coast between the islands and the Spanish mainland.

After 1399 it became a trading post, principally for the sale of local agricultural produce and raw materials destined for Spain, South of France, Italy, North Africa, Puerto Rico and other closer destinations. Because of its inaccessibility it was generally easier to move supplies by boat than overland to the port of Palma.

Fiesta time in Sóller. This one is re-enacting a battle scene from the 15th century when Christians defeated the Moors after 600 years of rule   *GW*

The construction of several towers along this coast, including Torre Picada, are testimony to the frequent and continous attacks by Arab bandits and pirates since the 13th century. The Es Firo festival celebrates a rebuffed pirate attack.

From the Middle Ages onwards Sóller had a huge fleet of merchant, fishing vessels and passenger ferries.

The port was rebuilt in the 18th century, and the splendid quays were used from 1936–39 by Franco as a major military base. It later became the centre of learning for the submarine service.

After the civil war the shipping trade was in decline but tourism created new oportunities. The whole region has been transformed by the construction of hotels, restaurants, bars and other trades, though the charm and originality of this port remains.

A small naval fleet remained until recently and the port is becoming more accommodating to yachtsmen.

Sights ashore locally

The attractive old rural town of Sóller – the name derived from the Arabic Sulliar, meaning 'golden valley' – was set well back from the sea as a first defence against pirate raids. It was long known for its oranges and lemons, which were exported in the famous *balancelles* (small, single-masted vessels). Even with the loss of that trade to Valencia the orange groves surrounding the little town remain. Sóller is linked to its port by a vintage tramway, an excursion highly recommended, as is a trip on the Victorian train which connects Sóller to Palma. Sóller, along with numerous other places in the western Mediterranean, claims to have been the birthplace of Christopher Columbus.

Bay of Sóller. Note dredger at work in bay

Further information is available from the tourist office in Sóller: Calle Calonge Oliver No.10 ☎/*Fax* 971 63 30 42. Open between March and October 1000–1300 and 1500–1830 weekdays, Sat 1000–1300.

Tickets for bus excursions may be found at change offices, car rental and tourist agencies in the port.

Local events

The fiesta and pageant of Nuestra Señora de la Victoria is held on the second Sunday in May to commemorate a victory over Moorish pirates in 1561; 15–16 July sees the Fiesta de la Virgen del Carmen with a waterborne procession; 25 July a fiesta in honour of Santiago (St James), and 24 August a fiesta in honour of San Bartolomé.

Eating out

A number of hotels and many restaurants, bars and cafés around the harbour.

Visitors' berths are restricted at Sóller   GW

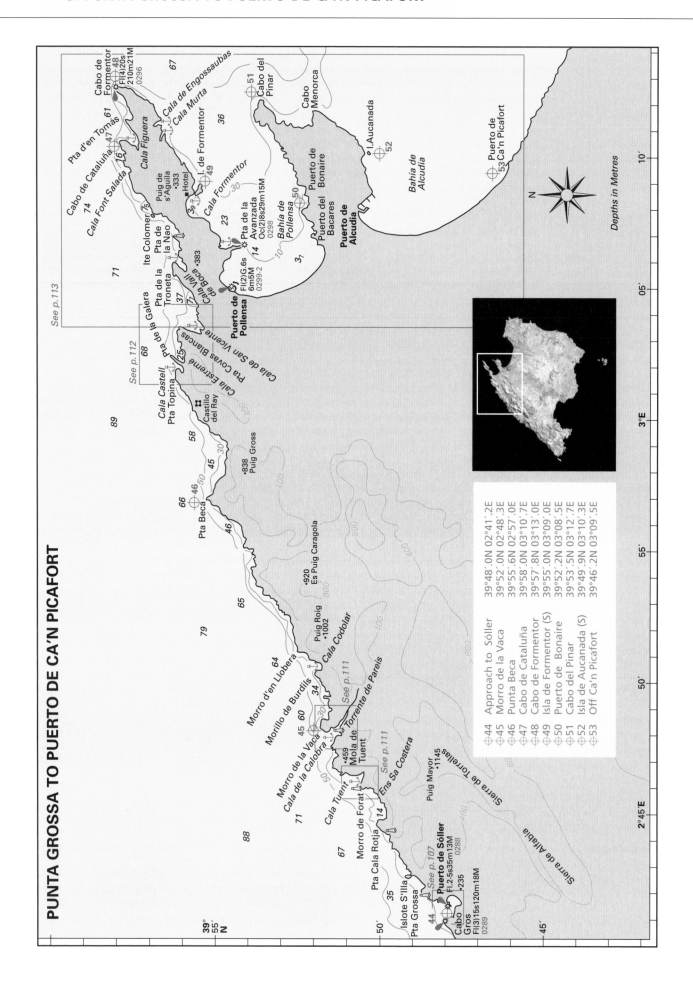

PUNTA GROSSA TO PUERTO DE CA'N PICAFORT

Depths in Metres

⊕44	Approach to Sóller	39°48'.0N 02°41'.2E
⊕45	Morro de la Vaca	39°52'.0N 02°48'.3E
⊕46	Punta Beca	39°55'.6N 02°57'.0E
⊕47	Cabo de Cataluña	39°58'.0N 03°10'.7E
⊕48	Cabo de Formentor	39°57'.8N 03°13'.0E
⊕49	Isla de Formentor (S)	39°55'.0N 03°09'.0E
⊕50	Puerto de Bonaire	39°52'.2N 03°08'.5E
⊕51	Cabo del Pinar	39°53'.5N 03°12'.7E
⊕52	Isla de Aucanada (S)	39°49'.9N 03°10'.3E
⊕53	Off Ca'n Picafort	39°46'.2N 03°09'.5E

3. Punta Grossa to Puerto de Ca'n Picafort

⚓ **ENSENADA SA COSTERA**

39°49′.8N 02°45′E

A wide, deep bay and a pleasant anchorage in settled conditions. Rocks line the shore but the water is usually very clear; approach carefully with a bow lookout, to anchor in 12–15m in the SW corner, open to N and NE. Puig Mayor (1,445m), the highest point on Mallorca with radio towers (F.R) and two radomes on its summit, lies just over 2 miles inland.

⚓ **CALA TUENT**

39°50′.6N 02°46′.4E

A small *cala* with a wide sand and stone beach, amidst spectacular surroundings 4.8 miles NE of Puerto de Sóller. Morro de Forat, close SW, has a ruined watchtower and offlying rocks. Anchor in 5–10m over sand and rock, open to NW and N. There are a few houses and a restaurant on the slopes overlooking the *cala* and a very winding road.

⚓ **CALA DE LA CALOBRA (TORRENTE DE PAREIS)**

39°51′.4N 02°48′.1E

A large and spectacular *cala* just S of Morro de la Vaca, with several mini bays and a slit in the high rocky cliffs behind, through which the Torrente de Pareis (more often a gentle stream) enters the sea. Anchor in 5–10m over sand and stones, open to NW and N. Tourist ferries land their passengers near the hotel overlooking the SW beach and should not be impeded.

The Torrente de Pareis is considered one of the sights of Mallorca and is a popular destination by road and sea, resulting in the usual restaurants and beach cafés. A tunnel through the rock links the two beaches.

⊕45 39°52′.0N 02°48′.3E Morro de la Vaca

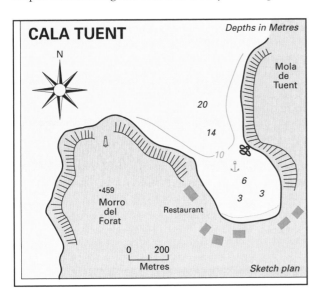

Cala de la Calobra (Torrente de Pareis) from SE

Cala Tuent viewed from NW

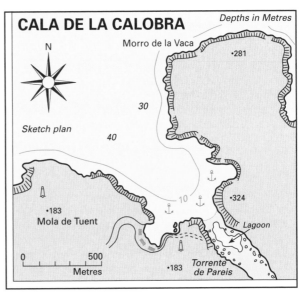

III. MALLORCA

Cala de la Calobra viewed from NW

Cala Estremé

⚓ CALA CODOLAR
39°51'.8N 02°50'.6E

A small *cala* surrounded by high cliffs close E of Morillo de Burdils. The water is deep (10m or so) up to the shore and the bottom is very rocky. If anchoring, it is essential to use a tripline.

⊕46 39°55'.6N 02°57'.0E Punta Beca

⚓ CALA CASTELL
39°56'N 03°02'.1E

A narrow *cala* open to the NE, separated from Cala Estreme by Punta de la Galera, a narrow rocky peninsula. Punta Topina close W, is a distinctive wedge shape when seen from the NE. Anchor in 5m over rock in the centre of the *cala* or in 3m over sand near the beach. Rocks line the eastern side. There is a small building behind the beach at the head of the *cala*, and a road leading inland.

⚓ CALA ESTREMÉ
39°56'N 03°02'.5E

Close E of Punta de la Galera and less sheltered than its neighbour, Cala Castell. Anchor over rock and sand near the small beach, open to NE and E.

⚓ CALA DE SAN VICENTE
39°55'.4N 03°03'.6E

A large *cala* backed by holiday developments. At its head there are two sandy beaches separated by a rocky point with a hole in it, fringed by hotels and apartments plus the usual cafés and restaurants. Anchor off either beach in 5m over sand. There is a very small stone quay in the SW corner of the western *cala*. A fiesta in honour of La Virgen del Mar is held on the first Sunday in July.

Cala de San Vicente

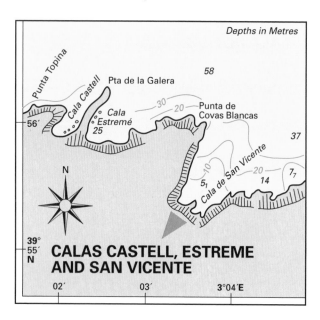

ANCHORAGES ON THE NORTHEAST COAST OF MALLORCA

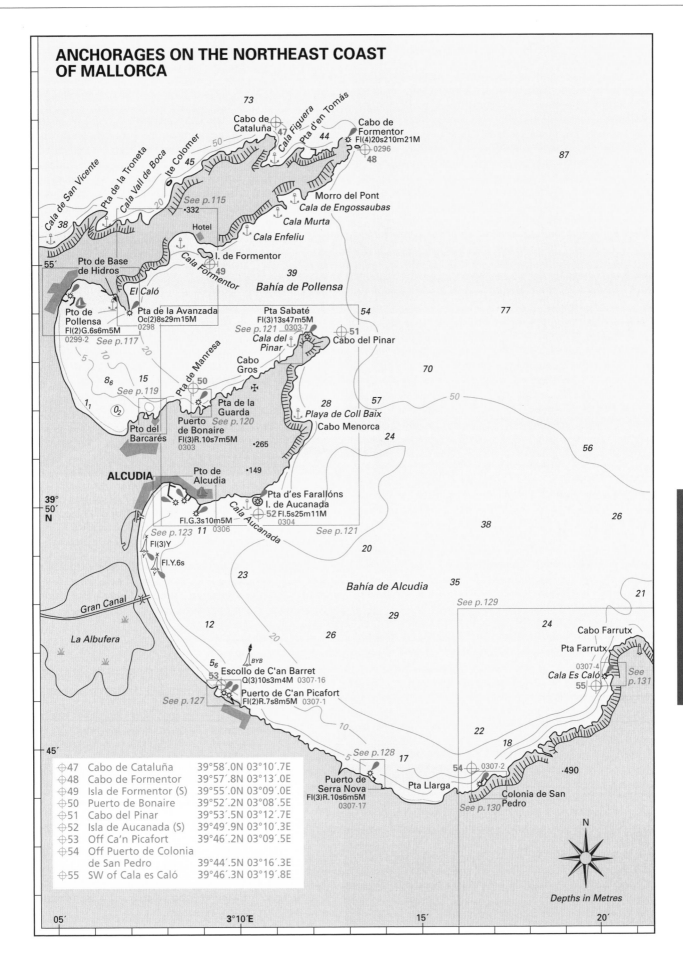

73

Cabo de Cataluña ⊕47

Cala Figuera

Pta d'en Tomás

44

Cabo de Formentor
Fl(4)20s210m21M
✿ 0296
⊕48

87

Pta de la Troneta

Ite Colomer

50

45

Cala Vall de Boca

Cala de San Vicente

Morro del Pont
Cala de Engossaubas

See p.115
•332

20

38

Hotel

Cala Murta

Cala Enfeliu

55'

Pto de Base de Hidros

Cala Formentor

I. de Formentor
⊕49

39

Bahía de Pollensa

77

Pto de Pollensa
Fl(2)G.6s6m5M
0299·2

El Caló

Pta de la Avanzada
Oc(2)8s29m15M
0298

Pta Sabaté
Fl(3)13s47m5M
See p.121   0303·7

54

⊕51
Cabo del Pinar

See p.117

Cala del Pinar

5   10   20

15

8₆

Pta de Manresa ⊕50

Cabo Gros

Cabo del Pinar

70

See p.119

1₁   (0₂)

Pto del Barcarés

Pta de la Guarda

Puerto de Bonaire
Fl(3)R.10s7m5M
0303

See p.120

28   57

⊕ *Playa de Coll Baix*

Cabo Menorca

24

50

56

•265

•149

ALCUDIA

Pto de Alcudia

Pta d'es Farallóns
I. de Aucanada
⊕52 Fl.5s25m11M
0304

38

26

39°
50'
N

Fl.G.3s10m5M
0306   11

Cala Aucanada

See p.121

See p.123

20

Fl(3)Y

Bahía de Alcudia

35

21

FI.Y.6s

23

See p.129

29

24

Gran Canal

12

26

Cabo Farrutx

Pta Farrutx

La Albufera

0307·4

Cala Es Caló
⊕55

See p.131

5₆
BYB

⊕53
Escollo de C'an Barret
Q(3)10s3m4M 0307·16

Puerto de C'an Picafort
Fl(2)R.7s8m5M 0307·1

See p.127

10

22

18

5
See p.128
17

Puerto de Serra Nova
Fl(3)R.10s6m5M
0307·17

Pta Llarga

54 ⊕ 0307·2

•490

45'

Colonia de San Pedro

See p.130

⊕47	Cabo de Cataluña	39°58'.0N 03°10'.7E
⊕48	Cabo de Formentor	39°57'.8N 03°13'.0E
⊕49	Isla de Formentor (S)	39°55'.0N 03°09'.0E
⊕50	Puerto de Bonaire	39°52'.2N 03°08'.5E
⊕51	Cabo del Pinar	39°53'.5N 03°12'.7E
⊕52	Isla de Aucanada (S)	39°49'.9N 03°10'.3E
⊕53	Off Ca'n Picafort	39°46'.2N 03°09'.5E
⊕54	Off Puerto de Colonia de San Pedro	39°44'.5N 03°16'.3E
⊕55	SW of Cala es Caló	39°46'.3N 03°19'.8E

N

Depths in Metres

05'   3°10'E   15'   20'

III. MALLORCA

⚓ CALA VALL DE BOCA
39°55′.8N 03°05′.9E

A narrow *cala* with a small stony beach between high rocky cliffs. Anchor in ±5m over rock, open to N and NE. There is an overland track to Puerto de Pollensa.

⊕47 39°58′.0N 03°10′.7E Cabo de Cataluña

Cala Val de Boca. Spectacular view looking from NE between the cliffs

⚓ CALA FIGUERA
39°57′.2N 03°10′.7E

A large deserted *cala* 1.6M W of Cabo de Formentor, surrounded by rocky hills and cliffs and with a small stone and sand beach at its head. Anchor in 5m over sand and rock, open to N and NE. There is a rough road leading up from the beach but little else.

This is one of three Cala Figueras around the coast of Mallorca, the others being at the SW end of the Bahía de Palma and on the SE coast near Punta Salinas.

Rounding Cabo de Formentor looking SW: Cala de Engossaubas to the left

⊕48 39°57′.8N 03°13′.0E Cabo de Formentor

⚓ CALA DE ENGOSSAUBAS (CALA EN GOSSALBA)
39°56′.5N 03°11′.4E

A very beautiful and deserted *cala* 1.7M SW of the tip of Cabo de Formentor, reasonably wide and completely unspoilt, between high steep cliffs. Anchor close to the head in 2.5m over sand, or further out in 6m over weed and rock. Open to SE round to SW though an E or even NE swell may work in. Ashore there is a track up to the road.

Cala Murta: always crystal-clear waters

⚓ CALA MURTA
39°56′.4N 03°11′E

Another pleasant and unspoilt small *cala* with rocky sides (37m) and a stony beach. There is a small castle-like rock at the entrance and very clear water. Anchor in 3–5m over sand.

⚓ CALA ENFELIU
39°55′.8N 03°09′.9E

A tiny *cala* with rocky sides and a small stony beach. Enter with care to anchor in 3–5m over rock and sand, open to NE–SE–SW.

⊕49 39°55′.0N 03°09′.0E Isla de Formentor (S end)

⚓ CALA FORMENTOR (CALA PINO)
39°55′.6N 03°08′.4E

This used to be a very popular open anchorage NW of Isla de Formentor (34m). The narrow passage inside Isla de Formentor now has a depth of only 1m.

The whole *cala* has been laid with buoys and it is now forbidden to anchor inside the (approximately) 15m contour. Anchoring is permitted outside the bay but there is little protection in that area from wind and swell from any direction.

Mooring charges were €15 per day for a 10m yacht during summer 2005.

Cala Formentor looking NW over Isla de Formentor. Note mooring buoys

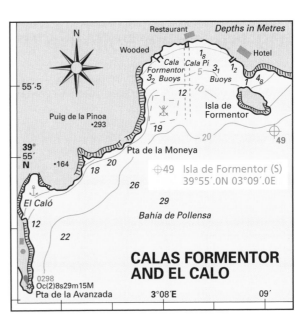

The beaches are popular with day tourists, speedboats, jet-skis and water-skiers weaving amongst the anchored yachts. Some areas may be buoyed off for bathers. As a contrast to the five-star hotel there are various beach bars and restaurants. The small jetties and quays in the NW corner are privately owned.

⚓ EL CALÓ
39°54´.7N 03°06´.7E

A small *cala* close E of the root of Punta de la Avanzada. Anchor in ±5m over sand.

Looking across Pta de la Avanzada towards Puerto de Pollensa

⚓ BEHIND PUNTA DE LA AVANZADA
39°54´.3N 03°06´.4E

A well sheltered anchorage close W of Punta de la Avanzada (Oc(2)8s29m15M, octagonal stone tower on building 18m) and only a mile E of Puerto de Pollensa. Anchor in +3m over sand and weed (but allow for the fact that the bottom is uneven). Apart from the considerable daytime disturbance from speedboats and jet-skis, the anchorage is calm. Unfortunately the old castle on the promontory, known as La Fortaleza, is privately owned and explorations ashore are said to be unwelcome.

PUERTO DE BASE DE HIDROS (SEAPLANE BASE)
39°54´.5N 03°6´.1E

This small and very shallow harbour belongs to the Spanish Navy and is a seaplane base. For obvious reasons it does not welcome yachts.

Anchorage SW of Pta de la Avanzada: note seaplane base right and buoyed exclusion zone along the coast

M9 Puerto de Pollensa (Pollença)

A very friendly and sheltered harbour with
berthing for 375 yachts, 100 miles from Barcelona

Location
    39°54′.1N 03°05′.1E
Distances
    Barcelona 100M
    Menorca 35M
Communications
    VHF: Ch 09
    Real Club Náutico de Pollensa ☎ 971 86 46 35
    Fax 971 86 46 36
    Email oficina@rcnpp.net
    www.rcnpp.net

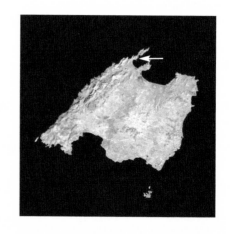

The harbour/marina

A good-sized yacht and fishing harbour with 375
berths. Puerto de Pollensa is at the head of a
beautiful wide bay surrounded by spectacular
mountains. The approach and harbour are both
somewhat shallow, but should present no problems
other than in strong E winds. The bay is open to the
sea from NE through E to SE, and in heavy winds or
swell from these directions, the head of the bay is
best avoided. The anchorage behind Punta de
Avanzada provides a sheltered alternative, though
during gales from the N quadrant violent gusts may
be experienced.

PILOTAGE

Approach

From S Cross the wide Bahía de Alcudia towards
Cabo del Pinar and Punta Sabaté – conspicuous,
with high rocky cliffs (Fl(3)9s47m5M, white
triangular tower, black band 12m). Cabo de
Formentor will be seen beyond. Round Punta Negra
onto a westerly course towards Punta de la
Avanzada (Oc(2)8s29m15M, octagonal stone tower
on building 18m), after which Puerto de Pollensa
will open up.

From N Round the almost vertical rocky cliffs of
Cabo de Formentor (Fl(4)20s210m21M, white
tower and house 22m), then follow the coast SW
past the lower Punta de la Avanzada. Puerto de
Pollensa will be seen once past this headland.

Anchorage in the approach

See *Anchorage behind Punta de la Avanzada* above.
Alternatively anchor in the bay NE of the harbour in
2–3m over sand and weed (though some patches
carry less than 2m so a careful watch on the depth is
necessary while manoeuvring). Holding is good once
the anchor has dug in. Mooring blocks and
associated ground tackle, often without mooring
buoys, may be encountered almost anywhere in the
bay N of a line between the NE end of the

breakwater and the entrance to the Base de Hidros.
They are usually visible in the shallow water and it
is possible to anchor safely amongst the more widely
spaced. The area is zoned for more moorings during
2006, after which anchoring will be prohibited and
a charge made.

Less protection can be had SW of the harbour
towards the two training walls (see plan) in 2m+
over sand, mud and weed. There are some moorings
in this area. In strong SE winds the best shelter will
be found close W of Puerto de Bonaire, some 3.5M
across the bay, in 4–6m over sand.

Puerto de Pollensa from NE: protected in the bay and in
spectacular surroundings   *GW*

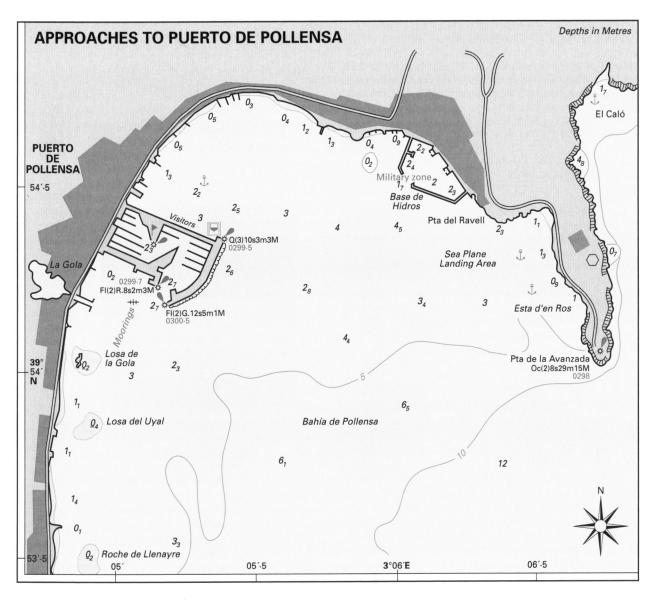

APPROACHES TO PUERTO DE POLLENSA

Depths in Metres

Entrance

Approach the head of the NE breakwater from E or SE, leaving it 30–40m to starboard on entry. There are shoals close SW of the entrance (see plan) and the wreck of a yacht is noted on some charts, unmarked at 39°54′.1N 03°05′.01E just S of the entrance, apparently covered by only 1m of water. The fuel berth at the end of the SW mole doubles as a reception quay. There is a 4-knot speed limit.

Berthing

The *club náutico* visitors' berths are on the outside of the N quay, exposed to NE and E. Mooring lines are provided, tailed to the quay.

Inside the harbour there is a Port Authority quay on the N side of the SW mole, and visitors may also use the outer section of the nearby pontoon (see plan). These berths also have mooring lines with water and electricity.

Facilities

Water Taps on quays and pontoons. There is a tap by Hotel Diana's swimming pool – and a place for a dinghy!

Electricity 220v AC points on all quays and pontoons, plus some 380v points.

Fuel Diesel and petrol pumps on the head of the SW mole.

Provisions Two supermarkets and other specialist food shops able to supply all normal requirements. An open-air market on Wednesday mornings in Puerto de Pollensa and Sunday in Pollensa town nearby, where there are also good shops.

Ice At the fuel berth, the Réal Club Náutico bar and a shop opposite the harbour.

Chandleries Náutica Brúixola SL ☎ 971 53 11 93 *Fax* 53 48 18 and others. Maritime International ☎ 971 86 72 99 *Fax* 971 86 69 96 offer a total boat care and maintenance service as well as selling chandlery from an office/shop close to the marina.

Repairs Astilleros Cabanellas boatyard on the SW mole can handle all normal work. A 50-tonne lift at the NE breakwater elbow. A 1-tonne crane on the NE breakwater and 4-tonne crane at the boatyard. A small

III. MALLORCA

slipway in the interior of the harbour and a larger one, with cradle able to take vessels up to 21m, at the boatyard.

Engineers At the boatyard. Motonautica Bonaire ☎ 971 53 04 62/89 23 01 *Fax* 971 53 04 66 are official service agents for Mercury/MerCruiser, Sole Diesel, Tohatsu, Volvo Penta and Yamaha.

Sailmaking and repairs Wilson Yachts ☎ 971 86 40 67 *Fax* 971 86 40 59; Plana Velámenes ☎/*Fax* 971 86 60 61.

Yacht club The Club Náutico de Puerto de Pollensa has a smart, modern clubhouse on the NE breakwater with lounge, terrace, bar, restaurant, swimming pool and showers.

Showers At the *club náutico* free to visitors using their berths, otherwise a small fee is charged.

Launderette Near the harbour.

Banks In Puerto de Pollensa and Pollensa town.

Hospital/medical services In Puerto de Pollensa and Pollensa town 3 miles inland.

Transport

Car hire/taxis In Puerto de Pollensa and Pollensa town.

Buses Frequent service to Pollensa town, several times daily to Palma.

Sites ashore locally

There are good walks around the harbour, particularly among the hills to the N with some dramatic views over the N coast of Mallorca. Two recommended hikes are across the Peninsula de Formentera to Cala de San Vicente and further NE to Cala Vall de Boca.

Pollensa town – built, like Sóller, some distance inland from its harbour – is attractive with good shops and some interesting ancient buildings. Its name comes from the Latin *pollentia* meaning powerful, though it is now agreed that the famous Roman city of Pollentia was actually sited near Alcudia. Nearby at Campanet are spectacular caves, well worth a visit with 50-million-year-old stalactites and stalagmites.

Local events

Fiestas are held on 17 January (San Antonio) and 20 January (San Sebastian) with the usual processions; on Good Friday, in mid-July, with the week-long Fiesta de la Virgen del Carmen; and on 2 August in honour of Nuestra Señora de los Angeles, incorporating a mock battle between Moors and Christians as in Sóller.

Eating out

Many eating establishments – Pollensa is a popular tourist resort. Restaurant and bar at the *club náutico*.

M10 Puerto del Barcarés

A small shallow harbour of little interest to yachts, but with possibilities for anchoring in the approach

Location
39°51´.85N 03°07´.2E

Communications
Puerto del Barcarés ☎ 971 53 18 67

The harbour

Puerto del Barcarés is a tiny harbour limited to small fishing boats and yachts drawing less than 1m and is in no way a port, though in the right conditions it would be possible to anchor off and visit by dinghy. The light was removed years ago but the structure is still there and now painted white. There are no facilities other than a single water tap on the quay.

Puerto del Barcarés from NW: shallows easily seen left of small harbour

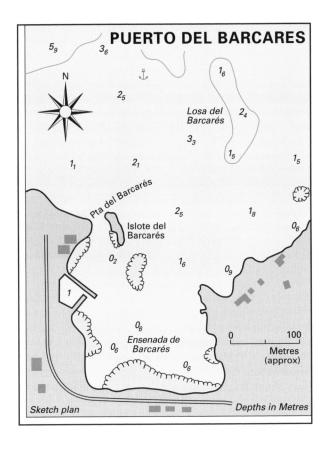

PUERTO DEL BARCARES

Losa del
Barcarés

Pta del Barcarés

Islote del
Barcarés

Ensenada de
Barcarés

0   100

Metres
(approx)

Sketch plan   Depths in Metres

M11 Puerto/Marina de Bonaire (Cocodrilo)

A well sheltered marina on the S side of Bahía de Pollensa with 352 moorings up to 17m, most occupied by local boats. It is easy to approach and is pleasantly located in a deeply forested region of the bay

Location
39°52´.1N 03°08´.5E

Communications
VHF Ch 09
Marina de Bonaire ☎ 971 54 69 55
Fax 971 54 85 64 *Email* marinabonaire@terra.es

PILOTAGE

Approach

Punta del Barcarés lies near the SW corner of the Bahía de Pollensa, W of Punta de Manresa and some 3 miles SE of Puerto de Pollensa. There are shoals in the approach, including the 1.5m Losa del Barcarés 400m NE of the entrance and an unnamed breaking patch SE of Islote del Bacarés (itself only a low rocky ledge).

Anchorage in the approach

Anchor N of Islote del Bacarés in 2–5m over sand and weed, open to W–N–NE.

Entrance

(Inadvisable except by dinghy).

Swing wide of the unnamed shoal mentioned above to round the N mole at slow speed. The entrance is no more than 2.5m wide and less than 1m deep.

Berthing

There is a dinghy slipway opposite the entrance.

Facilities

Water A tap on the quay

The harbour

Formerly known as Port del Cocodrilo, and still called by that name on several road signs locally and some charts, Puerto de Bonaire is an attractive, purpose-built yacht harbour amongst pleasantly wooded surroundings, believed to be on the site of one of the original Phoenician landings. The harbour is simple to approach and enter and offers excellent shelter. Most of the 352 berths for yachts up to 17m

Puerto de Bonaire: an attractive purpose-built marina

III. MALLORCA

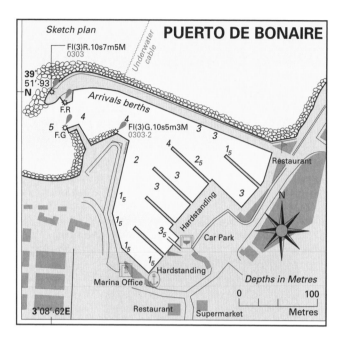

Puerto de Bonaire from within the marina   *GW*

are permanently occupied. Unlike many similar harbours in the Islas Baleares there is no commercial or fishing usage.

In December 2001, during a hurricane of over 100 knots, the sea wall was breached and partially destroyed, the restaurant at the breakwater root was blown away and 22 boats sank. Extensive reconstruction has included the raising of the sea wall by 2m and reshaping the entrance, providing excellent shelter and comfort.

PILOTAGE

Approach

⊕50 39°52′.2N 03°08′.5E Puerto de Bonaire

From S Cross the wide Bahía de Alcudia towards Cabo del Pinar and Punta Sabaté – conspicuous, with high rocky cliffs (Fl(3)9s47m5M, white triangular tower, black band 12m). Round Punta Negra to follow the S coast of the Bahía de Pollensa past Cabo Gros and Punta de la Guarda. Puerto de Bonaire lies 0.5M further W.

From N Round the almost vertical rocky cliffs of Cabo de Formentor (Fl(4)20s210m21M, white tower and house 22m), then steer SW towards Punta de Manresa, a low, dark rocky point surmounted by a castle. Puerto de Bonaire lies 0.5M E of this headland.

Anchorage in the approach

Anchor in the bay W of the harbour entrance in 5m over sand, open to the northern quadrant.

Entrance

The entrance is relatively narrow with a distinct dogleg. Approach on a southerly course, slowly closing the coast W of the N breakwater until the W mole comes into view. Then swing E and NE to remain in the centre of the channel. The reception quay is to port immediately inside the entrance.

If entering at night (quite feasible in settled conditions) note that the light on the N breakwater is some distance from the end of the rubble breakwater. A bow lookout with a strong torch is recommended. In summer there may be F.R and F.G lights on the spurs each side of the entrance.

Berthing

Berth at the reception quay until directed elsewhere by marina staff, preferably having already called on VHF Ch 09.

Facilities

Water Taps on quays and pontoons.
Electricity 220v AC points on quays and pontoons.
Fuel Available end of S jetty.
Provisions Small supermarket just S of the harbour (opposite a restaurant) and many shops in Alcudia a mile SW.
Ice From the bar/restaurant at the root of the N breakwater.
Chandlery Next to the marina office.
Repairs Workshops near the marina office. Motonautica Bonaire ☎ 971 53 04 62 *Fax* 971 53 04 66. A 30-tonne lift in the S part of the harbour. Slipway next to the travel-lift.
Engineers Engineering workshop near the marina office and Motonautica Bonaire (see above).
Electronic & radio repairs Enquire at the marina office.
Showers Near the marina office.
Launderette By the shower block.
Hospital/medical services In Alcudia.
Banks In Alcudia.

Transport

Car hire/taxis From Alcudia. Enquire at the marina office.

Sites ashore locally

There are excellent walks in the area and good views from Punta de Manresa, while the old Roman city of Alcudia is just over a mile away.

Eating out

Bar/restaurant at the root of the N breakwater and another S of the harbour. Others in the vicinity.

ANCHORAGES ON PENINSULA CABO DEL PINAR

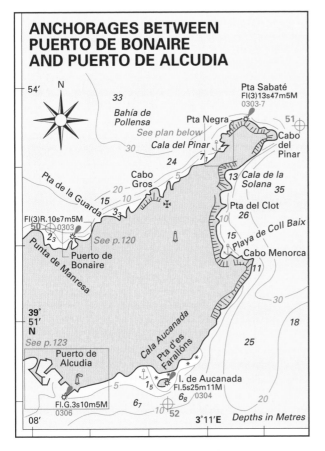

ANCHORAGES BETWEEN PUERTO DE BONAIRE AND PUERTO DE ALCUDIA

⊕50	Puerto de Bonaire	39°52´.2N 03°08´.5E
⊕51	Cabo del Pinar	39°53´.5N 03°12´.7E
⊕52	Isla de Aucanada (S)	39°49´.9N 03°10´.3E

⚓ CALA DEL PINAR (SES CALETAS)

39°53´.3N 03°11´.3E

An anchorage behind Punta Negra on the N side of the peninsula Cabo del Pinar, consisting of a double

Looking E over Cala del Pinar to Pta Sabate and Cabo del Pinar

Playa de Coll Baix with Cabo Menorca looming left

cala plus a smaller one to the N. Cabo del Pinar is a military area, with landing in the *calas* forbidden and access sometimes restricted by buoys. Anchor in 5–7m (less if it is permitted to enter the calas) over sand and weed. Holding is patchy. It is a popular place for day visitors from Pollensa and can become crowded.

⊕51 39°53´.5N 03°12´.7E Cabo del Pinar

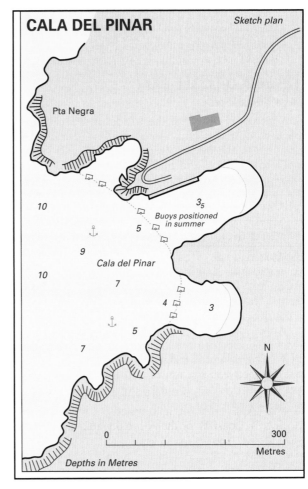

III. MALLORCA

Bahía de Alcudia viewed from N, with Isla de Aucanada left

⚓ PLAYA DE COLL BAIX

39°51´.9N 03°11´.4E

An open anchorage on the S side of the peninsula beneath dramatic cliffs off a small sand and stone beach. Anchor in 5m over rock, sand and stones, open to N–NE–E and to swell from the SE. Ashore there is a track to the road but nothing else.

⊕52 39°49´.9N 03°10´.3E Isla de Aucanada (S)

⚓ CALA AUCANADA

39°50´.3N 03°09´.9E

A wide but shallow bay 600m WNW of Isla Aucanada (Fl.5s25m11M, white tower and house 15m). The surrounding land is generally flat – quite a contrast if coming from the N.

Approach from the S or SW to anchor in 1.5m+ over sand, open to the S quadrant. The beach close NW of the island is fringed by reefs and the narrow passage between the island and Punta Aucanada is very shallow. There is a road down to the point and a few houses.

Isla de Aucanada looking W with anchorage behind

M12 Puerto de Alcudia (Marina Alcúdiamar)

A very sheltered marina with easy access and berthing for over 700 yachts but shallow at the N end of the harbour. A commercial and naval port lie just outside the marina

Location
39°50′.3N 03°08′.2E

Communications
Pilots (*Alcudia Prácticos*) VHF Ch 11, 13, 14, 16
Marina Alcúdiamar VHF Ch 09 ☎ 971 54 60 00/-04
Fax 971 54 89 20
Email alcudiamar@alcudiamar.es
www.alcudiamar.es

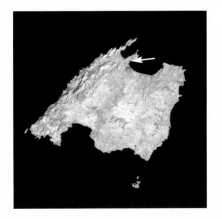

The marina

Alcúdiamar, a large, well-equipped but rather shallow marina able to accommodate 730 yachts of up to 25m, lies NW of a small commercial port handling cargo ships and ferries, with a small naval zone sandwiched between the two. The marina is easy to approach and enter and well sheltered once inside, though public access to the many restaurants and cafés on the W breakwater means that security is virtually nil. It shares its location with an old fishing harbour but this is no longer busy.

Work is underway (2006) at the commercial harbour to extend facilities to take larger vessels, possibly including cruise liners.

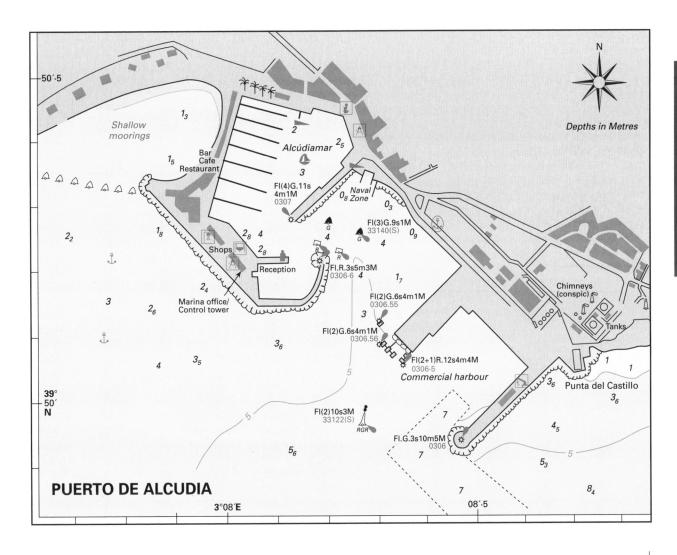

PUERTO DE ALCUDIA

PILOTAGE

Approach

From S The high headland of Cabo de Pera (Fl(2+3)20s76m16M, white tower on white building with dark corners and red roof 21m) and the even higher (272m) Cabo del Freu, which has a long low rocky projection at its foot, are both unmistakeable. Follow the coast NW towards Cabo Farrutx, passing the islet of Farayó de Aubarca (23m high and about 750m offshore) en route. There is good water on either side of the island.

On rounding Cabo Farrutx (unlit, though there are red lights on Puig Tudosa 1.5M to the S) the Bahía de Alcudia opens up, with Puerto de Alcudia in the NW corner. Pass *outside* Isla de Aucanada (Fl.5s25m11M, white tower and house 15m) and leave the head of the SE breakwater at least 50m to starboard. The two tall chimneys near the root of the breakwater are conspicuous.

From N Cross the Bahía de Pollensa and round first the steep reddish-cliffed Cabo del Pinar and then the even higher, but not so prominent, Cabo Menorca. Follow the coast (now becoming low and flat) at 500m to pass *outside* Isla de Aucanada and proceed as above.

Puerto de Alcudia and SW anchorage looking N into Bahía de Pollensa

Note The approach and entrance to the yacht harbour are relatively shallow and can be dangerous in heavy seas from E and SE. The area is prone to silting up and charted depths should not be relied upon.

Submarines occasionally exercise in the Bahía de Alcudia and its approaches. Commercial ships may be anchored S of the harbour.

Anchorage in the approach

Anchor SW of the marina in 2–4m over sand and weed, open to SE and S, keeping well clear of the entrance. Some moorings have been laid out to about 100m from the breakwater.

Entrance

Leave the head of the SE (commercial) breakwater (Fl.G.3s10m5M) a good 50m to starboard and also the buoy (Fl(2)10s3M) just to starboard. Keep well clear of any commercial ship or ferry movement by leaving the RGR buoy to starboard. Then steer N to pass between the marina breakwater light (Fl.R.3s5m1M) and the starboard hand buoy (Fl(3)G.9s1M). When halfway between the two lights, come round to port, leaving the breakwater end 50m or so to port to approach the marina entrance on a westerly heading. Depth at the entrance is dredged to 4m but silting can occur after strong winds, so proceed with caution. There is a 3-knot speed limit in the harbour.

Berthing

There is a reception area on the S side of the fuelling quay, but it is preferable to contact the marina office on VHF Ch 09 before arrival so that a permanent berth can be allocated. Anchoring is not allowed inside the yacht harbour.

Facilities

Water Taps on quays and pontoons, and at the fuelling berth.

Electricity 220v AC at all berths plus 380v AC at berths over 14m.

Fuel Diesel and petrol pumps on the inner arm of the SW breakwater.

Gas No Calor gas cylinders can be refilled in Mallorca now, but Náutica Mahón stocks Camping Gaz.

Provisions Small supermarket on the SW breakwater, many more in Puerto de Alcudia and Alcudia town. A produce market Sunday and Tuesday mornings in Alcudia town.

Ice From the fuel berth.

Chandleries Enmartor ☎ 971 548415, EMO's Ship-Shop ☎/Fax 971 54 71 10 and others.

Repairs Construcciones Navales Benassar SA boatyard ☎/Fax 971 54 67 00. All repair work can also be undertaken by Náutica Mahón ☎ 971 54 67 50 *Fax* 971 54 67 54 which has its offices in the marina complex. A 150-tonne lift and an 80-tonne lift are available on the SW breakwater. An 8-tonne mobile crane is also available. Small slipway in shallow (0.7m) water on the N side of the yacht harbour.

Engineers Náutica Mahón (see *Repairs* above) and Motonáutica Alcudia ☎ 971 54 61 30. The latter is the official service agent for MerCruiser, Tohatsu, Volvo Penta, Yanmar. Europa Marine Services (Balearics) S.L. ☎ 971 54 92 15 can service inboard/outboard engines and refrigeration units.

Electronic & radio repairs Náutica Mahón (see above) and others.

Sailmaker Plana Velámenes ☎/Fax 971 86 60 61.

Rigging Yacht-Rigger ☎ 908 43 59 75.

Showers On the SW breakwater.

Laundry In the marina.

Banks In Puerto de Alcudia and Alcudia town.

Hospital/medical services Medical services via marina office, hospital in Alcudia town.

Transport

Car hire/taxis In both Puerto de Alcudia and Alcudia town. A taxi rank at the root of the SW breakwater.

Buses Bus service to Alcudia town, Palma and elsewhere.

Ferries Regular service to Ciudadela in Menorca and Port Vendres in France.

History

Both the port and the old town a mile inland date back to Phoenician times, the latter a typical settlement site on a hilly peninsula served by two harbours on opposite sides of the isthmus. In due course the Romans took it over, calling the area Pollentia ('powerful') and making it the capital of the island; however, the Vandals occupied the town after the fall of Rome and destroyed most of the Roman buildings. Little evidence is left of the Moorish occupation except the name, Al Kudia, which means 'the hill'. After the Christian re-conquest, walls were built around the town.

Sights ashore locally

Sections of the walls can still be seen, together with the remains of the Roman theatre. In addition to the theatre (on the road between the harbour and the town), St Martin's cave, the castle and the museum are worth visiting.

For those who are interested in birds, the Albufera Nature Reserve behind the beach to the SW is a most important site. Follow the coast road S for about 3 miles, cross the Gran Canal and the entrance to the park is clearly labelled. There is an entry fee, but bird hides, etc. are provided. The Bahía de Alcudia is a popular tourist area, largely due to its excellent beaches.

Local events

Fiestas are held on 29 June in honour of San Pedro, with land and sea processions. On 2 July the Romería a la Virgen de la Victória includes a pilgrimage to the Santuari de la Victória on a peak 3 miles away, and on 25 July a fiesta in honour of Santiago (St James), the patron saint of the town, includes a parade on horseback.

Eating out

Many restaurants and cafés line the marina. There is a 4-star hotel in the NW corner of the marina, offering special rates for visiting yachtsmen.

III. MALLORCA

Post-storm seascape in the Bay of Pollensa looking SE towards Alcudia Old Town   *GW*

M13 Puerto de Ca'n Picafort

A small harbour with 470 yacht berths, easy to enter and offering excellent protection. It is 4M S of Alcúdimar with superb beaches on either side

Location
39°46′.1N 03°09′.6E

Communications
VHF Ch 09
Puerto Deportivo de Ca'n Picafort ☎/*Fax* 971 85 00 10
Club Náutico Ca'n Picafort ☎/*Fax* 971 85 01 85
Email pdcanpicafort@futurnet.es

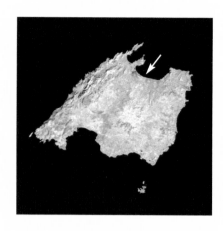

The harbour

Ca'n Picafort is a fairly small yacht harbour able to take 470 boats up to 12m, built onto a small, old fishing harbour. It is backed by a popular tourist resort of fairly recent origin, the first hotel having been built in 1933 when building controls were lifted.

Approach is straightforward, but entrance is dangerous with even moderate seas from the E or NE quadrant, due to shoaling water around the entrance. These are well marked.

PILOTAGE

Approach

⊕53 39°46′.2N 03°09′.5E Off Ca'n Picafort

For outer approaches see *Puerto de Alcudia* and page 124.

From S Round the high (432m) Cabo Farrutx on to a course just S of W. Puerto de Ca'n Picafort lies 9 miles away, near the S end of the hotels which line much of the Bahía de Alcudia. There is a day-mark (see *Lights* in *Appendix*) close to the harbour entrance, but it may be lost against the high-rise buildings behind.

From N After rounding Cabo Menorca head SSW across the Bahía de Alcudia, Puerto de Ca'n Picafort lies 6 miles away, identified as above.

Anchorage in the approach

The bottom is rocky near the harbour. Anchor in 5m over sand, 700m from the shore and some 1000m NW of the harbour with the two No.3 beacons in line, open to NE and E. Sound carefully.

Entrance

A dangerous breaking reef, Escollo de Ca'n Barret, marked by an E cardinal beacon (Q(3)10s3m4M, BYB post on wide yellow base, ♦ topmark) lies 300m WNW of the entrance.

Puerto de Ca'n Picafort. Seas breaking over the Escollo de Ca'n Barret reef

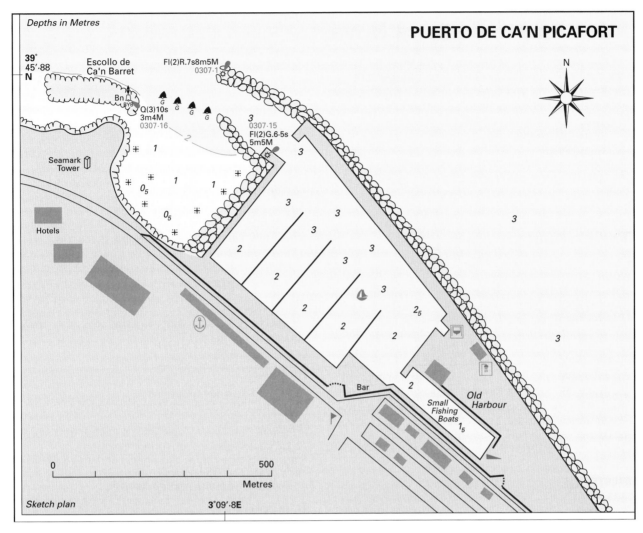

Depths in Metres

PUERTO DE CA'N PICAFORT

39°
45'·88
N

Escollo de
Ca'n Barret

Fl(2)R.7s8m5M
0307·15

Bn

Q(3)10s
3m4M
0307·16

Fl(2)G.6·5s
5m5M
0307·15

Seamark
Tower

Hotels

Bar

Small
Fishing
Boats

Old
Harbour

0   500
Metres

Sketch plan

3°09'·8E

Approach the head of the NE breakwater on a southerly course at slow speed, watching the depth-sounder. A line of four green buoys indicate the W side of the channel (Nov 2005), though these were red in previous years. Round the breakwater at about 20m and turn sharply to port to line up for the centre of the entrance, where at least 3m should be found. Entrance after dark is not recommended.

Berthing

Secure to the inner side of the NE breakwater until a berth can be allocated. The harbour office will be found near the root of the W mole.

Facilities

Water Taps on quays and pontoons. Check quality before filling tanks.
Electricity 220v AC points on quays and pontoons, 380v on hardstanding.
Fuel Still no fuel pumps (Nov 2005).
Provisions Many shops and supermarkets in the town. Market on Tuesday afternoons in Calle Cervantes.
Ice Available from bars and the *club náutico*.
Repairs Basic boatyard services near the 20-tonne travel-lift beside the old harbour. An 8-tonne mobile crane. A small slipway at the head of the old harbour.
Yacht club The Club Náutico de Ca'n Picafort has a lounge and bar.

Showers Shower block near the travel-lift.
Laundry In the town.
Banks In the town.
Hospital/medical services Doctor in the town, otherwise in Alcudia.

Transport

Car hire/taxis In the town.
Buses Bus service to Alcudia, Palma and elsewhere.

Sites ashore locally

The name Picafort is from the Spanish words meaning 'hew strongly', presumably referring to the cutting of stone from nearby quarries. The Necropolis de Son Real (a Bronze Age cemetery dating back to 700BC) is only ten minutes' walk along the shore to the SE. There are excellent beaches on either side of the harbour which understandably become crowded in summer.

Local Events

The fiesta of Mare de Deu d'Agost is held on 15 August each year.

Eating out

An outdoor bar near the old harbour and many restaurants and cafés in the town.

M14 Puerto de Serra Nova

A tiny harbour with berths mostly for small boats. An exceptionally narrow entrance, with silting in the approach: hardly worth mentioning, except that plans for greater things have been submitted

Location
    39°44´.4N 03°13´.4E
Communications
    Puerto de Serra Nova ☎/*Fax* 971 85 40 30

The harbour

Puerto de Serra Nova is another tiny harbour which hardly rates 'port' status. It was built as the first stage of a large yacht harbour to complement the 'urbanisation' of Son Serra Nova, but plans are on hold for the project with little prospect of expansion in the near future. Currently the harbour and surroundings are bleak and facilities very limited.

Approach is straightforward but it would be dangerous with heavy seas from the northern quadrant. Entrance is limited to small vessels no more than 9m in length and drawing less than 2m. The entrance is formed by two huge concrete blocks, making it very narrow and intimidating, and recent visits indicate a depth of less than 2m (Nov 2005).

PILOTAGE

Approach

For outer approaches see *Puerto de Alcudia* and page 124.

From S Round the high (432m) Cabo Farrutx and follow the coast westwards at a distance of 500m once past Colonia de San Pedro. Puerto de Serra Nova lies 3 miles beyond, at the northern end of an area of scattered houses backed by pine forest.

From N After passing Cabo Menorca, head S across the Bahía de Alcudia to close the coast close NW of the harbour, which lies at the northern end of the area of scattered houses and pine forest. The surrounding countryside is generally flat.

Anchorage in the approach

Anchor in 5m over sand about 400m from the shore, N of the harbour entrance, open to NW–N–NE.

Entrance

Approach the head of the NW breakwater at slow speed on a southwesterly course. The entrance, which lies a short distance beyond, is narrow – 10m or less – and room to manoeuvre once inside is very restricted. In bad weather the entrance can be closed by a metal barrier.

Berthing

Secure in a vacant slot as available and await allocation of a berth. The harbour shoals towards its head.

Facilities

Water Taps around the harbour.
Electricity 220v AC points around the harbour.
Fuel No fuel available.
Provisions The nearest shops are in the village of Son Serra 1.25 miles inland.
Repairs A 3-tonne crane and slipway at the *club náutico*.
Yacht club The Club Náutico Serra Nova has a small clubhouse with bar near the W mole.

Transport

Car hire/taxis Taxi from Ca'n Picafort by telephone.
Buses Bus service along the main road a mile inland.

Eating out

Friendly bar at the *club náutico* and a café or two in the 'urbanisation'. No restaurants nearby.

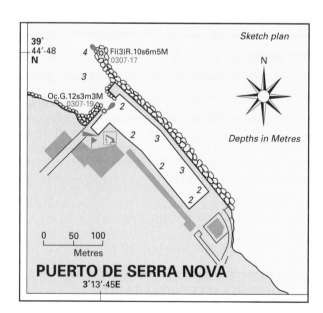

Puerto de Serra Nova: insignificant except that there are plans for expansion of this harbour into a major marina

4. Puerto de Colonia de San Pedro to Porto Cristo

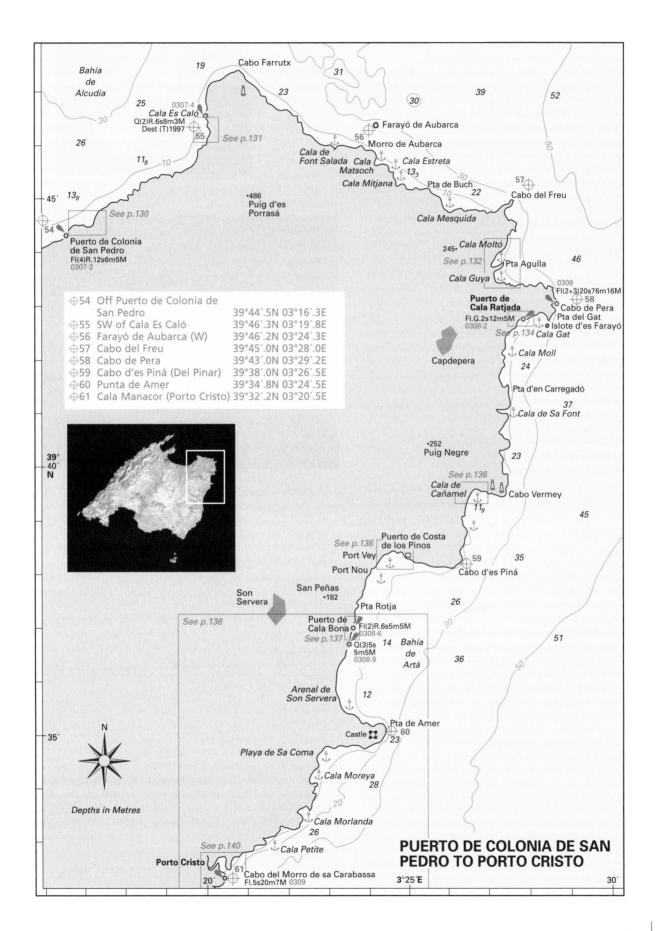

Bahía
de
Alcudia

19   Cabo Farrutx

31

23

39

52

25   0307·4
Cala Es Caló
Q(2)R.6s8m3M
Dest (T)1997

30

55   See p.131

56   ○ Farayó de Aubarca

26   Morro de Aubarca

11₉   10

Cala de
Font Salada   Cala   Cala Estreta
Matsoch   13₃
Cala Mitjana   Pta de Buch   22   57
Cabo del Freu

45´   13₈   •486
Puig d'es
Porrasá

30

10

Cala Mesquida

54   Puerto de Colonia
de San Pedro
Fl(4)R.12s6m5M
0307·2

245•   Cala Moltó
See p.132   46
Pta Agulla
Cala Guya

0308
Fl(2+3)20s76m16M
58
Cabo de Pera
Pta del Gat
Puerto de
Cala Ratjada   ○ Islote d'es Farayó
Fl.G.2s12m5M   See p.134   Cala Gat
0308·2

Capdepera   ⊥ Cala Moll

24

Pta d'en Carregadó

37
⊥Cala de Sa Font

•252
Puig Negre   23

See p.136
Cala de
Cañamel   Cabo Vermey
11₉

45

Puerto de Costa
See p.136   de los Pinos
Port Vey   35
Port Nou   59
Cabo d'es Piná

San Peñas   26
•182
Son
Servera   Pta Rotja
See p.138   Puerto de   51
Cala Bona   Fl(2)R.6s5m5M
0308·6
See p.137   14   Bahía
Q(3)5s   de
5m5M   Artá   36
0308·9

Arenal de   12
Son Servera

Pta de Amer
Castle   60
23

Playa de Sa Coma

⊥ Cala Moreya
28

⊥ Cala Morlanda
26

See p.140   ⊥ Cala Petite
Porto Cristo   61
20´   Cabo del Morro de sa Carabassa
Fl.5s20m7M 0309   3°25´E   30´

⊕54 Off Puerto de Colonia de
San Pedro   39°44´.5N 03°16´.3E
⊕55 SW of Cala Es Caló   39°46´.3N 03°19´.8E
⊕56 Farayó de Aubarca (W)   39°46´.2N 03°24´.3E
⊕57 Cabo del Freu   39°45´.0N 03°28´.0E
⊕58 Cabo de Pera   39°43´.0N 03°29´.2E
⊕59 Cabo d'es Piná (Del Pinar)   39°38´.0N 03°26´.5E
⊕60 Punta de Amer   39°34´.8N 03°24´.5E
⊕61 Cala Manacor (Porto Cristo)   39°32´.2N 03°20´.5E

39°
40´
N

35´

N

Depths in Metres

**PUERTO DE COLONIA DE SAN
PEDRO TO PORTO CRISTO**

III. MALLORCA

M15 Puerto de Colonia de San Pedro (Sant Pere)

A recently completed private marina in the E of
Alcudia Bay, located within a nature park, with
berths for over 300 yachts from 6 to 20m

Location
39°44´.3N 03°16´.2E

Communications
VHF: Ch 09
Club Náutico ☎ 971 58 91 47 *Fax* 971 58 91 18
Email info@clubnautic-coloniadesantpere.com
www.clubnautic-coloniadesantpere.com

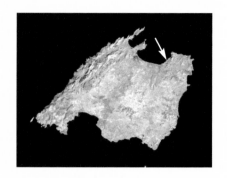

The harbour/marina

A new, privately funded marina, which has recently
been completed after many delays. There are berths
and services for 308 craft up to 20m. Although
privately owned by the local *club náutico* members,
visitors are welcome to use any empty berths. Set in
an area of natural beauty, and much of the
surrounding countryside is protected.

PILOTAGE

Approach

⊕54 39°44´.5N 03°16´.3E Approach to Puerto de Colonia de
San Pedro

From S Round the high (432m) Cabo Farrutx and
follow the coast westwards at a distance of 500m for
4M and the port will be clearly seen.

From N After passing Cabo Menorca, head S across
the Bahía de Alcudia to close the coast near to the
harbour. The immediate surrounding countryside is
flat with mountains as a backdrop.

Anchorage in the approach

Whilst it is possible to anchor W of the entrance in
6m, the nature of the bottom – rocky ledges with
many crevices – gives very poor holding or a foul
anchor so a tripline is essential. There are shallow
rocks extending out to 75m from the shore.

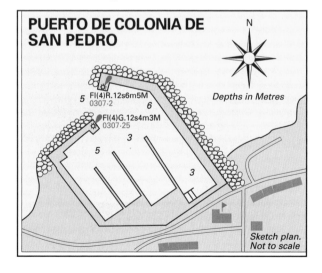

Puerto de Colonia de San Pedro viewed from NE

Anchoring was discouraged immediately E of the
harbour in 2005, though the small bay 0.5M further
NW looks inviting.

Entrance

Approach the head of the N breakwater on a S
course, rounding and entering when the NE part of
the breakwater is abeam and in transit.

Berthing

Secure in a vacant slot as available and await
allocation of a berth.

Facilities

Water Water tap near the slipway at the head of the harbour.
Electricity On each berth
Fuel Is not available.
Provisions A few shops in the village.
Yacht club The Club Náutico de Colonia de San Pedro
across the road from the harbour has a bar and
restaurant.
Repairs 35-tonne travel hoist. A slipway at the *club
náutico*.

Eating out

There are several restaurants and cafés including the
bar and restaurant at the *club náutico*.

ANCHORAGES BETWEEN PUERTO DE COLONIA AND PUERTO DE CALA RATJADA

⊕55 39°46′.3N 03°19′.8E Cala Es Caló (SW)

⚓ CALA ES CALÓ
39°46′.5N 03°20′E

An isolated anchorage 1.2 miles SW of Cabo Farrutx set against a dramatic rocky backdrop, Cala Es Caló offers a useful anchorage if waiting to round the cape. There is a short mole but no harbour. The single light was destroyed some years ago and has not functioned since. There are no facilities and only a track ashore.

Approach from W or NW to anchor in 5–6m over sand, weed and stones S or SE of the molehead, open to W and NW with some fetch from SW and S. Holding is poor in places. The short mole has underwater projections near its head and its E (inner) side is sometimes used by fishing vessels,

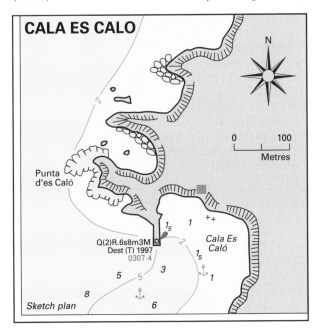

which must not be obstructed. Nets may also be laid in the vicinity.

There are good walks in the surrounding hills, and for the fit the climb to the top of Atalaya de Morey (432m), overlooking Cabo Farrutx, is rewarding. The Cueva (cave) des Vells Marins some 600m S of the anchorage, is also worth visiting.

⚓ CALA DE FONT SALADA
39°46′N 03°23′.2E

One of several similar *calas* in a large shallow bay. Anchor off a white sandy beach in 4–6m over sand, exposed to NW–N–NE. A track leads to a road some distance inland.

⊕56 39°46′.2N 03°24′.3E Farayó de Aubarca (W side)

FARAYÓ DE AUBARCA
39°46′.3N 03°24′.5E

A small nobbly islet 23m high and some 750m offshore, off the headland of Morro de Aubarca, which is topped by a watchtower. There is good water on either side: the inshore passage has depths of 20m or more and is free of dangers.

⚓ CALAS MATSOCH, ESTRETA AND MITJANA
Around 39°45′.5N 03°24′.8E

Three small open anchorages off narrow white sand and stone beaches, backed by sand dunes. Anchor in 3–5m over hard sand, open NW–N–E. All three can be reached by road and are frequented by tourists. Cala Mitjana has a beach café.

⚓ CALA MESQUIDA
39°44′.8N 03°26′.1E

An open anchorage off a long white sandy beach, with a growing tourist resort behind. Anchor in 3–5m over sand, open through N, NE and E and to swell from the NW. Water and basic provisions are available.

Cala Es Caló viewed from SW, nestling on S side of Cabo Farrutx

Cala Torta: between Cala Mitjana and Cala Mesquida, S of Pta de Buch   *GW*

⊕57 39°45′.0N 03°28′.0E Cabo del Freu

⚓ CALAS MOLTÓ AND GUYA (CALAS MOLTA AND DE S'AGULLA)

39°43′.6N 03°27′.3E

Two *calas* either side of a narrow rocky promontory terminating in Punta Agulla, Cala Moltó has a very small beach and no facilites whereas Cala Guya has a much longer sandy beach, which is popular with holidaymakers. There is a growing tourist development on its S shore.

Anchor in 3–5m over sand off either beach, taking particular care in Cala Moltó to avoid a pipeline running NE towards Menorca. Cala Moltó is open to the NE, Cala Guya to NE and E.

⚓ CALA GAT (CAT)

39°42′.7N 03°28′.3E

A *cala* tucked well into the NW side of Punta del Gat with Islote d'es Farayó to the E and Puerto de Cala Ratjada to the W. Cliffed and wooded slopes are overlooked by several houses, including the

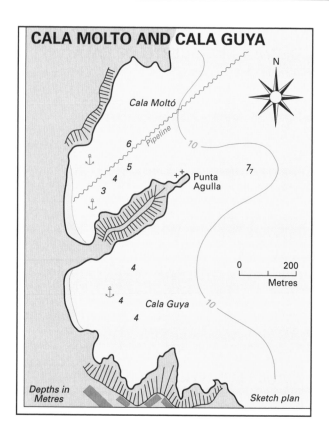

conspicuous Palacio Torre Ciega, on a hill 200m to the W. Anchor in 3–5m over sand, weed and rock, open through SW to SE. Although there is a channel carrying 4m between Punta del Gat and Islote d'es Farayó, it is not recommended without local knowledge. Foul ground extends some distance to the S of the island.

⊕58 39°43′.0N 03°29′.2E Cabo de Pera

View from SE over Cala Guya. Cala Moltó far side of Punto Agulla

M16 Puerto de Cala Ratjada

A small and very friendly harbour tucked under Cabo de Pera, offering berthing and facilities for 100 small yachts inside and larger vessels on the sheltered outer mole. The closest harbour to Menorca (23 miles away)

Location
39°42′.7N 03°27′.9E

Communications
Port Authority ☎ / *Fax* 971 56 50 67
Club Náutico de Cala Ratjada ☎ 971 56 40 19
Fax 971 81 90 08
Email clubnautico@calaratjada.e.telefonica

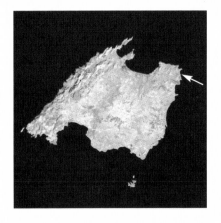

The harbour/marina

Once a little fishing harbour but now a thriving (and rather pleasant) tourist resort with a strong German influence. The vast majority of local boats are small and the *club náutico* pontoons can only take craft up to 12m or so. However, yachts up to 20m can lie alongside the breakwater outside the harbour proper, which is well sheltered in most conditions. Menorca is only 23 miles to the E, making Puerto de Cala Ratjada a popular destination or departure point for the inter-island passage.

Approach is straightforward but the entrance to the inner harbour is narrow and the harbour congested with fishing craft. Strong winds from between E and S create a heavy swell in both entrance and harbour, and the outside berths might become untenable.

PILOTAGE

Approach

From S The coast is very broken, with high rocky cliffs backed by even higher tree-covered hills. Cabo Vermey is high (252m sloping down to 185m) and has a rounded profile of reddish rocks with two towers on the top. Puerto de Cala Ratjada lies 4.4 miles N of this headland and about 0.8 miles W of Cabo de Pera (Fl(2+3)20s76m16M, white tower on white building with dark corners and red roof 21m).

From N Cross the wide Bahía de Alcudia towards Cabo Farrutx, a high sloping promontory (unlit, though there are red lights on Puig Tudosa 1.5M to the S). Follow the coast SE to Cabo del Freu (⊕57) – a low, narrow, pointed promontory, also unlit – passing en route Farayó de Aubarca islet (⊕56, 23m high and about 750m offshore). There is good water on either side of the island.

III. MALLORCA

Puerto de Cala Ratjada looking N

PUERTO DE CALA RATJADA

Cabo de Pera (⊕58) 2.1 miles SSE of Cabo del Freu is easily identified by its lighthouse. Follow its steep rocky cliffs SW to round Islote d'es Farayó off Punta del Gat, after which the harbour will be seen 0.7M to the W.

Anchorage in the approach

Anchor 500m SW of the end of the breakwater in 5m over sand, open to E through SE to S. Closer to the entrance the bottom is of rock, stone and weed and unsuitable for anchoring. There are a few sand patches opposite the breakwater head in 2–5m, but they may be occupied by moorings.

Entrance

Round the end of the breakwater at 30–40m to seek a berth on the inner side. There is a 3-knot speed limit. A rock carrying less than 3m has been reported 90–100m SSW of the breakwater head.

Sea levels

The level of the water increases by about 0.5m with onshore winds and decreases by the same amount with offshore winds.

Berthing

Visitors normally berth on the inner side of the breakwater, lying alongside rather than stern-to, due to the poor holding. In the summer, rafts may be four or five deep. Unfortunately for visiting yachtsmen a new fast catamaran service operates here, plying between Ciudadela and Ratjada. This uses the inshore section of the outer breakwater, (which has reduced the visitor space by half) and this has exacerbated the problems of finding a berth at both ports.

Yachts are no longer allowed to secure to the sides of the breakwater spur (fishermen's quay), even on the S side, which in any case has rocks along its base and some timber projections. Should it be necessary to lay an anchor be certain to use a tripping line – the bottom is very rough, consisting of broken rocks with many crevices and holes. Smaller yachts may occasionally be found a berth on the pontoons off the *club náutico*. Enquire at their office on the W side of the harbour.

If arriving between Friday evening and Sunday evening it may be possible to moor alongside a fishing boat on the eastern arm of the harbour – but note that most depart at 0600 on Monday morning.

Facilities

Water Points on all quays and pontoons.
Electricity 220v AC points on the pontoons and at visitors' berths on the inner side of the breakwater.

Fuel Diesel from pumps at the head of the breakwater spur (fishermen's quay), not open on Sundays and public holidays. Petrol from a garage ¾ mile NW of the harbour.

Provisions Several supermarkets and specialist food shops in the town, with more in Capdepera about 1½ miles away. Markets are Saturdays in Puerto de Cala Ratjada and Wednesdays in Capdepera.

Ice There is an ice factory at the back of the town just S of the *plaza*.

Chandlery Small chandlery/hardware store on the E side of the harbour.

Repairs No boatyard as such, though basic repairs can be carried out. Two cranes 10 and 7.5-tonnes are by the *club náutico* on the W side of the harbour. The slipway for fishing craft in the NE corner of the harbour may be available for yachts. There are two cradles, maximum draught 2m. Other slipways around the harbour.

Engineers Ask advice from local fishermen.

Yacht club The Club Náutico de Cala Ratjada is small, but has showers and a bar.

Showers At the *club náutico*.

Laundry In the town.

Banks In the town, with credit card facilities.

Hospital/medical services In the town.

Transport

Car hire/taxis In the town.

Buses Bus service to Capdepera and onward to Palma, etc.

Ferries Tourist ferries make daily trips to a number of popular beaches in the area.

Sights ashore locally

Little of the original town has survived the tourist building boom, but both Artá 5 miles inland and Capdepera 1½ miles away have retained many of their old buildings, the latter including an interesting castle with particularly good views.

The Cuevas (caves) de Artá at Cabo Vermey are well worth visiting and the garden museum of Sa Torre Cega has an interesting collection of sculptures.

Restored windmills abound in the area – most have been converted from water pumps for the agricultural area to electricity generators, though many do both. They are no longer in active use, because of supplies from the grid and mains water systems.

Local specialities

An enclave of Moors remained in this area much longer than elsewhere and the local people show more traces of Moorish descent than do those in other parts of the island. They also practise the old Moorish art of palmetto (palm work).

Local events

A fiesta is held at Puerto de Cala Ratjada in mid-August in honour of San Roc, patron saint of the town, and events include sailing races. On 24 August Capdepera honours its patron saint, San Bartolomé, this time with horse races among the revelry.

Eating out

Many eating houses of all descriptions, with the harbour surrounded by pleasant cafés and restaurants.

Restored windmills: once used for pumping water and generating electicity, rather than as mills

ANCHORAGES BETWEEN PUERTO DE CALA RATAJA AND PUERTO DE COSTA DE LOS PINOS

⚓ CALA MOLL
39°42´.3N 03°27´.5E

A wide bay off a popular sandy beach ¾ mile SW of Puerto de Cala Ratjada, Cala Moll has low rocky sides and is largely surrounded by buildings. Anchor about 150m off the beach in 2.5m over sand, open to the E quadrant. The small Islote Forana lies to the SE and should be left on the landward side.

⚓ CALA DE SA FONT (CALA DE SAN GERONI)
39°40´.9N 03°27´.3E

A sizeable, attractive *cala* with a fine sandy beach and some apartment buildings nearby. Anchor off the beach in 5m over sand and stone, open to the E quadrant. Some facilities ashore, otherwise Capdepera is less than 2 miles by road.

Cala de Sa Font viewed from E

III. MALLORCA

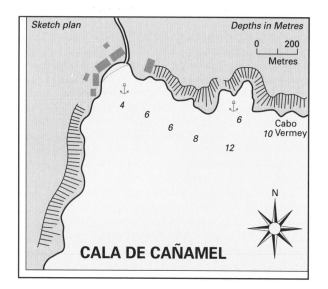

Cala de Cañamel looking W, with Cabo Vermey dominating right of picture

⚓ CALA DE CAÑAMEL

39°39′.4N 03°26′.6E

Rather an open anchorage in a bay just S and W of Cabo Vermey (reddish, with little vegetation) and the famous Cuevas (caves) de Artá. The sandy beach at the head of the *cala* is backed by hotels and apartments, but a good deal of greenery has been retained. A river flows through the beach on its northern side. Anchor in 3–5m of very clear water over sand, open to E, SE and S. The bottom shelves gradually and in heavy weather waves break some distance offshore. There are some shops in the tourist complex, including a small supermarket.

A second anchorage, with less swell but having room for only two boats, will be found in a very small *cala* halfway to Cabo Vermey. A spherical yellow buoy (Fl(5)Y.20s) is positioned 1.4 miles E of the cape itself.

⊕59 39°38′.0N 03°26′.5E Cabo d'es Piná (Del Pinar)

PUERTO DE COSTA DE LOS PINOS

A jetty rather than a port, but with a pleasant anchorage with easy access ashore nearby

Location
39°38′.2N 03°24′.8E

The jetty and anchorage

A very small, shallow facility that is not much more than a broad quay with a short protective extension. Built as an amenity for guests of the four-star Hotel Golf Punta Rotja, the 'Puerto' offers little shelter and can take only the smallest craft. The bay is often used for water-skiing, etc. but it nevertheless makes a pleasant anchorage.

PILOTAGE

Approach

The jetty and anchorage lie close W of Cabo d'es Piná (Cabo d'es Ratx), itself some 5.4 miles S of Cabo de Pera and 3.6 miles N of Punta de Amer. The square, white hotel overlooking the harbour will be seen for many miles.

Anchorage in the approach

Anchor in 2–4m over sand and weed W of the molehead, open to S and W. The bottom is uneven

with some rocks and a careful watch on the depth sounder will be necessary.

Entrance

Approach the NW corner of the quay, sounding continuously.

Berthing

Secure as space permits. There are a few projecting underwater rocks. Officials may appear, otherwise visit the hotel reception desk.

Facilities

Water Tap on the quay.
Provisions Supermarket behind the hotel.
Repairs Two small dinghy slipways.

Eating out

A choice of restaurants and cafés.

ANCHORAGES OFF PUERTO DE COSTA DE LOS PINOS

The long stretch of sandy beaches and small *calas* between Puerto de Costa de los Pinos and Puerto de Cala Bona make good anchorages in settled weather. Port Vey (Vell) and Port Nou are marked on the plan at the beginning of this section on page 129. Far from being ports, these are pleasant anchorages off the open beach. Anchor in 3–4m over sand and weed. A few houses, hotels, shops and cafés line the road behind the beach.

M17 Puerto de Cala Bona

A small (and usually full) port, with little room for visitors

Location
39°36´.9N 03°23´.7E

Communications
 Puerto de Cala Bona ☎/*Fax* 971 58 62 56

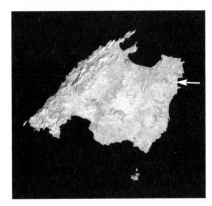

The harbour

Originally a small fishing harbour with an even tinier inner harbour, Puerto de Cala Bona has been improved by the construction of two outer breakwaters. Even so it is not large, with a total of 187 berths and limited facilities. The approach is straightforward but should not be attempted in strong onshore winds. The harbour is home to a number of glass-bottomed and other tourist excursion boats.

Puerto de Cala Bona: still a small harbour, despite the extensions

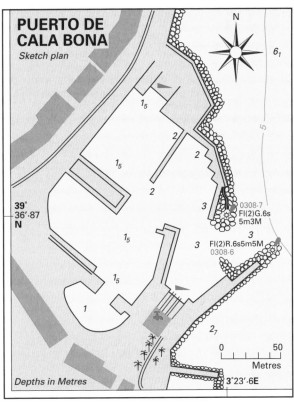

PILOTAGE

Approach

From S Punta de Amer is a low, rocky-cliffed promontory with a small castle on its summit. The wide Bahía de Artá stretches northwards from it as far as Cabo d'es Piná and the harbour is located near its centre, at the northern end of the heavily built up area.

From N The high, rounded profile of Cabo Vermey, which has reddish rocks, is recognisable as is the dark-cliffed Cabo d'es Piná. S of Cabo d'es Piná lies the wide Bahía de Artá, with Puerto de Cala Bona near its centre, at the northern end of the heavily built up area.

Anchorage in the approach

There are sand patches off the harbour entrance in 5m+, but it would be distinctly exposed.

Entrance

There are a number of rocky breakwaters close S of the harbour, established to retain sand on the beaches, so ensure that the harbour entrance is identified beyond all doubt. Enter at slow speed on a southwesterly course. Once inside there is little room to manoeuvre and parts are shallow.

Berthing

Secure bow or stern-to on the inside of the S breakwater. This position is exposed to wind or swell from E or NE but well protected from the SE quadrant.

Facilities

Water In containers from the fishermen's co-operative near the old inner harbour, or from one of the bars or restaurants.
Electricity A few 220v AC points around the harbour.
Fuel No fuel pumps. There is a service station outside the town.
Provisions Shops and supermarkets to the S of the harbour, more in Son Servera, 2 miles inland. Friday market in Son Servera.
Ice From the fishermen's co-operative or from one of the bars or restaurants.
Repairs Three slipways around the harbour, but little more than dinghy size.
Banks To the S of the harbour and in Son Servera.
Hospital/medical services In Son Servera.

Transport

Car hire/taxis In the town.
Buses Bus service to Son Servera and beyond.

Eating out

Many eating places around the harbour.

ANCHORAGES FROM PUERTO DE CALA BONA TO PORTO CRISTO

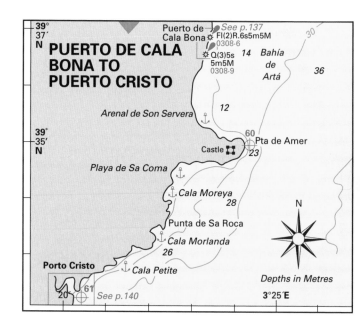

⊕60 Punta de Amer   39°34'.8N 03°24'.5E
⊕61 Cala Manacor (Porto Cristo) 39°32'.2N 03°20'.5E

CALA MILLOR
39°36'.3N 03°23'.4E

The large holiday development of Cala Millor lies half a mile S of Cala Bona. A small lit pier (Q(3)5s5m5M black column, yellow band with ✦ topmark) is present. It is not recommended to moor there but is included here in case the light confuses passing yachtsmen.

⚓ ARENAL DE SON SERVERA
39°35'.6N 03°23'.3E

A long sand and stone beach immediately N of Punta de Amer. Anchor in 5m over sand and rock near the southern end of the Cala Millor holiday development. There are numerous restaurants and cafés ashore plus a few shops.

⊕60 39°34'.8N 03°24'.5E Punta de Amer

⚓ PLAYA DE SA COMA
39°34'.5N 03°22'.8E

A wide and often crowded sandy beach close S of Punta de Amer. Anchor in 2–4m over sand, with some rock and weed further out, open to SW–S–E.

⚓ CALA MOREYA
39°34'.1N 03°22'.6E

A sandy bay close S of Playa de Sa Coma but surrounded by the much denser development of the S'Illot holiday town. Anchor in 2–4m over sand. Open to the E sector.

Cala Morlanda viewed from NE across Punta de Sa Roca

⚓ CALA MORLANDA

39°33′.4N 03°22′.3E

A double *cala* at the S end of the S'Illot holiday development but still largely unspoilt, with rocky sides and two small stony beaches. Anchor in 4–5m over sand. Open to the E.

⚓ CALA PETITE

39°32′.9N 03°21′.4E

A narrow, dog-legged *cala* with space for no more than two boats, enclosed by rocky cliffs and with nothing ashore beyond a rough track. Anchor in 3–6m over sand and rock in the centre of the *cala*, using two anchors to restrict swinging room, open to the E and SE.

There are a number of isolated rocks awash just off the small beach.

Cala Petite, bottom RH, looking SW to Porto Cristo

M18 Porto Cristo (Port de Manacor)

A very sheltered harbour with a total of 500 berths up to 16m, tucked well into the Cap de Estoy river

Location
39°32′.1N 03°20′.4E

Communications
Puerto de Porto Cristo VHF Ch 16
☎ 971 82 04 19
Club Náutico de Porto Cristo VHF Ch 09
☎ 971 82 12 53 *Fax* 971 82 06 50
Email lequio18@yahoo.es
www.cnpc@maptel.es

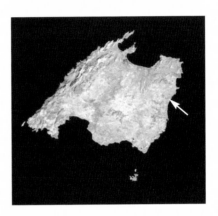

The harbour

A long and well-sheltered inlet with several doglegs, which has managed to retain a good deal of its charm despite the growth of the town. Approach and entrance present no problems other than in strong onshore winds. There are a total of 497 berths, with facilities on both banks of the river: at *club náutico* on the SE side, and the public quays on the NW side. Even so, the harbour is often full in summer and berths cannot be reserved in advance.

PILOTAGE

Approach

⊕61 39°32′.2N 03°20′.5E Cala Manacor (Porto Cristo approach)

From S The coast from Porto Colom is of low rocky cliffs which are broken by many calas, all very similar and difficult to identify. However, at Porto Cristo the conspicuous lighthouse tower on Cabo del Morro, with black and white vertical stripes is easily seen.

From N Cross the wide Bahía de Artá which terminates on its S side at Punta de Amer, which is relatively low but prominent. Porto Cristo lies 4 miles to the SW and can be identified as above.

III. MALLORCA

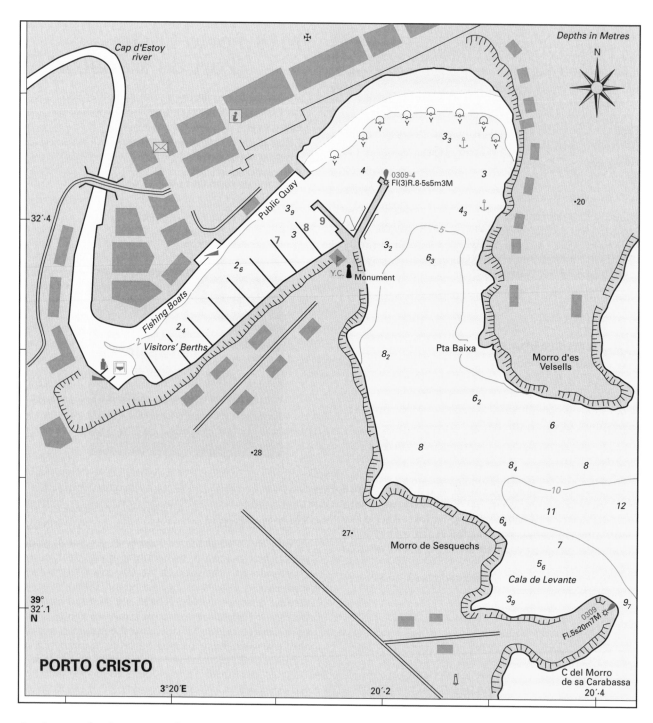

Anchorage in the approach

It is possible to anchor under the cliffs on the E side of the channel opposite the monument, or further N outside a line of yellow buoys marking the bathing area, in 3–5m over sand, mud and weed. Both spots can be roly, due either to swell or to wash from passing speedboats, and may be affected by a circular current in low pressure weather. Anchoring in the harbour itself is not permitted.

Entrance

The entrance channel is both wide and deep. Keep to the centre or slightly to starboard before rounding the NE mole into the yacht harbour (this mole is not completely solid but includes a bridge near the shore). Strong currents can occur when the river Cap d'Estoy is in spate and in heavy weather a strong surge may build up. In pleasant conditions it is not unusual to find swimmers and snorkellers virtually under the bow! A series of yellow buoys with a connecting line lies some way off the bathing beach. There is a 3-knot speed limit.

Berthing

The *club náutico* reserves the three easternmost pontoons (7, 8, 9) for visiting yachts. Moorings and lazy lines are provided and a berthing master is usually on duty. However the harbour is often full in summer, so it is advisable to call on VHF Ch 09 to check whether a berth will be available, even though

Porto Cristo: a very safe and sheltered harbour

they cannot be reserved before arrival. The visitors' pontoons have 3m or more at the outer ends, shoaling towards the quay.

If there is no space available at the *club náutico* it may be possible to lie stern-to on the Port Authority public quay opposite, SW of the beach. There are the usual lazy lines running out from the quay.

Facilities

Water Water points on the quay, pontoons and at the *club náutico*.

Electricity 220v AC points on quays and pontoons.

Fuel Diesel and petrol from pumps next to the travel-lift.

Provisions Shops of all types in the town including several small supermarkets, but a long walk round from the yacht pontoons (alternatively use the dinghy). Produce/fish markets Sunday in Porto Cristo and Monday in Manacor 6 miles inland.

Ice Delivered to the quay daily, also from the *club náutico* bar.

Chandlery Two well-stocked chandleries either side of the channel N of the boatyard.

Repairs A 50-tonne travel-lift and 12.5-tonne crane in the boatyard. Small slipways on both sides of the harbour. Jaume Vermell Náutica boatyard ☎ 971 82 20 22 *Fax* 82 20 21 at the SW end of the harbour has most facilities including a very protected winter lay-up area.

Engineers At the boatyard. Marina Marbella Balear SA ☎ 971 82 05 90 is official service agent for Mercury/MerCruiser and Volvo Penta.

Yacht club The Club Náutico de Porto Cristo has a smart clubhouse with bar, restaurant, swimming pool, terrace, showers, etc.

Showers At the *club náutico*.

Launderettes In the town.

Banks Several in the town, mostly with credit card facilities.

Hospital/medical services Medical services in Porto Cristo, hospital in Manacor 6 miles inland.

Transport

Car hire/taxis In the town.

Buses Regular service to Manacor, Palma, etc.

Sights ashore locally

The area is famous for the caves discovered by M E A Martel in 1896, and for an unsuccessful landing by Communist forces during the civil war. There are two monuments to this landing, one near the root of the NE mole and another at the NW end of the town. It was also favoured by the kings of Mallorca for their summer holidays.

The spectacular Cuevas del Drach (Caves of the Dragon) and Cuevas del Hams S of the town should not be missed (open 1000 to 1700). There is also a wildlife park nearby. Spectacular views of the coast can be seen from the tower SW of the lighthouse.

Local event

The Fiesta de la Virgen del Carmen, with waterborne processions, is held on 16 July.

Eating out

A large number of restaurants, cafés and bars.

5. Cala Murta to Cala Marmols

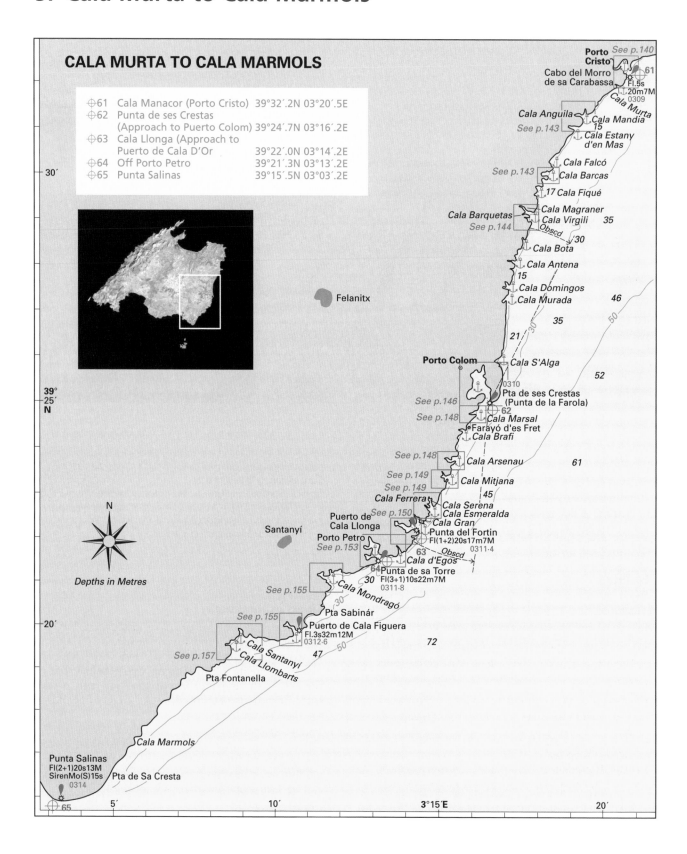

CALA MURTA TO CALA MARMOLS

⊕61 Cala Manacor (Porto Cristo) 39°32′.2N 03°20′.5E
⊕62 Punta de ses Crestas
       (Approach to Puerto Colom) 39°24′.7N 03°16′.2E
⊕63 Cala Llonga (Approach to
       Puerto de Cala D'Or   39°22′.0N 03°14′.2E
⊕64 Off Porto Petro   39°21′.3N 03°13′.2E
⊕65 Punta Salinas   39°15′.5N 03°03′.2E

See p.140
See p.143
See p.143
See p.144
See p.146
See p.148
See p.148
See p.149
See p.149
See p.150
See p.153
See p.155
See p.155
See p.157

Porto
Cristo
Cabo del Morro
de sa Carabassa
Fl.5s
20m7M
0309
Cala Murta
Cala Anguila
Cala Mandia
15
Cala Estany
d'en Mas
Cala Falcó
Cala Barcas
17 Cala Fiqué
Cala Magraner
Cala Barquetas
Cala Virgili
35
Obscd
'30
Cala Bota
Cala Antena
15
Cala Domingos
Cala Murada
46
35
50
21
Porto Colom
Cala S'Alga
0310
52
Pta de ses Crestas
(Punta de la Farola)
62
Cala Marsal
Farayó d'es Fret
Cala Brafi
Cala Arsenau
61
Cala Mitjana
45
Cala Ferrera
Cala Serena
Cala Esmeralda
Puerto de
Cala Llonga
Cala Gran
Punta del Fortin
Fl(1+2)20s17m7M
0311·4
Porto Petro
63
Cala d'Egos
Obscd
Punta de sa Torre
64
30
Fl(3+1)10s22m7M
0311·8
Cala Mondragó
30
Pta Sabinár
Puerto de Cala Figuera
Fl.3s32m12M
0312·6
72
Cala Santanyí
47
50
Cala Llombarts
Pta Fontanella
Cala Marmols
Punta Salinas
Fl(2+1)20s13M
SirenMo(S)15s
0314
Pta de Sa Cresta
65

Felanitx

Santanyí

N

Depths in Metres

30′
39°
25′
N
20′
5′
10′
3°15′E
20′

⚓ CALA MURTA
39°31′.9N 03°20′.1E

A narrow *cala* between steep rocky sides, with some new buildings to the N. Anchor in 3–5m over sand, open to the E and SE.

⚓ CALAS ANGUILA AND MANDIA
39°31′.3N 03°19′.1E

A small double *cala* with sandy beaches. A holiday development, Porto Cristo Nova, lies on the N side and there are others to the S. Anchor off either beach in 3–5m over sand, open to the E. Several nearby restaurants and cafés.

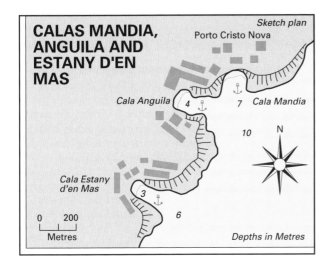

⚓ CALA ESTANY D'EN MAS
39°31′N 03°18′.9E

A small *cala* with rocky sides, the northern one almost completely covered with low-rise buildings. Anchor in 2–4m over sand off the crowded beach, open to the E and SE. Beach bars and *chiringhito* (summer beach restaurant).

Calas Mandia (right), Anguila (centre), and Cala Estany d'en Mas (left)

Cala Barcas: there are several nearby *calas* with good anchoring

⚓ CALA FALCÓ
39°30′.2N 03°18′.2E

A very open, totally deserted *cala*, with a track to the Cuevas del Pirata about a mile inland. Anchor in 2–5m over sand off the small stony beach, open to the eastern quadrant.

⚓ CALA BARCAS
39°29′.9N 03°17′.9E

A wide, square, undeveloped *cala*, the two sandy beaches at its head separated by a stretch of dark rocks. There is a shallow rocky outcrop projecting from the cliffs to the N, which have many sea caves. Keep to the centre of the entrance to anchor off either beach in 3–5m over sand, open to the NE and E. There is only a very rough track ashore, but the *cala* is popular with tourist boats and can become crowded in summer.

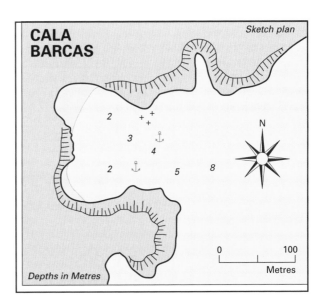

III. MALLORCA

⚓ CALA FIQUÉ (CALA SERRAT)

39°29'.6N 03°17'.7E

More accurately three very small, deserted *calas* with rocky headlands between. Anchor in 3–5m over sand, open to the eastern quadrant.

⚓ CALAS MAGRANER, BARQUETAS AND VIRGILI

39°29'.0N 03°17'.4E

Twin *calas* with sandy beaches, offering good protection near their heads. Anchor in 2–4m over sand; also just S of the projecting headland in Cala Virgili, in 3.5m. Other than a small grey hut on the northern headland there are no buildings, and the development shown behind the *calas* on several local maps does not appear to have taken place. Tracks ashore lead inland but few tourists seem to venture here.

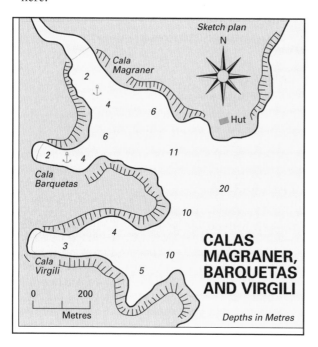

Calas Magraner (right), Barquetas and Virgili, (left) viewed from SE

tourist development. Anchor in 3–5m over sand, open through NE–E–SE. There are several large hotels close N, and the southern arm is backed by a restaurant with a distinctive conical roof.

⚓ CALA MURADA

39°27'.3N 03°16'.8E

A curved *cala* with a sandy beach at its southern end and dense housing on the point: once again, the beach is often crowded. Anchor off the beach in 3–5m over sand and weed, open to the NE and E. Protection is best close to the beach, where there is a bar/restaurant.

⚓ CALA S'ALGA

39°25'.8N 03°16'.6E

A large open *cala* with rocky sides and a very small stony beach, one mile N of the entrance to Porto Colom. Anchor in 3–5m over sand and weed, open to NE and E. There is a road across the headland to Porto Colom where supplies are available.

⚓ CALA BOTA

39°28'.4N 03°17'.3E

A small undeveloped *cala*, its mouth partially obstructed by a breaking rocky shoal running out from the southern cliffs, Cala Bota should be approached with extreme care. Enter from the NE with a lookout on the bow, to anchor in 4–5m over sand and weed, open to the E and SE.

⚓ CALA ANTENA

39°28'N 03°17'E

A small *cala* between high rocky sides, with some sizeable sea caves and a high-rise tourist complex to the S. Anchor off the beach in 3–5m over sand, open to the eastern quadrant.

⚓ CALA DOMINGOS

39°27'.5N 03°16'.8E

A double *cala* with two fine (and frequently crowded) sandy beaches, inevitably surrounded by

The conspicuous banded lighthouse on Punta de ses Crestas guards the eastern side of the entrance to Porto Colom

M19 Porto Colom

A large natural and well protected harbour with berthing for 250 yachts and many mooring buoys. One of the most pleasant places to visit in Mallorca

Location
39°25′N 03°16′.2E (entrance)
39°25′.4N 03°15′.8E (public pontoons)

Communications
VHF Ch 09
Club Náutico de Porto Colom ☎ 971 82 46 58
Fax 971 82 53 99
Email tomeu.tejedor@zagal.es

The harbour and anchorage

A large natural harbour with moorings for over 200 vessels in the Club Náutico de Porto Colom, operating in the NW corner of the harbour. With many more mooring buoys laid S of the port, anchoring is now technically prohibited, though many yachts do still anchor away from the port as described below. The port is well protected with a deep and narrow entrance, though much of the interior is relatively shallow: under 2.5m.

Although there is a low-rise housing development, particularly to the S of the harbour, the area is surprisingly undeveloped.

The *club náutico* staff are not particularly friendly or helpful but since there are usually no berths available for visitors this is not important. By contrast, the Port Authority staff are very helpful and have their office close to the fuelling berth.

Approaches to Colom: note buoys laid SW of port where anchoring is prohibited

III. MALLORCA

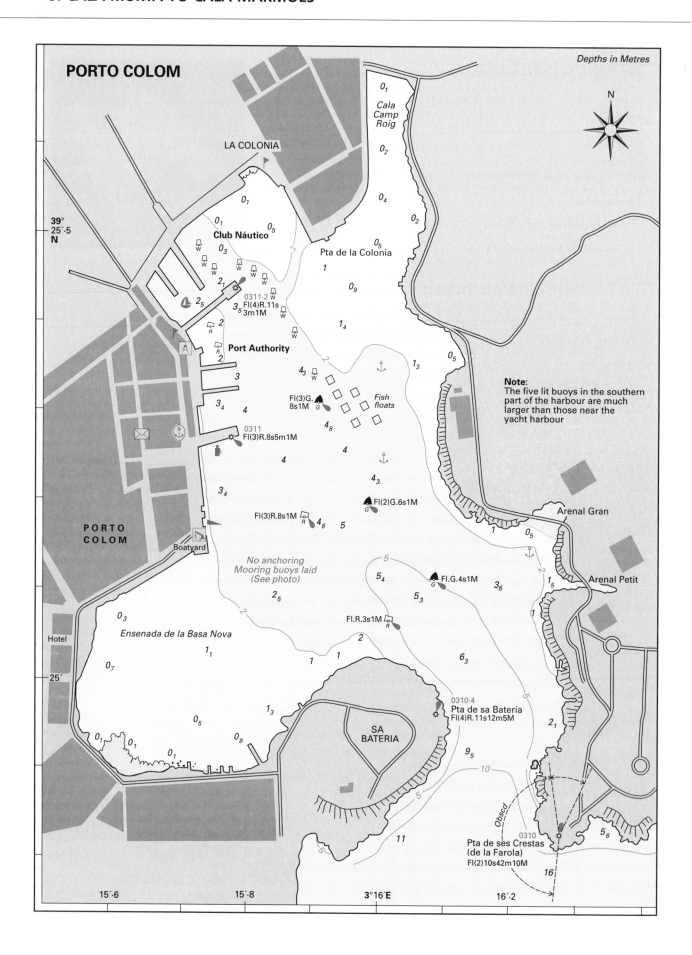

PORTO COLOM

Depths in Metres

LA COLONIA

Cala Camp Roig

0_1
0_2
0_4
0_2
0_5
Pta de la Colonia

39°
25′·5
N

0_1
0_1
0_5
Club Náutico
0_3
w w w
w w
2_1
2_5
0311·2
Fl(4)R.11s
3m1M
3_5
0_9
1_4
1
w w w
w

2
R
2
R
2
Port Authority
w

3
3_4
4
4_3
Fl(3)G.
8s1M
G
Fish floats
4_8
1_3
0_5

Note:
The five lit buoys in the southern part of the harbour are much larger than those near the yacht harbour

0311
Fl(3)R.8s5m1M

4
4
4_3
Fl(2)G.6s1M
G

Arenal Gran

3_4
Fl(3)R.8s1M
R
4_6
5

PORTO COLOM

Boatyard

No anchoring
Mooring buoys laid
(See photo)

2_5
Fl.G.4s1M
G
5_4
5_3
3_6
1_5
Arenal Petit
1
0_5

Fl.R.3s1M
R

0_3
Ensenada de la Basa Nova
1_1
1
2
6_3

Hotel

0_7
1_3

25′

0_5

0_1
0_1
0_1
0_8

SA BATERIA

0310·4
Pta de sa Batería
Fl(4)R.11s12m5M

9_5

10

2_1
5_6

11

Obscd

0310
Pta de ses Crestas
(de la Farola)
Fl(2)10s42m10M

16

5

15′·6
15′·8
3°16′E
16′·2

Porto Colom looking NW. Mooring buoys, Club Náutico top and two Port Authority pontoons centre. The wide fuelling jetty left

PILOTAGE

Approach

⊕62 39°24′.7N 03°16′.2E Pta de ses Crestas (Approach to Porto Colom)

From S The coast from Porto Petro and beyond is of low rocky cliffs broken by many calas. The distinctive lighthouse on Punta de ses Crestas (Fl(2)10s42m10M, ⊕62) white round tower with three black bands on white building with red roof 25m) on the E side of the entrance can be seen from many miles off, though if sailing close inshore the light itself will be obscured when bearing more than 006°. There is a small islet, Farayó d'es Fret (11m), 0.8 miles SW of the entrance.

From N The coast from Porto Cristo also consists of low rocky cliffs broken by many calas. When very close inshore the lighthouse on Punta de ses Crestas (see above) is obscured when bearing less than 207° but is otherwise clearly seen from many miles. The entrance itself does not open until around this headland.

Entrance and buoyed channel

The entrance is deep and unobstructed, other than a small rocky islet against the eastern shore. As the harbour widens out, follow the (unlit) buoyed channel to remain in depths of 4–5m. Unlit fish cages may be anchored to the E of the channel.

Much of the harbour is shallow and all manoeuvring outside the buoyed channel should be done with one eye on the depth-sounder, particularly since some of the banks appear to be unusually steep-sided.

Berthing

Secure bow or stern-to the S side of the yacht harbour S mole, or to one of the two Port Authority pontoons close S. The former has no more than 2.2m at its outer end and all three shoal towards the shore. Lazy lines are tailed to both mole and pontoons. None of these berths are viable in strong SE winds. Another option is on the fuel jetty, which is close to the harbour office.

The area S of the fuel jetty is now completely full of Port Authority moorings and although yachts do still anchor E of the channel, the harbourmaster discourages this when there are vacant moorings. The charge for the mooring buoys includes showers and water from the jetty tap (although reported to be very brackish in summer).

Anchorages

These are becoming scarce in the harbour as buoys are being laid in order to facilitate higher charges. One possibility is close to Arenal Gran and Arenal Petit, though S and SE swell affects the area. Another place is NE of the fish farm floats.

Facilities

Water Taps on yacht harbour mole and pontoons, Port Authority pontoons and near the Port Authority office. Also a tap by the fuel berth, for which a charge is made. Yachtsmen are advised not to drink the water, which in any case tastes very bad. This is probably a seasonal problem, as in many other ports.

Electricity 220v AC points on yacht harbour mole and pontoons, and on the public pontoons.

Fuel Diesel from pumps on the S side of the W mole (claimed to have 4m alongside). Petrol from a garage near the root of the mole.

Provisions Two supermarkets near the Ensenada de la Basa Nova, S of the yacht pontoons. Many other shops in the town.

Ice From the *club náutico* and from the above filling station.

Chandlery Near the *club náutico*.

Repairs A boatyard on the corner N of the Ensenada de la Basa Nova capable of straightforward work in wood or GRP. Also engine repairs. 10-tonne and 5-tonne mobile cranes at the boatyard. A 1.5m slipway at the boatyard and several others around the harbour.

Yacht clubs The Club Náutico de Porto Colom at the NW corner of the harbour has a bar, lounge, terrace and showers. The Club Náutico de Pescadores is NE of the harbour.

Showers By the Port Authority office just N of the W mole, and at the *club náutico*.

Post *office* A mobile post office visits a site near the Port Authority office (see plan) between 1150 and 1220, weekdays only. Times appear to change periodically.

Hospital/medical services Medical services in the town, hospital in Manacor 11 miles away.

Transport

Car hire/taxis In the town.

Buses Bus service to Felanitx, Manacor and beyond.

Sights ashore locally

The Monastery of San Salvador 4 miles inland is interesting and has a fine view, as has the ruined Castillo de San Tueri 3 miles inland.

Local event

A fiesta in honour of the Virgen del Carmen is held on 16 July, when the local fishing boats parade around the harbour dressed overall.

Eating out

The usual range of restaurants, cafés and bars.

III. MALLORCA

ANCHORAGES FRO PORTO COLOM TO PUERTO DE CALA LLONGA

⚓ CALA MARSAL AND CALÓ D'EN MANUELL

39°24'.6N 03°15'.8E

A double *cala* with rocky cliffs close S of Porto Colom. Cala Marsal has a sandy beach at its head. Anchor in 3–5m over sand off the beach, open to NE and E, or tuck into Caló d'en Manuell which has a sand and rock bottom, open to the SE. Both *calas* are surrounded by apartment blocks and hotels.

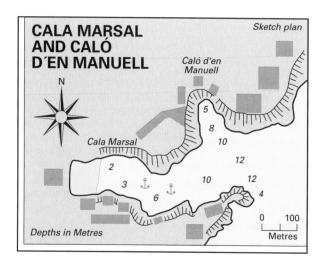

Cala Arsenau viewed from SE

⚓ CALA BRAFI

39°24'.2N 03°15'.5E

A small, narrow, dog-legged *cala* between rocky cliffs, with a stone boathouse at its head but no other buildings nearby. Anchor in 3–4m over sand, stone and weed. The small islet of Farayó d'es Fret lies close NE of the *cala*. It consists of a flat shelf of rock just above sea-level, with a narrow, vertical-sided 11m high rock on the top. In time erosion will probably displace this and convert it into a dangerous breaking ledge.

⚓ CALA ARSENAU (CALA SA NAU OR CALA DE RAS)

39°23'.6N 03°15'.2E

A narrow, angled *cala* offering relatively good protection, particularly near its head where there is a sandy beach, boathouse and café. There are breaking rocks close to the headland N of the *cala*. Anchor in 3–6m over sand and weed, open to the E and (depending on position) NE. One option is to take a sternline ashore to the northern bank behind the central promontory. In settled conditions Cala Arsenau makes a feasible overnight anchorage.

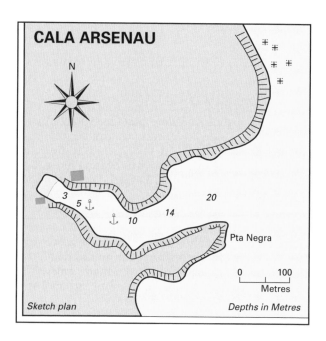

Cala Mitjana looking N with Cala Arsenau beyond. One of the most attractive anchorages in the Islands

⚓ CALA MITJANA

39°23'.2N 03°15'E

A very attractive triple *cala* with two sandy beaches and room for at least ten yachts. A tall white flagstaff (often with flags) stands on the N side of the

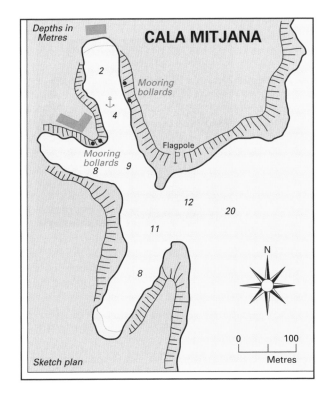

⚓ **CALAS SERENA, FERRERA AND ESMERALDA**
39°22´.6N 03°14´.5E

A treble *cala* with sandy beaches surrounded by hotels and apartments, with a prominent island off the northern headland and breaking rocks to the S. There is an isolated shoal patch carrying 3.5–4m in the centre of the entrance.

Anchor in 3–6m over sand and weed, open (depending on position) to SE and either E or S. Supermarkets and other shops nearby plus innumerable restaurants and cafés.

entrance and a pink-roofed building occupies the central headland. Swing wide of the rocky promontory below the flagstaff – a blind turn.

Anchor in 5m or less over sand and weed in the northern arm, setting a second anchor to limit swinging room, or take a line to the bollards set into the cliffs (see plan). This spot offers all-round protection.

Looking NW into Cala Esmeralda (left) with Cala Ferrera (centre) and Cala Serena (right)

M20 Puerto de Cala Llonga (Marina de Cala d'Or)

A well protected harbour, easy to enter in most conditions and with berthing for over 500 vessels in very pleasant surroundings

Location
39°22′.2N 03°14′.2E

Communications
Marina (Puerto Deportivo Marina) VHF Ch 09
Marina Cala d'Or ☎ 971 65 70 70
Fax 971 65 70 68
Club Náutico de Cala d'Or ☎ 971 64 82 03
Fax 64 81 30
Email marinacalador@ctv.es

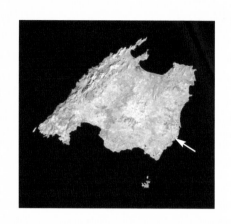

The marina

A single entrance from the sea leads to three calas, Cala Gran, Cala d'Or and Cala Llonga. Confusingly, the Marina Cala d'Or is located in the southernmost, Cala Llonga, rather than in Cala d'Or itself. Developers have not spoiled the very special nature of this place: it retains much of its original charm, and is still counted amongst the most beautiful *calas* on the coast of Mallorca.

The 565-berth Marina Cala d'Or is well protected, with good facilities and helpful staff but, as in most of Mallorca, is not cheap. It is often full in summer and a call on VHF Ch 09 prior to arrival would be wise. Approach and entrance are straightforward and good shelter is obtained, though in an E or SE wind a heavy swell enters all three calas.

⊕63 Cala Llonga (Approach to Puerto de Cala D'Or 39°22′.0N 03°14′.2E

PUERTO DE CALA LLONGA (MARINA CALA D'OR), CALA D'OR AND CALA GRAN

Depths in Metres

View W into Cala Llonga

Cala Llonga Marina viewed from SE

PILOTAGE

Approach

⊕63 39°22´.0N 03°14´.2E Cala Llonga (Approach to Puerto de Cala D'or)

From S Low rocky cliffs broken by two small *calas* extend northwards from Porto Petro. The low, square pinkish-brown fort on Punta del Fortin with its nearby lighthouse (Fl(1+2)20s17m5M, round white column on square white base, both with vertical black stripes, 6m) are easily identified.

From N There are five small *calas* in the low rocky cliffs that extend from Porto Colom southwards. Again the fort and lighthouse are easy to identify.

Anchorages in the approach

- *Cala Gran* Anchor in 5–6m over sand and weed in the middle of the *cala*, opposite a small squarish *cala* on the starboard side, open to the S and to swell from the SE and E. There is a fine sandy beach which is buoyed-off for bathing.

Anchorage in Cala Gran, Cala D'Or   *GW*

- *Cala d'Or* This *cala* is sometimes closed in the summer by means of buoys, when anchoring is prohibited. Otherwise anchor in the centre of the *cala* in 3–5m over sand and weed patches off a small sandy beach, open to E and SE and to swell from the E. This is the least sheltered of the three calas.
- *Cala Llonga* Anchor in the entrance to Caló d'es Pous in 2.5m over sand and weed, well out of the marina approach channel, open to the E.

Entrance

The outer entrance is straightforward with good depths. After passing the light structure on the N side of the entrance to Cala Llonga (Fl.G.5s9m5M, green column on white base 6m) and crossing the 5m contour, the buoyed channel into the marina will open up. A minimum depth of 2.5m should be found in the channel.

Berthing

Secure temporarily to the fuelling berth at the end of the marina S mole, having already called on VHF Ch 09. In this case a berth may be allocated over the radio.

Facilities

Water On the pontoons and the marina S mole.

Electricity 220v AC points on all pontoons, some 380v points.

Fuel Fuelling berth at the end of the marina S mole.

Provisions Supermarket and other shops nearby, with more at Porto Petro about 1 mile away. Produce markets on Wednesday and Saturday mornings in Santanyí, about 7 miles away by road.

Ice From the supermarket.

Chandlery In the marina complex.

Repairs Small repairs to GRP and wood hulls and engineering jobs can be handled by the marina boatyard. Outside contractors are not allowed to work in the marina without permission. A 50-tonne travel-lift at the marina plus a new one at the head of the *cala* and a 5-tonne crane.

Sail repairs Can be arranged via the marina office.

Yacht club The Club Náutico de Cala d'Or has a clubhouse on the NE side of Cala Llonga with bar, lounge, terraces and showers.

Showers In the marina complex and the *club náutico*.
Laundry In the nearby tourist complex.
Banks Several in the nearby tourist complex.
Medical services In Cala d'Or and Santanyí.

Transport

Car hire/taxis In the town.
Buses Bus service to Santanyí, Palma, etc.

Sights ashore locally

The old fort on the headland is worth the walk. The unusual Punta de Fortin light structure can be seen from here.

Local event

A fiesta with waterborne processions is held on 15 August in honour of the area's patron saint, Santa Maria del Mar.

Eating out

Many restaurants, cafés and bars.

ANCHORAGES S OF PUERTO DE CALA LLONGA

⚓ CALA D'EGOS

39°21′.5N 03°13′.5E

A twisty, rocky-cliffed *cala*, surrounded by mainly luxurious detached houses plus a large hotel overlooking the beach at its head. Anchor in 3–5m over sand and weed, open to SE and S.

⚓ CALA DEL LLAMP

39°21′.5N 03°13′.2E

A small *cala* between rocky cliffs on the NE side of the entrance to Porto Petro. Anchor near the head in 3m over stone and weed, open to SE and S. The area is also occupied by very luxurious detached houses, many with large gardens and pools.

Entrance to Porto Petro: Cala d'els Homos Morts and Cala de Sa Torre E on left, Cala del Llamp and Cala dels Mats right; Porto Petro centre

M21 Porto Petro
(and anchorages in approaches)

A small and friendly harbour which has recently been expanded to berth 230 vessels up to 15m. Anchoring in the approaches and adjoining *calas* is also an option

Location
39°21′.5N 03°13′E
Communications
VHF Ch 09
Port Authority ☎/*Fax* 971 65 70 12
Yacht harbour (Real Club Náutico Porto Petro)
☎ 971 65 76 57 *Fax* 971 65 92 16
Email rcnportopetro@btlink.net

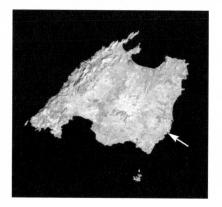

The harbour

A small but attractive yacht and fishing harbour occupying only one corner of a good-sized *cala* amidst relatively undeveloped surroundings and good anchorages. Porto Petro yacht harbour can berth 230 or so vessels up to 15m. In the past depth was a problem with much of the yacht harbour having less than 2m, but dredging has approximately doubled previous figures (and charges have increased to match!). A new mole has been built NE from the rocky headland S of the harbour, increasing the number of deeper berths and blocking any southeasterly swell.

There is a sailing school and a branch of the Club Méditerranée in the *cala*. Facilities for visitors are still improving, but as usual the small yacht harbour is frequently crowded in summer. A preliminary call on VHF Ch 09 is advisable.

PILOTAGE

Approach

⊕64 39°21′.3N 03°13′.2E Off Porto Petro

From S Porto Petro lies 9.5 miles NE of Punta Salinas (Fl(2+1)20s17m13M, white tower and building, narrow stone bands 17m), much of the coastline between comprising rough cliffs with few *calas* of any size until Calas Llombarts and Santanyí are reached. From Puerto de Cala Figuera with its conspicuous lighthouse (Fl.3s32m12M, white octagonal tower with vertical black stripes 6m) the coast is of low rocky cliffs. There is one small bay and a large deep *cala* before Porto Petro is reached. The Torre de Porto Petro and lighthouse (Fl(3+1)10s22m7M, white tower on square base with two vertical black stripes 9m) are obscured from W of S, and the entrance will be visible before they are seen.

From N From Cala Llonga and its low, square pinkish-brown fort and nearby lighthouse (Fl(1+2)20s17m5M, round white column on square white base, both with vertical black stripes, 6m) the coast is of low rocky cliffs broken by two small calas. The Torre de Porto Petro is very conspicuous from this direction, as is the lighthouse described above.

Anchorages in the approach

There are several possible anchorages: in Cala d'els Homos Morts and Cala de Sa Torre (4–6m over sand and weed, open to the E), in the main part of the *cala* (4–12m over sand, stones and weed, open to the SE), or, for very shallow-draught craft, off the beach N of the yacht harbour. All anchorages may be affected by swell from S, SE or E and a tripline is recommended as the bottom is foul in places. There are now large yellow visitors' buoys laid in Cala dels Mats, and anchoring is no longer permitted, though there may still be just enough room to anchor outside them. For Cala del Llamp see above.

Entrance

The *cala* entrance is wide and unencumbered. Buoys are sometimes laid in the approach to the yacht harbour, otherwise remain near the middle of the *cala* until the S mole is abeam before swinging to

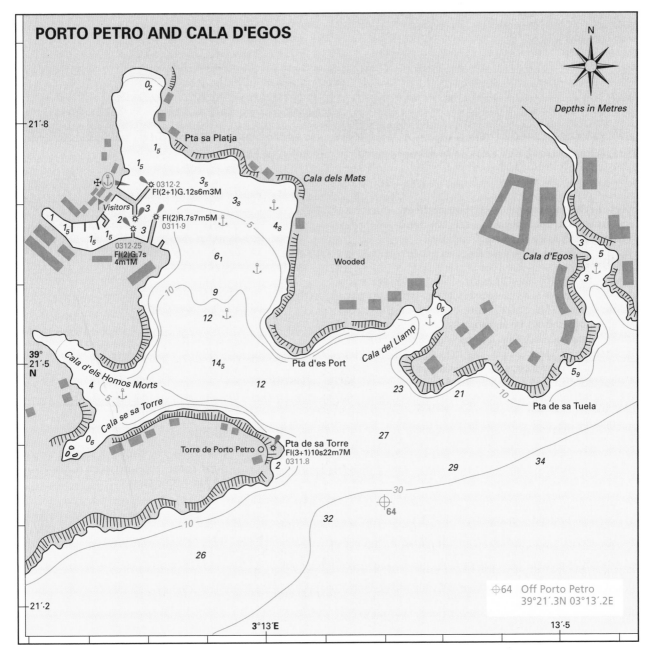

Porto Petro looking NE over Cala dels Mats. Puerto de Cala Llonga just visible beyond the peninsula

pass between it and the hammerhead. On no account venture beyond the N end of the hammerhead as depths shoal rapidly.

Berthing

Contact the harbour office on VHF Ch 09 prior to arrival, otherwise look for a vacant berth on the visitors' quay (see plan) and enquire at the *club náutico*. 3m should be found between the outer and inner S moles, 2.5–3m against the S arm of the hammerhead and 2.5m in the visitors' berths opposite. Otherwise watch the depth-sounder whilst manoeuvring. The angle enclosed by the N arm of the hammerhead is reserved for fishing and commerical tourist boats and the shallow inner harbour is private.

Facilities

Water All water connectors ashore are of the push-in adaptor type. It seems that the authorities do not like people visiting by dinghy and filling containers, but prefer them to berth to take on water (for which, of course, they make a charge).

Electricity 220v AC on quays plus a few 380v points. A deposit is normally required before the cable is connected.

Fuel No fuel available (late 2005).

Provisioning Small supermarket nearby plus other shops in the village able to meet all day-to-day requirements. Produce markets Wednesday and Saturday mornings in Santanyí, some 5M away.

Ice From a café near the root of the mole.

Repairs Basic work on engines, woodwork and GRP possible. Enquire at the Réal Club Náutico. A shallow slipway N of the hammerhead mole.

Yacht club The Réal Club Náutico Porto Petro has a small clubhouse on the quay overlooking the yacht harbour.

Showers At the Réal Club Náutico. A small charge is made if not berthed in the yacht harbour.

Laundry In Cala d'Or.

Banks In Cala d'Or and Santanyí, the latter about 5 miles away by road.

Medical services In Cala d'Or and Santanyí.

Transport

Car hire/taxis Enquire at the *club náutico*.

Buses Bus service to Santanyí, Palma, etc.

Sights ashore locally

A visit to the old town of Santanyí should prove interesting. A '*petit train*' runs between Cala d'Or, Porto Petro and Cala Mondragó.

Local events

Fiestas are held on 25 July in honour of San Jaime, with horseback processions, and on 30 November in honour of San Andrés.

Eating out

Several restaurants, cafés and bars.

⚓ CALA MONDRAGÓ
39°21′N 03°11′.5E

A wide, attractive and largely unspoilt *cala* between low rocky cliffs, Cala Mondragó has four arms, two of which are buoyed off in summer for swimmers. Anchor in 4–8m over sand and some weed. There are café/bars on both the tourist beaches.

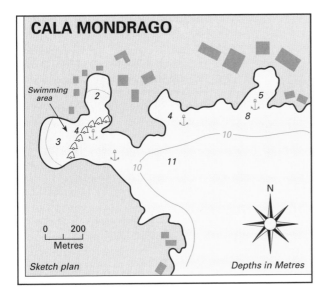

Cala Mondragó viewed from SW, showing nearby bays

M22 Puerto de Cala Figuera (de Santanyí)

A very tiny harbour offering good shelter but with visitors' berths for only 6 vessels. Cabrera is 15M from here

Location
39°19′.8N 03°10′.5E

Communications
Puerto de Cala Figuera ☎ 971 64 52 42

The harbour

A very small, attractive harbour devoted to fishing and a small day tourist trade. There is little space for yachts in the sheltered areas although six berths are reserved for visitors stern-to at the short mole. These would become untenable with strong wind or swell from E, SE or S, as would the anchorage further out. For this reason the *cala* is only suitable for a night stop in settled weather. The approach is straightforward but the entrance can be difficult to locate as it is narrow and lies between cliffs. Facilities are very limited.

III. MALLORCA

Puerto de Cala Figuera: small harbour with little space for visitors

PILOTAGE

From S Puerto de Cala Figuera lies 7 miles NW of Punta Salinas (Fl(2+1)20s 17m13M, white tower and building, narrow stone bands 17m), much of the coastline comprises rough cliffs with few *calas* of any size until Cala Llombarts is reached. The entrance to Cala Figuera can be identified in the close approach by the lighthouse (Fl.3s32m12M, white octagonal tower with vertical black stripes 6m) in front of a brownish stone watchtower on the NE side of the entrance.

From N From Porto Petro the coast is of low, broken rocky cliffs with a wide, deep indentation at Cala Mondragó. If sailing close inshore the lighthouse and tower at Cala Figuera are screened by hills and not visible until the closer approach.

Anchorage in the approach

Anchor in the middle of the *cala* well clear of the mole in 4–8m over muddy sand and rock, possibly with a line ashore to limit swinging, open to E and SE. If space and draught permit, anchorage may be found N of the mole, but this area is usually taken up by large fishing boats. Holding is reported to be poor in places.

Entrance

The red column on the end of the molehead can be seen from outside the entrance. Follow an S-shaped course, remaining near the centre of the *cala* and swinging wide of the foul ground extending from the two rocky points (see plan). The wind can be fluky between the high cliffs and the seas heavy and confused, making it difficult for craft with limited auxiliary power.

Berthing

Six berths are reserved for visiting yachts on the SE side of the mole, which require laying an anchor ahead and taking a stern line ashore. Holding is poor with weed on soft, shallow, muddy sand over rock, and plenty of scope is required. The inner end of the small breakwater to which visiting yachts may secure shoals to below 2m near the root and there is a rock with 0.3m over it close to the root. This position is completely exposed to onshore winds from between E and SE, which bring in a nasty swell and the *cala* is therefore only suitable as a night stop in very settled conditions.

Yachts are not normally permitted to berth at the fishermen's quay inside the mole, though from Friday evening to Sunday evening it may be possible to lie alongside a fishing boat – which will probably wish to leave at 0600 on Monday morning. A small yacht can sometimes find a slot in the narrow northern arm. The western arm is very tight and is further obstructed by lines across the harbour. Plans to create a yacht harbour have been shelved for now.

Moorings

There are a few moorings in the northern arm but they are private and usually occupied.

Facilities

Water Tap at the (wholesale) fish market near the root of the mole.

Electricity Not available.

Fuel Diesel from a pump near the root of the mole. Petrol by can from a filling station at Santanyí some 2½ miles inland.

Provisions Supermarket 10 minutes' walk up the hill S of the harbour. A few small shops provide everyday requirements. There are many more shops in Santanyí and a market is held there on Wednesday and Saturday mornings.

Ice From one of the restaurants.

Repairs A 5-tonne crane on the fishermen's quay. Small slipway at the head of the western arm.

Banks In Santanyí.

Medical services In the village and at Santanyí, 2½ miles inland.

Transport

Car hire/taxis In Santanyí.

Buses Summer service to Santanyí and beyond.

Sights ashore locally

See *Porto Petro* above.

Local events

Puerto de Cala Figuera is one of many harbours in Mallorca to honour Nuestra Señora del Carmen on 16 July with a fiesta including waterborne processions.

Eating out

Several restaurants and some café/bars near the harbour.

ANCHORAGES BETWEEN PUERTO DE CALA FIGUERA AND PUERTO COLONIA DE SANT JORDI

⚓ CALA SANTANYÍ
39°19′.7N 03°08′.9E

A *cala* surrounded by houses and hotels, its sandy beach roped off for swimming. There is a small tower on the E side of entrance and a small island on the W side, plus some breaking rocks inshore. Anchor in the middle of the *cala* in 5–10m over sand, open to E and SE. In addition to the many swimmers there is a windsurfing school.

Cala Santanyí (right) viewed from SE, with Cala Llombarts

Cala Llombarts from SE. The sea undercutting rock and creating caves is typical in this area

⚓ CALA LLOMBARTS
39°19′.5N 03°08′.6E

A double *cala*, though the northern arm is much the smaller, with rocky sides and a roped-off beach to the S. Mooring buoys have been laid, but it is not known if these are permanent. There is foul ground off the headland between the two. Anchor in 4–6m over sand and weed, open to E, SE and possibly S.

⚓ CALA MARMOLS
39°17′.3N 03°05′.6E

A small and completely deserted *cala* between rocky cliffs, just over 2 miles NE of Punta Salinas. Anchor in 3–6m over sand, open from E round to S.

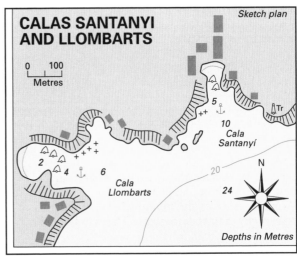

CALAS SANTANYI AND LLOMBARTS

Sketch plan

0   100
Metres

5

10
Cala Santanyí

Tr

2
4

6

Cala Llombarts

20

24

N

Depths in Metres

III. MALLORCA

6. Punta (Cap) Salinas to Bahía de Palma

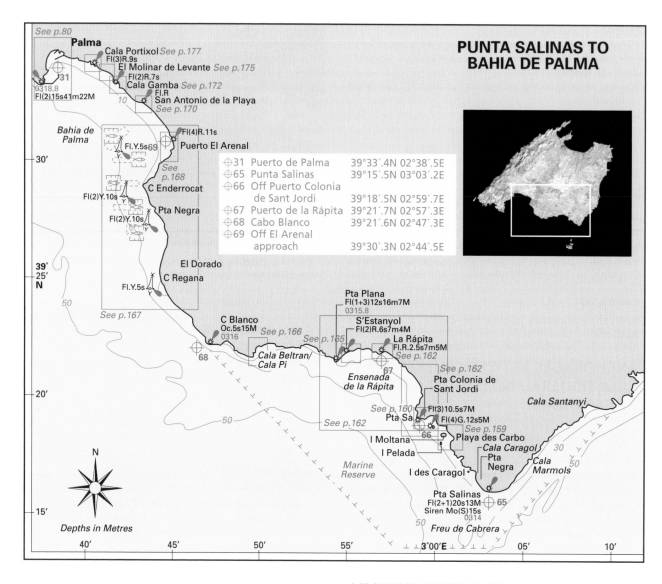

Within the map:

See p.80

Palma
Cala Portixol *See p.177*
Fl(3)R.9s
El Molinar de Levante *See p.175*
Fl(2)R.7s
Cala Gamba *See p.172*
Fl.R
San Antonio de la Playa
See p.170

31
0318.8
Fl(2)15s41m22M
10

Bahía de Palma

Fl(4)R.11s
Fl.Y.5s 69
Puerto El Arenal

30'

See p.168

C Enderrocat
Fl(2)Y.10s
Pta Negra
Fl(2)Y.10s

El Dorado
C Regana
Fl.Y.5s

39° 25' N

50

See p.167

⊕31	Puerto de Palma	39°33'.4N 02°38'.5E
⊕65	Punta Salinas	39°15'.5N 03°03'.2E
⊕66	Off Puerto Colonia de Sant Jordi	39°18'.5N 02°59'.7E
⊕67	Puerto de la Rápita	39°21'.7N 02°57'.3E
⊕68	Cabo Blanco	39°21'.6N 02°47'.3E
⊕69	Off El Arenal approach	39°30'.3N 02°44'.5E

Pta Plana
Fl(1+3)12s16m7M
0315.8

S'Estanyol
Fl(2)R.6s7m4M

La Rápita
Fl.R.2.5s7m5M
See p.162

C Blanco
Oc.5s15M
0316
See p.166
See p.165

68

Cala Beltran/
Cala Pi

Ensenada de la Rápita
67

See p.162

Pta Colonia de Sant Jordi

See p.160

See p.162

Fl(3)10.5s7M
Pta Sa
Fl(4)G.12s5M
See p.159

I Moltana
66
Playa des Carbo

20'

I Pelada

Cala Caragol
Pta Negra

Marine Reserve

I des Caragol

Cala Santanyi

Cala Marmols

30

50

Pta Salinas
Fl(2+1)20s13M
Siren Mo(S)15s
0314

65

15'

Depths in Metres

Freu de Cabrera

50

40' 45' 50' 55' **3°00'E** 05' 10'

N

PUNTA SALINAS TO BAHIA DE PALMA

⊕65 39°15'.5N 03°03'.2E Pta Salinas

PUNTA SALINAS
39°16'N 03°03'.5E

A low, flat, wooded promontory edged by stony beaches and marked by a conspicuous lighthouse (Fl(2+1)20s17m13M, white tower and building with narrow stone bands 17m).

⚓ CALA CARAGOL
39°16'.7N 03°02'.5E

A wide bay one mile NW of Punta Salinas and backed by pine woods, Cala Caragol has a particularly fine beach bounded to the SE by the low rocky Punta Negra and to the NW by Islote Caragol. Anchor in 2–5m over sand and weed, open to the S sector. The bay is often full of yachts during summer, but otherwise appears little visited. There are a few houses and a rough road.

Punta Salinas looking NW over the lighthouse

Close to Punta Salinas lie these salt pans, worked since
before Roman times   *GH*

Approaches to Puerto Colonia de Sant Jordi viewed NW
over Isla de na Guardia

⚓ CALA ENTUGORES
39°17´.4N 03°01´.8E

Much smaller and narrower than its neighbour, Cala
Entugores has no beach and is very shallow. Enter
carefully watching the depth-sounder – it is reported
to shoal to below 2.5m not far from the entrance.
Anchor as depth dictates, open to S and W.

ANCHORAGES BETWEEN ISLA PELADA AND ISLA DE NA GUARDIA
⚓ PLAYA DES CARBÓ
39°18´.6N 03°00´.8E
⚓ PLAYA DE SA ROQUETAS
39°18´.3N 03°01´.1E

Playa des Carbó and Sa Roquetas (RH) with Islas Pelada and
Moltana shown, viewed from SSE

Less than 1M NW of Cala Entugores lies a long
sandy beach with a spit running out to several small
islands and rocky shoals close to the shore. These are
Isla Pelada, Isla Moltana and Isla de na Guardia, the
latter being the only one lit (Fl(4)G.12s7m5M),
marking the approach to Puerto Colonia de Sant
Jordi. Do not attempt to pass between these islands
and the mainland with a keeled yacht (see plan).

Anchor in the northern bay (Playa des Carbó) in
3–4m over mainly sand, or further S (Playa de sa
Roquetas) in 2–4m over sand and weed. There can
be considerable disturbance from jet-skis and small
speedboats in both anchorages.

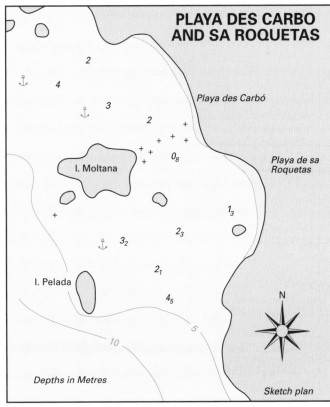

PLAYA DES CARBO
AND SA ROQUETAS

Playa des Carbó

Playa de sa
Roquetas

I. Moltana

I. Pelada

Depths in Metres

Sketch plan

III. MALLORCA

M23 Puerto Colonia de Sant Jordi (Puerto de Campos)

A small friendly fishing harbour with berths for over 300 vessels, usually full with local craft

Location
39°19′N 03°00′E
Communications
Puerto Colonia de Sant Jordi ☎/*Fax* 971 65 51 48

The harbour

A medium-sized fishing and yachting harbour, with 322 berths, mostly for small vessels. Much of the harbour is shallow and occupied by local craft. This is still basically a fishing port with nets being mended on the quayside. Facilities are limited but do include fuel, water and reasonable shopping. The approach is between low islands, some unmarked, and care is necessary.

Tourist ferries taking visitors to Cabrera berth inshore of the fuelling pontoon and leave the harbour at speed. This is a particular hazard if coming in by dinghy.

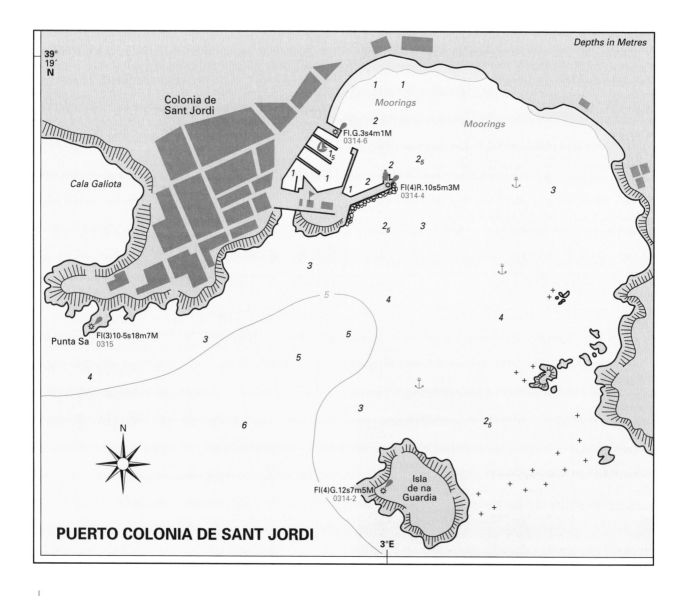

Puerto Colonia de Sant Jordi and the anchorage E of the port

PILOTAGE

Approach

⊕66 39°18′.5N 02°59′.7E Off Puerto Colonia de Sant Jordi

From W From Cabo Blanco – a high promontory of steep light brown cliffs topped by a lighthouse (Oc.5s95m15M, white tower and building 12m) and an old watchtower – the coast is of low rocky cliffs with a long sandy bay, Playa del Trench, followed by more low rocky cliffs and the houses and apartment blocks of Colonia de Sant Jordi. Punta Sa may be identified by its conspicuous lighthouse (Fl(3)10.5s18m7M, white round tower with three black bands 12m) on the very end of the headland, though it is partially hidden if viewed from further N. The low and inconspicuous Isla Corberana some 550m offshore presents a potential hazard, particularly when sailing at night, though there is good water on either side.

From E Round the low, tree-covered Punta Salinas with its lighthouse (Fl(2+1)20s17m13M, white tower and building with narrow stone bands 17m) and follow the coast past several sandy bays and low inconspicuous islands until S of the lighthouse on Punta Sa (see above). Do not attempt to pass inside either Isla Moltona or Isla de na Guardia.

Anchorage in the approach

The NE part of the bay between the harbour entrance and Isla de na Guardia is occupied by moorings; anchor further SW in 3–5m over sand and weed, open to SW and S, but with partial shelter from the SE. Areas of the bottom are foul and a trip line is advisable.

Entrance

From a point S of the lighthouse on Punta Sa, enter the bay on a NE course leaving Isla de la Guardia to starboard. Depths shoal as the harbour is approached, so sound carefully. Note that the end of the SE breakwater projects some distance beyond the light structure (though entry at night is not recommended).

Berthing

Much of the inner harbour has depths of less than 1.5m, though the fuel berth and the southern side of the marina S mole are reported to have 2m. Secure at the fuel berth and consult harbour staff.

Facilities

Water Taps on quays and pontoons, and at the fuel berth.
Electricity 220v AC on quays and pontoons.
Fuel Diesel and petrol pumps inside the end of the S breakwater, but no more than 2m depth. Access can be difficult due to nearby tourist boats.
Provisions Supermarket and other shops in the town.
Ice From the fuel berth.
Repairs Small boatyard W of the *club náutico*. Two slipways, both very shallow. Engineer at the yard.
Yacht club The Club Náutico de Sant Jordi has a small clubhouse at the S end of the harbour.
Laundry In the town.
Banks In the town.
Medical services Basic medical services available.

Transport

Car hire/taxis In the town.
Buses Bus service to Ses Salinas and on to Palma, etc.

ANCHORAGES BETWEEN PUERTO COLONIA DE SANT JORDI AND PUERTO DE LA RÁPITA

The headland SW of Puerto Colonia de Sant Jordi SE has several anchorages and offlying islands as follows.

⚓ ENSENADA DE LA RÁPITA, SE CORNER
39°19′.7N 02°59′.4E

A well-sheltered anchorage close N of the headland on which Colonia Sant Jordi stands, and S of Playa del Trench. Anchor in 3m or more over sand and weed NE of an old and dilapidated quay, open to

Ensenada de la Rápita: Isla Gabina can just be seen right of picture

NW (short fetch) and W. There is a fine beach to the E and a large hotel near the root of the quay.

⚓ BAY S OF ISLA GABINA
39°20′N 02°59′.5E

Similar to the above, but with much less shelter from the SW.

⚓ PLAYA DEL TRENCH
39°20′.8N 02°59′E

An open bay anchorage off a fine sandy beach. Anchor in 3m+ over sand and weed. A submarine cable runs in a WSW direction from Punta de sas Covetas at the N end of the beach.

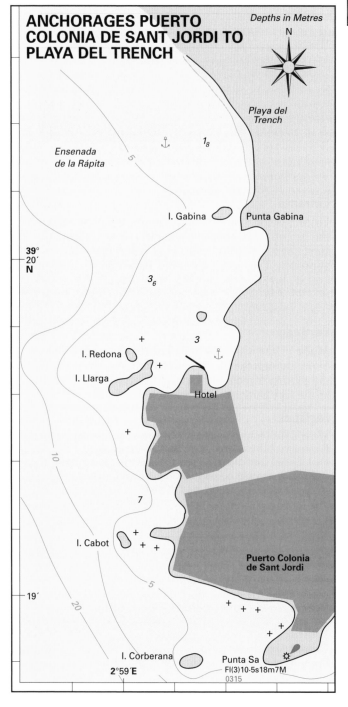

M24 Puerto de la Rápita

A large, safe and friendly yacht habour with berthing for 460 yachts just W of the finest beach in Mallorca: Playa del Trench. A good departure point for Isla de Cabrera

Location
39°21′.7N 02°57′.4E

Distances
Cabrera 12M

Communications
VHF Ch 09
Club Náutico de la Rápita ☎ 971 64 00 01
Fax 971 64 08 21
Email velarapita@webhouse.es

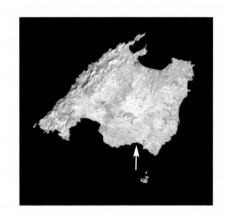

The port

Puerto de la Rápita is a large and modern artificial yacht harbour with 460 berths and excellent facilities, situated at the NW end of the long Playa del Trench. It is easy to enter and offers good protection once inside, though a heavy swell from SE or S could make the final approach dangerous due to shoaling water.

Puerto de la Rápita is a favourite departure point for Isla de Cabrera, just 12 miles S, and the marina staff are happy to help visitors apply for the necessary permit. (For details of Isla and *Puerto de Cabrera* see following chapter.)

PILOTAGE

Approach
⊕67 39°21′.7N 02°57′.3E S Puerto de la Rápita

From W Round Punta Plana (Fl(1+3)12s16m7M, white tower with black bands on building 12m) and pass Puerto de S'Estanyol in the NW corner of the bay; a NE course should then be set towards the far end of the houses of La Rápita. On closer approach the harbour breakwater will be seen with an old watchtower (18m) behind.

From E Allow Punta Sa (Fl(3)10.5s18m7M, white round tower with three black bands 12m) an offing

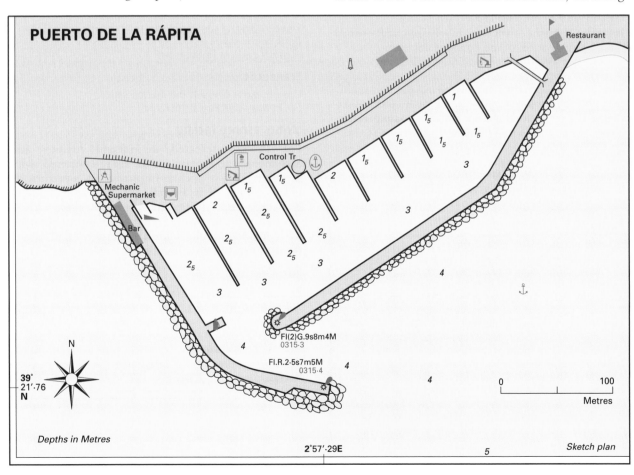

PUERTO DE LA RÁPITA

Depths in Metres

2°57′·29E

Sketch plan

III. MALLORCA

Puerto de la Rápita looking N. A lot of development underway around the port during 2005

of at least ½ mile in order to clear Isla Corberana, then steer NW into the wide Ensenada de la Rápita towards the houses of La Rápita. On nearing the harbour, the breakwater and watchtower will come into view.

Anchorage in the approach

In calm weather anchor in 4–5m over sand, 200–300m E or SE of the harbour entrance.

Entrance

The entrance presents no problems day or night, though a heavy swell from the SE or S could make the final approach dangerous due to shoaling water. There is a 2-knot speed limit in the harbour.

Berthing

Secure stern-to at the reception quay inside the SW breakwater until allocated a berth. Alternatively call the marina office on VHF Ch 09 before arrival.

Facilities

Water Taps on pontoons and quays, and at the visitors' quay. However, the water is sometimes brackish so check before filling tanks. It has been reported that the water at the fuel berth is of better quality.
Electricity 220v AC and some 380v AC points on quays and pontoons, and at the visitors' quay.
Fuel Diesel and petrol at the fuel berth.
Provisioning Small supermarket at the W end of the harbour, more shops in the town ½ mile away.
Ice From a machine near the marina supermarket.
Chandlery Two at the W end of the harbour.
Repairs Boatyard in the NW area of the marina. A 50-tonne travel-lift in the boatyard area and 7-tonne crane at the NE end of the harbour. The wide slipway nearby has been rendered inaccessible by a fixed walkway.

Engineers Cosme Oliver ☎ 971 64 01 99 *Fax* 971 64 00 21 at the W end of the harbour are official service agents for Caterpillar, Honda, Perkins, Tohatsu, Vetus, Volvo Penta and Yamaha.
Yacht club The Club Náutico de la Rápita has a large and well-appointed clubhouse with a bar and terrace restaurant at the E end of the harbour.
Showers Several shower blocks opposite the control tower.
Bank In the town.
Medical services In the town.

Transport

Car hire/taxis Consult the marina office.
Buses Bus service to Palma, etc.

Sights ashore locally

For those interested in ancient history and archaeological remains, this area is littered with interesting 'finds' such as Capicorp Vey, a prehistoric village, Sollerich (a burial cave) and Son Herue, a Bronze Age burial site. The village of Campos is well worth a visit, set in the countryside and surrounded by considerable agricultural activity and many beautiful restored windmills.

Local event

A fiesta in honour of Nuestra Señora del Carmen is held on 16 July.

Eating out

Several restaurants in the town, plus a restaurant at the *club náutico* and a café/bar at the W end of the harbour.

M25 Puerto de S'Estanyol de Migjorn (El Estañol)

A small harbour less than 2M W of Puerto de la Rápita, but usually full with local vessels

Location
39°21´.7N 02°55´.3E

Communications
VHF Ch 09
Club Náutico de S'Estanyol ☎ 971 64 00 85
Fax 971 64 06 82
Email cne@cnestanyol.com
www.cnestanyol.com

The harbour

A small, square, artificial harbour close E of Punta Plana, occupied by fishing boats and a few yachts under 12m or so. Approach and entrance are not usually difficult but would be dangerous in strong winds and swell from SE or S due to shallow water in the approach. Facilities are fair and everyday shopping requirements can be met in the strip of coastal development which joins up with La Rápita to the E.

Ambitious plans to more than double the size of the harbour by means of a new breakwater enclosure have been under discussion for years. Work had still not started in Nov 2005 and it is unlikely that permission will be granted (as in other places, because of environmental concerns).

PILOTAGE

Approach

From W Once past Punta Plana, Puerto de S'Estanyol lies 0.6 miles NNE of the headland past a small, low-lying island which should be left to port.

From E Heading NW through Ensenada de la Rápita, Puerto de S'Estanyol lies 0.6 miles NNE of the headland.

Entrance

Approach the eastern corner of the harbour heading NW to round the head of the S breakwater at slow speed. The entrance is narrow and may be partially blocked by moored boats. There is a 2-knot speed limit. Note that the close approach and entrance are shallow, making it dangerous in heavy swell from S or SE.

Berthing

Secure to the inner side of the S breakwater as space permits and visit the harbour office for allocation of a berth. Depths are 2.5–3m near the breakwater head shoaling to 2m or so at the elbow.

Puerto de S'Estanyol. Some development around the port, but plans for a much larger marina have been shelved for now due to environmental concern

III. MALLORCA

PUERTO DE S'ESTANYOL

Facilities

Water Taps on quays and pontoons.
Electricity 220v AC points at foot of lamp-posts and at normal supply points.
Fuel Diesel pump at the head of the N mole, petrol pump at its root (i.e. by can only).
Provisioning Everyday supplies from a supermarket and other shops in the nearby town.
Ice From the bar.
Repairs A 12.5-tonne crane, and slipway near the root of the N mole. Motor mechanic available for engine repairs.
Yacht club The Club Náutico S'Estanyol has a small clubhouse with restaurant, bar, terrace and two tennis courts.
Showers In the W corner of the harbour.
Bank In La Rápita, about 1½ miles away.
Hospital/medical services In Lluchmayor, 8 miles inland.

Transport

Car hire/taxis Consult the harbour office.
Buses Bus service to Palma, etc.

Eating out

A few restaurants and several café/bars.

ANCHORAGES W OF PUERTO DE S'ESTANYOL

⚓ CALA PI

39°21′.6N 02°50′.1E (entrance to *cala*).

A beautiful and very popular *cala* between high cliffs, but extremely narrow and often crowded (avoid weekends when charter yachts are setting out or returning). There is a conspicuous stone tower on the headland SE of the entrance. Anchor in 2–8m over sand and some weed either using a stern anchor or taking a line ashore, to restrict swinging. At about 3.5m depth beware an isolated rock, with 1.3m clearance, close to the cliff where rope tails from old shorelines abound. There is also a substantial

Cala Pi right and the smaller Cala Beltran left, viewed from the N

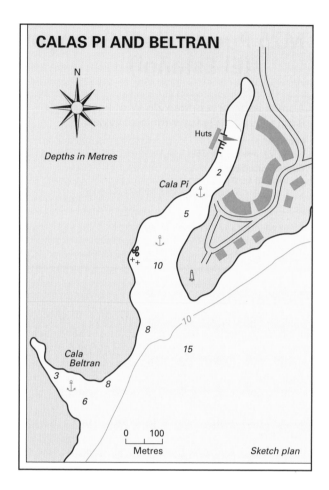

mooring block and ground tackle in the centre of the *cala* at this same depth, which may be a mooring in season but could be used as a swing limiter in low season. There are fishermen's huts and a rough slipway by the sandy beach at the head of the *cala*, and a small tourist development with cafés and restaurants, etc. to the E.

⚓ CALA BELTRAN

39°21′.6N 02°50′E

A small *cala* between rocky cliffs just W of Cala Pi, where it is possible to anchor in 3–5m over sand, open to E and SE.

⊕68 39°21′.6N 02°47′.3E Cabo Blanco

BAHÍA DE PALMA MARINE RESERVE

A marine reserve area has been created off Cabo Enderrocat, 3M N of Cabo Blanco, with four lightbuoys indicating the extremities. Vessels should keep outside these buoys.

Buoys
34190(S) **Buoy A** 39°24′.7N 02°43′.8E Fl.Y.5s5M pillar with × topmark (S marker)
34191(S) **Buoy 2** 39°25′.5N 02°43′.6E Fl(2)Y.10s3M can with × topmark
34192(S) **Buoy 1** 39°28′.4N 02°42′.2E Fl(2)Y.10s3M can with × topmark
34193(S) **Buoy C** 39°29′.9N 02°42′.1E Fl.Y.5s5M pillar with × topmark. (N marker)

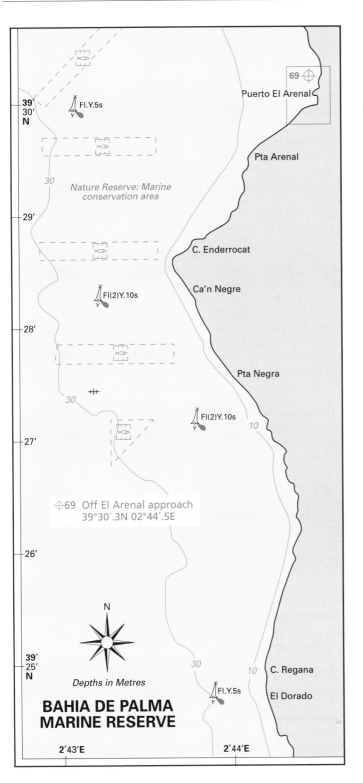

Depths in Metres

**BAHIA DE PALMA
MARINE RESERVE**

⊕69 Off El Arenal approach
39°30′.3N 02°44′.5E

M26 Puerto El Arenal

A large yacht harbour at the SE end of the Playa de Arenal, with berthing for over 600 yachts up to 25m

Location
39°30′.2N 02°44′.9E

Communications
VHF Ch 09
Club Náutico El Arenal ☎ 971 44 01 42/44 02 67
Fax 971 44 05 68
Email administracion@cnarenal.com
www.cnarenal.com

The harbour

A large, modern yacht harbour with 667 berths for vessels up to 25m and with 3m+ depths throughout. Built at the SE end of another spectacular and popular beach: Playa de Arenal, the new harbour is built alongside the small old harbour which has now been improved.

To the S a low rocky coast is backed initially by large houses and, further on, by unspoilt open countryside.

The harbour offers first class facilities including a lovely clubhouse with restaurant and pool and is far enough away from the tourist areas not to suffer from traffic or other noise. El Arenal is now full of charter craft and has become very expensive – even the Cabrera permit is now charged for! This is a useful place for a crew change as the airport is close by.

Approach and entrance are normally without problem, but heavy winds and swell from the SW quadrant could render the close approach and entrance dangerous.

Puerto El Arenal is one of many suitable departure points for Isla de Cabrera and the *club náutico* are happy to help visitors apply for the necessary permit.

For details of Isla and Puerto de Cabrera see following chapter.

III. MALLORCA

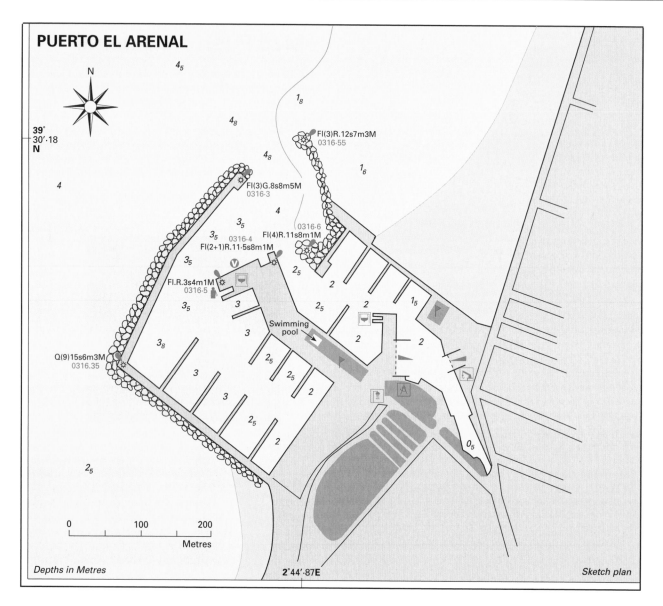

PUERTO EL ARENAL

Depths in Metres

2°44'·87E

Sketch plan

PILOTAGE

Approach

⊕69 39°30'.3N 02°44'.5E Off El Arenal

For outer approach see *Puerto Colonia de Sant Jordi* on page 161.

From W (as above) Round the very prominent Punta Cala Figuera which has a lighthouse (Fl(4)20s45m15M, white round tower with black diagonal stripes on building 24m) and radio masts on its steep cliffs. Cross the Bahía de Palma heading just N of E towards Cabo Enderrocat, with an inconspicuous tower on its summit, at the northern end of a line of high cliffs. El Arenal lies 2 miles NE of this headland, at the SE end of a sandy beach backed by solid high-rise development.

From E From Cabo Blanco follow the cliffs NNW round Cabo Enderrocat, keeping well clear of the new Marine Reserve buoys. El Arenal lies 2 miles NE off this headland, at the SE end of a sandy beach backed by solid high-rise development.

Anchorage in the approach

Anchor either side of the harbour in 3m+ over sand and weed, open SW–W–NW.

Entrance

The entrance is easily seen and without hazards, other than those posed by (or to) stray bathers, snorkellers, sailboards and pedalos. The entrance is regularly dredged to 4–5m with 3m throughout the yacht harbour. It is still wise to keep close to the southern breakwater head on entering. There is a 2-knot speed limit.

Berthing

Visitors lie stern-to against the head of the central mole, between the slipway and the fuel berth. Lazy lines are provided, tailed to the quay.

Facilities

Water Water points on the pontoons and quays.
Electricity 220v AC available on all quays and pontoons plus some 380v points.
Fuel Diesel and petrol from pumps at the W end of the central mole.

Puerto El Arenal looking SE

Provisions Everyday supplies from nearby shops and supermarkets, with many more in Palma 6 miles away. Hypermarket less than 5 miles away on the road between Palma and the airport. A market is held in the town on Tuesday and Friday, with a clothes market on Thursdays.

Ice From the *club náutico* bar.

Chandlery Just outside the main gate to the harbour.

Repairs Layup area on the central mole with some services available. Fully fledged boatyards in Palma. For repairs and general maintenance Renav is recommended locally. A 50-tonne travel-lift at the W end of the central mole. A smaller lift and 3-tonne mobile crane in the old harbour. Two slipways in the old harbour and one at the end of the central mole. Engineers available through the *club náutico*.

Yacht club The Club Náutico El Arenal has an elegant clubhouse with restaurant, TV room, bar, terraces, large swimming pool and laundry. Use of the club facilities, including the pool, is a bonus here. The old clubhouse to the NE also has a restaurant and is used by fishermen and dinghy sailors.

Showers At the E and SE corners of the harbour area.

Banks In the town.

Medical services In the town. Hospital in Palma 6 miles away.

Transport

Car hire/taxis In the town.

Buses Frequent bus service to Palma.

Ferries From Palma to the other islands and mainland Spain.

Air services Busy international airport 3 miles away.

Sights ashore locally

Palma and all its charms are only a short bus ride away.

Eating out

Many restaurants, cafés and bars along the beach.

ANCHORAGES NW OF PUERTO EL ARENAL IN THE BAY OF PALMA

⚓ BAHÍA DE PALMA, NE SIDE

In settled weather it is possible to anchor off the shore virtually anywhere between El Arenal and Palma itself; the coast is in the main gently sloping, with wide sandy beaches. Anchor to suit draught off the open beach. If swimming buoys are laid, ensure you do not encroach on them. Vessels doing so are fined heavily.

Bahía de Palma looking NW over Puerto de San Antonio. Palma beyond

III. MALLORCA

M27 Puerto de San Antonio de la Playa (Ca'n Pastilla)

Offering excellent protection and facilities for nearly 400 berths up to 15m, this new port is close to the airport and its accompanying noise, being directly under the flight path

Location
39°31′.8N 02°43′.0E

Communications
VHF Ch 09
Club Marítimo San Antonio de la Playa ☎ 971 74 50 76/ 26 35 12 *Fax* 971 26 16 38.
Email cmsap@cmsap.com
www.cmsap.com

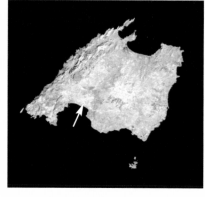

The harbour/marina

A good-sized yacht harbour with nearly 400 berths, handy for the airport (though paying the price with a good deal of aircraft noise) and with better than average facilities. It is easy to approach and enter in normal conditions though with strong onshore winds and swell it could become dangerous due to shallows in the close approach.

Puerto de San Antonio de la Playa lies very close to the large tourist resort of Ca'n Pastilla with its many high-rise hotels and apartment blocks, and is occasionally referred to by this name. An excellent sandy beach stretches for over 2 miles to the SE.

PILOTAGE

Approach

⊕70 39°31′.7N 2°43′.0E Puerto de San Antonio

For outer approach see *Puerto Colonia de Sant Jordi* on page 161.

From W (as above) Round the very prominent Punta de Cala Figuera which has a lighthouse (Fl(4)20s45m15M, white round tower with black diagonal stripes on building 24m) and radio masts on its steep cliffs. Cross the Bahía de Palma on a NE course; planes taking off and landing from Palma airport give a good indication of the position of this harbour. In the closer approach the long sandy Playa del Arenal, which is backed by a line of high-rise buildings, will be seen. Near the NW end of this beach is a separate group of high-rise buildings with the harbour in front. The small, low Islote Galera which has reefs extending 100m SW, lies 0.5 miles NW of the harbour entrance.

From E Round cabos Blanco and Enderrocat into Bahía de Palma. Once past the Marine Reserve, Puerto San Antonio lies almost 3.3 miles distant.

Anchorage in the approach

Anchor SE of the entrance in 5m over sand, or in nearby Cala Estancia (39°32′.1N 2°42′.8E), a small *cala* just W of the port. This is protected by two short breakwaters but is shallow (1–1.5m) and open to the S. A particularly large hotel overlooks it from the W and there is a busy road nearby.

Entrance

An extension to the N end of the SW breakwater has improved protection, particularly at the visitors' quay, but has turned the entrance into an S-bend. Observe the 2-knot speed limit.

PUERTO DE SAN ANTONIO DE LA PLAYA

0   100
Metres

Ca'n Pastilla

1₅
1₅
2
2
2
2
2₅
2
2₅
2₅
3
3
3
3
3
0316·72
Fl(4)G.11s6m3M
3
3
Visitors
2
39°
31′·91
N
3
Fl(4)R.11s8m5M
0316·7
4
4
4

N

Sketch plan   2°42′·97E   *Depths in Metres*

Puerto de San Antonio de la Playa looking N. It is very close to the airport

Berthing

Preferably call ahead on VHF Ch 09 to check that a berth will be available. Otherwise secure to the inner side of the SW breakwater and visit the harbour office at the *club marítimo* building. There is no more than 2.5m at the visitors' quay, shoaling to 1.5m in places.

Note The visitors' berth becomes virtually untenable in conditions likely to create a swell from the southerly quadrant due to reflection from the eastern breakwater. Also the marina staff are loathe to allow visitors to use empty berths in the marina as they are all private. It is recommended that this port be avoided during strong S winds.

Facilities

Water Taps on all quays and pontoons, including the visitors' quay.

Electricity 220v AC points on all quays and pontoons, including the visitors' quay. 380v AC in the boatyard.

Fuel Diesel and petrol from pumps at the head of the E breakwater; the green column marking the starboard side of the entrance emerges from the fuel cabin's roof.

Provisions Many shops and supermarkets nearby, with more in Palma 3 miles away. Hypermarket about 2 miles away on the road between Palma and the airport. Market Tuesdays and Thursdays in Ca'n Pastilla.

Ice From the bar.

Chandlery Near the harbour. Several large chandleries in Palma.

Repairs Boatyard on the W side of the harbour, equal to most work. Otherwise large boatyards in Palma. A 60-tonne travel-lift in the boatyard, 6-tonne mobile crane and several smaller ones. A small slipway near the club maritimo building.

Engineers, electronic & radio repairs at the boatyard. Several Sailmakers in Palma.

Yacht club The Club Marítimo San Antonio de la Playa has a large clubhouse with restaurant, bar, terrace, showers, etc.

Showers Below the *club marítimo* building.

Laundrette In Ca'n Pastilla.

Banks In Ca'n Pastilla, directly behind the yacht harbour.

Medical services In Ca'n Pastilla. Hospital in Palma 3½ miles away.

Transport

Car hire/taxis In the town.

Buses Frequent bus service to Palma.

Ferries From Palma to the other islands and mainland Spain.

Air services Busy international airport 3 miles away.

Sights ashore locally

A short distance from Palma, with a regular bus service.

Eating out

Restaurant at the *club marítimo* and many more restaurants, cafés, and bars in the town.

M28 Puerto de Cala Gamba

A small shallow well protected harbour with 275 berths, occupied with local vessels. Silting has reduced depths in the entrance to around 1.5m (Nov 2005)

Location
39°32′.8N 2°41′.8E

Communications
VHF Ch 09
Club Náutico Cala Gamba ☎ 971 26 18 49
Fax 971 49 19 00
Email info@cncalagamba.com

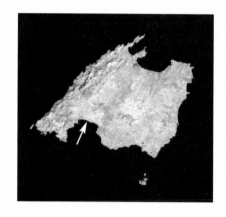

The harbour

The addition of new breakwaters and pontoons has turned this pleasant little fishing harbour into a flourishing yacht harbour with 275 berths, but both depth and facilities are still limited. Much of the harbour carries less than 2m, though 2.5m may be found against parts of the SW breakwater. The entrance in late 2005 was reduced to 1.5m. It cannot be entered with any swell from SE, S or SW due to very shallow water in the approach, but otherwise approach and entry offer no difficulties. The noise generated by nearby Palma airport is considerable.

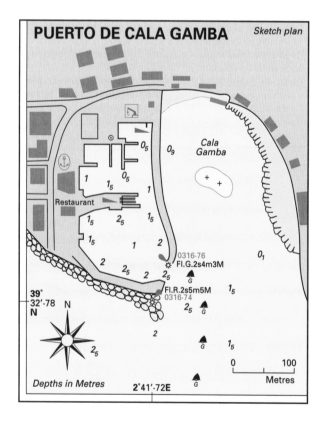

PUERTO DE CALA GAMBA   *Sketch plan*

Restaurant

Cala Gamba

0316·76
☼ Fl.G.2s4m3M

Fl.R.2s5m5M
0316·74

39°
32′·78 N
N

0   100
Metres

Depths in Metres   2°41′·72E

PILOTAGE

Approach
⊕71 39°32′.7N 2°41′.7E Puerto de Cala Gamba

For outer approaches see *Puerto de San Antonio de la Playa* on page 170.

From W Puerto de Cala Gamba lies 1.3 miles NW of Puerto de San Antonio de la Playa and slightly N of the airport main runway. A tall, solid, black and white buoy with an × topmark (Fl.Y.3s3M) 650m S of the harbour entrance marks the water inlet for a power station, the chimney of which will be seen. A W cardinal beacon with ⌀ topmark (Fl(9)15s5m5M) marks the end of a short breakwater 550m NW of the harbour, with a second W cardinal beacon, also (Fl(9)15s5m5M), a further 600m to the NW. All three must be passed on the seaward side. Four small conical green buoys and a conical red buoy are the stb entrance channel markers to the harbour.

From E Steer NNW from Cabo Enderrocat, being certain to leave both Islote Galera, 0.5 miles NW of Puerto de San Antonio de la Playa, and the black and white buoy to starboard.

Anchorage in the approach

Anchor in 4m over stones 400m S of the entrance and some 250m N of the buoy mentioned above. Holding is poor.

Entrance

Approach cautiously heading NE. Though dredged from time to time the entrance channel is narrow and subject to silting.

Berthing

Seek a vacant berth as draught permits and visit the *club náutico* office for allocation of a visitors' berth.

Puerto de Cala Gamba: shallows to N of harbour can be seen clearly

Facilities

Water Taps on quays and pontoons.
Electricity 220v AC points on quays and pontoons.
Fuel Not available.
Provisions Some small shops nearby, supermarkets and more shops a little further inland and all the resources of Palma 2½ miles away. Hypermarket on the road between Palma and the airport.
Ice From the *club náutico* bar.
Repairs Local craftsmen can carry out simple work. Fully equipped boatyards in Palma. 5-tonne and 1-tonne cranes near the root of the E breakwater. A slipway on the central mole and another in the NE corner.
Yacht club The Club Náutico Cala Gamba has a clubhouse overlooking the harbour with restaurant, bar, showers, etc.
Showers At the *club náutico.*
Banks Nearby.
Hospital/medical services In Palma, 2½ miles away.

Transport

Car hire/taxis Locally or in Palma.
Buses Frequent bus service to Palma.
Ferries From Palma to the other islands and mainland Spain.
Air services Busy international airport 2 miles away.

Eating out

Numerous restaurants, cafés and bars nearby.

M29 Puerto del Molinar de Levante (Caló d'en Rigo)

A small fishing harbour in a quaint old village, with berths for 140 craft drawing not much more than half a metre as the entrance is silted

Location
39°33′.4N 2°40′.5E

Communications
Club Marítimo Molinar de Levante ☎ 971 27 34 79
Fax 971 25 04 06

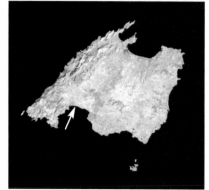

The harbour

A very small fishing harbour built in Caló d'en Rigo, only suitable for craft drawing around half a metre (due to reduced depths in the entrance) and under 9m in length. It is almost exclusively occupied by small speedboats. Facilities are limited to everyday requirements. Approach and entrance are easy but would be dangerous with swell from the southern quadrant.

PILOTAGE

Approach

See *Puerto de Cala Portixol* and page 176 below. Puerto del Molinar de Levante lies 0.3 miles to the SE.

Anchorage in the approach

Anchor in 2.5m over sand and mud, 400m SE of the harbour entrance, open SE–SW–NW.

Entrance

Approach the E side of the harbour at slow speed, watching the depth carefully, until the entrance opens up to port.

Berthing

Seek a vacant berth and visit the *club náutico* office for allocation of a visitors' berth.

Puerto del Molinar. Note silting in entrance

View NW over Puerto del Molinar (bottom left) and Puerto de Cala Portixol. Puerto de Palma in background

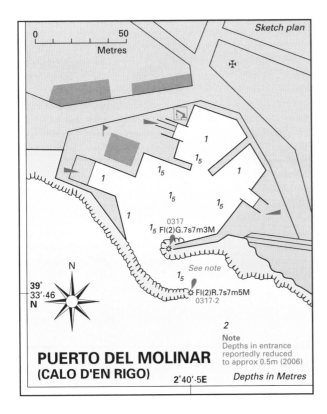

PUERTO DEL MOLINAR
(CALO D'EN RIGO)

Note
Depths in entrance reportedly reduced to approx 0.5m (2006)

Depths in Metres

2°40'·5E

39° 33'·46 N

Facilities

Water Taps around the harbour.
Electricity 220v AC points around the harbour.
Fuel Not available.
Provisioning Shops and supermarkets in El Molinar.
Ice From the Club Marítimo bar.
Chandlery Small chandlery shop nearby.
Repairs Crane On the N side of the harbour and three slipways around the harbour.
Yacht club The Club Marítimo Molinar de Levante has a clubhouse with restaurant and bar on the W side of the harbour.
Banks In El Molinar.
Hospital/medical services In Palma, 1½ miles away.

Transport

See *Puerto de Cala Portixol*, following.

Sights ashore locally

The surrounding area is, as yet, relatively unspoilt with some attractive older houses and a lofty brick church directly behind the harbour.

Eating out

A wide selection of restaurants/cafés nearby.

M30 Puerto de Cala Portixol

A large and very safe fishing and yacht harbour less than 2M from Palma with berths for 300 vessels, but it is usually full with local boats and has little space for visitors

Location
39°33′.5N 2°40′.1E

Communications
Club Náutico Portixol ☎ 971 24 24 24

The harbour

An old fishing harbour in a semicircular cove, converted into a combined fishing and yachting harbour by the addition of extra breakwaters and other facilities. Berthing available for 300 vessels, but restricted to not much more than 12m. No space is reserved for visitors. Much of the harbour has depths less than 2m. Traffic noise from the nearby motorway is distinctly audible, as is the nearby airport.

As with the harbours to the SE, approach and entrance are straightforward other than in heavy swell from the S quadrant, when shoals in the approach could render it dangerous.

PILOTAGE

Approach

⊕72 39°33′.4N 2°40′.1E Off Puerto de Cala Portixol

From W Round the very prominent Punta de Cala Figuera which has a lighthouse (Fl(4)20s45m15M, white round tower with black diagonal stripes on building 24m) and radio masts on its steep cliffs. Cross the Bahía de Palma heading NE towards Palma Cathedral, a very large building with small twin spires. From a position 0.8 miles off Puerto de Palma S breakwater, the very much smaller breakwaters of Puerto de Cala Portixol will be seen 1.5 miles ahead.

From E Round Cabo Blanco, which is high with steep light brown cliffs topped by a lighthouse (Oc.5s95m15M, white tower and building 12m) and an old watchtower, and set a course NW until the buildings of Palma come into view. Puerto de Cala Portixol will be seen to starboard when still a mile short of the entrance to Puerto de Palma.

Puerto de Cala Portixol: berthing for smaller yachts

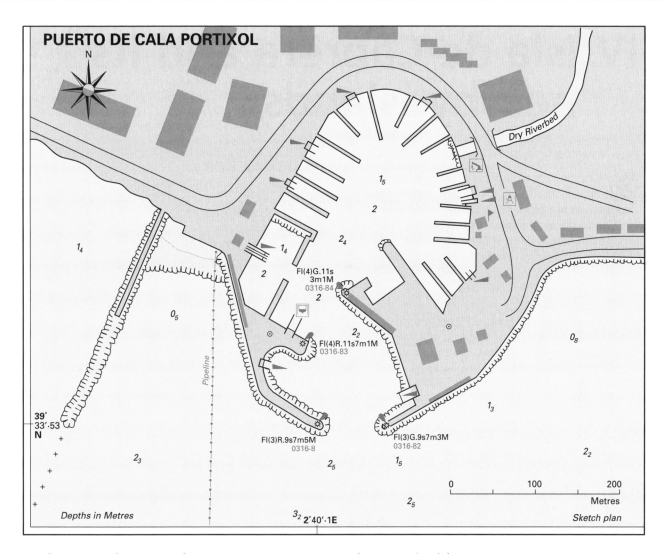

PUERTO DE CALA PORTIXOL

N

Dry Riverbed

1_5

2

2_4

1_4

2

Fl(4)G.11s
3m1M
0316·84

2

1_4

1_4

0_5

Pipeline

2

2_2

Fl(4)R.11s7m1M
0316·83

0_8

39°
33′·53
N

Fl(3)R.9s7m5M
0316·8

2_3

2_5

Fl(3)G.9s7m3M
0316·82

1_5

1_3

2_2

0   100   200
Metres

Depths in Metres

2_5

3_2 2°40′·1E

Sketch plan

Anchorage in the approach

See *Cala Portixolet* below.

Entrance

Approach and enter on a northerly course between the outer breakwaters and then the inner moles, to enter the main harbour. There is a 2-knot speed limit.

Berthing

Local yachts berth on the W side of the harbour just inside the inner mole, but it is unlikely that there will be a space available.

Facilities

Water Water taps around the harbour.
Electricity 220v AC points around the harbour.
Fuel Not available.
Provisions Some shops nearby, with a vast range in Palma, less than 2 miles away.
Ice Ice machine at the *club náutico*.
Chandlery Two chandlery/fishing tackle shops on the road opposite the harbour gate.
Repairs Simple work possible. Fully equipped boatyards in Palma. A 4-tonne crane to the NE of the harbour. Nine slipways, mostly very small.
Yacht club The Club Náutico Portixol has a pleasant clubhouse on the E of the harbour with restaurant, bar, terrace, etc.

Showers At the *club náutico*.
Banks In Palma.
Hospital/medical services In Palma.

Transport

Car hire/taxis In Palma.
Buses Frequent bus service to Palma.
Ferries From Palma to the other islands and mainland Spain.
Air services Busy international airport 3 miles away.

Sights ashore locally

As for Palma.

Eating out

Many eating houses in the area.

⚓ CALA PORTIXOLET

39°33′.6N 2°40′.4E

A shallow and somewhat bleak anchorage, with the rocky breakwaters of Puerto de Cala Portixol on one side and a road backed by houses at the head. Anchor in 1.5m over sand, open to the southern quadrant.

IV. Isla de Cabrera and its nearby islands

As a National Park, Cabrera is a restricted zone of great natural interest due to its rich wildlife and several rare species of flora, fauna and birdlife unique to the archipelago. The island may only be visited if a permit has first been acquired through its offices in Mallorca. There are 50 buoys in the harbour, available to permit holders and limited to one or two nights. Unsupervised walks are limited to the foreshore and castle but other walks are conducted by the park ranger. There are virtually no facilities but the rugged beauty, rich wildlife and tranquillity of the island await those who are prepared to accept these inconveniences

NAVIGATIONAL INFORMATION FOR APPROACHES TO CABRERA

Since a permit obtained from the main islands is required to visit, approaches from the S are unlikely. The only dangers approaching from the S side are the unlit rocks around Islotes Estels on the southernmost tip. To the N, Isla Conejera and the passages between the island and Cabrera are described in this volume.

Magnetic variation

Negligible: 0°47′W (decreasing 6′E annually).

Approach and coastal passage charts
See *Appendix* for full list of Balearic charts.
Approach lights
0338 **Punta Anciola** 39°07′.8N 02°55′.4E Fl(3)15s121m19M
Red and white chequered tower on white building 21m 277.5°-vis-169°
0338.3 **Cabo Llebeig** 39°09′.7N 02°55′.1E Fl(4)14.5s74m7M
Black and white chequered angular tower 7m
0340 **Isla Horadada** 39°12′.5N 02°58′.8E Fl(2)12s42m13M
White round tower, five black bands, on white round house 13m 047°-vis-0001°

ISLA DE CABRERA WAYPOINTS
⊕73	Puerto de Cabrera	39°09′.5N 02°55′.6E
⊕74	Between Pta de Sa Corrent &	
	Isla Redonda	39°09′.8N 02°58′.4E
⊕75	Off Islote Imperial (SE)	39°07′.5N 02°57′.7E
⊕76	Pta Anciola	39°07′.6N 02°55′.0E
⊕77	Cabo Llebeig	39°09′.7N 02°54′.9E
⊕78	Pta de la Escala	39°11′.0N 02°57′.0E
⊕79	Isla Horadada	39°12′.6N 02°58′.7E

INTRODUCTION

Cabrera is a rugged and hilly island with numerous offlying islets, stretching NNE like giant stepping stones towards Mallorca, just over 5 miles away.

The archipelago was declared a National Maritime and Terrestial Park in April 1991 by the Spanish government in order to preserve the rare indigenous plant and animal life. Access is restricted and a permit must be obtained before visiting (see below). The main island measures some 3 miles in each direction, indented by several deep bays and rising to 172m at Alto de Picamoscas. There is an excellent sheltered bay on the NW side, known as Puerto de Cabrera despite having no port facilities beyond a couple of short jetties. Anchoring is forbidden but fifty visitors' moorings have been laid. Access to the many other small, secluded anchorages is also restricted.

The only other island in the group of any size is Isla Conejera, measuring about 1 mile by 0.6 miles and separated from Isla de Cabrera by a channel 0.7 miles wide and more than 20m deep. Seven smaller islands lie N of Isla de Cabrera with others close inshore to the S. In general Isla de Cabrera and its islets are all steep-to, and in most places deep water runs close inshore.

No tourist developments, no jet-skis, no noise and only other seafarers for company: this place is as near to heaven as it gets in the Baleares!

WILDLIFE

There are several species of fauna, flora and lizards unique to the archipelago, which is also a haven for seabirds including the rare Audouins gull (see *Flora and Fauna* in the *General Introduction* above) and birds of prey such as the osprey and both peregrine and Eleonora's falcon. The surrounding waters are home to fish, turtles, dolphins, whales and a variety of corals. Booklets describing the history and wildlife of the Cabrera group are available in several languages from the Cabrera National Park Office (see below).

Permits

The National Park is administered by ICONA, the Instituto Nacional para la Conservación de la Naturaleza, whose head office is at Calle Ciudad de Queretaro s/n, 07007 Palma de Mallorca. Permits, which are dated and can be applied for between three and twenty days in advance, are issued by the Cabrera National Park Office at Plaza España 8, 07002 Palma ☎ 971 72 50 10/72 53 84 *Fax* 971 72

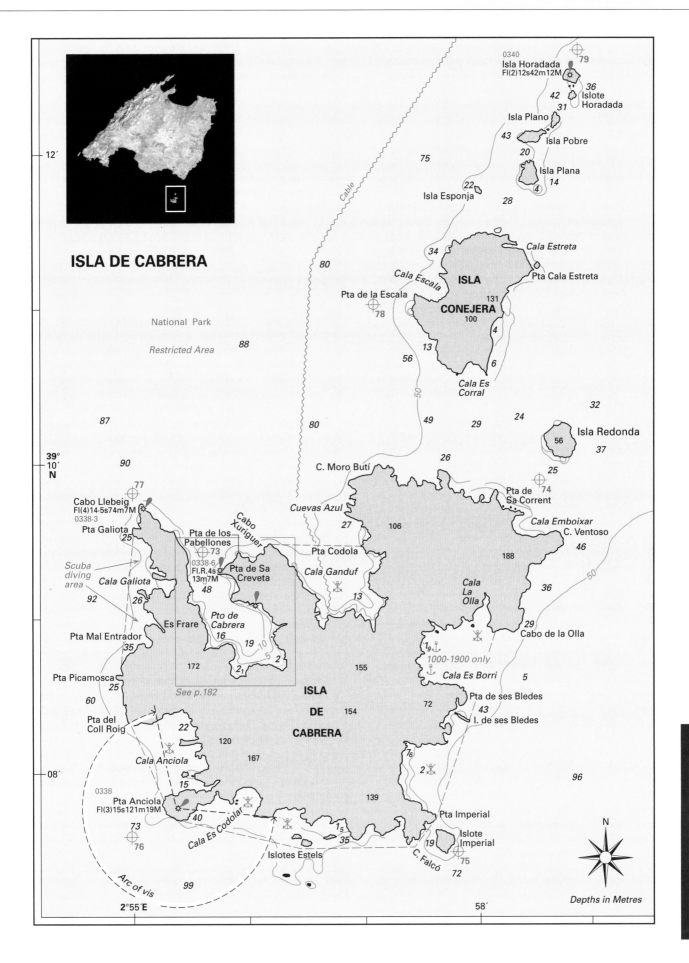

ISLA DE CABRERA

12′

National Park

Restricted Area

0340
Isla Horadada
Fl(2)12s42m12M
79
36
Islote
Horadada
42
31
Isla Plano
43
Isla Pobre
20
Isla Plana
14
Isla Esponja
22
4
28

75

Cable

80

88

87

90

Cala Estreta

Cala Escala
ISLA
CONEJERA
Pta de la Escala
78
131
100
4
13
56
6
Cala Es
Corral

50

32
Isla Redonda
56
37
24
25

39°
10′
N

49
29
26
C. Moro Butí
Pta de
Sa Corrent
74

80

77
Cabo Llebeig
Fl(4)14·5s74m7M
0338·3
Pta Galiota
25

Cabo
Xuriguer
Pta de los
Pabellones
73
0338·6
Fl.R.4s
13m7M
48
Pta de Sa
Creveta

Cuevas Azul
27
106
Pta Codola
Cala Ganduf
13

Cala Emboixar
C. Ventoso
46
188

Cala
La
Olla
36

Scuba
diving
area
Cala Galiota
92
26

Es Frare
Pto de
Cabrera
16
19

10
2

29
Cabo de la Olla
1g
1000-1900 only
Cala Es Borri
5

Pta Mal Entrador
35

172
2 1
2
155

ISLA
DE
CABRERA
154
72
Pta de ses Bledes
43
I. de ses Bledes
7 6

Pta Picamosca
25
60

Pta del
Coll Roig
22
120
167
Cala Anciola
15

0338
Pta Anciola
Fl(3)15s121m19M
40
73
76

Cala Es Codolar
Islotes Estels
35
5
139

2
7

96

Pta Imperial
19
Islote
Imperial
75
C. Falcó
72

Arc of vis
99

2°55′E

08′

58′

N

Depths in Metres

IV. ISLA DE CABRERA

See p.182

55 85 (closed at weekends and bank holidays). Nearby yacht clubs, marinas and harbourmasters in Mallorca will provide a blank Solicitud de Autorizacion and, when completed, will fax it through (a small fee is sometimes charged for this service, though the permit itself is free). Details of the yacht (registration document), skipper (passport and certificate of competence), owner and number aboard are required. A scuba-diving permit is available from the same office, though fishing is strictly prohibited. Animals may not be landed from boats and all rubbish must be taken back aboard.

No more than fifty yachts can use the harbour, Puerto de Cabrera, at any one time and visits are limited to one night in July and August, two nights in June and September and up to seven nights for the rest of the year. The permit is dated, and only valid for the date(s) shown, but if not all the buoys are occupied it may be possible to remain an extra night. (Equally, if all fifty buoys are already allocated a last minute application will be refused.) Weekends are inevitably in greatest demand.

Although sailing around the island in certain areas is allowed, nights have to be spent in the harbour on the allocated buoy.

Each permit is accompanied by a map with details of permitted daytime (1000–1900) anchorages –

currently two areas in the entrance to Puerto de Cabrera and Cala Es Borri on the E coast – and prohibited areas, which at present include Cala Ganduf, Cala Anciola, Cala Es Codolar and others on the S coast: Cala La Olla and Cala Emboixar. Even so, brief details of these *calas* are included below in case the restrictions are lifted. There is a 5-knot speed limit in the entire Maritime Park area and a 2-knot speed limit in the harbour.

The boundary of the National Park is indicated by five pillar buoys, all lit and with × topmarks, in positions 39°13′.5N 02°58′E (Fl.Y.2s5M); 39°13′.5N 03°00′E (Fl(2)Y.5M); 39°06′.5N 03°00′E (Fl.Y. 2s5M); 39°06′.5N 02°53′.5E (Fl(2)Y.5M); and 39°10′N 02°53′.5E (Fl(3)Y.5M).

HISTORY

It is probable that Isla de Cabrera (Goat Island) and Isla Conejera (Rabbit Island) were inhabited in prehistoric times: traces of an ancient building have been identified at Clot des Guix, and Roman and Byzantine ceramics and coins have also been found. The castle overlooking Puerto de Cabrera is thought to date back to the end of the 14th century and was probably built as a defence against pirates. During the Peninsular Wars some 9,000 French prisoners were interned on the island, where nearly two-thirds died of disease and starvation. They are buried near the castle and a memorial was erected in 1847 in the centre of the island.

Recent history

Prior to the first world war the island was privately owned, but was requisitioned by the Spanish government in 1915 to prevent it falling into enemy hands. A small army garrison was established (which still exists) and at various times the area has been used as a gunnery range. Landing on any of the smaller islands could be *dangerous*, due to the presence of unexploded shells or other ammunition (as well as being contrary to the rules of the park).

Tourist offices

Sightseeing is limited on Cabrera as it is a National Park, but there is a Park Information Office in the harbour (see harbour plan below). Their head office is in Palma, where permits are issued, details of which are above.

Embassies

None on Cabrera, but see *Appendix* for contact details of embassies on the other islands.

ISLA DE CABRERA NATURE RESERVE

C1 Puerto de Cabrera

This is a large sheltered bay laid with 50 buoys for which a permit must be obtained prior to entry (see note on Permits under *Tourist Offices* above)

Location
39°09'.3N 02°55'.6E

Communications
Park Information Office VHF Ch 09
☎ 971 72 50 10 *Fax* 971 72 55 85

The harbour

A large natural harbour which can be entered under virtually any conditions apart from in strong NW winds, which are rare. Shelter is good, though a swell rolls in with N or NW winds. Gusts blowing down into the harbour from the surrounding hills can also be fierce. However, in normal conditions it is one of the few truly peaceful spots in the Balearics, without jet-skis, waterskiers and speedboats, though tourist ferries from Palma and Colonia de San Jordi arrive daily in the summer.

PILOTAGE

⊕73 39°09'.5N 02°55'.6E Puerto de Cabrera

Approach

From N When approaching from this direction the chain of islands running N/S does not appear separated from Isla de Cabrera itself until quite close. Leave these islands to port, heading for a position slightly E of Cabo Lleibeig (Fl(4)14.5s 74m7M, black and white chequered angular tower 7m). The entrance lies close under this headland, with Punta de Sa Creveta (Fl.R.4s13m7M, red and white chequered angular tower 5m) to the E.

From W The hills of Isla de Cabrera can be seen from some distance away, with the line of smaller islands running towards the N visible on closer approach. Set a course to round Cabo Lleibeig, the NW tip of the island, after which the entrance will open up beyond.

From E or NE Pass either side of Isla Redonda to round Cabo Moro Butí and cross the wide and deep Cala Ganduf towards Cabo Xuriguer and Punta de los Pabellones. The entrance will open up on rounding Punta de Sa Creveta beyond.

Puerto de Cabrera. The peace and tranquility here is palpable

IV. ISLA DE CABRERA

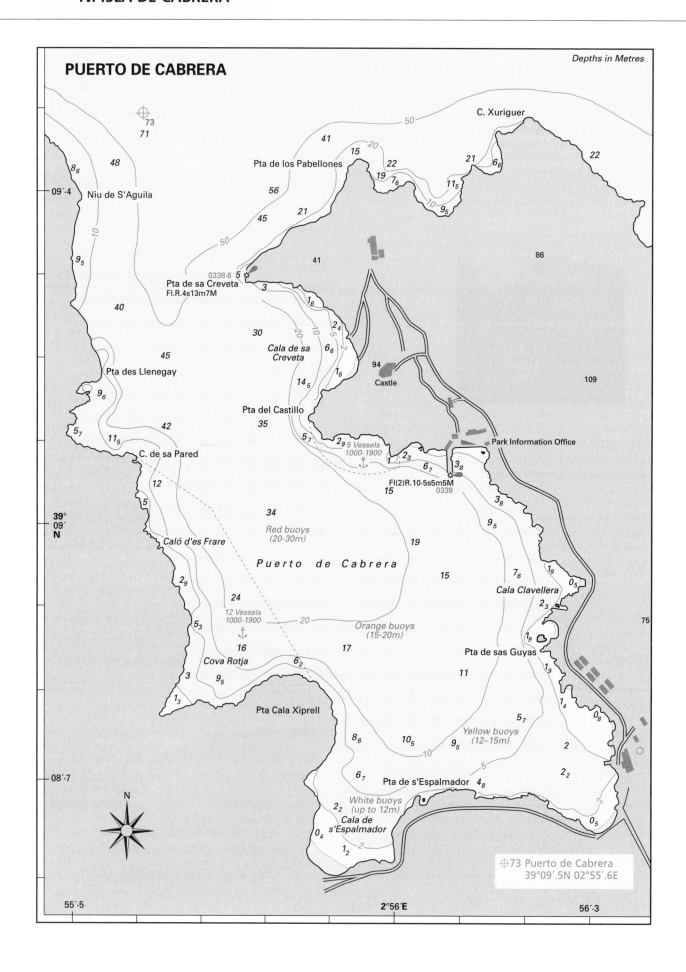

PUERTO DE CABRERA

Depths in Metres

C. Xuriguer

Pta de los Pabellones

Niu de S'Aguila

Pta de sa Creveta
Fl.R.4s13m7M

Cala de sa
Creveta

Pta del Castillo

Castle

Park Information Office

Fl(2)R.10·5s5m5M
0339

Pta des Llenegay

C. de sa Pared

Caló d'es Frare

*Red buoys
(20-30m)*

Puerto de Cabrera

Cala Clavellera

*Orange buoys
(15-20m)*

Pta de sas Guyas

Cova Rotja

12 Vessels
1000-1900

5 Vessels
1000-1900

Pta Cala Xiprell

*Yellow buoys
(12–15m)*

Pta de s'Espalmador

*White buoys
(up to 12m)*

Cala de
s'Espalmador

⊕73 Puerto de Cabrera
39°09′.5N 02°55′.6E

N

Currents

Strong wind-induced currents may be experienced around the islands, the direction and strength dependent on that of the wind.

Entrance

The entrance, which is deep but relatively narrow, lies between Cabo Llebeig and Punta de Sa Creveta. Wind conditions in both the entrance and harbour can be very fluky due to the high surrounding hills. Mooring buoys lie S of a line between Cabo de sa Pared and Punta del Castillo. As well as the 5-knot speed limit in the entire Maritime Park area there is a 2-knot speed limit in the harbour itself.

Berthing

Lying alongside the jetty is only possible with a military permit or in an emergency.

Moorings

Secure to one of the fifty visitors' moorings, colour-coded according to yacht size as follows:

White   up to 12m
Yellow   12–15m
Orange   15–20m
Red   20–30m

No charge is made for mooring use. Smaller yacht moorings are tucked into Cala de s'Espalmador and are the most sheltered but also furthest from the main (NE) jetty, the only place where landing is permitted.

Secure to the mooring by putting a loop of line through the eye on the end of the mooring rope and paying out until the pick-up buoy is back in the water. If it is left out of the water the guard will correct it.

Anchoring

Anchoring in the harbour is generally forbidden. However, a current relaxation to the rule allows for 12 vessels to anchor between the hours of 1000 and 1900 on the W side of the harbour between C. de sa Pared and Pta Cala Xiprell and for five craft on the E side in the cove SE of Pta del Castillo, as marked on the plan.

A third anchorage available between these hours lies in Cala Es Borri, on the E side of the island, described below.

Formalities

A guard visits each yacht every evening to check that a valid permit is held. Landing by dinghy is only allowed at the main jetty, and the permit must be shown at the Park Information Office on embarking ashore. Scuba permits should also be presented before diving.

Facility

Water Small quantities of non-drinking water can usually be collected from the army *cantina* (take containers).

Sights ashore

It was once possible to roam over the island unsupervised, but yachtsmen, having landed on the main jetty, are now restricted to the road by the foreshore and a walk to the castle. All other walks (minimum four people) are conducted by Park Rangers at designated times available from the Park Information Office.

The walk up the steep track leading to the castle ruins will be rewarded with spectacular views and it is also possible to visit the memorial to the French prisoners of war.

The Cuevas Azul (Blue Caves) in Cala Ganduf some 600m S-SW of Cabo Moro Butí are also most attractive but are only accessible by sea. Anchoring in the *cala* is not permitted, but at some 1.4 miles from the buoys in Puerto de Cabrera, a visit by dinghy is feasible.

There are a few houses near the S mole, some used by the owners of the sheep and pigs pastured on the island which keep the vegetation down.

Eating out

The army *cantina* welcomes visitors and has a bar, though food is not available.

ANCHORAGES AROUND CABRERA

⚓ CALA ES BORRI
39°08'.7N 02°57'.5E

This is the only anchorage currently available to yachts, apart from those within Puerto de Cabrera (above). All are restricted to use between 1000 and 1900 daily. Anchor in the central and southern parts of the bay. Cala Es Borri is actually the small inlet at its SW corner. No more than twenty boats can be present at any one time in the *cala*.

Anchor as space permits in 5m+ over sand and rock, open to the E quadrant and to swell from the S. There is a fine sandy beach in Cala Es Borri itself.

Calas and features around Isla de Cabrera

Anchoring is prohibited in the *calas* listed below. Some, as noted, can be sailed in, whereas others can only be admired from afar. These brief details are included for interest.

CALA GANDUF
39°09'.2N 02°56'.7E

A protected and deep bay with several separate indentations, open for sailing, but nothing more.

Passage between Isla de Cabrera and Isla Redonda

⊕74 39°09'.8N 02°58'.4E Between Pta de Sa Corrent and Isla Redonda

An 800m wide passage with a minimum depth of 21m. Transit in a NW-SE direction.

CALA EMBOIXAR

39°09´.6N 02°58´.3E

An attractive small bay under cliffs, with a rocky ledge looking like a breakwater to the NW. Open for sailing, but not for anchoring. There are two small beaches, one rocky and one of sand.

CABO VENTOSO (CAP VENTÓS)

39°09´.5N 02°58´.6E

A high (188m), steep, rocky-cliffed promontory with good water at its base.

CALA LA OLLA

39°09´.0N 02°57´.9E

An interesting *cala* amidst wild scenery at the mouth of the eastern of two small calas, themselves at the northern end of a wide bay. Sailing (only) allowed in the *cala*. Several islets lie close to the W.

⚓ CALA ES BORRI

39°08´.7N 02°57´.5E

This *cala* is restricted, currently allowing anchoring between the hours of 1000 and 1900 daily. Note, however, that restricted anchoring zones change from time to time.

Cala Es Borri looking N. Isla Redonda in view over peninsula with Isla Conejera left top of photo. Isla Plana and Mallorca just in view

⊕75 39°07´.5N 02°57´.7E Off Islote Imperial (SE)

Passage between Islote Imperial and Isla de Cabrera

A 100m wide, 18m deep, passage between dramatic cliffs, for use in settled weather.

Sailing is permitted along the S coast from Islote Imperial W to Punta Anciola.

ISLOTES ESTELS

39°07´.3N 02°56´.4E (Southernmost: Estels de Fuera)

Five scattered, rocky islands up to 750m off the S coast of Isla de Cabrera.

PUNTA ANCIOLA

39°07´.8N 02°55´.3E

⊕76 39°07´.6N 02°55´.0E Pta Anciola

A rounded headland connected to Isla Cabrera by a low, narrow neck. The paintwork on its lighthouse (Fl(3)15s121m19M, red and white chequered tower on white building 21m) may well be unique.

N OF PUNTA MAL ENTRADOR

39°09´.1N 02°55´.1E

A small bay open to the western quadrant. This area is currently reserved for licensed scuba diving.

CALA GALIOTA
39°09′.2N 02°55′.3E

An attractive *cala* under high cliffs. As above, Cala Galiota is also part of an area restricted for licensed Scuba diving.

CABO LLEBEIG 39°09′.7N 02°55′.1E
⊕77 39°09′.7N 02°54′.9E Cabo Llebeig

A large (60m) conspicuous rocky hummock with a not very prominent lighthouse (Fl(4)14.5s74m7M, black and white chequered angular tower 7m).

The smaller islands of the Isla de Cabrera group

ISLA REDONDA
Centred on 39°10′.1N 02°58′.6E

A roughly circular island some 450m in diameter and 56m high. No anchorages or landing allowed.

Passage between Isla Redonda and Isla Conejera

A 1,000m-wide passage with a minimum depth of 20m.

ISLA CONEJERA (ILLA DES CONILLS)
Centred on 39°11′.1N 02°57′.9E

The second-largest island at 1 mile long by 0.6 miles wide and reaching 131m high. There are potential landing places on the E coast and several *calas* (see below) but their use is currently prohibited.

CALA ES CORRAL, ISLA CONEJERA
39°10′.6N 02°57′.9E

Two small *calas* side by side at the S end of the island. There are two small offlying islets on either side.

⊕78 39°11′.0N 02°57′.0E Pta de la Escala

Passage between Isla Conejera and Isla Esponja or Isla Plana

A passage 400m wide, with a minimum depth of 11m if midway between Isla Conejera and the two smaller islands.

ISLA ESPONJA
39°11′.7N 02°57′.9E

200m by 40m, and 23m high, Isla Esponja is steep-to and inaccessible.

ISLA PLANA
39°11′.8N 02°58′.4E

400m by 125m, 26m high.

Passage between Isla Plana and Isla Pobre

A 150m wide passage with depths shoaling to 2.5m.

ISLA POBRE
39°12′.1N 02°58′.4E

400m by 100m, 27m high.

Passage between Isla Pobre and Isla Plano

Foul.

ISLA PLANO (ILLOT PLÁ)
39°12′.2N 02°58′.6E

200m by 100m, 27m high.

Passage between Isla Plano and Islote Horadada

A passage 200m wide with 12m minimum depth.

ISLOTE HORADADA (ILLOT FORADADA OR FORADAT)
39°12′.3N 02°58′.8E

100m by 80m, 12m high.

Passage between Islote Horadada and Isla Horadada

Foul.

ISLA HORADADA (ILLA FORADADA OR FORADAT)
39°12′.5N 02°58′.8E

210m by 120m and 42m high, with a lighthouse (Fl(2)12s42m13M, white round tower with five black bands on white round house 13m) on its summit.

⊕79 39°12′.6N 02°58′.7E Isla Horadada N

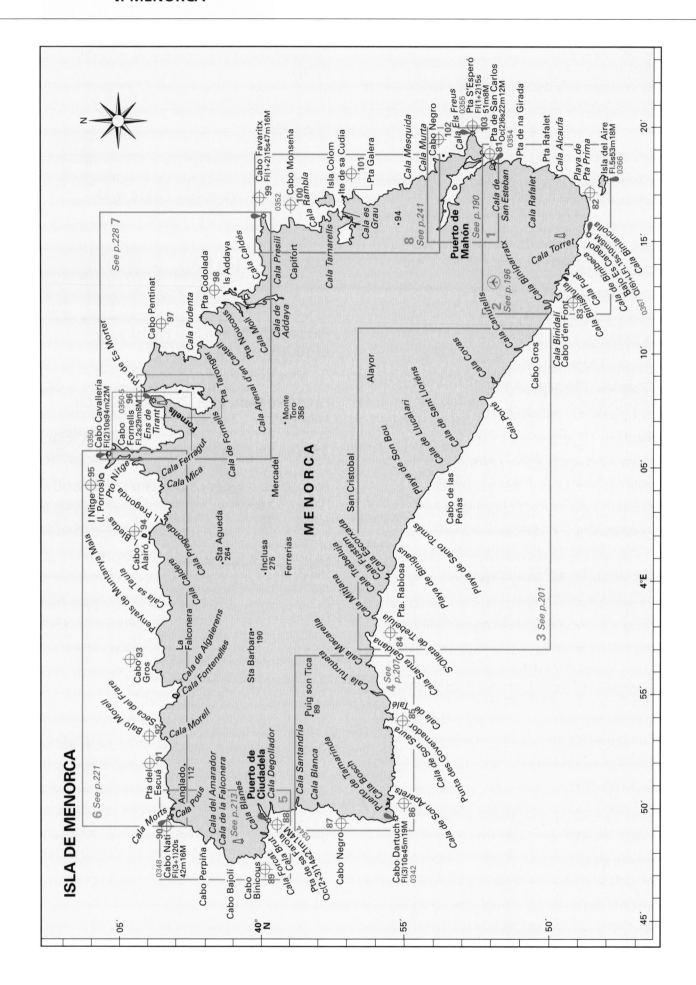

V. Menorca

SECTIONS

The coastline is considered in a clockwise direction around the island beginning at Puerto de Mahón

MENORCA WAYPOINTS

⊕81	Puerto de Mahón fairway	39°52′.0N 04°18′.6E
⊕82	Isla del Aire Passage	39°48′.4N 04°17′.0E
⊕83	Off Cabo D'en Font	39°49′.1N 04°12′.1E
⊕84	Cala Santa Galdana	39°56′.0N 03°57′.4E
⊕85	Cala Son Saura	39°55′.1N 03°53′.6E
⊕86	Puerto de Tamarinda	39°55′.4N 03°50′.1E
⊕87	Off Cabo Negro	39°57′.2N 03°49′.1E
⊕88	Puerto de Ciudadela	39°59′.6N 03°49′.5E
⊕89	Cabo Binicous (de Banyos)	40°00′.0N 03°47′.1E
⊕90	Cabo Nati	40°03′.1N 03°49′.0E
⊕91	Punta del Escuá	40°03′.8N 03°52′.0E
⊕92	Bajo Morell rock	40°04′.0N 03°53′.0E
⊕93	Off Cabo Gros	40°04′.7N 03°56′.0E
⊕94	Isla Bledas N	40°04′.7N 04°01′.9E
⊕95	Off Isla Nitge	40°05′.8N 04°04′.1E
⊕96	Puerto de Fornells	40°04′.0N 04°08′.0E
⊕97	Cabo Pentinat	40°03′.6N 04°10′.6E
⊕98	Addaya Approach	40°01′.4N 04°12′.4E
⊕99	Cabo Favaritx	39°59′.8N 04°16′.4E
⊕100	Cabo Monseña	39°59′.1N 04°16′.4E
⊕101	Punta Galera	39°56′.7N 04°17′.5E
⊕102	Cabo Negro	39°54′.0N 04°18′.7E
⊕103	Punta S'Esperó	39°52′.6N 04°19′.9E

The oldest of the Balearic islands, Menorca abounds in ancient monuments and relics. It also boasts the largest natural harbour, Mahón, offering excellent berthing and nautical facilities as well as historical sites to visit. There is a strong British influence because of their previous occupations of the island. There are 4 other ports, and numerous delightful bays in which to sojourn, only a few miles apart.

NAVIGATIONAL INFORMATION FOR APPROACHES TO MENORCA

Menorca is an excellent departure point when heading E and NE to France, Italy or to Corsica and Sardinia. Space for berthing in Puerto de Mahón while awaiting favourable winds can be found, even in summer. Unlike the other islands, it is less crowded and often cheaper.

Magnetic variation

Negligable: 0°23′W decreasing 6′E annually

Approach and coastal passage charts

(See *Appendix* for full list of Balearic charts).

Imray	M3
Admiralty	1703, 2833
Spanish	48E, 6A, 428A
French	5505, 7117

Approach lights

0355 **Punta S'Esperó** 39°52′.7N 04°19′.7E Fl(1+2)15s51m8M White round tower, two black bands, on white building 11m

0354 **Punta de San Carlos** 39°52′N 04°18′.5E Oc(2)6s22m12M White round tower, three black bands, on square white base 15m 183°-vis-143°

0366 **Isla del Aire** 39°48′N 04°17′.6E Fl.5s53m18M White tower, black bands, on white building 38m 197°-vis-111°

0367 **Bajo d'es Caragol** 39°48′.6N 04°15′.3E Q(6)+LFl.15s10m5M South cardinal beacon with s topmark 10m

0342 **Cabo Dartuch (D'Artrutx)** 39°55′.4N 03°49′.5E Fl(3)10s45m19M White tower, three black bands, on white building 34m 267°-vis-158°

0348 **Cabo Nati** 40°03′.1N 03°49′.5E Fl(3+1)20s42m16M White tower, aluminium cupola, on white building with red roof 19m 039°-vis-162°

Note The characteristics of Cabo Nati are very similar to those of Cabo Formentor, Mallorca

0350 **Cabo Cavallería** 40°05′.3N 04°05′.5E Fl(2)10s94m22M White tower and building 15m 074°-vis-292° Racon

0352 **Cabo Favaritx** 39°59′.8N 4°16′E Fl(1+2)15s47m16M White tower, black diagonal stripes, on white building 28m

Ancient monastery with a church built in 1595 on the highest point in Menorca, Mount Toro

INTRODUCTION

Twenty miles ENE of Mallorca lies Menorca. It is the most easterly of the Islas Baleares and is 26 miles long and 11 miles wide. It is not as mountainous as the other two main islands, being for the most part a low plateau with a few small hills near the N coast and the lone Monte Toro (358m) near the centre of the island. This 'mountain' can be seen from afar and makes a useful landmark.

Geologically the island is interesting, in that it consists of two parts. That N of a line drawn from near Cala Morell to Mahón is the oldest part of the Islas Baleares and was apparently originally joined to Corsica, mainland Europe and Catalonia. The southern part of the island was created later by a process of overlaying and folding: part of the same upheaval which formed the Alps. Menorca was also the first of the Baleares to become separated as an island, but this was much later. It lies in the path of the NW *tramontana* or *mestral* gales and is sometimes referred to as the 'Windy Isle'. The N coast is dangerous when this wind is blowing and should be given a wide berth.

Viewed from offshore many parts of Menorca have a barren appearance, due to the rocky cliffs, despite a considerable amount of arable and wooded land behind the coast. However, these cliffs are broken by innumerable *calas* which offer many attractive anchorages.

Puerto de Mahón (Maó) on the E coast is the major port and can be entered under most conditions. On the W coast lies the much smaller (and often very crowded) Puerto de Ciudadela, which offers shelter in all conditions other than westerly or southwesterly gales. The remaining harbours should not be entered with strong onshore winds and are mostly very uncomfortable, if not downright dangerous, at such times. Cala de Addaya is a notable exception, offering excellent shelter once inside, though the entrance itself may become impassable.

Menorca has noticeably fewer tourist developments than the other Islas Baleares, and where such facilities exist they generally cater more for the 'quality' than the 'quantity' market. It is certainly less commercialised than the other islands. Mahón is, to a certain extent, an exception because it has been an important naval base for many years and has absorbed the influences, habits and behaviour of the various occupying forces (including the British who were there for much of the 18th century). The island population is currently some 60,000, of whom more than a third live in either Mahón or Ciudadela. Local industries of long standing include leatherwork (mainly shoes), jewellery, and the production of a hard mature cheese which is enjoyed throughout Spain.

Although not as spectacularly beautiful as much of Mallorca, Menorca has its own attractions and has much to offer those who prefer to avoid major centres of tourism.

For the serious navigator interested in cruising around the coast of Menorca the book *Menorca; Atlas Náutico* by Alfonso Buenaventura is an absolute must, as it shows the coastline in 67 chartlets in extreme detail.

There is a growing tendency in some of the calas, as in mainland Spain, to exclude pleasure craft entirely by laying swimmer buoys in high season. In general this applies mainly to *calas* having adjacent hotels: the bigger the hotel, it seems, the greater the exclusion.

HISTORY

Menorca has the greatest concentration of prehistoric remains in the entire Mediterranean, including what is claimed to be the oldest building in Europe. There are a number of Neolithic caves and villages on the island and many megalithic monuments such as *talayots* (towers), *navetas* (burial mounds) and *taulas* (T-shaped monuments) – probably built for religious and funerary purposes by the Bronze Age civilisation which inhabited the land before the Iberians established themselves. Unfortunately very little has been discovered about this Bronze Age tribe, or about the construction and use of the 400 or so large buildings and monuments which are scattered around the island.

In due course, as in large parts of the Mediterranean basin, Menorca saw successive waves of invasion and colonisation by Phoenicians, Carthaginians, Greeks, Romans, Vandals, Byzantines, Visigoths and Moors. During the occupation by the Carthaginians the towns of Maguén (Mahón) and Yamma (Ciudadela) were founded, though doubtless both inlets had been used by seafarers since time immemorial. The period of Roman occupation from 123BC to AD427 was relatively peaceful and prosperous, Mahón

Prehistoric remains at Torralba d'en Salord, near Cala en Porter   GW

becoming Municipio Flavio Magontano and Ciudadela, Lamnona. Amongst other legacies, the Romans built the island's first road system.

The successive waves of invasion and colonisation by Vandals, Byzantines and Visigoths left fewer permanent traces. After many years of raids, the island was finally occupied by the Moors in about 913. They remained until driven out by King Alfonso III of Aragon in 1287, by which time Menorca was the last Muslim territory in eastern Spain, although in theory it had owed allegiance to the crown of Aragon since 1232. The common prefix 'Bini', as in Binidalí and Binibeca, is from the Arabic, meaning 'belonging to the son of'.

The following centuries were even more difficult for the islanders, with devastating pirate raids, droughts and epidemics. In 1535 Mahón lost much of its population to a raid by the Turkish pirate Barbarossa, in 1558 it was the turn of Ciudadela, which withstood a nine-day siege before being overrun and almost completely destroyed by a force of 15,000 Turks.

Due to the strategic position of Mahón as a naval base in the western Mediterranean, it was coveted by all maritime nations and Menorca changed hands frequently. In 1708 it was occupied by the British, who had supported the Carlist cause in the War of the Spanish Succession, and in 1713 the island was officially ceded by the Treaty of Utrecht (as was Gibraltar). One of their most lasting legacies was the road built by the Governor, Sir Richard Kane, from Ciudadela to Mahón – the first good road linking the two towns since Roman times – and his moving of the capital from Ciudadela to Mahón in 1722. The island remained in British hands for more than forty years, during which Mahón grew as a fortified naval base and the island prospered.

In 1756 a French army landed near Ciudadela and marched across the island to lay siege to the fortress of San Felipe, near Mahón, which was eventually forced to surrender. It was following this episode that the unfortunate Admiral Byng was executed by firing squad at Portsmouth, on the quarterdeck of HMS *Monarque*, for failing to engage the French fleet and thereby lift the siege. This provoked Voltaire's famous quip: '*Dans ce pays-ci, il est bon de tuer de temps en temps un amiral pour encourager les autres.*' ('In this country, it is wise from time to time to kill an admiral in order to encourage the others').

However, the French only held the island until 1763 when it was returned to Britain by the Treaty of Paris.

Richelieu, who had commanded the successful French invasion in 1756, had a sauce called *mahon-ésa* – based on the local *aïoli* (*alioli*) sauce – served at the victory banquet in Paris. This delicacy, which his chef had invented while on the island, has become the ubiquitous 'mayonnaise'.

In 1782 a Franco-Spanish force once more laid siege to the garrison, which after another heroic resistance was forced to surrender. Not surprisingly one of the first things the victors did was to demolish the fortress, first built in the 1500s as a defence against Corsairs. Sixteen years later the British recaptured the island but had to return it to Spain in 1802 under the Treaty of Amiens. A direct result of this ongoing rivalry was the construction of forts and other large defensive works in and around the port of Mahón, many of which are still to be seen. Under Spanish rule the island reverted to a simple pastoral and fishing existence, though in 1830 the French were permitted to establish a base at Mahón for use during their campaign in Algeria. The limited opportunities and employment for young people during the 19th century encouraged emigration, particularly to the W coast of America. During the Spanish Civil War Menorca remained in the hands of the Republicans and much damage was done to the island's churches.

Recent history

Only recently has any attempt been made to cater for the tourist trade, but today considerable development can be seen, bringing not only income but outside influences and values into the lives of the islanders.

TOURIST INFORMATION

Places of interest in Menorca

In addition to the places of interest described in the harbour sections there are many other sites inland which can be visited by taxi, bus or on foot. One not to be missed is Monte Toro, near the village of Es Mercadal, for the panoramic view, the church (built in 1595) and the restored 17th-century monastery founded by Augustine monks. The name Monte Toro comes not from the Spanish 'Bull Mount', but from Arabic 'The Highest (point)' which indeed it is, at 358 metres.

Of the many Megalithic remains, the following are easy to reach from the two main harbours:

- 1 mile S of Mahón, the *taula* and *talayot* of Trapuco: a megalithic tower and monument
- 2 miles SW of Mahón, the *talayot* of Torellonet (near the airport)
- 5 miles W of Mahón, the Torralba group of *taulas* (T-shaped monuments)
- 3 miles E of Ciudadela, the *naveta* burial mound at Nau d'es Tudóns (claimed to be the oldest building in Europe)
- 4 miles E of Ciudadela, the *poblado* and *taulas* of Torre Llafuda
- 4 miles S of Ciudadela, the *talayot* of Son Olivaret.

The Euro-Map of Mallorca, Menorca, Ibiza published by GeoCenter International shows many of the historic and prehistoric sites, as does a multilingual map available locally.

For details of tourist offices see *General Introduction*.

Embassies

For details of embassies see *Appendix*.

1. Puerto de Mahón to Punta de San Carlos

ME1 Puerto de Mahón (Maó)

A long and deep *cala* leads into a natural and well protected harbour hosting a naval base, fishing fleet and many yachting facilities along its shores, with berthing for over 1,000 vessels

Location
39°52´.1N 04°18´.6E

Communications
Pilots (Mahón Prácticos) VHF Ch 12, 14, 16, 20, 27
Port authority ☎ 971 22 81 50 *Fax* 971 72 69 48
Puerto de Mahón ☎ 971 35 48 44
Fax 971 35 43 27
Email portsdebaleares@portsdebalears.com
www.portsdebalears.com
See text for further internet information on other options

The port

An attractive and interesting commercial, naval, fishing and yachting port up a long deep *cala*. The approach and entrance are straightforward and entry can be made in storm conditions, with good shelter available once inside. There are excellent facilities for yachtsmen including a first-class, expensive yacht club and many lesser facilities.

PILOTAGE

Approach

⊕81 39°52´.10N 4°18´.6E Puerto de Mahón fairway

From S The tall lighthouse on Isla del Aire (Fl.5s53m18M, white tower with black bands on white building 38m), 4M S of the *cala* entrance is easily identified and the island can safely be left on either side. The few hazards between Isla del Aire

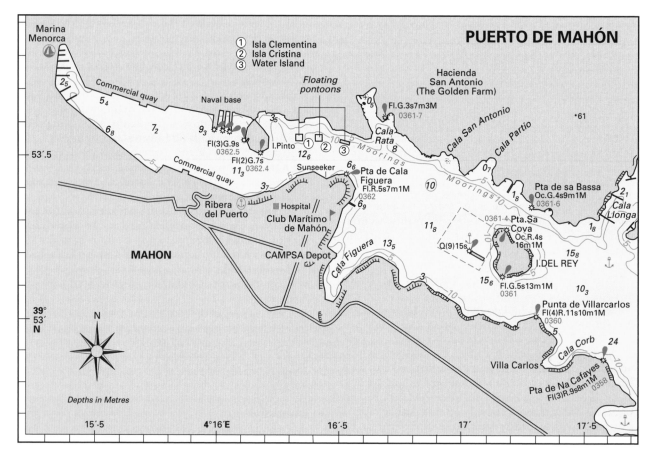

and Puerto de Mahón will be avoided by following a track at least 250m off Punta Rafalet and Punta de Na Girada. The lighthouse (Oc(2)6s22m12M, white tower with three black bands on square white base 15m) and nearby radio towers on Punta de San Carlos are also conspicuous, and the high (78m) peninsula of La Mola ahead easily recognised. The harbour entrance lies between the two.

From N From Cabo Favaritx (Fl(1+2)15s47m16M, white tower with black diagonal stripes on white building 28m) southwards the coast is very broken; Isla Colom may be recognised if sailing inshore. The high peninsula of La Mola (78m) with buildings on its summit and a lighthouse on Punta del Esperó (Fl(1+2)15s51m8M, white tower with two black bands on white building 11m) are conspicuous from this direction. The entrance to Puerto de Mahón lies just beyond.

Currents

There is normally a SW current past the entrance to Puerto de Mahón. N or NE winds increase its speed while winds from S or SW either slow or reverse the flow.

Anchorages in the approach

Just S of the entrance lies Cala de San Esteban. To the N lie Clot de la Mola and Cala Taulera. Clot de la Mola is a small horseshoe bay with 10m over rock and stone, exposed to the S quadrant. Cala Taulera, in contrast, is a long narrow inlet between La Mola and Isla del Lazareto, offering total protection in 6m or less over sand though shallow along its N edge. If coming from the E, turn in close past Laja de Fuera buoy to avoid the spit running out from the S end of Isla del Lazareto. The *cala* can easily accommodate

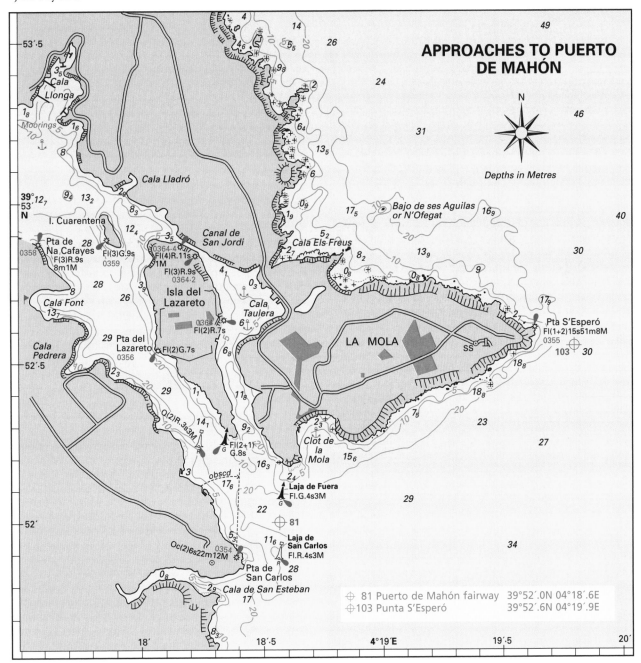

APPROACHES TO PUERTO DE MAHÓN

Depths in Metres

| ⊕ 81 Puerto de Mahón fairway | 39°52′.0N 04°18′.6E |
| ⊕ 103 Punta S'Esperó | 39°52′.6N 04°19′.9E |

Approach to Mahón looking NW. Pta de San Carlos left, La Mola right and Isla del Lazareto all clearly seen, along with buoys

twenty or thirty yachts at anchor and is popular with both visitors and locals even though a charge is sometimes made. Avoid the W side of the *cala* as this is used, at speed, by the tourist boats. An artificial channel, the Canal de San Jordi (sometimes referred to as Canal del Lazareto) provides a 'back door' into the harbour. The canal has a minimum depth of 3m and there are no overhead wires.

Cala Taulera viewed from SSW over Isla del Lazareto

Entrance

Enter Puerto de Mahón on a NW course between the high peninsula of La Mola to starboard and the low rocky-cliffed Punta de San Carlos to port. Lit buoys mark the channel, which is used by commercial vessels of some size and should offer a yacht no difficulties, day or night, provided the buoyage is complied with. However, note that Mahón is a naval, ferry and commercial port and that these vessels have right of way over yachts and small craft. A 3-knot speed limit is in force throughout the *cala* and harbour, but beware of speeding ferries, port officials and motor craft who ignore it.

Sea levels

The sea level falls prior to and during strong winds from SW, W and NW.

Note: charted depths

Editions of BA charts 2833 pre 1997 show incorrect depths for Mahón. Subsequent editions have been corrected.

Berthing options

Other than a very few visitors' berths offered by the *club marítimo* and Sunseeker Menorca, nearly all yacht berthing in the port is now controlled by Ribera del Puerto SL, licensed by the harbour authorities to administer visitors' berths and moorings. They have four principal berthing areas:

Cala Llonga looking SE over entrance to Mahón

a. Stern-to on the quayside just E of their office (see plan), lines tailed to quay.

b. Two floating 'islands' Isla Clementina and Isla Cristina, moored E of Isla Pinto. They can take 25 and 18 yachts respectively, moored stern-to (lazy lines are provided). A rubbish collection service is provided and electricity is available. Water is now dispensed from a third small island to the E of the above pair – it is not for mooring to; simply fill up with water and leave. Sometimes a long hose is rigged to the floating islands for convenience.

c. Five pontoons in Cala Llonga, able to take 100 yachts up to 15m. Rubbish collection is laid on and water, electricity and showers are available.

d. The designated anchorage area, just W of Isla del Rey, now has a long pontoon, with lazy lines attached, which smaller craft (up to 15m) are encouraged to use instead of anchoring. Anchoring in the area is now reserved for 20m+ boats. The pontoon is now lit with Q(9)15s2m1M on a 1m yellow structure.

Ribera yacht berthing VHF Ch 09
Ribera del Puerto sl ☎ 971 35 48 44 *Fax* 971 35 43 27
Email ribera@riberadelpuerto.com
www.riberadelpuerto.com

- **Sunseeker Menorca** They have a small pontoon and some stern-to berths on the quay outside their office just W of Punta de Cala Figuera and another small pontoon down by the floating restaurant. Although very busy in high season they are always worth contacting for possible berths.

Sunseeker Menorca ☎ 971 35 33 20 *Fax* 971 35 33 50
Email sales@sunseeker.com
www.sunseeker.com

- **Club Marítimo de Mahón** Their mooring area extends from the Punta de Cala Figuera down to their fuelling berth near the S end of Cala Figuera. They have a small pier and floating pontoons but all their moorings are occupied by local members

and there is seldom room for visitors. Anchoring is no longer permitted in the *cala*.

Club Marítimo ☎ 971 36 50 22 *Fax* 971 36 07 62
Email cmahon@terra.es
www.clubmaritimomahon.com

- **Marina Menorca** A newish yacht harbour in the extreme W end of the harbour. It has berths for at least 100 yachts of up to 15m, though many of the slots will be for smaller boats with less draught. Water and electricity are available on the pontoons. This is the furthest marina from the city. Staff are on duty from 0800 to 2100 daily.

VHF Ch 09 or Ch 69
☎ 971 35 98 21
www.marinamenorca.com

- **Pedro's Boat Centre** has a large hardstanding area. It has a fleet of fast RIBs and is always willing to help out in emergencies, though not offering berthing as previously.

☎ 971 36 69 53 *Fax* 971 36 24 55
www.pedrosboatcentre.com

- **Public Quay** The Port Authority, which runs the public quay not already leased to the firms mentioned above, will not allow yachts to berth on the quay as it is now for commercial and ferry traffic only.

- Several private moorings lie along the *cala* between the Commercial Quay and Marina Menorca. It is sometimes possible to find an empty berth in this area and negotiate a price if the owner returns.

Mooring buoys

Private moorings occupy most of the northern shore, with some visitors' moorings (bright yellow) off Cala Llonga, around Cala Partio and off Cala Rata, extending westwards toward Isla Clementina. All are administered by Ribera del Puerto SL. A rubbish collection service is provided and there is a dinghy landing stage E of the Ribera del Puerto office (a floating restaurant is currently moored to the end of the pontoon).

There are new mooring areas in Cala Font (Fons) and Cala Corp (Corb) which are understood to be administered by Ribera.

Anchorages within the cala

- In Cala Taulera just inside the entrance to the harbour (see *Anchorages in the approach*) for which a charge is sometimes made

- In the designated anchorage close W of Isla del Rey (see plan) for craft over 20m. Again there is a fee, but this includes rubbish collection and use of a dinghy landing stage in Cala Figuera

- In the mouth of Cala Llonga, outside the moorings.

Prohibited anchorages

Anchoring is prohibited everywhere other than the three areas mentioned above.

Viewed from S, Cala Fonts, Cala Llonga, Cala Pedrera

Facilities

Water At the Club Marítimo; on the quay near both the Sunseeker Menorca and Ribera del Puerto offices; at the western end of the commercial quay; on Isla Clementina and its sister island; on the pontoons in Cala Llonga; on the pontoons at Marina Menorca; from the Club Náutico de Villacarlos at the head of Cala Font. Water is metered other than on the commercial quay, where it is coin-operated. The minimum charge can be quite high for small quantities.

Electricity At the Sunseeker Menorca berths, on Isla Clementina and the pontoons in Cala Llonga, and Marina Menorca.

Fuel Diesel and paraffin from the CAMPSA depot on the W side of Cala Figuera (where bunkering facilities are also available). At first sight the CAMPSA depot does not look like a fuel station. Diesel and petrol from the Club Marítimo.

Viewed from S: Cala Figuera across to Cala Rata. Rafts and moorings on far side of bay

Bottled gas Camping Gaz is readily available in chandleries and hardware stores.

Provisioning Small supermarket behind the Ribera del Puerto office. Larger one near the CAMPSA depot and another just up the hill from Cala Fonts. The largest supermarkets are on the industrial estates outside the town. General shops of every description are to be found in Mahón. Excellent produce and fish markets near the large church of Santa María, open every morning except Sunday.

Ice From the Club Marítimo and Sunseeker Menorca as well as nearby bars and supermarkets.

Chandlery There are several chandlers around the commercial quay area. Some items from Sunseeker Menorca. It is possible to berth for an hour or so near the chandleries on the commerial quay to load heavy items.

Charts From the chandlers; however, there is no official Spanish chart agent in Menorca.

Repairs Major repairs to wood, GRP and aluminium hulls can be undertaken by local yards. Both Ribera del Puerto and Sunseeker Menorca are willing to assist in arranging repairs or maintenance. Pedro's Boat Centre, opposite the new Marina Menorca, has a large area of hardstanding.

There are two travel-lifts (50 and 35-tonne capacity) and a mobile crane at Pedro's Boat Centre. Several more cranes on the commercial quays. Sunseeker Menorca has a 12-ton crane, the Club Marítimo has 10 and 2-tonne models, also a slipway. There is a slipway on the W side of Cala Figuera, 20-tonnes and 14m maximum (enquire at Ribera del Puerto or Sunseeker Menorca regarding its use).

Engineers Many around the harbour, including the English-run Marine & Auto Power ☎ 971 35 44 38 and MenMar ☎ 971 35 48 35 *Fax* 971 35 33 50.
Official service agents include the following (telephone and fax numbers should be prefixed 971).)
Sunseeker Menorca ☎ 35 33 20 *Fax* 36 50 95 – Volvo Penta; Auto Recambios Union ☎ 36 01 13 – Yamaha; Motonáutica Menorca ☎ 36 89 17 *Fax* 35 27 25 – Detroit diesel, Honda, Man, Mariner, Perkins; NauticCentreMenorca ☎ 36 05 50 *Fax* 35 12 50 – Ecosse, Mercury/MerCruiser, Solé diesel, Yanmar; Nautic Reynes ☎ 36 59 52 *Fax* 35 34 98 – Force, Mariner, Mercury/MerCruiser, Yanmar; Pedro's Boat Centre ☎ 36 69 68 *Fax* 36 24 55 – Mercury/MerCruiser.

Electronic & radio repairs Enquire at Ribera del Puerto or Sunseeker Menorca.

Sailmaker At the Club Marítimo.

Yacht clubs The Club Marítimo de Mahón has now completed rebuilding and is a magnificent building with showers, toilets, restaurant and all facilities. The Club Náutico de Villacarlos *Fax* 36 58 84 at the head of Cala Font is a smaller concern, offering a bar and water but no berths.

Showers At the Club Marítimo and Ribera del Puerto building. Also on the pontoons in Cala Llonga and on Isla Clementina (outdoor shower). Showers in a portacabin are also available at Marina Menorca.

Launderette Several in the town, also at the Club Marítimo and in the Ribera del Puerto building.

Banks Several banks in the town, mostly with credit card facilities.

Hospital In the town.

Looking W across Isla Pinto to Marina Menorca and the
commercial port   *GW*

Transport

Car hire/taxis Numerous car hire and taxi companies.
Buses Bus service to Ciudadela and elsewhere.
Ferries To Palma and mainland Spain.
Air services Smallish international airport, with services
direct to major capitals, less than 3 miles SW of
Mahón.

History

The whole area is steeped in history, some of it from
the British occupation.

The ancient Portús Magonis (Mahón) was once
thought to have been named after Mago, the
younger brother of Hannibal, who founded it in
about 206BC. There is, however, no evidence for this
and the name could also have come from the
Phoenician *maguén* meaning 'shield' or 'fortress',
which would have been equally apt. Due to its
excellent harbour and its position in the centre of the
Mediterranean, Mahón has been a prize that many
nations have coveted, and traces of the long British
occupation during the 18th century are
unmistakable. Many of the older streets and houses
with sash windows have a very English appearance,
and various English words have gained a place in the
Menorquín language. There is even a gin distillery
near the harbour. The island changed hands six
times between 1708 and 1802 and each time it was
Mahón that was the prize.

During the last period of British occupation Lord
Nelson, who was in temporary command of the
Mediterranean Fleet, spent a few days at the Golden
Farm on the N side of the harbour, sometime
between 12 and 22 October 1799. Local tradition
declares (without evidence) that Lady Hamilton was
a guest in the house at the same time. Villa El
Fonduco, near the SE side of Cala Figuera and now
a hotel, was the residence of Lord Collingwood
while he was Flag Officer in Mahón during the early
19th century.

Sights ashore locally

Among places of interest near Mahón, the Golden
Farm (now a terracotta colour, not yellow!) should
be visited for the view – the house is privately owned
and not open to the public. The church of Santa
María with its superb early 19th-century organ, and
the Casa Mercadel Museum are in the town itself.
For those interested in the underwater world there is
an aquarium near the ferry wharf. The old
fortifications around the mouth of the harbour are
worth exploring, and the fort of Isabel II at La Mola
is open for guided walks, lasting two and a half
hours, at 1000 and 1700 at a price of €4. It is quite
difficult to get to the gate where the tickets are sold
by road without a car, but for yachts anchored in
Cala Taulera simply land on the small beach and
walk the 100m to the ticket office. Apparently the
Vickers cannons are a highlight of the tour. The
prehistoric *taula* (T-shaped monument) and *talayot*
(ancient tower) at Trepuco, about a mile to the S, are
typical of many throughout the island. If prepared to
stroll a little further, the village of San Luis, founded
by the French and still with a definite Gallic feel, is
on the same road.

Local events

Fiestas are held on 5–6 January with the arrival by
boat of Los Reyes Magos (the Three Wise Men) with
toys for the children, followed by a procession. On
Good Friday there is a procession and medieval
parade. On 15–16 July a sea procession is held in
honour of Our Lady of Carmen, and on 7–8
September the fiesta of Nuestra Señora de Gracia
includes processions, music, sailing races and other
sports. In the third week of September a fair is held
to showcase local products.

Eating out

A wide selection of restaurants and many quayside
bars and cafés. Bar/restaurant at Cala Llonga. A
walk up the steps near the Commercial Quay takes
you into town where there are many excellent eating
places, some friendly family run businesses, and
other more expensive restaurants.

2. Punta de San Carlos to Cala Binidalí

⚓ CALA DE SAN ESTEBAN (SANT ESTEVE)
39°51′.9N 04°18′.4E

A narrow but deeply indented *cala* surrounded by a fringe of houses, just S of Puerto de Mahón and easily identified by Punta de San Carlos lighthouse (Oc(2)6s22m12M, white tower with three black bands on square white base 15m), two radio masts and a large house all close N of the entrance. Depths of 2m or more lead almost to its head: favour the deeper N side and sound carefully as the bottom is rocky. Good protection is gained deeper in the *cala*.

⚓ CALA RAFALET
39°50′.4N 04°18′.1E

One of the most beautiful of the islands' small calas, narrow with steep rocky cliffs and ideal for a fantastic yacht photograph. Investigate by dinghy first and approach with great caution to anchor in 4–6m, open to the E quadrant. The narrow valley running inland from the head of the *cala* is most attractive and shows signs of ancient cave dwellers. There is a track to the main road and a housing estate on the high ground several hundred metres to the S. A *talayot* (ancient tower) lies 1½ miles to the NW.

⚓ CALA ALCAUFA (D'ALCAUFAR)
39°49′.7N 04°17′.9E

One of the first *calas* to be developed, with many houses on the N side but virtually nothing to the S. Easy to identify by virtue of a large pale stone tower just S of the entrance. Enter, leaving Illot d'es Torn to starboard and anchor in 2–4m over rock and sand, open to the SE. Holding is poor. There are many moorings and space to anchor is restricted – it may be necessary to moor fore-and-aft or take a line ashore. There are a few shops, restaurants and bars in the village.

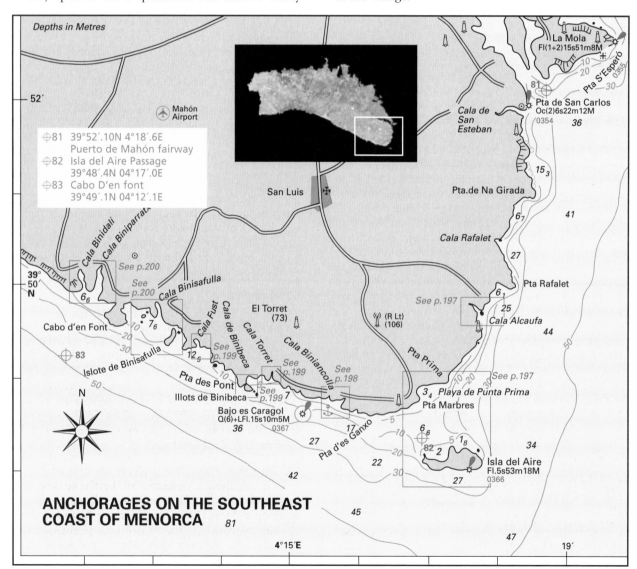

ANCHORAGES ON THE SOUTHEAST COAST OF MENORCA

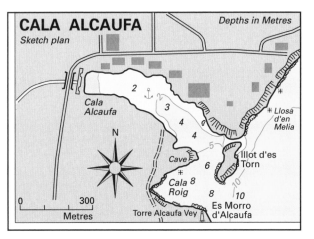

CALA ALCAUFA
Sketch plan

Depths in Metres

Cala
Alcaufa

N

Cave

Cala
Roig

Llosa
d'en
Melia

Illot d'es
s Torn

Es Morro
d'Alcaufa

Torre Alcaufa Vey

0   300
Metres

V. MENORCA

⚓ **PLAYA DE PUNTA PRIMA (ENSENADA ARENAL DE ALCAUFA)**

39°48′.8N 04°17′.1E

An exposed anchorage in a wide bay off a superb sandy beach. Anchor in 2m+ of turquoise water. Somewhat protected from the S by Isla del Aire. The bay is backed by houses and apartment blocks together with the usual shops, bars and restaurants. A submarine cable runs in a SE direction from a point near the head of the bay.

The British landed here under Admiral Sir John Leake and General Stanhope when they captured the island in 1708. Later it was used again by Spanish troops under the Duc de Crillon, landing in 1781 to recapture the island.

Cala Alcaufa viewed from SE. Often deserted even in summer

Playa de Punta Prima

⊕82 Isla del Aire Passage 39°48′.4N 04°17′.0E

F.R.
Ro Mast
(160)

To San Luis

Pta Prima

Depths in Metres

N

Torre Alcaufa
Nou

Playa de
Punta Prima

Pta d'es
Gancho

Pta
Marbres

Underwater cable

82

Escollo
del
Aire

Pta Llebeig

I.del Aire

Pta
Mitans

Fl.5s53m18M
0366

**PLAYA DE PUNTA PRIMA
AND ISLA DEL AIRE**

Sketch plan

39°48′N

4°17′.6E

0   500
Metres

⚓ **ISLA DEL AIRE**

Bisected by 39°48′.1N 04°17′.4E

A low, flat island just over 1,000m long by 400m wide but much of it less than 4m high, with a couple of hillocks (18m) and (20m) to the SE, one topped by a lighthouse (Fl.5s53m18M white tower, black bands, on white building 38m).

Anchor in a bay on the NW side of the island in 2–4m over sand, weed and some rocks, about 150m W of the landing pier from which there is a track to the lighthouse. Watch for rocky pinnacles and use a tripline.

The island is uninhabited – other than by rabbits and a unique race of black lizards (*Lacerta lilfordi*) – but is visited by tourist boats during summer. It is said that the lizards particularly enjoy tomatoes and will approach quite close if pieces are offered.

Admiral Byng's unsuccessful battle against the French fleet under Galissonnière took place off Isla del Aire in May 1756. This is where Byng failed to close and engage the enemy and fled to Gibraltar. He was court-martialled and executed, as Voltaire said: '*pour encourager les autres*' ('to encourage the others').

Isla del Aire viewed from SE. Note anchorage N side of island

Passage between Isla del Aire and Menorca

⊕82 39°48′.4N 04°17′.0E Isla del Aire passage

An unimpeded passage 1,000m wide exists between Isla del Aire and Menorca with a minimum central depth of 6.6m. Yachts drawing 2–5m or less can follow the Menorcan coast at 200m. The sandy bottom can usually be seen quite clearly.

⚓ CALA BINIANCOLLA

39°48′.7N 04°15′.7E

A small *cala* with low rocky sides and a village at its head, suitable for small yachts only. A large, conspicuous apartment block stands behind the hamlet and can be seen from afar. If approaching

from the W give the rocky Bajo Es Caragol a generous berth, and enter with care to avoid the outlying rocks on either side. Anchor in sand, rock and weed in ±3m. There are restaurants and cafés in the village.

BAJO ES CARAGOL

39°48′.6N 04°15′.2E

A breaking, rocky bank about 800m SW of Cala Biniancolla, marked by a S cardinal beacon (Q(6)+LFl.15s10m5M with ⊽ topmark) at its NW corner. Although there is good water about halfway between the beacon and the shore, the *bajo* should be given a generous berth as rocks extend up to 100m E and S.

Biniancolla viewed from S. Rocky patches just visible

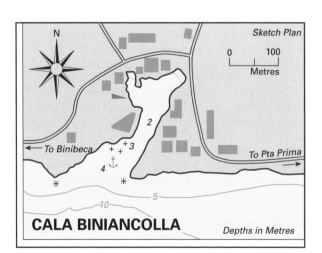

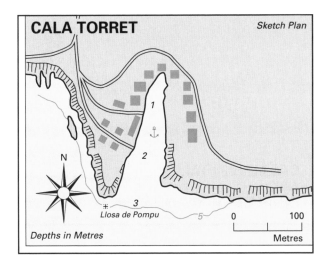

⚓ **CALA TORRET**

39°49´N 04°14´.8E

A small, developed *cala* surrounded by houses, only suitable for smaller yachts in good weather. The El Torret tower on the skyline about ¾ mile NE is a useful mark, as is a line of arched doorways along the W side of the *cala*. Enter with care and anchor in the middle of the *cala*, open SE through to SW. The usual cafés, restaurants and small shops will be found ashore.

⚓ **CALA DE BINIBECA (BINIBEQUER)**

39°48´.9N 04°14´.4E

A large, well-known 'developed' *cala* tucked behind Punta des Pont and the Illots de Binibeca, and overlooked by the tourist development of Binibeca Nou. Approach and entrance are straightforward: anchor near the middle in 3–7m over hard sand and weed, open from E to S. There is an excellent beach, very crowded in the season, with a pier, slipway and dinghy crane a short walk E. A *club náutico*, restaurants, shops and a hotel will be found in Binibeca Nou.

⚓ **CALA FUST (D'EN FUST)**

39°49´.3N 04°13´.7E

Occasionally, and confusingly, referred to as Binibeca Vell, Cala Fust is small with many houses and a conspicuous church spire to the E (the village of Binibeca Vell). It is suitable only for smaller yachts. There is an awash rock (Llosa d'en Fust) close E of the entrance. Local fishing craft are moored at the shallow head of the *cala*. There are the usual facilities ashore and some good examples of local rural architecture in Binibeca Vell.

Cala Torret right and Binibeca left, viewed from S

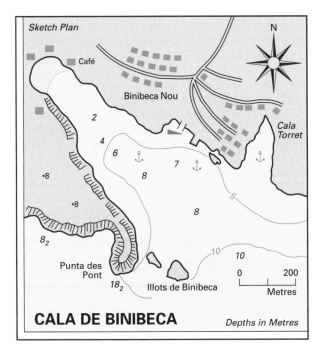

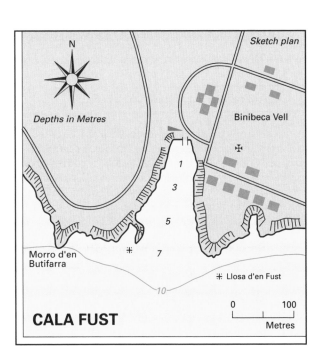

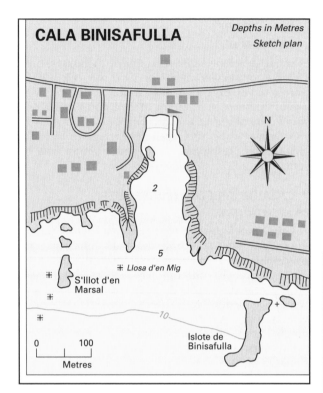

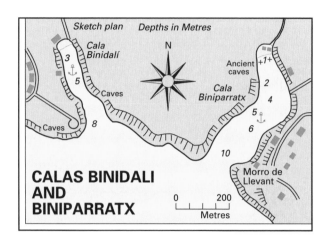

Cala Biniparratx from S

Cala Binisafulla from S

⊕83 39°49´.1N 04°12´.1E Off Cabo d'en Font

⚓ CALA BINIPARRATX
39°49´.8N 04°12´.1E

An attractive small *cala* with high rocky sides, easy to approach and enter. Though inconspicuous from offshore, Cabo d'en Fonts (some 750m to the E) is prominent. Anchor just short of the 'elbow' in 4–6m over sand and rock. There are rocky patches beyond the corner, and depths shoal rapidly towards the sandy beach. A few houses stand on the E bank of the *cala*, but there are no real facilities.

⚓ CALA BINIDALÍ
39°49´.9N 04°12´.0E

A pretty but very small *cala* just W of Cala Biniparratx, with high rocky cliffs, a sandy beach and a few houses well set back. Strictly a fair-weather anchorage but now closed off by buoys for most of the summer. When open the approach and entrance present no problems; use one or two anchors in 3–5m over sand and rock with possibly a line ashore. The head is shallow. There are no facilities.

⚓ CALA BINISAFULLA (BINISAFULLER)
39°49´.5N 04°13´.1E

A medium-sized *cala* with some adjacent houses but not overdeveloped. Approach with care because of a number of islets and awash rocks: a course from near the SW corner of Illot de Binisafuller clears all dangers. Anchor in 2.5m over sand and weed. Cala Binisafulla is in line with the airport runway so it can be noisy.

CABO D'EN FONT (ES CAP D'EN FONT)
39°49´.5N 4°12´.6E

A low (12m) but prominent rocky-cliffed headland covered with houses. Several rocky islets lie to the SE.

3. Cabo Gros to Cala Santa Galdana

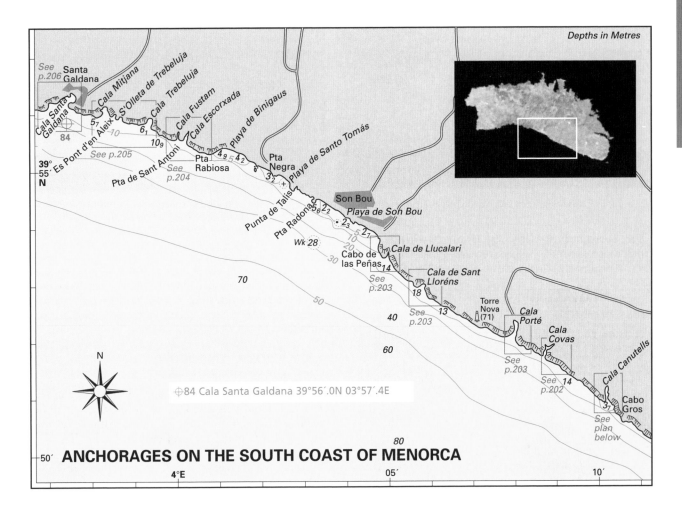

Depths in Metres

ANCHORAGES ON THE SOUTH COAST OF MENORCA

⊕84 Cala Santa Galdana 39°56´.0N 03°57´.4E

V. MENORCA

CABO GROS

39°50´.6N 04°10´.5E

A high (39m), rocky-cliffed headland with some houses on the top. Even so it is not very prominent and can only be seen if coasting close in. There are some prehistoric caves cut into the cliffs, including a very large one on the W face.

⚓ CALA CANUTELLS

39°50´.8N 04°10´.1E

A large and attractive S-shaped *cala* between sloping rocky cliffs, with a large tourist development to the E and many local craft on permanent moorings. Enter down the centre of the *cala*, keeping well clear of the awash rock at the western entrance point, and anchor as space permits in 4–6m over sand. The upper part of the *cala* is very shallow, with a shelving sandy beach at its head which is deservedly popular with tourists. There is a café/restaurant on the beach and at the top of the hill (200m past the café) there is a supermarket, hotel, post, car hire and an English-speaking doctor in attendance every day.

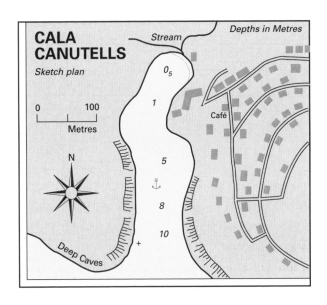

CALA CANUTELLS

Sketch plan

Depths in Metres

Stream

Café

Deep Caves

Cala Canutells viewed from SW: caves visible left of picture

Cala Covas: one of the most spectacular in the Islands, surrounded by caves, many of which were dwellings in prehistoric times

The surrounding cliffs are riddled with caves, including two tall, arched recesses close W of the entrance and the Covas d'es Castella 800m to the E.

⚓ CALA COVAS (COVES)

39°51′.7N 04°08′.6E

Considered the most spectacular and beautiful anchorage in the Islas Baleares, Cala Covas is surrounded by nearly 150 caves, some of which were occupied during prehistoric times. The entrance between two high rocky cliffs lies ¾ mile E of Cala Porté, which is easily identified by the huge housing development to its E. Anchor in 3–5m with two anchors or a line ashore to limit swinging: there are several convenient posts on the W side of the small central promontory (see plan), but investigate first by dinghy as there are fringing rocks. Much of the bottom is rocky, making a tripline advisable. The anchorage is open to SW and S, depending on the spot chosen.

The *cala* is deserted except for two houses, but large numbers of tourists visit the beaches every day in summer and litter has been a problem. There are several freshwater springs and a road inland, but no facilities.

⚓ CALA PORTÉ (EN PORTER)

39°52′.1N 04°07′.9E

A large *cala* lying between high (48m) rocky cliffs. The valley and hillside to the N and E are covered by holiday homes, hotels, shops, cafés, restaurants and discos, which make the *cala* easy to locate. The 8m Torre Nova tower stands about ¾ mile NW.

Anchor in 3m+ over sand, open to the S and SW. A line (sometimes two lines) of buoys may be laid to mark off the bathing area in front of the beach. There are two beach cafés, and most everyday requirements are available in the tourist area.

It is worth walking along the cliffs on the eastern side of the entrance to Cova d'en Xeroni, a

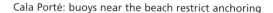

Cala Porté: buoys near the beach restrict anchoring

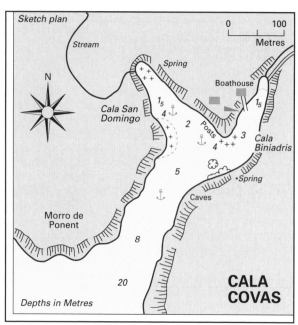

Sketch plan

Stream

Spring

N

Boathouse

Cala San Domingo

1 5

4 ⚓

Posts

2

+ 3

⚓

4 + +

Cala Biniadris

5

Spring

⚓

Caves

Morro de Ponent

8

20

0   100

Metres

CALA COVAS

Depths in Metres

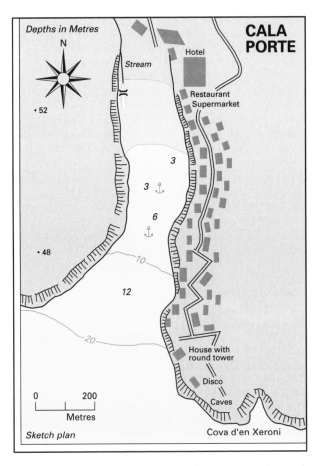

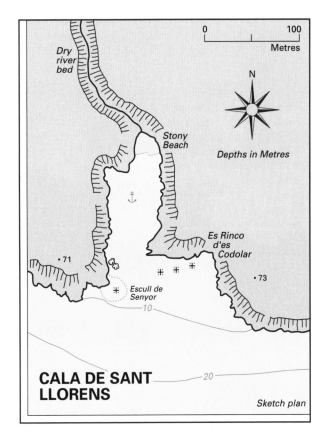

succession of natural caves with openings through the cliffs, now occupied by a bar and restaurant (and a nightly disco). There are several important *talayots* (towers) and other ancient ruins on the road to Alayor.

TORRE NOVA
39°52′.3N 04°07′.0E

A ruined ancient lookout tower 8m high on the edge of a 63m rocky cliff, about ¾ mile NW of Cala Porté. It is not very conspicuous.

⚓ CALA DE SANT LLORÉNS (SANT LLORENÇ)
39°52′.9N 4°05′.7E

A very small, deserted *cala* surrounded by sheer rocky cliffs with a steep-sided river valley behind. Only suitable for use by small yachts in settled conditions. Care is necessary in the approach due to several fringing rocks. Moor with two anchors over sand and rock.

⚓ CALA DE LLUCALARI
39°53′.4N 4°04′.9E

A very small, deserted *cala* similar to Cala de Sant Llorens, with high sloping rocky sides. It is tucked behind Cabo de las Peñas (Cap de ses Penyes) and backed by a dried-up river valley with a track inland. Its use is limited to small yachts in good weather. Anchor in the centre of the *cala* in 3–4m over rock and sand. There is a small rocky beach but no facilities.

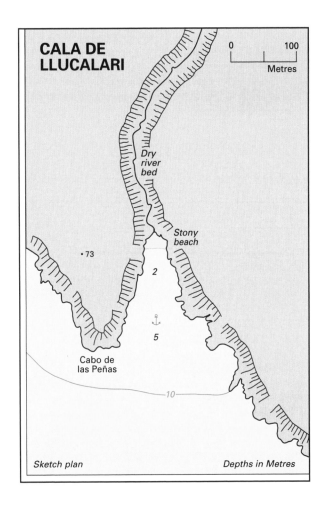

Cala de Llucalari from SE: narrow with a stony beach

⚓ PLAYA DE SON BOU, PLAYA DE SANTO TOMÁS (PLAYA DE TALIS OR ATALIX) AND PLAYA DE BINIGAUS

Stretching from 39°53′.8N 4°04′.6E to 39°55′.3N 4°01′.1E

A 3-mile stretch of sandy beaches between Cabo de las Peñas (Cap de ses Penyes) and Punta Rabiosa, broken only by the low rocky promontories of Punta Radona, Punta de Talis and Punta Negra. They are backed by apartment blocks and hotels and a number of tourist developments, including those of San Jaime Mediterráneo and Santo Tomás.

The 10m contour runs some 400m offshore, making it possible to anchor over sand almost anywhere along this stretch of open coast. There are two small islands and some rocks close inshore.

The San Jaime Mediterráneo resort at Son Bou includes a bank amongst its facilities, as well as a supermarket and the usual bars and restaurants. Santo Tomás has beach bars, restaurants, supermarkets and gift shops.

The ruins of an early Christian church dating from the 5th century overlook the eastern end of the Son Bou beach while two *talayots* (towers) lie near the road from Santo Tomás to Ferrerías, together with other ancient remains. There is a spring at the NW end of Playa de Binigaus, which is generally less built up than the other beaches mentioned above.

⚓ CALA ESCORXADA

39°55′.5N 04°00′.2E

A deserted *cala* with low rocky cliffs and a large sandy beach, about ¾ mile NW of the end of Playa de Binigaus. Anchor in 2–5m over sand. Ashore there is a track to San Cristóbal but nothing else.

⚓ CALA FUSTAM

39°55′.5N 04°00′.0E

A smaller and narrower version of Cala Escorxada lying 300m further NW, on the other side of Punta de Sant Antoni. Moor with two anchors in 3–4m over sand, open from SE to SW. The sandy beach is not as large as that at Cala Escorxada, but the *cala* is very pretty and totally deserted. Again there is nothing ashore other than the track to San Cristóbal.

Cala Fustam (left) and Cala Escorxada, viewed from SE

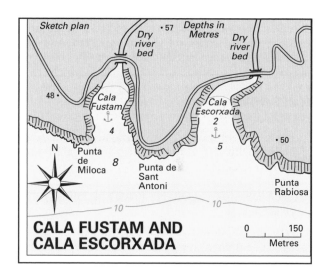

West of Cala Fustam is Cala Trebeluja and then Cala Mitjana. (both page 205). Between them lie S'Olleta de Trebeluja and Es Pont d'en Aleix. These are little more than breaks in the cliff line. Although charts show them to be anchorages they are most suited to entering and exploration by dinghy.

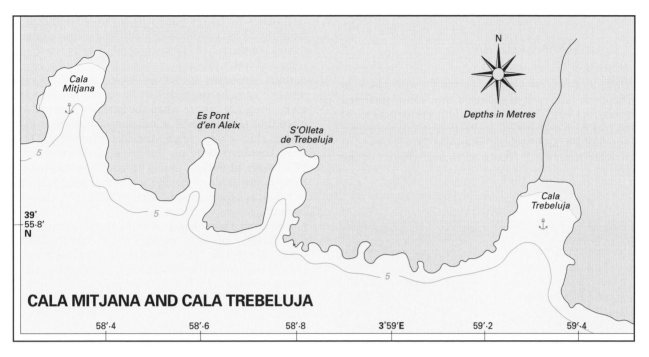

CALA MITJANA AND CALA TREBELUJA

Cala Trebuluja

Cala Mitjana from the SW

⚓ CALA TREBELUJA (TREBELÚJER)
39°55′.7N 03°59′.3E

A large, wide cala with a pinkish sandy beach. there are high (64m) sloping rocky caves on the southeast side and lower, tree-covered cliffs on the northwest side. Anchor in 4–6m over sand. A small freshwater river enters the NW corner of the cala. It has a low sand bar over which a dinghy can be pulled or carried, allowing one to row a mile upstream with the chance of seeing turtles, fish and various birds. There is a track to San Cristóbal but otherwise the *cala* is deserted.

⚓ CALA MITJANA
39°56′N 03°58′.3E

A large *cala* more than 100m wide, surrounded by rocky cliffs but with two good sandy beaches, lying just under ¾ mile E of Cala Santa Galdana (easily recognised by its large hotels and apartment blocks). Anchor in 3–6m over sand and weed. A track connects with the road to Ferrerías.

⊕84 39°56′.0N 03°57′.4E Cala Santa Galdana

⚓ CALA SANTA GALDANA
39°56′.2N 03°57′.5E

Once one of the most beautiful large *calas* in Menorca, and still the largest and most sheltered anchorage on the S coast. The construction of several high-rise hotels make it easy to recognise, especially if approaching from the W. However, if arriving from the E little is seen until abreast of the entrance.

A series of buoys linked by a thin line stretches from the central promontory across the *cala* to near the end of the beach, protecting the bathing area but seriously restricting the anchorage. Anchor as space permits, probably in 5m or more, over sand and weed. It may be necessary to lie to two anchors or take a long line ashore when the harbour is crowded. Note that in strong SW winds the swell rolls in and makes this a very uncomfortable anchorage. The river Barranco de Cala Santa Galdana enters the NW corner of the *cala* and is navigable by dinghy for more than ½ mile. A bridge some 10m long and 3m in height spans its mouth, with a smallcraft pontoon beyond.

The long sandy beach is crowded in season and the shouts of the bathers echo around the surrounding cliffs. There is also a lot of noise during the evening from bars and discos, but these usually cease around 2200. Restaurants, cafés, bars, supermarkets and tourist shops flourish in the resort.

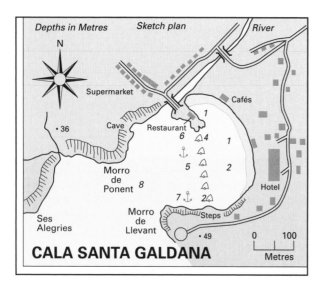

Cala Santa Galdana from SW. An excellent anchorage in clear waters, though the buoys placed to protect swimmers restrict the anchoring to deeper water

4. Cala Macarella to Cala Santandria

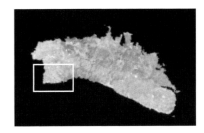

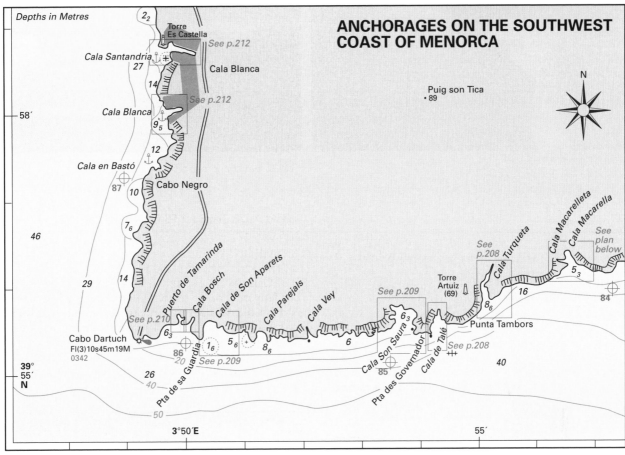

ANCHORAGES ON THE SOUTHWEST COAST OF MENORCA

⚓ CALA MACARELLA AND CALA MACARELLETA
39°56′.1E 03°56′.3E

A large double *cala* with two sandy beaches, surrounded by sloping rocky cliffs, scrub and trees, and easy to spot just under a mile W of Cala Santa Galdana. Anchor in 3–6m over sand and a few weed patches. The anchorage is often crowded and it may be necessary to use two anchors or to take a line ashore. Cala Macarelleta has a mooring stone complete with ring, but keep clear of the W end of the *cala* which is roped off for swimmers.

Three tracks bring in day tourists and there is a popular camp site nearby (caves overlooking the *calas* may also be inhabited in summer). The stream flowing into Cala Macarella is embanked with what could be Moorish masonry; the water appears clean and is recommended locally. There is a café/bar on the beach and an ancient ruined village to the W. These calas, together with those further E, were used as hideouts by Barbary pirates in medieval times.

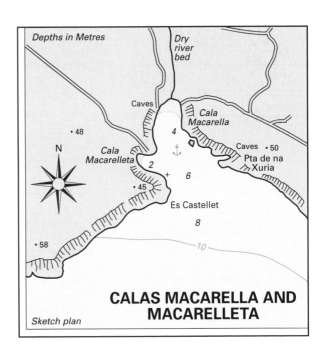

CALAS MACARELLA AND MACARELLETA
Sketch plan

V. MENORCA

Calas Macarella and Macarelleta

Cala Turqueta and the caves around its entrance

⚓ CALA TURQUETA

39°55'.7N 03°54'.9E

A small, attractive *cala* surrounded by scrub and pine-covered rocky cliffs and with a sandy beach at its head. It lies a mile W of Cala Macarella and the same distance from Cala de Son Saura. The conspicuous Torre de Artuiz lies just W of the entrance. Anchor in 3m+ over sand with weed patches, taking a line ashore if necessary (there is a mooring ring on the E side). Two tracks at the head of the *cala* lead inland. Peace in the *cala* is somewhat spoiled in the middle of the day by a procession of tourist craft coming from Ciudadela and disgorging hundreds of tourists on to the tiny beach. Calm returns in the evening.

⚓ CALA DE TALÉ (D'ES TALAIER)

39°55'.5N 03°54'.1E

A small and often deserted *cala* with a low rocky shore backed by scrub and pine woods, about ½ mile E of Cala Son Saura and separated from it by Punta des Governador. Enter with care as there is a small islet on the W side of the entrance and a lone rock awash close inshore to the E. Anchor in 2m+ over sand, open to SE and S. Space is very limited and it may be necessary to lie to two anchors. There is a sandy beach at the head of the *cala* and a track inland.

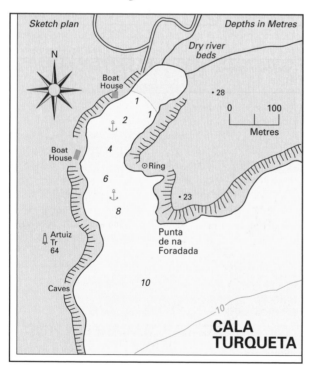

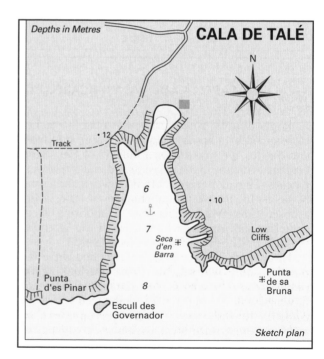

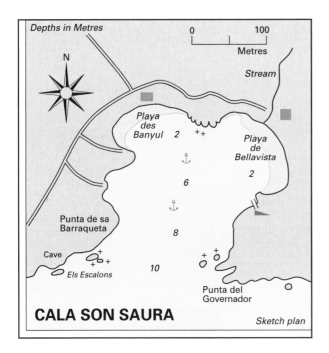

CALA SON SAURA

Sketch plan

Ashore there is a long pinkish sandy beach divided into two parts (Playa de Bellavista to the E and Playa des Banyul to the W), by a low rocky area, with a small stream crossing the eastern beach after wet weather. There is a small fishing boat slipway, a few houses well set back and a road leading inland, but nothing else.

⚓ CALA VEY (DE SON VELL) AND CALA PAREJALS

39°55´.3N 03°52´.1E

Two small *calas* with rocky sides on the much-indented stretch of coast between Cala Son Saura and Cala de Son Aparets. There are numerous inshore rocks and islets, and the area should only be explored with considerable care and by experienced navigators.

⚓ CALA DE SON APARETS (PLAYA DE SON XORIGUER)

39°55´.4N 03°50´.6E

A large rounded bay surrounded by low rocky cliffs, behind which lie houses and some apartment blocks. The *cala* is easy to find, being a little under a mile E of Cabo Dartuch and close E of Puerto de Tamarinda and Punta de sa Guardia (na Cap de Porc). On the approach watch out for the isolated Bajo Dartuch (Seca de na Cap de Porc) which lies 400m E of the W entrance point and carries 1.6m, but otherwise there are no hazards. Anchor in 2m+ over sand and weed. The beach is good but often very crowded and in season the swimmers' buoys are laid out to the 5m contour (the major part of the *cala*). There are several beach cafés and roads inland. The Puerto de Tamarinda tourist complex is a short walk away.

Cala de Talé and Cala Son Saura (larger bay on left) viewed from SE

⊕85 39°55´.1N 3°53´.6E Cala Son Saura

⚓ CALA SON SAURA

39°55´.5N 03°53´.6E

A large, semi-enclosed bay surrounded by a low, sloping rocky foreshore with dark pine trees and scrub behind. It lies close W of Punta Governador (Gobernadó) and is easily recognized by its sheer size – the entrance is 500m wide and it broadens out further inside. There are two small islets on the W of the entrance and two isolated rocks near the E side, but the bay itself is clear. Anchor in 3–8m over sand and weed.

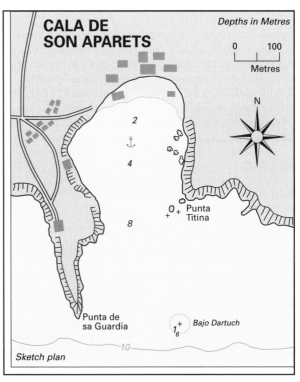

CALA DE SON APARETS

Sketch plan

V. MENORCA

⚓ CALA BOSCH (EN BOSC)

39°55′.5N 03°50′.2E

A small *cala* with low rocky edges and a crowded sandy beach at its head, just E of Puerto de Tamarinda and W of Punta de sa Guardia (na Cap de Porc). Anchor in 2m+ over sand and weed, keeping clear of the swimmers' buoys off the beach. In season swimmers' buoys exclude craft from entry into this *cala* as they stretch from headland to headland. There are low-rise tourist apartments behind the *cala* and it is only a step across to the Puerto de Tamarinda tourist complex where there are shops and other facilities.

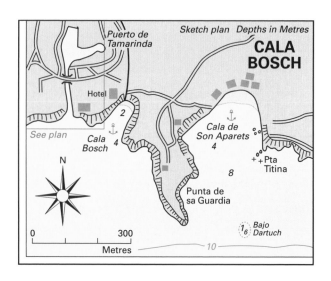

ME2 Puerto de Tamarinda (Marina Cala'n Bosch)

A small harbour with 264 moorings accessed via a narrow canal, but with a bridge restricting height to 10m. Only suitable for motor boats and dinghies

Location
39°55′.5N 03°50′.1E

Communications
Club Deportivo Cala'n Bosch ☎ 971 38 71 70/38 52 38
Fax 971 38 71 71
Email darbosch@teleline.es

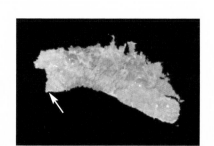

The harbour

A small man-made lagoon dredged from a low-lying area. Approached via a narrow channel spanned by a footbridge reminiscent of a willow-pattern plate, Puerto de Tamarinda is inaccessible to sailing vessels needing more than 10m height above water. However, it makes an interesting visit by dinghy and is suited to medium-sized motor yachts, speedboats and smaller sailing craft. It is also used by sailboarders. The harbour is surrounded by a growing tourist development with all the related facilities.

PILOTAGE

Approach

⊕86 39°55′.4N 3°50′.1E Puerto de Tamarinda

From E Follow the coast past a series of small calas. The large Cala de Son Aparets is easily recognized, being separated by a low rocky promontory (Punta de sa Guardia) from the narrow Cala Bosch, behind which stands a group of apartment blocks. 200m W of this *cala* lies the entrance to Puerto de Tamarinda. The entrance is not obvious until close by.

From N and W Approach the prominent Cabo Dartuch with its black-and-white-banded lighthouse

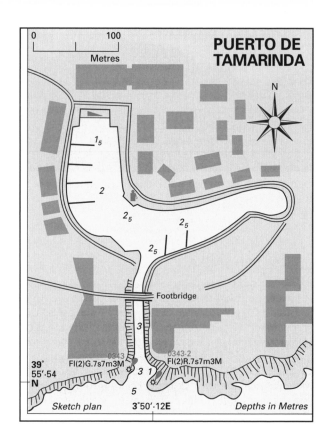

Cabo Dartuch with its distinctive lighthouse, viewed from S. Cala Bosch and Puerto de Tamarinda just behind peninsula centre of picture

(Fl(3)10s45m19M, white tower with three black bands on white building 34m surrounded by a low white wall). The entrance to Puerto de Tamarinda lies around 1,000m ENE of the lighthouse and W of Cala Bosch, which will be recognised by its narrow sandy beach surrounded by apartment blocks.

Anchorages in the approach

Anchor in Cala Bosch or Cala de Son Aparets (see above) if possible; later in the season the *calas* are closed off with swimmer buoys.

Entrance

The entrance is less than 10m wide – too narrow for anything larger than dinghies to pass each other, and much too narrow to turn. It is therefore essential to check that the way is clear before committing oneself. Approach heading N into the channel with its conspicuous white footbridge and enter at slow speed. The water is often muddy and depths are unreliable, so keep a close eye on the echo-sounder. If in any doubt about mast clearance it would be wise to anchor in Cala Bosch and walk round to measure the bridge. In strong winds and swell from the southerly quadrant it would be dangerous to attempt entry into Puerto de Tamarinda.

Berthing

Secure in any vacant berth: the harbour is unlikely to be full. An official will allocate one in due course.

Facilities

Water At the base of some of the pontoons, otherwise from one of the cafés.
Electricity On some (but not all) of the pontoons.
Fuel Available.
Provisioning Small supermarket and other shops in the complex, a chemist and tourist shops.
Ice From the nearby bars and cafés.
Repairs A very wide slipway at the head of the harbour.
Bank In the tourist complex.
Hospital/medical services In Ciudadela, about 4½ miles away.

Transport

Taxis By telephone from Ciudadela, or enquire in the tourist complex.
Buses Buses to Ciudadela.

Sight ashore locally

There is a *talayot* (ancient tower) at Son Olivaret about a mile N on the road to Ciudadela.

Eating out

A choice of restaurants, cafés and bars within the tourist complex.

PUERTO TAMARINDA TO CALA SANTANDRIA

CABO DARTUCH (CAP D'ARTRUTX)
39°55′.3N 03°49′.5E

A prominent headland of low (10m) dark cliffs surmounted by a conspicuous lighthouse (Fl(3)10s 45m19M, white tower with three black bands on white building 34m surrounded by a low white wall). The headland is steep-to.

⊕87 39°57′.2N 3°49′.1E Off Cabo Negro

CABO NEGRO (CAP NEGRE)
39°57′.1N 03°49′.5E

A relatively inconspicuous headland of black rock, 12m high and steep-to. Easily seen if coasting close inshore.

Puerto de Tamarinda with its quaint bridge, Cala Bosch to right just out of picture

⚓ CALA EN BASTÓ

39°57′.4N 03°49′.7E

A very small *cala* close N of Cabo Negro and about 2 miles N of Cabo Dartuch, surrounded by low (8m) black rocky cliffs and to be used with extreme caution. A small breaking rock lies on the S side of the entrance. The *cala*, which is open from W to N, has no beach and is generally deserted.

⚓ CALA BLANCA

39°58′N 3°50′E

A narrow *cala* between low rocky sides, Cala Blanca is easy to identify due to an unusual building with deep verandas on its northern side and a huge white apartment block/hotel in the background. Anchor in 4–8m over sand. In high season swimmers' buoys virtually exclude craft from this *cala*. The sandy beach at its head is often crowded, and there are hotels, restaurants, cafés and houses nearby. The Caves of Parella a few hundred metres inland are worth visiting.

⚓ CALA SANTANDRIA

39°58′.8N 03°49′.9E

A long *cala* with several shorter branches, Cala Santandria lies between low, pinkish, rocky cliffs just over a mile S of Puerto de Ciudadela. The entrance is not easily picked out, but the Torre Es Castella (a restored defensive tower) on the N headland helps. A small islet off the E side of the entrance is the only hazard on entering. Anchor in 3m+ over sand and weed as space permits, either lying to two anchors or taking a line ashore. Two cables run down the centre of the *cala*, so care is needed when picking a spot. This anchorage has been reported as uncomfortable even in light winds and it is difficult to keep clear of the cables.

Lines of buoys mark off all three bathing beaches with their bars and cafés. Supermarkets, hotels and restaurants are located slightly further back. There are pleasant walks on either side of the *cala* and the Torre Es Castella is worth a visit. Maréchal Richelieu, commander of the French invasion, landed here with his troops on 18 April 1756, en route to capture Ciudadela.

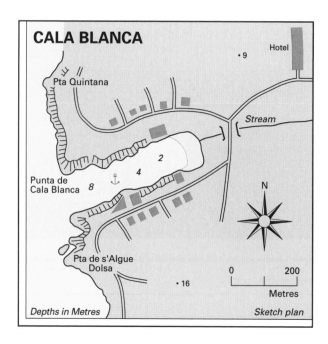

Cala Santandria viewed from W

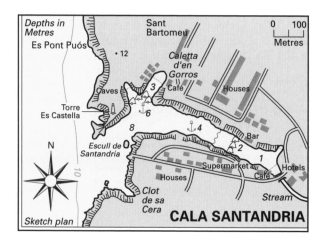

⚓ CALA DEGOLLADOR

39°59′.6N 03°49′.7E

A narrow *cala* just S of the entrance to Puerto de Ciudadela, surrounded by low rocky cliffs and with two popular (and often crowded) sandy beaches at its head. Islote de la Galera, a small islet 4m high, lies in the middle of the entrance with a 4.1m shoal extending 80m northwards. Anchor in 4m+ over sand with weed patches. It may be necessary to use two anchors to restrict swinging room as the *cala* is very narrow (see plan below).

Cala Degollador forms a useful alternative to Ciudadela when the latter is crowded, and has all its shoreside facilities within easy reach. Plans for turning the *cala* into a yacht harbour behind protective breakwaters seem to have been shelved. An alternative proposal is to build a marina in Cala d'en Busquets on the N side of Puerto de Ciudadela.

5. Punta Degollador to Cabo Nati

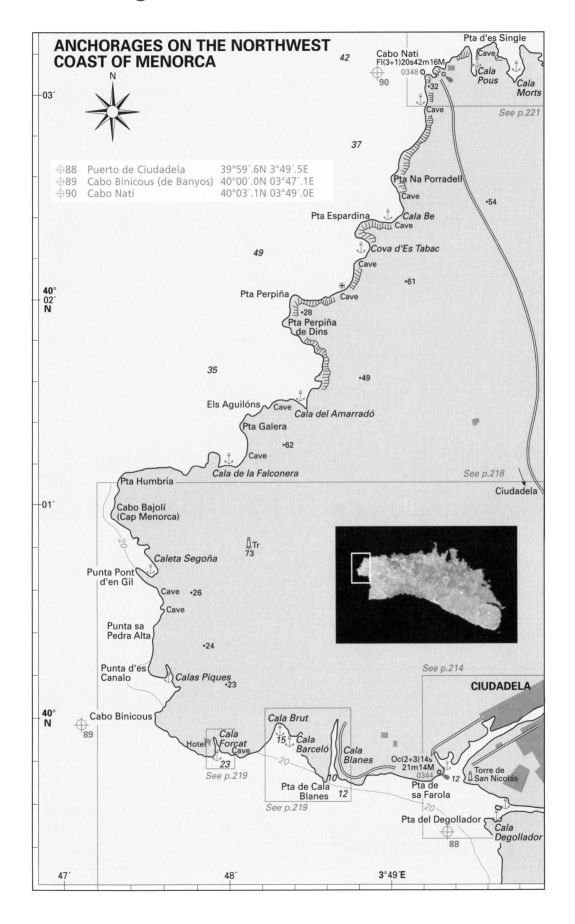

ANCHORAGES ON THE NORTHWEST
COAST OF MENORCA

N

⊕88 Puerto de Ciudadela   39°59'.6N 3°49'.5E
⊕89 Cabo Binicous (de Banyos) 40°00'.0N 03°47'.1E
⊕90 Cabo Nati   40°03'.1N 03°49'.0E

03'

40°
02'
N

40°
01'

40°
N

Pta d'es Single
Cabo Nati
Fl(3+1)20s42m16M
0348
90
·32
Cave
Cala
Pous
Cala
Morts
Cave
See p.221

42

37

Pta Na Porradell
Cave
·54

Pta Espardina
Cala Be
Cave

49
Cova d'Es Tabac
Cave
·61

Pta Perpiña
Cave
·28
Pta Perpiña
de Dins

35
·49

Els Aguilóns
Cave
Cala del Amarradó
Pta Galera
·62
Cave
Cala de la Falconera
See p.218

Pta Humbria
Ciudadela

Cabo Bajolí
(Cap Menorca)

20

Tr
73
Caleta Segoña

Punta Pont
d'en Gil
Cave ·26
Cave

Punta sa
Pedra Alta
·24

Punta d'és
Canalo
Calas Piques
·23

See p.214

CIUDADELA

Cabo Binicous
89

Hotel
Cala
Forcat
Cave
23
See p.219

Cala Brut
15
Cala
Barceló
Cala
Blanes
10
Pta de Cala
Blanes 12
See p.219

Oc(2+3)14s
21m14M
0344
12
Torre de
San Nicolás

Pta de
sa Farola
20
Pta del Degollador
Cala
Degollador
88

47'   48'   3°49'E

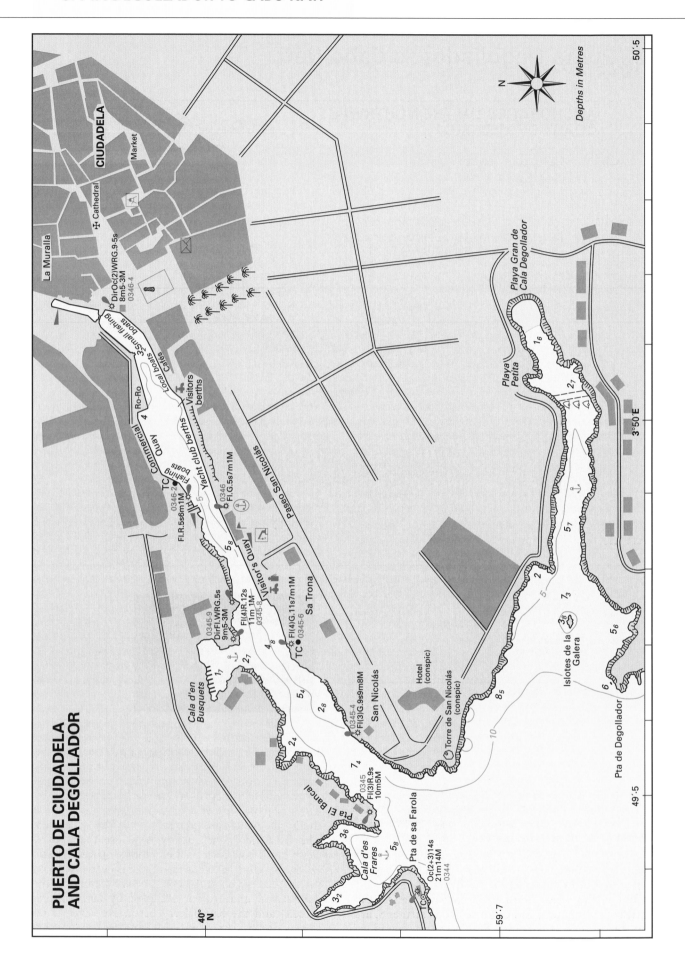

PUERTO DE CIUDADELA AND CALA DEGOLLADOR

CIUDADELA

La Muralla

Cathedral

Market

DirOc(2)WRG.9.5s
8m5-3M
0346.4

Small fishing boats

Local boats

Cafés

Visitors berths

Ro-Ro

Commercial Quay

TC

Fishing boats

Yacht club berths

0346.2
Fl.R.5s6m1M

0346
Fl.G.5s7m1M

Paseo San Nicolás

Cala d'en Busquets

0345.9
DirFl.WRG.5s
9m5-3M

Fl(4)R.12s
11m 1M
0345.8

Fl(4)G.11s7m1M
0345.6

TC

Sa Trona

Visitor's Quay

San Nicolás

0345.4
Fl(3)G.9s9m8M

Hotel
(conspic)

Torre de San Nicolás
(conspic)

Pta El Bancal

0345
Fl(3)R.9s
10m5M

Pta de sa Farola

Cala d'es Frares

Oc(2+3)14s
21m14M
0344

TC

Playa Gran de
Cala Degollador

Playa Petita

Islotes de la
Galera

Pta de Degollador

N

Depths in Metres

3°50'E

50'·5

49'·5

59'·7

40°
N

ME3 Puerto de Ciudadela (Ciutadella)

A natural harbour up a long *cala,* with berthing for 100 vessels

Location
39°59′.8N 03°49′.5E

Communications
Port Authority (Puerto de Ciudadela)
VHF Ch 09, 14, 16
Club Náutico de Ciudadela ☎ 971 38 39 18
Fax 971 38 58 71
Email cnciutadella@cncuitadella.com
www.cnciutadella.com

The harbour

A most attractive natural harbour consisting of a long narrow *cala* leading to a small inner area edged with ancient quays. Only in the last decade has a new public quay for visitors been added nearer the entrance.

Approach and entrance are straightforward but, from some angles and in some light conditions, it is virtually impossible to see the entrance itself until very close in. Entry is not advisable in strong SW winds as seas break across its mouth. Once inside, good shelter is available, but swell finds its way up the *cala* with winds from SW or W. During the summer season both harbour and town become very crowded.

PILOTAGE

Approach

⊕88 39°59′.6N 3°49′.5E Puerto de Ciudadela

From S or SW Cabo Dartuch, a low rocky-cliffed promontory topped by a very conspicuous lighthouse (Fl(3)10s45m19M, white tower with three black bands on white building 34m surrounded by low white wall), is easily recognised. The entrance to Puerto de Ciudadela lies 4.4 miles to the N and there are no offshore hazards. The buildings of Ciudadela (in particular the Torre de San Nicolás) together with the large curved hotel behind, can be seen from afar.

From N or NW Cabo Nati and its conspicuous lighthouse (Fl(3+1)20s 42m16M, aluminium cupola on white tower above white building with a red roof 13m), Cabo Bajolí with its 10m tower and 20m brick signal station, and Cabo Binicous further S, are all prominent headlands. Follow them round at 400m until heading ESE, when the buildings of Ciudadela will be seen less than 2 miles away.

Anchorages in the approach

There are several nearby *cala* anchorages, the largest of which is Cala Degollador some 400m to the S (description given previously). N and W of the entrance lie Cala d'es Frares, Cala Blanes and Cala Brut (see below).

Entrance

The entrance can be difficult to identify until close in, but the Punta de Sa Farola lighthouse on the N side and the Torre de San Nicolás to the S are good landmarks. SW gales produce breaking seas across the entrance and swell inside the harbour. In these conditions an alternative destination should be sought. See also the note regarding sea levels below. Due to the steep cliffs on either side the wind can be very variable and fluky.

There are three sets of six lights set up (marked TC on plan) for harbour traffic control. They are 3 vertical red, and vertical green, white, green. If the 3 red lights are lit you must clear the harbour channel within a maximum of 10 minutes. If the GWG plus flashing red are on then access to the channel is prohibited to all craft except for those expressly authorised. When lights are off, navigation is open to any user and to enter the harbour simply follow the centre line of the *cala.*

Sea levels

The level of the sea rises with a SW wind and falls with N and NE winds by as much as 0.5m. Under certain meteorological conditions, usually when a depression and spring tide coincide, a phenomenon known as *resaca* or *seiche* occurs, causing the level to rise and fall by as much as 1.5m every ten or fifteen minutes, an oscillation which may continue for several days. Local fishermen often give warning when they expect it to occur.

Berthing

Although there are a variety of berthing possibilities, Puerto de Ciudadela is often full to capacity during the summer. On the starboard side just short of the *club náutico* is a stretch of quay capable of taking seven or eight yachts in line, rafted two or three deep. Although owned by the Port Authority this is franchised to the *club náutico,* who admister the area and collect mooring fees.

Beyond the *club náutico* local yachts and smallcraft lie bow or stern-to, with Port Authority moorings for a few visiting yachts, also stern-to, at the far end just short of where the harbour narrows. The Iris Jet service from Ratjada uses the quay on the N side which was previously used by fishermen. The fishermen consequently now use the S quay (with much bad grace as their storage spaces are still on the N quay!) which means there is even less room for visitors. Much of the port side is taken up by the commercial quay (often occupied by large fishing vessels) and the RoRo ferry berth. However, if no ship is due, yachts may be allowed to lie alongside overnight. The wash caused by ships passing can cause surge problems on the western quay,

Ciudadela viewed from SW. Cala Degollador to right. The 17th C torre de San Nicholas seen centre of picture and Cala d'es Frares left

particularly if rafts have grown to more than three yachts deep, in which case the outer yachts will be told to leave in order to clear the channel.

Anchorage in the harbour

It is currently possible to anchor in the entrance to the small Cala d'en Busquets on the N side of the harbour (see plan). Bow and stern anchors are likely to be needed. The *cala* itself is full of moorings.

Facilities

Water At all three quays listed above.
Electricity On the *club náutico* and Port Authority quays.
Fuel Diesel and petrol pumps on the *club náutico* quay.
Provisions A good selection of supermarkets and specialist food shops. A small open-air market in the town, with a fish market in its centre.
Ice From nearby bars.
Chandlery About 200m E of *club náutico* on Paseo San Nicolas. Menorca Yachting ☎ 971 48 20 44 *Fax* 971 48 20 12 on the waterfront above the restaurant, Sa' Figura is also willing to assist yachtsmen in need.
Repairs Small boatyard by the slipway W of the commercial quay. Cranes on the commercial quay and at the *club náutico* (5 tonnes). Slipway at the W end of the commercial quay. The slightly rustic cradle can handle up to 5 tonnes.
Engineers Centre Nautic Ciudadela ☎ 971 38 26 16 *Fax* 971 38 56 79 are agents for Ecosse, Volvo Penta and Yanmar.
Yacht club The Club Náutico de Ciudadela has a fine clubhouse fronting the harbour with bar, lounge, terrace, restaurant and showers.
Showers At the *club náutico*. A small charge is made, payable at the bar.
Laundry In the town.
Banks Several in the town, with credit card facilities.
Hospital/medical services In the town.

Transport

Car hire/taxis Available in the town.
Buses Bus service to Mahón, Fornells and elsewhere.
Ferries Car ferries to Alcudia, Mallorca.

History

Ciudadela harbour has been in use since prehistoric times, long before the Phoenicians settled in 1600-1200BC and gave it its first name, Yamma, meaning 'western' or 'west town'. The Greeks and Romans followed, and Pliny the Elder referred to it as Iama or Iamnona. The next name on record was that of the Arabs, to whom it was Medina Minurka. With the expulsion of the Arabs by the Aragonese it received its current name of Ciudadela meaning 'little city', though very little from that time remains due to repeated attacks by pirates and Corsairs. The most notorious assault was led by the Turkish pirate

Looking up the *cala* to visitors' berths   *GW*

Ancient walls of Ciudadela   *GW*

Sights ashore locally

The fascinating old town is unspoilt and can answer most needs. It is a delight to explore, with pavement cafés under the arches of Ses Voltes and a contrast between the palaces of the old families fronting the open squares and the tiny houses of the artisans, packed apparently at random (intended, it is said, to confuse the all-too-frequent intruders with a succession of blind alleys and unexpected turns). The 14th-century cathedral merits a special visit, but Ciudadela is a town oozing antiquity and interest on every side.

Three miles out of Ciudadela, just off the road to Mahón, lies the Naveta d'es Tudóns, which lays claim to being the oldest building in Europe and is undoubtedly the oldest in Spain. The Naveta (so-called because the ground plan resembles a ship) is built of large stone blocks and has two storeys. It measures 14m by 6.5m and was used over many centuries as a communal tomb.

Barbarossa who, in 1558, laid siege to the town and, when it fell, destroyed its buildings and took many of the inhabitants away as slaves. Even so, Ciudadela remained the capital of the island (and the see of a bishop) until 1722 when the British transferred the administration to Mahón, the better natural harbour.

Local speciality

Ciudadela's final distinction lies in its fiesta of San Juán on 23–24 June, famed for its daring equestrian displays to which the usual drinking and merrymaking are only a sideshow. The build-up to the fiesta begins the previous Sunday and it can be guaranteed that there will not be a free berth in the harbour. On 2 July the Fiesta Patriótica is celebrated, commemorating the town's resistance to Turkish pirates in 1558.

Eating out

Many restaurants, cafés and bars.

Ciudadela looking NE across Pta de sa Farola. Yachts on the visitors' quay further up the *cala* can just be seen on the right   *GW*

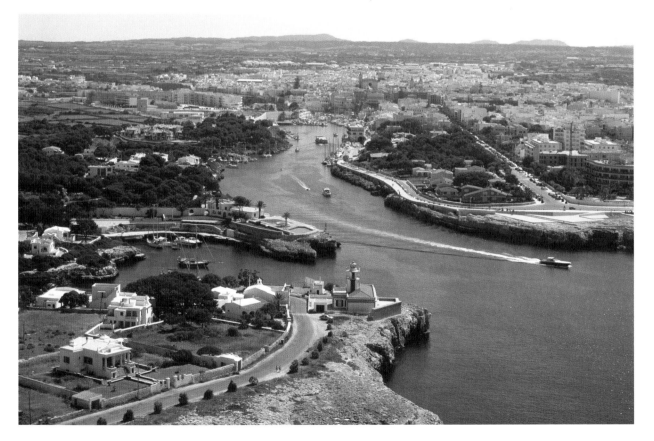

ANCHORAGES W AND NW OF PUERTO DE CIUDADELA

⚓ CALA D'ES FRARES
39°59´.8N 03°49´.4E

A short double *cala* on the N side of the entrance to Puerto de Ciudadela, surrounded by low (6m) sloping rocky cliffs. Anchor near the entrance in ±4m over sand. The W arm of the *cala* has a small sandy beach.

⚓ CALA BLANES
39°59´.7N 03°48´.7E

A long narrow *cala* between low (9m) undercut cliffs leading to a crowded sandy beach, about ½ mile W of Punta de Sa Farola lighthouse and the entrance to Puerto de Ciudadela. There is a large hotel with a small white tower on its roof near the head of the *cala* which can be seen from the entrance. Anchor in 5m+ over sand and weed, open to the S: it may be necessary to use two anchors or to take a line to one of the rings ashore. In summer a line of buoys marks

Cala Brut (left of centre), Cala Barceló (centre) and Cala Blanes (right) viewed from S

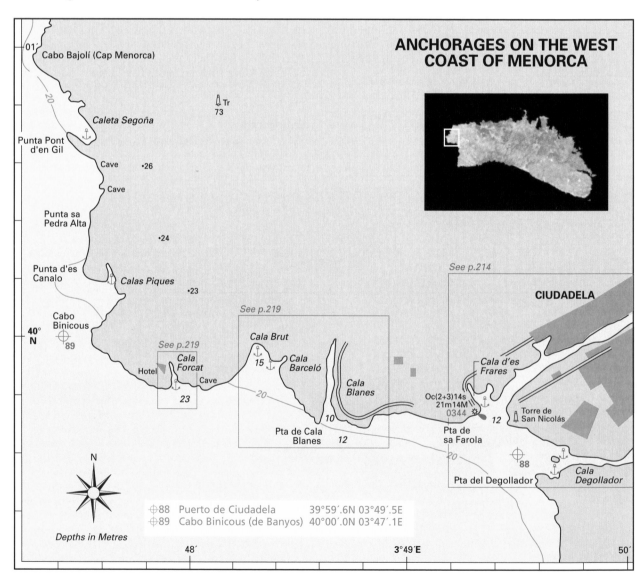

ANCHORAGES ON THE WEST COAST OF MENORCA

⊕88 Puerto de Ciudadela   39°59´.6N 03°49´.5E
⊕89 Cabo Binicous (de Banyos) 40°00´.0N 03°47´.1E

Depths in Metres

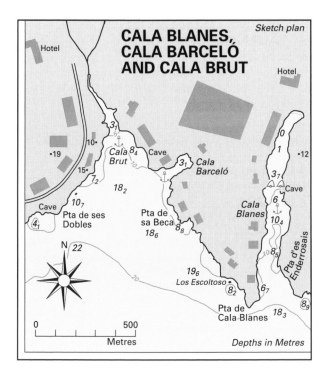

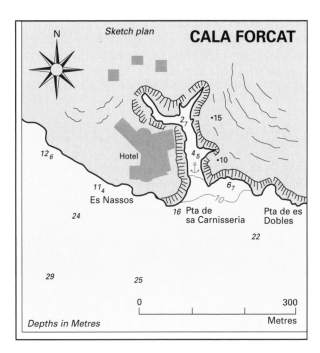

off the bathing area and virtually excludes craft from using this *cala*.

A tourist resort is growing around Cala Blanes, complete with the usual hotels, restaurants, beach bars, etc. Most day-to-day items can be purchased in the resort, though it may be simpler (and cheaper) to go into Ciudadela.

Cala Forcat bottom right, looking NW over Cabo Binicous (left). Calas Piques and Caleta Segoña on far side of peninsula

⚓ CALA BARCELÓ
39°59′.9N 03°48′.5E

A very small, almost circular *cala* surrounded by 10m rocky cliffs, open to the SW. Mooring buoys occupy most of the space available. There is no beach or other attractions.

⚓ CALA BRUT
40°00′N 03°48′.4E

A small narrow *cala* at the head of a wider inlet about 0.75M W of the entrance to Puerto de Ciudadela. Anchor in 5–10m over sand in the entrance to the *cala*. There are rocky bathing terraces on either side and a large hotel near the head. Again note that in high season swimmers' buoys exclude craft from most of this *cala*.

⚓ CALA FORCAT
39°59′.9N 03°48′.1E

A very small Y-shaped *cala* dwarfed by an immense reddish-orange hotel, Cala Forcat is suitable only for smaller yachts and dinghies. It is surrounded by low (10m) rocky cliffs and is open to the S. Anchor in 4–5m over sand and rock, using two anchors. All the usual facilities of a large modern hotel are available.

⊕89 40°00′.0N 03°47′.1E Cabo Binicous (de Banyos)

CABO BINICOUS (CAP DE BANYOS) TO CABO NATI

The anchorages between Cabo Binicous (Cap de Banyos) and Cabo Nati should not be attempted in anything less than settled weather and by experienced navigators. Most are deep and surrounded by high rocky cliffs (24–64m) and there are no beaches, houses or roads. The bottom is mostly rocky and 10–15m deep.

PUNTA PONT D'EN GIL

40°00′.7N 3°47′.6E

A long, thin, rocky-cliffed point with a large natural arch leading through into Cala Segoña. The arch is about 10m high and 8m wide and can be used with care by dinghies and small motor boats.

⚓ CALETA SEGOÑA (CIGONYA)

40°00′.7N 3°47′.7E

Just N of Punta Pont d'en Gil there is a natural archway leading through the rocky outcrop.

CABO BAJOLÍ (CAP MENORCA)

40°01′.1N 03°47′.5E

A large headland, high inland (72m), sloping down in a W direction to dark, rocky, steep-to cliffs. A disused semaphore signal station is located on the highest point.

⚓ CALA DE LA FALCONERA (ES POP MOSQUER)

40°01′.4N 03°48′.0E

A small *cala* under very high cliffs on the N side of Cabo Bajolí.

⚓ CALA DEL AMARRADÓ (RACO DE S'ALMARRADOR)

40°01′.7N 03°48′.4E

A very small *cala* open to W and NW.

⚓ COVA D'ES TABAC

40°02′.3N 03°48′.9E

Close S of Punta Espardina, open to SW and W.

⚓ CALA BE (COVA DE SON SALOMÓ)

40°02′.4N 03°49′.0E

An open *cala* with a sandy bottom and some caves, open to the W and NW.

Rugged coastline looking ESE from Cabo Nati, with several calas

6. Cala Pous to Isla Nitge

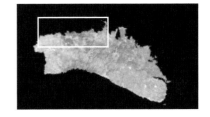

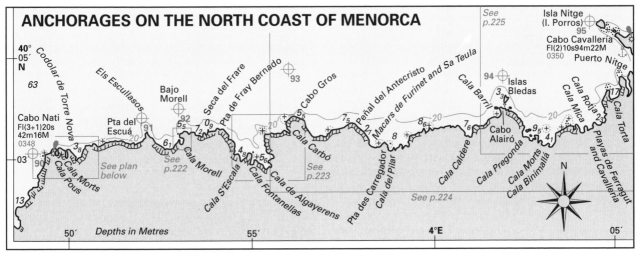

ANCHORAGES ON THE NORTH COAST OF MENORCA

⊕90 40°03'.1N 03°49'.0E Cabo Nati

CABO NATI

40°03'.1N 03°49'.2E

A prominent 32m headland of dark cliffs sloping to the NW, with a conspicuous white lighthouse (Fl(3+1)20s42m16M, aluminium cupola on white tower above a white building with a red roof 13m) set inside a white-walled enclosure a hundred metres or so inland. The cliffs are steep-to, but with several small rocky islets close inshore. A road runs from the lighthouse to Ciudadela.

⚓ CALA POUS

40°03'.2N 03°49'.6E

A small, narrow, rocky *cala* amidst rugged surroundings 300m NE of Cabo Nati lighthouse, with a small high islet on the E side of the entrance. The inlet lies between 30m sloping cliffs and has a small stony beach at its head. Anchor over rock, weed and sand.

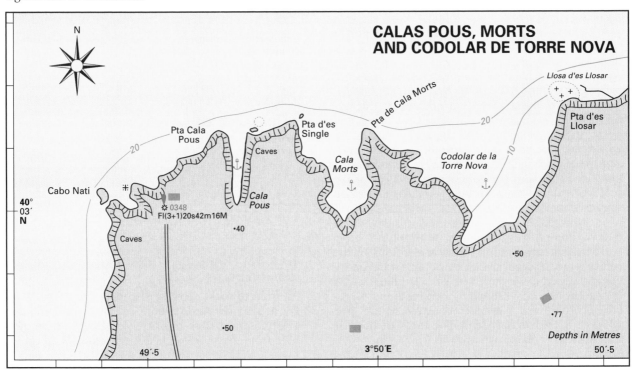

CALAS POUS, MORTS AND CODOLAR DE TORRE NOVA

⚓ CALA MORTS

40°03´.2N 03°49´.8E

A larger, wider *cala*, again between 30m rocky cliffs and with a stony beach at its head, separated from Cala Pous by Punta d'es Single. Two conspicuous islets to the W of the entrance and a *talayot* (ancient tower) on the skyline, make identification easy. Anchor in sand, rock and weed, open to the N sector. There are a great many *talayots*, large and small, but nothing else.

⚓ CODOLAR DE LA TORRE NOVA

40°03´.1N 03°50´.2E

A large, open deserted *cala* with 40m rocky cliffs, some rocky beaches and several caves, one of which can be entered by dinghy. There are several rocky islets off Punta d'es Llosar on the E side of the entrance and two *talayots* (ancient towers) on the skyline. Anchor in 10m or less over sand, rock and weed, open to the N.

⊕91 40°03´.8N 3°52´.0E Punta del Escuá

PUNTA DEL ESCUÁ AND ELS ESCULLASOS

40°03´.5N 03°52´.1E

Three small rocky islets lie close inshore under the high (79m) sloping cliffs of Punta del Escuá (Punta de s'Escullar). 100m to the N lie two breaking rocks (Els Escullasos) with foul ground extending for 100m around them.

⚓ CALA MORELL

40°03´.4N 03°52´.9E

This small, almost landlocked *cala* with sloping rocky cliffs gives a very beautiful anchorage. The entrance is difficult to spot until well into the outer bay. If coming from the W, on rounding Els Escullasos a group of white houses will be seen above Punta d'es Elefant on the SW side of the entrance. Coming from the E a few houses on Punta de Cala Morell will be seen. The *cala* only opens after this point is astern. Allow generous clearance to Seca d'es Frare and Bajo d'en Morell (see below).

Anchor in 4–6m over sand and weed near the centre of the *cala*, avoiding the unmarked 0.3m reef on the E side (see plan) and the swimmers' buoys which take up the E third of the *cala* and now actually enclose the reef. Most people anchor with a long line to the western shore (if tying to a ring make sure it is a secure one!). Holding is patchy and a few summer moorings are usually laid for local boats. If winds from the N sector are forecast it is adviseable to leave immediately, as a nasty swell rolls in.

There is a small sandy beach at the head of the *cala* where a seasonal stream enters, and a miniature quay, slipway, crane and boat park for dinghies. A restaurant and basic shopping can be found in the village. There are a number of caves in the area which are second only in importance to those at Cala Covas. A main road leads to Ciudadela.

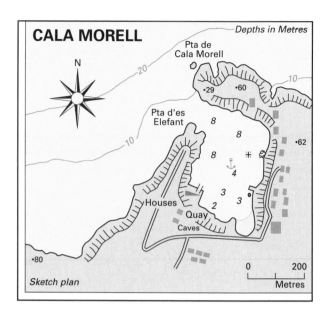

Cala Morell: a very pleasant and safe anchorage in most conditions

⊕92 40°04´.0N 3°53´.0E Bajo Morell Rock N

BAJO (BAIX D'EN) MORELL

40°03´.7N 03°53´.0E

This breaking rock lies 400m N–NE of Punta de Cala Morell with foul ground reaching for 100m around it. There are two other similar rocks very close inshore. There is a passage 150m wide and 16m deep between the *bajo* and the shore; use with caution.

SECA DEL FRARE (DE CORNIOLA)

40°03´.7N 03°53´.7E

An isolated rock, carrying less than 1m, 250m W of Pta de Fray Bernardo (Punta de Fra Bernat) and not to be confused with a rocky islet, Escull des Frares, 50m from the shore some 200m to the SW.

Cala S'Escala right, with Cala Fontanellas just behind the rock and the larger Cala de Algayerens beyond

⚓ CALA S'ESCALA (CODOLAR DE BINIATRAM)

40°03´.1N 03°54´.7E

An open bay surrounded by a sloping rocky shore with a stony beach, Cala S'Escala can be identified by the bleak Escull de ses Vinjoles Island (14m) off the headland to the E. Anchor over sand and rock, open to the N quadrant. There is a track leading inland but otherwise the bay is deserted.

⚓ CALA FONTANELLAS

40°03´.1N 03°55´E

A pleasant anchorage surrounded by green shrub-covered hills, with a small sand and rock beach. Escull de ses Vinjoles (14m) lies on the NW side of the entrance. Anchor over sand, rock and weed near the head of the *cala*, which is open to the N but also feels swell from NW and NE. A few seasonal moorings may be laid for local boats.

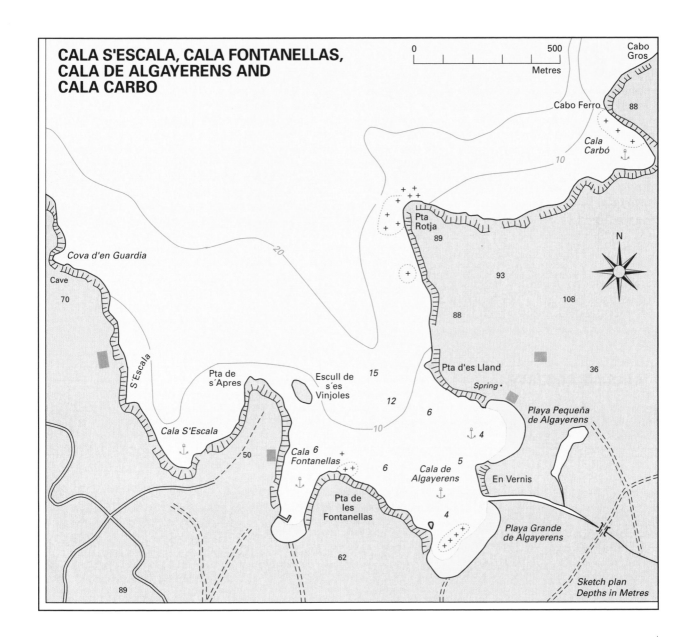

CALA S'ESCALA, CALA FONTANELLAS, CALA DE ALGAYERENS AND CALA CARBO

There are one or two houses in the vicinity and fishermen's huts on the N side. Much of the beach at the head of the *cala* is taken up by a short stone quay and slipway for the use of small motorboats kept on the foreshore.

⚓ CALA DE ALGAYERENS (D'ALGAIARENS)

40°03′N 03°55′.3E

A wide bay with two good beaches, Playa Grande de Algayerens (Platja des Tancats) to the SE and Playa Pequeña de Algayerens (Platja des Bot) to the NE, divided by an angular headland. If approaching from the N keep well off Punta Rotja which has foul ground extending up to 200m from its base. Anchor off either beach over sand with weed patches in 2–6m. A rocky reef lies close to the beach of Playa de Grande Algayerens.

There is a boathouse on Playa de Pequeña Algayerens with a spring, the Font d'en Cumar, nearby, but no houses. Several roads and tracks allow visitors to reach the beaches which are popular in summer. A large lagoon with much wildlife lies inland.

⚓ CALA CARBÓ (CARABÓ)

40°03′.5N 03°55′.7E

A small rocky *cala* tucked under the W side of Cabo Gros. Enter with care as awash rocks line most of the NE side and parts of the SW. Anchor over sand, stones and rock. The ruins of an important prehistoric village are ashore.

⊕93 40°04′.7N 03°56′.0E Off Cabo Gros

CABO GROS

40°03′.8N 03°56′.1E

Cabo Gros (96m) has steep cliffs and several small islets and awash rocks close in, particularly to the NW. Both it and Peñal del Anticristo 1.2 miles further E are composed of the same distinctive rust-red rock as Punta Rotja. It is sometimes erroneously referred to as Falconera, which is actually the high

Cala Carbó

peak (205m) which lies a mile SSE. A ruined prehistoric village and wall lie S of the headland, not far from Cala Carbó.

NORTH MENORCA MARINE RESERVE

Reserve area shown on plan below

From Cabo Gros E to Punta de Es Morter (just E of Fornells) there is a marine reserve. The area marked by three light buoys (see plan) is a fishing exclusion zone.

36690(S) **Buoy A** 40°04′.3N 3°56′E Fl.Y.5s5M with × topmark
36695(S) **Buoy No.1** 40°04′.2N 3°58′E Fl(2)Y.10s3M with × topmark
36697(S) **Buoy No.2** 40°04′.4N 4°01′.6E Fl(2)Y.10s3M with × topmark

From Peñal del Anticristo to Isla Bledas is a *Reserva Integral* within which no underwater activity of any kind is permitted (including, according to the latest Spanish charts, anchoring). The affected anchorages would be Macar de Furinet, Cala Caldere and Cala Barril. These are, however, included below in case they become available again.

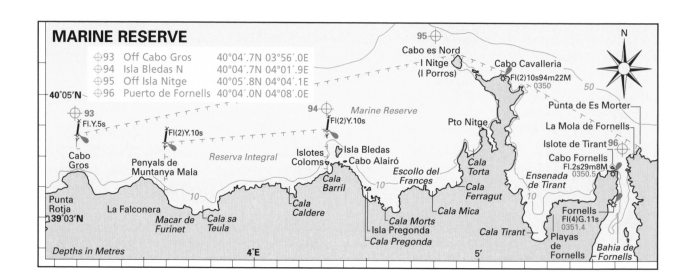

MARINE RESERVE

⊕93   Off Cabo Gros   40°04′.7N 03°56′.0E
⊕94   Isla Bledas N   40°04′.7N 04°01′.9E
⊕95   Off Isla Nitge   40°05′.8N 04°04′.1E
⊕96   Puerto de Fornells 40°04′.0N 04°08′.0E

⚓ MACARS DE FURINET AND SA TEULA

40°03´.5N 03°58´.4E (see anchoring note above)

Two ends of an open bay surrounded by sandy and rocky cliffs, to be used with care. There are rocks off the W beach (Macar de Furinet), while Punta des Carregador to the E has rocks and islets extending at least 100m NW. Anchor off either beach over sand and rock, open to the N quadrant. There is a hut behind the stony E beach but otherwise the area is deserted.

⚓ CALA DEL PINAR

40°03´.3N 03°58´.7E

A small bay between high (69m), sloping reddish cliffs. Numerous awash rocks and small islets line the coast to the east, but an approach on a southerly course leaving Illa d'es Pilar 150m to port clears all dangers. Anchor over sand and rock, open to NW round to NE.

⚓ CALA CALDERE

40°03´.6N 04°00´.9E (see anchoring note above)

A wide *cala* with sloping reddish cliffs on either side and scrub-covered hills (57m) above. There are two awash rocks close inshore, one each side of the *cala*, and at its head a sandy beach crossed by a stream bed. Anchor off the beach over sand and rock, open to the NW and N. There is a track leading inland with a few houses and two prehistoric *navetas* (burial mounds) at Sant Jordi about ½ mile away.

⚓ CALA BARRIL

40°03´.8N 04°01´.7E (see anchoring note above)

An anchorage off a rock and sand beach close W of Cabo Alairó (Cap de s'Alarió) and the Isla Bledas (Illa Bledas), easy to locate by a track embanked with a stone wall. Careful navigation is necessary due to a small island, an awash rock and an islet to port of the approach. From a position 200m N of Isla de'sColoms, avoiding an awash rock (Baix d'es Coloms) 120m to the NW of the *isla*, enter on a southerly course between the *isla* and Cabo Alairó, aiming for the centre of the beach at the head of the *cala*.

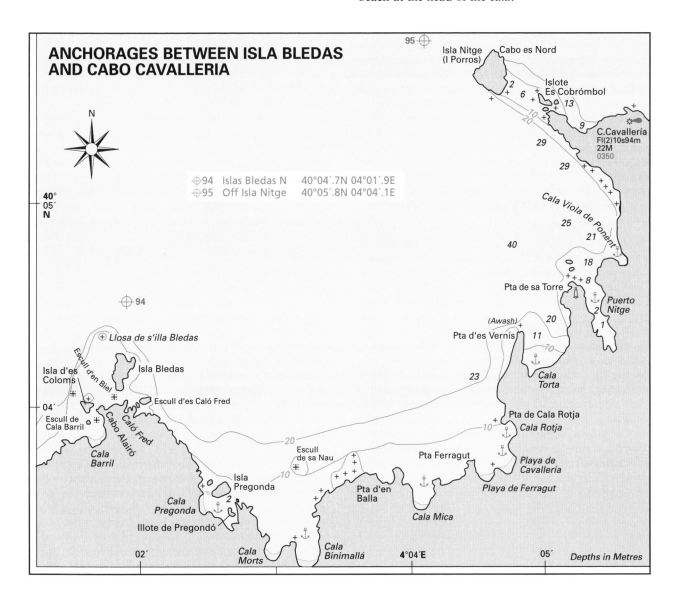

ISLA BLEDAS

40°04´.2N 04°02´.0E

Normally pass north of the Nature Reserve buoy to the north of Ilsa Bledas – although an offing of at least 250m will clear the isolated Llosa de s'illa Bledas, which lies 120m NW of the northwestern point of the isla.

There is said to be a fair-weather passage 100m wide and 5m deep inside Isla Bledas but this area is reported as a maze of barely submerged rocks. Rock hoppers should rely on eyeball navigation if attempting this passage.

⚓ CALÓ FRED

40°03´.9N 04°02´.1E

A very small *cala* hidden away behind the Escull d'es Caló Fred, only for use by experienced navigators in good weather. More a place to explore than to anchor, the *cala* is open to the NE, has a rocky bottom and no beach. There are just a few houses and a road ashore.

⚓ CALA PREGONDA

40°03´.4N 04°02´.6E

A pleasant anchorage in a large bay and partially protected by rocky islets, Cala Pregonda has become popular and is no longer deserted. If coming from the NE having rounded Isla Nitge (Porros), a direct course for the entrance clears Escull de sa Nau – an awash rock off Cala Binimallá. Enter the *cala* on a SW course between Isla Pregonda and the smaller Illot de Pregondó. Anchor off the beach in ±4m over sand. The wide sandy beach has a few houses and a road behind, and there is a second smaller beach to the E.

⚓ CALA MORTS AND PLAYA DE BINIMALLÁ

40°03´.3N 04°03´.0E

A wide bay with two sandy beaches divided by a rocky promontory. The W bay (Cala Morts) has two islets and an awash rock at its mouth and is not recommended. The E beach has some small rocks close inshore near its centre but is otherwise clear. Approach on a southerly course leaving the awash rock Escull de sa Nau 100m to starboard (it breaks in all but the calmest weather), and two similar rocks close inshore to port. Then favour the E side of the bay, taking care to avoid a shallow patch extending NE from the promontory which divides the two beaches. Anchor over sand and weed in 4m or less.

There is a lagoon behind the beach backed by sloping, scrub-covered hills, with one or two houses, a beach bar/restaurant and a track inland.

⚓ CALA MICA

40°03´.5N 04°04´.0E

A wide and deep *cala* with a sandy beach. It has a number of islets and awash rocks both in the approach (up to 200m from the shore) and fringing either side of the entrance. Anchor near the middle of the *cala* over sand, weed and rocks. There is very little ashore: a house and a track inland, and some of the surrounding hills are terraced.

⚓ PLAYA DE FERRAGUT, PLAYA DE CAVALLERÍA AND CALA ROTJA

40°03´.6N 04°04´.5E

Three possible anchorages in a large bay broken by rocky outcrops. Approach Playa de Ferragut on a S course to anchor off the beach over sand and weed. At the E end of the beach there are two small rocky islets dividing it from Playa de Cavallería, which is popular with visitors in summer. Take care on final approach to this latter as there is an isolated awash rock 200m off the middle of the beach (see plan) – favour the E end, to anchor over sand and rock.

Beyond the distinctive reddish point known as Punta de Cala Rotja (Rotja means 'red'), lies the *cala* of that name. Approach on an E course to anchor off the beach avoiding a patch of rocky islets. Various tracks run inland but there is little else.

⚓ CALA TORTA

40°04´.2N 04°04´.9E

A large open *cala* between dark rocky cliffs, with a large conspicuous tower built by the British in the 18th century on Punta de sa Torre, to the E. On the W side Punta d'es Vernís has an islet and an awash rock off its point. Approach and entrance are straightforward – anchor off the small stony beach in the SW corner over sand, weed and rock. The *cala* is deserted and only has footpaths leading to it.

⚓ PUERTO NITGE (PORT SA NITJA)

40°04´.5N 04°05´.2E

Not a port, but a long, narrow inlet on the W side of the peninsula of Cabo Cavalleria. It was a Phoenician harbour around 1600BC and is typical of the sites they often chose: a low, defensible promontory with the possibility of launching or anchoring boats on both sides, so that irrespective of wind direction they could escape, defend or attack as necessary. The Romans occupied the *cala* in their turn (circa 200BC), establishing a small settlement which is mentioned by Pliny in his *Natural History*.

Puerto Nitge is tucked in on the W side of Cabo Cavalleriá with Isla Nitge (Illa d'els Porros), and its large round tower just W of the entrance. Approach and entrance are straightforward, but without local knowledge it is advisable to pass outside the two islets lying off Punta de sa Torre even though a 50m passage carrying 5m depths exists between the islets and the point.

Favour the E side of the entrance as rocks fringe the W point, and watch the echo-sounder carefully –

the inner part of the inlet has silted up – though 2m can usually be carried for 200m, and 1m for the same distance again. Anchor in 2m+ over sand, weed and rock, open to the NW and N. The sides of the *cala* are of dark rock and the surroundings somewhat low and windswept.

There are three short piers or jetties in the upper part of the *cala*, used by small motor and fishing boats, and some seasonal moorings may be laid. A stream, largely blocked by a sandbank, flows into the SW corner. A few houses and fishermen's huts lie to the E with a large farm to the S. There is a road out to the lighthouse on Cabo Cavalleriá. A large-scale plan of Puerto Nitge appears on Spanish chart 4262.

⚓ CALA VIOLA DE PONENT

40°04′.6N 04°05′.3E

This tiny *cala,* which lies near the E side of the entrance to Puerto Nitge, might be visited by experienced navigators in good conditions, but has a number of isolated rocks, on the NE side of the *cala*. Open to the W and NW.

⊕95 40°05′.8N 04°04′.1E Off Isla Nitge

Passage inside Isla Nitge (Illa d'els Porros)

40°05′.5N 04°04′.5E

There is a passage 150m wide with a minimum depth of 6m between Isla Nitge and Cabo Cavallería with its offlying rocks and islets. Head NNE (or SSW), equidistant between Isla Nitge and Islote Es Cobrómbol, keeping to the centre of the passage as the sides are lined with just-covered and awash isolated rocks.

A very narrow fishermen's passage, the Pas d'es Cobrómbol, exists between the islet of that name and Menorca. However, it should not be attempted without local knowledge or first making a detailed recce by dinghy.

Looking W from Ensenada de Tirant towards Isla Bledas and Cabo Gros

7. Cabo Cavallería to Cabo Favaritx

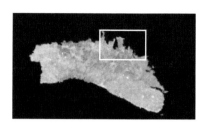

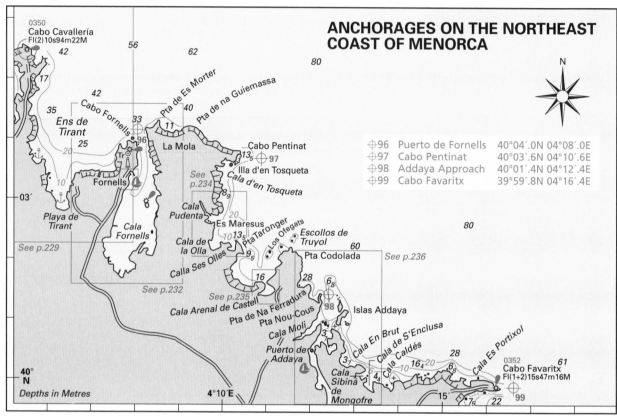

ANCHORAGES ON THE NORTHEAST COAST OF MENORCA

⊕96	Puerto de Fornells	40°04′.0N 04°08′.0E
⊕97	Cabo Pentinat	40°03′.6N 04°10′.6E
⊕98	Addaya Approach	40°01′.4N 04°12′.4E
⊕99	Cabo Favaritx	39°59′.8N 04°16′.4E

CABO CAVALLERÍA

40°05′.4N 04°05′.5E

A very prominent and conspicuous peninsula and headland sloping from 80m at the N end down to 5m where it joins Menorca. A lighthouse (Fl(2)10s94m22M, white tower and building 15m) stands on the NE point. There is very deep water up to the cliffs but watch out for the one 6.5m outlier, Llosa dels Ocelliers, just N of the lighthouse.

ANCHORAGES BETWEEN CABO CAVALLERÍA AND PLAYA DE TIRANT

A series of anchorages open to NE through to SE edge the E side of the peninsula of Cabo Cavallería. All have isolated rocks close inshore and a rock and sand bottom, and should be used only with great care in settled conditions. From Cova des Vell Mari southwards they appear on the large-scale Bahía de Tirant and Cala Fornells insert on BA 2833.

⚓ CALA S'OLLA

40°05′.1N 04°05′.7E

A wide, high-cliffed (74m) *cala* close E of Cabo Cavallería lighthouse, which is deep close inshore.

⚓ CALA VIOLA DE LLEVANT

40°04′.5N 04°05′.7E

Two awash rocks on the S side of the entrance.

⚓ COVA DES VELL MARI

40°04′.2N 04°05′.7E

Surrounded by low rocky cliffs open N through to E.

⚓ CALA MACAR GRAN

40°03′.5N 04°05′.8E

A wide shallow bay with some offshore rocks, open from N to NE.

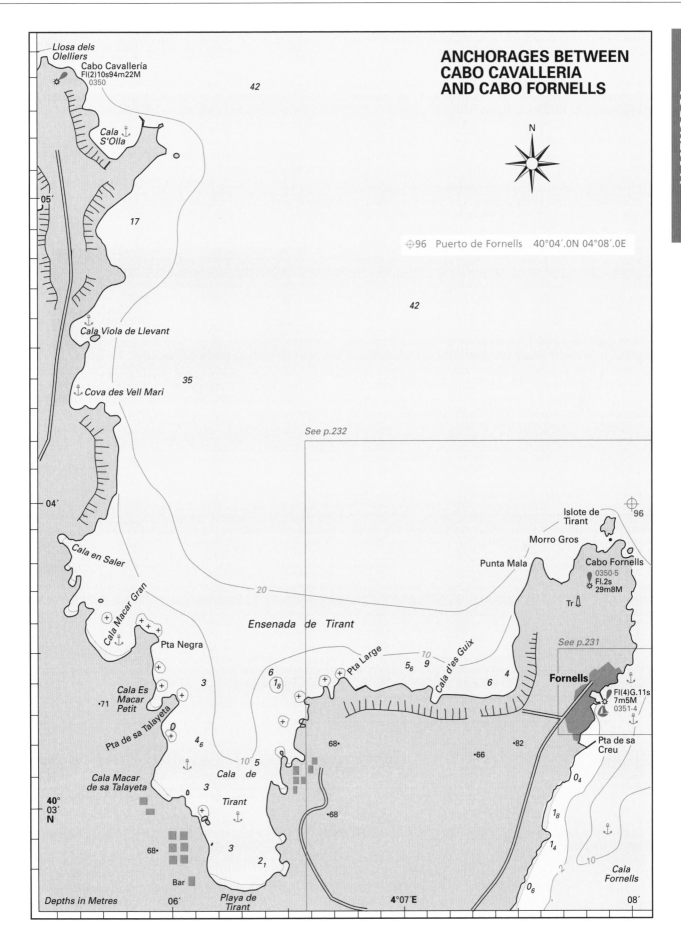

ANCHORAGES BETWEEN CABO CAVALLERIA AND CABO FORNELLS

N

⊕96   Puerto de Fornells   40°04′.0N 04°08′.0E

Llosa dels Olelliers
Cabo Cavallería
Fl(2)10s94m22M
0350

42

Cala S'Olla

05′

17

Cala Viola de Llevant

35

Cova des Vell Mari

42

See p.232

Islote de Tirant

⊕96

04′

Morro Gros

Punta Mala

Cabo Fornells
0350·5
Fl.2s
29m8M

Tr

Cala en Saler

20

Ensenada de Tirant

See p.231

Cala Macar Gran

Pta Negra

Pta Large

10

5 6   9

Cala d'es Guix

6   4

Fornells

Fl(4)G.11s
7m5M
0351·4

6
1 8

Cala Es Macar Petit

•71

3

Pta de sa Talayeta

4 6

68•

•82

Pta de sa Creu

10 5

Cala   de

•66

0 4

Cala Macar de sa Talayeta

3

Tirant

•68

1 8

**40°
03′
N**

3

1 4

68•

2 1

2

Cala Fornells

Bar

0 6

10

06′

Playa de Tirant

4°07′E

08′

V. MENORCA

⚓ CALA MACAR DE SA TALAYETA (TAILERA)

40°03´.0N 04°06´.0E

A wide bay with a large sandy beach backed by houses, open to N through E. (Cala Macar de sa Talayeta is incorrectly identified on BA chart 2761 inset as Cala Es Macar Petit).

⚓ PLAYA DE TIRANT

40°02´.9N 04°06´.3E

A large deep bay surrounded by low scrub-covered hills and an increasing number of housing developments. Approach on a S course towards the centre of the beach and anchor in 4–5m over sand, open to the N with swell from the NE. The long sandy beach is sometimes crowded – there is a café, and a good road inland. The huge lagoon behind has much wildlife.

CABO FORNELLS

40°03´.8N 04°07´.8E

This rocky headland has a lighthouse (Fl.2s29m8M, white tower with black band on white building 6m), and a small fort a little further inland. This fort, built by the British in 1801, has recently been restored and houses a small museum. Islote de Tirant (20m) lies close off its point with foul ground between it and the headland.

ME4 Puerto de Fornells

A narrow entrance gives excellent shelter in this long *cala* leading to several mooring possibilities for yachts, including 88 berths and several anchorages

Location
  40°03´.9N 04°08´.1E (entrance)

Communications
  Club Náutico de Fornells ☎ 971 37 63 28
  Fax 971 37 63 58
  Email nauticfornells@compusoft.es
  www.nauticfornells.com

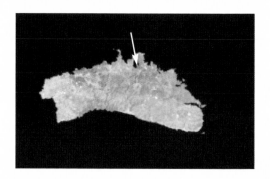

Fornells viewed from N over Islote de Tirant. Isla Sargantana centre

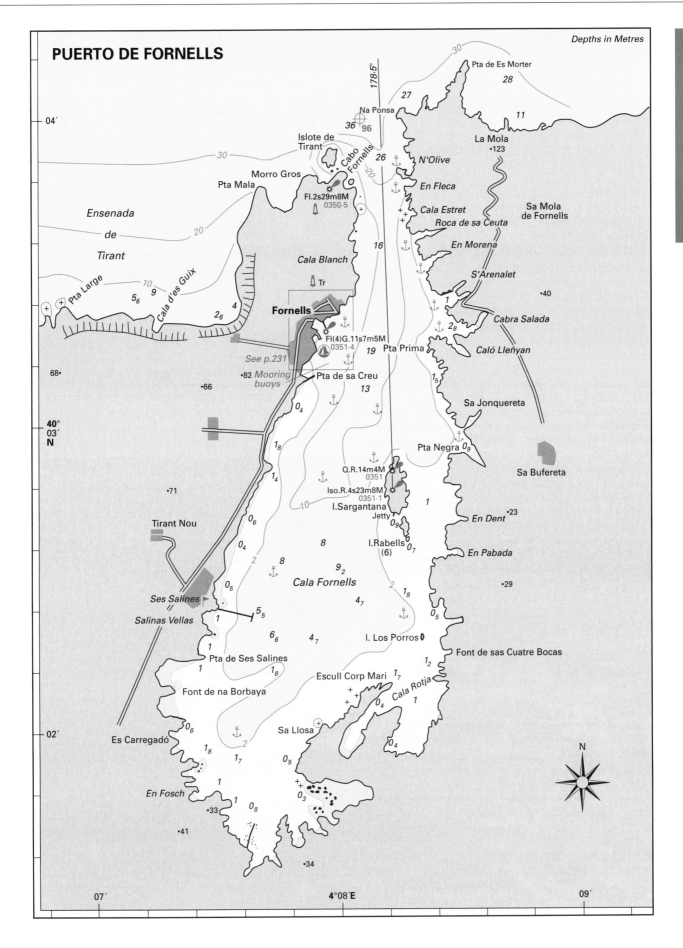

PUERTO DE FORNELLS

Depths in Metres

V. MENORCA

Pta de Es Morter
28
27
11
178·5
Na Ponsa
36 96
La Mola
•123
26
N'Olive
Islote de
Tirant
Cabo
Fornells
Morro Gros
Pta Mala
En Fleca
Sa Mola
de Fornells
Fl.2s29m8M
0350·5
Cala Estret
Roca de sa Ceuta
Ensenada
de
Tirant
20
16
En Morena
S'Arenalet
Cala Blanch
Tr
•40
Pta Large
Cala d'es Guix
30
10 9
5 6
1
Cabra Salada
Fornells
4
2 6
Caló Lleñyan
Fl(4)G.11s7m5M
0351·4
2 8
19
Pta Prima
See p.231
•82 Mooring
buoys
Pta de sa Creu
68•
•66
13
1 5
0 4
Sa Jonquereta
**40°
03′
N**
1 8
Pta Negra 0 9
•71
1 4
Sa Bufereta
Q.R.14m4M
0351
Iso.R.4s23m8M
0351·1
Tirant Nou
I.Sargantana
Jetty
0 9
En Dent •23
1
0 6
En Pabada
0 4
2
8
I.Rabells 0 7
(6)
•29
Ses Salines
0 5
8
Cala Fornells
9 2
2
1 8
Salinas Vellas
1
5 5
4 7
0 5
6 6
4 7
I. Los Porros
Font de sas Cuatre Bocas
Pta de Ses Salines
1
1 8
1 2
Font de na Borbaya
Escull Corp Mari
1 7
Cala Rotja
1
0 4
0 6
Es Carregadó
2
Sa Llosa
0 4
1 8
1 7
0 5
N
En Fosch
1
0 3
1
0 8
•33
•41
•34

The harbour

A narrow, deep entrance channel gives access to an inland area of water some 2 miles long by up to 0.7 miles wide, with a small and shallow harbour near the entrance. Approach and entrance are straightforward and there is a large area where yachts can anchor in solitude, though holding is very poor in places. A swell finds its way into the anchorage with gales from N and NW.

PILOTAGE

Approach

⊕96 40°04´.0N 04°08´.0E Puerto de Fornells

From W The very prominent Cabo Cavallería with its conspicuous lighthouse projects nearly 2 miles out to sea and has two outlying islands to its NW. Immediately to the E of this promontory lies the deeply indented Bahía de Tirant which is separated from Puerto de Fornells by another promontory, Cabo Fornells (41m). This is much smaller than Cabo Cavallería and has a very conspicuous isolated tower on its top. To the E of the entrance lies La Mola (123m) and Punta de Es Morter, composed of

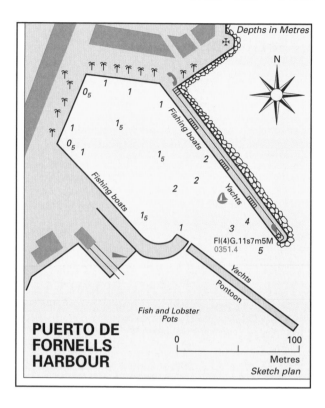

PUERTO DE FORNELLS HARBOUR

Puerto de Fornells harbour looking NE, with yachts anchored off. Shallows in the area can be clearly seen

steep, angular cliffs falling to a gentler slope below. Approach when the entrance bears due S.

From E After rounding Cabo Pantinat (25m) follow the coast past Punta de na Guiemassa (50m) to Punta de Es Morter with the lofty La Mola (123m) behind. On rounding Punta de Es Morter the entrance lies to the S.

Entrance

When positive identification of the entrance has been made, approach on a course due S. Isla Sargantana with its two white beacon towers will be visible in the middle of the bay just over a mile away. Line up the towers on 178.5° to enter (or alternatively keep the island bearing 180°). The sides of the entrance channel are steep-to.

Entrance at night should present no problems providing the leading lights are identified before entering the channel and followed until opposite or beyond the small harbour.

Anchorages

There are many possible anchorages in Cala Fornells (see plan), though holding is poor in the more popular areas due to over-use and elsewhere because of beds of long, dense, grassy weed. For close access to the town, anchor about 100m E or SE of the harbour in 5m over soft mud and weed. An area just S of the harbour is used to moor lobster-keep boxes, which float just level with the water and are difficult to see.

SW of the harbour is shallow with many moorings but it is reported that there is excellent holding in mud just S of the moorings off Punta de Ses Salines.

The area between Punta Prima and the Isla Sargantana used to be taken up with fish farms but these have now been removed and the *cala* just to the N of Punta Negra is available for anchoring in 2.5m over sand/weed. It is also possible to anchor further N off Calo Lleñyan in 4m but both these anchorages should be used with caution as holding has been reported as poor, but reasonably good equidistant between the harbour and Isla Sargantana in about 8m over mud and weed.

The Club Náutico de Fornells has its clubhouse and dinghy jetty at Ses Salines in the SW part of the bay, near which there are several further anchorages particularly favoured by those who carry sailing dinghies or windsurfers.

If entering and anchoring after dark, follow the leading lights until the single harbour light (Fl(4)G.11s7m5M) bears 230°, alter course onto 215°, and drop anchor in 8m or so when the light bears due W.

Berthing

The harbour is small with room for fewer than twenty yachts not exceeding 10m or so; check by dinghy first as it becomes very crowded in summer and there is little chance of a vacant berth. If space permits, berth stern-to the NE mole or on the pontoon extending from the SW quay. Several buoys have been laid just N of the stone mole; these are available for visitors and from here it is only a very short row into town. Berthing is inexpensive here and anchoring is still free.

Facilities

Water and electricity On the southern pontoon and all berths.
Fuel No fuel available.
Provisions Supermarket and other shops in the village. It may be possible to buy fish at the co-operative SW of the harbour.
Ice From the fishermen's co-op SW of the harbour (likely to be icebox quality only) or from a bar opposite the N corner of the harbour.
Chandlery A small chandlery near the harbour.
Repairs Carried out on local craft at the head of the wide shallow slipway which lies SW of the harbour. Crane available but no information on specifications.
Yacht club The Club Náutico de Fornells, located at Ses Salines about 1¼ miles S of the harbour and main anchorage, has a bar, restaurant, lounge, terrace and showers.
Bank In the village (open mornings only).
Post office In the village.

Transport

Car hire/taxis One car rental company in the village.
Buses Buses to Mahón and Ciudadela.

History

The fishing village of Fornells (pronounced Fornays) dates back to time immemorial, but its claim to historic fame comes from having been used as one of the secondary invasion ports during the first British expedition of 1798. They had intended to land at Fornells, but a headwind prevented this so the first landing took place at Addaya. When the wind changed the following day Commodore Duckworth captured Fornells.

Sights ashore locally

Most of the surroundings are of unspoilt natural beauty and development is restricted to a few areas. The village is small and picturesque but offers simple facilities.

The anchorage is surrounded by some enjoyable walks, such as to the defence tower and museum on Cabo Fornells or, for the really energetic, up to La Mola (123m) on the E side of the entrance. Both offer excellent views. Isla Sargantana makes an interesting dinghy expedition, partly to observe the unique breed of lizard which has evolved there (though you have to be an expert to know the difference). At the S end of Cala Fornells are the ruins of an ancient Christian church.

Local event

A fiesta is held in Fornells during the last week of July in honour of San Antonio.

Eating out

Many restaurants and cafés. Fornells has long been famous for its lobsters, served either with *mahonésa* or as *caldereta de langosta* (lobster stew).

ANCHORAGES AND FEATURES E OF PUERTO DE FORNELLS

PUNTA DE ES MORTER (DES MURTER), PUNTA DE NA GUIEMASSA AND CABO PENTINAT

(See plan page 228)
40°04′.2N 04°08′.5E to 40°03′.7N 04°10′.5E

A 1.7-mile-wide promontory with three distinct headlands, the westernmost backed by the heights of La Mola (123m). As a whole the headland slopes downwards from W to E and steep-to other than two rocks awash close inshore off Punta Na Guiemassa. However, when rounding Cabo Pentinat (Punta d'en Pentinar), you should give the point a berth of at least 200m to avoid Lloses d'en Pentinar, awash rocks that lie 100m NE of the point and two smaller awash rocks E of the point. There is also a lot of turbulence around the headland.

⚓ CALA D'EN TOSQUETA

40°03′.4N 4°10′E

A well-protected *cala* tucked away under Cabo Pentinat, with a sand and shingle beach and rocky cliffs. Approach leaving Illa d'en Tosqueta to starboard (rocks also extend off the headland to the NE) to anchor off the beach over sand and rock, open to the SE. A second beach lies 100m SW and there are two more further S. There is a fine view from the headland and two caves to explore. Cala d'en Tosqueta is a popular anchorage which often becomes crowded in summer.

⊕97 40°03′.6N 04°10′.6E Cabo Pentinat

⚓ CALA PUDENTA AND ES MARESUS

40°02′.5N 04°09′.8E

A smallish double *cala* with low rocky sides and small sandy beaches. The approach is straightforward, but look out for two awash rocks either side of Es Maresus. Anchor in sand over 3m or less, open to NE through SE. There is a spring behind the NW beach, a track inland and a parking area, but little else.

View looking WNW over Peninsula La Mola. Cala de la Olla with Cala Pudenta on right, Isla Sargantana in the background

Arenal d'en Castell

⚓ CALA DE LA OLLA (ARENAL DE SON SAURA)

40°02′.2N 04°09′.8E

A nearly circular *cala* with a large sandy beach and sloping rocky sides. A small islet lies off the NW corner, and there are awash rocks close inshore on the NW and SE sides. Anchor in 3–5m over sand. There is an extensive tourist development on the eastern headland, and a large lagoon with much wildlife about ¼ mile to the SW.

⚓ CALA SES OLLES

40°02′.1N 04°10′.1E

A small, rounded *cala* close E of Cala de la Olla, surrounded by low cliffs and with no beach. Enter with care sounding carefully: an awash rock, Escull d'en Tarouger, and several islets lie up to 150m off the point on the E side of the entrance and there are some small rocks close to the shore to the SW. Anchor in 3–6m over rock, open N and NE and to swell from the E. There is a large tourist development between the two calas.

⚓ ARENAL D'EN CASTELL

40°01′.5N 04°10′.9E

A large, almost circular bay with a long sandy beach, surrounded by large apartment blocks, hotels and houses. If approaching from the E, round Punta Codolada with a least offing of 400m and continue due W until the entrance bears 160° before turning S. This avoids three small islets off the headland, plus the low rocks to the W known as Los Ofegats (Esculls d'es Augegats). In most conditions the latter's breaking crests will be clearly visible.

Anchor off the beach in 4–8m over sand and weed, open only to the N. There are small-craft moorings on the W side of the bay and the N part has a rocky bottom. There is a considerable amount of development behind the beach, with all the usual tourist shops, restaurants and cafés.

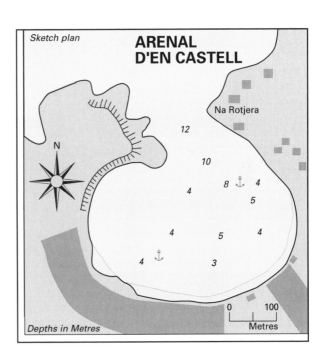

PUNTA CODOLADA

40°02′.1N 04°11′.5E

A low rocky headland with outlying rocks and islets but it can be identified when coming from the E by an isolated white house 200m from the point. The island na Joanassa lies close N of the point, with two rocks, Escollos de Truyol, some 350m N of the point. If rounding to visit Arenal d'en Castell keep well clear of Los Ofegats, lying some 550m SW of the point (see *Arenal d'en Castell* above).

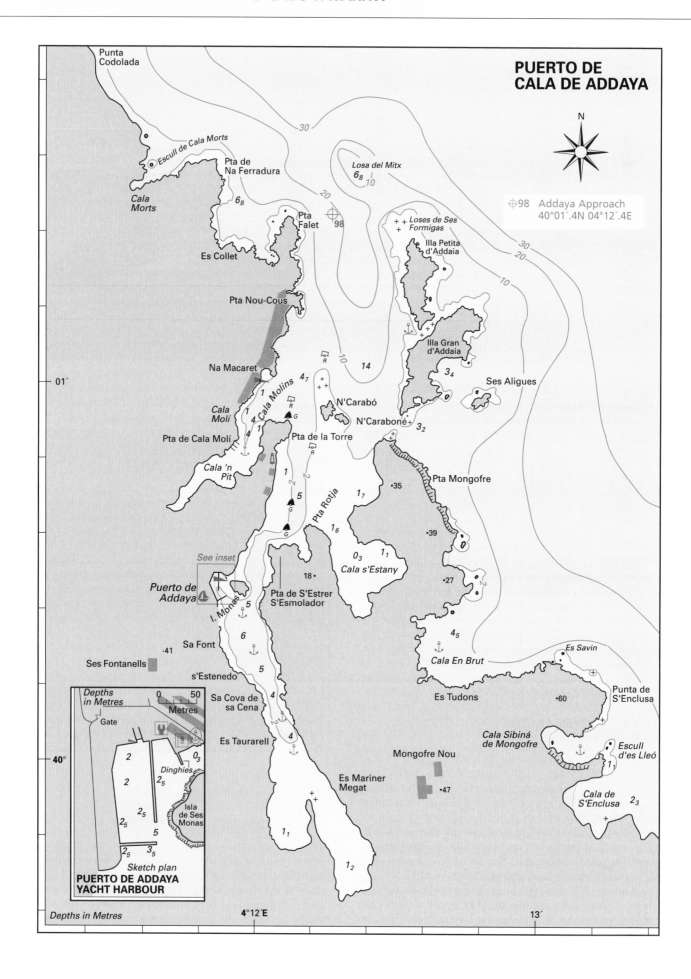

PUERTO DE
CALA DE ADDAYA

N

⊕98 Addaya Approach
40°01´.4N 04°12´.4E

Punta
Codolada

Escull de Cala Morts

Pta de
Na Ferradura

Cala
Morts

6₈

Es Collet

Pta
Falet

98

Losa del Mitx

6₈

Loses de Ses
Formigas

Illa Petita
d'Addaia

Pta Nou-Cous

Na Macaret

Cala Molins

4₇

Illa Gran
d'Addaia

3₄

Ses Aligues

Cala
Molí

N'Carabó

N'Caraboné

3₂

Pta de Cala Molí

Pta de la Torre

Cala 'n
Pit

Pta Rotja

Pta Mongofre

•35

5

1₇

•39

1₆

Cala s'Estany

1₁

0₃

•27

See inset

18 •

Puerto de
Addaya

I. Monas

Pta de S'Estrer
S'Esmolador

4₅

Cala En Brut

Es Savin

Sa Font

6

Es Tudons

Punta de
S'Enclusa

•60

•41

Ses Fontanells

s'Estenedo

5

Sa Cova de
sa Cena

4

Cala Sibiná
de Mongofre

Escull
d'es Lleó

Es Taurarell

4

Es Mariner
Megat

Mongofre Nou

•47

Cala de
S'Enclusa

2₃

1₁

1₂

Depths
in Metres

0   50
Metres

Gate

2

2

0₃

Dinghies

2₅

2₅

2₅

5

Isla
de Ses
Monas

2₅

3₅

Sketch plan
PUERTO DE ADDAYA
YACHT HARBOUR

40°

01´

Depths in Metres

4°12´E

13´

ME5 Puerto (Deportivo) de Cala de Addaya

A very safe friendly harbour deep in a long *cala*, with berthing for 150 vessels. Requires accurate navigation to enter with larger vessels. Berthing for 150 vessels up to 20m in a beautiful location

Location
> 40°01′N 04°12′.3E (entrance)
> 40°00′.4N 04°12′E (yacht harbour)

Communications
> **Puerto Deportivo de Addaya** VHF Ch 09
> Marina office ☎/*Fax* 971 18 88 71

The harbour and anchorage

A long, narrow estuary, its entrance guarded by a line of islands, Cala de Addaya (or Addaia) is a very pleasant, secluded and sheltered anchorage with a small and helpful yacht harbour in one corner. Considerable tourist development is taking place around the *cala* overlooking the yacht harbour, together with a yacht club building and sports club.

The entrance to the *cala* requires care and in some light conditions it is difficult to see. Entrance would be impossible in strong winds from NW round to E, though vessels already in the lagoon would be both safe and comfortable.

Facilities are limited, but adequate for everyday needs.

Cala Molí moorings for shallow-draught vessels. Shallows easily seen here

PILOTAGE

Approach
⊕98 40°01′.4N 4°12′.4E Addaya Approach

From NW Round the wide promotory comprising Punta de Es Morter, Punta de Na Guiemassa and Cabo Pentinat, which are without offlying hazards, then head SSE for Punta Codolada 1.8 miles away. There are a number of *calas* in the intervening bay. On rounding Punta Codolada, leaving it at least 400m to starboard, the Islas Addaya (Illes d'Addaia) will open up ahead, with Punta de Na Ferradura and Punta d'en Falet to starboard. In heavy weather Losa del Mitx (Losa d'Emmig), a rock with 6.8m depth, may break about 550m offshore but at other times it poses no threat. Aim to pass Punta d'en Falet about 200–300m off, rounding the headland at this distance to take a S and then SW course into the

channel between Punta Nou-Cous (mis-spelt Punta Na Cous on BA 2833 and 2761, as well as being somewhat misplaced) and Illa Petita d'Addaia (see plan).

From SE After rounding Cabo Favaritx, a low headland with a conspicuous lighthouse of black and white diagonal stripes, steer 300° towards a position off Punta Codolada. Stand on well past the Islas Addaia and the offlying Loses de Ses Formigas rocks, only heading in towards the coast when Punta d'en Falet bears 235° or less. Close the headland to a distance of 300m before taking a S and then SSW course into the channel between Punta Nou-Cous and Illa Petita d'Addaia (see plan).

Note Although fishermen use the passage between Punta Mongofre and the Islas Addaya as a short cut if heading E, it is far from straightforward and requires local knowledge.

Anchorage in the approach

There is a good daytime anchorage just W of the gap between Illa Gran d'Addaia and Illa Petita d'Addaia in 5m+ over rock and weed, open to the N and NW.

Entrance

Once past Punta Nou-Cous the channel is buoyed approximately as on the plan, though the buoys may be positioned slightly differently each season. Head for Punta de la Torre (low, with houses and a car park; the tower itself is well back from the point), passing one small red port-hand buoy (not always on station, and note that both the existence and/or positions of some of the inner channel buoys appear somewhat erratic: see warning following). If in doubt favour the W side of the channel: the chief danger is posed by rocks N of the islets of N'Carabó and N'Caraboné.

A slightly larger red buoy is laid in summer off Punta de la Torre and should be left to port. A green starboard-hand buoy sits within a stone's throw of the headland. Turning to port through this 'gate', a red buoy may be seen ahead marking the SW side of N'Carabó and this should be left fairly close to port. One or more green buoys show the extent of the shoals and mudbank fringing the E side of Punta de la Torre (some indication is also given by the extent of smallcraft moorings). Proceed slowly towards Punta de S'Estrer in the centre of the channel. (Note that the shallows can be clearly seen in most conditions but a good lookout is recommended.)

A little short of Punta de S'Estrer a mudbank, normally marked by two small green buoys, extends out from the W shore putting an S-bend in the channel. If these two buoys are *not* in place, once past the tower (see plan) steer for the centre of Punta de S'Estrer ahead, turning W only when depths off the headland begin to shoal. In calm conditions the mudbank will be clearly visible as a brownish patch, but should a mistake be made the bottom is soft and the position sheltered.

Keep to the centre of the gap between Illa de ses Monas and the eastern bank before turning into the yacht harbour or coming to anchor in the lagoon

beyond. Round Isla Monas about 50m off and Puerto Deportivo de Addaya will open to the NW.

Warning

The channel buoys mentioned previously may not be laid until well into the season (May or June) and are unlit. If cruising the area for the first time earlier in the year do not attempt the entrance unless conditions are favourable. If the buoys are not in position proceed very slowly as described, with a lookout on the bow and a careful watch on the echo-sounder.

Night approach, without good local knowledge, is not advisable: for preference a first visit should be made in light winds and good visibility.

Berthing

Visitors normally berth bow or stern-to outside the S pontoon, though space is at a premium during the high season, and if in doubt about space or depth anchor off and investigate by dinghy. Alternatively consult the yacht harbour staff on VHF Ch 09.

Puerto Deportivo de Addaya is one of the Balearics' smallest (and many would say nicest) marinas, with just over 150 berths covering all sizes up to about 20 metres. As with everywhere in the islands there are plans to expand but they are unlikely to be approved.

Anchorages

Anchor in 6m or less in the lagoon S of Isla Monas, which has good holding and all-round shelter. It is also possible to anchor further up the *cala* (see plan) in 4 to 6m, N of the narrows. (Note: a mud bank sticks out from the E shore almost to the centre of the narrows so keep to the W side). The inner lagoon is silting and depths are now reported as being less than 2m: proceed with caution and keep a good lookout at the bow. Much of the bottom is weed covered and holding is thus suspect. The land around the *cala* is privately owned.

There is a small pontoon directly in front of the harbour office where crews of anchored yachts may land by dinghy. There has been no charge for anchoring, though this is being considered.

Owners of shallow-draught yachts may wish to investigate Cala Molí (Molins) on the W side of Punta de la Torre. Proceed with care (the bottom is uneven and there are many moorings). The birdwatching is excellent.

Moorings

There are a number of mooring buoys in the lagoon but all are private.

Facilities

Water On the pontoons; yachts anchored off are charged to come in and fill tanks. If asked politely the harbour staff usually allow portable carriers to be filled gratis.

Electricity 220v AC points on the pontoons.

Fuel Not available, though it may be possible to arrange small quantities via the harbour office.

Provisions The supermarket up the hill to the W of the harbour, plus shops at Na Macaret (W of Cala Molí) can provide everyday requirements.

Puerto de Cala de Addaya from NE, tucked in behind Isla Monas

Ice From the harbour office.

Repairs Mardaya SC ☎ 971 18 88 05 *Fax* 971 37 22 90, based at the yacht harbour, can handle repairs, maintenance, painting, etc. A cross between a travel-lift and a trailer, since it uses the slipway, of approximately 10-tonne capacity. Also a shallow slipway on the N side of the harbour.

Engineers Addaya Motor Servicios ☎/*Fax* 971 18 87 96, based at the yacht harbour.

Sailmaker Mardaya SC handle canvas work.

Yacht club A yacht club is planned.

Showers By the harbour office. Free if berthed in the yacht harbour, otherwise € 2.

Launderette Up the hill from the harbour.

Banks In Mahón, though there is an exchange bureau up the hill from the harbour.

Hospital/medical services In Mahón.

Transport

Car hire/taxis Car hire agency nearby, ☎ 971 367111 or can be arranged from Mahón.

Buses Bus service to Mahón and elsewhere along the nearby main road (ask for directions in the harbour office).

History

The harbour has been in use since Roman times and many amphoras and other remains have been found. The last British expedition to Menorca landed near Na Macaret on 7 November 1798 under the command of General Sir Charles Stuart, mainly because the three frigates and troop transports were unable to enter Fornells in adverse winds. The Highland Scots troops were amazed to find the hills covered with heather similar to that at home. In five days the 3,000 British troops captured Menorca from 3,600 Spanish without the loss of a single British soldier. In 1861 three Dutch ships carrying bullion (the warship *Wasaner* and two escorts, the *Sint Laurens* and *Sint Joris*) were wrecked off Cala de Addaya.

Sights ashore locally

There is a small sandy beach off the holiday village of Na Macaret, where there are restaurants and basic shops.

Mahón is less than 10 miles away by bus.

Eating out

Restaurants and cafés up the hill from the harbour and a bar in the harbour itself.

ANCHORAGES E AND SE OF PUERTO DE ADDAYA

⚓ CALA EN BRUT
40°00'.3N 4°12'.7E

An open bay on the E side and S of Punta Mongofre, surrounded by high sloping rocks, recognisable by a conspicuous white building with a tower on the hill behind. There are a few islets close inshore on the N side. Anchor over sand.

⚓ CALA SIBINÁ (SIVINAR, SAVINAR) DE MONGOFRE AND CALA DE S'ENCLUSA
40°00'N 4°13'.1E

Twin *calas* surrounded by high (40m to 63m) rough hills and separated by a rocky point. Cala Sibiná is the smaller of the two and has rocks awash close inshore on both sides of the entrance. Cala de S'Enclusa has an islet with an outlying rock, Llosa de S'Enclusa, E of the entrance and a single breaking rock in the SE part of the *cala* itself. Both *calas* are mainly sand and are open to the N and NE. A conspicuous white building with a tower and red roof, stands on the hill to the E. There are several sandy beaches and some tracks inland, but otherwise nothing (see plan page 236).

⚓ CALA CALDÉS
39°59'.8N 4°13'.7E

A small *cala* at the mouth of a narrow valley with high (30 to 70m) hills each side and a small stony beach. A group of five rocky islets lies to the W of the entrance and four awash rocks plus an islet to the E. Enter on a S course midway between the two groups to anchor off the beach over sand and rock, open to the N. There is one small house in the valley with a track inland.

⚓ CALA ES BARRANC GROS
40°00'.0N 4°15'.2E

A large open *cala* amongst rocky cliffs and hills, with a smaller *cala* in the SW corner in which there is a sand and stone beach. Several islets lie close inshore on either side of the entrance. Anchor off the beach over rock with sand patches. The road from Cabo Favaritx to Mahón lies only 200m inland.

⚓ CALA ES PORTIXOL
40°00'N 4°15'.5E

A small round *cala* with an islet in the middle of the entrance, surrounded by low rocky cliffs and sloping hills (15 to 21m). Inshore islets line either side of the entrance; enter with care favouring the E side, and anchor off the beach, taking care to avoid three awash rocks in the S centre of the *cala*. Open to the N. There is a small sandy beach backed by sand dunes in the SE corner, and the road to Mahón 100m inland.

View SE over Cabo Favaritx

8. Cabo Favaritx to Punta S'Esperó

⊕99 39°59′.8N 04°16′.4E Cabo Favaritx

CABO FAVARITX

39°59′.8N 04°16′.2E

A very prominent low (12m), broken rocky headland with a conspicuous lighthouse (Fl(1+2) 15s47m16M, white tower with black diagonal stripes on white building 28m) set slightly back from the point itself. It is steep-to but with two islets on its S side.

⚓ CALA PRESILI

39°59′.4N 04°15′.4E
(Incorrectly identified as Cala Algaret on BA 2833)

A very open *cala* with sandy beach, dunes and small sloping hills behind. Anchor off the beach over sand and stone, open to the NE through SE. Three rocks with some 2m over them are reported to lie about 100m off the beach. If approaching from the S see the note regarding Punta de las Picas and Cabo Monseña, below.

Cala Presili looking NW

PUNTA DE LAS PICAS

39°59′.2N 04°15′.7E

Punta de las Picas (Cap de ses Piques) is a wide headland with offliers and awash rocks some 150m offshore. An islet, Escull d'en Tortuga (39°59′.1N 04°15′.8E), lies 350m to the W of the point with clear water all around it.

⚓ CALA MORELLA NOU

39°59′N 04°15′.7E

A *cala* with two sandy beaches separated by a rocky point. Enter on a SW course between the islets and reefs off Cabo Monseña (Cap Monsenyar Vives) to

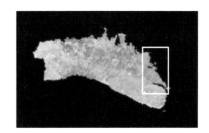

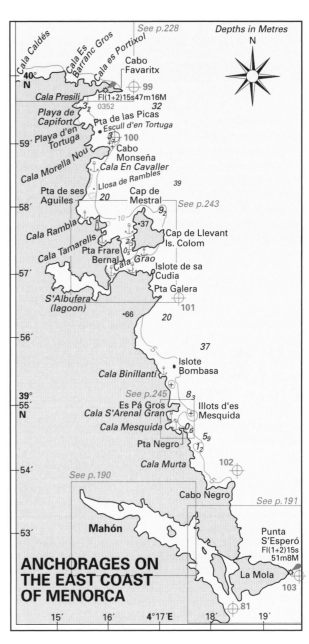

ANCHORAGES ON THE EAST COAST OF MENORCA

⊕99	Cabo Favaritx	39°59′.8N 04°16′.4E
⊕100	Cabo Monsena	39°59′.1N 04°16′.4E
⊕101	Punta Galera	39°56′.7N 04°17′.5E
⊕102	Cabo Negro	39°54′.0N 04°18′.7E
⊕103	Punta S'Espero	39°52′.6N 04°19′.9E

port, and Punta de las Picas (Cap de Ses Piques) to starboard. The latter has a small island, Escull d'en Tortuga, some 350m offshore which should be left to starboard. Anchor off either beach in sand. There is a track inland and a few houses.

⊕100 39°59′.1N 04°16′.4E Cabo Monseña

CABO MONSEÑA
39°59'N 04°16′.1E

Cabo Monseña (Cap de Mossèn Vives) is a narrow headland with a reef of awash rocks, Baix des Ferros, running off some 450m to the NE. It is advisable to keep at least 600m off this point especially in rough weather, to avoid the overfalls.

⚓ CALA EN CAVALLER
39°58′.7N 04°15′.7E

A small *cala* just S of Cabo Monseña, with a sand and shingle beach and a small islet on the S side of the entrance. Enter on a NW course, keeping closer to the S side to avoid a couple of groups of awash rocks extending some 100m from the cliffs, on the N side. Anchor off the beach: open to E and SE. A tree-lined valley with sloping rocky sides runs inland. If approaching from the N see Cabo Monseña and Punta de las Picas, above.

⚓ CALA RAMBLA (CALA SA TORRETA)
39°58′N 04°15′.5E

A large double *cala* with low rocky cliffs on either side and the Llosa de Rambles reef some 400m N of the entrance. Enter on a SW course to anchor over sand off the W beach, open to N and NE. The E side of the *cala* has some awash rocks scattered across its entrance though there is a good sandy beach behind. There is a single house between the beaches and a track inland. A standing *taula* and a *talayot* (ancient monument and tower) and burial ground will be found just over 0.5M inland, together with a ruined village at Sa Torre Blanca.

ISLA COLOM NORTH END
39°58′.0N 04°16′.6E

An almost deserted island with rocky cliffs, Isla Colom is 0.6M long by 0.5M at its widest point and up to 42m high. The NE coast between Cap de Mestral and Cap de Llevant has many rocky outliers, many just below the surface. One, Llosa des Cap de Mestral, is no less than 450m N of the central headland and a similar distance NNE of Cap de Mestral itself. Some 75m N of Cap de Llevant, (although it has been reported further offshore by several people who have grounded there) lies Llosa de ses Eugos, a rock with only 1.3m over. It is

Looking W, Menorca centre and Isla Colom right. Left is Cala Grao with S'Albufera lagoon behind. Left foreground is Islota de sa Cudia

ANCHORAGES AND PASSAGES BETWEEN ISLA COLOM AND MENORCA [14]

recommended that an offing of at least three cables (550m) is maintained along this section of the island coast. There are two attractive small beaches to which daily boat trips are run from Es Grao, and one large house, Lloc de s'Illa, plus a hut. Inevitably, the island has its own unique species of lizard.

Passage inside Isla Colom

A dog-legged passage between Isla Colom and Menorca, little more than 1m deep and about 100m wide makes a short cut for shallow draught vessels. However, the passage is prone to shifting sands following gales and depths are unreliable.

ANCHORAGES BEHIND ISLA COLOM

Apart from Mahón and Addaya, the anchorages behind Isla Colom offer the best shelter on the NE coast. They are, however, open to the NW and to swell from the N, and are therefore not suitable in heavy weather or in winds with a N component, since the two anchorages that might be thought to give all-round shelter (Cala Tamarells d'es Nord and S'Arenal d'es Moro) are too small to provide adequate swinging room in a blow.

The next four anchorages all have an interesting phenomenon: sandy weed-covered tufts stick up abruptly giving unreliable depth readings. Clumps of weed can be as high as 3m, reducing depths displayed on the echo-sounder to practically nothing. For reliable depths avoid these areas.

⚓ CALA TAMARELLS D'ES NORD
39°57'.8N 04°15'.8E

The N, and smaller, of a pair of *calas* divided by a rocky promontory. The conspicuous Torre Rambla (Es Colomar) stands on the N side of the entrance. Rocky islets and awash rocks lie close inshore around this point and off the central promontory – favour the S side of the entrance to anchor in ±5m over sand and rock. Shelter is good from all directions, but there is restricted swinging room even for a single yacht and it may be necessary to moor using two anchors at the bow.

⚓ CALA TAMARELLS D'ES SUD
39°57'.6N 04°16'E

A much larger anchorage than its twin to the N, with better protection than might be expected. There are offlying rocks around both headlands as well as the central promontory – keep to the S and W sides where there are a couple of sandy beaches. Anchor in 5–8m over sand and rock. Depths reduced to 2m have been reported, with an uneven bottom.

⚓ S'ARENAL D'ES MORO, ISLA COLOM
39°57'.8N 04°16'.5E

A small *cala* on the NW side of Isla Colom surrounded by sloping, scrub-covered hills. A small islet, Illot d'es Moro (also called Islote Pardals), lies just off the N side of the sandy beach, which itself has an offlying ridge of rock, carrying less than 1m. Anchor in 5–7m over sand and weed in good shelter. There is little swinging room and in all but the lightest winds it may be necessary to moor using two anchors at the bow. S'Arenal d'es Moro is a popular spot with daytime visitors but is deserted at night.

⚓ CALA DE S'ISLA, ISLA COLOM
39°57'.5N 04°16'.4E

A small, shallow, but very pretty *cala* just NE of the passage between Isla Colom and Menorca, surrounded by low sloping hills and with a house set back from the NE corner. A large rock just below water level lies in the central part of the anchorage, while the S side is fringed with rocks merging into those of the SW headland. Approach the centre of the *cala* with care on an E course to anchor in the outer part of the bay in 3m over sand. Like the beach further N, Cala de s'Isla is a popular destination for tourist boats from Cala Grao but is very quiet at night.

⚓ MACAR DE DINS, ISLA COLOM
39°57'.3N 04°16'.6E

Strictly a fair-weather stop on the S side of Isla Colom, off a small beach with rocks awash near its centre. In settled northerly weather it is possible to anchor almost anywhere between Macar de Dins and the SW promontory.

⚓ CALA GRAO (CALA DE LA ALBUFERA)
39°57'.1N 04°16'.1E

A popular anchorage in a large, rounded *cala* scattered with moorings and overlooked by the holiday village of Es Grao. Approach and enter on a W course keeping near the centre of the *cala*, which shoals rapidly towards the beach – keep an eye on the echo-sounder after crossing the 10m line. See also note below. Anchor in 3m+ off the beach, open to the E. There are slipways and quays for dinghies and small boats. Es Grao has a supermarket, restaurants and cafés (which also sell ice).

A broad stream leading from the vast Albufera lagoon drains into the SW corner of the *cala* and would make an interesting dinghy excursion. The lagoon and marshes, which extend more than a mile inland, are a wildlife and nature reserve.

⚓ CALETA AVELLANA (CALA VELLANA)
39°57'.1N 4°16'.5E

A small *cala* between sloping rocky sides close E of Cala Grao, with an isolated rock in the middle of the entrance.

Note This rock, with about 1.2m over, has been reported some 100m further N than the position shown on the chart, which can be a problem if a little too far S when entering Cala Grao. Approach from slightly W of N sounding carefully to anchor over sand, weed and rock.

⊕101 39°56'.7N 04°17'.5E Punta Galera

⚓ CALA BINILLANTÍ
39°55'.5N 04°17'.0E

A very small, deserted *cala* inshore of Islote Bombasa (En Bombarda) and N of Punta Sansá. Approach on a SW course and anchor off the beach. Do not confuse Cala Binillantí with one of a series of five even smaller *calas* to the N.

⚓ CALA S'ARENAL GRAN (GRAU)
39°54'.9N 04°17'.3E

This large *cala* lies immediately N of Cala Mesquida and Punta de sa Torre (topped by a large pale stone tower), and S of Punta Pá Gros. Tfreuo the E lies Islota Mesquida. Punta Pá Gros has groups of offlying rocky islets of which the outermost, the Illots d'es Mesquida, are 400m offshore. Leave all these islets to starboard on the approach and anchor over sand off the N end of the beach, open to the E and SE. The S part of the beach has rocky outcrops running out into the *cala*. There are a few houses and a road, but no facilities.

⚓ CALA MESQUIDA
39°54'.8N 04°17'.3E

An angular *cala* with a small beach, close S of Cala S'Arenal Gran and Punta de sa Torre and its prominent tower (which has the proportions of a

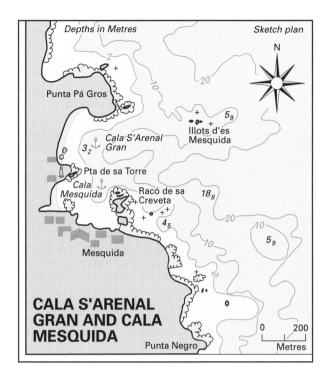

Depths in Metres · Sketch plan · N

Punta Pá Gros

Illots d'es Mesquida

Cala S'Arenal Gran

Pta de sa Torre

Cala Mesquida

Racó de sa Creveta

Mesquida

CALA S'ARENAL GRAN AND CALA MESQUIDA

Punta Negro

0   200

Metres

⊕102 39°54´.0N 04°18´.7E Cabo Negro

CABO NEGRO (CAP NEGRE)
39°54´N 04°18´.5E

A high (37m), prominent point of black rock with steep sides sloping seawards. A small islet and awash rock lie close to the promontory, which has some sea caves.

⚓ CALA ELS FREUS
39°52´.9N 04°18´.7E

A narrow *cala* on the N side of the isthmus of La Mola, which is foul on its S side. Bajo de las Aguilas (N'Ofegat), a low islet with awash rocks, guards the approach 500m to the ENE (see plan page 191).

⊕103 39°52´.6N 04°19´.9E Punta S'Espero

PUNTA S'ESPERÓ
39°52´.6N 04°19´.7E

A high (78m), conspicuous, flat-topped promontory with sheer cliffs, sloping gently downwards towards Puerto de Mahón. A large fort and other conspicuous buildings occupy the plateau, with a lighthouse (Fl(1+2)15s51m8M, white round tower with two black bands on white building 11m) at the eastern tip. There are two awash rocks close to this point but it is otherwise steep-to.

medieval castle keep). Leave the Illots d'es Mesquida to starboard and steer SW towards the small beach, leaving Racó de sa Creveta and its associated rocks to port. If approaching from the S keep at least 500m offshore until due E of Punta de sa Torre before heading in. Anchor between Racó de sa Creveta and the tower in 5–6m over sand and rock. Do not approach the beach without a previous recce by dinghy, as a reef runs most of the way across it in a NW direction from the rocks near the further buildings. A shallow river flows into the head of the *cala*. There is a dinghy harbour and slipway in the SE corner, in front of a café/restaurant backed by several streets of houses.

It was here that the heavy siege train of the Duc de Richelieu was finally landed in April 1756. It had originally been landed at Ciudadela, but was held up by the destruction of the road to Mahón and was re-embarked.

PUNTA NEGRO
39°54´.3N 4°17´.8E

A low (12m) headland with houses on its summit, not to be confused with the much more prominent Cabo Negro (37m) 0.7M to the SE. Rocks lie SE off the point.

⚓ CALA MURTA (ES MURTAR)
39°54´.2N 04°17´.7E

A wide *cala* just S of Punta Negro, with a series of rocky beaches and many houses to the N. Approach the middle of the *cala* on a W course to anchor in the NW corner over rock and sand, open to the E and SE. Care is necessary because the coast is foul in parts.

Looking SE over Isla Colom to Cala Grao and S'Albufera lagoon. Es Grao is on the left

Appendix

1. List of Lights

IBIZA

IB1 PUERTO DE IBIZA (EIVISSA)
Approach
0262 **Islote Dado Grande** 38°53´.5N 1°27´.2E Fl(2)10s13m6M Black tower, red band, ⁑ topmark 6m
0264 **Islote Botafoch** 38°54´.2N 1°27´.2E Oc.WR.7s31m14M Siren(2)10s White tower above a white house 16m 034°-R-045°(over Islas Malvines and Esponja)-W-034°(obscured over N Llados by Isla Grossa)
Entrance
0263 **Botafoch breakwater head** 38°54´.2N 1°26´.9E Fl.G.3s5m7M Green post 4m
0264.4 **NE (Marina Botafoch) breakwater head** 38°54´.7N 1°27´E Fl(2+1)G.11s6m3M Green column, red band, on white base displaying green ▲ 3m
0264.5 **T-jetty hd** 38°54´.7N 1°27´E Fl(2)R.5s2m1M Black post 1m
0264.6 **Marina Botafoch, inner mole** 38°54´.7N 1°27´E Fl(2)G.5s2m1M Green post 1m
0265 **SW breakwater** 38°54´.7N 1°26´.6E Fl(2)R.7s12m5M White truncated conical tower on building, red cupola 11m Obsc W of Islotes Malvins
0265.6 **Puerto Deportivo Ibiza Nueva, S mole** 38°54´.8N 1°26´.6E Fl(2)G.7s12m1M Green column on white base 11m
0265.8 **Puerto Deportivo Ibiza Nueva, N mole** 38°54´.8N 1°26´.7E Fl(4)R.11s7m1M Red tower on office building 6m
0265.9 **SW head** 38°54´.9N 1°26´.6E Fl(2+1)G.21s5m1M Green column, red band 4m
0266 **Contramuelle, NE corner** 38°54´.8N 1°26´.3E Fl(3)R.9s6m1M Red post 4m
0266.2 **NW corner** 38°54´.7N 1°26´.4E Fl(4)R.11s6m1M Red post
0267 **Commercial mole, E corner** 38°54´.8N 1°26´.4E Fl(2+1)G.8s6m1M Green pole red band 4m
0267.2 **Commercial mole, W corner** 38°54´.8N 1°26´.3E Fl(4)G.11s6m1M Green metal column 4m

PASSAGES BETWEEN IBIZA AND ESPALMADOR
0260 **Islote Ahorcados, S end (Illa des Penjat)** 38°48´.9N 1°24´.7E Oc(1+2)14s27m12M White tower, three black bands, on white building 17m
0258 **Bajo de'n Pou** 38°48´.4N 1°25´.2E Q.9m4M N cardinal beacon, ↥ topmark 9m
0254 **Los Puercos or Los Pou** 38°48´N 1°25´.3E Fl(3+1)20s28m11M White tower, two black bands, 27m
0256 **Isla Espardel, N point** 38°48´.2N 1°28´.6E Fl(3)7.5s37m8M White truncated conical tower 16m
32540(S) **Boya Bajo Ahorcades** 38°48´.7N 1°24´.5E Q(6)+LFl.15s5M ⚐ card

IB2 PUERTO DE SAN ANTONIO
Approach
0274 **Isla Conejera** 38°59´.7N 1°12´.9E Fl(4)20s85m18M White tower and building 18m

0273 **Punta Xinxó** 38°58´.5N 1°17´.1E Fl(2)G.7s9m5M Green column on white base displaying green ▲ 8m 075°-vis-275°
Entrance
0273.3 **N breakwater head** 38°58´.6N 1°17´.8E Fl(2)R.7s11m3M Red column on white base displaying red ■ 9m
Club Náutico pontoons 38°58´.8N 1°18´.2E F.R.3.5m1M Blue metal posts at end of each of the five *club náutico* pontoons
Buoys
32465(S) **Buoy 1** 38°58´.5N 01°17´.7E Fl(3)G.9s3M lateral stbd ▲ topmark
32475(S) **Buoy 2** 38°58´.4N 01°17´.9E Fl(4)G.11s1M lateral stbd ▲ topmark
32480(S) **Buoy 3** 38°58´.7N 01°18´.3E Fl.G.5s1M lateral stbd ▲ topmark

IB3 PUERTO DE SANTA EULALIA DEL RIO (SANTA EULARIA DES RIU)
Approach
31970(S) **Buoy** 38°58´.7N 1°35´.5E Fl(2)5s5M ⁑ topmark
Entrance
0267.8 **Dique de Abrigo head** 38°58´.9N 1°32´.3E Fl(3)G.9s11m5M Green pyramidal tower 6m
0267.85 **Contradique head** Fl(3)R.9s4m3M Red pyramidal tower 3m

FORMENTERA

F1 PUERTO DE SABINA
Approach
0252 **Isla Sabina** 38°44´.2N 1°25´E Fl(4)16s13m7M White truncated conical tower 11m
Entrance
0253 **Dique de Abrigo** 38°44´.2N 1°25´.2E Fl(2)G.6s11m3M Green column on white base displaying green ▲, 8m
0253.2 **Dique Pesquera head** Fl(4)R.15s5m1M Red tower 3m

MALLORCA

M1 PUERTO DE PALMA DE MALLORCA
Approach
0330 **Punta de Cala Figuera** 39°27´.5N 2°31´.4E Fl(4)20s45m15M Siren(2)12s Aero RC White round tower, black diagonal stripes, on building 24m
0316 **Cabo Blanco** 39°21´.9E 2°47´.3E Oc.5s95m15M White tower and building 12m 336°-vis-115°
0318.8 **Puerto de Palma** 39°32´.7N 2°37´.9E Fl(2)15s41m22M Square brown stone tower, visible outside Bahía de Palma 327°-040°
Entrance
0318 **S breakwater head** 39°33´.2N 2°38´.4E Fl.R.5s19m7M Red column on white hut displaying red ■ 13m F.R. on radio masts 4.5M E and E–SE
0318.3 **S breakwater outer elbow** 39°33´.1N 2°38´.4E Q(3)10s16m5M E cardinal tower 10m Obscd inside harbour Siren Mo(P)30s
0318.6 **S breakwater inner elbow** 39°32´.7N 2°37´.9E Q(6)+LFl.15s16m5M S card tower 8m

0319 **Muelles de Poniente** 39°33'.3N 2°38'.0E
Fl(2+1)R.12s5m3M Red pyramidal column, green band
4m

0320 **W mole N elbow** 39°33'.3N 2°37'.8E Fl(2)R.7s7m1M
Red metal column 5m

0328.42 **Club de Mar central mole, S head** 39°33'.4N
2°37'.7E FlY5s5m1M Yellow post 4m

0328.39 **Club de Mar N mole, S head** 39°33'.5N 2°37'.8E
Fl(2+1)R.12s5m1M Red column 4m

0322 **NE breakwater, SW corner** 39°33'.6N 2°38'.1E
Fl.G.5s17m5M Green column on white hut displaying
green ▲ 15m

0322.2 **NE breakwater, NW corner** 39°33'.7N 2°38'.1E
Fl.G.3s8m3M Green tower 6m

0328.38 **Club de Mar N mole, N head** 39°33'.6N 2°37'.8E
Fl(4)R.11s5m3M Red metal post 4m

0328.36 **Pantalán del Mediterraneo, S head** 39°33'.7N
2°37'.8E Fl(2+1)R.15s2m1M Red metal post 1m

0328.34 **Pantalán del Mediterraneo, N head** 39°33'.8N
2°37'.8E Fl.R.3s5m1M Red metal column 4m

0328.08 **Réal Club Náutico, S extremity** 39°33'.9N 2°38'E
Fl(2+1)R.12s6m1M Red post, green band 5m

0323 **NE breakwater spur, W corner** 39°33'.8N 2°38'.1E
Fl(2)G.7s7m1M Green post 5m

Numerous other lights exist in the NE of the harbour.

M2 PUERTO DE CALA NOVA

0328.7 **S breakwater** 39°32'.9N 2°36'E Fl(2)R.7s7m5M Red
post 3m

0328.75 **N mole** 39°33'N 2°36'E Fl(2)G.7s7m3M Green post
2m

M3 PUERTO PORTALS

0328.8 **S breakwater** 39°31'.8N 2°33'.9E Fl(3)G.14s9m4M
Green column on white base displaying green ▲ 6m

0328.85 **N mole** 39°31'.9N 2°34'E Fl(3)R.14s4m3M Red
column 2m

M4 PUERTO DE PALMA NOVA

0329 **S mole** 39°31'.5N 2°32'.6E Fl(4)G.11s7m5M Green
column on white base displaying green ▲ 6m

0329.2 **N mole** 39°31'.5N 2°32'.6E Fl(4)R.11s6m3M Red
column on white base displaying red ■ 6m

M5 PORTO ADRIANO

Approach

0332 **Islote El Toro** 39°27'.8N 2°28'.4E Fl.5s31m8M White
round tower 7m

Entrance

0332.5 **W breakwater** 39°29'.4N 2°28'.6E Fl(2)G.6.5s6m5M
Green column, white top 3m

0332.6 **E mole** 39°29'.4N 2°28'.7E Fl(2)R.10s4m3M Red metal
post 2m

M6 PUERTO DE SANTA PONSA

0333 **NW breakwater** 39°30'.9N 2°28'E Fl(3)G.8s10m5M
Green column on white base displaying green ▲ 5m

0333.2 **Punta de la Caleta** 39°30'.8N 2°28'E Fl(3)R.8s10m3M
Red column on red base 4m

M7 PUERTO DE ANDRAITX

Approach

0334 **Cabo de la Mola** 39°32'N 2°21'.9E Fl(1+3)12s128m12M
White column, black bands, on white square tower 10m

Entrance

0336 **Outer breakwater** 39°32'.6N 2°22'.8E Fl(4)R.12s12m5M
Stone tower, red top 9m

35191(S) **Buoy No.1** 39°32'.6N 2°22'.9E Fl(4)G.12s3M Green
pillar buoy

35192(S) **Buoy No.1** 39°32'.7N 2°22'.9E Fl.R.4s1M Red pillar
buoy

35193(S) **Buoy No.2** 39°32'.7N 2°23'E Fl(2)R.6s1M Red pillar
buoy,

35195(S **Buoy No.2** 39°32'.6N 2°22'.9E Fl.G.4s1M Green pillar
buoy

35197(S) **Buoy No.3** 39°32'.7N 2°23'E Fl(2)G.6s1M Green
pillar buoy

35198(S) **Buoy No.4** 39°32'.7N 2°23'.1E Fl(3)G.12s1M Green
pillar buoy

0336.6 **YC Dique de Abrigo head** 39°32'.8N 2°23'.1E
Fl(3)R.8s6m1M Red column on white hut displaying red
square 4m

0336.7 **YC Spur W head** 39°32'.8N 2°23'.1E Fl.G.4s3m1M
Green post 2m

0336.8 **YC Spur E head** 39°32'.8N 2°23'.2E Fl(4)R.12s6m1M
Red column 3m

0337 **S mole** 39°32'.8N 2°23'.2E Fl(4)G.12s7m1M Green
column on white base.

Note The fish keeps may be marked by one or more yellow
lights (Fl.Y.4s) and several unlit reflectors, but they are out
of the channel to the N.

ISLA DRAGONERA AND THE DRAGONERA PASSAGE

0282 **Cabo Llebeitx** 39°34'.5N 2°18'.3E Fl.7.5s130m20M
Masonry tower on stone building with red roof 15m
313°-vis-150°

0284 **Cabo Tramontana** 39°36'N 2°20'.4E Fl(2)12s67m14M
Round masonry tower on stone building with red roof
15m 095°-vis-230° and 346°-vis-027°

0286 **Isla Mitjana** 39°35'.2N 2°20'.6E Q(9)15s10m3M⯑ Y
beacon, black band 5m

M8 PUERTO DE SÓLLER

Approach

0289 **Cabo Gros** 39°47'.9N 2°41'E Fl(3)15s120m18M White
tower and house, red roof 22m 054°-vis-232°

Entrance

0288 **Punta de Sa Creu** 39°47'.9N 2°41'.4E Fl.2.5s35m13M
White conical tower, three black bands 13m 088°-vis-
160°

0290 **Ldg Lts on 126.5° Front** 39°47'.6N 2°41'.9E Q.R.49m5M
Aluminium ◆ on white round tower 7m

0290.1 **Rear 36m from front,** Iso.R.4s60m5M Aluminium ◆
on white round tower 7m

0291 **Dique E head** 39°47'.8N 2°41'.6E Fl.R.4s7m5M Red post
2m

0292 **NW Mole head** 39°47'.9N 2°41'.7E Fl(2+1)R.12s6m3M
Red post, green band 5m

0293.2 **Commercial mole head** 39°47'.9N 2°41'.8E
Fl(2)R.6s6m1M Red post 5m

0293 **Commercial mole elbow** 39°47'.9N 2°41'.7E
Fl.G.3s6m1M Green post 5m

M9 PUERTO DE POLLENSA

Approach

0296 **Cabo Formentor** 39°57'.7N 3°12'.8E Fl(4)20s210m21M
White tower and house 22m

0303.7 **Punta Sabaté (Cabo del Pinar)** 39°53'.6N 3°11'.8E
Fl(3)13s47m5M White tower, black band 15m

0298 **Punta de la Avanzada** 39°54'.1N 3°06'.7E
Oc(2)8s29m15M Octagonal stone tower on building 18m
234°-vis-272°

Entrance

0299.2 **Brkwt hd** 39°54'.4N 3°05'.1E Fl(2)G.6s6m5M Green
tower, white base and top 4m

0301 **Dique de Abrigo head** 39°54'.1N 3°05'.1E
Fl(2)G.6s6m5M Green tower, white top and base 4m

0299.5 **Dique de Abrigo elbow** 39°54'.3N 3°05'.3E
Q(3)G.10s3m3M ◊ on black beacon, yellow band 2m

0299.7 **Contradique head** 39°54'.2N 3°05'.1E Fl(2)R.8s2m3M
Red column 1m

0300 **Service mole S head** 39°54'.3N 3°05'.2E Fl(3)R.9s2m1M
Red column 1m, synchronised with 0300.2

0300.2 **Service mole N head** Fl(3)R.9s2m1M Red column 1m,
synchronised with 0300.

0300.5 **Yacht Club Spur** Fl(3)G.12s5m1M Green tower white
base and top 4m

M10 PUERTO DE BACARES

The light was withdrawn in 1997 but the structure is still
there and now painted white.

M11 PUERTO MARINA DE BONAIRE
Approach
0296 **Cabo Formentor** 39°57'.7N 3°12'.8E Fl(4)20s210m21M White tower and house 22m
0303.7 **Punta Sabaté (Cabo del Pinar)** 39°53'.6N 3°11'.8E Fl(3)13s47m5M White tower, black band 12m
Entrance
0303 **N breakwater** 39°52'.1N 3°08'.7E Fl(3)R.10s7m5M Red column, white base and top 4m
0303.2 **W mole** 39°52'.1N 3°08'.7E Fl(3)G.10s5m3M Green column on white base 4m

M12 PUERTO DE ALCUDIA
Approach
0304 **Isla Aucanada** 39°50'.2N 3°10'.3E Fl.5s25m11M White tower and house 15m F.R. on chimney 4M W-SW
Commercial harbour
0306 **SE (commercial) breakwater** 39°50'N 3°08'.5E Fl.G.3s10m5M Green column on white base 5m
33122(S) **Buoy** 39°50'N 03°08'.3E Fl(2)10s3M RGR pillar with topmark
0306.5 **W mole SE head** 39°50'.1N 03°08'.4E Fl(2+1)R.12s4m3M Red tower with green band 3m
0306.55 **Pile** Fl(2)G.6s4m1M Green post 2m synchronised with 0306.56
0306.56 **W mole NW head** Fl(2)G.6s4m1M Green post 1m synchronised with 0306.55 Fl(2)G.6s4m1M Green post 2m
Marina and fishing harbour
33140(S) **Buoy** 39°50'.3N 3°08'.3E Fl(3)G.9s1M
0306.6 **Dique SE head** 39°50'.3N 3°08'.2E Fl.R.3s5m3M Red pyramidal tower 4m
0307 **Old N mole** 39°50'.3N 3°08'.2E Fl(4)G.11s4m1M Green pyramidal tower 3m

M13 PUERTO DE CA'N PICAFORT
Approach
0307.16 **Escollo de Ca'n Barret** 39°46'.1N 3°09'.5E Q(3)10s3m4M Black column, yellow band, 3m
Entrance
0307.1 **E breakwater** 39°46'.1N 3°09' Fl(2)R.7s8m5M Red pyramidal tower 4m
0307.15 **W mole** 39°46'.1N 3°09'.6E Fl(2)G.6.5s5m5M Green tower 4m
Beacons
Seventeen pairs of tall day-marks, about 1000m apart and numbered from N to S, were erected along the coast from a point just S of the Gran Canal to the NE of Colonia de San Pedro. Though some pairs are now missing, the remaining beacons are still useful navigationally.
Beacon Nos 1 and 2 mark an area of obstructions 1.5 miles NW of the harbour. Beacon No 4 (which is white with a red top, but does not display its number) is located just W of the entrance to Ca'n Picafort. Some of the remaining beacons are white, others natural stone.

M14 PUERTO DE SERRA NOVA
0307.17 **NE breakwater** 39°44'.4N 3°13'.5E Fl(3)R.10s6m5M Red column 2m
0307.19 **W mole** 39°44'.4N 3°13'.4E Oc.G.8s3m3M Green column 2m

M15 PUERTO DE COLONIA DE SAN PEDRO
0307.2 **Breakwater head** 39°44'.3N 3°16'.4E Fl(4)R.12s6m5M Red column 3m
0307.25 **W mole head** 39°44'.3N 3°16'.5E Fl(4)G.12s4m3M Green column 3m

M16 PUERTO DE CALA RATJADA
Approach
0308 **Cabo de Pera** 39°43'N 3°28'.7E Fl(2+3)20s76m16M White tower on white building with dark corners and red roof 21m 148°-vis-010°
Entrance
0308.2 **Breakwater head** 39°42'.6N 3°27'.9E Fl.G.2s12m5M Green post 3m
0308.3 **Breakwater spur (fishermen's quay)** 39°42'.7N 3°27'.9E Fl(2)G.6s6m1M Green post 5m
0308.32 **W mole** 39°42'.7N 3°27'.9E Fl.R.3s6m3M Red post on white base 5m

0308.34 **NW mole** 39°42'.7N 3°27'.9E Fl(2)R.6s6m1M Red post 5m

M17 PUERTO DE CALA BONA
0308.6 **S breakwater** 39°36'.8N 3°23'.6E Fl(2)R.6s5m4M Red column on white base displaying red ■ 2m
0308.7 **N breakwater** 39°36'.8N 3°23'.6E Fl(2)G.6s5m3M Green column on white base displaying green ▲ 2m

M18 PORTO CRISTO
0309 **Cabo del Morro de sa Carabassa** 39°32'.2N 3°20'.5E Fl.5s20m7M White tower, black vertical stripes 6m
0309.4 **NE mole** 39°32'.5N 3°20'.3E Fl(3)R.8.5s5m3M Red octagonal column 2m

M19 PORTO COLOM
Approach
0310 **Punta de ses Crestas (Punta de la Farola)** 39°24'.9N 3°16'.3E Fl(2)10s42m10M White round tower, black bands, on white building with red roof 25m 207°-vis-006°
Entrance
0310.4 **Punta de sa Batería** 39°25'.0N 3°16'.2E Fl(4)R.11s12m5M Red tower on white base 7m
0311 **W mole** 39°25'.3N 3°15'.8E Fl(3)R.8s5m1M Red tower on white base with red square 3m
0311.2 **Yacht harbour S mole** 39°25'.5N 3°15'.8E Fl(4)R.11s3m1M Red column 2m
33622(S) **Buoy 1** 39°25'.2N 3°16'.1E Fl.G.4s1M Green pillar, ▲ topmark
33624(S) **Buoy 2** 39°25'.1N 3°16'.1E Fl.R.3s1M Red pillar, ■ topmark
33625(S) **Buoy 3** 39°25'.3N 3°16'E Fl(2)G.6s1M Green pillar, ▲ topmark
33626(S) **Buoy 4** 39°25'.2N 3°15'.9E Fl(2)R.6s1M Red pillar, ■ topmark
33628(S) **Buoy 5** 39°25'.4N 3°15'.9E Fl(3)G.8s1M Green pillar, ▲ topmark
Buoys
In addition to the starboard-hand buoys, ten unlit white buoys with green triangular topmarks indicate the starboard side of the dredged channel into the yacht harbour, and two white buoys with red triangular topmarks mark a shoal near the root of the yacht harbour S mole. A line of yellow buoys marks the swimming area off the beach at Arenal Gran.

M20 PUERTO DE CALA LLONGA
0311.4 **Punta del Fortin** 39°22'.1N 3°14'.1E Fl(1+2)20s17m7M Round white column on square white base, both with vertical black stripes 6m
0311.45 **Cala Llonga N side** 39°22'.2N 3°13'.9E Fl.G.5s9m5M Green column on white base 6m
0311.5 **Marina S mole** 39°22'.2N 3°13'.7E Fl.R.5s5m1M Red column on white base 3m

M21 PORTO PETRO
0311.8 **Punta de sa Torre** 39°21'.4N 3°13'E Fl(3+1)10s22m7M White tower on square base with two vertical black stripes 9m
0311.9 **Yacht harbour S mole** 39°21'.7N 3°12'.8E Fl(2)R.7s7m5M Red column 3m
0312.2 **Yacht harbour hammerhead, N end** 39°21'.8N 3°12'.8E Fl(2+1)G.12s6m3M Green column with red band on white base
0312.25 **Yacht harbour hammerhead, S end** 39°21'.7N 3°12'.7E Fl(2)G.7s4m1M Green post 3m

M22 PUERTO DE CALA FIGUERA
0312.6 **Torre D'en Beu** 39°19'.8N 3°10'.7E Fl.3s32m12M White octagonal tower, vertical black stripes 6m
0313 **Molehead** 39°20'N 3°10'.3E Fl(3)R.8s6m5M Red column on white base displaying red ■ 5m

M23 PUERTO COLONIA DE SANT JORDI
Approach
0315 **Punta Sa** 39°18'.8N 2°59'.7E Fl(3)10.5s18m7M White round tower, three black bands 12m
0314.2 **Isla de na Guardia** 39°18'.7N 3°00'E Fl(4)G.12s7m5M Green tower on white base 5m

Entrance

0314.4 SE **Breakwater head** 39°19'N 3°00'E Fl(4)R.10s5m3M
Red column on white base

0314.6 **Marina N mole** 39°19'N 2°59'.9E Fl.G.3s4m1M Green
column on white base 3m

0315.8 **Punta Plana** 39°21.2N 2°54.9E Fl(1+3)12s16m7M
White round tower, black bands 12m

M24 PUERTO DE LA RÁPITA

Approach

0315.8 **Punta Plana** 39°21'.2N 2°54'.9E Fl(1+3)12s16m7M
White tower, black bands, on building 12m

Entrance

0315.4 **W breakwater head** 39°21'.8N 2°57'.4E
Fl.R.2.5s7m5M Red column 6m

0315.5 **E breakwater head** Fl.G.4.5s8m3M Green column 6m

M25 PUERTO DE S'ESTANYOL

Approach

0315.8 **Punta Plana** 39°21'.2N 2°54'.9E Fl(1+3)12s16m7M
White tower, black bands, on building 12m

Entrance

0315.6 **S breakwater** 39°21'.7N 2°55'.3E Fl(2)R.6s7m5M Red
column on white base 6m

0315.7 **N Mole head** 39°21'.7N 2°55'.2E Fl(2)G.7s8m1M
Halfway up black lamp post 8m

M26 PUERTO EL ARENAL

0316.3 **Dique de Abrigo head** 39°30'.2N 2°44'.8E
Fl(3)G.8s8m5M Green column, with white top and base
4m

0316.35 **Dique de Abrigo elbow** 39°30'N 2°44'.7E
Q(9)15s6m3M Yellow tower black band 2m

0316.55 **Contradique head** 39°30'.2N
2°44'.9EFl(3)R.12s7m3M Red post 4m

0316.6 **Contradique spur** Fl(4)R.11s8m1M Red tower on
white base 6m

0316.4 **Interior mole NE corner** 39°30'.1N 2°44'.9E
Fl(2+1)R.11.5s8m1M Red column, green band, white top
7m

0316.5 **Interior mole SW corner** Fl.R.3s4m1M Red tower 3m

M27 PUERTO DE SAN ANTONIO DE LA PLAYA

0316.7 **W breakwater head** 39°32'N 2°43'.E Fl(4)R.11s8m5M
Red column on white base 6m

0316.72 **E breakwater head** Fl(4)G.11s6m3M Green column
on building 5m

M28 PUERTO DE CALA GAMBA

0316.74 **Dique de Abrigo** 39°32'.8N 2°41'.7E Fl.R.2s5m5M
Red post 3m

0316.76 **Contradique head** Fl.G.2s4m3M Green post 3m

M29 PUERTO DEL MOLINAR DE LEVANTE

0317.2 **SW breakwater head** 39°33'.5N 2°40'.5E
Fl(2)R.7s7m5M Red tower 4m

M30 PUERTO DE CALA PORTIXOL

0316.8 **SW breakwater** 39°33'.5N 2°40'.1E Fl(3)R.9s7m5M
Red column on white base displaying red ■ 6m

0316.82 **SE breakwater** 39°33'.5N 2°40'.2E Fl(3)G.9s7m3M
Green column on white base displaying green ▲ 6m

0316.83 **SW inner mole** 39°33'.6N 2°40'.1E Fl(4)R.11s7m1M
Red column on white base displaying red ■ 4m

0316.84 **SE inner mole** 39°33'.6N 2°40'.1E Fl(4)G.11s7m1M
Green column on white base displaying green ▲ 5m

CABRERA

C1 PUERTO DE CABRERA

Approach

0338.3 **Cabo Llebeig** 39°09'.7N 2°55'.1E Fl(4)14.5s74m7M
Black and white chequered angular tower 7m

Entrance

0338.6 **Punta de Sa Creueta** 39°09'.3N 2°55'.8E
Fl.R.4s13m7M White angular tower 5m

0339 **Jetty** 39°09'.1N 2°56'.1E Fl(2)R.10.5s5m5M Red column
on building 4m

MENORCA

ME1 PUERTO DE MAHÓN

Approach

0366 **Isla del Aire** 39°48'N 4°17'.6E Fl.5s53m18M White
tower, black bands, on white building 38m 197°-vis-111°

0355 **Punta S'Esperó** 39°52'.7N 4°19'.7E Fl(1+2)15s51m8M
White round tower, two black bands, on white building
11m

0352 **Cabo Favaritx** 39°59'.8N 4°16'E Fl(1+2)15s47m16M
White tower, black diagonal stripes, on white building
28m

Entrance

0354 **Punta de San Carlos** 39°52'N 4°18'.5E Oc(2)6s22m12M
White round tower, three black bands, on square white
base 15m 183°-vis-143°

35970(S) **Laja de San Carlos** 39°51'.9N 4°18'.6E Fl.R.4s3M
Red pillar buoy, ■ topmark

35990(S) **Laja de Fuera** 39°52'.1N 4°18'.6E Fl.G.4s3M Green
pillar buoy, ▲ topmark

36010(S) **Punta San Felipet** 39°52'.3N 4°18'.4E Q(2)G.3s3M
Green pillar buoy, ▲ topmark

36030(S) **Laja del Moro** 39°52'.3N 4°18'.3E Q(2)R.3s3M Red
pillar buoy, ■ topmark

0356 **Punta del Lazareto** 39°52'.6N 4°18'.2E Fl(2)G.7s13m3M
White column displaying green ▲ 9m

0359 **Isla Cuarentena or Plana** 39°53'N 4°18'E
Fl(3)G.9s9m3M Green column, white top and base 6m

0358 **Punta de Na Cafayes** 39°53'N 4°17'.7E Fl(3)R.9s8m1M
Red column on white hut displaying red ■

0360 **Punta de Villacarlos** 39°53'.1N 4°17'.4E
Fl(4)R.11s10m1M Red column on white hut displaying
red ■ 4m

0361 **Isla del Rey or del Hospital, S side** 39°53'.2N 4°17'.3E
Fl.G.5s13m1M White column displaying green ▲ 13m

0361.2 **Pontoon head** 39°53'.2N 4°17'.1E Q(9).15s2m1M
Yellow column, black band 1m

0361.4 **Isla del Rey, N side (Punta Sa Cova)** 39°53'.3N
4°17'.3E Oc.R.4s16m1M Red tower 6m

0361.6 **Punta de Sa Bassa** 39°53'.4N 4°17'.4E Oc.G.4s9m1M
Green ▲ on green metal tripod on white hut 3m

0361.7 **Cala Rata** 39°53'.6N 4°16'.8E Fl.G.5s7m3M
Green ▲ on green post

0362 **Punta de Cala Figuera** 39°53'.5N 4°16'.6E Fl.R.5s7m1M
Red ■ on red metal post 5m

0362.4 **Isla Pinta, S side** 39°53'.6N 4°16'.3E Fl(2)G.7s4m1M
Green ▲ on green metal post 3m F.R on tower 650m
N-NW

0362.5 **Isla Pinta, W side** 39°53'.6N 4°16'.2E Fl(3)G.9s4m1M
Green ▲ on green metal post 3m

0363 **Naval base, E jetty** 39°53'.6N 4°16'.2E Oc(2)G.6s7m1M
Green ▲ on green metal post 3m

0363.2 **Naval base, central jetty** 39°53'.6N 4°16'.1E
Q.G.4m1M Green ▲ on green metal post 3m

0363.4 **Naval base, W jetty** 39°53'.7N 4°16'.1E
Fl(4)G.11s4m1M Green ▲ on green metal post 3m

0364.2 **Canal de San Jordi E end** 39°52'.9N 4°18'.3E
Q(2)R.6s7m1M Red tower 6m

0364.4 **Canal de San Jordi W end** Fl(4)R.11s7m1M Red tower
6m

0364 **Isla del Llatzeret E coast** 39°52'.6N 4°18'.4E
Fl(2)R.7s7m1M Red round tower

ME2 PUERTO DE TAMARINDA

0343 **Entrance canal (E)** 39°55'.6N 03°50'.1E Fl(2)G.7s7m3M
Green column on white base with green ▲ 5m

0343.2 **Entrance canal (W)** Fl(2)R.7s7m3M Red column white
base with red ■ 5m

ME3 PUERTO CIUDADELA

Approach

0342 **Cabo Dartuch (D'Artruitx)** 39°55'.4N 3°49'.5E
Fl(3)10s45m19M White tower, three black bands, on
white building 34m 267°-vis-158°

0348 **Cabo Nati** 40°03'.2N 3°49'.5E Fl(3+1)20s42m16M White
tower, aluminium cupola, on white building with red
roof 13m 039°-vis-162°

Entrance

0344 **Punta de Sa Farola** 39°59′.8N 3°49′.4E
Oc(2+3)14s21m14M White tower, black vertical stripes,
on white building 13m 004°-vis-094°

0345 **Punta El Bancal** 39°59′.9N 3°49′.5E Fl(3)R.9s10m5M
Red tower on white base displaying red ■

0345.4 **San Nicolás** 39°59′.9N 3°49′.6E Fl(3)G.9s10m3M
Green square structure on white base displaying
green ▲ 4m

0345.6 **Sa Trona** 39°59′.9N 3°49′.7E Fl(4)G.11s7m1M Green
square structure on white base displaying green
▲ 4m

0345.9 **Cala d'en Busquets, Dir Lt** 40°N 3°49′.8E
DirFl.WRG.5s9m5-3M White square tower, green lantern
3m (044°-W-046° marks centre of channel, red sector to
the N, green sector to the S)

0345.8 **Cala d'en Busquets, E light** 40°N 3°49′.8E
Fl(4)R.12s11m1M Red column on white base displaying
red ■ 4m

0346.2 **Slipway** 40°00′.1N 3°49′.9E Fl.R.5s6m1M Red tripod
on white base displaying red ■ 5m

0346 **Club Náutico** 40°00′.0N 3°49′.9E Fl.G.5s7m1M Green
column on white hut displaying green ▲ 5m

0346.4 **La Muralla** 40°00′.1N 3°50′.2E
DirOc(2)WRG.9.5s8m5-3M White square tower 6m.
(064°-W-065° marks centre of channel, red sector to the
N, green sector to the S)

ME4 PUERTO DE FORNELLS

0350.5 **Cabo Fornells (Cap de Sa Paret)** 40°03′.8N 4°08′E
Fl.2s29m8M White tower, black band, on white building
6m

0351 **Ldg Lts 178.5° (Isla Sargantana)** *Front* 40°02′.9N
4°08′.2E Q.R.14m7M White pyramidal tower 6m

0351.1 *Rear* 110m from front Iso.R.4s23m8M White
pyramidal tower 9m

0351.4 **Harbour, NE mole** 40°03′.3N 4°08′E Fl(4)G.11s7m5M
Green column 6m

ME5 PUERTO DE CALA DE ADDAYA

No lights.

2. Waypoints

IBIZA WAYPOINTS

⊕1	E Approach to Puerto de Ibiza	38°53′.7N 01°27′.5E
⊕2	Puerto de Ibiza	38°53′.9N 01°26′.7E
⊕3	Isla Sal Rossa	38°52′.2N 01°24′.8E
⊕4	Freu Grande channel	38°48′.6N 01°25′.6E
⊕5	Punta Rama	38°49′.5N 01°22′.0E
⊕6	Cabo Llentrisca	38°51′.0N 01°14′.7E
⊕7	Isla Vedrá W	38°51′.7N 01°10′.8E
⊕8	Islote Espardel W	38°57′.5N 01°10′.4E
⊕9	Isla Conejera NW	38°59′.7N 01°12′.5E
⊕10	Puerto de San Antonio	38°58′.8N 01°17′.0E
⊕11	Islas Margaritas (Margalides) W	39°03′.0N 01°18′.6E
⊕12	Cabo Eubarca W	39°04′.6N 01°21′.4E
⊕13	Isla Murada	39°05′.8N 01°25′.9E
⊕14	Punta Charracó	39°06′.7N 01°29′.4E
⊕15	Punta Moscarté	39°07′.4N 01°32′.0E
⊕16	Islas Hormigas	39°06′.3N 01°35′.5E
⊕17	Punta Grosa	39°05′.0N 01°37′.0E
⊕18	Between Punta Valls and Isla Tagomago	39°02′.2N 01°37′.7E
⊕19	Isla de Santa Eulalia	38°58′.8N 01°35′.3E
⊕20	Puerto de Santa Eulalia	38°58′.6N 01°32′.5E
⊕21	Cabo y Escollo Llibrell	38°56′.6N 01°32′.0E
⊕22	Lladó del Norta	38°55′.4N 01°29′.5E

FORMENTERA WAYPOINTS

⊕23	Puerto de Sabina	38°44′.2N 01°25′.3E
⊕24	Isla del Gastabí (SW)	38°46′.3N 01°24′.7E
⊕25	Pta Single Mal	38°39′.8N 01°36′.0E
⊕26	Cabo Berbería	38°37′.7N 01°23′.2E
⊕27	Pta Gabina	38°43′.1N 01°22′.1E
⊕28–30	unallocated	

MALLORCA WAYPOINTS

⊕31	Puerto de Palma	39°33′.4N 02°38′.5E
⊕32	Puerto de Cala Nova	39°32′.8N 02°36′.1E
⊕33	Las Illetas	39°31′.8N 02°35′.5E
⊕34	Puerto Portals	39°31′.5N 02°33′.8E
⊕35	Isla del Sech	39°28′.7N 02°32′.8E
⊕36	Punta de Cala Figuera	39°27′.2N 02°31′.5E
⊕37	Islote el Toro	39°27′.5N 02°28′.0E
⊕38	Isla Malgrats	39°29′.5N 02°26′.5E
⊕39	Cabo de la Mola	39°31′.6N 02°21′.4E
⊕40	Isla Dragonera (S)	39°33′.8N 02°18′.5E
⊕41	Punta de na Foradada	39°38′.5N 02°25′.2E
⊕42	Punta S'Aliga	39°42′.4N 02°31′.5E
⊕43	Peninsula de la Foradada	39°45′.6N 02°37′.2E
⊕44	Approach to Sóller	39°48′.0N 02°41′.2E
⊕45	Morro de la Vaca	39°52′.0N 02°48′.3E
⊕46	Punta Beca	39°55′.6N 02°57′.0E
⊕47	Cabo de Cataluña	39°58′.0N 03°10′.7E
⊕48	Cabo de Formentor	39°57′.8N 03°13′.0E
⊕49	Isla de Formentor (S)	39°55′.0N 03°09′.0E
⊕50	Puerto de Bonaire	39°52′.2N 03°08′.5E
⊕51	Cabo del Pinar	39°53′.5N 03°12′.7E
⊕52	Isla de Aucanada (S)	39°49′.9N 03°10′.3E
⊕53	Off Ca'n Picafort	39°46′.2N 03°09′.5E
⊕54	Off Puerto de Colonia de San Pedro	39°44′.5N 03°16′.3E
⊕55	SW of Cala es Calo	39°46′.3N 03°19′.8E
⊕56	Farayó de Aubarca (W)	39°46′.2N 03°24′.3E
⊕57	Cabo del Freu	39°45′.0N 03°28′.0E
⊕58	Cabo de Pera	39°43′.0N 03°29′.2E
⊕59	Cabo d'es Piná (Del Pinar)	39°38′.0N 03°26′.5E
⊕60	Punta de Amer	39°34′.8N 03°24′.5E
⊕61	Cala Manacor (Porto Cristo)	39°32′.2N 03°20′.5E
⊕62	Punta de ses Crestas (Approach to Puerto Colom)	39°24′.7N 03°16′.2E
⊕63	Cala Llonga (Approach to Puerto de Cala D'or)	39°22′.0N 03°14′.2E
⊕64	Off Porto Petro	39°21′.3N 03°13′.2E
⊕65	Punta Salinas	39°15′.5N 03°03′.2E
⊕66	Off Puerto Colonia de Sant Jordi	39°18′.5N 02°59′.7E
⊕67	Puerto de la Rápita	39°21′.7N 02°57′.3E
⊕68	Cabo Blanco	39°21′.6N 02°47′.0E
⊕69	Off El Arenal	39°30′.3N 02°44′.5E
⊕70	Puerto de San Antonio	39°31′.7N 02°43′.0E
⊕71	Puerto de Cala Gamba	39°32′.7N 02°41′.7E
⊕72	Off Puerto de Cala Portixol	39°33′.4N 02°40′.1E

ISLA DE CABRERA WAYPOINTS

⊕73	Puerto de Cabrera	39°09′.5N 02°55′.6E
⊕74	Between Pta de Sa Corrent & Isla Redonda	39°09′.8N 02°58′.4E
⊕75	Off Islote Imperial (SE)	39°07′.5N 02°57′.7E
⊕76	Pta Anciola	39°07′.6N 02°55′.0E
⊕77	Cabo Llebeig	39°09′.7N 02°54′.9E
⊕78	Pta de la Escala	39°11′.0N 02°57′.0E
⊕79	Isla Horadada	39°12′.6N 02°58′.7E
⊕80	unallocated	

MENORCA WAYPOINTS

⊕81	Puerto de Mahón fairway	39°52′.0N 04°18′.6E
⊕82	Isla del Aire Passage	39°48′.4N 04°17′.0E
⊕83	Off Cabo D'en Font	39°49′.1N 04°12′.1E
⊕84	Cala Santa Galdana	39°56′.0N 03°57′.4E
⊕85	Cala Son Saura	39°55′.1N 03°53′.6E
⊕86	Puerto de Tamarinda	39°55′.4N 03°50′.1E
⊕87	Cabo Negro	39°57′.2N 03°49′.1E

⊕88	Puerto de Ciudadela	39°59′.6N 03°49′.5E
⊕89	Cabo Binicous (de Banyos)	40°00′.0N 03°47′.1E
⊕90	Cabo Nati	40°03′.1N 03°49′.0E
⊕91	Punta del Escuá	40°03′.8N 03°52′.0E
⊕92	Bajo Morell rock	40°04′.0N 03°53′.0E
⊕93	Off Cabo Gros	40°04′.7N 03°56′.0E
⊕94	Isla Bledas N	40°04′.7N 04°01′.9E
⊕95	Off Isla Nitge	40°05′.8N 04°04′.1E
⊕96	Puerto de Fornells	40°04′.0N 04°08′.0E
⊕97	Cabo Pentinat	40°03′.6N 04°10′.6E
⊕98	Addaya Approach	40°01′.4N 04°12′.4E
⊕99	Cabo Favaritx	39°59′.8N 04°16′.4E
⊕100	Cabo Monseña	39°59′.1N 04°16′.4E
⊕101	Punta Galera	39°56′.7N 04°17′.5E
⊕102	Off Cabo Negro	39°54′.0N 04°18′.7E
⊕103	Punta S'Esperó	39°52′.6N 04°19′.9E

3. Charts

Charts and other publications may be corrected annually by reference to the Admiralty *List of Lights and Fog Signals* Volume D (NP 77) or weekly via the *Admiralty Notices to Mariners*.

Note A few charts appear twice in the following list under different island headings. The index diagrams only show large-scale charts where the diagram's scale permits.

BRITISH ADMIRALTY CHARTS

Chart	Title	Scale
Approaches from the Spanish coast		
1701	Cabo de San Antonio to Villaneuva y Geltrú including Islas de Ibiza and Formentara	300,000
Ibiza		
1702	Ibiza, Formentera and southern Mallorca	300,000
2834	Islas Baleares, Ibiza and Formentera	120,000
	Channels between Ibiza and Formentera	50,000
	San Antonio Abad	20,000
	Ibiza	10,000
Mallorca		
1703	Mallorca and Menorca	300,000
2831	Mallorca: Punta Salinas to Cabo de Formentor including Canal de Menorca	120,000
	Puerto de Alcudia	20,000
2832	Mallorca – Punta Salinas to Punta Beca including Isla de Cabrera	120,000
3034	Approaches to Palma	25,000
3035	Palma	10,000
Menorca		
1703	Mallorca and Menorca	300,000
2761	Menorca	60,000
2762	Mahón	7,500

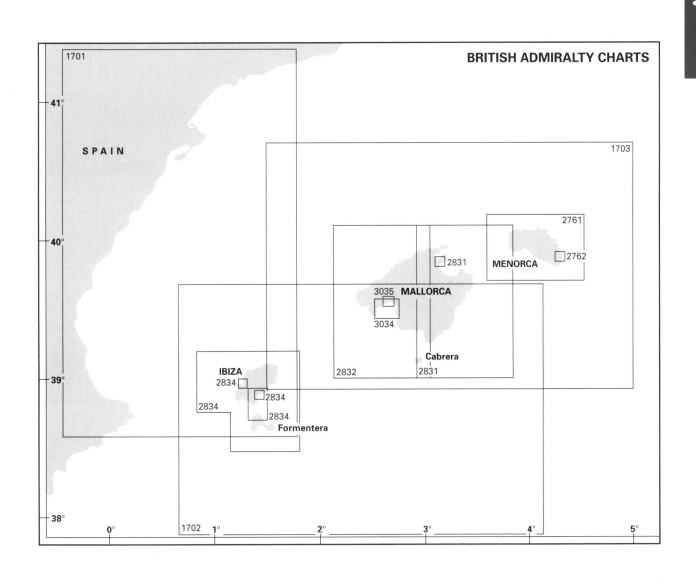

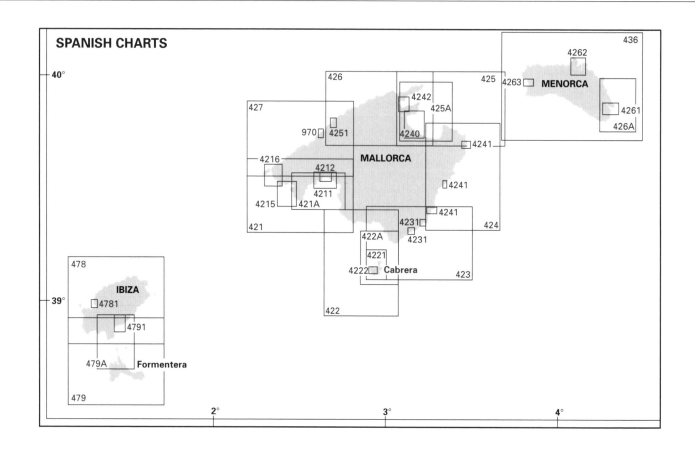

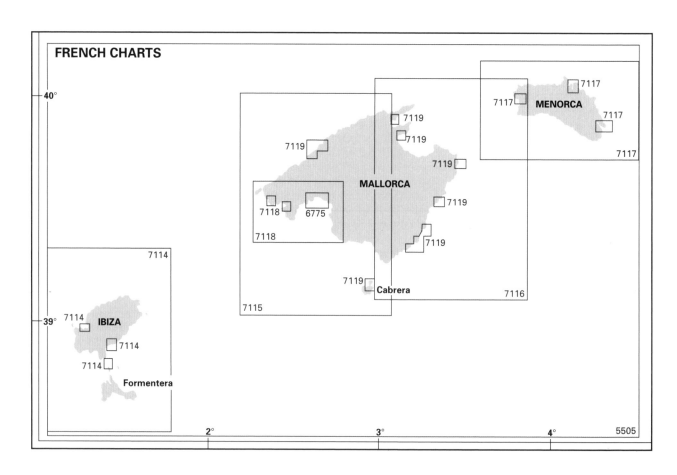

SPANISH CHARTS

Ibiza

478	De Cabo Negret a Cabo Berberia	50,000
479	De Cabo Berberia a Punta Arabi	50,000
479A	Freus entre Ibiza y Formentera	25,000
4781	Puerto de San Antonio Abad	5,000
4791	Puerto de Ibiza	10,000

Mallorca

48E	Islas de Mallorca y Menorca	175,000
421	De isla Dragonera a Cabo Blanco	50,000
421A	Bahía de Palma. De islote El Toro a Cabo Regana	25,000
422	De Cabo Regana a Punta Salinas	50,000
422A	Freu de Cabrera	25,000
423	De Punta Plana a Porto Colom con la Isla de Cabrera y adyacentes	50,000
424	De cala Llonga a Cabo Farrutx	50,000
425	De Cabo Pera a Cabo Formentor	50,000
425A	Bahía de Alcudia	25,000
426	De la Bahía de Alcudia al Puerto de Sóller	50,000
427	De Cala de la Calobra a Isla Dragonera	50,000
4211	Bahía de Palma. De las Illetas a islote Galera	10,000
4215	Ensenada de Santa Ponsa	10,000
4216	Freu de Dragonera y Puerto de Andraitx	15,000
4221	Isla de Cabrera y adyacentes	12,500
4222	Puerto de Cabrera	5,000
4231	Porto Petro y Cala Llonga	7,500
	Cala Figuera	2,500
4240	Bahía de Alcudia	12,500
4241	Porto Colom	5,000
	Porto Cristo o Cala Manacor	5,000
	Cala Ratjada	5,000
4242	Bahía de Pollença	7,500
4251	Puerto de Pollensa	7,500

Menorca

48E	Islas de Mallorca y Menorca	175,000
426A	Approaches Puerto de Mahón	25,000
428A	De Punta Binibeca a Cabo Favaritx	25,000
436	Isla de Menorca	60,000
4261	Puerto de Mahón	7,500
4262	Puerto de Farnells y Bahía de Tirant	10,000
4263	Puerto de Ciudadela	5,000

FRENCH CHARTS

Ibiza

5505	Iles Baléares	319,000
7114	Ibiza et Formentera	
	Cartouche: A – Ibiza et Formentera	100,000
	Cartouche: B – San Antonio Abad	20,000
	Cartouche: C – Puerto de Ibiza	10,000
	Cartouche: D – Passages entre Ibiza et Espalmador Abords de Puerto de Ibiza	30,000

Mallorca

5505	Iles Baléares	319,000
6775	Baie de Palma – De Las Illetas à l'îlot Galera	10,000
7115	Mallorca – Partie Ouest – De Punta Beca à Punta Salinas	100,000
7116	Mallorca – Partie Est –De Punta Salinas à Cabo de Formentor	100,000
7118	Abords de Palma – De Isla Dragonera à Cabo Blanco	40,000
	Cartouche: A – Puerto de Andraitx	10,000
	Cartouche: B – Cala de Santa Ponsa	10,000
7119	Ports et mouillages de Mallorca et Cabrera	
	Cartouche: A – Puerto de Pollensa	12,500
	Cartouche: B – Puerto de Alcudia	10,000
	Cartouche: C – Puerto de Sóller	10,000
	Cartouche: D – Puerto Colom	15,000
	Cartouche: E – Cala Ratjada	10,000
	Cartouche: F – Surgidero de la Foradada	12,500
	Cartouche: G – Cala Figuera	5,000
	Cartouche: H – Puerto Cristó ou Calá Manacor	5,000
	Cartouche: I – Puerto de Cabrera	12,500
	Cartouche: J – Porto Petro et Cala Llonga	12,000

Menorca

5505	Iles Baléares	319,000
7117	Menorca – Ports et Mouillages de Menorca	
	Cartouche: Menorca	100,000
	Cartouche: A – Puerto de Ciudadela	10,000
	Cartouche: B – Bahía de Tirant et Cala Fornells	15,000
	Cartouche: C – Puerto de Máhon	15,000

NAVICARTE CHARTS
(PUBLISHED BY EDITIONS GRAFOCARTE)

E01	Majorque Est – Minorque
E02	Majorque Ouest – Ibiza – Formentera

IMRAY

M3	Islas Baleares	356,000

4. Further reading
PILOTS AND TOURIST GUIDES

Many navigational publications are reprinted annually, in which case the latest edition should be carried. Others, including most cruising guides, are updated by means of supplements available from the publishers. Further corrections or amendments are always welcome.

Admiralty publications

Mediterranean Pilot Vol I (NP 45) and supplement covers the S and E coasts of Spain, the Islas Baleares, Sardinia, Sicily and the N coast of Africa

List of Lights and Fog Signals Vol E (NP 78) (Mediterranean, Black and Red Seas)

List of Radio Signals

Vol 1, Part 1 (NP281/1) Coast Radio Stations (Europe, Africa and Asia)

Vol 2 (NP 282) Radio Navigational Aids, Electronic Position Fixing Systems and Radio Time Signals

Vol 3 Part 1 (NP 283/1) Radio Weather Services and Navigational Warnings (Europe, Africa and Asia)

Vol 4 (NP 284) Meteorological Observation Stations

Vol 5 (NP 285) Global Maritime Distress and Safety Systems (GMDSS)

Vol 6, Part 2 (NP 286/2) Vessel Traffic Services, Port Operations and Pilot Services (The Mediterranean, Africa and Asia)

NP 289 Small Craft United Kingdom and the Mediterranean (including Azores and the Canary Islands)

English language

Imray Mediterranean Almanac Rod Heikell (Imray Laurie Norie & Wilson Ltd). A biennial almanac with second year supplement, packed with information. Particularly good value for yachts on passage when not every cruising guide is likely to be carried.

Mediterranean Cruising Handbook Rod Heikell (Imray Laurie Norie & Wilson Ltd). General information on cruising areas, passages etc. some of which is now slightly out of date.

Guia del Navegante – La Costa de España y el Algarve (PubliNáutic Rilnvest SL, revised annually) in colloquial English with a Spanish translation. Not a full scale pilot book, but an excellent source of up-to-date information on local services and facilites (partly via the advertisements) with phone numbers, etc.

Guia Náutica Turistica y Deportiva de España by the Asamblea de Capitánes de Yate. An expensive and colourful guide book covering all the Spanish coasts and including some useful data on harbours but no pilotage information. The plans are in outline only. Written in Spanish with a partial English translation. Because symbols are lavishly used, much of it can be understood with only a limited knowledge of Spanish.

Guia Náutica de España. Tomo II, Costa del Azahar, Blanca and Baleares. One of a series of books featuring attractive colour pictures, some of which are out of date, and some text. Written in Spanish but an English version is sometimes available.

El Mercado Náutico (The Boat Market). A free newspaper published every two or three months and available from yacht clubs, marina offices, etc. Written in Spanish, English and German it includes, amongst other things, a useful (though by no means comprehensive) listing of current marina prices.

Menorca. Atlas Náutico Alfonso Buenaventure. A book of 67 double page chartlets showing the coastline of Menorca in extreme detail – a must for anyone thinking of cruising around Menorca.

*Nuevos Aeroguias – El Litoral de Mallorca (*Editorial Planeta S.A) It has aerial photographs of the whole coastline of Mallorca. Ensure you get a recent edition as most shops only hold the old one.

North Africa RCC/Graham Hutt (Imray)

French

Votre Livre de Bord – Méditerranée (Bloc Marine) French almanac covering the Mediterranean, including details of weather forecasts transmitted from France and Monaco. An English/French version is also published which translates some, though by no means all, the text. Published annually.

Ports & Mouillages – Baléares (SHOM). French guide in a series which also covers western Italy, Sardinia and the Lesser Antilles. Colour photos and plans.

Les Guides Nautiques – Baléares J C Alvarez (Edition Eskis). Written in French in colloquial style, lacking in detail and with basic plans.

German

Spanische Gewässer, Lissabon bis Golfe du Lion K Neumann (Delius Klasing). A seamanlike guide and semi-pilot book, which includes sketch plans of most harbours. Harbour data is limited but it contains much good general advice on sailing in this area.

Die Baleares Bernhard Bartholmes (Edition Maritim). Well laid-out with good detail and some excellent, though out of date, aerial photographs.

Häfen und Anker Plätze Gerd Radspieler. A useful book but with very basic plans and lacking in detail.

Background

The Birth of Europe Michael Andrew (BBC Books). An excellent and comprehensive work which explains in simple terms how the Mediterranean and surrounding countries developed over the ages from 3000 BC.

The First Eden, David Attenborough (William Collins). A fascinating study of 'The Mediterranean World and Man'.

The Inner Sea Robert Fox (Sinclair-Stevenson, 1991). An account of the countries surrounding the Mediterranean and the forces which shaped them, written by a well known BBC journalist.

Sea of Seas H Scott (van Nostrand). A half-guidebook half-storybook on the western Mediterranean. Very out of date and now out of print, but a delight to read.

TRAVELLERS' GUIDES

Essential Mallorca, Ibiza and Menorca Tony Kelly (Automobile Association, 2004). A handy, pocket-sized tourist guide with a little bit of everything – what to see, where to shop, restaurant recommendations, countryside and wildlife, etc. Excellent colour photos. Highly recommended and very user friendly, this series is available at some UK airports and via www.theAA.com/bookshop

The AA Map & Guide to Mallorca, Twinpack series Tony Kelly (AA publishing 2005). Similar in size and content to *Essential Mallorca*, it includes, 'Top 25 sights', 'Where to: eat, shop, etc.' and 'Practical Matters'. It comes with an OS map of the island. Also highly recommended, as is *Twinpack Menorca* and the AA *Spiral Guide Mallorca* (Carol Baker 2001).

Baedeker's Majorca (which also covers Menorca) and *Baedeker's Ibiza* Peter M Nahm (Automobile Association, 1994). Serious, informed guides, well illustrated and particularly strong on culture – history, architecture, etc. – though with some notable omissions and many errors in the index. A pocket in the plastic cover carries an island map.

Landscapes of Ibiza Han Losse; *Landscapes of Mallorca* Valerie Crespí-Green; *Landscapes of Menorca* Rodney Ansell (Sunflower Books, 1995, 1994 & 1996). Three pocket-sized volumes of car tours, walks and picnic suggestions, plus some public transport schedules.

The Rough Guide: Mallorca & Menorca Phil Lee (Rough Guides, distributed by the Penguin Group, 1996). A new addition to the worldwide series for land-based budget travellers, but useful to anyone wanting practical information. Town plans, no photographs. Also 46 pages on the Islas Baleares in the Spain volume (1994).

The Balearic Islands Helen Thurston (Batsford, 1977). Not so much a travel guide as a detailed history of the influences which have shaped the islands over the centuries. Slightly out of date but highly readable.

The Balearic Islands (Nagel Publishers, 1969). Thumbnail descriptions of places in the Islas Baleares, with historic details and suggestions for visits. Companion volume on Spain. Getting distinctly out of date.

Mallorca and Menorca Berlitz Travel Guide. By 1995 this book had reached its 24th edition – what more can one say!

PERIOD ACCOUNTS

Jogging Round Majorca Gordon West (Black Swan Books, 1994). First published in 1929 when 'jogging' meant a leisurely stroll, this is a charming glimpse of the island before tourism arrived. Also available on cassette. Highly recommended.

A Cottage in Majorca Lady Margaret Kinloch (Skeffinton, 1936). Another mirror into the past written with great affection. Long out of print, so not an easy book to track down.

Majorca Observed Robert Graves and Paul Hogarth (Cassells, 1965). Probably the most famous author to live and write in Mallorca before mass tourism.

ROAD MAPS

Road maps are indispensable when making a journey inland. As usual, Michelin produce an excellent road map which is available throughout the islands.

Euro-Map – Mallorca, Menorca, Ibiza (GeoCenter International). Detailed but comprehensible road map giving contours, place names (sometimes both Castilian and local versions) historic sites, street plan of Palma, etc. Scale 1:150,000. Useful for any form of travel.

The Firestone road map of the Islas Baleares is also reported to be excellent, but may be difficult to obtain in the UK.

COOKERY BOOKS

Mediterranean Seafood Alan Davidson. Penguin. A handbook with all the names of Mediterranean fish, crustaceans and molluscs in several languages and over 200 recipes from Mediterranean countries. Indispensable in the markets and fishing harbours with their unfamiliar fish. The recipes are practical and do not require ingredients exotic to the Mediterranean.

Mediterranean Cookery Claudia Roden. It contains 250 delicious and easy recipes of traditional Mediterranean cooking prepared with locally available ingredients.

5. Spanish glossary

The following limited glossary relates to the weather, the abbreviations to be found on Spanish charts and some words likely to be useful on entering port. For a list containing many words commonly used in connection with sailing, see Webb & Manton, *Yachtsman's Ten Language Dictionary* (Adlard Coles Nautical).

WEATHER

On the radio, if there is a storm warning the forecast starts *aviso temporal*. If, as usual, there is no storm warning, the forecast starts *no hay temporal*. Many words are similar to the English and their meanings can be guessed. The following may be less familiar:

Viento (wind)
calm calm
ventolina light air
flojito light breeze
flojo gentle breeze
bonancible moderate breeze
fresquito fresh breeze
fresco strong breeze
frescachón near gale
temporal fuerte gale
temporal duro strong gale
temporal muy duro storm
borrasca violent storm
huracán, temporal huracanado hurricane
tempestad, borrasca thunderstorm

El cielo (the sky)
nube cloud
nubes altas, bajas high, low clouds
nubloso cloudy
cubierto covered, overcast
claro, despejado clear
Names of cloud types in Spanish are based on the same Latin words as the names used in English.

El mar (sea state)
calma calm
marizada ripples
marejadilla slight sea (choppy)
marejada rough sea
fuerte marejada very rough
mar corta short seas
mar gruesa steep seas

Visibilidad (visibility)
buena, bueno, buen good
regular moderate
malo, mala, mal poor
calima haze
neblina mist
bruma sea mist
niebla fog
Precipitación Precipitation
aguacero shower
llovizna drizzle
lluvia rain
aguanieve sleet
nieve snow
granizada hail

Sistemas del Tiempo Weather Systems
anticiclón anticyclone
depresión, borrasca depression
vaguada trough
cresta, dorsal ridge
cuna wedge
frente front
frío cold
cálido warm
ocluido occluded
bajando falling
subiendo rising

LIGHTS AND CHARTS – MAJOR TERMS AND ABBREVIATIONS

A	*amarilla*	yellow
Alt	*alternativa*	alternative
Ag Nv	*aguas navegables*	navegable waters
Ang	*angulo*	angle
Ant	*anterior*	anterior, earlier, forward
Apag	*apagado*	extinguished
Arrc	*arrecife*	reef
At	*atenuada*	attenuated
B	*blanca*	white
Ba	*bahía*	bay
	bajamar escorada	chart datum
Bal	*baliza*	buoy, beacon
Bal. E	*baliza elástica*	plastic (elastic) buoy
Bco	*banco*	bank
Bo	*bajo*	shoal, under, below, low
Boc	*bocina*	horn, trumpet
Br	*babor*	port (i.e. left)
C	*campana*	bell
Card	*cardinal*	cardinal
Cañ	*cañon*	canyon
	boya de castillete	pillar buoy
cil	*cilíndrico*	cylindrical
C	*cabo*	cape
Cha	*chimenea*	chimney
Cno	*castillo*	castle
cón	*cónico*	conical
Ct	*centellante*	quick flashing (50{80/minute)
CtI	*centellante interrumpida*	interrupted quick flashing
cuad	*cuadrangular*	quadrangular
D	*destello*	flash
Desap	*desaparecida*	disappeared
Dest	*destruida*	destroyed
	dique	breakwater, jetty
Dir	*direccional*	directional
DL	*destello largo*	long flash
E	*este*	east
edif	*edificio*	building
	ensenada	cove, inlet
Er	*estribor*	starboard
Est	*esférico*	spherical
Esp	*especial*	special
Est sñ	*estación de señales*	signal station
ext	*exterior*	exterior
Extr	*extremo*	end, head (of pier etc.)
F	*fija*	fixed
Fca	*fabrica*	factory
FD	*fija y destello*	fixed and flashing
FGpD	*fija y grupo de destellos*	fixed and group flashing
Flot	*flotador*	float
Fondn	*fondeadero*	anchorage
GpCt	*grupo de centellos*	group quick flashing
GpD	*grupo de destellos*	group flashing
GpOc	*grupo de ocultaciones*	group occulting
GpRp	*grupo de centellos rápidos*	group very quick flashing
hel	*helicoidales*	helicoidal
hor	*horizontal*	horizontal
Hund	*hundida*	submerged, sunk
I	*interrumpido*	interrupted
Igla	*iglesia*	church
Inf	*inferior*	inferior, lower
Intens	*intensificado*	intensified
Irreg	*irregular*	irregular
Iso	*isofase*	isophase
L	*luz*	light
La	*lateral*	lateral
	levante	eastern
M	*millas*	miles
Mte	*monte*	mountain
Mto	*monumento*	monument
N	*norte*	north

Naut	*nautófono*	foghorn
NE	*nordeste*	northeast
No	*número*	number
NW	*noroeste*	northwest
Obst	*obstrucción*	obstruction
ocas	*ocasional*	occasional
oct	*octagonal*	octagonal
oc	*oculta*	obscured
Oc	*ocultación sectores*	obscured sectors
Pe A	*peligro aislado*	isolated danger
	poniente	western
Post	*posterior*	posterior, later
Ppal	*principal*	principal
	prohibido	prohibited
Obston	*obstrucción*	obstruction
Prov	*provisional*	provisional
prom	*prominente*	prominent, conspicuous
Pta	*punta*	point
Pto	*puerto*	port
PTO	*puerto deportivo*	yacht harbour
	puerto pesquero	fishing harbour
	puerto de Marina de Guerra	naval harbour
R	*roja*	red
Ra	*estación radar*	radar station
Ra+	*radar + suffix*	radar + suffix (Ra Ref etc.)
RC	*radiofaro circular*	non-directional radiobeacon
RD	*radiofaro dirigido*	directional radiobeacon
rect	*rectangular*	rectangular
Ra	*rocas*	rocks
Rp	*centeneallante rápida*	very quick flashing (80-160/min)
RpI	*cent. rápida interrumpida*	interrupted very quick flashing
RW	*radiofaro giratorio*	rotating radiobeacon
s	*segundos*	seconds
S	*sur*	south
SE	*sudeste*	southeast
sil	*silencio*	silence
Silb	*silbato*	whistle
Sincro	*sincronizda con*	synchronized with
Sir	*sirena*	siren
son	*sonido*	sound, noise, report
Sto/a	*Santo, Santa*	Saint
SW	*sudoeste*	southwest
T	*temporal*	temporary
Te	*torre*	tower
trans	*transversal*	transversal
triang	*triangular*	triangular
troncoc	*troncocónico*	truncated cone
troncop	*troncopiramidal*	truncated pyramid
TSH	*antena de radio*	radio mast
TV	*antena de TV*	TV mast
U	*centellante Ultra-rápida*	ultra quick flashing (+160/min)
UI	*cent. Ultra-rápida interrumpido*	interrupted ultra quick flashing
V	*verde*	green
Vis	*visible*	visible
	vivero	shellfish raft or bed
W	*oeste*	west

PORTS AND HARBOURS

'puerto' is applied to any landing place from a beach to a container port.

a popa stern-to
a proa bows-to
abrigo shelter
al costado alongside
amarrar to moor
amarradero mooring
ancho breadth (see also manga)
anclar to anchor

botar to launch (a yacht)
boya de amarre mooring buoy
cabo warp, line (also cape)
calado draught
compuerta lock, basin
dársena dock, harbour
dique breakwater, jetty
escala ladder
escalera steps
esclusa lock
escollera jetty
eslora total length overall
espigón spur, spike, mole
fábrica factory
ferrocarril railway
fondear to anchor or moor
fondeadero anchorage
fondeo mooring buoy
fondo depth (bottom)
grua crane
guia mooring lazy-line (lit. guide)
nudo knot (i.e. speed)
longitud length (see also eslora), longitude
lonja fish market (wholesale)
manga beam (i.e. width)
muelle mole, jetty, quay
noray bollard
pantalán jetty, pontoon
parar to stop
pila estaca pile
pontón pontoon
práctico pilot (i.e. pilot boat)
profundidad depth
rampa slipway
rompeolas breakwater
varadero slipway, hardstanding
varar to lift (a yacht)
vertedero (verto) spoil ground

Direction
babor port
estribor starboard
norte north
este east
sur south
oeste west

Around the port
aceite oil (including engine oil)
agua potable drinking water
aseos toilet block
astiller shipyard
duchas showers
efectos navales chandlery
electricidad electricity
gasoleo diesel diesel
hielo (cubitos) ice (cubes)
lavandería laundry
lavandería automática launderette
luz electricity (lit. light)
manguera hosepipe
parafina, petróleo, keroseno paraffin, kerosene
gasolina petrol
velero sailmaker (also sailing ship)

Phrases useful on arrival
Donde puedo amarrar? Where can I moor?
A donde debo ir? Where should I go?
Que es la profundidad? What is the depth?
Cuantos metros? What is your length?
Para cuantas noches? For how many nights?

Formalities
aduana customs
capitán de puerto harbourmaster
derechos dues, rights
dueño, propietario owner
guardia civil police
patrón skipper (not owner)
título certificate

Documentation

It has been found useful to have the following list available for registering at each port or marina to be visited:

Nombre de Yate Yacht's name
Bandera Flag
Lista y folio Yacht's number
Reg. bruto Registered weight
Tipo Type of vessel
Palos Number of masts
Motor, marca y potencia Engine make and capacity
Eslora total L.O.A.
Maga Beam
Calado Draught
Puerto base Home port
No. cabinas No. of cabins
Seguro Insurance company
Proprietario Skipper
Nacionalidad Nationality
Telefono Telephone
Pasaporte Passport
Tripulante y pasajero Passengers on board

6. Charter regulations

Any EU-flag yacht applying to charter in Spanish waters must be either VAT paid or exempt (the latter most commonly due to age). Non-EU flag vessels must have a valid Temporary Import Licence and may also have to conform to other regulations.

Applying for a charter licence can be a tortuous business. Firstly the Director General de Transportes at the Conselleria d'Obres Publiques i Ordenacio del Territorio must be approached with a pre-authorisation application. This obtained, the application itself is sent to the Capitanias Maritimas together with ships' papers and proof of passenger insurance and registration as a commercial activity. A safety and seaworthiness inspection will be carried out. Finally a fiscal representative must be appointed and tax paid on revenue generated.

It will probably be found simpler to make the application through one of the companies specialising in this type of work. Try NETWORK, Edificio Torremar, Passeo Marítimo, 44 - 07015 Palma de Mallorca ☎ 971 403903/403703 Fax 971 400216, who will also deal with VAT and legal matters.

7. Repair and maintenance facilities in Palma de Mallorca

All telephone and fax number have a prefix of 971.
Companies are normally listed alphabetically.
Chandleries Yacht Centre Palma ☎ 715612 *Fax* 711246 at the Club de Mar, also Náutica Seameermar ☎ 737092 *Fax* 450382, La Central ☎ 731838 and others.
Merca Nautic ☎ 736563, 288521 Fax 735081 sells secondhand (as well as new) equipment.
Liferaft servicing
    GDR ☎ 760798 Fax 759688.
Charts Admiralty
    Rapid Transit Service ☎ 403703, 403903 Fax 400216
    Spanish – Librería Fondevila ☎ 725616 *Fax* 713326
    Casa del Mapa ☎ 466061 Fax 771616.
Generators
    Salva ☎ 730303 *Fax* 453910.
Ropes and rigging
    Lliñas ☎ 466686, Parts Palma SL ☎ 732040 *Fax* 450718
    Sails & Canvas ☎/Fax 733937
    Yachtech ☎ 458942 *Fax* 732478
Repairs
Audax Marina ☎ 720474/639303943 *Fax* 720475
    audaxmarina.com Repair yard at the Réal Club Náutico
    info@audaxmarina.com

Astilleros de Mallorca boatyard ☎ 710645 *Fax* 721368: a shipyard with four slipways able to take yachts up to 100m, on the Contramuelle Mollet opposite the Réal Club Náutico
Boat Yard Palma ☎ 718302 Fax 718611 and Carpinser ☎ 725079 on the Muelles Viejo and Nuevo near the root of the NE breakwater, and several others.
150-tonne travel-lift at Boat Yard Palma, 90 and 30-tonne lifts on the Muelle Viejo, 60-tonne lift at Réal Club Náutico. A 9-tonne crane at the Réal Club Náutico, 5-tonne crane at Club de Mar, plus many others in the commercial areas of the port. A commercial slipway in the Dársena de Porto Pi able to handle 350 tonnes, for which a docking plan is required. Several in the shipyard E of the Réal Club Náutico
Engineers
    C-Tec SA ☎ 405712, Marine Machine ☎ 462660
    Fax 463693
    Talleres Guidet ☎ 718643 *Fax* 720577
Official service agents include:
C-Tec SA (see above) – Caterpillar, Man
Commercial Morey ☎ 753333 *Fax* 756149
    Mercury/MerCruiser, Suzuki
Ecosse Diesels ☎ 733957 Ecosse Diesels
Finanzauto SA ☎ 971 756600 *Fax* 758966 Caterpillar
Harald Schmidt ☎/*Fax* 780042 Mercedes, Sole Diesel, Yanmar
Juan Frau Navarro ☎ 260599 Yanmar
Magic Boats ☎ 757426 Ecosse Diesels
Marine Machine (see above) Ford/Lehman, Perkins, Sabre, Volvo Penta
Mecanautica ☎ 971 281929 Sole Diesel
Euroservice Mallorca ☎/*Fax* 719376 Caterpillar, Volvo Penta
Náutica Seameermar ☎ 737092 *Fax* 450382 Volvo Penta
Pressure Marine ☎ 753272 *Fax* 201316 Mariner
Salva ☎ 730303 *Fax* 453910 Bukh, Caterpillar, Cummins, Man
Talleres Noray ☎/*Fax* 723839 Mercedes
Volvo Penta España SA ☎ 971 430343 Volvo Penta
Metalwork
    Ruben Doñaque ☎ 760796 *Fax* 202313
    Talleres Guidet (see above in Engineers).
    Hydraulics Yachtech ☎ 458942 *Fax* 732478.
Refrigeration, air conditioning and pumps
    Palma Yachts SL ☎ 450366 *Fax* 289099
    Anfra Tecnica SL ☎ 242626 *Fax* 271210
Electronic & radio repairs, autopilots, watermakers etc
    C-Tec SA ☎ 405712
    Dahlberg SA ☎ 469961 *Fax* 469469
    Yacht Electronic Services ☎ 400213, 700427 *Fax* 405873
    Vetus Mallorca ☎ 713050 *Fax* 713054
    DanBrit ☎ 677201 www.danbrit.com
Sailmakers and canvaswork
    North Sails España SA ☎ 725752 *Fax* 718374
    Sails & Canvas ☎/*Fax* 733937
    Velas Ferrá SA ☎ 467413 *Fax* 463982
    Velería Orion ☎ 757688, 757781
    Velera J Matheu ☎ 273887.

8. Official addresses

SPANISH NATIONAL EMBASSIES AND CONSULATES

UK 39 Chesham Place, London SW1X 8SB ☎ 020 7235 5555
    Fax 020 7259 5392
Consulate 20 Draycott Place, London SW3 2RZ ☎ 020 7589
    8989 *Fax* 020 7581 7888
US 2375 Pennsylvania Avenue NW, Washington, DC 20037
    ☎ 202 452 0100/728 2340 *Fax* 202 833 5670
    email embespus@mail.mae.es
Consulate 150 E. 58th St, New York, NY 10155
    ☎ 212 355 4080/2/5/6 Fax 644 3751/90
    email spainconsulny@mail.mae.es

BRITISH AND AMERICAN EMBASSIES IN MADRID

UK Calle Fernando el Santo 16, 28010 Madrid
    ☎ 91 700 8200/524 9700 *Fax* 91 700 8309
    www.madridconsulate@ukinspain.com
US Calle Serrano 75, 28006 Madrid
    ☎ 91 587 2240/5872240 *Fax* 91 587 2243/2303

APPENDIX

APPENDIX

BRITISH REPRESENTATION IN ISLAS BALEARES

Mallorca British Consulate, Plaza Mayor 3D, 07002 Palma de
Mallorca, ☎ 971 712445, 716048 *Fax* 971 717520 *email*
consulate@palma.mail.fco.gov.uk

Menorca British Vice-Consulate, SA Casa Nova, Cami de
Biniatap 30, 07720 Es Castell, Menorca ☎ 971 367818
Fax 971 354690 www.fco.gov.uk

Ibiza British Vice-Consulate, Avenida Isidoro Macabich
45-1, Apartado 307, 07800 Ibiza ☎ 971 301816/8
Fax 971 301972 *email* BritishConsulate.Ibiza@fco.gov.uk

AMERICAN REPRESENTATION IN ISLAS BALEARES

Mallorca Vice-Consulate, Edificio Reina Constanza, Porto Pi,
8,9D 07015 Palma de Mallorca ☎ 971 403707/403905
Fax 971 403971

SPANISH NATIONAL TOURIST OFFICES

UK PO Box 4009 London W1A 6NB ☎ +44 020 74868077
Fax 020 74868034 *email* info.londres@tourspain.es
www.tourspain.co.uk

US 666 Fifth Avenue, New York, NY 10103
☎ 212 265 8822/6577246 *Fax* 212 2658864
email oetny@tourspain.es
www.okspain.org

Index

Choccywoccydoodah

Chocolate, Cake and Curses

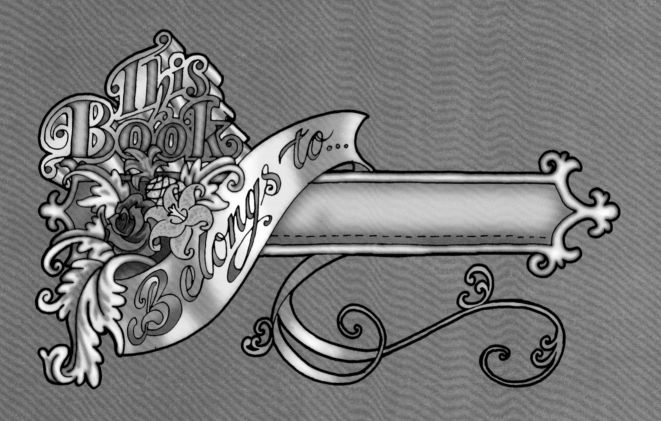

This Book Belongs to...

preface

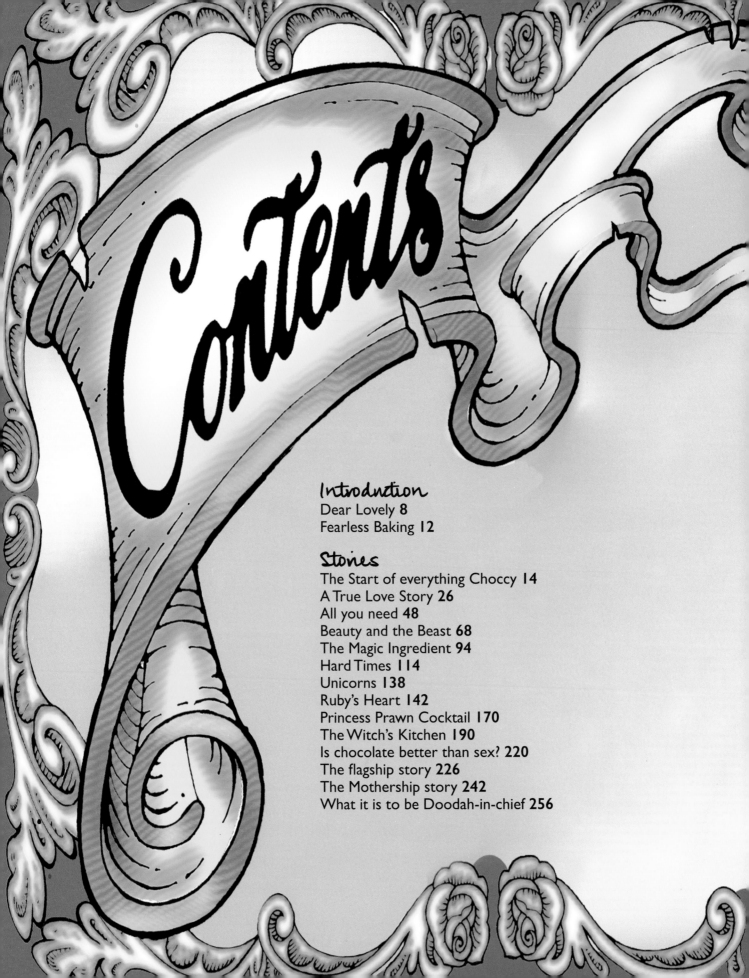

Contents

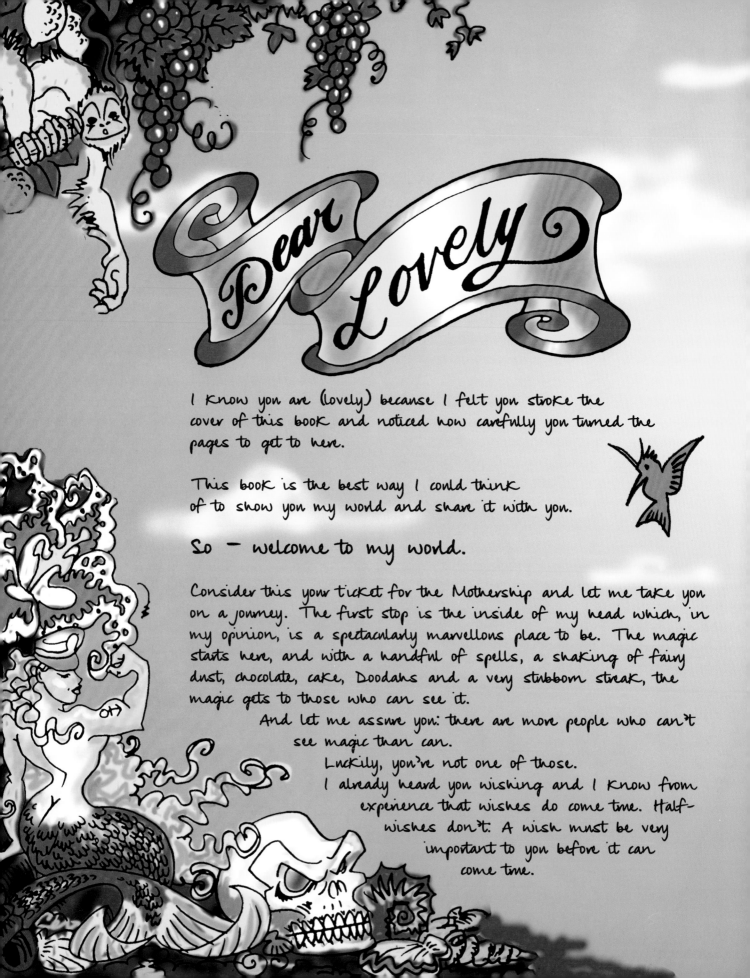

Dear Lovely

I know you are (lovely) because I felt you stroke the
cover of this book and noticed how carefully you turned the
pages to get to here.

This book is the best way I could think
of to show you my world and share it with you.

So — welcome to my world.

Consider this your ticket for the Mothership and let me take you
on a journey. The first stop is the inside of my head which, in
my opinion, is a spectacularly marvellous place to be. The magic
starts here, and with a handful of spells, a shaking of fairy
dust, chocolate, cake, Doodahs and a very stubborn streak, the
magic gets to those who can see it.

    And let me assure you: there are more people who can't
    see magic than can.

        Luckily, you're not one of those.

        I already heard you wishing and I know from
            experience that wishes do come true. Half-
              wishes don't. A wish must be very
                important to you before it can
                  come true.

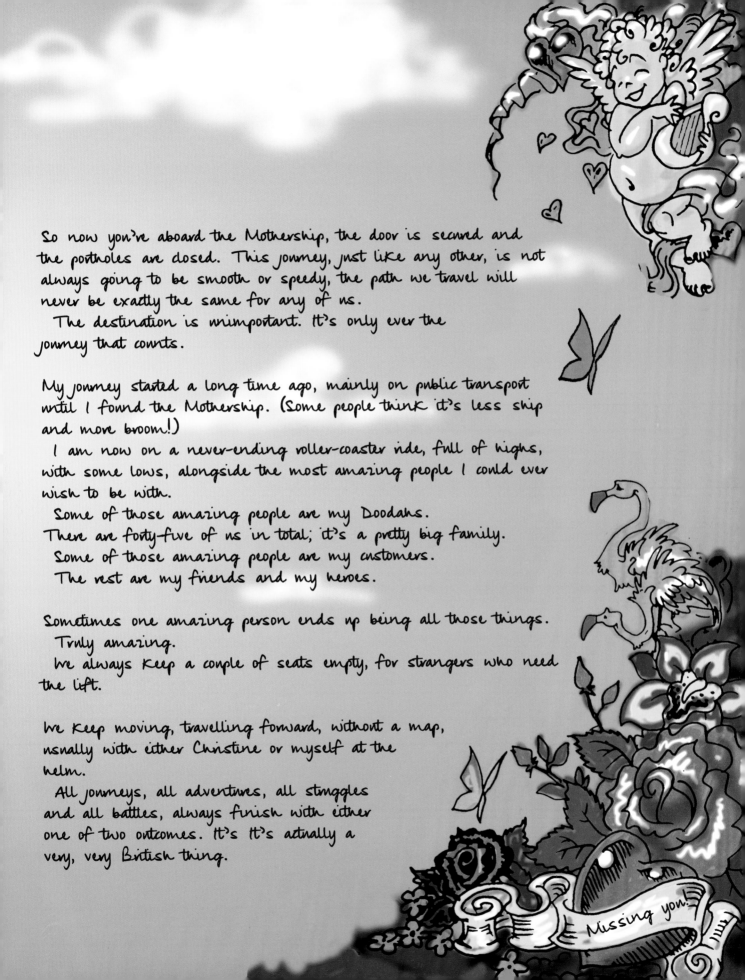

So now you've aboard the Mothership, the door is secured and the portholes are closed. This journey, just like any other, is not always going to be smooth or speedy, the path we travel will never be exactly the same for any of us.

The destination is unimportant. It's only ever the journey that counts.

My journey started a long time ago, mainly on public transport until I found the Mothership. (Some people think it's less ship and more broom!)

I am now on a never-ending roller-coaster ride, full of highs, with some lows, alongside the most amazing people I could ever wish to be with.

Some of those amazing people are my Doodahs.
There are forty-five of us in total; it's a pretty big family.
Some of those amazing people are my customers.
The rest are my friends and my heroes.

Sometimes one amazing person ends up being all those things.
Truly amazing.
We always keep a couple of seats empty, for strangers who need the lift.

We keep moving, travelling forward, without a map, usually with either Christine or myself at the helm.
All journeys, all adventures, all struggles and all battles, always finish with either one of two outcomes. It's It's actually a very, very British thing.

Missing you!

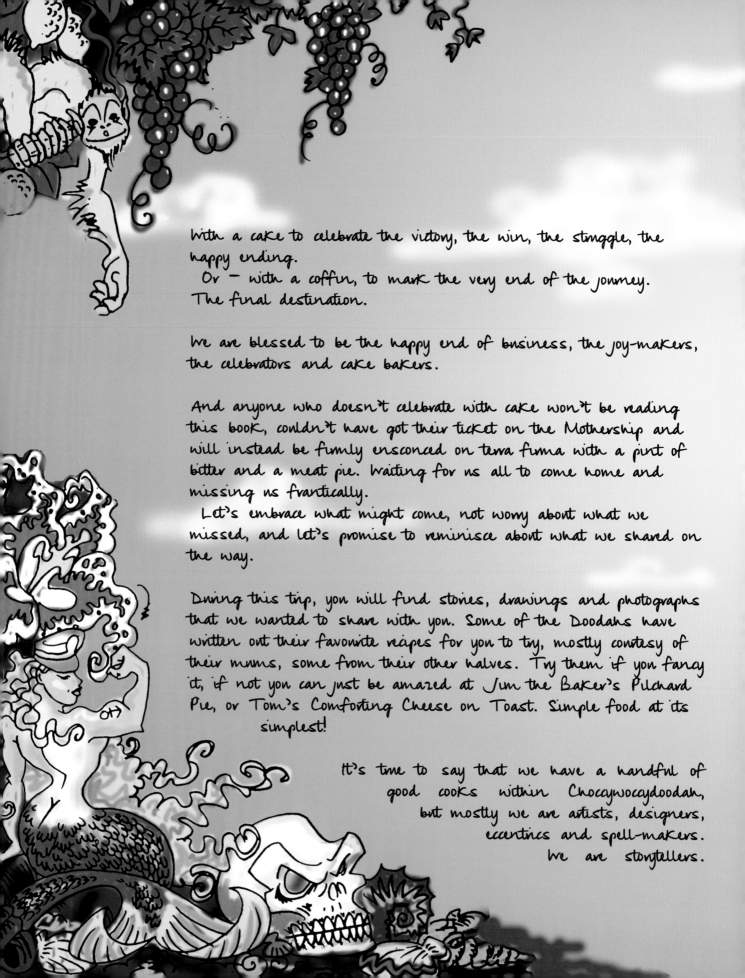

With a cake to celebrate the victory, the win, the struggle, the happy ending.
  Or — with a coffin, to mark the very end of the journey. The final destination.

We are blessed to be the happy end of business, the joy-makers, the celebrators and cake bakers.

And anyone who doesn't celebrate with cake won't be reading this book, couldn't have got their ticket on the Mothership and will instead be firmly ensconced on terra firma with a pint of bitter and a meat pie. Waiting for us all to come home and missing us frantically.
  Let's embrace what might come, not worry about what we missed, and let's promise to reminisce about what we shared on the way.

During this trip, you will find stories, drawings and photographs that we wanted to share with you. Some of the Doodahs have written out their favourite recipes for you to try, mostly courtesy of their mums, some from their other halves. Try them if you fancy it, if not you can just be amazed at Jim the Baker's Pilchard Pie, or Tom's Comforting Cheese on Toast. Simple food at its simplest!

It's time to say that we have a handful of good cooks within Choccywoccydoodah, but mostly we are artists, designers, eccentrics and spell-makers. We are storytellers.

We know how to make cake, how to make chocolate and how to make joy. We make happy endings. And because that's what we do, we don't expect you to, so our chocolate and cake techniques and our recipes will remain our secret.

However, we would love to welcome you into our world, we love most of you dearly and want you to share our journey.

After having this adventure together, I hope you emerge out into the daylight sparkling in fairy dust, spells memorised and ready to embark on your own journey, no matter what is thrown at you. Our paths will surely cross and crisscross.

Any book should be well loved, parts of it more than others. A well-read book should provide you with quotes, it should be creased and thumbed, it should be kept where you can easily reach it.

Because this is now your book, not mine any more.

I have deliberately made certain that there are pages for you to write on, pictures for you to colour, notes for you to send. Best of all, I hope that the spell I put on it, and in it, inspires you to be the best that you can be. And leave what you can't be where it belongs.
Behind you.

Christine

I'm a rule breaker, I can't stand being told what to do. I've spent my life baking and making delicious things to eat without following recipes. I've never owned kitchen scales. I've never decided what a portion should be. Big people eat a lot, little people eat a little. Duh.

Liberate your kitchen, throw out your scales, put on your oven gauntlets and create joy.

The basic principle of sugar, butter, eggs and self-raising flour is cake. Sugar, butter and plain flour is biscuit. How complicated does it need to be?
Baking is not about being prissy, it's not about going to the shops for ingredients, it's not about rules.

It is about using up the odds and sods in your cupboard, it is about experimenting and it is all about being fearless.

I do however have an observation. Not everyone can bake. They don't even want to. And that is entirely fine by me. I can't fix cars and I don't even want to. But I've never met anyone who can't eat.

And that's what baking is all about.

Feel free to use my recipes as you will. They are guidelines, not laws. If you cock up, try again.

If it tastes delicious and looks awful, in my world that's a massive success. If it tastes awful but looks delicious — well, just try again. Or ask someone else to. There's no harm in getting your mum/partner/brother or colleague to bake you a cake. I do, all the time.

Christie x.

I'm Christine Taylor and my business partner is another Christine, Christine Garratt.

We have been friends for ages, in and out of each other's lives and families for as long as I can remember.

We both had careers in London: I was a graphic designer in an agency and the other Christine was a tax analyst for American ex-pats in an oil company.

One day we decided we wanted a change. A change of career, pace, lifestyle and town. We pooled our money and our resources and bought a small (actually, really tiny) cafe in Brighton.

We thought it would be easy.

We knew nothing.

Serving the public and catering — two of the hardest jobs in existence.

The third hardest part of our chosen new career was that the cafe only sat fifteen people. We were always full, always busy and always poor.

We needed more tables and chairs to earn enough money to make even a small profit.
(I feel I should point out that despite working our tits off and being as poor as church mice, life was

rancously entertaining. The cafe customers, the staff and both of us all performed and out-performed each other in our tiny little space with hysterical laughter and shenanigans almost out-stripping our reputation for good food and amazing milkshakes. It's another story for another time.)

Then, unexpectedly, the shop next door to our cafe became vacant.
And — there was an internal connecting door.
All we would need to do was open the door and fill the space with tables and chairs.

So we took on the lease.

And celebrated.

Our celebrations didn't last long however.
The council informed us that they would not look kindly on losing an established retail premises.
We already had the key.
To a shop we no longer wanted.

We got drunk.

In fact, we drank a very large bottle of gin between us.
At the bottom of that bottle, we found a plan.
Drunk and jolly, in
desperate need
of

chocolate, we realised that if we had to have a key to a shop door, that shop should sell chocolate.

And it should be called Choccywoccydoodah.

(Pronounced drunk as Sschoccywoccydoodaaaaaah)

The second part of our plan was that when we had made everyone fat, including ourselves, we would open a diet shop.
And that shop would be called Chubbywubbydoodah.
Actually, we still might. We certainly got fat.

Reap what you sow.

Stone cold sober, we still thought it was a marvellous plan.
So, at the end of every day, the cafe till would be emptied and a little of our takings would be set aside to be used for the purchase of chocolate.

We found out one of our Saturday regulars was a sales rep for a Belgian chocolate manufacturer. She introduced us to clever people who made delicious chocolates and an unconventional convent of nuns who hand-made truffles.
Gradually, we acquired stock. Little by little, we bought every decent piece of handmade chocolate we could find.

When the cafe closed in the evenings, Christine and I would bake cakes, roast chickens and make soup for the following day.
Then we would nip next door and build cabinets, shelves, window displays and paint our new shop.
It took us three months.

We announced our opening date, 26th October 1994, to all our cafe customers, who were keenly following our progress.

The 24th of October was spent filling the shelves, displaying our wares and boxing our gorgeous, handmade by nuns, chocolate truffles.

When we stepped back, smiling confidently, to admire our handiwork, we were appalled.
The shop looked half empty.
We had obviously eaten far more than we realised and purchased far less than we realised. Although, we had eaten a lot.

No time for gin.

We hit the kitchen and baked for 24 hours non-stop.

Cake after cake, enrobed in chocolate.
As the hours went by we became more delirious and the cakes became more fantastical.
The shelves, the counter, the displays, all groaned under the weight of the crazy cakes.
Wobbly, tall cakes with cherries spilling from the top.
Whisky-soaked (an accident) white chocolate cakes.
Fat, short cakes piled high with pistachio creams.
Chocolate cake on every surface.
We opened the doors to our new emporium, as promised, on 26 October 1994.

And we sold out of cakes.

Bacon & egg Breakfast Muffins

Bits i need	food
Oven	7 Slices of bread (anything is good)
Bread knife	6 Medium eggs
Rolling pin	12 Slices of Streaky bacon (smoked is)
knife	Spoonful of butter Tasty
Bowl	Salt & pepper
Muffin tin	

Pre heat oven to 190°, Melt butter & grease the muffin Tin (save some butter for later)

Fry Bacon until crispy but still limp. (keeps cooking in the oven)

Cut off the bread crusts & flatten the bread bread with a rolling pin or glass. The bread needs to be bigger ✻

Push the bread into the muffin tin, Make Sure all edges are pressed in to round out & flatten the bread.

Use the left over butter to brush onto the tips of the bread.

Put in the bacon (messy & floppy looks good)

Crack an egg into each muffin Case & add S & P

Put into the oven for 15 minutes. 20 mins <u>MAX</u>

white of egg <u>JUST</u> needs to be cooked, Runny yolk!

Loosen with a knife & plate up!

Eat them <u>Now</u>! with Some brown Sauce.

✻ one Slice of bread extra in case of holes!
  Just Squidge in more bread to fill.

Dan Flowergirl

Clever clever fingers!
Flowers, skulls, cakes,
creative cook.

This is Dan's perfect
hangover recipe.

A True Love Story

In a small village in suburban England there is a delightful and traditional tearooms. The lady that owns the tearooms is called Tuppenny Teapot.

She worked in the tearooms for years and years, familiar with her customers, watching their families grow, but never getting married or having a family of her own.

Her most familiar and reliable customer was an old sailor, who she served with cups of tea every day for many years. He had an old dog and a bad limp and out of kindness she used to let the dog sit under the cafe table.

One day, sitting alone in front of her fire in her tiny flat, she realised she was lonely. And getting older. She thought about the old sailor, who was much younger when she served him with his first cup of tea.

And the thought suddenly struck her — he didn't come into the tearooms every day for a cup of tea — he came to see her.
   The thought lit up her heart and filled her with joy as she realised the obvious truth. They had both been so shy, so polite, for so long, how would it now be possible to let him know that she knew he loved her?

And, that she cared for him...

Ah! she thought, I will bake him a cake. But then she remembered she had never seen him eat anything.

He simply had a cup of tea, just to be able to talk to her, every day.

Miss Teapot decided to sleep on it.

The following morning she had a plan.

She would make him a most delicious treat to have with his cup of tea that very day. Something chewy, something soft, something hard, something fruity, something fluffy, something crunchy, all smothered in delicious milk chocolate.

She melted a big bowl of the very best milk chocolate and then she added marshmallows, fudge, honeycomb, jellybeans, nutty nougat and coconut ice.

The chocolate was full of love.

That afternoon, the old sailor came in as normal and asked for a cup of tea.
   He noticed that Tupperry's (he had always thought of her as his lucky tuppence) cheeks were rosier than ever. And her bright blue eyes were more twinkly than usual. But he never, ever, expected to receive such a beautiful chocolate treat. Made especially for him, with love.

Very shortly after that the old sailor, with a new spring in his step, married his only ever one true love, Miss Tupperry Teapot.

The dog was delighted. The customers were delighted. And I am delighted to say they live happily ever after.
   As we all know, the path of love never runs smooth and because of that, the chocolate bar of love has always been known as Rocky Road.

ROCKY ROAD

It's perfectly acceptable to buy all your ingredients for this, if you don't have time to make each individual item. It's as easy or as hard as you want to make it.

milk chocolate
chunks of honeycomb
nut brittle
fudge
coconut ice
marshmallows
nougat

VARIATIONS:

Add jelly beans or wine gums. We do.

Line your favourite baking tray with baking parchment.

Melt a big bowl of milk chocolate slowly in the microwave.

Fill the bowl with the remaining ingredients.

Pour into the lined baking tray.

Pop into the fridge to set.

True love. Meant for sharing.

Fearless Baking...

(Well, seeing as it's you!)
MARSHMALLOWS BY GAVIN

These are very, very nice. You do need a sugar thermometer (a digital one is best). So I would say it's for confident cooks. Make it with whatever colour and flavour combo you fancy. I've made caramel ones and rhubarb ones.

a little oil, for greasing
25g powdered gelatine
2–3 drops red food colouring,
    optional (or any colour you like)
1 tsp vanilla extract
500g granulated sugar
2 large free-range egg whites
3 tbsp each icing sugar and
    cornflour, mixed together

Line a 35.5 x 23cm rectangular dish with clingfilm, then oil the clingfilm. Brush oil over a spatula.

Measure 125ml boiling water into a jug and pour the gelatine in. Stir to dissolve. Add the drops of food colouring and mix in along with the vanilla extract. Put the sugar into a pan with 250ml cold water. Heat gently to dissolve the sugar then turn up the heat and let it bubble until the temperature reaches 122°C.

Meanwhile, using a freestanding mixer, whisk the egg whites in a spotlessly clean bowl until the mixture stands in stiff peaks.

When the sugar mixture reaches 122°C, take the pan off the heat and carefully stir in the gelatine mixture.

With the mixer running on slow, pour the sugar and gelatine mixture carefully and slowly on to the beaten egg whites. The egg whites may collapse a little but never fear.

Once you've added all the sugar to the egg whites, turn up the mixer to high and whisk the living daylights out of it, for at least 10 minutes, until it has cooled a little. It will get bigger and become glossy and very, very sticky.

Tip the mixture out, using the oiled spatula to ease it into the corners, and let it settle in the tin. Leave uncovered in a cool spot overnight.

Lift the marshmallow out of the tin and onto a board. Cut it into whatever sized pieces you like. Dredge each piece in the icing sugar mixture to make handling them easier.

Store airtight in dry conditions. They will last for a week.

COCONUT ICE

A really good, easy recipe for kids to get messy with.

170g tin condensed milk
225g icing sugar, sieved
175g desiccated coconut
1 tiny drop red food colouring

VARIATIONS:

Try dipping the chunks of
coconut ice into melted
chocolate, then leave to set.

Use cocoa powder instead of
the red food colouring.

Add glacé cherries and
pistachio nuts.

Spoon the condensed milk into a bowl and add the icing
sugar. Mix together, then stir in the coconut.

Put half the mixture into another bowl. Add the drop of
red food colouring to one bowl and mix well to colour it
pink.

Line a small plastic box or baking tray, around 20 x 15cm,
with the white coconut mix, pressing it in so it's level on
top. Press the pink coconut mix on top to make a layered
bar.

Cover and leave at room temperature for at least
2 hours to firm up.

Cut into chunks and devour. Store in an airtight container
for up to 3 weeks.

FUDGE

Another reasonably easy recipe, but it does involve boiling sugar.
So it's not one I would recommend for children to make, only to eat.

300ml milk
350g caster sugar
100g unsalted butter
1 tsp vanilla extract

VARIATIONS:

Add fruit or nuts.

Dip the chunks into melted chocolate and put on baking parchment to set.

Replace some of the milk with Baileys Irish Cream.

Line a 15 x 22.5cm baking tin with coated baking parchment.

Pour the milk into a heavy bottomed pan and add the sugar and butter and heat gently. Wait for the sugar to dissolve and the butter to melt. Keep stirring the mix. When it has all melted, bring to the boil.

Turn the heat down and allow the mixture to simmer for 15 minutes stirring every now and again. It should be a soft, thick and golden consistency.

To test, put a little cold water onto a cold saucer. Spoon a little bit of the mixture into the water. If the mixture sets to a fudge-like consistency, it's done. Remove from the heat and beat in the vanilla extract, or any other flavourings and ingredients.

Carry on beating for a couple of minutes, then pour the mixture into the lined baking tin.

Leave to cool at room temperature and cut into chunks.

This is a brilliant recipe even when it goes wrong. If you over cook the recipe and end up burning the sugar, add some more milk and butter, warm through slowly and use it as butterscotch sauce.

If it doesn't set firm enough, where you haven't cooked it for long enough, return the mixture to the pan and add some chopped chocolate. Warm it through gently over a low heat and pour it over ice cream.

HONEYCOMB (cinder toffee)

Not for children to make on their own, as it involves boiling sugar. And if you're a dotty adult, be careful. Sugar burns and really hurts — I have proof. This is a recipe I had to practice at.

200g caster sugar
5 tbsp golden syrup
2 tsp bicarbonate of soda

Line a 15 x 22.5cm baking tin with baking parchment, shiny side up.

Put the sugar and syrup together in a deep and heavy bottomed pan. Place over a gentle heat, stirring all the time. Do not let the mixture bubble until it's completely smooth, with no grains of sugar in sight.

Turn up the heat at this point and cook until the mixture becomes a golden amber colour. This happens very quickly so watch it carefully.

Immediately turn off the heat, add the bicarbonate of soda and stir it in with a wooden spoon. The mixture will foam right up.

Pour the mixture into the lined baking tin with great care. It will continue to bubble in the tin. The honeycomb will set in about an hour, maybe an hour and a half.

When it's hard and cool, break into chunks and eat.

Store airtight, at room temperature.

Delicious but not good for your teeth.

NUTTY NOUGAT

Not easy. But delicious.

sheets of edible rice paper
150ml water
225g powdered glucose
450g caster sugar
2 large egg whites
150g toasted hazelnuts

VARIATIONS:

Replace hazelnuts
with almonds.

Add glacé fruit.

Dip in chocolate.

Line a baking tin with coated baking parchment, shiny side down. Layer the rice paper on the parchment.

Put the water, glucose and sugar in a large, heavy bottomed saucepan. Slowly bring to the boil, stirring all the time. Turn the heat down and simmer for 10 minutes. If you are using a sugar thermometer it should read 120°C. Turn the heat off.

Beat the egg whites into peaks. It's always quicker to do this with a food mixer, but it can be done by hand with a whisk.

When the sugar thermometer reaches 110°C, turn the heat back on and monitor the temperature. When it reaches 149°C, pour a quarter of the syrup into the egg whites in a slow, steady stream, whilst continuing to whisk on a slow speed.

When the syrup reaches 149°C again, turn off the heat and pour it slowly and steadily into the egg whites, still whisking. Continue to gently whisk for 30 minutes, scraping down the sides of the bowl from time to time.

Add the hazelnuts to the nougat mixture and stir through.

Pour the mixture onto the rice paper. Put more rice paper on the top of the poured mixture to cover it. Place in the fridge overnight to set. Cut into slices, wrap in baking parchment and keep airtight.

Jem's Lovely Potatoes

Hello, this is Dave. At the age of 24, as I scraped some burnt cheese sauce into the bin, I vowed never to cook again. And I pretty much haven't. Fortunatly I married a man who loves to cook, and I love to eat his cooking. Everyones a winner!!!

This is a recipie for potatoes, normally served at our chistmas party.

Ingredients :- As many potatoes as you like
Salt
Sugar (for par boiling)

For cooking:- whole clove of garlic
lots of salt, lots of freshly ground black pepper, mustard seeds, mixed herbs, rosemary, whole cumin, oregano, cor coriander seeds, oil.

Method

Method - wash & peel potatoes, chop into numerous (?) bite size chunks. Put into large pan, fill with cold water till it covers the potatoes. Put in a liberal dash of salt and a tablespoon of sugar. Bring to boil, and boil for 10 minutes. Strain well. Whilst boiling, you can prepare the garlic by peeling & chopping it finely, then steep it in oil. Lay the potatoes in a baking tray (or 2), one layer deep, drizzle some oil over & mix it in. Shake over the rest of the herbs and finally spoon over the garlic. Bake in the oven at 180° for 1 hr. After 30 mins, take them out & give them a shake. After 1 hour, they made need a little longer until they are golden & crispy.

Dave Pop!

Married to architect Jem,
proud parent of Trevor
and Gef Schnauzers,
Captain Creative of
Choccywoccydoodah.
His potato recipe is actually
Jem's speciality, as Dave
can't cook. Won't cook.

nce upon a time, in a country called Sussexonia, lived three princesses. Princess Tiara was the oldest daughter, named after her mother's favourite head-dress. The middle daughter was called Princess Ruby after her mother's favourite jewels. The baby of the family was named Princess Prawn Cocktail after her mother's favourite crisp flavour. The family affectionately referred to her as Prawn, but on official duty she was known more formally as Princess Cocktail.

The girls were aged twenty-eight, twenty-five and twenty-two respectively. They all lived at home with the King and the Queen, who they knew simply as Mum and Dad.

Nearly everyone was really happy. The Kingdom was small, peaceful and very pretty.

The princesses led a very busy life, working in the Kingdom, singing and organising vintage fairs that travelled from town to town.

The only princess who was a bit unhappy was Prawn.

There were certain archaic laws in place that her father had never seen fit to change. One being that until Princess Tiara got married, neither of her sisters could. They couldn't even leave home or go to university. The oldest had to come first. Poor Prawn was desperate to go to India with her boyfriend and explore the landscape he told her about. He was from Mumbai and painted colour with his words, music with his hands and respect with his deeds.

Abdhul would never let Prawn leave home and cross her parents. He said they must be patient.

Princess Tiara was a lively girl. She loved her dogs and horses, she adored her family and she was inseparable from her best friend, Bellinki, who practically lived at the palace. She showed no signs of romantic attachment to any of the local princes, or to any of the local boys at all.

Princess Prawn confided in her other sister Princess Ruby.

Ruby was the family beauty, not interested in too much apart from clothes, make-up and her kittens. But she was very aware that a famous film star, Jimmy Hipp, was very interested in

her. And she quite liked the idea of living in Hollywood with people who had similar interests to her.

So Ruby listened quite intently and genuinely gave their predicament some serious thought. Which was interesting for her, as she didn't know she could have serious thoughts.

Ruby and Prawn decided to set up a secret matchmaking service for their sister. And because they both loved her dearly, they went to a lot of trouble to choose her potential beau.

They invited the bravest soldier in the land, a hero amongst heroes, so brave the King himself had personally given him many medals.
When Tiara was left alone with him, she asked him if he would like to go horse riding with her.
It turns out the only thing in the world that this heroic soldier was scared of was horses.
So Tiara and Bellinki went out on the horses on their own.

The next potential match was a Russian prince. So handsome, so dashing, so charming that women would literally swoon into his arms.
However, Tiara in her high heels stood nearly six foot six. And even in his highest Cuban heel, Prince Borshch stood only four foot ten.
When Tiara tried to put him in her pocket, both Princesses Prawn and Ruby knew this was not a match made in heaven.

Men came to the palace from all over the world to meet Princess Tiara.
By now the Queen had guessed her younger daughters' plans, and although she approved she could easily see that none of the eager courtiers were right for

her precious oldest daughter, who would one day be Queen herself.

What could be done?
  Then one day, out of the blue, a jolly whistling postman turned up at the Palace with a package for Princess Tiara.
  A huge uproar ensued as all the servants and the cats and the dogs ran through the palace calling for Tiara to come and sign for her unexpected parcel.
  As usual she was in the stables, mucking out the horses with Bellinki and talking about music festivals. Should they have one in the palace gardens?

The postman handed Tiara the parcel and told her to check it before she accepted it. She looked at him intently, noticing his kind eyes and strong postmanly hands. She ripped the tape from the box and pulled out an amazing chocolate cake.
  Not just any old chocolate cake, but one from the best chocolate shop in the land, Choccywoccydoodah.
  On top of the cake was a beautiful handmade heart that read

'Marry me'.

Tiara's face flushed, her eyes got teary and she kissed the postman. He returned the gesture and then wished her all the luck in the world as he
    passed a small handwritten card to Tiara.

     Ruby, Prawn and the entire household admired the cake.
      Who could have sent such a perfect, delicious and apt gift to Princess Tiara?
  Who could have understood that that would be the best way to Princess Tiara's heart?

Nobody noticed Bellinki's absence. No one saw her making her way to the King and Queen's quarters, pale and tense. Nobody guessed what was about to happen.

Princess Tiara read the little note that came with the cake.

She drew herself up to her full height, picked up her cake and looked hard at her little sisters. 'If all goes well with Dad, will you be my bridesmaids?'

The girls squealed and pinched each other. 'Of course!'

Tiara then took off her riding boots, hung up her riding hat, and made her way into the palace.

She looked majestic, striding through the corridors of her family home with an entourage of palace servants, cats and dogs following her. All agreed they could see that she was going to be a very regal Queen and they felt very proud.

But who was to be the new King?

When Princess Tiara finally reached her parents' quarters in the Palace and flung open the door, the determination on her face was clear for everyone to see.

In the middle of the room, stood the King, the Queen and Bellinki.

They all stared at her.

And then the King, Tiara's beloved father, a man whom she knew to be both gentle and wise, hurried over to her and gave her an enormous bear hug.

The Queen threw her arms around Tiara's waist and danced with her across the room.

Bellinki smiled at her and nodded her head, just a little.

The following day there was a very important Royal Announcement made by the King himself.

He stood on the special Royal Announcement balcony with his family, the Queen proudly holding his hand.

Thousands of Sussexonian people stood waiting for their King to speak.

He said:

'For many years I have ignored the archaic marriage laws of this country.

'I love my daughters and have loved living as a family under

this great old building's roof.

'But it's time for me to make modern changes, not just for my children, but for all our children.

'Love is all. Without it we are nothing. Rich or poor, believer or non-believer.

'Love is all you need.' I have amended the silly old marriage laws as from this day forward.

'And the first happy newly legal announcement from the palace is that my darling daughter Princess Tiara is to be betrothed to her own darling Bellinki.

'The wedding will be in fourteen days and the entire nation is invited!'

Not everyone was as happy as the Royal family, but then, that hardly ever happens anyway. But almost everyone was as happy and the great celebrations were organised.

In Brighton, in the little chocolate shop there, where Bellinki had trusted everyone to keep her secret, the phone rang.

Stephen answered then passed the phone to Henry. 'It's the Queen,' he whispered.

And Henry and the Queen designed the most magnificent wedding cake, big enough to feed nearly everyone.

All you need is love.

Back at the Palace, Princess Prawn and Princess Ruby were making their own plans. But nothing that couldn't wait until after the wedding ...

BANANA SPLIT

Very easy.

1 banana
1 scoop each vanilla, chocolate
  and strawberry ice cream
as much raspberry coulis as you like
double cream, whipped
1 cherry

Split the banana lengthways and put in a long dish. Place the scoops of vanilla, chocolate and strawberry ice cream down the centre.

Drizzle with raspberry coulis. Smother with the whipped cream. Top with a cherry.

Eat.

CHOCOLATE SUNDAE

Very easy. Break the rules and mix it up.

vanilla ice cream
chocolate ice cream
chocolate sauce (see page 266)
chocolate brownie, chopped into
　chunks (see page 234)
whipped cream

To decorate
chopped nuts, Maltesers or Flake

Layer scoops of the vanilla and chocolate ice cream, the chocolate sauce and the chocolate brownie in a tall sundae glass until it's full. Top with a spoonful of whipped cream.

Finish with chopped nuts or Maltesers or a Flake.

Eat.

BEST ICE-CREAM SUNDAE
FOR GROWN-UPS

Easy. Go easy.

1 tin stoned black cherries, drained
a generous glass of vodka
good-quality vanilla ice cream
dark chocolate, grated
double cream, whipped

Soak the cherries and the vodka in a bowl overnight. When you're ready to make the sundaes, spoon the cherries and vodka evenly into a cocktail glass, reserving a cherry for each helping.

Top each with ice cream.

Add the grated chocolate.

Top with whipped cream.

Pop a cherry on top of each.

Squiffy.

DARK CHOCOLATE ICE CREAM

Easy if you're disciplined. Fantastic served with shards of nut brittle (see page 272).

2 eggs, plus 2 large egg yolks
75g caster sugar
250ml single cream
200g dark chocolate, chopped
250ml double cream

VARIATIONS:

Vary the recipe by adding nuts or fruit.

Beat the eggs, egg yolks and sugar together in a bowl.

Put the single cream and dark chocolate together in a heavy bottomed pan and place over a very gentle heat. Bring to the boil, stirring constantly.

Beat the chocolate mixture vigorously into the egg mixture. Let the mixture cool, stirring it from time to time. If it separates, beat it vigorously again.

Whip the double cream in a separate bowl until thick and fold it into the cool chocolate mixture. Pour the mixture into a sealable plastic tub and cover. Freeze for 1½ hours, then take out of the freezer and beat again. Freeze overnight.

Before serving, put the ice cream in the fridge for 15–20 minutes to soften.

DOG BISCUITS

We are famous for our love of dogs and our love of chocolate. However, chocolate is poisonous to dogs so instead we make these for our beloved best friends. They are intended as a treat, not as a way of life. This is quite easy.

butter, for greasing
225g plain flour
110g rolled oats
1 tbsp cornflour
50g soft margarine
1 chicken stock cube
1 tsp yeast extract
1 large egg
splash of milk
1 suitably shaped biscuit cutter

Preheat the oven to 170°C/150°C fan oven/325°F/gas mark 3½. Grease and flour a large baking tray.

In a large bowl, combine the plain flour, oats, cornflour and margarine and gently work all the ingredients together with a table knife to roughly chop the margarine into the dry mixture.

Next add the stock cube, and rub all the ingredients together until the mixture resembles breadcrumbs. Then add the yeast extract, one egg and stir. Draw the mixture together with your hands and lightly knead. If it is too dry, add a splash of milk.

Flour a flat surface, and roll out to the thickness of a pound coin. Stamp out as many biscuit shapes as you can, re-rolling any off-cuts until all the dough has been used up. Place the biscuits on the tray and pop into the oven and bake for 15 minutes or until golden.

Lift onto a rack to cool. Store in an airtight tin or jar.

By swapping chicken stock cube for Parmesan cheese and seasoning with black pepper these are excellent human savoury biscuits.

Daveed's Perfect Cookie Recipe

200 grms of soft brown Sugar
4 tblspoon of golden Syrup
250 grms of butter
340 grms of plain flour
½ teaspoon of Bicarbonate of Soda
120 grms of chocolate chips
   pinch of ground cinnamon.

Cooking time

10-12 min @ C° 180

★ melt the butter with the Sugar, golden Syrup & Cinnamon

★ Sift the flour & Bicarb into a bowl, create a well in the middle

★ Pour the melted butter mix into the well and mix until you get a soft, and a little sticky, texture. add the chocolate chips

★ Roll out some clingfilm flat on the counter

★ Pour your mix onto the clingfilm and make a thick long sausage. Roll it into a tight roll. Place in the freezer for a few hours

★ When you want freshly baked Cookies, simply take the sausage out of the freezer and cut thick slices. Place on a baking tray lined with parchment paper (don't forget to remove the clingfilm) with plenty of space between them as they expand quite a lot.

★ Cook for 10-12 min in a preheated oven @ 180 C°

enjoy 👍

Daveed the French Fancy

Troubleshooter,
troublemaker and
King of cookies.

Original recipe created
for a Countess with a
craving for a cookie.

Beauty and the Beast

Some people think they don't deserve to be loved.
Some people aren't loved.
Some people don't know how to love.
This is not a story about those people.

As we all know, nearly everyone is loved, or was loved, has loved or is loving.
Parents love their children; who else will?
Lovers love each other, they don't even see the rest of us in the same world.

Husbands love their wives or their husbands, sometimes their mistresses and their best friends.
Especially after a drink.
Wives love husbands or wives, families and sometimes a tempting visiting stranger.
Friends love friends.
Owners love their dogs and are loved unconditionally in return.
Sometimes love passes through, sometimes it crashes in, sometimes it is one-sided and unrequited.
Sometimes love lasts for ever, through whole generations, through storms and disasters, loss and win, battle and triumph. A great love.

And this is the love that Beauty sought.
Beauty was born with film-star looks into a modest family. His dad was a car mechanic and his mum was adorable, but

dotty. He had no brothers or sisters, as he was an unexpected surprise from the stork when his parents were both quite old.

A lovely surprise, found where the stork had dropped him, long, long after his parents had given up on the idea of ever being able to have children.

Beauty lived in a tower block on an estate about four doors down from his parents. Near enough to get to them if they needed him, far enough away that they could not see his comings and goings.

The estate was full of gangsters and tough guys, families and old people.

Everyone knew everyone else.

There was no such thing as minding your own business.

Everybody's business was everybody else's business.

Beauty's real name was George, but when he was born he truly was so beautiful that his mum called him Bean. Everyone on the estate asked her what on earth that meant, she explained it meant Beauty and the name stuck.

In fact, everyone agreed that he really was absolutely beautiful.

As he got older, he became more handsome and on the estate, within his own group of friends, Beauty was just a boy with an ordinary name.

His friends were called Billybullyboy, Whitehawker, Chelsea, Paragon and Rumplestiltskin. Beauty sometimes counted his blessings that he didn't end up as just George. He would have felt really awkward.

Like many only children Beauty was the sun in the universe of his parents' eyes. He was the star that their world orbited around.

Every accomplishment, every achievement and every failure was closely monitored.

Not just by his mum and dad, but by the whole estate.

As were everybody's kids.

He was photographed, filmed, recorded and every school report was pored over.

Being an only child sometimes made him lonely and a little envious.

Beauty often daydreamed about having a brother, or a sister, someone to talk to, to make plans with, to share dreams with, to fight with.

Although he was popular with his friends, when they all went home he was very much left to his own devices.

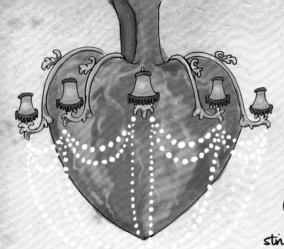

He spent a lot of time dreaming about the future, a time when he would have someone to love, someone of his own, someone for ever.

As he got older, because of his crazily good looks, Beauty had a lot of girlfriends. He got a job selling lovely cars which also made him very popular with the boys.

When he was younger he took his popularity in his stride.

He didn't know any different.

As he got older he became more cynical and could easily see that some people courted his friendship because of his looks and his cars. Not because they loved him, or even liked him.

He did talk to his mum and dad about it, but it just made them sad.

And so he wasted years trying to have a good time, pretending to have a good time and feeling more and more that he was the good time. And he was being had completely.

More than anything, Beauty wanted to feel love.

Not the love he felt for his parents, although he loved them dearly.

Not the love he felt for his animals, although he loved them dearly too.

Not the love he felt for all the people he grew up with on the estate, although he truly did love them all.

He wanted to understand how it would feel to love someone so much that their happiness was more important to you than your own.

He wanted to sleep badly, eat badly, work badly because his emotions were in such turmoil over someone else.

He had read of such love. He had heard great songs written about such love. He had seen such love between his parents, especially as his adorable mother became dottier and dottier every day, slowly retreating into her own world, leaving all her loved ones in another world entirely.

His dad never once lost his patience, lost his love or lost his wife. He would tenderly chaperone her everywhere, seeing to her needs and keeping her cheerful.

They would sit together night after night watching the telly, holding hands and drinking hot chocolate. Their love was great.

Where do I find such love? Beauty asked his dad and mum time and time again.

His mum told him that when she was a girl, it was a knight's duty to confront an enemy or a monster or a huge fear, defeat it, or kill it, to win the hand of a fair maiden. Kingdoms were fought for and lost in such quests.

Marriages were made, children were born and great loves grew out of these confrontations.

And some Knights were princes. Some from faraway Kingdoms and some from quite near.

But his mum lived in another world entirely.

Beauty thought this through.

In the olden days he could see that working: saving a damsel from a dragon, or fighting a great battle on horseback to defend a Kingdom.

But now, with iPhones and Ferraris, TV at all times and not that many Kingdoms to fight for, how would that work?

How would that guarantee love?

And so life went on.

Neither happy nor unhappy.

Not adored or adoring.

On another estate, just across the motorway, there lived another family whose youngest daughter also yearned for such love.

She had met Beauty many times at school dances and when her estate had organised fights with his estate.

Ddraig had done everything she could to be noticed by Beauty but he never noticed her.

Years passed, Ddraig turned away many boys and even turned down marriage proposals. For years, from when they were both small children, her heart belonged to Beauty, although he never knew it.

Both Ddraig's brothers had long since got married and between them had four children. Her sisters were also either married or in mad love affairs.

Ddraig had tried love, had sought love and had rejected lovers time and time again.

She wanted Beauty and only Beauty.

And now life was passing her by.

The rest of Ddraig's family were a bit concerned about her.

Although she herself wasn't blessed with great beauty and she was very, very fond of her food, Ddraig had a wicked sense of humour, was always willing to try anything and showed great courage in terrible situations. In other words, she was a good catch for someone who didn't want a dull life.

Her obsession with Beauty got on her family's nerves. He hadn't even noticed her and they told her she could do so much better.

Finally, her mother, Bwyell Frwdyr, who ruled the estate on which she lived with fierce love, decided to do something about it.

She was much feared and much respected. Nobody ever crossed her or questioned her decisions. This particular decision was not something that most mothers would ever risk but Bwyell Frwdyr had been pushed to the outer edges of her patience and was unafraid of the consequences of her actions.

Bwyell Frwdyr summoned her crazy sister Swynwraig to the estate for a family discussion.

Swynwraig was a very famous sorceress, world renowned for her ability to infiltrate minds, cast spells and sometimes get it very badly wrong. However, she knew she could not ever get it wrong for family. And if she did, Bwyell Frwdyr would kill her.

Swynwraig was a wild-looking woman, with masses of tangled red hair, brightly coloured clothes, and a small red moustache.

She could look into your very soul.

Whether you wanted her to, or not.

The powerful sisters spent a very long night discussing Ddraig and Beauty.

By morning, they had a plan.

Ddraig was called into the kitchen and they talked her through the plan.

At first, she was a little shocked.

Then amused.

And finally she agreed.

They all walked together to the local recreation park.

By the broken swings, next to the abandoned fridges and old mattresses, Swynwraig uttered her spell.

Ddraig was transformed.

In her place was a massive red dragon, as big as a big house, with long eyelashes and a little bit on the tubby side.

Bwyell Frwdyr and Swynwraig showed the Dragon her reflection in the duck pond.

She liked it.

And so the plan was underway.

Dragon made her way across her own estate to the motorway.

She could see Beauty's estate but knew she must bide her time.

She attracted great crowds of people who had never seen a dragon before.

However, her mother and her aunt rode on her back, keeping troublemakers away and offering lifts to anyone waiting at a bus stop.

The whole estate fell in love with the dragon, and everyone tried to pat and pet her.

As she was a girl with a big appetite which had just increased a hundred-fold, the only difficulty was finding enough food.

Even if she ate the entire contents of her mum's house it would not fill her up.

Someone who knew her mum told her that all the big supermarkets threw away tons of perfectly good food every day, just because the packaging was damaged. So she feasted in the supermarket skips and was able to eat all her favourite foods.

Everyone was very relieved as no one wanted to defend their party from a hungry dragon, especially when that dragon was Bwyell Frwdyr's daughter.

Eventually, when night fell, Ddraig crossed the motorway into the neighbouring estate and made her way to Beauty's tower block.

Pressing her eye against the window of his bedroom she could see him fast asleep in bed.

He looked gorgeous.

She curled up around the bottom of the tower block and waited for morning.

Straight after breakfast, Beauty decided to get in his car and take a spin around the estate, before heading into work.

Dragon stood at the entrance to the underground car park with her mouth wide open.

And she could open her mouth really, really wide.

It was so simple.

Beauty drove straight in before he ever knew what happened.

And by the time he came to his senses he was right in the dragon's belly.

This belly was not like any other dragon's belly that had ever existed.

It was fully furnished with the most exquisite taste.

Beautiful velvet and silk soft furnishings, a state-of-the-art entertainment centre, a library of the best books ever written. The space was huge.

And every time Dragon opened her mouth, the view was breathtaking.

Ddraig had got her wish. Beauty now lived next to her heart. He kept her belly full and her heart happy.

And Beauty finally understood what a great love felt like.

During their long conversations on their journeys together walking around both their estates, Beauty finally admitted he had found the perfect woman.

They were meant to be.

Dragon knew that Beauty had fallen in love with her when he arranged for a cake to be displayed in the window of her favourite shop in the world, Choccywoccydoodah.

The cake read 'Ddraig, will you marry me?'

She said yes. At last.

She then ate the cake in one go. It was delicious. All of it, even the cake board and wrapping. She also ate a significant amount of the shop, at least half of the chocolate and most of the cakes on display.

She did manage to spit out the poor customers who didn't get out of the way quickly enough but Beauty happily invited them to the wedding to say sorry.

Everyone said yes and everyone was happy.

On important occasions, such as their wedding day, their children's naming ceremonies, high days and holidays, Dragon transformed back into Ddraig.

Both estates loved her.

Both estates loved him.

They had a truly great love.

And they loved each other most when Beauty was inside Dragon's belly, next to her heart, gazing at the stars through her open mouth.

George and the Dragon.

Ddraig had got her wish. Beauty now lived next to her heart. He kept her belly full and her heart happy.

☆ Sausage and Egg Picnic Pie ☆

Ingredients

- 5 x Medium Free-range Eggs
- 1 x Packet of sage and Onion stuffing
- 2 x Packets of 375g sheet ready-rolled Puff Pastry.
- 800g Good quality Pork Sausages
- ½ x tsp garlic powder
- ½ x tsp Black Pepper
- ½ x tsp Chopped thyme.

Method.

1) Preheat the oven to 200°C / Fan 180°C / Gas Mark 6.
Place 4 eggs in a Pan of Cold water and bring to boil, then simmer for 3 mins, then plunge eggs into a bowl of cold water and leave to cool completely before removing the shells.

2) Split the sausages, remove skins, then place in a large bowl, add garlic, thyme and ground black pepper. Boil Kettle and add water to stuffing mix as instructions on packet, when cool add mix to Sausages. Best way to mix is with your hands, until very well combined.

3) Roll out one sheet of puff pastry, greece a flan dish about 12" wide, cover with Pastry and leave excess pastry hanging over edge. Blanch cook base, for about 5 mins, then add small amount of meet mix to dish, then place boiled eggs evenly spaced around dish then gently pack meet around over eggs evenly, overing eggs with out any gaps.

4) Roll out remaining sheet of puff Pastry and cut long strips to form the lattice work on top of flan, join base and top Pastry with the remaining egg, (beaten egg) then glace lattice with beaten egg.

5) Finilly bake in oven for 45 mins until golden brown, then leave to stand for 10 mins. ☆ Baker!

Doodah's favourite recipes

Denise Sweetie Wrappery

This recipe was invented by Denise as she juggled children and life.
It made her children big and strong, along with being juggled.

BRIGHTON (CHOCOLATE) ROCKS

If you can make meringues, you can do this. I can't make either.

2 large egg whites
100g caster sugar
75g flaked almonds, toasted
2 tbsp cocoa powder
50g milk, dark or white chocolate

Preheat the oven to 200°C/180°C fan oven/400°F/ gas mark 6. Line a baking tray with baking parchment.

Whisk the egg whites in a spotlessly clean, greasefree bowl until stiff. Add the sugar a little at a time, continuing to whisk the mixture constantly until all the sugar has dissolved.

Reserve a few almonds for topping the rocks, then fold in the remainder with the cocoa using a large metal spoon.

Place small spoonfuls of the mixture onto the baking tray and bake for 15 minutes. Do this in batches or on another tray if you have too much mixture for one tray. Cool on the tray then lift each one up to loosen and leave them on the parchment to decorate.

Break the chocolate into pieces and put into a small bowl. Melt on a low setting in the microwave, in short bursts, stirring after each burst. Drizzle over the rocks and scatter over the remaining almonds then put to one side to set the chocolate.

Store at room temperature in an airtight box.

CANDIED ORANGE PEEL

Again, a boiling sugar recipe, so not for children. It is very easy though and very delicious.
Use for decoration or a really intense flavour on cakes, puddings and ducks.

500g white granulated sugar
300ml small glass orange juice
4 oranges

Line a large baking sheet with baking parchment, shiny side up.

Put the sugar and orange juice into a heavy bottomed pan and cook gently, without stirring, until the sugar has completely dissolved.

Peel the oranges using a peeler then cut the peel into strips and chunks.

Drop the pieces into the sugar mixture and bring to the boil, then simmer at the lowest temperature for 2–3 hours until the peel is tender.

Lift the orange peel from the pan, piece by piece and using a slotted spoon, and place onto the baking parchment.

It will stay sticky. Keep in an airtight container at room temperature.

Dip each piece in a bowl of 200g melted dark chocolate and leave to set on a parchment-lined tray. Then half dip in 200g melted milk chocolate and leave to set. Next half dip the other end in melted white chocolate and leave to set.

Very moreish.

CHOCOLATE GANACHE

So easy.

100g chocolate
100ml single cream
50g salted butter, chopped

Break the chocolate into pieces and put in a heavy bottomed pan with the cream. Warm through gently.

Stir the two ingredients together. When they are blended, smooth and starting to thicken, remove from the heat and add the chopped butter, stirring hard.

If you allow it to cool it will set firm to use for the handmade truffles. If you use it when slightly warm, to pour over a 15cm cake for instance, it will cool and have a glossy finish.

The quantities are easy to scale up. Use whatever chocolate is your favourite – milk, white or dark.

Add flavour by mixing in alcohol, nuts or fruit zest at the same time as stirring in the butter.

CHOCOLATE PALMIERS

Totally child-friendly and easy to make.

1 sheet ready-rolled puff pastry
50g milk or dark chocolate, grated
1 medium egg, beaten, or milk,
    to glaze

Preheat the oven to 240°C/220°C fan oven/475°F/ gas mark 9.

Unroll the pastry on a board. Sprinkle the chocolate all over.

Roll the pastry up, like a Swiss roll, from one side to the middle.

Then repeat, rolling from the other side to the middle, so that you have two tight rolls that sit next to each other, joined.

Brush with egg or milk. Slice into 1cm slices. Place them flat on a baking sheet, well spaced apart.

Bake for 10 minutes, or until golden brown. Eat when cool.

POSH SALTY NUTS

Easy.

Your favourite salted nuts, arranged in little piles, drizzled
with your favourite chocolate, topped with sea salt.

Great with beer, or full-bodied red wine.

CHOCOLATE WALNUT WHIRLS

Makes 15 Biscuits

- You Will Need -

FOR THE BISCUITS:

- 200G Butter
- 75G Caster Sugar
- 175G Plain Flour
- 1 1/2 tbspn Cocoa powder
- 4 Cups of Cornflakes
- 15 Whole Walnuts

FOR THE ICING:

- 1 Cup of Icing Sugar
- 2 Tbspn Cocoa Powder
- 3 Tbspn water

- INSTRUCTIONS -

- Preheat the oven to 180°c / gas mark 4.

- Cream the butter & sugar together in a bowl until light & fluffy. Add the cocoa & flour, mixing till combined. Add your cornflakes in last (try not to crunch them up too much!)

- Using a tablespoon, dollop spoonfuls of the mixture on to a baking tray lined with parchment. Keep them well spaced apart.

- Bake for 15 - 20 minutes.

- Make the icing by combining all the ingredients. Mix until smooth.

- Let the biscuits cool a little before topping with icing & a walnut!
  These are quite crumbly so don't remove from the tray until cool.

My Mum makes these for me every single birthday. I love them because they are slightly savoury, meaning I can eat more than one at once, mmmm!

Enjoy!

Chocolate is the Magic Ingredient in any Spell

To make converture perform and turn into delicious chocolate anything it has to be tempered.

This is an excellent word for this process and applies both to the chocolate and the chocolatier. Both must be feeling patient, seductive, confident and loved by the other. Or it simply will not work.

Working with chocolate is unlike working with any other medium.

It behaves as it wants to, but if you love it and are passionate about it, it will perform for you like no other food.

If you are irritable or fearful or inattentive, it will create the sweet illusion of softly melting into the confectionery you desire, but at the last minute, will turn its back on you and bloom or cloud.

At Choccywoccydoodah we make everything by hand.

Every cake mix is beaten by hand, every cake tin is washed by hand.

Each slab of chocolate, each mendiant, each chocolate figure is created by a person.

We temper our converture by hand in small quantities, using our instinct and experience. This allows us to make small batches of beautifully designed chocolate every day, to suit our mood, to suit our customers' moods and to suit chocolate's mood. So we all enjoy good temper.

We all love what we do here. Genuinely, utterly and passionately.

Designing the product, trialling it amongst ourselves and then to our customers, producing it and selling it. Small batches of beloved chocolate made by someone, for someone.

A world away from an automated conveyer belt of

identical chocolate bars made possible by a button pusher.
And when it's made, it's checked, finished and wrapped, entirely by hand.

The Sweetie Wrappers work closely with the chocolatiers in the same room, equally as immersed in making chocolate and cake beautiful as the chocolatiers themselves.

They wrap, ribbon, label and tag the finished confections before kissing them goodbye and sending them to our shops.

Choccywoccydoodah's chocolatiers work in our studio.

The environment and atmosphere is creative, bustling and lively. Music plays, telephones ring and everyone chats.

In the hot kitchen and wafting down the street as you approach the studio, is the most delicious aroma of baking. Mainly chocolate cake but sometimes the citrusy tones of Sicilian lemon oil lead you to Jim's bakery door.

Jim, and now Archie, his right-hand man, work in an isolated kitchen producing heat and cakes day in, day out. The heat cannot escape into the chocolaterie areas otherwise it will affect the chocolate-tempering process. Hence they work alone.

In the chocolaterie, the air is thick with the smell of molten chocolate. Probably the most delicious smell that exists, definitely the most delicious food that exists.

It's a very close team. Dave Pop is at the helm with a fourteen-year career so far, the newest Sweetie Wrapper is six months old and everyone else is in between.

It takes three years' training, patience, trials and errors to become a really proficient Choccywoccydoodah chocolatier. Longer, if the end goal is to be as good as Dave. Fourteen years, to be precise.

Our techniques and recipes are our secret. Everyone who works in studio signs a confidentiality agreement before they cross the threshold. And we all take our skills, our secrets, our responsibility to be the best we can, very seriously.

Nearly twenty years ago, when Choccywoccydoodah was just a twinkle in my eye, I melted my first bowl of couverture.

I didn't understand the tempering process, but I had no fear of my most favourite food and plunged both hands into the bowl, up to my wrists. The chocolate was fragrant, barely warm, thick as double cream and welcomed my hands like an old friend.

I worked the chocolate, played with the chocolate, and created good things to eat with the chocolate. And realised, once you start, you must stay immersed. It is impossible to work with chocolate if you can't stand it on your hands. And if you can't keep yourself from washing your hands, you will ruin the chocolate and set yourself on the road to insanity.

Chocolate and I quickly established ourselves as lifelong friends, mutually committed to bringing pleasure to those around us. I think I love chocolate more than it loves me, although when I see how it clings so closely to my hips, I do wonder.

When you are finished with your batch, then of course, you must wash your hands. (Which will be soft, because the cocoa butter in chocolate is a dream for skin. The most unlined, fresh-faced, clear complexions I have ever seen belong to chocolatiers. It's the cocoa butter.)

And then, you repeat the process.

And should you ever get the opportunity to work with us in studio, one of the first things you will have to do is immerse your hands in chocolate and create.

Half of those who try it will love it. The other half will realise it's not the job for them.

Tempered chocolate should be glossy, snappy, and melt in your mouth at body temperature. It's an art as well as a science, but it's also a state of mind.

I do truly believe that chocolate is partly food, partly magic.

Couverture is untempered chocolate. It's delicious.

It can be purchased from any supermarket, in the baking section in small quantities. Look at the ingredients, aim for 28-32 per cent cocoa butter for white chocolate, 29-34 per cent cocoa solids for milk chocolate and 60-70 per cent cocoa solids for dark chocolate. I have bought supermarket own brand for when I've worked on chocolate at home, with very pleasing results.

We buy our couverture from Belgium, from a company called Barry Callebaut.

There are cheaper and more expensive varieties of couverture available on the market, but having tried most of them, we are confident our customers' preference is for Barry Callebaut. It is gorgeous.

If you are following a recipe, allow at least twice as much chocolate as the recipe dictates. This allows you the opportunity of cocking up and the worst that can happen is that you have to eat surplus chocolate.

The easiest way to temper couverture is by using a microwave.

Break two-thirds of your couverture into even-sized pieces, place in a microwaveable bowl, ideally plastic.

Put the microwave on moderate for a twenty-second burst.

Remove and stir the chocolate for twenty seconds.

Continue this until the chocolate warms up and starts melting.

Moving the chocolate constantly between each burst is very important.

Once the chocolate is mostly molten, fluid, and warm (never, ever, hot) break up the remaining chocolate into small pieces, and bit by bit, add it to the molten chocolate.

Stir until it's completely melted. It will take a few minutes.

From the middle of the bowl take a little dab of chocolate and put it on your bottom lip.

If it's warmer than your lip, it's too warm to use and you must add a little more broken couverture.

If it's the same temperature, it's perfect and you must work with it immediately. If it's cooler than your lip, return it to the microwave for a very short burst, stir like crazy and try again.

Chocolate can be tempered twice. After that, it will never temper.

It will remain ill-tempered.

For those of you who enjoy working with measurements and exact instruction, when tempering, bring the temperature of couverture up to 41°C, stirring constantly.

Reduce the temperature immediately to 29°C by adding cold couverture, still stirring constantly.

Raise the temperature slightly to 31°C and now the couverture is ready to use. Immediately.

And if that doesn't put the fear of God into both you and chocolate, you are a better chocolatier than me.

I still prefer the more seductive, instinctive route to good temper, including a good chat, some mutual admiration and respect. It has never let me down yet.

But — I'm not good at following instructions, I'm too bloody-minded to do as I'm told and far too rebellious to bow to conformity.

In the UK we eat more chocolate per head than any other nation.

Yet our own national chocolate brands contain more dairy fat and sugar than most other chocolate. (I'm not including the USA, whose chocolate doesn't always contain cocoa)

Chocolate is the great British comfort food.

It's what we were raised on, it's our national habit.

And over the last decade, as a nation, we have become more discerning.

We know the difference between a good quality chocolate, well refined with a significant cocoa percentage and our childhood comfort food.

But sometimes, even as grown ups, we need the familiar fix of childhood favourites.

And if you want a KitKat with your cuppa, then really, only a KitKat will do.

Good chocolate is not just about cocoa solid percentages.

Good chocolate comes from good cocoa beans, harvested well and processed well. The resulting couverture then must be well tempered and coupled with equally delicious ingredients.

Otherwise it's just poor chocolate with a high cocoa solid percentage.

Dark chocolate is the purest form of chocolate and is now recognised universally for its positive attributes.

50 grams a day is the ideal portion.

It reduces blood pressure and is more effective than taking an aspirin a day.

It contains more antioxidants than most other food, or drink.

French dentists recommend finishing a meal with dark chocolate to prevent cavities.

It contains potassium, magnesium, iron, calcium, vitamins A, B1, C, D and E.

It contains theobromine, which makes humans happy.

Once eaten it releases serotonin into our system, making us all naturally happy.

When humans have sex, fall in love, or eat chocolate, phenylethylamine is released from our brains into our blood stream. Chocolate is an aphrodisiac.

It is addictive.

If you suffer from indigestion, soothe it away with dark chocolate.

If you have a sore throat, or a persistent cough, dark chocolate will really help.

If you are diabetic, a small portion of good quality dark chocolate is the best option for you. It contains little sugar, no dairy fat or processed fats.

Chocolate helps with pre-menstrual tension. A lot.

The melting point for chocolate is body temperature and as we become one, the intensity of chocolate increases. By the time we have savoured and melted chocolate in our mouth, the flavours are eleven times more intense than when we popped the chocolate into our mouth.

Chocolate should rarely be chewed.

It should be melted, considered and swallowed.

The correct name for cocoa is Theobroma Cacao.
This translates as 'Food of the Gods'. Welcome to church.

CHOCOLATE CAKE

Quite straight forward, a good cake to start with if you're inexperienced.

200g salted butter, plus extra
    for greasing
200g golden caster sugar
4 large eggs
100g ground almonds
200g dark chocolate, melted
100g self-raising flour
1 tsp baking powder
50g cocoa powder
250ml double cream, whipped

For the filling and topping
200ml double cream
200g dark chocolate
100g salted butter, chopped
icing sugar, to dust

Preheat the oven to 170°C/150°C fan oven/325°F/gas mark 3½. Grease and line two 15cm round sandwich cake tins.

Cream the butter and sugar together in a bowl until fluffy. Beat in the eggs and ground almonds. Stir in the molten chocolate.

Sift the flour, baking powder and cocoa together, then fold into the chocolatey mixture, a little at a time. Finally, fold in the whipped cream.

Divide the mixture between the sandwich tins. Bake for 15–20 minutes or until bouncy to the touch. The cake should be sticky. Leave to stand in the tins for 15 minutes then put on a wire rack to cool.

When the cake is completely cool, make the topping and filling.

Break up the chocolate and put it into a heavy bottomed pan with the cream. Heat gently, stirring the two ingredients together until the chocolate has melted and the mixture thickens.

Remove from the heat and cool slightly. The best way to do this is to put it in a clean bowl. Add the butter a knob at a time and beat in. Use to fill and top the cake. Shake icing sugar over the top.

To vary the flavour of the topping, add alcohol at the point of cooling. Or grate the zest of any citrus fruit into and onto the topping.

Delicious.

CELEBRATION REFRIGERATOR CAKE

This isn't difficult, but you do need patience. I soak my dried fruit for six months, so if you have leftovers from this recipe you could start a Kilner jar of boozy fruit, stored at room temperature.

200g salted butter, chopped, plus a little extra for greasing
250g mixed dried fruit
125g glacé cherries
100g stoned dates
100g ready-to-eat apricots
50g chopped crystallised ginger, optional
300–500ml mug of alcohol – we like whisky, brandy or rum
200g flaked almonds, toasted
100g whole almonds, toasted
100g hazelnuts, toasted
I tsp ground mixed spice
750g dark chocolate
500ml whipping cream (use UHT for longer life)

To decorate
icing sugar
a handful of holly leaves for the winter, and nasturtiums for the summer

Grease and line a 25cm round cake tin with baking parchment.

Soak the fruit and the alcohol together in a bowl for at least 24 hours. Stir it every now and again so that it gets an even soaking. Add the nuts and spices and mix again.

Break the chocolate into pieces and put into a heavy bottomed pan with the cream. Allow to melt over a low heat. Beat in the butter.

Add the fruit and nuts to the chocolate in the pan, over a very gentle heat, and stir together.

Pile the chocolatey mixture into the cake tin, banging the tin a couple of times on your work surface to get the air out.

Stamp the mixture down so it's level. I use a sheet of greaseproof paper and a pan lid to do this.

Refrigerate for at least 24 hours.

Release the cake from the tin and peel off the paper. Put on a plate and shower with icing sugar. Decorate with the holly in the winter and nasturtiums in the summer.

Store airtight at room temperature – not in the fridge!

We like this variation, too. Replace the nuts with broken ginger snaps or digestive biscuits. Instead of the dried fruit, just use cherries soaked in vodka for several days and big chunks of crystallised ginger. You'll need to work with the same weight, 625g. Swap in 400g toasted flaked almonds for the nuts.

CHILLI CHOCOLATE CAKE

This is a straightforward recipe if you make cakes already. A good one to start with if you don't. The cake should have heat that emerges after you've eaten it, so don't be tempted to add more chilli for impact. It's delicious, not frightening.

200g butter, plus a little extra
    for greasing
200g golden caster sugar
4 large eggs
100g ground almonds
200g dark chocolate, melted
100g self-raising flour
1 tsp baking powder
50g dark cocoa powder
1 tsp hot chilli powder
250ml double cream, whipped
    until thick

For the simple filling and topping
200ml double cream
200g dark chocolate
100g salted butter, chopped
icing sugar, to dust
1 whole fresh chilli, to place on top

Grease and line two 15cm-round sandwich cake tins with greaseproof paper. Preheat the oven to 170°C/150°C fan oven/325°F/gas mark 3½.

Cream the butter and sugar together in a bowl until fluffy. Beat in the eggs with the ground almonds.

Stir in the melted chocolate, then sift over the flour, baking powder, cocoa and chilli. Fold carefully into the chocolatey mixture. Finally, fold in the whipped cream.

Divide the mixture evenly between the sandwich tins. Bake for 15–20 minutes, or until the top feels bouncy when touched lightly. The cake should be sticky.

Leave to stand in the tins for 15 minutes to cool, then tip out onto a wire rack and cool completely.

Make the topping and filling once the cake is completely cool. Break the chocolate into pieces and put in a heavy bottomed pan with the cream. Heat gently and stir together until the chocolate has melted and the mixture is starting to thicken. Remove from the heat and cool slightly. The best way to do this is to spoon it into a clean bowl. Add the butter, a knob at a time, and beat in.

Use half to fill the cake and the other half to top the cake. Dust with icing sugar and top with the fresh chilli. This final touch acts as both decoration and warning. Store dry and airtight.

CHOCCYWOCCYCOFFEE CAKE

It's quite simple, but if you've inexperienced, try the Chocolate Cake (page 102) first, then this one.

For the cake
200g salted butter, plus extra
    for greasing
200g demerara sugar
8 heaped tsp instant coffee
    dissolved in 2 tbsp boiling water
100g ground almonds
4 large eggs
75g self-raising flour
1 tsp baking powder
25g cocoa powder

For the filling and topping
200g icing sugar
4 tsp instant coffee dissolved in
    1 dessertspoon boiling water
4 tsp cocoa powder dissolved in
    1 dessertspoon boiling water
100g salted butter, chopped
a little grated chocolate (be as
    greedy as you like)
a few chopped walnuts

Preheat the oven to 170°C/150°C fan oven/325°F/gas mark 3½. Grease and line a 20cm, deep round cake tin with greaseproof paper.

Cream the butter and sugar together in a bowl. Add the instant coffee and beat in. Stir in the ground almonds. Beat in the eggs, one at a time.

Sift the flour, baking powder and cocoa together, then fold into the cake mixture a little at a time. Spoon into the cake tin and bake for 30 minutes or until a skewer pushed into the middle comes out clean.

Cool in the tin for 10 minutes, then pop onto a cooling rack to finish cooling.

Sieve the icing sugar into a bowl and add the warm instant coffee and cocoa mixtures. Beat hard.

Drop the butter in a knob at a time and stir hard until completely smooth. Use to fill and smother all over the cake. Finish with the grated chocolate and chopped walnuts.

Store in airtight conditions.

NUNS' NAUGHTY SECRETS

Really easy. Even if it goes wrong, no one will ever know... Unless you tell them.

This makes a lot. You'll be pleased you made a lot.

200g good quality almond
  marzipan
100g toasted whole hazelnuts
500g ready to eat apricots
  (these could be soaked in brandy
  first, optional)
500g milk or dark chocolate

VARIATION:

Use dates instead
of apricots.

Spread out your baking parchment, shiny side up, on your work surface.

Roll out thimble-sized pieces of marzipan and push a toasted hazelnut into the centre of each roll. Then stuff each roll into an apricot.

Melt the chocolate.

Drop an apricot into the chocolate and then retrieve the apricot with a fork, placing it on the baking parchment. Repeat the process until you've run out of ingredients.

If your chocolate has gone off temper, melt a little more chocolate and drizzle over the top of the chocolate-dipped apricot, then sprinkle chopped nuts, or grated chocolate or icing sugar over. They will look yummy.

Store these at room temperature in an airtight container.

INGREDIENTS

DIGESTIVE BISCUITS
COCOA POWDER
Jelly Babes
Vanilla SUGAR
Raisins or SULTANAS
BUTTER
MILK

SWEET HARMONY

BRAKE BISCUITS IN SMALL PEACES, CUT JELLY BABES IN PEACES, THEN ADD COCOA POWDER, RAISINS AND LITLE DE VANILLA SUGAR, THEN MELT DOWN BUTTER AND THEN ADD MILK AND THEN MIXED UP ALL. ALL MIXTURE PUT ON GREASEPROOF AND WRAPED UP AND ITS READY TO EAT. :)

Doodah's favourite recipes

Guntis and Janis,
big brother,
little brother

Far from home, far from
mum, this recipe keeps
them from being homesick.
And reminds them of
family far away.

The Queen of Queens

The Queen of Queens decreed that the government of the day were useless and called an emergency meeting.

She pulled together all the other queens, her bridesmaids, all the head teachers in the whole country, and all the best artisanal builders from across the globe.

She didn't bother with any politicians or bankers or committees.

It was a three-day meeting, in the palace ballroom, with accommodation and catering and tents in the palace garden for those who couldn't get a bedroom.

Across the nation, the Queen of Queens' subjects were struggling. A huge calamity had befallen everyone and although everyone knew whose fault it was, the jolly good people of the land were too polite to point the finger or get cross.

Money had run out. Mainly because the oldest man in all history was in charge of counting the money in and counting the money out. It transpired he could only count to nine before he fell asleep, and as a result, no financial transactions, money paid in, or money paid out, were ever greater than nine guineas.

The team that worked for him, who were younger and far more awake, were unable to resist temptation, so they took home all the numbers above nine. And led a very good life, spending the guineas with great enthusiasm and speed.

Everyone guessed what had happened, but in such a close community, nobody wanted to accuse their neighbours' children of stealing from the nation. Or worse still, own up to the fact that their own children seemed quite rich, had treated them to a holiday on the moon, and did, in fact, work for the oldest man in all history.

And when it transpired that the government, between them, could only count to eight, it was down to the Queen of Queens to put two and two together.

With no money, there was shoddy housing, or even no housing at all, no work and no national treats.
  It was a horrible state of affairs.

Prior to this calamity, the whole Empire had been a terribly pleasant place to live.
  The weather was always perfect, not too hot and not too cold. The rolling hills and valleys of the landscape were always lush and green.

The towns and villages were bustling, the shops were full and busy.

The countryside was well kept and the farmers took their responsibilities very seriously, both to grow enough food for the nation and to maintain the landscape to the highest of standards.

Travelling people, both native and from abroad, were welcomed with open arms into every community. New stories to be shared, new customs to be learnt, new recipes to be tried and new friends to be made.

But now, there seemed to be a big grey cloud over everything.

Not just in the sky, but also in people's hearts.

There was plenty of work, but not enough money to pay people a decent wage. People's homes were looking tatty at best, completely ramshackle at worst.

The population balance altered as crowds of young people went to where there seemed to be most work.

Some areas were so overpopulated, there wasn't enough room for everyone. Other areas were so empty and neglected, they just fell into rack and ruin. Everyone was irritable.

Nobody looked forward to the arrival of the travellers any more. More people meant more problems.

The gloom was everywhere. It seeped into everyone's life, it stopped people singing, nobody danced for joy and it seemed like every day was just one long, hard slog.

Except of course, for the people who had taken everyone else's money. Nobody dared to say they were greedy, or even that they were thieves.

But everyone, including the Queen of Queens, could see that the situation was very, very wrong.

So many people who had worked so hard, who had contributed to their country's well-being, had to watch as the greedy people squandered money that should never have been theirs.

On the first day of the big meeting at the Palace, the Queen of Queens said (very loudly), 'Although I am the Queen of Queens and would normally expect anybody who talks to me to do so with good manners and a certain amount of reverence, over the next three days I want everyone here to talk to me truthfully and tell me how they feel.'

She explained, at length, that her bridesmaids were there to write down everything that anybody said. The head teachers were there because they were responsible for every child in the nation. They were clever, they could do sums, they lived in their communities and every day they dealt with the real problems of hungry children, children who didn't have a home and parents who no longer knew where to turn.

The artisans were there, because after all the sums had been done (scheduled into day two) they would know how much the budgets were for improving housing, providing shelter and giving people back their pride in their towns.

And all the queens were there to make sure that the plans, when made, would be carried out.

On day one the head teachers filled a hundred blackboards with their workings out. They divided everyone into teams and worked out people's strengths and weaknesses. They very quickly assessed almost every situation and gave each bridesmaid a clear and simple report.

On day two the artisanal builders read the reports of how many houses needed to be built. They looked at the money they had to build the houses. They also wanted to build or repair hospitals and schools, so a quick discussion was set up to prioritise these most important projects.

But the head teachers, who had tried and tried to make the sums work out differently, had to break the news to the artisanal builders that there was hardly any money at all in the whole empire.

Maybe there was enough to repair some important buildings, but definitely not enough to build anything new.

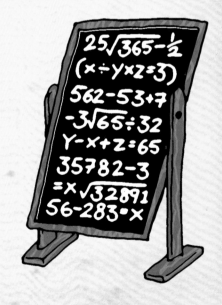

Everyone agreed to sleep on it, a new day would bring new ideas.

And so, on day three things started to happen.
Ideas were being written down to be turned into reality.

Imaginative, creative, and brave plans were put forward.
The people's simple wishes were being listened to and acted upon.

I may not have mentioned that the Queen of Queens' Empire, compared to say, Queen Elizabeth's Empire, was very small.
Even the people were very small.
The houses and towns were very small.
But they did not know this, neither did they feel small.
Although, in the same way that I know they were small, they knew that we were big.
Which is how we became involved in their master plan.

One of the most respected artisans, a lady called Pippapipefixer, when she was very, very young, had a job as a tooth fairy.
One of her greatest believers, in fact, the only big person who had opened his eyes when she was delving under his pillow, was a boy called Tom.
Pippapipefixer had personally collected every single one of Tom's baby teeth.
She still had, to this very day, all the little notes and drawings he left her.
And from a great distance, Pippapipefixer watched Tom grow up.
She watched his trials and tribulations, his achievements and his failures.
She even went to his graduation ceremony, which, of course, he never knew. Although, he did wonder how the cobwebby gossamer strands of captured rainbows and sunshine came to be on his mortar board.
(Incidentally, because you're probably wondering, Tom had very strong baby teeth and they were used to make a piano keyboard, which is now one of the most famous concert pianos in the whole empire. Strangely, Tom can also play the piano very well.)

Pippapipefixer knew that Tom had
worked on a building site in the big people's world.

She knew that he wasn't happy there and looked, every day, for a job
where he would be happy.

And on the day that Tom got taken on as a trainee Doodah at
Choccywoccydoodah, Pippapipefixer drank four thimbles of Tom's celebratory
beer, without Tom ever knowing. Even though she was so drunk she
fell into the beer glass and nearly got swallowed by Tom.

She watched Tom as he became cleverer and cleverer. She admired his
attention to detail, his precision, his ability to draw straight lines and
perfect circles.

And she knew, during this horrendous time of crisis, that somehow,
Tom could help.

But now?

And even more worrying, how could she talk to him?

As we all know, the little people can never talk to the big people and
the big people can only talk to the little people when they are very young,
very drunk or very mad.

Pippapipefixer was nothing if not resourceful.

She wrote Tom a note and she left it under his pillow.

But when Tom came to change his sheets and plump his pillow he
hardly noticed the tiny scrap of paper under it. He simply threw it in
the bin.

Pippapipefixer tried again.

This time she wrote her note on a poster-sized piece of paper, then
during the night she wrote across Tom's nose, right at the very end, in
her neatest writing 'look under your pillow carefully'.

When Tom got up and stumbled sleepily to the bathroom, he glanced in
the mirror before tackling his morning shave.

He was horrified.

The biggest blackhead he had ever seen was perched at the end of his nose.

Fully awake, he pulled his shaving mirror towards his face, switched the light on and turned the mirror to its magnifying side.

And then Tom blinked and blinked.

He shouted for his flatmates.

They came running with buckets, convinced he was on fire.

But then they all read the tiny, tiny writing.

Everyone made a dash for Tom's bed.

Tom got there first and under his pillow he found a postage-stamp-sized piece of paper covered in more tiny writing. He found a magnifying glass and sent everyone out of his room.

He needed thinking time and he needed a private moment for a joyous little celebration.

The tooth fairy was real and what's more, she remembered him, just as he had never, ever forgotten staring into the tiny, scared face of the littlest person he could imagine, who he had actually witnessed stuffing his baby tooth into her rucksack. Whoa!

And now it seemed the tooth fairy needed his help. Tom thought long and hard.

He made plans, did elaborate sketches and then he went to work where he discussed his thoughts, plans and drawings.

That night, he wrote his own letter to Pippapipefixer.

The following day Tom set to work creating the most astonishing small town of chocolate houses, chocolate schools, chocolate shops and a chocolate hospital.

The houses had chocolate vegetable patches, candy roofs, liquorice curtains and chocolate garden gnomes.

There were four-bedroom houses with landscaped gardens, two-bedroom houses with window boxes (Tom understood that not everyone is into gardening) and three-bedroom houses with chocolate kennels for chocolate dogs.

The schools had clock towers, jellybean walls and dolly mixture window frames.

The playgrounds were cobbled in chocolate beans and had soft play areas made from marshmallows.

The hospital walls were made from buttery toffee popcorn enrobed in fine milk chocolate. The wards were light and airy as Tom created big windows framed with sugar strands.

The chocolate shops sold everything a little person could ever need. Chocolate clothes and shoes, bread and cakes, fruit and vegetables.

Each chocolate building was unique, every wall and tile, every window and doormat had been designed, created and finished with love.

And Tom had deliberately not built a single bank.

And when the small town was complete, Tom spoke quietly to Jennyflowergirl.

That night, Jennyflowergirl waited for all the Doodahs to hustle and bustle out of the door and go home. It took longer than usual simply because the little chocolate town was so beautiful and everyone wanted to add a tiny something extra to each building.

Jennyflowergirl waited patiently until the air was still and the night was very quiet. She didn't turn on the lights, she simply worked with the moonlight streaming through the windows.

She covered the flowers and the trees with fairy dust. She made the windows sparkle and the rooftops shimmer with sugar frost.

Door knockers gleamed and butterflies glittered.

The very air itself was full of Jennyflowergirl's fairy dust.

And when she had finished, she sat very quietly, as agreed with Tom, with her eyes closed.
Gradually she drifted off to sleep.
The tiny bumps and bangs, the hushed whinnies of reindeer, the muted clop of hooves didn't wake her.

At one minute past midnight, Tom rang Jennyflowergirl on her mobile phone, making her jump out of her skin.

'Oh, Tom,' she said, a little bit scared. 'Oh, Tom. The beautiful houses, the beautiful schools, the shops and the hospital. They've all gone.'

She even cried a little bit.

'Well done,' said Tom. 'We pulled it off, Jennyflowergirl.'

Then Jennyflowergirl went home.

Meanwhile, the Queen of Queens stood on her balcony, which gave the best view of her principality and watched as a new small town nestled itself down into the rolling green hills of her countryside.

Starlight and fairy dust shimmered above the new houses.

Tomorrow, she thought, tomorrow will be a brand new day.

We have homes, we have schools, we have shops and we have a hospital.

And what's more, if the people are hungry, they have food.

Delicious food.

And if we can do that, we can do anything.

Faerie ✖ Times

FAERIETOWN REBUILT
IN A SINGLE NIGHT!!!!!!
SEE PAGES 2,3,4,5,6,7,8.

QUEEN OF QUEENS
ANNOUNCES
NATIONAL HOLIDAY

'MY MATE TOM'
an exclusive by
Pippapipefixer.

CHOCCY BANOFFEE PIE

Sooo easy. Sooo messy. It'll last for up to a day in the fridge.

a little butter for greasing
250g milk chocolate
250g Rice Krispies
6 bananas
3 x 397ml tins Carnation caramel
600ml double cream
50g flaked almonds, toasted

Grease and line a 20cm pie dish or shallow quiche tin with greaseproof paper.

Break the milk chocolate into pieces and put in a heatproof bowl. Melt in the microwave on low, in short bursts, 30 seconds at a time. Stir really thoroughly between each burst.

Cool a little. When the chocolate is lukewarm and still liquid, stir in the Rice Krispies. Spoon the mixture into the prepared tin and pop into the fridge to set.

Chop up the bananas and spread over the base. Pour over the caramel, then pop back in the fridge for 20 minutes.

Whip the cream in a bowl until the mixture is thick with soft peaks. Pile it on top of the bananas, and toss a handful of the toasted almonds on top.

Then eat.

CHOCCY CHESTNUT ROULADE

This requires a bit of experience. It's a great Christmas cake alternative.

For the roulade
a little butter for greasing
2 large eggs
2 tbsp caster sugar
2 tbsp orange juice
400g can chestnut purée
400g milk or dark chocolate,
   melted

For the filling
200ml double cream, whipped
zest of 1 orange, grated
100g dark chocolate, melted
250g cream cheese
chopped mixed nuts

icing sugar, to dust

Preheat the oven to 170°C/150°C fan oven/325°F/gas mark 3½. Grease and line a 20 x 25cm Swiss roll tin with greaseproof paper or use a similar-sized baking sheet with a lip all the way round.

Beat the eggs and sugar together. Add in the orange juice and chestnut purée, then stir in the chocolate.

Spoon into the prepared tin and bake for about 20 minutes, or until it feels springy to touch. Cool, then cover with a sheet of damp greaseproof paper and refrigerate for 2 hours.

Make the filling, just by mixing all the ingredients together in a bowl.

Take the cake out of the fridge. Generously dust icing sugar over a clean sheet of greaseproof paper. Carefully turn the cake out onto this. Remove the top layer of paper then spread the filling over the cake, leaving a gap at the front edge.

Roll the cake like a Swiss roll, placing your hands under the greaseproof paper and gently rolling away from yourself, peeling the paper away from the cake as you go. Lift onto a plate and dust over more icing sugar.

Store the cake in the fridge and eat within 24 hours.

DRIPPING CHOCOLATE MILLEFEUILLE

Easy. This is a huge, showyoffy pudding I make for dinner parties when I would prefer to be with my guests rather than in the kitchen. Or when I'm asked to make pudding for someone else's party. It makes people gasp.

3 sheets ready-made puff pastry
strawberry jam
1.2l double cream, whipped
  until thick
500g blueberries
500g raspberries
6 kiwi fruit, sliced
1kg strawberries, mostly sliced, plus
  a few extra whole strawberries
500g milk, white or dark chocolate,
  melted
icing sugar, to dust

If you want to create smaller versions, just use one sheet of puff pastry and cut it into three.
It will still have ridiculous height.

I vary the fruit and jam, but never the size.

It lasts for a good couple of days in the fridge and I have never had leftovers.

Bake the puff pastry sheets on flat baking sheets, following the instructions on the pack and using the same oven temperature. Leave them in the fridge overnight.

Place one baked pastry sheet top-side down onto a large flat serving dish.

Spread the flat side with strawberry jam. Pile half the whipped cream on top and cover the pastry. Throw on the blueberries, raspberries and half the kiwi slices, letting them spill out of the pastry.

Flatten the next sheet of cooked puff pastry by turning it upside down and pushing on it gently to break the top crust of pastry. Place it top-side down on the fruit and cream. Spread the surface with strawberry jam.

Pile on the rest of the whipped cream. Throw on the strawberries and remaining kiwi slices. Again, don't worry about the fruit spilling out or the cream splurging everywhere.

Put the last sheet of puff pastry onto the cream and fruit layer, top-side up.

Dip the reserved strawberries in the melted chocolate and set aside. Pour the rest of it over the top of the pastry and let it drip.

Finish with a shake of icing sugar and the chocolate-dipped strawberries.

EASY PEASY HANDMADE TRUFFLES

Easy Peasy.

exactly the same ingredients as
   Chocolate Ganache (page 86)
   but use 4 times the amount of
   flavouring, such as rum

For coating
chopped nuts, grated chocolate,
   melted chocolate or cocoa
   powder and icing sugar, all in
   separate bowls

Line a 15 x 22.5cm baking tin with greaseproof paper.

Make the ganache mixture and pour into the baking tin.
The mixture should be at least 2.5cm deep.

Cover the tin with clingfilm and pop in the fridge for at
least 2 hours or overnight to let the truffles set firm. The
clingfilm prevents the chocolate from absorbing any other
food aromas in the fridge.

When the mixture is set, chop it up into rough 2.5cm
squares or oblongs. If you want to vary the shapes, roll
each square with very clean hands between your palms
until it's shaped into a round ball – it'll feel a bit sticky –
then roll it in one of your favourite toppings, such as nuts
or icing sugar.

Job done.

Store these easy peasy truffles in an airtight container in
the fridge and they'll last for at least a week.

*Who are we kidding? They'll be demolished in
a day!*

S'MORES

This is a very exciting biscuit to eat and make, especially if you are a child. It's quite easy, with a little supervision.

big marshmallows
big cookies
milk chocolate

VARIATIONS:

Sandwich two cookies together with marshmallow and dip one end in melted milk chocolate and the other end in melted white chocolate.

Sprinkle sugar strands over the chocolate before it sets.

Use peanut butter instead of the marshmallow.

Pop the marshmallows into a bowl and microwave very briefly until they melt slightly.

Spoon onto the cookies. Leave to set.

Melt the chocolate in a bowl in the microwave, in short bursts, stirring frantically. When it's gloopy, lumpy and barely warm it's ready to use.

Spoon the chocolate over the marshmallowed cookies.

Leave it to set.

If you have leftover chocolate you could double dip the cookies. Yummmmmm.

Fearless Baking...

Henry's Grannies 'Green Magic'

My Grannie is my favourite cook — everything she makes tastes amazing. This is my favourite taste sensation that she came up with — its brilliant on toast — with salads, cheeses and spread on smoked salmon — amazing!

— YOU NEED —

- 3 Medium or 2 Large <u>Ripe</u> Avocados
- ½ Onion or 1 shallot — chopped fine
- 2 Cloves of Garlic — chopped fine
- Dessert Spoon of Lemon Juice
- Sprinkling of Lemon rind (Grated)
- Dollop of olive oil
- 6 Sundried tomatoes — chopped fine

Whizz altogether and season with Salt & Pepper to taste. Easy!

It <u>makes</u> a lunchtime salad!

enjoy!

Henry Hotter

Lookalike for Harry Potter, but hotter and Christine's personal assistant.

An excellent grandson and keeper of Gran's best kept secrets. (And now so are you.)

The happiest creatures ever born
Are the spiral horned Unicorns
Gatekeepers on Earth and caretakers of space
Born to watch over the human race.

Rarely seen and usually invisible
Sightings are made that are totally plausible
You can even ask her Royal Highness the Queen
About all the unicorns she has seen.

If you've seen one, your luck must be in
If you've seen two, try for a lottery win
If you've seen more, you're in heaven I'm guessing
As a herd of unicorns is known as a Blessing.

Not the wisest of creatures, nor the most silly
Here to teach us how to live happily
How to love and be loved in return,
Lessons in joy for us all to learn.

Wild and regal, joyful and beautiful
Their single purpose is to be dutiful
Guardians of the human race
Making the world a better place.

Once Princess Tiara had married her only true love, Bellinki, and the whole nation had celebrated for three days and two nights with time off work to do so, Princess Ruby finally felt she could spread her own wings and fly.

A great beauty and a social butterfly, Ruby had always assumed that the world loved her, completely and unconditionally.
   Her family did love her, truly and dearly.
   But they loved her even though she was a little bit vain, a little bit selfish and a little bit dim. Sometimes.

Now that Princess Tiara was happily married, now that the laws of the land had been changed for the better, Princess Ruby could focus her attention completely on her favourite subject. Herself.

Her first scheme was to try marriage out for herself. One of the many beaus that Princess Ruby and Princess Prawn had tried to set Princess Tiara up with had made it very obvious he preferred Ruby. He was spectacularly handsome and claimed to be rolling in money following the success of his fast-food restaurants.
   Ruby asked Prawn to contact him. He immediately texted Ruby and dating was soon underway.
   Ruby didn't really feel inclined to do the whole 'getting to know you' thing as she wasn't really interested in other people.
   However, she liked the idea of a wedding, leaving home and being filthy rich.

Gustavo was grateful to Ruby for this and it seemed right from the start they were compatible, if not in love.

So they got married, in great style, but sadly for Ruby, because the nation had just enjoyed a Royal wedding, complete with royal hangover, no one could summon the same enthusiasm for a second Royal wedding so quickly.

For once, Ruby's beauty didn't make her the centre of press attention, or the nation's attention. Everyone was still basking in the warm glow of Princess Tiara's wedding to Bellinki.

Ruby was devastated and it didn't take long before things started to sour.

Gustavo thought Ruby was too precious and too spoilt.

Ruby thought Gustavo was just rude. Especially when he asked for money.

Which he did with growing frequency, saying he couldn't keep up with her ability to shop.

In fact, three weeks after the wedding Ruby flounced back to the castle, back to her servants and back to her cats.

The King and Queen were dismayed but Ruby had always been precocious and they quite liked her being back home.

The week after that divorce papers were filed on Ruby. Unreasonable behaviour.

And Gustavo asked for half of Ruby's income, half of her belongings and half of her future predicted income.

His business was going bankrupt and he blamed Ruby. All his employees blamed Ruby too.

Princess Ruby gathered her wits, her experts and her solicitors about her.

It was the biggest cat fight of her life and she still lost a third of everything. She became the poorest princess.

Although she still lived in a palace and still had jewels and servants, Princess Ruby was bitter.

It never occurred to her that someone would marry her for her money, not her beauty. That someone would not love her as much as she loved herself.

Ruby felt ridiculed and foolish.

She decided to make a plan and get away from her sympathetic family and unsympathetic subjects.

She ordered airline tickets to take her to Hollywood, she ordered three of her best friends and seventeen of her devoted servants to pack their cases and she ordered four tabby kittens from the local pet shop. She needed to stroke something fluffy to keep her calm whilst a storm of organisation took place around her.

Before she got on the aeroplane, Ruby called Hollywood film star, Jimmy Hipp. Jimmy arranged for Ruby and her entourage to be met at the airport and whisked to one of his amazing mansions in LA.

Ruby's new home.

Quite a brave move for Ruby, who had never left Sussexonia or been so far from her family, although she was twenty-five and not nearly as naive as her family would like to believe, except for the King, who in his wisdom, understood his daughter very well and loved her for her shortcomings.

Her beauty dazzled everyone she met, she was constantly forgiven for her silly comments, her vanity and her tendency to covet other people's things.

In fact, as a teenager she had a very brief career in shoplifting and burglary, where she just took everything she liked the look of, because — well — just because.

Her victims, who loved the Royal Family, didn't make a fuss about it. They just wrote polite notes to the King and Queen, who arranged for their belongings to be returned, with a box of handmade chocolates from the infamous chocolatere, Choccywoccydoodah.

Generally, that smoothed things over and everyone was happy.

At least the police were never called.

The Queen spoke firmly to Princess Ruby and explained that stealing was a terrible thing. Ruby cried and was sorry, but she was more sorry that she couldn't have all the lovely things she craved. Even though her room was full of the loveliest things in the nation, she wanted more and more.

And most especially if someone else had them.

But she did at least stop her criminal activity.

Jimmy Hipp, Hollywood film star, was completely dazzled by Princess Ruby.

He had followed her every move. Every event she attended, every ribbon she had ever snipped at local fêtes had been photographed and every photograph had been saved by Jimmy.

Although he had only ever seen her in Hello! magazine and on TV, his heart was entirely hers.

People all over the world loved Jimmy Hipp.

Women, men, girls and boys watched his films and wanted to melt into his arms. A heartthrob of global stature, his face advertised razors, his bum advertised pants, his teeth were dazzled by toothpaste, his hair was dandruff-free.

If Jimmy Hipp was seen in a car, that car became the best-selling car of the week.

If he was photographed in a restaurant, that restaurant was booked up six months in advance.

He was the wealthiest and most desirable man in Hollywood.

He could have anyone he wanted.

But he only wanted Princess Ruby.

And finally, after a decade of yearning, Jimmy met Ruby at LAX.

She was more beautiful than he imagined in real life.

More fragrant, English, cool, polite, chic and aloof.

His heart literally hurt, he loved her so much.

And when Jimmy took Ruby and her sizeable entourage back to his house, she took one long look around and decided she might as well love Jimmy too.

The house was crammed with treasures, beautiful art, precious historical artefacts. The pool was carved from shimmering marble with fountains spurting pink champagne into cascading pools.

Ruby quivered with almost overwhelming desire to own the house and everything in it.

Within a month, they were engaged to be married.

The whole of Sussexonia and Hollywood went mad with excitement.

A wedding date was set, exactly six weeks from when they met.

A private Lear jet was sent to pick up the King and Queen, Princesses Tiara, Bellinki and Prawn Cocktail. Almost all of Sussexonia waved the family off as they taxied down the runway in the flashy private jet, on their way to Hollywood.

The wedding was enormous, with a thousand guests, five hundred of whom were journalists. Helicopters buzzed above and the surrounding hillsides were crammed with uninvited journalists and their telephoto lenses.

Princess Ruby was ecstatic.

Jimmy Hipp was the happiest man on the planet.

The guests, the journalists and the caterers left the happy couple at midnight.

For the first time Jimmy and Ruby climbed the stairs together to go to bed.

They kissed passionately and with the promise of more to come, Ruby slipped away to the bathroom with her wedding night trousseau.

Ruby perfumed her skin, brushed her hair until it was like satin, powdered her face and cleavage, then dressed in the most alluring negligee that ever existed. Made entirely by Royal Sussexonian spiders, the negligee was a shimmering web of translucent silk decorated with dragonflies made from precious jewels.

Ruby had never looked more beautiful, she thought, as she gazed at herself in the mirror.

Meanwhile Jimmy had downed half a bottle of bourbon, brushed his teeth and positioned himself to look his very best, reclining on the bed on a gorgeous faux bear skin.

Jimmy was very fond of bourbon but worked to a discipline of never drinking it for breakfast.

Ruby entered the room.

The light in the room seemed to change, such was the power of her beauty.

Jimmy's joy was complete.

His expression was rapturous.

And then he died.

He never felt a thing. His poor heart had simply exploded with joy.

Ah well, thought Ruby. I didn't really know him.

At least I've got the beautiful house, the jewels, the art, the exquisite swimming pool full of pink champagne to comfort me.

A year went by, life for the people of Sussexonia chugged along in its normal happy way and Princess Ruby split her time between Hollywood and home.

The King was concerned for Ruby.
  Although she was now a widow, she didn't seem particularly changed, or particularly unhappy.
  Far from having a broken heart, it occurred to him that his precious daughter might not have a heart at all. Unless you could count the enormous heart-shaped ruby she wore on a chain around her neck.

On the day each of his daughters were born the King bought them a gift.
  Princess Tiara received a tiara, Ruby received a ruby and Prawn Cocktail got a lifetime supply of crisps. Any flavour, as the King was, by nature, a thoughtful man who understood prawn cocktail was not to everyone's taste.

Eventually Ruby spent most of her time back in Sussexonia.
  Her feelings towards Gustavo were less bitter and she sometimes enjoyed a milkshake or chicken sandwich from one of his drive-through restaurants.
  One day she spotted him, in his restaurant car park, climbing out of a powder blue Bentley sports car with a dazzling blonde on his arm.
  She seethed.
  Princess Ruby decided she wanted Gustavo back. On her own terms and with a pre-nup. And what she wanted, she always got.
  This time the wedding was low key.
  Ruby wore crimson velvet and her hair was piled high on her head.
  Her diamond engagement ring was so big it made her finger ache.
  Her matching pale pink Bentley sports car was a wedding present from Gustavo.
  Gustavo couldn't believe his luck.
  A successful fast-food business, bailed out by his divorce from Princess Ruby

first time round, then millions of pounds' worth of publicity because of his famous wife, second time round.

And second time round Gustavo pampered Ruby, whatever she wanted, whatever she needed, whatever, she got.

But Ruby, having got Gustavo, on her own terms, second time round, didn't want him any more than the first time.

Once again she moved back to the palace.

And then she divorced him. The pre-nup protected only her interests, not his.

So this time, Ruby made a fortune.

Another fortune.

Once more the King and Queen were concerned about their middle daughter.

She shrugged off her third marriage and seemed to content herself with counting her money and admiring her belongings.

They suggested she take a little time out to travel the country, visit far-flung relatives and take the opportunity to think about the future.

She agreed.

She packed for a year.

And off she went in her pale pink Bentley sports car with a loyal team of servants, kittens and best friends following in a convoy of articulated lorries and mid-range cars.

Then, one quiet Sunday just as the King and Queen were about to share a gigantic slab of buttery toffee popcorn enrobed in milk chocolate and watch Antiques Roadshow, the family phone rang.

The Queen answered.

She went pale.

She said very little, which was highly unusual, and she sat down very abruptly, chocolate, popcorn and telly, completely forgotten.

'My dearest husband,' she said, 'Ruby called us to let us know she has remarried and will be bringing her new husband to visit us tomorrow.'

'Oh!' said the King. 'And who is this lucky chap?'

'The oldest man in all history,' said the Queen. 'The oldest and the richest man in all history.'

The King felt a twitch in his eye and a very cold feeling washed over him.

The Queen quietly wept and shovelled a huge mouthful of comforting chocolate in her mouth.

Tiara and Prawn were far more philosophical.

They knew their sister had remarried to increase her wealth and get her hands on unimaginably rare things of beauty and curiosity, which everyone knew the oldest man in history collected.

They also reasoned that Ruby was probably just another part of that collection for the old man.

Of course, the oldest man in all history was not the wisest man in all history and although the overwhelming beauty of Ruby did not kill him on his wedding night, it did the night after.

Although he was briefly also the happiest and oldest man in all history.

So the Royal family of Sussexonia never got to meet Ruby's fourth husband. They did, however, attend his funeral out of very Royal politeness.

By now Ruby was the most wealthy woman in the Empire.

Lots of people and charities asked her for donations.

Artists, scholars and intelligent, curious people asked her if they might view her rare collections.

Men queued up around the entire nation to ask for her hand.

She said no to everyone.

Ruby did not care for sharing.

Princess Ruby was gradually changing.

Her easy beauty and clear skin, her shiny hair and ready laugh were fading. Her softness was hardening.

Her family still loved her, but everyone admitted within the castle walls, they were worried.

The nation no longer took her to their hearts.

It's very hard to love someone who isn't loveable.

The King became deeply troubled. Winter had arrived and with it, his mood became darker.

He summoned Ruby to his private office. He expressed his worry and she told him to mind his own business.

The King became angry and raised his voice. Ruby raised hers several shrill octaves higher than the King's.

Dogs fled under beds.

Horses kicked in the stables.

Servants hid in cupboards.

The Queen and Princesses Tiara and Prawn got in the family car and went to Bluewater for some retail therapy, despite swirling snow and icy roads.

Even then, the reverberations of Ruby's shrill screams could be heard bouncing off the wintry landscape.

Finally, the good and wise, loving King snapped.

He pulled the heart-shaped ruby from Ruby's throat and roared at her, 'This is the only heart you have, Ruby. As hard as this stone, as cruel as the diamond cut and as cold as this jewel. Where is your love? Do you even know what love is?'

Ruby stopped mid-scream.

Tears welled up in her eyes. 'I do, Daddy,' she said. 'My family used to love me.'

The King hurled the ruby out of the nearest window. 'They still do,' he said, furious at her selfish response. 'But who do you love? Just Ruby.'

Princess Ruby fled down the corridors of the palace.

The halls were silent as the servants hid away and all the animals cowered.

She threw herself on her old childhood bed and wept and wept and wept.

So did the King.

Everyone forgot the ruby heart laying in the snow.

The following day, a traveller from a distant land came to the side door of the palace and knocked very politely.

One of the kitchen staff answered.

The stranger wondered if there were any jobs? Perhaps in the kitchen?

The stranger was asked to wait while Chef was fetched.

A cup of strong tea was brought out from the kitchen, with a bowl of sweet dried fruit.

After introductions, the stranger, whose name was Curtis, was told to sit on a garden bench and drink his tea.

He couldn't be allowed into the Palace until he had security clearance.

Curtis understood this from his experience at the Kremlin.

The thought made him shudder, but he knew his long journey had brought him to a better place. A place where he could be free and where he might be appreciated for the kind man he was.

As he walked to the bench, he spotted the huge red ruby heart.

His own heart quickened. He put the ruby in his pocket, hardly daring to breathe.

Yes!

In the snow a perfect heart imprint remained.

Thinking quickly, Curtis opened his rucksack and got out the tools of his trade.

Some milk couverture, a little stirrer and a little pot of red glitter made from distant dreams and fairy magic.

He put the couverture in the bowl containing the sweet dried fruit.

He then balanced the bowl on his steaming cup of tea.

And he stirred and stirred until the couverture melted.

The fruit became enrobed in chocolate.

The heady smell contrasted with the frosty weather and wafted towards the palace windows.

When the chocolate reached its perfect point, Curtis poured it into the perfect heart imprint in the snow. It was a perfect match.

Within two minutes the chocolate had set and Curtis covered it with his sparkling red glitter of distant dreams.

Carefully he removed the chocolate heart from the snow and gently nestled it in his money pouch, which was completely empty.

Then he sat on the garden bench and prayed he had not been forgotten.

Meanwhile, in her childhood room, with a view of the garden, Ruby had cried all night and all morning. Even the sight of her sister's snowman dressed in their father's best robes didn't stop her crying.

Her eyes were red and swollen.

Her nose was flaky and sore.

Her lips were cracked.

Her hair was wild and red and tangled.

She had snot smeared across her cheek and all over her sleeves.

What did make her stop crying was the waft of molten chocolate coming in through her window.

She stuck her head out, spotted Curtis and really rudely shouted 'And who exactly are you? And what is that delicious smell?'

Curtis, much relieved at not being forgotten, would be forgiven for not realising he was addressing a princess.

He walked across the garden and stood underneath her open window.

His face was earnest and solemn, his English not perfect.

He was hungry, but would never have been able to eat.

He struggled to find the right words that might get him a job and perhaps a home.

'All I have in the world are three hearts. One that has been broken, one that I have found and one that I have made. I will gladly give you all three in exchange for a place in your home.'

Princess Ruby disappeared from the window and without even checking in the mirror, appeared minutes later at the palace side door.

'Show me,' she demanded, 'show me your hearts.'

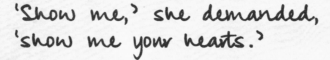

Curtis fished in his pocket for the ruby and placed it in Ruby's hands.

'No,' she said. 'You can keep it. This heart is too hard, too cold.'

Then Curtis revealed his chocolate heart, glistening and aromatic.

Ruby snatched it from him and took a huge bite.

She was starving! No supper, no breakfast, no elevenses and chocolate was her favourite food.

The heart melted in her mouth and in her hands.

Colour came back into her face.

She could feel herself smile.

She offered Curtis the last bite of the most delicious thing she had ever tasted.

Curtis took the morsel of chocolate from her and his big warm hands touched hers. He finished the chocolate.

Princess Ruby had a strange look on her face.

By now, half the palace were out in the garden, watching events unfurl.

The Queen shouted for somebody to shut the bloody back door, it was cold.

The air changed. Ruby started to look more and more beautiful, despite the snot on her sleeves and her swollen eyes.

Curtis couldn't take his eyes off her. To him she was like a rare bird, captured and caged. He realised he wanted to set her free.

He also thought she was a servant.

'Do you know,' Ruby said, 'I have never, ever shared anything before? Ever, in my whole life?'

A ripple of agreement went around the garden and through the people hanging from windows.

'Curtis, said Ruby, you mentioned three hearts. One that I have given you, one that I have eaten and one that is broken. Come into the kitchen and sit with me. Share your troubles with me. I want to hear about your broken heart.'

So Curtis did.

He sat with the most beautiful and wilful woman in the whole kingdom and told her everything.

And Ruby fell in love.

Curtis, of course, could not work at the palace, it was not befitting for the fiancé of Princess Ruby, even if he was a most talented chocolatier.

And everyone at the Palace loved chocolate as much as they loved Curtis.

Instead, he went to where all the most talented chocolatiers in the world went.

Obviously.

He joined Choccywoccydoodah and works there still.

A modest prince among men, earning his keep and making the most delicious confections for his precious Ruby, the whole nation and his mother, who despite everything, he missed very much. (The ruby also went to his mother who sold it to the Kremlin. It now adorns the hand of the mistress of a Russian oligarch. Another story for another time.)

Curtis also made Ruby give away everything she owned.

So they both had exactly the same.

Nothing.

It worked.

And when Ruby trembles with desire at the sight of a pair of shoes, or a bag, Curtis whispers into her ear, 'Just remember, you are my socks and I am all the shoes you need'

Which always makes Ruby remember what it was like to want, want, want.

But now, with Curtis, she will never forget what it is she needs.

To love. And be loved in return.

If you are Socks then I am Shoes

CHOCCYTOFFEE SHORTCAKE

Like Millionaires, but for everyone. This is easy for a baker and a good recipe for someone who wants to get into baking. If you don't have a chance to make the filling, buy a tin of Carnation caramel instead.

For the shortcake base
100g butter, plus extra for greasing
50g caster sugar
100g plain flour
25g ground rice
25g cornflour

For the toffee filling
100g butter
50g light brown soft sugar
250g condensed milk

For the topping
250g milk chocolate

Grease and line a 15 x 20cm deep baking tray with greaseproof paper.

Make the base. Cream the butter and sugar together in a bowl. Add the dry ingredients and rub them in using your hands.

When the mixture looks like crumbs, knead it together to make a dough. Press the mixture into the baking tin using your hands. Prick it all over with a fork and set aside for 1 hour before you bake it.

Preheat the oven to 170°C/150°C fan oven/325°F/gas mark 3½.

Bake for 20 minutes until pale golden. Cool in the tin whilst making the filling.

Put the butter, sugar and condensed milk in a heavy bottomed pan and bring to the boil. Boil for 5 minutes, stirring constantly until it's a pale gold colour. Cool for a few minutes then spread over the shortcake. Leave to set. (Alternatively, open the tin of Carnation caramel, spread over the shortcake and top with the melted chocolate immediately.)

Melt the milk chocolate in the microwave on the lowest setting in short bursts, checking regularly.

Pour the chocolate over the cooled caramel. Divide into portions with a sharp knife, when the chocolate is still soft, but don't break up the cake until it's completely set. Once set, use a knife to cut into pieces.

Store it in your belly, or in an airtight container until your belly is ready.

CHOCOLATE BREAD PUDDING

Very easy. Not to be confused with bread and butter pudding. Great warm with custard or cold on a picnic.

a large stale loaf
whatever dried fruit you have in
  the pantry
200g chocolate buttons or grated
  chocolate
200g caster sugar
2 tsp cinnamon or mixed spice
600ml full-fat milk

Roughly tear the bread into shreds using your hands and put in a big bowl. Add the dried fruit, chocolate, most of the sugar and the spice. Pour the milk over the top.

Mush everything about until the whole mixture is wet. Leave it to stand in the fridge for at least an hour or overnight.

Preheat the oven to 170°C/150°C fan oven/325°F/ gas mark 3½. Line a 22.5 x 15cm roasting tin with baking parchment.

Pile it into a roasting tin, packing it down densely with the back of a spoon. Sprinkle the rest of the sugar over the top.

Bake for 1½ hours or until it looks and feels crusty. Leave to cool for at least 45 minutes before cutting it into big chunks and serving. Store airtight at room temperature.

HENRY AND DAVEED'S HUNKY CHUNKY MONKEY

Henry and Daveed made this up as a café alternative to our Chunky Monkey Bar sold in the shop. This must be easy as Henry can make it! It's messy and the measurements can be varied to taste.

a handful of salted peanuts
a handful of digestive biscuits,
   shortbread or ginger snaps,
   crushed
half a handful of dried banana chips
a large mug of melted milk
   chocolate
half a mug of white chocolate
sea salt

Put the peanuts, biscuits, banana chips and melted chocolate into a large bowl. Give it a good stir.

Spoon rough cookie-size dollops onto a tray lined with baking parchment. Refrigerate for half an hour.

Then, melt the white chocolate in a bowl in a microwave, in short bursts, giving it a gentle stir between each burst. Drizzle the chocolate over each dollop and sprinkle sea salt on top.

Put back into the fridge for about 10 minutes.

Store in an airtight container, good for ages... best eaten pronto.

Yum.

Fearless Baking...

This is also delicious with chopped dates or dried vine fruits in place of the salted peanuts.

You can also replace a spoonful of chocolate with a spoonful of nutella... yummers.

Jenna's Home Made Country Cottage Pie

Base

Base

500g Mince Beef.

1 Red Onion.

2 Carrots

1 Oxo stock Cube.

½ Pint of Water

Topping

4 Large White Potatoes

2 Parsnips

2 TBSP of horseradish.

Handful of Grated Mature Cheese

Knob of Butter

Dash of Milk.

Base

\# Heat a tbsp of olive oil in A frying Pan, and add The Chopped Onion and Carrot

\# When The Onions start to Brown, Add the Mince and Brown.

\# Crumble The Oxo Cube, then add Water.

\# Season with Salt + lots of Black Pepper.

For The Topping

\# Chop Both the potatoes and Parsnips and add them to Boiling Salted Water.

\# Wait until Soft, then Drain.

\# Add Butter, Milk and horseradish and Mash It!

To finish

\# Drain excess fat from the Base sauce, and Simmer.

\# Pour the Sauce into an oven proof Dish, and Layer ontop the Mash Mixture

\# Sprinkle with the Cheese, and Pop in the oven for 30 minutes on 200°c!

— ENJOY XX

— ENJOY XX

Doodah's favourite recipes

Jenna,
Captain of the
Flagship, London

Comfort food recipe from
mum. Sometimes now
made for mum.
Comforting.

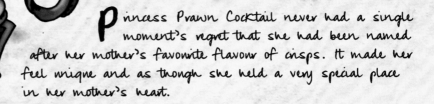

Princess Prawn Cocktail never had a single moment's regret that she had been named after her mother's favourite flavour of crisps. It made her feel unique and as though she held a very special place in her mother's heart.

The baby of the family, nicknamed Prawn, always struggling to be heard above her noisier sisters, to achieve as much as her boisterous sisters and get as much attention as her demanding sisters.
By nature, she was thoughtful and quiet.
Her beauty wasn't as obvious as her sisters', but anyone who spent time with her ended up mesmerised by her big blue eyes, pale, dewy skin and shiny hair.

The people of Sussexonia loved her deeply.
She never let the Royal family down, she worked tirelessly for charity and she never put on airs and graces. And she was very quiet.

When she was twenty years old she met a beautiful Indian prince called Abdhul. Abdhul was also a very quiet and thoughtful boy, a little younger than Prawn.

Prawn was very passionate about elephants. So much so that her private charity sponsored elephant sanctuaries in both Africa and India, although of course, until Tiara got married, according to the ancient laws of the land, she would never be able to visit either country.
Abdhul was also passionate about elephants and had decided to make saving and breeding elephants his life's work.

Such magnificent, intelligent and spiritual animals, well-loved by most of the planet, and yet treated cruelly by a small percentage.

Abdhul's parents, the Maharani and Maharajah, were devoted to their only child and proud that he was so passionate about elephants.
It was the Maharajah who contacted Princess Prawn's father, the King and suggested that their children should meet.
The men went to Oxford University together before they were Kings and had a lifelong friendship since.

The Maharajah loved the Sussexonia Royal family and when he visited them to pay his respect to the Queen after she gave birth to Prawn Cocktail, he hatched a little plan.

He decided that if his baby, shortly to be born, was a boy, he would do everything in his power to make their match.

He thought it would be a match made in heaven.

The Maharani, however, did not feel the same.

She had great respect for the Sussexonia Royal family, but hated the English weather. She thought the landscape was too small and too green.

The clothes and the costumes were dull.

The music and dancing was terrible.

She tried to avoid visiting.

She could not help but think, what sort of person could thrive in such a wet, green, culturally colourless world?

But she did truly love her husband and, mostly, had great respect for his thoughts.

Sometimes he made quite brilliant plans.

And — she occasionally forgot this — she loved English food.

Whenever her husband visited his friend the King she arranged for great boxes of chocolate and cake to be collected from Choccywoccydoodah to come back with him.

She ordered dozens of Cornish pasties to be frozen and sent to her on the Royal Indian plane with the Maharajah. Vegetarian, of course.

Her other big weakness was Tiptree strawberry jam. She ordered it a case at a time.

And when the King or Queen of Sussexonia visited her, they filled their plane likewise.

To the delight of both the Maharajah and the King, from the very first moment their children met, they liked each other.

They would walk round the palace gardens together, hand in hand, talking and sometimes, not talking at all.

They would sit in the grand rooms of the palace looking at ancient paintings of elephants.

Abdhul told Prawn about his country, the colour, the heat, the noises and smells, the food, the poverty and the wealth. He was a talented storyteller, he spoke with his voice and with his hands and sometimes, in a very British garden, with dew under her feet and daffodils in her hand, Prawn would be transported to India by his words.

Prince Abdhul was very slight.

Shorter than Prawn, who was the shortest person in her family.

He was very beautiful, he had delicate features, tiny hands and tiny feet.

Princess Prawn quite liked being the bigger of the two.

It made a change.

She never got tired of looking at Abdul, she knew his face better than her own, from his fine arched eyebrows and long, long, black eyelashes to his perfect mouth and perfect teeth.

He, in turn, adored Prawn.

He loved her intensity, her constant gaze from her big blue eyes and her gentleness.

He loved her so much that, the minute they were separated, he developed a craving for Prawn Cocktail crisps.

Poor Prince Abdul was utterly terrified of her older sisters, however, and Prawn protected him completely from their loud confidence and occasional rude remarks.

It did seem to everyone, even the Maharani, that maybe this could be a match made in heaven.

As soon as Princess Tiara had got happily married and after Princess Ruby eventually found her one and only true love, Princess Prawn and Prince Abdul decided to get married.

They had patiently and quietly waited three long years.

Both families planned enormous celebrations, one in India and one in Sussexonia.

But the quiet pair wouldn't agree to that.

They wanted a small ceremony, with a handful of guests, delicious food and good music.

Because Prawn had never been away from home, she wanted the wedding to take place in India.

The Maharani felt quite triumphant and although it nearly killed her, she organised the wedding exactly as requested.

Of course, she ordered the wedding cake from Choccywoccydoodah in Sussexonia.

It could come on the plane with the King, Queen, Tiara, Bellinki and Ruby. Thank goodness, Curtis would be accompanying it, should anything go wrong or drop off.

The day before the wedding Prince Abdul had arranged to meet Princess Prawn Cocktail at his own elephant park.

They were going to ride elephants and look at the landscape, maybe talk, maybe not.

She put on her riding boots, her jodhpurs and a clean crisp shirt.

Abdul's servants settled her on a gentle, slow old elephant who would obey the Princess.

She rode around for a few minutes on her own, waiting for Abdul, utterly, utterly content.

Through the gates of the elephant park came a huge bull elephant, on the top of which was a tiny, beautiful, colourful and sparkling girl.

Dressed in a glittering sari, barefoot, with bangles round her wrists and ankles.

Princess Prawn found the sight breathtaking and wished she had her iPhone to take pictures. She had left it in her bedroom.

The elephant and the girl slowly made their way to Prawn who was still comfortably saddled on her own elephant.

As the bull elephant got nearer Prawn could see the girl was not a girl, but Abdul.

Abdul looked so beautiful, so shy, so perfect, that Prawn felt a bit tearful.

'Darling Prawn,' said Abdul, 'I did not want to marry you tomorrow with any secrets in my heart. And sometimes, my heart wants me to dress in beautiful saris and wear beautiful jewels. It sets my heart free. I hope it does not break yours, my love.'

Prawn replied 'You are everything to me. My soul is your soul. My heart is your heart. My dresses could now be your dresses. That is all. How can the cut of a cloth dictate who we are? Does a bull elephant feel ashamed in a pink blanket? Does his lady wife assume something is wrong? No. Of course not. And nor do I.'

They rode for half a day, sometimes talking, sometimes not talking.

Abdul explained that his mother had advised him to reveal his dressing-up tendencies. 'When I wear a sari she says I am the daughter she never had. When I don't she says I am the best son she ever had. My father also accepts me as I am, a prince, passionate about elephants, ladies' clothes and most of all you.'

Prawn knew her family would feel the same.

The rest of the day they rested under the cool shade of trees, sharing a picnic with their elephants.

They knew they would not go back to the palace that night.

They lay in each other's arms under the stars and slept soundly, with the elephants keeping a watchful eye on them.

The King and Queen grew worried when Abdhul and Prawn did not appear for dinner.

The Maharani, however, was serene and reassuring. No need to worry, she said.

So nobody did.

The following day, the wedding party walked to the temple for the wedding ceremony.

Way off in the distance the silhouette of two elephants could be seen, ponderously swaying their way towards the same temple.

As everyone got closer they could see Prince Abdhul, dressed in a crisp shirt, with jodhpurs and riding boots, holding hands with Princess Prawn Cocktail, dressed in a glittery sari, barefoot with bangles on her wrists and ankles.

A match made in heaven.

After the very private ceremony the wedding picnic was laid out in the palace gardens, under huge colourful fringed umbrellas.

It was delicious.

And finally the Maharani and Maharajah revealed the astonishing wedding cake they had commissioned for the happy couple.

At the centre of the colourful cake, which was adorned with bright flowers and birds, was a sculpted sash, upon which Tom, at Choccywoccydoodah, had painted:

'You set my heart free'

And the Maharani knew what kind of person thrived in such a wet, green landscape in Sussexonia. A perfect person.

(It did not pass either Princess Tiara or Princess Ruby's attention that Abdhul was dressed in women's clothing on his wedding day. They heartily approved.)

MASHED POTATO CAKE (gluten free)

Not so easy. We have had varying degrees of success with this recipe, the egg whites have to be stiff.

125g unsalted butter, plus a little
   extra for greasing
400g caster sugar
250g warm mashed potato
100g dark chocolate, melted
1½ tsp bicarbonate of soda,
   dissolved in 4 dessertspoons of
   warm water
4 large eggs, separated
a pinch of salt
a dash of vanilla extract
125ml milk

For the filling
4 tbsp Nutella

Preheat the oven to 210°C /190°C fan oven/410°F/ gas mark 6½. Grease and line two 15cm cake tins with greaseproof paper.

Cream the butter and sugar together in a large bowl using an electric hand whisk until the mixture is light and fluffy.

Beat in the mashed potato and melted chocolate. Add the dissolved bicarbonate of soda and beat again, making sure it's all mixed in.

Beat the egg yolks in a separate bowl until they look creamy then add to the mixture in the large bowl, along with the salt and vanilla. Pour in the milk gradually, stirring all the time.

Whisk the egg whites in a spotlessly clean, greasefree bowl until stiff. The beaters need to be clean, too, otherwise the egg whites won't whip up. When the whites are ready you should be able to hold them over your head without them falling out.

Fold the egg whites into the mixture using a large metal spoon, taking care not to beat out the air.

Divide the mixture between the two cake tins and bake for 30 minutes, or until a skewer pushed into the centre comes out clean.

Transfer to a wire rack to cool and, once cool, spread one half with the Nutella then top with the other half and tuck in.

SALMON WITH WHITE CHOCOLATE

This is easy. Accompany with green salad.

4 salmon fillets
4 slices of lemon
150ml single cream
50g white chocolate buttons
chopped chives
whole pink peppercorns

Preheat the oven to 180°C/160°C fan oven/350°F/ gas mark 4.

Top each piece of salmon with a lemon slice, wrap in greaseproof paper, and fold into a parcel. Bake in a roasting tin for 15 minutes.

Place the cream, chocolate and chives into a heavy bottomed pan. Heat gently to melt the chocolate and do not allow the mixture to boil.

Keep the mixture warm over a gentle heat for a couple of minutes.

Serve salmon still wrapped in greaseproof. Spoon the sauce over the salmon and scatter over pink peppercorns to taste.

SAVOURY CHOCOLATE DIPPING POTS

Easy and dramatic.

Serve molten chocolate in ramekins, on a tray surrounded by pretzels, tortillas, kettle crisps, bread straws, cocktail sausages, cheese cubes and crispy cold bacon.

You can add a kick to the chocolate with a little sprinkling of chilli flakes.

SWEET CHOCOLATE DIPPING POTS

Easy.

Serve molten chocolate in ramekins on a tray surrounded by marshmallows, fudge, strawberries, cherries, coconut ice, mango and honeycomb.

Let the fun begin.

Muesli Muffins  by Jenny Banham

These are really easy to make, though mine
always come out more like rock cakes then
muffins :')

Makes about 20.......
8oz (225g) Wholemeal Flour.
2 tsp baking powder.
½ tsp bicarbonate of Soda
1 tsp salt
1 tsp mixed Spice
1 tsp Cinnamon
40z (100g) butter, melted
40oz (100g) soft brown Sugar
1 large egg
4 fl oz (125ml) milk
1 mug of muesli
2 large handfuls of raisins or mixed berries.

① Melt butter and leave to cool.
② mix milk and egg together.
③ Sift flour, baking powder, bicarbonate of Soda,
Salt & Spices into a bowl.
④ add sugar, muesli and dried fruit to the
bowl, make a well and add melted butter,
egg and milk .. Mix together........
⑤ Spoon mixture into cases and bake in
oven. for 10-12 mins, Gas mark 5 (190°c).....
⑥ take out and eat :') (when cool).

Doodah's favourite recipes

Jenny Flowergirl

The cleverest of all clever fingers, her fearsome reputation extends to muesli muffins for baby boy Sam, Doodah husband Paul and for throwing at the hens. Not us. (This time.)

A Long, A Long, time ago...

In a small leafy village in the middle of England a strange woman moved into a ramshackle house on the very edge of the very end of the village.

The house had stood empty for as long as anyone could remember.

It had a wonky roof, a wonky chimney, tiny windows, a wonky door and a really overgrown garden.

It was a sad and neglected house.

One evening, just as dusk descended on the village, a car drove through on the only road, with two men in the front and a strange old lady in the back.

Because there was only one road, because in those days nobody had a telly, everyone in the village knew a stranger had arrived.

Half an hour after the car arrived, it left.

The two men were still in the front.

A dim light could be seen from the windows of the wonky house.

The next day some of the village people knocked on the wonky house door.

They could see someone peeking out of the window but no one ever came to the door.

Eventually people got fed up with being ignored and decided to leave the stranger alone.

The children in the village would hang around the garden gate of the wonky house to try and see who lived there.

A shadowy figure could be seen within the house, bent over, with ratty

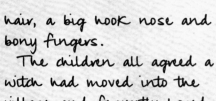

hair, a big hook nose and
bony fingers.

The children all agreed a
witch had moved into the
village and fervently hoped
she wouldn't cast an evil spell
on them, or worse, eat them.

A dark cloud seemed to hover
over the wonky house.

Sometimes, very late at night the villagers were startled
by the sounds of wailing and shouting in a language they didn't
understand, coming from the little house.

The children assumed the witch was making spells and shivered in
their beds.

Eventually, the village returned to its normal routine and took no notice
of the witch in her wonky house.

Occasionally she would be seen trundling her shopping from the bus
stop in the village to her house.

She was always stooped, never looked at anyone, always wore a big
scarf wrapped around her head.

Sometimes the children called out after her, cruel words and names.

They always ran away in case she turned them into frogs.

Winter came to the village. The leaves fell off the trees, the
flowers all died back and the air chilled.

It was dark when the children came home from school.

Three curious little girls lingered at the gate and looked
into the witch's house.

They could see quite clearly into the kitchen as the light
was on and it was dark outside.

There appeared to be a cake on the kitchen table and
the kitchen looked warm and friendly, with a huge
armchair in the corner and an open fire.

The witch saw them and opened the window.

The smell that wafted out was delicious.

The witch spoke, but the girls couldn't

understand what she said and fled in terror.

They thought she might be trying to lure them inside to eat them.

Well, Bella and Popular did.

The third girl, Homely, thought that the witch might have offered them cake, but couldn't be sure.

What she was sure of was that the kitchen looked most unlike a witch's kitchen.

No cauldrons, no black cat and no pointy hats.

She kept her thoughts to herself.

As winter settled in, the village became used to the delicious smells that wafted over it.

Some of the older villagers made an effort to talk to the witch when she got off the bus. They said she came from a foreign country and was still learning English.

Sometimes the older villagers seemed upset and wanted to say more, but never did.

When spring arrived and daylight poured over the village into the evenings, people spent time in their gardens and talked over their fences.

The winter had been long and most people had forgotten about the witch.

Very easy to do as she lived on the very edge of the village.

One day, the little girl Homely decided to walk to the outskirt of the village, without her friends. She deliberately walked to the gate of the wonky house.

She couldn't believe her eyes.

Someone had tidied the garden, planted hollyhocks and rambling roses, a vegetable patch of cabbages and runner beans. Daisies and buttercups covered the lawn.

It was beautiful.

The house had been painted shell pink: the walls, the doors, the windows and the garden gate itself.

As she stared and stared, the kitchen window opened and the witch looked out at her.

The witch's face was no longer bony, her nose looked much smaller

against her plump cheeks. Her hair was dark and shiny. She seemed straighter and taller.

When she saw the little girl she smiled and the sun came out.

The little girl smiled back.

All three little girls, Bella, Popular and Homely, decided to go back to the witch's house, a few days later.

On the kitchen window sill was a giant apple pie, cooling.

Through the window they could see the kitchen table, covered in a flowery tablecloth, with plates of toffee apples, biscuits and cake.

The smell wafted through the garden and into the village.

More children joined the three little girls. Oh, how all those children wanted the biscuits and toffee apples! Even the cruel children had fallen in love with the wonky house and its delicious smelling kitchen.

After a while, the front door opened.

A beautiful plump lady in an apron with flour on her hands brought out a tray of toffee apples. She smiled broadly at the children, put the tray on the garden wall and indicated they could help themselves.

And they did.

Crisp, tart apples on sticks, dipped in caramel, with biscuity bits, then chocolate, then a crisp shell of burnt sugar.

Those children had never tasted anything like it.

Ever.

When they finished, they all called thank you through the open kitchen window and drifted off home.

Apart from Homely. She returned the empty tray through the kitchen window and told the beautiful witch that the toffee apples were the tastiest things the children have eaten.

The beautiful witch smiled her most bewitching smile and her eyes filled with tears.

She turned away and Homely knew it was time for her to leave.

When Homely got home, desperate to share her story with her mother, she found her mother anxiously pacing the garden path, waiting and watching for Homely's return.

Fear struck Homely's heart.

Her mother was the postmistress of the village and always got everyone's bad news first.

During the Terrible War, she was the one who had to deliver the yellow telegrams announcing the death or loss of someone's father, brother, or son.

One day, a telegram arrived and it didn't need to be delivered.

Homely's father had been killed in action.

That awful, not too distant day, as Homely made her way home from school, her mother had been pacing the garden path, waiting for Homely to come home.

All thoughts of toffee apples flew out of Homely's head as she prepared herself for more awful news.

However, she suddenly realised that her mother didn't look sad — she looked teary but happy as she ushered Homely into the house, lickettysplit.

It was great news, her mother told her.

Great news and before she delivered the news, she needed to share it with someone who could keep it a secret.

Homely solemnly swore to keep the secret but begged her mother to tell all and quickly.

Homely's mother, Thoughtful, had visited the witch when she arrived in the village.

However, the witch wouldn't open the door.

Thoughtful had important letters and documents for her, so she couldn't just leave it be.

She went back day after day after day, after work.

When she got no reply to her knocking she would always leave a little token of friendship on the doorstep. Sometimes a flower, or a candle, or a packet of biscuits.

Every day she visited she noticed that her small gifts were taken in.

Eventually the witch trusted her enough to open the door.

Thoughtful gave her the important papers and immediately understood the witch would not be able to read them as she spoke very little English.

She recognised terror in the witch's eyes as she received the legal and official documents.

Thoughtful offered to read them for her and help her to understand.

The witch was not a witch at all.

Her name was Liebe.

She was born, raised and married in the country that fought England in the Terrible War.

However, her people were considered to be enemies of the State and many, many of them were placed in prison camps or worse.

Liebe and her husband had their children taken away by soldiers whilst they were packing suitcases to flee the country.

Liebe's husband was shot there and then for his treachery and Liebe was placed on a crowded cattle train with hundreds of her kinfolk.

The train ended up in one of the most terrible prison camps ever known.

But Liebe survived, only just, until the end of the war.

She was one of very few who did.

She asked her rescuers to put her somewhere safe, as far away from her homeland as they could.

So they placed her in the little English village, far from home, to start a new life.

At first she was terrified, waiting for the knock on the door, waiting to be taken away. She received plenty of knocks on her door, but no one came to take her away.

Gradually, slowly, eventually, she realised nobody ever would take her away.

And the tiniest little bud of friendship with Thoughtful began.

Slowly she told her story, first in her own language, then with sign language and eventually in faltering English.

Officially, she was now English.

Her paperwork made her a citizen of the country she had chosen and she was both proud and relieved to be so.

But every day, her heart broke and her strength to build a new life faltered as she thought of her children.

Her son, Celeste would be fifteen now, her daughter, Verehrt, would be thirteen.

The last time she saw them they were twelve and ten.

Too young to die, but so many children had.

Late at night, she would cry and cry, calling for her children in her sleep.

Thoughtful would come and sit with Liebe, holding her pitifully thin hands and weeping with her for her children.

The village elders, who understood better than anyone the evils of war, would talk to Thoughtful when they came to the little post office in her front room.

Some were set against Liebe, because she wasn't English, but most were anxious to help.

Thoughtful used her skills as postmistress to write to everyone she could think of who might be able to help find out about Liebe's children.

She wrote over two hundred letters.

It took many, many months.

And she received very few replies.

Thoughtful never told Liebe about the letters she wrote.

She was not hopeful about finding the children and didn't want to make the cracks in Liebe's heart even wider.

In the meantime, the elders of the village, most of whom were passionate about gardening, did what they could.

As they sowed their gardens, they would pop round to Liebe's house and do a little of her garden.

She would return the favour with a cake or some biscuits.

Mr Elderly Painter, now retired, loved her sachertorte, and decided to paint Liebe's house in the hope that she would make him one.

She did.

And she loved the beautiful shell pink paint he had found in his loft.

Slowly, Liebe's appetite returned as her fight for life returned and her spirit grew as her hair grew.

But still her heart ached and sometimes her grief was too much for her to bear.

The children of the village often gathered round her gate, curious and questioning.

Liebe couldn't ever bring herself to look at them, she missed her own so much.

The best she could do was to bake her children's favourite biscuits, make their favourite toffee apples and hope the village children would like them.

But today — this day — Thoughtful had received a letter.

A letter from an official body in America who had traced Liebe's children.

They survived the prison camps.

They were lucky, they were strong and they had been taken in by a family who had fled to America from Liebe's hometown.

The children and their new family had been trying to trace Liebe, never thinking for one minute she would be alive.

Thoughtful had sent a telegram to Liebe's children, telling them her address.

She had got an immediate telegram back, to say that the children and their kind hosts were leaving America immediately for England.

They would be in the village in three weeks.

Homely and Thoughtful laughed and cried and laughed and wondered, should they tell Liebe?

Or should they wait?

If something went wrong, Liebe would never recover from any more bad news.

But — it was such tremendously good news — surely Liebe should know?

They decided to keep it to themselves, just in case.

So many bad things had happened to so many people for such a long period of time, they felt that if this went wrong, only Thoughtful and Homely would have to cope with the news.

Over the next three weeks they made bunting, asked the elders to keep the gardens and verges looking lovely and collected ingredients for baking.

The elders knew there was something afoot.

In the end, a week before Liebe's children were due, Thoughtful trusted them with her secret.

The elders decided to tell Liebe that someone very important was going to visit the village and they asked her to bake all their favourite dishes that she had introduced to the village.

And to make plenty of toffee apples.

The baking ingredients were all sent to Liebe's kitchen.

On the Wednesday of that week, when all the children were at school, Thoughtful received a telegram.

Gelebte and Verehrt would be in the village by tea time.

She shut up the post office in her front room.

She left a cryptic note on the door for the elders to read and understand.

She started the walk to the outskirts of the village, to Liebe's house.

But Liebe was not at home.

Her kitchen window was open, her kitchen table groaned under the weight of her splendid baking, but she was not there.

Thoughtful ran back to her house, searching the village as she went, hoping that Liebe hadn't got on a bus to go to the big town.

Her heart was thudding.

And then, in the distance, on the only road in or out of the village, she saw a small figure with shiny black hair and a basket on her arm.

Thoughtful carried on running to catch up with Liebe, but she wasn't much used to exercise and had to stop.

She shouted Liebe's name again and again.

Thoughtful was sure that Liebe could hear her, but she didn't stop walking along the dusty village road.

Schoolchildren passed her on their way home from school and smiled at her.

They said she smiled back, but looked distracted.

Just as Thoughtful nearly caught up with Liebe, she bumped into Homely.

She didn't even have enough time to tell Homely the news when a very old and

noisy taxi trundled down towards the village.

Liebe put her basket down and stood stock still in the middle of the road.

The air changed.

The schoolchildren and the elders, Thoughtful and Homely became silent and still.

The taxi doors opened and two quite big children with shiny black hair got out.

They went to their mother and all three hugged silently for a very long time.

Two elderly people also got out of the taxi and it drove away, leaving the strangers on the road.

Thoughtful walked over to the strangers and bade them welcome.

The village erupted into cheers and laughter, the schoolchildren were whooping and calling to each other.

There were many tears running down many cheeks, smooth and wrinkled, young and old.

Slowly, Liebe turned around to face the village, with her children and walked with them, towards her little house.

The villagers lined the road and waved the bunting and shouted their best wishes at Liebe and her family.

Liebe smiled and smiled and smiled.

Apart from Liebe and her two children, everyone else gathered in the post office, in the garden of the post office and spilled onto the road.

The two older strangers stayed with the villagers, leaving Liebe to enjoy her children alone.

Everyone had a glass of beer. Even the small children had a sip of beer.

Secretly though, everyone was thinking about all the marvellous baking Liebe had done.

Far too much for just two children, in fact, plenty for the whole village.

An hour later,

 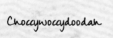

Liebe walked up to the post office, found Thoughtful, and asked her to invite everyone down to the wonky house.

In good time the whole village made their way to the very, very, edge of the village.

Some carried chairs, some carried tables, some brought beer.

Pots of tea were made as people passed their houses, crockery was piled into shopping bags with table cloths and pints of milk.

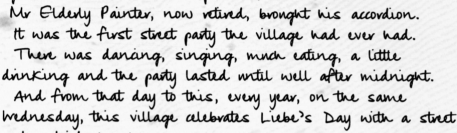

Mr Elderly Painter, now retired, brought his accordion.

It was the first street party the village had ever had.

There was dancing, singing, much eating, a little drinking and the party lasted until well after midnight.

And from that day to this, every year, on the same Wednesday, this village celebrates Liebe's Day with a street party outside her house.

Her children and her grandchildren bake for a week, but the speciality is still the most amazing toffee apples.

Before the party started, but after Liebe and her children had walked to her wonky house, Homely walked back up the road to retrieve the basket Liebe had placed in front of the taxi.

When she looked inside she found two toffee apples.

One had been decorated with ' Geliebte' and the other 'Verehrt'.

Ah, she thought, we were right. She is a witch.

Then she ate them.

CHOCOLATE APPLES

This is very very easy and child friendly.

milk chocolate – 1kg will coat 8 or
    9 small to medium apples
apples
chopsticks or kebab sticks

VARIATIONS:

Fill small bowls with different
toppings ready to dip the
chocolatey apple in.

Biscuit crumbs or sugar strands,
chunks of crystallised ginger,
cinnamon.

Or, wait for the chocolate to
set, then double dip into melted
white or dark chocolate.

Sprinkle a little sea salt on the
chocolate.

Or, add chopped chunks of
fudge, a
generous pinch of chilli powder
and mini marshmallows to the
big bowl of melted
milk chocolate.

Or, keep it simple and pipe
names onto the apples for place
settings or gifts.

Line a tray with greaseproof paper.

Melt the chocolate gently in the microwave, in short
bursts. Stir vigorously between each burst. When the
chocolate is gloopy and still lumpy, it's time to use it.

Put the sticks into the apples and plunge the apple into
the chocolate. Leave on the greaseproof to set.

I find the apples stay good for up to a week if they're not
damaged before dipping.

Store airtight at room temperature.

APPLE STRUDEL

Very easy.

8 eating apples, chopped
100g caster sugar
100g sultanas
1 tsp cinnamon (optional)
100g butter, melted, plus an extra
  50g knob
8 sheets ready-made filo pastry
icing sugar

Line a baking sheet with greaseproof paper. Preheat the oven to 200°C/180°C fan oven 400°F/gas mark 6.

Put the apples, sugar, sultanas and cinnamon in a frying pan, with a knob of butter and pop the pan over a medium heat. Cook for about 5 minutes until the apples caramelise slightly, tossing the pan every now and again. Be careful they don't overcook otherwise they'll lose their shape.

Leave the mixture to cool.

Unwrap the filo pastry on a board and layer the sheets on top of each other, higgledy piggledy, brushing a little melted butter between each sheet.

Pile the cooled apple mixture onto the pastry and fold the sheets around the mixture into a rough parcel. Use the melted butter as glue to stick them down.

Brush the last of the butter over the top of the parcel, then sieve over icing sugar. Bake for 30 minutes or until crisp and golden brown.

Leave to cool slightly. Sieve more icing sugar over just before serving and serve with cream or ice cream.

CHOCOLATE KRISPY POMPOMS

Messy. Great fun. Easy. This also works with cornflakes. These are great for hanging on Christmas trees, or wishing trees.

200g milk chocolate
200g white chocolate
Rice Krispies, medium-sized box

You'll also need cellophane and ribbons

Line a baking tray with greaseproof paper.

Melt both types of chocolate separately in big bowls in the microwave, on low, in short bursts, stirring after each burst.

Add half the Rice Krispies to each bowl and stir each until all the Krispies are covered and the mixture is dense.

Place a dessertspoon of the milk chocolate mixture on the lined baking tray. Repeat until you've used half the mixture.

Place a dessertspoon of the white mixture onto the milk mixture, tamping it down a little with the back of a spoon.

Put another spoon of milk chocolate mixture on top of each, then again with the white mixture. The stripes will not be completely even and it doesn't matter that they will look a bit messy.

Pop in the fridge for 2 hours to set completely. Wrap each pompom in cellophane with a long length of ribbon to tie to the tree.

Eat the bits left on the tray. It's the least you deserve.

DARK STUFF

This is quite grown up, not as easy as brittle. As it requires boiling sugar, I suggest it's only made by a sensible grown-up.

150g salted butter, plus extra
   for greasing
150g brown sugar
1 tsp mixed spice
a handful of sultanas
a handful of mixed nuts
240ml of milk
200g dark chocolate, chopped

Grease and line a 22.5 x 30cm baking tin with baking parchment, shiny side up.

Put the sugar and butter in a heavy bottomed pan. Stir the mixture, allowing the butter to melt and sugar to dissolve then bring to the boil.

Add the spice, fruit and nuts.

When the mixture is amber golden, carefully pour in the milk. Stir. When it thickens, turn off the heat and add the chocolate, stirring.

Pour the mixture onto the lined baking tin.

Refrigerate for an hour or so.

Cut into chunks. Store in an airtight box.

DRINKING CHOCOLATE

Very easy.

large mug
150g chocolate buttons
milk

Optional
whipped cream, marshmallows
brandy, rum, whisky, Baileys Irish
 Cream liqueur or Cointreau
chilli pepper
more chocolate
churros, for dunking (see page 236)

Put the chocolate buttons into the mug.

Pour the milk into a pan and bring to the boil. Pour over the chocolate.

Stir until the chocolate has melted.

Add from the list opposite.

SACHERTORTE

Sometimes I'm too impatient to wait for this to cool and set before I get it out of the tin. This always results in a disastrous-looking cake. I don't care though, I simply pour chocolate over it, stick it in the fridge to set and eat it in front of the TV. It's a brilliant recipe for a reasonably confident baker.

100g salted butter, softened,
   plus extra for greasing
200g dark chocolate
100g plain flour
1 level tsp baking powder
100g golden caster sugar
100g ground almonds
4 large eggs, separated

Preheat the oven to 190°C/170°C fan oven/375°F/ gas mark 5. Grease and line a 20cm cake tin with greaseproof paper.

Melt the chocolate. Put the flour, baking powder, sugar and ground almonds together in a large bowl. Add the butter and egg yolks and beat the mixture to a creamy consistency.

Pour in the chocolate gradually, beating all the time.

Whisk the egg whites then fold into the cake mixture, gradually, keeping the air in the mix.

Pour or spoon the mixture into the cake tin and bake for 40 minutes. It should feel springy but firm when baked.

Leave it to cool in the tin for 1½ hours before turning it out on to a plate.

To decorate, pour more melted chocolate over the top or dust with icing sugar.

Serve with thick, whipped cream.

TOFFEE APPLES

I love these, especially made with sour apples, but try not to use damaged apples or they won't last long.

Definitely not for children to make, because of the boiling sugar, but all children should eat once cool.

Very, very easy.

500g golden caster sugar
wooden kebab sticks or chopsticks
6–8 apples

VARIATIONS:

Now dip the toffee apple into grated chocolate.
Or sugar strands.
Or smashed-up biscuit.
Or roll it around in mini mallows.

Cover a board with a sheet of baking parchment.

Pour the sugar into a heavy bottomed pan. Place over a medium heat and allow to dissolve until it's golden, translucent and liquid. Don't stir.

While you're waiting, push the sticks into the core of the apples.

When the sugar is ready, turn off the heat and plunge the apple on the stick into it. Swizzle it around until the apple is pretty much coated. Put onto the baking parchment.

Repeat until you've run out.

Let the toffee set and cool before eating.

JIM. PILCHARD PIE

MUM MADE THIS ONCE A WEEK FOR MY BROTHER, SISTER AND ME; IT WAS A MUCH-LOOKED-FORWARD-TO TREAT AND EVEN TODAY, ALMOST WITHOUT FAIL, IT'S A STAPLE OF OUR (REBECCA + MY) WEEKLY DINING EXPERIENCE — OUR MONDAY NIGHT MEAL. ENJOY!

A FANCIFUL REPRESENTATION: THE PILCHARD DOESN'T POKE OUT OF THE TOPPING — THAT WOULD BE STARGAZY PIE, ANOTHER THING ENTIRELY.

INGREDIENTS: 1 X 400g TIN PILCHARDS IN TOMATO SAUCE
1 X TABLESPOON PLAIN FLOUR
MILK
APPROX 4 X MEDIUM-SIZED POTATOES (DEPENDING ON HOW THICK A TOPPING IS DESIRED)
1 X LARGE KNOB OF BUTTER (OR MARG.)

(FOR SAUCE, WILL NEED MORE BUTTER FOR MASH)

METHOD: FOR THE SAUCE — MELT BUTTER IN SAUCEPAN; MIX IN FLOUR TO FORM A ROUX; ADD SPLASH OF MILK AND STIR TILL YOU HAVE THICK SAUCE. ADD PILCHARDS IN TOMATO SAUCE AND MIX TOGETHER. POUR INTO OVEN-DISH.

FOR TOPPING — CUT UP POTATOES AND PLACE IN PAN WITH ENOUGH WATER TO COVER. BRING TO BOIL + CONTINUE BOILING FOR APPROX 20 MINS (OR UNTIL POTS ARE SOFT ENOUGH TO MASH). DRAIN THEM MASH, ADDING PLENTY OF BUTTER + PEPPER + DASH OF MILK.
SPREAD MASH OVER SAUCE TILL SAUCE IS COVERED + MARK ALL OVER WITH A FORK. BAKE IN PRE-HEATED OVEN 180°C FOR ABOUT 20 MINS TILL TOPPING IS CRISP + BROWNED. SERVE WITH BREAD + BUTTER OR — TO IMPRESS FRIENDS — PEAS. (I ALSO LIKE TO SMOTHER IN TABASCO) + KETCHUP.

AND I AM HIGH IN OMEGA 3's.

Doodah's favourite recipes

Jim the Baker

This recipe is Jim's favourite childhood recipe, made by his mum. Now made by Jim for his own daughter, Connie Albertine, and wife, Rebecca.

Is Chocolate better than Sex?

All chocolate is better than poor sex.
Even cheap chocolate is better than cheap sex.
Really good chocolate is as good as really good sex and there are many, many women out there who would rather get messy with a bar of chocolate than with a man.

Reasons to love chocolate:

Chocolate is completely reliable.
Never lets you down, doesn't judge you, walk out on you, or leave you unsatisfied.
Chocolate is predictably marvellous, time after time, hitting the spot and satisfying the need.
Sinful without sinning, decadent without showing off, and as rich as we can cope with or hope to be.
Good-quality chocolate actually can have health benefits too.
It has the highest levels of antioxidants in any food. It soothes sore throats, eases indigestion and acts as an instant mood levitator.
And what all chocolate lovers know is that good chocolate raises the levels of phenylethylamine in our system when we eat it.
The same hormone that we release when we have sex or fall in love.
In my experience this is most strongly felt and appreciated by women.

And the brilliant thing is that to recapture that feeling, all we need to do is eat more chocolate.

Easy.

Good chocolate is qualified by its cocoa percentage: the higher the cocoa solids the purer the chocolate. But for it to be a delicious, good chocolate, it needs to be a fine quality product, made from a well sourced cocoa bean, processed to a high standard and made into an irresistible, snappy, sexy confection.

Chocolate is an aphrodisiac.

It could be the prelude to fantastic sex.

Wine, music, warm molten chocolate... drink the wine, play the music and dip yourself in chocolate. Let your partner have dessert.

Chocolate and the human race have had an enduring love affair for centuries.

There's no sign of a divorce, no question of a seven-year itch and no shortage in the pipeline.

Sex is fleeting.

Chocolate is forever.

SIMPLY DESSERT

It's as difficult as you want it to be.

400g of your partner's favourite
   chocolate, melted and poured
   into an attractive jug
bed
sheets that you don't mind ruining,
   made on the bed
absolute privacy
a bottle of chilled champagne

Drink some champagne.

Take your clothes off, recline on the bed.

Take turns in pouring chocolate over yourselves and each
other.

Eat.

Maybe drink a little more champagne.

Delicious.

ESPRESSO

Easy.

With dunking buttons of chocolate.

The Flagship Story

I love a bit of romance
attached to a tragic tale.
And our rather gorgeous flagship shop in
Fonbert's Place, off Carnaby Street, provides exactly that.
In the very olden days, when Shakespeare was a London
face and the first Elizabeth was trying to persuade everyone she
was a modest queen, our capital city was blighted by the plague. Known
as the Black Death, it wiped out sizeable chunks of the population and
wreaked havoc on London. Because of the vast quantity of dead people,
and the awful risk of infection involved, burials could no longer be
a sombre, dignified and singular event. Mass burial pits had to be
dug and many thousands of dead people were laid
together with no great ceremony.

One of the largest of these mass graves was in
today's Soho.

Once the Black Death had been consumed by the
Great Fire of London, frightened Londoners returned
to resume their city lives, working, trading and of
course, shopping.

One of the most popular markets was in an
area called Carnaby, which is now still known
as Carnaby Street. The market and surrounding
area were built on the mass grave of Black Death
victims.

The area thrived and a well known local man,
Henry Fonbert, opened a school of arms in the area.

The school taught privileged children how to fence and ride, amongst
other things. It then went on to become a riding school and stables.
Years came and went, as did the stables, horses and all. But Fonbert's
Place still remains as a name and is home to our flagship shop.

The building went up in 1900 and was first used as a tobacco
factory, which is why the windows are so tall and the window ledges so

wide, because the tobacco was dried here before it got rolled into cigarettes.

The business was past owned by Ernest Shackleton, intrepid and heroic Antarctic explorer. (Another story for another time.)

During the course of its history, the building became many things, including a brewery. It seems very apt to me that it is now a chocolaterie.

I'm sort of hoping that eventually it becomes an incredibly decadent brothel.

I have stood in the basement of the building quietly and alone, a lot.

Listening for ghosts, hoping to catch whispers from the past.

I even got Keith, a gorgeous Irish man who worked on the building with us when we were struggling to get open, to come and stand with me.

Keith believes in ghosts and has kissed the Blarney Stone so I know if there were whispers, he'd have heard them.

Neither of us ever did. Such a shame.

The flagship shop is five floors of chocolate and joy, from the stockrooms to the office in the roof, with three floors of fun, cake and chocolate for our customers and visitors to explore.

Of course, the Secret Room can only be explored if it's been booked. Otherwise it's not really a secret at all.

CHOCOLATE BREAD AND BUTTER PUDDING

This is very simple comfort food. Serve with cream.

a little butter, for greasing
1 large brioche, sliced and buttered
coarse cut marmalade
100g dried vine fruit
175g dark chocolate, either buttons
   or grated
large glug of Cointreau
1 large egg
600ml full-fat milk
50g caster sugar

Preheat the oven to 180°C/160°C fan oven/350°F/ gas mark 4. Grease a 22.5 x 15cm deep dish.

Slice the brioche and spread with marmalade. Layer the brioche in the dish, sprinkling vine fruit then a little chocolate between each layer. Pour the Cointreau over the top.

Beat the egg, milk and sugar together in a large jug, then pour all over the brioche mixture and leave to stand for an hour.

Half fill a roasting pan with cold water, and put the dish in the roasting pan. Bake in the oven for around 25 minutes until golden brown with a slightly crusty top.

CHOCOLATE BROWNIES/BLONDIES

Brownies can be hit and miss, but this recipe is almost foolproof.

200g salted butter, plus extra
    for greasing
200g whole almonds or any other
    type of nut
2 tsp very strong liquid coffee
4 large eggs
200g ground almonds
300g dark chocolate buttons
200g golden caster sugar
4 drops vanilla extract
200g dark chocolate, melted

VARIATION:

Replace the dark chocolate and coffee with white chocolate to make blondies.

Preheat the oven to 200°C/180°C fan oven/400°F/ gas mark 6. Grease and line a 20 x 30cm baking tray with baking parchment.

Toast the almonds or nuts on a baking tray in the oven until golden brown. Cool.

Melt the butter in a pan over a gentle heat, then stir in the coffee.

In a separate bowl, mix the eggs, ground almonds, nuts, chocolate buttons, sugar, vanilla and lastly the butter mixture. Stir in the melted chocolate. Mix until creamy and thick. Don't over mix, it makes the brownie crumble.

Pour the mixture into the lined baking tray. Bake for 20–25 minutes, until the edges are crusty. The middle should be soft. Leave it to cool in the tin. Slice into squares.

CHURROS

Requires confidence. Delicious dunked in hot chocolate. Or dipped straight into molten chocolate.

2 tsp cinnamon
110g caster sugar
240ml water
a pinch of salt
vegetable oil, for frying, plus a
    little extra
225g self-raising flour

Mix the cinnamon and sugar together in a bowl.

Pour the water into a heavy bottomed pan. Add 2 tbsp of the sugar and cinnamon mixture, a pinch of salt and 2 tbsp oil. Bring to the boil.

As soon as the liquid comes to the boil, take the pan off the heat and stir in the flour, mixing well until it forms a ball of dough.

Spoon the dough into a piping bag fitted with a large star or round nozzle.

Fill a deep pan to just under halfway with vegetable oil and heat it up. Line a baking tray or large plate with kitchen towel.

Pinch a little bit of dough from the piping bag and drop it carefully in to the oil to check it's ready. If it's hot enough it should turn golden brown almost immediately.

Pipe the dough directly into the oil in 10cm-ish lengths. It might be easier to snip the dough from the end of the nozzle so that the oil doesn't splatter you.

Cook three churros at a time, until crisp and golden. Put the cooked churros on kitchen towel to absorb the excess cooking oil.

When the whole batch is done, roll them in the remaining sugar and cinnamon mix and serve straightaway.

DOG CAKE

Choccy has made something like a million birthday cakes, and all of them have been chocolate. Sadly these cannot be shared with our most loyal friends, our dogs, because of the chocolate. However, this recipe makes an amazing birthday cake for dogs. Of course, it does oblige you to throw a party. This is quite easy.

For the cake
butter for greasing
225g self-raising flour
225g rolled oats
1 tbsp cornflour
110g butter or soft margarine
1 chicken stock cube
2 large eggs
1 loaded tsp yeast extract
splash of milk

For the filling
cream cheese or peanut butter

VARIATION:

By swapping the chicken stock for Parmesan cheese and seasoning with freshly ground black pepper this is an excellent savoury cake which can be filled with any sandwich filling for a picnic, or left with a cream cheese filling

Preheat the oven to 170°C/150°C fan oven/325°F/ gas mark 3½. Grease and line a 10cm cake tin with greaseproof paper.

Mix all the dry ingredients together in a bowl. Add the butter and stock cube and rub in until the mixture looks like breadcrumbs.

Make a well in the centre and add both eggs and yeast extract and mix well with a spoon until it's a heavy, dense cake mix. If it's not moist enough you can add a splash of milk.

Spoon into the cake tin and bake for about 40 minutes. It should be golden brown, with the texture of a scone and firm on the outside.

Leave it to cool then cut it in half. Spread the base with the cream cheese or peanut butter and top with the other half.

Phil Lovedisco's Carbonara
(SKINNY!)

Despite lots of disco dancing I'm always on a diet. This is my version of a classic thats not quite as naughty!!

lots of spagetti
lots of garlic
lots of back smoked bacon (trim off fat)
2/3 large eggs
tiny bit of olive oil.
60 grm of parmasan cheese.

Put pasta on to boil, chop bacon and fry in pan gently add chopped garlic do not burn garlic or will taste bitter. Beat eggs and mix with half of cheese. Pour cooked pasta into bacon e garlic, take off heat. Mix in egg, hot pasta will cook eggs. Add rest of cheese AND Black Pepper

DELICIOUS!!

Doodah's favourite recipes

Phillovesdisco
Sweetie Wrapper
in Chief

Skinny carbonara because
Phil loves to be ironic.
His own recipe in his own
attempt to be as skinny
as his carbonara.

The Mothership Story

Like most Brighton residents, I am only here for the long weekend. Mine started in 1987 and I have yet to get to Sunday.

Everyone in Brighton has a story, but as this is not their book, I shall tell you only mine.

A long time ago, Christine Garratt (current financial director of Choccywoccydoodah) and I pooled our resources, packed our big old London bags and headed to Brighton to find a different life from our metropolitan one.

We arrived shortly before a hurricane. Oddly enough, the hurricane blew through south-east England on my birthday, sweeping away the landscape as we knew it, the cars, the trees, some buildings and our old lives.

The most horrible and memorable part of those few days, when Brighton was isolated from the rest of the country by devastation and fallen trees, was walking on dead sparrows. There were many thousands of them, killed by the storm. It was impossible to avoid either walking on the debris of people's lives, or dead sparrows.

As you have read by now, we bought a cafe. We had a hoot, but business people we were not. Not then, and not now.

We have absolutely promised ourselves that one day we shall write a business plan and with that we shall conquer the world. Or the bank manager.

But as of yet, we have always managed to find more interesting things to write.

Back to Brighton.

Just off the seafront is a ridiculous Indian Palace built by a ridiculous member of the Royal family for entertainment and entertaining. Quite a long time ago.

And as a result, the small fishing village of Brighthelmstone became Brighton and established itself as home to the dirty weekend, the gay capital of Europe, and the pleasure capital of the UK.

The palace is actually spectacular, one of my favourite buildings in the world and we are very privileged to have such a remarkable folly in our backyard.

The town is dearly divided into areas: Kemptown, Hanover, town centre, seafront, North Laines and the Lanes. There are other outposts such as Seven Dials, Brunswick, Fiveways, Moulsecoomb and Whitehawk.

Some are posh, some are not.

Some are architectural eyesores and some are architectural eye salve.

Within these areas, we have a hugely eclectic population of people.

Eccentric, bohemian, addled, addicted, gangsters, gays, artists, piss artists and entrepreneurs.

And for me, it is the people of Brighton who are most important, most enduring and responsible for the success and cock-ups of this schizophrenic town.

Brighton is small enough to be walked around, intimate enough that we can speak to each other as strangers, tolerant of most things, proud of our achievements and even prouder of our failures.

At least we tried.

Because of the marvellous Brighton population, because Brighton liked Choccywoccydoodah from the start, because Brightonians really enjoy cake, the Mothership will always be here, in Brighton.

The Mothership is the beating heart of Choccywoccydoodah, the brave beginning, the creative energy and the driving force. The Doodahs are the crew of this tiny ship and together we steer ourselves uncertainly to an unknown destiny, sure only of the adventure, the joy of

working together and the chocolate. We shall boldly go to where no chocolatiers have gone before us. But where that is, is anybody's guess.

You have now stepped into my world, which as it's the only place I exist in, makes this a true story.

Brighton is actually a very small planet, with a palace, a theatre, some shops, a beach, bars and great people. Good-time and bad-time people. Happy people and happy for the wrong reasons people. This planet is in a balloon, which is anchored to the south coast of England by a very long piece of string and a very wobbly drawing pin.

One day, the drawing pin will loosen, we shall float off and someone, somewhere, maybe in China, or a Brazilian rainforest, will catch the string, understand the situation and pin us back in temporarily, until the drawing pin loosens again.

I believe it's happened a hundred times already and will happen a hundred times more. And the utterly, fabulously marvellous thing about that is that everyone on planet Brighton is oblivious.

The balloon is intact and so are we.

The long weekenders.

The balloonatics.

I should mention that Brighton and Hove were originally two separate towns.

To create a city, the two towns were merged together. But only on paper. Spiritually, there are Brightonians and people from Hove, actually.

The Brightonians are generally more disgraceful whereas the people from Hove are generally more genteel. It's not a hard and fast rule, it only applies to about 99 per cent of each population.

CHOCOLATE MOUSSE

Sometimes practice makes perfect.

a measure of brandy
500ml whipping cream
2 large eggs
500g dark chocolate
6–8 martini or wine glasses,
   depending on size

VARIATION:

Add orange zest to the cream
stage of the mousse, with
Cointreau instead of brandy.

Top with sugar-coated grapes
(see page 251).

Top with candied orange peel
(see page 84).

Whip the brandy and cream together in a bowl until very
thick.

Separate the eggs and whisk the egg whites in a spotlessly
clean, greasefree bowl until stiff peaks form.

Gently melt the chocolate, but don't let it get hot. Beat
the egg yolks into the chocolate.

Fold the egg whites into the brandied cream. Add a little
of the chocolate, again using a folding motion.

Then add the egg white, cream and chocolate mixture
into the remaining chocolate mixture. Fold everything
together until the mixture is spoonable and gloopy.

Divide the mixture among 6 to 8 martini or wine glasses,
depending on the size. Refrigerate for at least 2 hours, or
overnight.

CHOCOLATE PIE

Easy.

500g of your favourite chocolate,
   melted and cooled a little
600ml whipped cream
1 ready-made sweet
   pastry case
grated rind of orange

Pour the chocolate over the whipped cream, folding the chocolate in slowly with a large metal spoon.

Pile the chocolate mixture into the pastry case.

Decorate with the orange rind.

Put it into the fridge to set.

It's very rich.

SUGAR-COATED GRAPES

Easy peasy.

a small bunch of grapes
1 egg white
caster sugar

Wash the grapes and snip into mini bunches of four or five. Dry them thoroughly.

Beat the egg white in a bowl and put the caster sugar into another.

Dip each bunch into the egg white, then caster sugar and leave to set at room temperature.

Perfect on top of the chocolate mousse (page 248).

TIFFIN

Tiffins rely on being made from leftovers, so measurements are unimportant. So long as you have enough chocolate to bind the ingredients together it will be a huge success and you can make chocolate, cinnamon or coconut variations. The ratio I work to, very roughly, is two thirds dry ingredients to one third chocolate. More chocolate is moreish, less chocolate is not.

stale cake (chocolate for chocolate
   or cinnamon tiffin, coconut
   for coconut tiffin)
broken biscuits
a little golden syrup
melted butter
enough molten milk chocolate to
   bind everything together (use
   white chocolate for
   coconut tiffin)

For Chocolate Tiffin:
sultanas or any dried fruit
White chocolate buttons or a
   broken up bar

For Cinnamon Tiffin:
dried fruit
1 heaped tsp cinnamon powder
broken walnuts or pecans,
   hazelnuts or almonds

For Coconut Tiffin:
glacé cherries
white chocolate buttons or a
   broken up bar
dessicated coconut, if you have it

Put all the ingredients together in a bowl and stir.

Push the ingredients into a lined baking tin and refrigerate for 2 hours.

Done.

You can sprinkle icing sugar or chocolate powder on top, or if you have leftover chocolate, drizzle that over.

Fearless
Baking...

Authentic Spanish Omelette

My first job when I left school was in a coffee shop in the Imperial Arcade in Brighton.
This was where I met 'Baker Boy' Jim, as he used to busk over the road in Churchill Square with his band called the Hot Diggity Dogs. He came in for coffee & the rest was history!!

The cafe was owned by a formidable South American lady who showed me how to make this basic Spanish omelette. It's great hot, or cold with lashings of mayonnaise.

Ingredients
Potatoes
Onion
Eggs
Extra Virgin Olive oil

Method

Thinly slice enough potatoes to fill a large frying pan & add a medium chopped onion. Fry in the oil on a medium heat until the potatoes are soft. Don't worry if there are slightly burned bits, I find it adds to the flavour!!

When its all cooked through, take the potato & onion mix out the pan making sure you drain out as much of the oil as you can.
Place to the side for the time being.
In another large bowl crack & beat some eggs. I usually use four eggs for my frying pan, though you can use more or less depending on the size of your omelette/pan.
Add salt & pepper to flavour.
Then add your potato & onion mix to your eggy mix & stir together.
Go back to your frying pan & add a small amount of oil on a medium heat.
Add your egg/pot/onion mix and flatten down to a patty shape. Cook it like this for a few minutes but don't let the bottom burn!
Pop a plate over your frying pan & flip over your omelette & cook the other side the same way.
Make sure the eggs are cooked in the middle & then you can serve.

Olé!!

Rebecca Flowergirl

This recipe has been a thread through Bex's life, from early romance to marriage, children and now Chocgywoccydoodah.

What it is to be a Doo...

My name is Christine Taylor, I am the creative director of Choccywoccydoodah and business partner of Christine Garratt, who is financial director of Choccywoccydoodah.

I am the pushy, loud and impractical half of the business. I thrive on the creativity of the company and am always looking for the next project.

I have a reputation for spending the company money on extravagant gestures and shop displays. I don't really worry my head about the staff getting paid, or the rent, or the bills.

Thank goodness for us all, Christine Garratt really does care.

She makes absolutely certain that staff are paid, always, during good times and more importantly, during hard times. And we have had our fair share of that.

Christine also worries about the staff's well-being, helps them to tackle and resolve issues that are too big for their shoulders, and keeps an eye on those who seem to be struggling, for whatever reason.

It's a good team effort, we have developed a proven strategy over many years of working together.

k-in-Chief

(or an Entrepreneur)

Some things only she needs to think about, some things only I need to think about. The things we both need to think about get resolved in a furious row.

One of our offices is four floors above the shop and during one of our famous negotiations a timid Doodah rang us from the shop floor.

Apparently our vitriolic verbal sparring could be heard in the shop and was frightening customers!

Only the customers though. The Doodahs have become used to our heated discussions and either slide away to not get caught in the crossfire, or buy tickets for the chocolaty equivalent of a Punch and Judy show.

Apart from the necessary rows, we also share a love of chocolate, cake, our great team of people and the ridiculous... We are Mrs Ying and Mrs Yang.

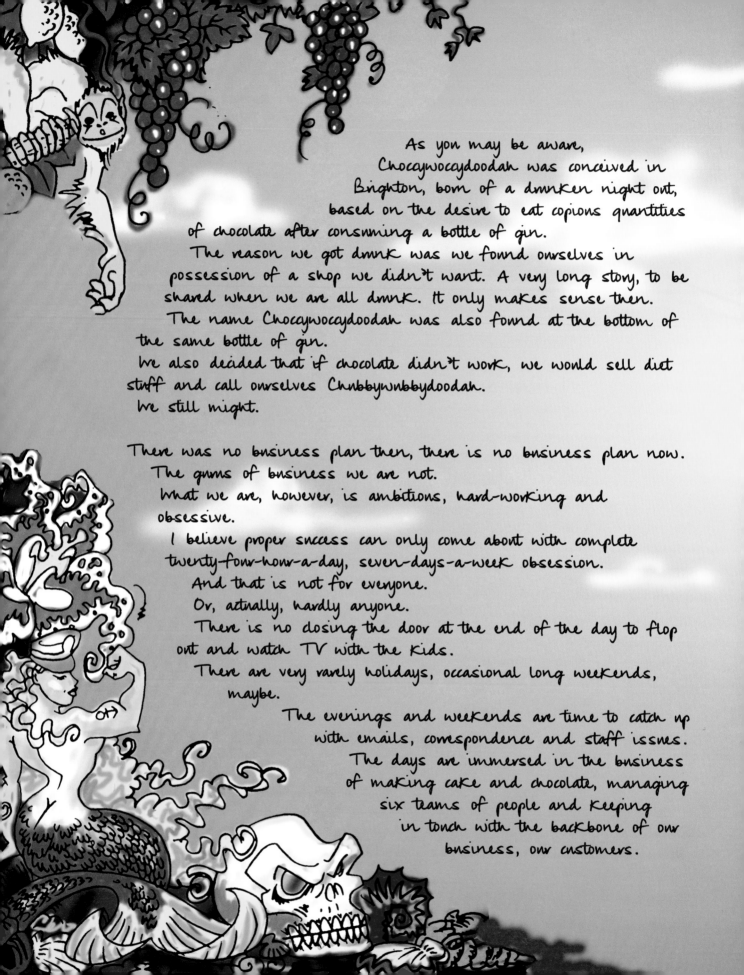

As you may be aware,
Choccywoccydoodah was conceived in
Brighton, born of a drunken night out,
based on the desire to eat copious quantities
of chocolate after consuming a bottle of gin.

The reason we got drunk was we found ourselves in possession of a shop we didn't want. A very long story, to be shared when we are all drunk. It only makes sense then.

The name Choccywoccydoodah was also found at the bottom of the same bottle of gin.

We also decided that if chocolate didn't work, we would sell diet stuff and call ourselves Chubbywubbydoodah.

We still might.

There was no business plan then, there is no business plan now.

The gurus of business we are not.

What we are, however, is ambitious, hard-working and obsessive.

I believe proper success can only come about with complete twenty-four-hour-a-day, seven-days-a-week obsession.

And that is not for everyone.

Or, actually, hardly anyone.

There is no closing the door at the end of the day to flop out and watch TV with the kids.

There are very rarely holidays, occasional long weekends, maybe.

The evenings and weekends are time to catch up with emails, correspondence and staff issues. The days are immersed in the business of making cake and chocolate, managing six teams of people and keeping in touch with the backbone of our business, our customers.

We have an open door policy for our staff and I make certain that I read almost every email that comes into the company.

And do you know what?

We love it.

There is no such thing as having it all, fifty-fifty work-life balance, it's total bollocks.

Choose your direction, tread your own path, make certain it's really what you want and commit 100 per cent. As I said, this life is not for everyone.

I am not the only entrepreneur who knows this is true.

We find our joy and pride in our accomplishments.

Not in having a celebrity client base, or a TV series, although both are very lovely.

What we are most proud of is our team.

Carefully chosen, all a little off centre, some so far off centre we have to tie them to the edge.

There are about forty-five of us now, all working together, enjoying what we do, making chocolate, creating cakes, selling chocolate, selling cakes and of course, we all eat chocolate and cake.

The standards we work to, the designs we produce, the boundaries we push and the fences we break down make me satisfied, but not proud.

It's the people I work with who get what I need them to do who make me proud.

We are a cross between a cult and a an asylum.

Dipped in chocolate.

The inspiration for what we do comes from everyday life, interspersed with

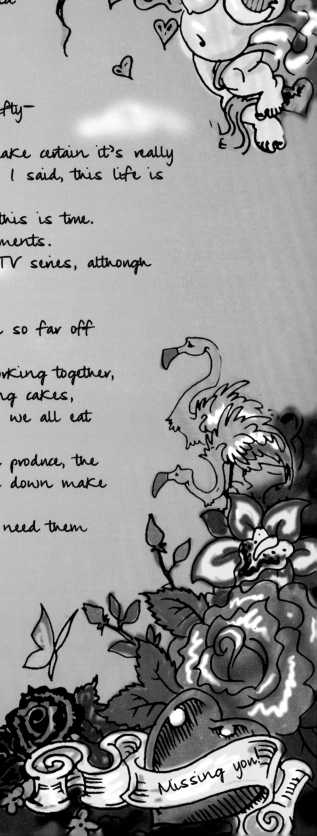

Missing you!

extraordinary moments.

My head is so full of projects yet to do, designs yet to make. I feel I should have a head like Tim Burton's Red Queen.

I employ artists and designers, the studio is full of creativity.

Creative people just are, it's a curse as well as a gift.

If we didn't work in chocolate we would still be doing this, maybe using dustbin lids instead.

Brighton is our blessing, as well as our hometown.

Our own planet and Mother to the Mothership.

The best thing about Brighton is the people.

They are eccentric, eclectic, proper bohemian, forgiving if they like you, supportive if they understand you and tough as old boots if you don't measure up.

With our massive population of artists, gays, gangsters, good timers and chancers, Brighton is unshockable.

And without Brighton, Choccywoccydoodah wouldn't exist.

Looking back, there is nothing I would change.

The tough experiences, the harsh decisions and the poverty that comes with starting a business from scratch, was crucial.

Without the mistakes, there couldn't be improvement.

It's either all good, or no good at all. And actually, it's all good.

The best and worst piece of advice I've ever been given is don't give in to fear, don't be frightened of risks.

Take it, or don't, is my advice to you. (Both the advice and the risks. It's easy to risk nothing, when you have nothing.)

Currently we are enjoying being on the telly: an approach out of the blue a few years ago resulted in cameras tagging along in our lives

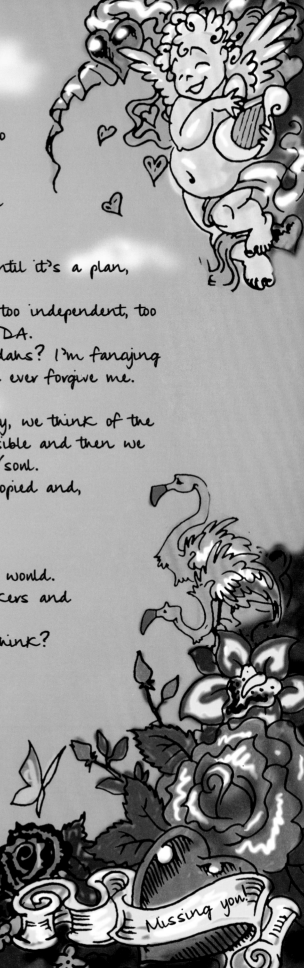

on an almost daily basis recording what we do and who we are.

Sometimes it's irritating, sometimes much worse than that, but mostly, we love it. Natural show-offs with a TV camera — who'd have thought it?

And the future — because it's never a plan until it's a plan, who can say?

We shall never be a chain store, we are way too independent, too much about people and not enough about EBITDA.

So maybe just one or two more Choccywoccydoodahs? I'm fancying New York, but wondering if Manchester would ever forgive me.

And my last thought: we are a design company, we think of the design, we invest in making the creation possible and then we produce and sell our original thoughts/designs/soul.

It is such irritating bad form for that to be copied and, worse still, copied badly.

If you like what we do, commission it.

Don't copy it.

And do question the morals of someone who would.

This should be a motto for all original thinkers and creators.

We make the world a better place, don't you think?

Choccywoccydoodah.
Quite a mouthful.

Missing you!

Stephens Scotch eggs

This recipe was taught to me by
my dad , Quick and easy
Scotch eggs

ingredients

6 x eggs
500g Sausage meat
3 small Garlic cloves - crushed
Dried Sage - 1 Tea spoon
      Salt + Pepper
1 x chopped Onion
250g Bread crumbs

1. Pre heat oven to 190°C
2. Boil 5 of the 6 eggs for 15 minutes
3. Mix the sausage meat with the chopped onions, crushed
   garlic , sage , salt and pepper
4. Shell the eggs - allow to cool
5. divide the sausage meat into 5 portions
6. Crack the last egg and beat in a bowl
7. Place the egg in the middle of the sausage meat
   and seal around the egg
8. roll the egg + meat in the beaten egg + then
   roll in bread crumbs
9. once you have done this twice to all eggs cook
   in oven for 20 minutes

Doodah's favourite recipes

Stephen, Customer Service and Webzeitgeist

Face and voice of customer service, Stephen also manages our website. Between those tasks he is the official Scotch egg maker for the Mothership. A recipe handed down from his Dad.

CHOCOLATE SAUCE (hot and sweet)

Follow the instructions and it's easy. Serve this warm, over fresh fruit or profiteroles, or poached pears.

25g brown sugar
50g butter
150g dark chocolate, broken up
250ml single cream
a measure of bourbon

VARIATION:

A strange, but delicious alternative is to crumble Stilton into the warm sauce, stirring until melted.

Put the sugar and butter into a heavy bottomed pan. Heat gently, stirring all the time until the sugar has dissolved.

Add the chocolate and the cream, stirring all the time.

When the mixture is fluid and warm, add the bourbon.

Serve in ramekins with salty crackers for dunking and a big glass of port.

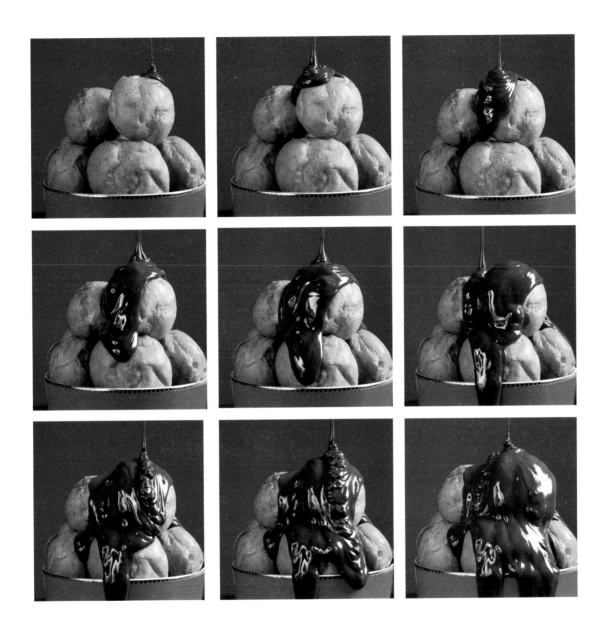

SAVOURY CHOCOLATE SAUCE

This is fairly easy. Pour over grilled chicken or grilled halloumi and serve with honeyed carrots and new potatoes.

50g salted butter
1 tbsp olive oil
1 garlic clove, crushed
1 small onion, chopped
2 red chillies, chopped and
    deseeded, add to taste
salt and pepper
150ml single cream
175g dark chocolate buttons

Melt the butter in a pan with the olive oil over a gentle heat. Add the garlic, onions, chopped chillies and some salt and pepper, then turn up the heat a little and fry everything together.

When the onions are soft, pour in the cream and pop the chocolate into the pan, too. Turn down the heat and carry on warming everything through gently until all the chocolate has melted.

DIPPED FRUIT

Easy. Magnificent.

strawberries
physalis
dried mango
cherries
a glass of champagne
icing sugar
molten chocolate, any flavour,
    gently melted in a microwave

Dip the fruit in champagne, then icing sugar, then chocolate.

Eat immediately, before the chocolate sets.

Yum.

CHOCOLATE CANAPÉS

~~Effortless~~. With great effect.

milk chocolate discs
whipped cream
fruit

or

dark chocolate discs
blue cheese
walnuts

Discs of milk chocolate topped with whipped cream and fruit.

Discs of dark chocolate topped with crumbled blue cheese and walnuts.

Incredibly simple, beautiful and absolutely delicious.

NUT BRITTLE

Any recipe, including this one, that requires boiling sugar as a method is too dangerous for a child to do. This must only be eaten when it's completely cool.

Very easy.

250g any salted nuts, or a mixture
250g light brown soft sugar

VARIATIONS:

This is very simple, very delicious and great to be eaten on its own, or as an accompaniment to ice cream.

Try dipping the ends of the shards into chocolate.

Line a baking tin with baking parchment, shiny side up.

Put the sugar in a heavy bottomed pan and place over a high heat. Don't stir until the sugar is liquid.

Add the nuts and stir constantly for 3 minutes.

Pour onto the baking parchment and leave to cool.

When cool, break into shards.

Store in an airtight tin or jar.

Tom's Amazing Cheesy Toast
(for hangovers)

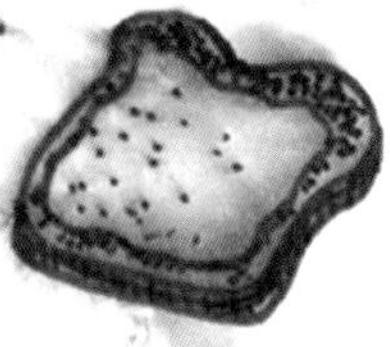

Ingredients:

1. cheese — I prefer mature cheddar but double gloucester or red leicester are reasonable alternatives.

2. bread — white is best

3. Herbs and spices

You will need a toaster and a grill.

step 1. Put bread in the toaster. minimum 2 slices. toast as you would for jam or such like.

step 2. Whilst bread is toasting, slice the cheese generously, enough to cover the toast.

step 3. Arrange the cheese on the toast. Avoid gaps, then sprinkle herbs or spices of your choice. My personal favourite combination is rosemary on one slice and cayenne pepper on the other.

step 4. place under the grill for 1-2 mins until cheese is bubbling.

step 5. Enjoy with cup of tea. mmmmm.

Messengers of the DEVIL

I've shared my journey so far with dozens of
fantastic people, some are still strapped into the
Mothership, some we dropped off at their chosen
destination and some have come to the very end
of their journey.
We miss them dreadfully.

The loved ones.
So - just so you all know -
Christine Garratt, who is co-founder of this marvellous ship
in which we all sail is also Captain of our Destiny and
provider of good sense. Without her we would all have sailed
away aimlessly on a ship of dreams and broken promises.
Big love to her.

All my Doodahs, past, present and future.
Dave, Daveed, Henry, Edward, Jim, Curtis, Tom, Jerry, Rebecca,
Janis, Dan, Stacey, Donna, Stephen, Flick, Mav, Jenna, Beth, AJ,
Mikaela, Jade, Mike, Phil, Stef, Denise, Chi, Barry, George, Arkadius,
Heather, Josie, Terry, Phillippa, Gemma, Rachel, George, Amanda, Antonio and more, always more.
The Doodahs are Choccys future.

I wouldn't be who I am without guidance, advice and support from some other co-travellers, people that
I've fallen in love with over years, tears and adventures.
Edward Taylor, Mark Cobley, Gavin Munro, The Darlings (not their real name, but they don't know
that), the infamous Glocklers. The Carrolls'. My mum, my sisters, Anne and Carolyn, my beloved
dad, no longer with me.
Charlie and Rita. Elizabeth, my nan. Barry, Ken and Ebo. The journey couldn't have started without
them, but finished for them way too early.

Then there are those that I'm eternally grateful to, Dave's mum, Mrs Pat Ratcliffe of Swansea.
Jeremy Diaper, our friend and husband to Dave.
The parents and families that I don't know, who belong to, nurture and are so proud of the Doodahs.
Quite rightly.
And you. Of course you. You make it all possible, enabling us to turn dreams into reality, chocolate into
cake, curses into spells. I am so grateful.

Then more formally, because it's proper, I'd like to thank Trevor Dolby for allowing me to publish a
book that is as near to handmade/homemade as we could get.
And thank you Robert Kirby, thank you Madeleine Kirby.

Me, Christine, the Doodahs and some Dontdahs, are still here on the Mothership; if you want to join
us, we've got spare seats and we are always on the lookout for the odd hitchhiker. Odd being the
key word. X

1 3 5 7 9 10 8 6 4 2

Preface
20 Vauxhall Bridge Road
London SW1V 2SA

Preface is part of the Penguin Random House group of companies whose addresses can be found at global.penguinrandomhouse.com.

Penguin
Random House
UK

First published by Preface in 2015

www.randomhouse.co.uk

A CIP catalogue record for this book is available from the British Library.

ISBN 978 1 848 09451 2

Written by Christine Taylor
Illustrated by Dave (Pop) Ratcliffe
Project Editor Henry Everett
Design by Two Associates

Illustrations © Dave Ratcliffe
Cover image © Nick Pate
Images © Dave Branfield p46-47, p92-93, p284-285.
All images for recipes by Christine © Gary Moyes and also p77, p133, p152-153, p177, p224-225.
Tino & Pip p6-7, p66-67, p134-135, p162-163, p188-189, p230-231, p262-263, p276-277, p288.
All images for Doodah recipes © Henry Everett and Peter Coventry and also p119, p246, p247.

Printed and bound by C&C Offset Printing Co., Ltd.